From Bismarck to De Gaulle

A History of Europe, 1870–1966

Francis T. Holohan

Gill and Macmillan

Published in Ireland by
Gill and Macmillan Ltd
Goldenbridge
Dublin 8
with associated companies throughout the world

0 7171 1513 5

Designed by Grainne Whelan Design
Print origination in Ireland by
Design and Art Facilities
Cover designed by Design Image

Acknowledgments

Cover pictures: Archiv fur Kunst und Geschichte, Berlin (Bismarck) and Scoop/Paris-Match (de Gaulle).

Pictures with text: BBC Hulton Picture Library, Imperial War Museum.

Contents

Foreword

This textbook on modern European history, 1870–1966, is written essentially for senior post primary students and treats of the main political, social and economic movements and events that have shaped our contemporary world.

Since a fully comprehensive history of modern Europe covering such a vast array of material within the confines of a single textbook would have been impractical, if not impossible, I decided to strike a balance between synthesising one hundred years of European history and maintaining a high level of narrative and analysis.

A special feature of this textbook is the introductory chapter which not only 'sets the scene' but elucidates the many abstract factors and forces which seek their tangible expression in the post 1870 period. In addition, a concluding section is devoted to chapters on cultural, scientific and technological developments which may be studied in their historical context.

For greater facility in reading and revising, the contents are logically structured. Examination type essays and questions at the end of each chapter provide a set of clarified thoughts around which additional reading may take place and which will contribute to a more rewarding study of history.

The student is also provided with a comprehensive glossary of historical concepts and terms, together with an extensive bibliography from which more 'in depth' reading on special areas may be pursued.

Francis T. Holohan

September 1987

Maps & Diagrams

EUROPE 1815–70

The proper study of mankind is man. . . .
Created half to rise, and half to fall;
Great lord of all things, yet a prey to all;
Sole judge of truth, in endless error hurled;
The glory, jest and riddle of the world!

Alexander Pope, *An Essay on Man*.

EUROPE AFTER NAPOLEON

As soon as Napoleon was finally defeated at Waterloo in June 1815 and sentenced to perpetual exile on the remote island of St Helena in the mid-Atlantic, the statesmen of Europe reassembled at Vienna and remade the map of Europe. They tore up the one Napoleon had made; and, after many disputes, left Europe almost as it had been in 1789, before the French Revolution and Napoleon had upset everything (map, p.2).

France was reduced to her old borders, and the Bourbon monarchy, in the person of Louis XVIII, was restored. Belgium and Holland were united in the kingdom of the Netherlands, and Norway and Sweden became the kingdom of Sweden. Tsarist Russia was guaranteed in her Baltic provinces and in eastern Poland. The Austrian (Hapsburg) empire was given a large share of northern Italy. The kingdom of Prussia was confirmed in western Poland and large slices of other German states. All those parts of Germany not falling under Prussia or Austria were left in a condition of disunity, ruled by petty kings, princes and dukes. Italy, similarly, was split up into a variety of petty statelets, and the country's name became no more than a geographical expression. In south-east Europe, known generally as the Balkans, the Turkish (Ottoman) empire was allowed to hold sway. Finally, the settlement of Vienna restored all the old rulers whom Napoleon had deposed or expelled.

In effect, the settlement was a reiteration of the old principle of the 'divine right' of monarchs to rule without any reference to the wishes of their subjects; but, more important, it was a denial of the principles enunciated by thinkers before and during the French Revolution: *liberty, equality, fraternity, democracy* and *nationality*.

THE FORCES OF CHANGE

Nationalism

The most potent and far-reaching development in the nineteenth century was the growth of nationalism. In essence, this is the belief that people linked together by such factors as a common heritage, language, religion or territory, should form a nation state as the ideal and only legitimate form of political organisation that allows for the full potential of cultural creativity and economic advance.

Nationalism derived much of its strength from the romantic movement in literature and art. Romanticism had arisen in part from a disillusionment with the eighteenth-century Enlightenment and its faith in reason, which had apparently led to revolution and wars; in part from a reaction against the drabness of industrial and urban life; and in part from a nostalgic look backwards by scholars and poets to past glories of the nation.

Although romanticism was essentially cultural, it was also political. Thus nationalism was romantic and most romantics were nationalists.

Before the French Revolution, wars, as a rule, did not arouse deep national emotions. National consciousness was almost non-existent among a largely illiterate peasantry, while the educated few were generally imbued with Renaissance learning and culture. But the impact of the French Revolution and the wars of Napoleon, coupled with the growth of

EUROPE AFTER THE CONGRESS OF VIENNA (1815)

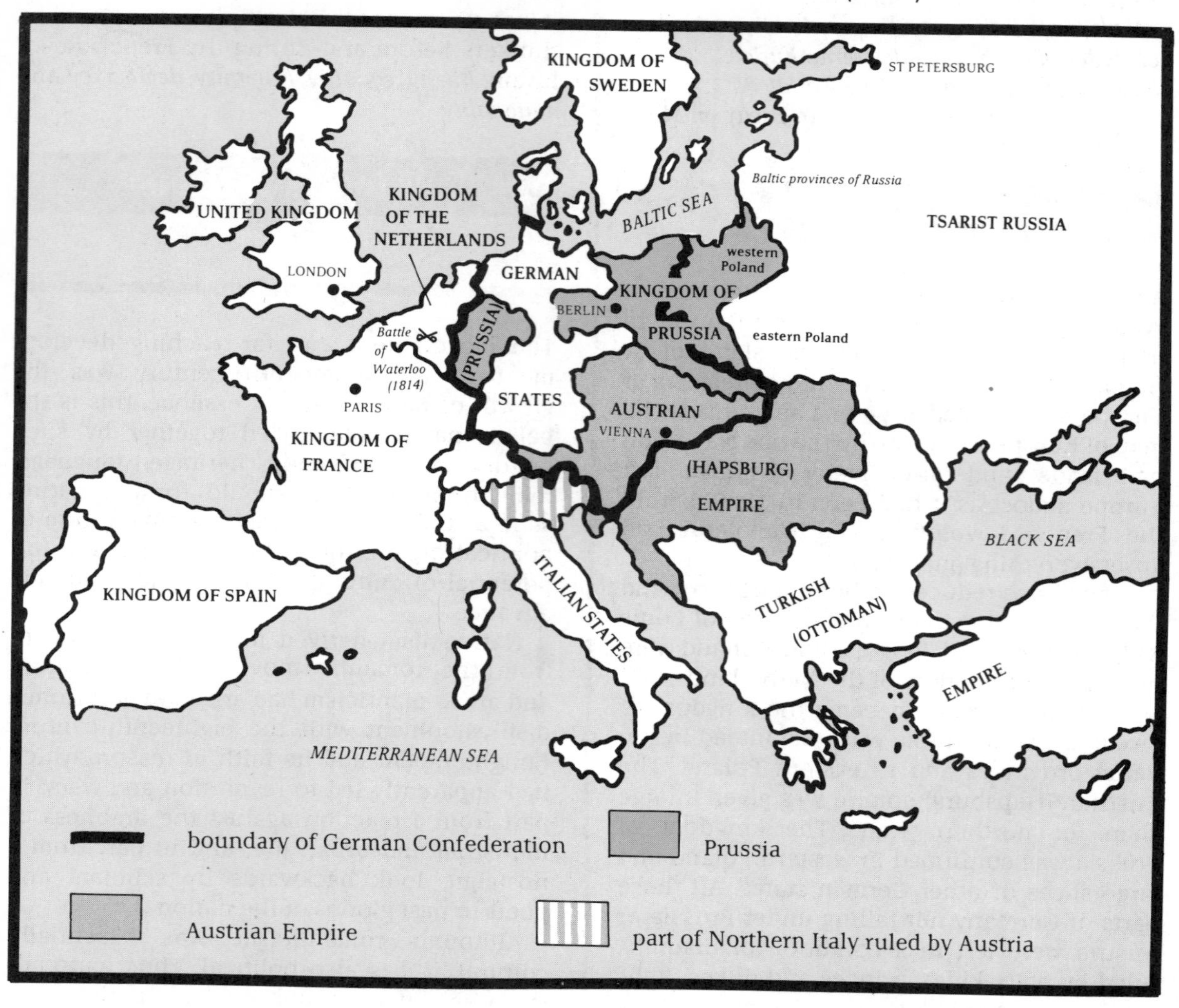

the romantic movement in literature and art, aroused national consciousness from Ireland to Greece. The map of Europe drawn up at Vienna in 1815 was doomed to failure since nationalist aspirations sought to reform European boundaries along lines of nationality. In the years between 1815 and 1870 nationalism triumphed in many parts of Europe.

Industrialism

Industrialism was another most important force for change. It first developed in England

New middle-class houses in London about 1860.

in the late eighteenth century and then spread to the continent.

In England, increasing demands for woollen cloth accelerated a series of inventions in textile machinery. This use of mechanised power to process large quantities of raw materials created the factory system with its machines, steam power, labour to tend the machines, and the necessary capital for investment. The need to transport raw materials to factories, and finished products to markets (via the ports), accelerated the construction of roads, canals, railways and ships.

Industrialism also led to profound changes in the structure of society. The increased mechanisation of agriculture resulted in a decrease in the number of people required on the land, while the concentration of industrial work in mines and factories led to large movements of people from rural areas into growing urban centres. Thus a new 'working class' came into existence, while at the same time, the development of industry and business brought new wealth and importance to the owners of industry and to the growing numbers of businessmen in banking, insurance and shipping. This rising social group, known collectively as the middle class, advocated the virtues of individualism and became increasingly associated with the doctrines of liberalism.

Liberalism

Liberalism arose from the economic conditions of the industrial revolution and the ideals of liberty proclaimed by the French Revolution. It was a mixture of economic and political ideas. The economic aspects of liberalism came from the writings of Adam Smith, Thomas Malthus and David Ricardo. They held that each man is the best judge of his own interests and that governments should not place any restrictions on individual enterprise since the economic law of supply and demand was the surest yardstick in the regulation of economic life. These men advocated the economic principle of *laissez-faire*, or the absence of government regulation in economic life.

Political liberalism found its greatest advocate in John Stuart Mill, who pleaded in his essay *On Liberty* for freedom of thought and discussion, and such freedom of action as does not interfere with the rights of others. Mill's greatest contribution to political liberalism lay in his claim that 'all mankind has no right to silence one dissenter'. A typical nineteenth-century liberal, therefore, would have favoured government that had only a limited power over the individual. This would best be guaranteed by an elected parliament, with ministers responsible to that assembly who must resign once a majority in the parliament disagreed with them.

Liberals were not necessarily democrats, that is, in favour of rule by all the people; many nineteenth-century liberals believed that the right to vote should be granted only to 'responsible' citizens, that is, citizens of property and education. However, by the twentieth century, mostly as a result of the educational and social advance of the masses, liberalism came to be associated with democracy.

Socialism

Side by side with the development of liberal thought, a different school of thought arose known as socialism. It was mainly concerned with economic considerations and emerged from three small streams in France, Britain and Germany.

French socialist thought had its origin in the writings of Rousseau, who had taught that in the original condition of nature all men were free and equal but that private property had created inequality. Social philosophers like Saint-Simon and Fourier maintained that all land, capital and the instruments of production should be held in common and that everyone should work according to his or her ability and be rewarded according to his or her service.

In nineteenth-century Britain a complete and advanced socialist programme was put forward by Robert Owen, a factory owner from New Lanark in Scotland. Owen was influenced by the terrible abuses of the industrial revolution and he began to doubt if equality could ever be achieved under the capitalist system; but he opposed revolution as a means of achieving socialism. Owen placed his hopes on education, trade unionism and co-operation, which would replace illiteracy, exploited labour and competition. In the early nineteenth century he set up a model factory in New Lanark to show that people worked best in good conditions. After paying himself and his workers a fixed sum, the rest of the proceeds were put back into the community. He hoped to persuade the government to set up villages of co-operation, in which people would form self-sufficient farming and factory communities. But such planned economic societies were not popular in the days of *laissez-faire* capitalism and Owen's projects died out.

German socialism began in the early nineteenth century when Karl Marlo advocated collective ownership, co-operative production and communal distribution, while Karl Rodbertus looked forward to the day when all people would be equal and everyone would be rewarded according to his service.

In the first half of the nineteenth century all three streams remained largely ineffective until Karl Marx gave socialism a scientific base.

Scientific Socialism: Marxism

The teachings of Karl Marx gave socialism a revolutionary purpose from which communism takes its rise. His ideas are best seen in his *Communist Manifesto*, which he drew up, in collaboration with his associate, Friedrich

Karl Marx in 1861. His analysis of economics and society led to scientific socialism, or communism.

Engels, in 1848. Marx claimed to have discovered the scientific laws of history, which develop inexorably by a dialectical process. According to Marx, all human progress came from man's economic needs. He showed how, from age to age, man had assumed more power over the forces of nature, and as a result of successive inventions — the wheel, the plough, currency, the factory system – great changes had occurred in man's relationship with his fellow man. In this way the political and social conditions at any given time merely reflected the prevailing economic conditions.

Marx held that the key to understanding history and politics lay in the idea of the class struggle. At every point in history the class of people that held economic power controlled the destinies of all other classes. In the feudal period the landowners dominated. When feudalism broke down with the emergence of trade and commerce, a new class, the owners of industry or the *capitalists*, came to dominate the workers in industry. This new middle class, which rose to power through trade and industry, Marx called the *bourgeoisie*, while those whom they exploited, the workers, he referred to as the *proletariat*. Marx held that as industrialisation developed in each country, the rural peasantry would drift from the land into the factories and mines, swelling the ranks of the proletariat, who would be unable to improve their lot under capitalism, because the bourgeoisie would continue to control the state apparatus — parliament, finance, the police and the army.

On the other hand, the capitalist class would also undergo change. In their efforts to maximise profits, the strong capitalists would 'gobble up' the weaker ones, so that monopoly capitalism would develop. Therefore, as the proletariat grew larger and poorer, the bourgeoisie would grow fewer and richer. There would then come a point when the 'law of increasing misery' would produce a proletarian revolution. Once the proletariat had overthrown the bourgeoisie, there would be no more wars because there would be no more classes. The means of production, distribution and exchange would then be communally owned in a classless society, which Marx called communism.

POLITICAL DEVELOPMENTS 1815–48

The first revolt against the map of Europe drawn up at Vienna in 1815 was the Greek insurrection against their Turkish masters in

THE BALKANS AND THE CRIMEA

1821. The Greek revolt fired the imagination of many Europeans who admired the culture and civilisation of ancient Greece and believed that the Greeks had a just case for independent nationhood. However, the problem was complicated by the attitudes of the great powers. The tsar of Russia was no lover of revolution, but he was prepared to support Greece since anything that might weaken the Ottoman empire would be to Russia's advantage. England and France, however, did not wish to let the tsar intervene because they feared Russian influence in the Near East, and especially in the Dardanelles, the narrow strait separating European and Asiatic Turkey (p.6). In 1827 Russia, England and France joined together to force Turkey to grant Greek independence. Outnumbered and isolated, the Turks granted full independence to Greece in 1830.

Meanwhile Balkan nationalism had triumphed to some degree. Serbia had secured a large measure of independence from the Turks, while the tiny state of Montenegro, secure behind her mountain barrier, had never really fallen under Turkish rule. Then in 1855, following the Crimean War (p.10), Romania achieved a measure of independence.

In France the restored Bourbon monarch, Louis XVIII, no longer claimed the 'divine right' to rule, and was willing to act as a constitutional monarch in co-operation with the Liberals in the Chamber of Deputies. When he died in 1824, Louis XVIII was succeeded by his brother Charles X, who believed with the ultra-royalists that the king's power should be increased. This made the middle class hostile, and when they won a large majority in the election of 1830, matters came to a head. Charles issued a series of decrees that dissolved the Chamber, reduced the electorate by 75 per cent, and called new elections. Revolution followed as workers joined the middle-class uprising. After three days of fighting, the army refused to act against the revolt, and Charles fled to England.

The wealthy middle class in France then took control of events. They wished to retain a constitutional monarch, and opposed the workers and radicals, who wanted a republic based on universal suffrage. The throne was offered to Louis Philippe, Duc d'Orléans, a relative of the deposed Bourbon, who promised to respect the constitution.

The 1830 uprising in Paris provided the impetus for revolution elsewhere in Europe. In Belgium, nationalists and middle-class liberals rebelled against the Dutch in that same year and declared their complete independence. But because Belgian independence was a violation of the Vienna settlement of 1815 (p.1), a conference of the great powers was called and in 1831 all five (Russia, Prussia, Austria, Britain and France) signed the Treaty of London. By this treaty the powers recognised Belgium's independence and agreed that the country must remain 'perpetually neutral'. The Dutch eventually recognised the treaty in 1839 (map, p.8).

Meanwhile, revolutions broke out in many German states (Brunswick, Saxony, Hesse-Kassel); in Italy (Modena, Parma); and in Poland. However, the conservative forces reacted in Prussia, Austria and Russia, and by 1835 they were firmly in control.

Britain was the only major country to escape revolution, although unrest in Ireland and Chartism (a movement for political reform) at home showed how fragile peace could be. Essentially, Britain's relative peace stemmed from the fact that despite heated opposition, reforms were carried through that blunted the edge of revolution.

In 1832 the Whig government of Lord Grey succeeded in getting the Reform Bill through the House of Lords and making it law. The first Reform Act accomplished two things. First, it lowered the property qualifications, thus enabling the upper middle class to vote. Secondly, it redistributed the seats in the House of Commons to allow representation from the growing industrial towns. Political

EVENTS IN EUROPE, 1848–1870

power was no longer the preserve of the aristocracy; it was now shared by merchants, manufacturers, business and professional people.

In 1833 slavery was abolished in the British Empire, the first Factory Act was passed, and many more reforms followed.

THE YEAR OF REVOLUTIONS: 1848

During the 1840s many social groups throughout Europe were discontented. The lower classes resented their exclusion from political power. In Germany and Italy desire for national unification was growing, while in the Hapsburg empire, Czechs, Croats and Hungarians were eager to achieve independence. These grievances were brought to a head by an economic depression in the mid-1840s that caused large-scale unemployment across Britain and continental Europe. In addition, potatoes and wheat — the staple diet of the poorer classes — were in short supply and prices soared. A potato blight swept across Europe from Poland to Ireland in 1845 and 1846. This combination of political discontent and economic distress caused a wave of revolutions in 1848.

France

Once again France led the way. On 21 February barricades were erected in the working-class districts of Paris, following a ban on a meeting for franchise reform, and rioting spread throughout the city. When the National Guard refused to fire on the people, Louis Philippe lost his nerve and on 24 February fled into exile. The revolutionary leaders (a mixture of middle-class liberals and working-class radicals) proclaimed the Second Republic. (The First Republic had been proclaimed in 1792 at the time of the great French Revolution.)

In December, elections were held and Prince Louis Napoleon, a nephew of Napoleon Bonaparte, was elected president of the republic by an overwhelming majority.

The Hapsburg Empire

The revolution in Paris sparked off outbursts throughout Europe. On 13 March, barricades went up in the streets of Vienna and the government hastily agreed to a democratically elected assembly. On 15 March the Hungarians, led by Lajos Kossuth, declared Home Rule. In Vienna the emperor Ferdinand was obliged to accept. Then a few days later the Czechs revolted in Prague and Ferdinand again agreed to Czech Home Rule. In addition, serfdom was abolished throughout the Hapsburg empire (map, p.8).

During that same month revolutions broke out across Italy. Austrian rulers were driven out of northern Italy; Venice declared itself a republic, and Pope Pius IX was forced to flee from Rome.

Yet, desite all these disturbances, the Hapsburg monarchy did not panic. The army remained loyal, and by June the tide had begun to turn. In Prague, Alfred Windischgrätz, an Austrian field-marshal, bombarded the city and suppressed an insurrection. In July, Josef Radetzky, the Austrian commander-in-chief in Lombardy, restored Hapsburg control of northern Italy. In September civil war broke out in Hungary when the Slavs refused to submit to Hungarian rule. In October, Windischgrätz forced the liberals in Vienna to surrender.

By 1849 the Hapsburg monarchy had successfully crushed all opposition. The Republic of Venice was brought to an end and Rome was restored to the Papacy. Although the Hungarians put up a fierce resistance, they succumbed when Tsar Nicholas I of Russia sent help and recaptured Budapest for the Hapsburgs. Meanwhile the old emperor, Ferdinand, had resigned in favour of his eighteen-year-old nephew, Franz Joseph. The new emperor, not feeling bound by his uncle's liberal promises, opposed all forms of constitutionalism and nationalism.

Germany

The revolution spread to Germany as well. On 15 March a revolt broke out in Berlin and King Frederick William IV of Prussia promised a constitution. Similar riots erupted in other German states and many governments fell. Elections were then held for an all-German National Assembly. In May, over 800 delegates met in Frankfurt to draw up a liberal constitution for a united Germany. Liberalism and nationalism had joined forces. However, from the beginning, the Frankfurt Assembly lacked any power to enforce its decisions, and since they were liberals and not democrats, their middle-class (limited) constitution lost them the support of the vast majority of disenfranchised Germans.

Meanwhile Frederick William had reasserted his authority in Prussia, and soon the rulers of other German states also succeeded in suppressing liberal revolts in their domains. In April 1849 the Frankfurt Assembly completed its constitution and offered the crown of a united Germany to Frederick William, who was to act as a constitutional monarch. But he contemptuously rejected a crown 'created by an assembly born of revolutionary seed' and the Frankfurt Assembly came to an inglorious end, its efforts to secure German unity a failure.

THE CRIMEAN WAR 1854–55

The only large-scale clash between the powers in the period from the 1815 Congress of Vienna to 1870 was the Crimean War, which pitted France and Britain against Russia.

When a dispute arose over whether France or Russia had the right to act as the protector of Christians in the Holy Land, the Sultan Abdul Mejid (in whose Turkish empire the Holy Land was situated) sided with the French. This action angered Tsar Nicholas I, who sought to intimidate the Sultan by sending Russian troops into the Turkish-controlled principalities of Moldavia and Wallachia (now Romania). The British, ever fearful of Russian expansion towards the Dardanelles, together with the French, decided to take up arms on behalf of the Turks (map, p.6).

The tsar, realising that he had overstepped the mark, withdrew his troops. But British hysteria was determined on war in order to 'teach the "bear" a lesson'; and France, under Napoleon III, saw an excellent opportunity to enhance her prestige in a short victorious war.

Almost all the fighting took place in the Crimea, a long peninsula jutting out from Russia into the Black Sea. In September 1854 thousands of British and French troops landed at Eupatoria and began to march on the Russian city of Sevastopol. On 20 September they crushed the Russians at the River Alma; on 25 October they again defeated the Russians at Balaklava, and were victorious once more on 5 November at Inkerman. However, they could not break through the Russian defences at Sevastopol and an eleven-month siege ensued. Cold, disease, lack of food, fuel and medicine reaped a terrible harvest of suffering and death. After a huge bombardment, the allied troops forced the Russians to evacuate the city in September 1855, and the new tsar, Alexander III, who had come to the throne in March, was willing to make peace.

In March 1856 a peace conference was held in Paris. By the Treaty of Paris the tsar had to cede parts of Bessarabia to Moldavia, thus losing control of the mouth of the Danube; the principalities of Moldavia and Wallachia were given self-government and became the nucleus of future Romania; and the tsar renounced his claim as exclusive protector of Christians in the Ottoman empire. But the most humiliating stipulation was that Russia must not maintain warships and fortifications on the Black Sea. Although this provision applied to all powers, it affected Russia more seriously since now her southern frontier was unprotected. From this moment onwards, the principal aim of Russian foreign policy was to revise this Black Sea clause and regain military rights there.

One of the wide tree-lined boulevards of Paris, built according to Haussman's plans during the period of the Second Empire.

THE POLITICAL REORGANISATION OF EUROPE

In the fifteen years between the end of the Crimean War (1855) and the Franco-Prussian War (1870), the European political system was radically reorganised. The changes were essentially brought about by a remarkable group of leaders whose policies reflected the rising tide of European nationalism.

France

When France elected Louis Napoleon as president of the Second Republic in 1848 (p.9), a new era was about to begin. He worked to acquire greater power for himself, and won support by trading on his famous name and stressing national prestige.

In 1851, Louis Napoleon arranged a *coup d'état* to overthrow the constitution and asked the nation to vote on whether he should be made emperor. The response was overwhelmingly affirmative. Accordingly, the Second Republic was transformed into the 'Second Empire', with Louis Napoleon taking the title of Emperor Napoleon III (the first empire had been created by his uncle in 1804 and came to an end with the restoration of the Bourbon monarchy in 1815, while the title Napoleon III was taken to preserve the fiction that the son of Napoleon I was the rightful ruler of France during the intervening years).

At heart Napoleon III was a despot, and parliament had very little real power. However, he was a shrewd politician and sugared the pill of despotism with a programme of economic development. Railroad construction was accelerated, iron ships replaced wooden ones, and in 1859 a French company began the ten-year task of building the Suez Canal to link the Mediterranean and the Red Sea. The great city planner, Baron Georges Haussmann, was given the task of modernising Paris. He helped create beautiful tree-lined boulevards, public squares and parks; and magnificent buildings and monuments replaced the crowded slums. Napoleon III created model farms for the peasants, strikes were legalised, hospitals built, and free medicine was distributed to the poorer classes.

But Napoleon III was not content to concern himself exclusively with domestic matters. He had a mystical belief in his destiny as a great world figure and was determined to earn glory abroad. In 1854 he led France into the Crimean War (p.10) and in 1861 intervened in Mexico when President Benito Juárez suspended payments on his country's foreign debt.

In 1863 Napoleon declared the Archduke Maximilian of Austria, the brother of Emperor Franz Joseph (p.80), emperor of Mexico. But when the American Civil War ended in 1866, the United States demanded the withdrawal of French troops from Mexico. In 1867 Napoleon pulled out his troops, and Maximilian, now deserted by the French, was captured and shot by the Mexicans.

Italy

The Congress of Vienna (p.1) had left Italy divided into a multiplicity of statelets. But Italian nationalism continued to grow, and expressed itself specifically in the writings of the patriot Giuseppe Mazzini, and more generally in the *Risorgimento* (Resurgence), a movement among middle-class liberals for Italian unification.

In 1852 Count Camillo de Cavour became prime minister of Piedmont-Sardinia. He proceeded to make the state a model of economic and political progress, and the national leader in the movement for Italian unification. In 1859 Cavour won the support of Napoleon III and they both went to war with Austria. Although Napoleon made a separate peace with Austria, revolutions throughout northern Italy continued and in 1860 all the country's northern provinces, except Venetia, united with Piedmont-Sardinia (map, p.8).

At this point a fiery leader named Giuseppe Garibaldi took matters into his own hands. In May 1860, with a volunteer army of over a thousand 'redshirts', he sailed from Genoa and conquered the kingdom of Sicily and Naples. He then prepared to march on Rome and take the papal states from the Pope. But Cavour, knowing that any attack on the Pontiff would incur the wrath of Austria and France, hurried south with an army which seized a large part of the papal states and prevented Garibaldi from attacking Rome. Cavour then persuaded Garibaldi to permit the unification of Sicily and Naples with Piedmont-Sardinia. In 1861, the Kingdom of Italy was formally proclaimed (although Rome remained outside it), and Victor Emmanuel II of Piedmont-Sardinia was installed as king.

In 1866, when Austria was defeated by Prussia in the seven weeks' war (p.16), Otto von Bismarck forced Austria to cede Venetia to Italy. Only Rome remained. But Napoleon III had sent troops to guard the Pope, so Victor Emmanuel counselled caution. Then in 1870, when France went to war with Prussia (p.18), Napoleon withdrew his troops from Rome. Victor Emmanuel, judging the time ripe, marched on Rome. The papal troops put up a feeble resistance and, on 20 September, the king of Italy entered Rome.

The following year, 1871, Victor Emmanuel

summoned the first parliament of a united Italy to meet in Rome. The constitution allowed for a parliament elected on a limited franchise and Victor Emmanuel became a constitutional monarch (p.73).

The period between 1870 and 1914 was one of progress and optimism. After 1871 it began to seem as if the age of major European wars was over. In one country after another democracy, literacy and trade union organisation spread downwards from the middle classes to the masses. At the same time, industrialisation and the resultant increase in the availability of goods and services seemed to usher in a period when poverty would be reduced and human well-being advanced.

This was also a great age of imperialism. Partly because of rising nationalism and partly as a result of the rapid growth of industry and commerce, there was a rush for colonies in which the European powers partitioned the continent of Africa, and much of Asia and Oceania were brought under European control.

These four decades also witnessed phenomenal advances in science, and it seemed to many that the universe would eventually be explained in materialistic terms. Medicine and public health progressed and, as the death rate dropped, Europe's population grew rapidly; huge numbers moved from the countryside into the expanding cities, while many others emigrated to the new lands of America and Australia.

But even as there was progress towards a peaceful, prosperous, expanding world, guided by science and supplied by machine industry, a darker side emerged. Working and living conditions in factories and cities were often below the level of human dignity, and political leaders attempted to improve the lot of the masses through social legislation. Progress was essentially confined to western Europe, for, in the east, especially in the Turkish and Russian empires, there was little industry, no democracy and scant attention was being paid to the needs or aspirations of the masses.

This was also a period of growing national consciousness when the nation state became the political and ideological goal of nearly all Europeans. Much of the continent was organised into nation states, but many races, especially in the Hapsburg and Ottoman empires, were frustrated in their demands for self-determination. These racial tensions in a Europe divided into two camps, in which powerful nation states strove to outbid each other in military might, made the latter half of the period a time of 'armed peace'.

Section One

Progressive and Imperialist Europe 1870–1914

The Franco-Prussian War and its Aftermath 1870–71

1

The unification of Germany was incidental, a by-product of Bismarck's never-ending pursuit of Prussian interests. . . .

David Thompson, *Europe Since Napoleon.*

THE CAUSE of the Franco-Prussian War in 1870 is related to the progress of German unification and the concept of a European 'balance of power'.

In the first half of the nineteenth century, Germany was not a united country. It was divided into thirty-nine independent states, of which the kingdom of Prussia in the north and the Austrian empire in the south, were the two strongest. The states were loosely connected through a German confederation, but this tenuous alliance had very little power because its decisions could be vetoed by any one of the states. Moreover, Prussia and Austria rarely agreed on anything since the rulers in Berlin and Vienna continually vied with each other for control of the confederation. Throughout the nineteenth century German nationalism gathered momentum so that the question became, not merely would Germany be united, but what form would that unity take (p.10).

THE AIMS OF BISMARCK

In 1862 William I, king of Prussia, appointed Otto von Bismarck as prime minister of Prussia. Bismarck was not a German nationalist as such, but a conservative aristocrat who wished to expand the power of his native Prussia; if German nationalism could serve him, he would not be opposed to channelling it to that end.

But two powers, Austria and France, would automatically oppose the possibility of the German states being swallowed up in a powerful Prussia. Austria regarded herself as the leader of the southern states and would oppose her exclusion from a new Germany under Prussian control. France had always regarded a disunited Germany as essential to her own security and had no intention of allowing a powerful neighbour to appear on the Rhine.

War with Austria

Bismarck's strategy was to prevent a united stand against him by Austria and France. To this end he secured French acquiescence in a Prussian war against Austria by making vague promises to Napoleon III whereby France would be allowed to 'rectify her frontiers' and 'expand to the Rhine'. Having secured French neutrality, Bismarck was ready to go to war. Victory over Austria came quickly. The Prussian army (equipped with a new rifle) utterly defeated the retreating Austrians at Sadowa in the summer of 1866.

Prussia declared the German confederation to be at an end. The German states to the north of the river Main joined in a north German confederation under Prussia's leadership. The states south of the Main were detached from Austrian influence and became independent. With one swift war, lasting only seven weeks, Bismarck had ended Austria as a factor in German affairs.

Bismarck's Diplomacy

The years between the defeat of Austria and the outbreak of war with France can be regarded as the period when Napoleon III played into Bismarck's hands.

When Napoleon suggested to the German chancellor that France should take the lands

THE FRANCO-PRUSSIAN WAR AND THE ESTABLISHMENT OF THE GERMAN EMPIRE

of the Rhine-Mainz and part of the Palatinate, Bismarck refused to give his consent and informed Bavaria, who controlled the Palatinate, so that when war did come in 1870, Bavaria and the southern German states joined Bismarck against France. When Napoleon proposed absorbing neutral Belgium, Bismarck informed Britain, the guarantor of Belgium's independence. This inflamed the British to the extent that her neutrality in the coming war was guaranteed. When Napoleon suggested purchasing Luxembourg from the king of Holland, Bismarck again turned it to his advantage by arousing indignation within Germany, and at an international conference Napoleon's proposal was turned down.

The immediate cause of the war arose out of the succession to the Spanish throne. In 1868 a revolution in Spain deposed Queen Isabella II, and the Cortes (Spain's parliament) offered the throne to Prince Leopold of Hohenzollern, a relative of William I. France, fearful of German influence south of the Pyrenees, demanded that Leopold should not accept. The crisis seemed to have passed when Leopold refused the offer, but the French were in a warlike mood and, with the greatest diplomatic folly, made a further demand that, in the future, a Hohenzollern prince would never accept the throne of Spain. The French ambassador was granted an interview with William I of Prussia, who was on holidays in the German spa of Ems. William would not give France such a guarantee and sent a telegram to Bismarck informing him of the incident.

Bismarck allowed a shortened version of the telegram to be published in the press, which gave the impression, in Germany, that the French had presented an ultimatum, and in France, that the king had insulted the French ambassador. Passions in both countries ran high, but especially in Paris, where crowds, demonstrating in the streets, were shouting 'On to Berlin'. Napoleon was ill and not inclined for battle, but he could not resist the national mood for war. France declared war on Prussia on 19 July 1870.

WAR

The French army was said to be ready 'down to the last gaiter button', equipped with a new bolt-action rifle, the *chassepot*, and a machine gun, the *mitrailleuse*. They also had experienced generals in MacMahon and Bazaine, while their emperor, Napoleon III, was a name to arouse and inspire all French people.

Nevertheless, French unpreparedness was soon evident. Supplies were inadequate and unevenly distributed. In some areas there was little or no ammunition for the guns, while elsewhere there was plenty of ammunition but no guns. Some units had too many officers; others had too few. The same was the case with soldiers and uniforms. Reservists were called up and ordered to report to their home depots, and not to the nearest military barracks, which caused confusion and delay. Finally, the railway system got choked up as civilian traffic continued despite the urgent need to rush troops to the front.

In contrast, the Prussian strategy moved with exemplary precision. All civilian traffic was stopped, while the commander in chief, Helmuth von Moltke, used the railway system to great effect in moving three German armies, totalling half a million troops, to the French frontier in record time.

Napoleon III, suffering from what later proved to be cancer of the stomach, personally took command of the French army. He planned to march towards the Rhine and invade Germany. But this only served to strengthen Bismarck's exhortation to all Germans to fight against France and to defend the threatened states along the Rhine. One French army under MacMahon, after winning a battle at Saarbrücken near the French border, went on to be defeated at the German frontier at Worth on 4 August. Two days later he was again defeated at Wissembourg and was forced to retreat. After encountering the Germans, a second French army under Bazaine was forced to seek refuge in the French fortress of Metz in Alsace. The Germans surrounded the city and fortress of Metz, thus 'locking up' a quarter of a million French troops.

Meanwhile Napoleon's army had joined up with MacMahon's, and they decided to march to Metz and relieve Bazaine and his troops.

Napoleon III (left) with Bismarck on the morning after the surrender of the French army at Sedan.

However, the Germans were prepared for them, and, under Moltke, led the French into a trap at the frontier fortress of Sedan. In the ensuing battle on 1–2 September, the two French armies under Napoleon and MacMahon were surrounded and forced to surrender. Twenty thousand Frenchmen were killed. The war was over. Napoleon abdicated and, following a short captivity under the Germans, was allowed to go into exile in England, where he died in 1873.

When news of the defeat at Sedan reached Paris, the National Assembly (parliament) met, and on 4 September proclaimed the Third Republic. It then formed an emergency provisional government under Léon Gambetta and decided to continue the war. The Germans followed up their victory at Sedan by forcing Bazaine and 180,000 men to surrender Metz on 27 October. The Germans were now free to march on Paris.

The siege of Paris

With the fall of Metz and the failure of Gambetta (who had left Paris in a balloon) to raise fresh armies to fight the invader, the provisional government knew that there was now no hope of victory. But the extreme republicans of Paris refused to accept defeat, and the Prussian troops intensified their siege of the city, which had begun on 23 September.

William I returns to Berlin in triumph as kaiser (emperor) of Germany.

Extreme hardship followed as food and fuel became scarce during the harsh winter of 1870–71. Finally, on 28 January 1871, starvation and not the Prussian guns made Paris surrender.

DECLARATION OF THE GERMAN EMPIRE

Ten days before the fall of Paris, the German empire had been proclaimed by the assembled German princes in the Hall of Mirrors at the Palace of Versailles. The southern German states, Württemberg, Bavaria, Baden and Hesse-Darmstadt, were given extra legal privileges (their own postal system and railways) to induce them to join. William I of Prussia accepted the crown as kaiser (emperor) of Germany:

> A choir consisting of men of the seventh, forty-seventh, and fifty-eighth regiments intoned the choral, 'Let all the world rejoice in the Lord . . .' A sermon was preached by the Reverend A. Rogge . . . and the Grand Duke of Baden stepped forth and exclaimed, 'Long Live His Majesty the Emperor.'

THE TREATY OF FRANKFURT 1871

Bismarck refused to negotiate with the provisional government and insisted that elections should be called for a new National Assembly. The elections in February 1871 returned a conservative assembly and Adolphe Thiers became premier of a republican administration.

The peace treaty between Germany and the new republican government, known as the Treaty of Frankfurt, was agreed to in February, but did not become public until May. Carried along on the tide of popular pressure and by the excitement aroused by a victory over the 'old enemy', Bismarck agreed to exact terms that were more harsh than he would have otherwise wished: (i) France had to pay a war indemnity of 5,000 million francs within three years; (ii) Germany would maintain an army of occupation in eastern France until such time as the indemnity was paid; (iii) in return for the French request to retain Belfort, the only part of the province of Alsace left to France, a triumphal march of German troops would be made through Paris; (iv) the north-eastern provinces of Alsace and Lorraine and the fortresses of Metz and Strasbourg were ceded to Germany (map, p.17).

The insistence on the acquisition of Alsace and Lorraine was inspired by national military and economic considerations. Over half the population of Alsace was German-speaking. The Vosges mountains would prove a better frontier than the river Rhine, and the iron ore of Lorraine would help the growth of German industrialisation, including her armaments. But the desire to take Alsace-Lorraine was also born of the need for a 'symbol of victory' over France, which would serve to unite the northern and the southern states in a new Germany. Nevertheless, the Germans underestimated the resentment that the French would feel at the loss of part of their national territory.

THE COMMUNE

The extreme republicans, imbued with the doctrines of Karl Marx, felt betrayed by the French government. The working classes of Paris regarded the capital as their sacred city of revolution, for it was here in 1789 that the great French Revolution had started. Their anger increased further when the results of the February election became known. More than 400 monarchists and only 150 republicans were elected, and this conservative chamber met at Bordeaux. Republican Paris was outraged and felt betrayed by the rest of France, especially since the head of the new government, Adolphe Thiers, was known to be unsympathetic to the working classes.

The new government's first task was to conclude a peace treaty with Germany, the terms of which were harsh and humiliating. But when the Parisians heard that a clause in the treaty allowed for a German triumphal march through the capital in return for France's retention of Belfort, they were infuriated. When the Assembly ratified the hated Treaty of Frankfurt, Paris again felt betrayed.

To make a bad situation worse, the Assembly continued to estrange itself from Paris by two further actions. First, it passed a decree that all debts and rents outstanding since the war must be paid within 48 hours. Secondly, the pay of 1.50 francs a day to the National Guard (who had defended Paris) was stopped. The combined effects of these two decrees dealt a heavy financial blow to the Parisian working and lower-middle classes. On 1 March the German troops held their triumphal march through the city. They were received with black flags, silent streets and a public day of mourning. When they left, bonfires were lit, and the pavements were scrubbed to purify the city. Then on 10 March the Assembly moved from Bordeaux; but because they feared the anger of the people of

Paris, they did not return to the capital, convening instead at Versailles.

The cumulative effects of these events created an insurrectionary mood. Thiers, feeling it necessary to show that his new government was master, sent troops into Paris on 18 March to recover 200 cannon, but they omitted to bring horses with which to tow away the guns. Huge crowds surrounded them; in the general riot, two generals were shot and mutilated and the regular troops deserted.

This incident made Thiers decide to take the city by force. On 26 March, the people of Paris elected a General Council of ninety members, known as the Paris Commune. This looked back to the Jacobin Paris Commune of 1793, which had helped to execute Louis XVI and had set up the first French Republic. The 1871 Commune therefore saw itself as part of a great tradition that would never betray the honour of Paris. It called for the setting up of local communes all over France to be run by the workers. In early April, government troops laid siege to Paris; their forces increased rapidly in number as Bismarck returned 400,000 French prisoners of war.

The second siege of Paris was much crueller than the first. The communard chief of police, Rigault, was bitterly anti-clerical, and rounded up many priests, including the Archbishop of Paris, who was shot. When the government troops began to enter Paris in May, the communards shot all prisoners and hostages. They also wreaked havoc on many of the city's most notable buildings, such as the Tuileries, the Hôtel de Ville and the Palais de Justice. The government troops were equally ferocious and had orders to shoot on sight women carrying bottles, since they might be used as petrol bombs. They also had orders to shoot communards who surrendered. The communards, knowing that no mercy would be given them, fought desperately. In 'Blood Week', 21–28 May, over 3,000 people, including 50 hostages, were killed.

When the fighting came to an end, the French government was victorious, but at a terrible price. More than 20,000 communards had been killed. The trials of other communards dragged on for five years and a further 13,000 were either imprisoned or sent to the French penal colony on Devil's Island off French Guiana. In one sense, Thiers had 'tamed' Paris, for never again did it attempt to decide the fate of France; but the scars remained on French society and politics. In addition to suffering a humiliating defeat at the hands of Bismarck, the French had to bear the shame of having fought each other in an almost primitive savagery.

Yet the Paris Commune's more lasting effects can be seen in the subsequent polarisation of society. The middle classes became more conservative and less sympathetic to the workers. On the other side, the workers became less moderate in their demands than they would otherwise have been. The trade union movement became more extreme and the labour movement split into various socialist factions. For these reasons, the class conflict was to become more bitter in France than in Germany or Britain, and Frenchmen began to close ranks only with the outbreak of war in 1914.

THE NEW BALANCE OF POWER

The Franco-Prussian war resulted in the creation of a federal empire of the German states. Capturing Alsace-Lorraine meant that Germany would benefit economically from the textiles of Alsace and the iron ore of Lorraine. Strategically, it meant that Germany now had a line of defence against France running through Strasbourg, Metz and the Vosges mountains. For France it meant the end of the Second Empire and the creation of the Third Republic, a republic that was born in the worst possible circumstances of defeat, humiliation and loss of territory. Moreover, it had led to a bitter civil war in Paris and ensuing class conflict in French politics. But most important of all, the Franco-Prussian War ensured that there could be no reconciliation between France and Germany after such a crushing defeat and the loss of the two north-eastern provinces, which included a population of one and a half million people, who continued to see themselves as French.

The German victory had upset the 'balance of power', that delicate equilibrium among European states. It now tilted dramatically in favour of the new Germany; but the manner in which it had been achieved was to determine Bismarck's diplomacy for the next twenty years (p.31).

The war brought repercussions elsewhere in Europe. When the French troops withdrew from Rome during the war, the Italian army, seizing the opportunity, invaded Rome, and papal rule came to an end. Rome became the capital of a united Italy; the Pope retired to the Vatican and refused to recognise the legitimacy of the Italian government. Relations between church and state in Italy remained troubled until eventually they were healed by the Lateran Treaty of 1929 (p.216).

The war also brought a decisive change in the attitude of the Hapsburg monarchy, who gave up all thoughts of revenge on Prussia and accepted the loss of Austrian influence over the southern German states. The way was thus opened for a reconciliation with Bismarck's Germany, for both empires were conservative and had an interest in maintaining the *status quo*.

Finally, the Franco-Prussian War convinced most leaders in Europe that a new age of materialism had dawned. Science and technology, symbolised in German munitions, railways and army efficiency, had triumphed. Soon other nations would seek to imitate the German example by building up large and efficient standing armies, and applying the fruits of technology to armaments production. The Franco-Prussian War had ushered in an age of 'armed peace'.

Study Assignments and Essays

1. *To what extent was the Franco-Prussian war dictated by the aims of Otto von Bismarck?*
2. *Treat of the main military engagements in the Franco-Prussian War.*
3. *Why were the French defeated in the Franco-Prussian War?*
4. *'The Treaty of Frankfurt made inevitable the permanent hostility of France and sowed the seeds of World War I.' Discuss.*
5. *'The Franco-Prussian War led to a new "balance of power" in Europe.' Discuss.*
6. *Write an essay on two of the following: (i) The Ems Telegram; (ii) Emperor Napoleon III as a military leader; (iii) The siege of Paris in 1870; (iv) The aims of the Paris Commune of 1871; (v) The significance of Alsace-Lorraine.*

The German Empire 1871 –1914 2

The nation did not recognise its saviour... he [Bismarck] had to save her by gripping her by the throat...

Johan Haller

THE CONSTITUTION

THE NEW German empire consisted of twenty-five states. In form it was a federation — each state continued to rule itself, except in certain matters reserved to the central (federal) government in Berlin. The federal government was responsible for relations with other countries, the conclusion of treaties, and the control of trade, banking, coinage and railways. It consisted of the kaiser, the chancellor, and two houses of parliament, the Bundesrat (Upper House) and the Reichstag (Lower House).

The kaiser was always to be the king of Prussia. He appointed the chancellor, and assembled and dismissed parliament; he was commander-in-chief of the armed forces and all laws had to receive his signature (together with the chancellor's) before they became effective.

The Bundesrat was made up of represen-

THE CONSTITUTION OF THE GERMAN EMPIRE

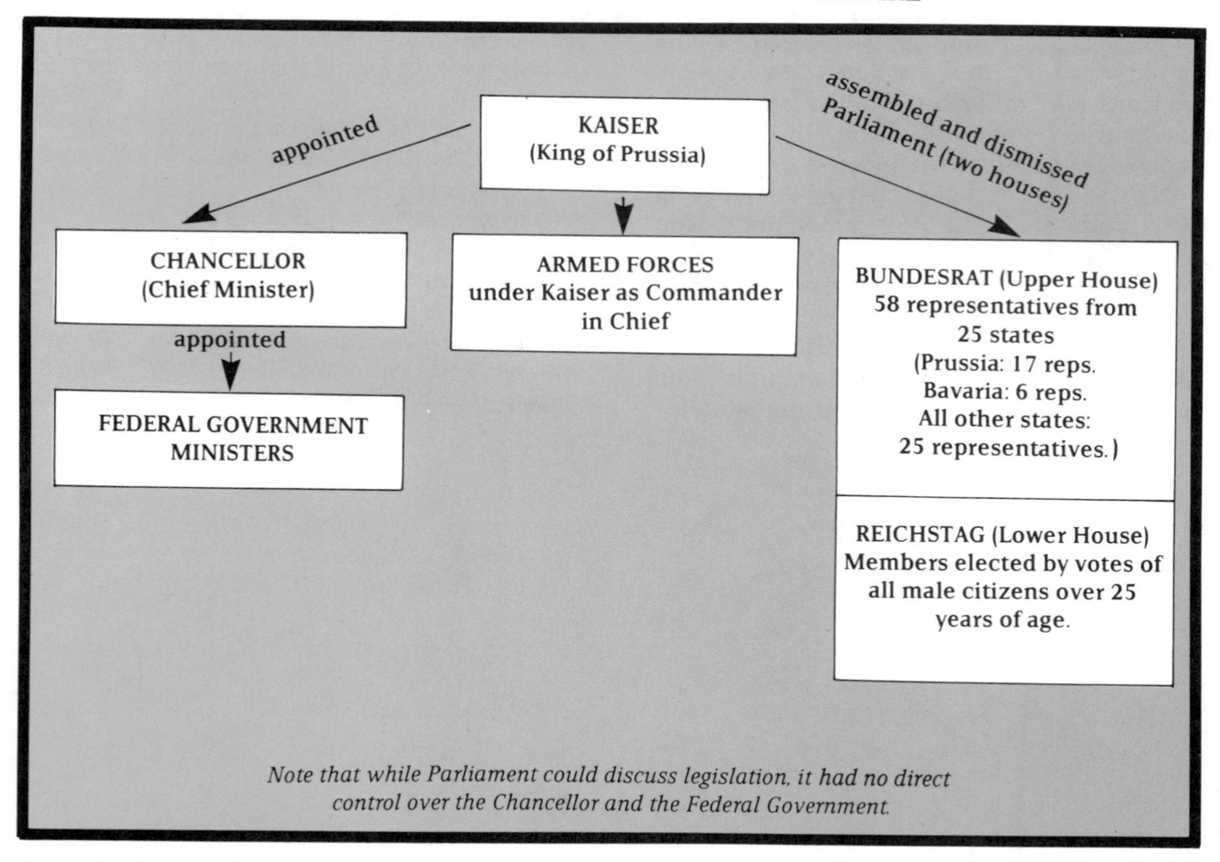

tatives from each of the twenty-five states; and their numbers were determined by each state's size and power. Prussia held seventeen of the fifty-eight representatives in the Bundesrat. The next largest group was Bavaria with six, while the majority of states had only one. Since a motion to alter the constitution could be defeated by fourteen votes, Prussia could always prevent constitutional change.

The Reichstag was composed of members elected by universal suffrage (males over twenty-five years of age), but, while it was democratically elected, the members had little role to play. Although they could introduce legislation, they could not force government ministers to resign, since these were responsible to the chancellor, not to the Reichstag. The chancellor (Otto von Bismarck from 1871 to 1890) was the emperor's chief minister. All other ministers were responsible to the chancellor, and he was answerable to the kaiser alone. Thus a strong chancellor, by manipulating the kaiser, could rule the empire single-handedly. This in effect is what Bismarck did for twenty years.

POLITICAL PARTIES

The political parties in the Reichstag fell into six main groups.

1. On the political right wing stood the *Conservatives*, who drew their support mainly from the Prussian landowning class and were closely associated with the Lutheran church. They believed in the solidarity of kingship and therefore advocated co-operation with the empires of Russia and Austria-Hungary and feared republicanism and socialism.
2. *The Free Conservatives* came next, and although they too had landowning support, they essentially represented the industrialists.
3. *The National Liberals* occupied the centre-right position. They drew their support from the protestant middle class, and were more nationalist than liberal.
4. In the middle came the *Centre Party*, comprising German catholics, and other catholic minorities, such as the Poles, and the French of Alsace-Lorraine. The party's membership came from different classes, ranging from the nobles of Bavaria to the peasants of the Rhineland and the industrial workers of the Ruhr.
5. The *Progressives* were on the left of centre and drew their support from the intelligentsia, small businessmen and artisans.
6. On the left, the *Social Democrats* were elected mainly by the rapidly growing industrial working class. Inspired by the writings of Karl Marx, they aimed to create a socialist state where private ownership would be abolished and all workers would share equally in the fruits of their labour.

ECONOMIC DEVELOPMENT

Agriculture

There were two different farming communities in Germany. East of the Elbe lay a region of large *junker* (landlord) estates, employing hired landless labourers. This was the great cereal-producing area. The *junkers* were very influential in German politics. In the west (especially the Rhineland) and the south lay a region populated by predominantly peasant farmers engaged in mixed agriculture and vine-growing.

After 1870 the drift from the land into industry was partially compensated for by imported casual labour from Poland and the Balkans. Between 1870 and 1914 agriculture progressed, mainly because of government assistance, increased mechanisation, and, after 1879, a policy of protection by high tariffs. The new sugar beet industry, especially, made remarkable progress: in 1870

Inside the Krupps steel works at Essen on the Ruhr about 1870.

production amounted to two-and-a-half million tons; by 1910 it had risen to nearly fourteen million tons. One important aspect of German agriculture was the establishment of rural co-operatives, which encouraged savings and provided credit. So successful were the co-operative banks that in 1876 the main German bank agreed to recognise them.

Industrialisation

The unification of Germany gave a tremendous boost to industrialisation. German manufacturers now had one large market at their disposal. The country's already large supplies of coal and iron were increased by the acquisition of Lorraine, while her cotton and textile industry, which flourished in the Rhineland and Lower Saxony, was supplemented by an already developed textile industry in Alsace.

Germany's greatest progress, however, occurred in the coal, metallurgical and engineering industries, while newer industries, such as chemicals and electrical engineering, also developed rapidly. In 1870 the country already had 27,000 kilometres of railway line — half in private hands, the rest owned by individual states. From then on, an imperial railway system was laid down, which effectively had been completed by 1914. Railway construction gave a tremendous boost to Germany's coal and iron industries: by 1914 she was producing 279 million tons of coal, while steel production, for the country's naval programme, had risen to 18.9 million tons. Industrial growth was greatly helped by the government's tariff policy, which sheltered industries from outside competition.

By 1914 Germany was, next to America, the world's greatest economic power. Her population had grown from fifty million to sixty-seven million, to make her Europe's most populous nation.

Trade

After 1870 exports rose rapidly, especially between 1900 and 1914. The bulk of German exports was concentrated on iron and steel products, particularly materials for railway construction in eastern Europe and South America. The products of her new chemical industries also found outlets overseas, especially in Britain and the United States.

BISMARCK'S DOMESTIC POLICIES

The Kulturkampf

The creation of the German empire in 1871 brought within its borders a population that was about one-third catholic, most of whom lived in the southern states, in the Polish area to the east, and in the west along the Rhine and in Alsace-Lorraine. Furthermore, the new empire, dominated by Lutheran Prussia, had been created at the expense of two catholic powers — Austria and France (map, p.17).

To protect their interests, German catholics organised themselves into a new political party, the Centre Party, which also attracted minorities, such as the Poles, the Danes and the French — all opposed to the empire. They demanded a firm guarantee of the freedom of the catholic church in the new Germany. Bismarck was irritated by their demands and the prospect of a strong opposition, which seemed to threaten his unfettered leadership. Moreover, he was aware of the international nature of the catholic church, and the danger that German catholics might take their direction from the papacy rather than from the imperial government.

At the first Vatican Council in 1870, Pope Pius IX proclaimed papal infallibility to be a doctrine of faith. This meant that catholics were bound to believe that when the Pope spoke *ex cathedra* on matters of faith or morals, he was divinely inspired and could not err. Bismarck and the Liberals maintained that the individual should give undivided loyalty to the state, and saw the papal pronouncement as a threat to this loyalty from a foreign ecclesiastical power. If German catholics accepted the Pope's prior authority, would this now come into conflict with the state's authority?

The declaration of papal infallibility divided catholics in Germany. Many German bishops and almost 50,000 of the laity refused to accept the doctrine and formed a group known as 'Old Catholics'. The Pope branded them as heretics, for which the punishment was excommunication. Many 'Old Catholics' held state appointments in education and the civil service and looked to the new government for support. The stage was thus set for what became known as the *Kulturkampf*, the struggle between two cultures — the international church and the national state.

Bismarck, suspicious of the power and attitude of the Centre Party, now saw an opportunity in the division caused by papal infallibility, to crush it. In 1872 the Jesuit order was banned and other religious groups were forbidden to teach in Germany. But the full attack did not come until the following year. In May 1873, with Bismarck's support, Adalbert Falk, Prussian minister for ecclesiastical affairs, introduced the May Laws.

1. Appointments of priests would be recognised only if they had graduated from a German university.
2. Papal jurisdiction over the catholic church in Prussia was ended, and a royal court was established with powers to dismiss unreliable clergy.

3. German education was taken out of the hands of the church and placed under state control.

4. The 'Pulpit Law' prohibited catholic clergy from raising political topics in their sermons.

5. Civil marriage was made compulsory, and was extended to all Germany in 1875.

Catholic reaction was swift. Pius IX cut off diplomatic relations with Berlin, declared the 'May Laws' null and void, and counselled a policy of civil disobedience. But Bismarck used the Pope's reaction as proof of the papacy's interference in German affairs; and, in justification for the *Kulturkampf*, the government fully enforced the laws in the face of catholic solidarity. By 1876 all bishops in Prussia were either in prison or in exile. By 1877, over one-third of the 4,600 catholic parishes were without a priest.

Despite its harshness, the *Kulturkampf* failed to break the catholic church or the Centre Party, which in 1871 held 57 out of 382 seats in the Reichstag. In the 1874 election it increased its representation to 90 seats.

Bismarck now realised that he had overreacted. Instead of uniting Germany against what he saw as foreign interference, he had succeeded only in dividing Germans. Not more than thirty out of some 10,000 priests had submitted; the Centre Party had grown stronger; the Prussian Lutheran conservatives had become critical of Bismarck's policies because the May Laws had also limited their influence; and his allies, the Liberals, disliked religious persecution.

When Pius IX died in 1878 and was replaced by the more conciliatory Leo XIII, Bismarck availed of the opportunity to end the struggle. Moreover, the Russian-Turkish War (p.104) and the growth of socialism at home were presenting far greater problems than the issue of German catholic loyalty. Bismarck came to realise that the Centre Party, instead of being an enemy, could replace the Liberals and help him in his fight against the rising tide of socialism. He shifted the blame for the worst excesses of the *Kulturkampf* onto his minister, Falk, and dismissed him in 1879.

Within the following ten years bishops were reinstated, all religious orders (except the Jesuits) were allowed to carry on their ministries, and the catholic church regained control of the education of its own priesthood. All that remained of the May Laws were state supervision of schools, the anti-Jesuit law (repealed in 1917) and compulsory civil marriage.

The Policy of Tariff Protection

Bismarck's retreat over the *Kulturkampf* coincided with a change in his policy towards the Liberals. In 1877 they had made it clear to him that unless they got a say in policy decisions, and perhaps a few ministerial appointments, they would not continue to support him in the Reichstag. Bismarck was prepared to give their leader, Rudolf von Bennigsen, the position of vice-chancellor, but since this was insufficient to satifsy the Liberals, in the following year they voted against Bismarck's anti-socialist legislation.

In 1879 Bismarck introduced trade protection. This abruptly ended the liberal alliance, a central policy of which was free trade. Bismarck's motives for this were partly financial and partly economic. Federal revenue was gathered partly from customs and partly from the contributions of the individual states. Bismarck disliked having to rely on the states since it gave them too much power. Now, with protectionism and the consequent increase in tariff revenues, he would become less dependent on them and thus reduce their power.

Secondly, there was increasing economic pressure to introduce tariff protection. By 1879 Russia, France and Austria-Hungary had introduced high tariffs in order to protect their own economies from free trade competition. Pressure for protection had come from German industrialists, afraid of competition from French textiles and British iron and steel.

Yet Bismarck was even more influenced by the German landowners' change of attitude. Before 1875, Germany had been an exporter of grain and the landowners had supported free trade. But by the late 1870s, with the advent of bigger and better ships, cheap grain from Canada and the United States was flooding the European market. Grain prices fell sharply and the landowners clamoured for protective tariffs. Bismarck, a Prussian landlord himself, was sympathetic to their interests and, in this alliance of 'steel and rye', saw an opportunity of gaining the support of the Conservative Party through the landlords. These two groups, combined with a more friendly Centre Party, would become his allies against the rising tide of socialism.

Bismarck and the Socialists

Germany's rapid industrialisation brought into being a large and growing number of workers who saw the country's wealth increasing while their share of it remained small. As an answer to their problems, the working classes turned towards socialism. Socialism preached not just reforms, but a complete reconstruction of the economy and society. In 1869 the various socialist groups in Germany joined together under the leadership of Ferdinand Lassalle to form the first real socialist party in Germany, the Social Democratic Party (SDP).

In 1875 the party met at Gotha and drew up a programme that condemned private property and advocated state ownership of all the means of production, distribution and exchange — industries, railways and banks. It denounced the profit motives of the capitalist economy and demanded that all profits should be shared among the workers. The Gotha manifesto contended that the socialists' loyalty was not to the state, which was the cause of their plight, but to the working classes of all countries.

In the 1877 election the SDP won twelve seats in the Reichstag, polling nine per cent of the votes. Bismarck's reaction was to see in the socialists a threat to the social order and stability of his newly created German empire. Perhaps his reaction was extreme, for with their level of support — drawn mainly from the growing industrial cities of Berlin, Essen and Duisburg – the socialists could hardly overthrow the state. But Bismarck had a horror of revolution and communism after the Paris Commune and the rise of nihilism in Russia (p.21). He became convinced that he must suppress the socialists before they had time to grow stronger. In May 1878 his opportunity came. Following two unsuccessful attempts to assassinate the Kaiser, Bismarck, using the events to blame the socialists, dissolved the Reichstag and fought the ensuing election on a campaign of anti-socialism. The electorate returned a conservative majority and Bismarck now was able to introduce an anti-socialist bill in the Reichstag:

> Associations which aim, by social-democratic, socialistic, or communistic agitation, at the destruction of the existing order of the state or society, are forbidden.

All socialist or communist associations, their meetings, offices and publications, could now be banned or closed down. In addition, the law empowered the government to forbid the right of assembly, to prohibit the collection of funds, and to expel or exile persons considered to be a danger to public peace.

In effect, these anti-socialist laws, which were extended four times over the following twelve years, drove the SDP underground. During the years of its enforcement, 1,350 publications were banned, 900 people were expelled and 1,500 imprisoned.

The law inevitably aroused intense bitterness and ultimately failed in its objective of crushing the socialist challenge. Socialists found several ways of evading the law through secret meetings; if they were expelled from one area, they agitated in the next area, thereby spreading socialist propaganda to regions it might not otherwise have reached. Exiled leaders continued to agitate from Switzerland, where the SDP's annual party congresses were held. Despite these repressive measures, the socialists kept on contesting elections and won more seats in the Reichstag. By 1890 their vote had trebled, and by 1912 the SDP had become the largest party in the Reichstag (p.36).

But Bismarck was too clever a politician to create martyrs, who would be counterproductive to his policy. Realising that the existence of genuine hardship among the working class had contributed to the growth of socialism, he decided that it might be more effective to try to kill it by kindness. He therefore determined to implement the more moderate aspects of the socialist programme. This, he hoped, would dampen the SDP's revolutionary ardour and demonstrate that the condition of the worker could be better served through peaceful persuasion in parliament than through violent agitation outside.

Having given a lead to Europe with manhood suffrage, Bismarck now made innovations in the field of social security. Laws were passed to protect workers against the three major threats to their social livelihood: sickness, accident and old age or incapacity. In 1883 a law introduced compulsory health insurance for wage-earners; two-thirds of the cost was to be borne by contributions from the workers themselves and one-third by the employers. The second law in 1884 introduced compulsory accident insurance. Bismarck intended that the government would contribute towards the cost as a demonstration of goodwill, but since the Liberals opposed the idea in the Reichstag, the employers had to bear the full cost. The third law in 1889 introduced old-age pensions at seventy years, and disability pensions for workers who were permanently incapacitated. Workers, employers and the government contributed to its cost.

Although these laws were the first of their kind in Europe and formed the foundation of the modern welfare state, they failed to allay socialist hostility since their practical value did not become apparent until some years later. Socialists believed that their interests would be better served if Bismarck eased the restrictions on trade unions so that they could freely bargain for a living wage. They also held that government intervention would be more appreciated if it was directed towards improving working conditions in the factories. Bismarck was not prepared to act on this issue and factory legislation had to await his departure from office in 1890 (p. 34).

The Problem of Minorities

The building of a strong Prussia under Frederick the Great in the eighteenth century, and of a united German empire by Bismarck's three wars in the nineteenth century, had created several national minorities in the new Germany. In North Schleswig the Danish population had been promised a plebiscite to determine whether they wished to remain within Germany or return to Denmark. Bismarck never fulfilled his promise, the result being the permanent opposition of the Danes of North Schleswig and poor relations between Germany and Denmark (map, p.17).

A large Polish population existed in the east of the new empire. Bismarck particularly disliked the Poles, not only because he regarded Slavs as inferior to Germans, but also because they were catholic and had opposed him during the *Kulturkampf* (p.27). Bismarck hoped to crush the Poles by depriving them of their natural leaders, who were members of the nobility or the church. The catholic primate, Cardinal Ledochowski, was imprisoned for alleged sedition in 1874 and his See was kept vacant for twelve years. The Polish landlords were deprived of their estates on every possible pretext and a fund was set up by the government to buy up these estates and transfer them to German ownership.

The remaining parts of Poland were within the borders of the Russian and Austro-Hungarian empires, and since conditions in these empires were extremely harsh, many Poles migrated into German-Poland. In 1886, Bismarck, alarmed by the large increase in the Polish population, expelled 34,000 Poles. In an effort to kill their national feeling, their language was suppressed and German became the language of education in schools. Despite these measures, the Poles retained their identity and eventually gained their independence by the Treaty of Versailles in 1919 (p.181).

But the most important minority problem arose from Germany's acquisition of Alsace-Lorraine following the Franco-Prussian War of 1870 (p.21). Of its population of one-and-a-half million, three-quarters were catholics who had opposed the *Kulturkampf*. Bismarck viewed this racial and religious minority with deep apprehension. Moreover, he believed that, given the opportunity, France would strike back in a war of revenge and attempt to recover the two lost provinces. To prevent this, Bismarck's foreign policy was tailored to keep France in isolation, not allowing her to gain allies for a war of retaliation (p.32).

The French minority of Alsace-Lorraine dictated Bismarck's diplomacy for the twenty years of his rule as chancellor. In addition to his foreign policy, Bismarck hoped to contain the problem domestically. Because Alsace-Lorraine was not given the status of a federal state within the German empire, it was not entitled to any representation in the Bundesrat (p.24). It was merely a province under the direct rule of a governor, who represented the emperor. The Germans monopolised the civil service posts and permanently stationed a large garrison of German troops in the province. All this served to confirm a feeling of subordination in the people of Alsace-Lorraine, and in the period up to 1914, some 400,000 citizens emigrated into the French Republic.

In 1874 Bismarck had given Alsace-Lorraine the right to elect deputies to the Reichstag and it continued to send fifteen deputies there, who joined with other national minorities in forming a group that held nearly ten per cent of the seats. This group was continually hostile to Bismarck.

BISMARCK'S FOREIGN POLICY

Dreikaiserbund

The emergence of the German empire changed the balance of power in Europe. The general reaction to this new state of affairs was unfavourable. France, implacably hostile, was determined to recover the lost provinces of Alsace-Lorraine. Britain feared for the safety of Belgium and Holland. Tsarist Russia was nervous about Bismarck's intentions in the Baltic region. But the fears of the great powers were unfounded. Bismarck had no territorial ambitions. 'Germany', he said, 'was a satisfied power.' He had made Germany great by war; now he intended to keep her great by peace.

Because of Germany's geographic position, she was particularly vulnerable to a two-front attack from France and Russia, or from a naval blockade by Britain. Recognising that France was likely to remain permanently antagonistic, Bismarck geared all his foreign relations towards keeping her in isolation. The best way of achieving this was for Germany to remain friendly with every other European power. Since Britain was pursuing a policy of non-entanglement in European affairs and Italy was a weak power, only Russia and Austria-Hungary remained.

In 1872 Bismarck brought the emperors of Germany, Austria-Hungary and Russia together in Berlin to show their common friendship. All three empires, ruled by monarchs, were conservative and undemocratic, regarding republicanism and socialism as their common enemies. In 1873 the League of the Three Emperors or *Dreikaiserbund* was formed. It was not a formal military alliance, merely a statement of common interests and a promise to consult each other on matters of European importance.

It seemed as if Bismarck had ensured the conservative stability of Europe with the *Dreikaiserbund*; but there was one problem. The two other members of the League had a conflict of interest in the Balkans (p.103). This came to a head following the Treaty of San Stefano (1878) whereby Russia had secured the creation of a new state of Bulgaria at the expense of Turkish possessions in the Balkans. Austria-Hungary, fearing the increase of Russian influence in the Balkans, which might encourage her own Slav subjects to rebel, was not prepared to accept the situation. Furthermore, Britain, always suspicious of any Russian advance towards the Mediterranean, was preparing for war.

In these conditions, Bismarck's diplomacy can be seen at its best. Since Bismarck and Germany had no ambition or interest in the Balkans, he realised that a war between the powers would put an end to German security. First, it would destroy the *Dreikaiserbund*, on which the peace of Europe rested. Secondly, in any war involving Russia, Austria-Hungary or Britain, France might offer her services to one side or the other in return for support in a war of revenge against Germany.

Bismarck acted quickly and decisively: he offered himself as an 'honest broker' and suggested that a Congress be held in Berlin to settle the problem (p.107). Although the problem was solved (temporarily) at Berlin in 1878, agreement was reached only because Russia had been outmanoeuvred by the other powers. Russia's resentment at having lost her gains in the Balkans was especially directed against Austria-Hungary and Germany.

This was a serious blow to the *Dreikaiserbund*, and to Bismarck's policy of keeping the peace in Europe, and France in isolation. The German chancellor believed that, sooner or later, Russia would again venture into the Balkans in accordance with her policy of extending her influence to the Mediterranean. He believed that Russian policy was a threat to peace, as a letter he wrote to the king of Bavaria in September 1879 reveals:

> I cannot resist the conclusion that in the future, perhaps even in the near future, the peace is threatened by Russia and Russia alone.

In this letter, Bismarck went on to argue that, while trying to preserve the *Dreikaiserbund*, a closer alliance with Austria-Hungary was necessary. One month later, in October 1879, a secret Dual Alliance was signed.

Alliances

The principal clause of this Dual Alliance stated:

> Should, contrary to their hope, and against the loyal desire of the two High Contracting Parties, one of the two Empires be attacked by Russia, the High Contracting Parties are bound to come to the assistance one of the other with the whole war strength of their Empires.

Another clause stated that if either empire was attacked by a power *other than* Russia (such as France), the empire that was not being attacked would remain neutral.

In 1882 the Dual Alliance was expanded into a Triple Alliance with the inclusion of Italy (p.76). In this new alliance, which again was secret, Germany and Austria-Hungary promised that:

> In case Italy . . . should be attacked by France for any reason whatsoever, the two other Contracting Parties shall be bound to lend help and assistance with all their forces. . . . The same obligation shall devolve upon Italy in case of any

aggression without direct provocation by France against Germany.

Bismarck never really put any faith in the inclusion of Italy because he did not regard her as a major power (p.76); nevertheless, Italy's inclusion effectively kept her away from an alliance with France.

The Reinsurance Treaty

Alexander II of Russia was assassinated in March 1881 and his successor, Alexander III, was anxious to reach better relations with Germany. In June 1881 Germany, Russia and Austria-Hungary agreed on a new *Dreikaiserbund* for three years. By its terms, which were secret at the time, it was agreed that if any one of the three became involved in a war with a fourth power, the others would remain neutral. This agreement pleased both Russia and Germany. Since Russia might be at war with Britain over the Balkans, she had now ensured German neutrality; and if Germany found herself at war with France, the Russians could not come to France's aid.

The *Dreikaiserbund* survived its three-year agreement, and in 1884 was renewed for a further three years. By the time it again came up for renewal in 1887, problems had arisen between Russia and Germany. In 1886 the Bulgarians ousted their king, Prince Alexander of Battenberg, a cousin of the tsar. To make matters worse, the Bulgarians offered the throne to a German, Prince Ferdinand of Saxe-Coburg. He was naturally acceptable to Germany and Austria-Hungary, but Russia refused to recognise his election. Thus, when the *Dreikaiserbund* came up for renewal in 1887, Russia refused to sign it. Bismarck was alarmed because an unfriendly Russia might find an ally in France and destroy his entire diplomacy. He therefore invited the tsar to Berlin.

Following discussions, Germany and Russia signed a secret Reinsurance Treaty. By its terms, the two nations agreed to stay neutral if either of them was at war with a third power. However, this guarantee of neutrality would not apply to Germany if Russia attacked Austria-Hungary, nor to Russia if Germany attacked France.

The Reinsurance Treaty therefore did not contradict Germany's obligations to Austria-Hungary under the terms of the Dual Alliance. In fact, Bismarck placed little confidence in the treaty, but he hoped that it would serve its purpose in keeping Russia away from France. However, Bismarck's tariff policies were severely restricting Russian exports of grain to Germany. Then when Bismarck refused to grant credit to Russia, which was badly needed for Russian industrialisation, the Russians turned to French bankers and were given financial help. Thus began an 'economic alliance' between Russia and France, which, after Bismarck's dismissal from office in 1890, turned into a formal alliance (p.117).

Colonial Policy

Bismarck had declared on several occasions that Germany had no interest in overseas expansion. He regarded Germany as a continental power and believed that the acquisition of colonies could easily disturb the delicate equilibrium he had established. Above all, colonies meant having a navy to protect them; and Bismarck fully realised that a German navy would arouse Britain's hostility since Britain had always regarded her own naval supremacy as the cornerstone of her security. Yet even Bismarck was unable to resist the public pressure caused by the general fever of imperialism that caught the imagination of Europeans in the 1880s (p.92).

In 1882 the German Colonial Society was founded to encourage overseas acquisitions. It received support from industrialists, merchants, missionaries and adventurers, each with separate motives, but all desirous of government support for colonial expansion. In 1883 an area known as German Southwest Africa (now Namibia) was declared a German protectorate. The following year Togo and the Cameroons became German colonies. In 1885 German East Africa (now Tanzania) was taken over. The feared confrontation with Britain did not materialise, and this fact prompted Bismarck to allow expansion in New Guinea and the Marshall Islands (maps, p.88 and p.97).

The colonies were a mixed blessing. Because of the unsuitable climate of Africa, there was very little emigration from Germany to her newly won colonies. At heart, Bismarck had no real interest in overseas colonies and, although they later proved to be a valuable source of raw materials, he contended that the cost of maintaining them was too high.

THE FALL OF BISMARCK

Bismarck's actual position of power stemmed from the fact that William I had given him a free hand. When the kaiser died at the age of 91 in March 1888, his successor, Frederick III, was already ill with cancer of the throat. He died in June and was succeeded by his 29-year-old son, William II.

The new kaiser had no intention of allowing Bismarck a free rein and from the beginning had it in mind to dismiss him. 'I will give the old man six months' breathing space, then I will rule myself,' he said to his friends.

The excuse came in 1890 when the old chancellor and the young kaiser clashed over the treatment of the socialists and the direction of German foreign policy. The anti-socialist law was now due for renewal and Bismarck wished to make it permanent, but he was opposed in the Reichstag by the Liberals and the Free Conservatives. In a stormy interview the kaiser, who wished to be known as 'the poor man's emperor', disagreed with him. To exacerbate the situation, the kaiser also opposed the renewal of the Reinsurance Treaty with Russia, which Bismarck desired. Instead, the kaiser proposed an alliance with Britain, where his grandmother, Queen Victoria, was monarch. Bismarck enraged the kaiser when he showed him a letter from the tsar of Russia wherein William was referred to as *'un garçon mal élevé et de mauvaise foi'* ('a bad-mannered youngster and not to be trusted'). The kaiser immediately demanded Bismarck's resignation. The career of the Iron Chancellor was brought to an end.

Bismarck returned to his estates at Friedrichsruh, but continued to entertain hopes of a recall to Berlin. When this did not materialise, he spent the rest of his days writing his memoirs and bitterly criticising William and his chancellors.

GERMANY UNDER KAISER WILLIAM II

With the fall of Bismarck, German domestic policies became less stable. Subsequent chancellors did not have Bismarck's ability, and the kaiser continually interfered in matters of state. William's next chancellor was General Georg Leo von Caprivi. He was a man of exceptional integrity but lacked political experience. The first problem to be tackled was the question of socialism. In 1891 the Social Democrats formally adopted Marxist theory, although in practice they were willing to work through parliament for the gradual dissolution of capitalism by peaceful means.

William hoped to turn the workers away from socialism by introducing a number of labour laws. Hours of work were reduced for women and children. Sundays were decreed to be a workers' holiday, and factory inspection was made more effective. Between 1892 and 1894 tariffs were lowered on imported foods, which greatly benefited workers. But despite these measures, the Social Democrats continued to grow, and by 1912 they formed the largest party in the Reichstag (p.36).

The Chancellorship of Hohenlohe 1894–1900

In 1894 Caprivi resigned when the Reichstag rejected an anti-socialist bill that he had introduced at William's behest. His successor was Chlodwig, Prince of Hohenlohe-Schillingsfürst, a Bavarian catholic who had a good relationship with William. However, at 75 years of age, and not having the temperament for argument in the Reichstag, his period in office saw a further decline in the chancellorship's authority, as William came more and more to direct government. All appointments, all bills, all diplomatic gestures, were made on the kaiser's orders. Statesmen who opposed him were eased out of office and replaced with subservient men of his own choice.

By 1897, William's personal rule was total. German nationalism and imperialism came to dominate his thinking, and three groups became increasingly significant. (i) The Colonial Society, founded in 1882 but not influential under Bismarck, now came to the fore and helped to create an atmosphere conducive to William's claim that Germany required 'a place in the sun'. (ii) The Pan-German League, founded in 1890, made a significant contribution to the development of German *Weltpolitik* (p.118). The activities of the League created distrust among other European powers, especially when it was backed by William's remarks. The Pan-German League not only advocated a fair share of colonies for Germany, but expansion in Europe as well. It especially advocated the incorporation of the German-speaking areas of the Hapsburg empire. It was believed that on the death of Emperor Franz Joseph (70 years old in 1900) the multiracial empire would break up and the German provinces would then unite into a *Grossdeutschland* or Greater Germany. (iii) The Navy League, founded in 1898, was used to convince the German people of the necessity for a large navy. It was an idea dear to William's heart, but he failed to recognise the repercussions that would follow the building of a German navy (p.118).

Bismarck (left) with the new Kaiser, William II.

The Chancellorship of Bülow 1900–09

In 1900 Hohenlohe resigned; he had come to realise that his authority was purely cosmetic. He was succeeded by Count Bernhard von Bülow, whose main desire was to stay in power by appealing to the kaiser's vanity. In 1906 Bülow arranged a coalition of conservatives, liberals and progressives which opposed the catholic Centre Party and the Social Democrats. However, this 'Bülow bloc' was compelled to take cognisance of the opposition. Concessions were made to the workers and individual Jesuits were allowed to work again in Germany (p.27).

In 1908 Bülow faced a humiliating crisis which brought about his downfall. In October the London *Daily Telegraph* published an article in which the kaiser claimed to have given the British the military plan that had won the Boer War (p.93). Bülow, who knew of the article before its publication, was obliged by

William II reviewing the troops outside Berlin about 1895.

the Reichstag to guarantee that in future the kaiser would be more prudent. Such a blow to the kaiser's vanity was enough to make him decide on Bülow's downfall. The opportunity arose in June 1909 when Bülow's proposal for an inheritance tax, to pay for increased expenditure on social reform and the armed forces, was defeated in the Reichstag. Bülow, knowing that the kaiser was not going to save him, resigned.

The Chancellorship of Bethmann-Hollweg 1909–14

The kaiser's fourth chancellor was Theobald von Bethmann-Hollweg. In 1911 he drafted a new constitution for Alsace-Lorraine, which gave the two provinces a certain degree of local autonomy. Yet, despite this, the great majority of the provinces' French population remained opposed to their incorporation into the German empire. In 1913 a Finance Law, to pay for army increases, imposed a levy on property and income. This tax was made as a concession to the socialists and fell heavily on the rich. But despite this, the rise of socialism continued, and many came to believe that only a strong monarchy and German patriotism could prevent the left from assuming power. Thus, the instability of German society affected her foreign policy in the pre-war years (p.121).

Study Assignments and Essays

1. *'Bismarck's constitution was a sham.' Do you agree?*
2. *'German economic development after 1871 was an unprecedented achievement.' Treat of the main features of Germany's economic development and analyse the factors that made it possible.*
3. *'Bismarck's domestic policies were essentially*

dictated by the need for German security.' Discuss.
4. 'The Dreikaiserbund *was ultimately doomed to failure.' Do you agree?*
5. Consider the following: (i) 'The Triple Alliance was purely defensive'; (ii) 'The Reinsurance Treaty was a contradiction.'

6. Write an essay on two of the following: (i) The origin and results of the Kulturkampf; *(ii) The role of the Centre Party in German affairs; (iii) Bismarck's social record; (iv) Bismarck's colonial policy; (v) The fate of Alsace-Lorraine within the German empire.*

The French Third Republic 1871–1914

3

History with us has become a sort of permanent Civil War. It teaches us to hate one another.

Fustel de Coulanges,
French historian 1830–89.

THE NATIONAL Assembly, elected in February 1871 to conclude peace terms with Prussia, was in favour of making France a monarchy. Four hundred of its six hundred and fifty deputies were monarchists, but they could not agree upon a king. One faction supported the Bourbon, the Comte de Chambord; another supported the Orléanist, the Comte de Paris. The ancestors of both these men had occupied the throne of France. (The last Bourbon king, Charles X, had been replaced, following the revolution of 1830, by the Orléanist, Louis Philippe.)

Adolphe Thiers, president of the Provisional Republic, reminded the Assembly: 'There is only one throne of France and two men cannot sit on it.' The failure of the monarchists to agree played into the hands of the minority who wanted a republic. Eventually a majority of deputies were won over to the idea of a republic, believing it to be the form of government that would least divide their fellow countrymen. Accordingly, in January 1875 the Assembly voted for the Third Republic by a majority of one vote.

The republic's constitution provided for a president, a Senate and a Chamber of Deputies. The president was to be elected for a seven-year term of office by the Senate and Chamber acting together. The Senate consisted of 400 members, all of whom had to be over forty years of age. There were seventy-five life members elected by the National Assembly, while the remainder were elected for a nine-year term. Each commune,

CONSTITUTION OF THE THIRD FRENCH REPUBLIC

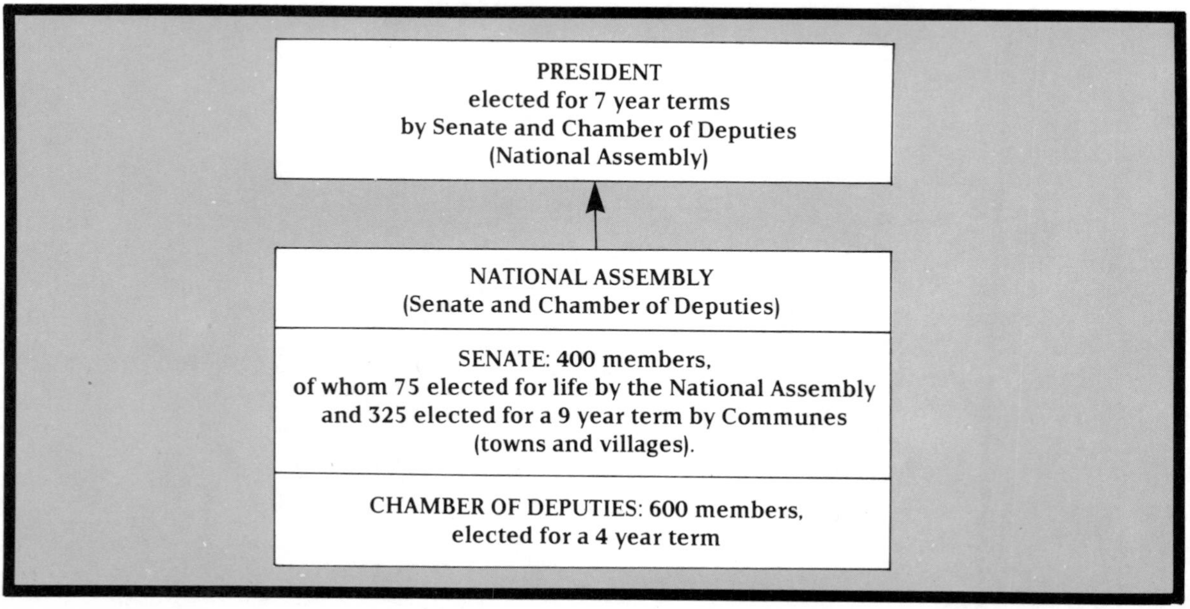

PRESIDENT
elected for 7 year terms
by Senate and Chamber of Deputies
(National Assembly)

↑

NATIONAL ASSEMBLY
(Senate and Chamber of Deputies)

SENATE: 400 members,
of whom 75 elected for life by the National Assembly
and 325 elected for a 9 year term by Communes
(towns and villages).

CHAMBER OF DEPUTIES: 600 members,
elected for a 4 year term

irrespective of population, elected one member. This meant that Senate membership was weighted in favour of the conservative rural areas, as opposed to the more radical cities and towns. The Chamber consisted of 600 members, each of whom had to be over twenty-five years of age; they were elected for a four-year term. The constitution, born in the most inauspicious circumstances, lasted for sixty-five years until it was destroyed by Hitler in 1940 (p.248).

POLITICS

During the 1870s the main political struggle in France was between republicans and monarchists.

When the battle had been won for a republic rather than a monarchy, the republicans split into two camps. Léon Gambetta and Jules Ferry led the conservative group, known as the Opportunists. Georges Clemenceau led another group, more inclined to reform, who were called the Radicals. Both Opportunists and Radicals appealed essentially to the peasantry and to the lower middle classes. On the right lay the various monarchist groups and the Bonapartists. On the left the socialists sought the support of the three million French industrial workers.

But the socialists too were fragmented. Some were willing to work within the system and fight for reforms. Others believed in a Marxist revolution and regarded those working through the Assembly as traitors to the cause of labour. Still others (the Syndicalists) saw change coming through the trade union weapon of strike action.

These divisions in French politics made political progress almost impossible. No single group could gain sufficient support and a shifting panorama of temporary coalitions dominated political life. Moreover, since the Assembly could be dissolved only every four years, governments could break up at will, without causing a general election. Thus, the system itself helped to promote a certain irresponsibility among deputies and parties, and the average life of governments up to 1914 was only about ten months.

Georges Clemenceau, leader of the Radicals and later a supporter of Dreyfus's attempts to clear his name.

SYMPTOMS OF INSTABILITY

By the mid-1880s republicans had become more confident about the future of the Third Republic. Yet a great deal of discontent remained, which came to a head during three crises that rocked the republic to its foundations: the Boulanger Crisis, the Panama Scandal, and the Dreyfus Affair.

The Boulanger Crisis

In 1886 General Georges Boulanger was appointed minister for war and was given the task of remodelling the army by bringing in universal conscription and purging it of monarchist army officers. Boulanger also made fighting speeches against Bismarck's Germany. These captured the imagination of the nationalists, who saw in him a leader who could revenge the defeat of 1870; they began to call him 'General Revanche' (Revenge). Yet many moderates were worried about Boulanger's recklessness and, following a change of government in 1887, he was dismissed.

Out of office, Boulanger became the darling of the discontented. Support for him began to grow and he was persuaded to stand for election in Paris in 1889. When he won, crowds surged into the streets shouting 'to the Elysée'. It seemed that with Paris behind him, Boulanger could take command as a dictator, but at the last moment, his courage failed him. When the government began legal proceedings against him for treason, Boulanger, fearing arrest, fled to Brussels. Two years later, when his mistress died of cancer, Boulanger shot himself and died on his lover's grave.

Though Boulangism had ended as a farce, it had been a powerful force and had shown the level of discontent that still existed against the Republic. The right had hoped to use Boulanger to destroy the Republic and avenge the defeat of 1870, while the left had hoped that he would better their economic and social conditions.

The Panama Scandal

No sooner had the Boulanger Crisis ended, than a new example of political corruption came to light. Already in 1881 a French company had begun the construction of the Panama Canal to link the Atlantic and Pacific Oceans. Ferdinand de Lesseps, who had constructed the Suez Canal, and Gustave Eiffel, the builder of the Eiffel Tower, were the principal agents in the enterprise. However, the project ran into many difficulties. The mosquito-ridden swamps transmitted incurable yellow fever, killing over twenty thousand men, while the work of digging through miles of rock proved almost beyond the endurance of human labour. After a few years the Panama Canal Company ran into financial difficulties, and in 1888 the government authorised the issue of lottery bonds to finance the venture. However, not enough money was raised and in February 1889 the company went bankrupt. The project had to be abandoned and some 800,000 Frenchmen had lost money.

During the next few years the company and the lottery was decried as a swindle organised by Jews and politicians. The scandal finally broke when it was held that the company had bribed many deputies in order to get authorisation for the issue of the lottery bonds. It was further reported in an anti-Jewish paper, *La Libre Parole*, that two German Jews, Baron Jacques de Reinach and Cornelius Hertz, had been responsible for much of the bribery. De Reinach committed suicide and Hertz fled the country. The government was forced to set up a committee of inquiry and charges were brought against ten politicians, although only one was finally convicted. De Lesseps and his son were given five years' imprisonment, and Georges Clemenceau, whose newspaper had been financed by Hertz, was forced to withdraw from public life. The scandal created cynicism in many quarters, while the enemies of the Republic were convinced that the republican regime was incurably corrupt.

The immediate outcome was a swing to the socialists in the election of 1893, but its most important result was an increase in anti-Jewish feeling, which helped to create the climate for the third and most damaging crisis the Republic had to face.

The Dreyfus Affair

L'affaire Dreyfus developed in the army, which was largely right-wing and monarchist. In 1894 the intelligence service of the war office discovered that there had been a leakage of military information to the German embassy, and a Jewish military officer, Captain Alfred Dreyfus, was arrested for espionage. While the case was being heard by secret court martial, there was an outcry in the anti-Jewish press. Dreyfus was found guilty and, in January 1895, was sent to the French penal settlement on Devil's Island in French Guiana.

Dreyfus's family were convinced that he was being made a scapegoat by anti-Jewish officers and went to work to find evidence that would clear him. At the same time, and quite independently, an intelligence officer, Colonel Picquart, had come across conclusive evidence that the *bordereau* (memorandum) on which Dreyfus's conviction had been based was in fact written by another officer, Major Ferdinand Esterhazy. Picquart duly informed his superior officers. But, alarmed at the discredit that would follow upon an admission that military justice had erred, they told Picquart that 'fresh evidence' of Dreyfus's guilt had been obtained since the trial. When Picquart continued to insist that the case be re-opened, he was posted to North Africa. The 'fresh evidence' was in fact a forgery by Picquart's successor, Colonel Henry.

From Tunisia, Picquart was able to communicate his findings to the vice-president of the Senate and to the prime minister; but both were determined to avoid another scandal. By now, however, a growing 'Dreyfusard' party was in being, determined to work for a re-opening of the case. The novelist Émile Zola took up his cause, and Clemenceau, in a series of articles in *L'Aurore*, demanded that the truth be told.

To satisfy public opinion, Esterhazy was tried by secret court martial in January 1898. He was acquitted in a matter of minutes and was hailed as a hero by enthusiastic crowds. The government and the war office believed that this would be the end of the matter, but they were very much mistaken. Two days later Zola published an open letter to the president, entitled *J'accuse*. In it he accused a number of generals of deliberately procuring Dreyfus's guilt on the basis of a second document that was not given to the defence; Zola declared that the court martial had been ordered to acquit Esterhazy.

Zola's letter, described as a 'revolutionary act of incomparable power', roused passions to fever heat and forced all French people to take sides. For many citizens, Dreyfus's guilt or innocence became an article of faith. To the anti-semitic right, Dreyfus was the symbol of the eternal Jewish traitor. The nationalists, the patriots, the catholics, and all who believed in stability and social order saw the affair as a deliberate plot by international Jewry to discredit the army and throw France into confusion and disorder. To the left Dreyfus was the symbol of the denial of justice. For reasons of state, injustice had been tolerated and the rule of law violated. If this was not righted, no citizen could henceforth feel secure.

Zola was tried and condemned for slander, to the delight of the crowds shouting 'death to Zola and death to the Jews'. But in the summer of 1898, new and sensational developments occurred. A new minister for war, Louis Cavaignac, decided to establish Dreyfus's guilt by disclosing the evidence in the Chamber. His hope was that this 'proof' would defeat the Dreyfusards, but the opposite occurred. Colonel Henry, under questioning by Cavaignac, confessed to the forgery and on being sent to prison, committed suicide. Esterhazy, watching developments, quietly slipped out of the country to England, where he lived under an assumed name — Comte de Voilemont — until his death in 1923.

France was in an uproar. Strikes, demonstrations and plots continued until a new government, under Waldeck-Rousseau,

Dreyfus before the court martial at Rennes in 1899.

determined to restore public order and dispose of the Dreyfus affair as quickly as possible, ordered a retrial.

In August 1899 the new court martial of Dreyfus, which by now had aroused world-wide attention, began at Rennes. In September the verdict was announced: a majority (five of the seven judges) found Dreyfus guilty of 'intelligence with the enemy with attenuating circumstances' and sentenced him to ten years' detention. Most people had expected him to be acquitted and a wave of indignation met the verdict. Soon afterwards, however, the president pardoned Dreyfus and by the end of the year the government had secured an amnesty for all concerned, their main object being to end the affair once and for all. But the Dreyfusards were not satisfied and continued to agitate until 1906 when the verdict of 1899 was quashed, but no retrial was ordered. Instead, the Chamber passed a special resolution for Dreyfus's rehabilitation; he was decorated with the Legion of Honour and he and Picquart were both promoted in rank.

The Dreyfus Affair had dragged on for twelve years and at times had dominated French politics. Yet, although the educated classes were passionately aroused, the great mass of French people soon lost interest in a question beyond their understanding, tending to dismiss it as a soliders' and politicians' quarrel of no concern to them. Nonetheless, it was of profound importance for the development of French politics. The eventual triumph of the Dreyfusards meant that the Republic was to revert back to militant anti-clericalism. It resulted in a defeat for the right and the consequent ascendancy of radicalism, marking the re-emergence of old hatreds and divisions.

THE CATHOLIC CHURCH

Since the catholic church had invariably associated itself with the monarchists and the right, it was seen by the left as a rival for the people's allegiance. The Waldeck-Rousseau government (1899–1902), composed of republicans and socialists, was determined to smash the church's power.

The first step was to end the church's control of education, which, according to the government, was turning France's youth against the Republic and all it cherished. A start already had been made in the 1880s under the premiership of Jules Ferry when, in a series of enactments, religious instruction was forbidden in all public schools, and members of religious orders were forbidden to teach in them. But since there were relatively few public schools, these measures had little effect. Half of the boys, and almost all girls, attended catholic parochial schools. Then in 1891, the Assumptionists, the most anti-republican of all the religious orders, were dissolved. The same year, an Association Act was passed, which allowed only those religious orders authorised by parliament to continue in existence.

Matters might have ended there had not the catholic clericals campaigned so bitterly against the coalition government in the national election of 1902. This further infuriated the coalition, which won the election anyhow, and Waldeck-Rousseau was replaced as premier by the radical Émile Combes.

In June 1902, Combes closed down all primary schools for girls run by religious sisters. In July he gave the remaining 3,000 parochial schools eight days to shut down, and despite riots and opposition, they were closed.

Under the Association Act, fifty-four congregations had requested authorisation; Combes now urged parliament to reject their application. They were dissolved and many of the 20,000 clerics fled abroad. Finally, in July 1904, Combes completed the destruction of the religious orders with an Act that forbade them to teach in any school, whether it was controlled by them or not.

Combes then did battle with the Holy See. In 1904 the new Pope, Pius X, protested against the state visit of Émile Loubet, the French president, to the king of Italy. The Vatican did not recognise the new Italian kingdom and resented the fact that France did. Combes called the Pope's protest 'an intolerable interference into France's conduct of her foreign affairs', and recalled the French ambassador to the Holy See. The Chamber of Deputies almost unanimously supported him in passing a new law separating church and state. This law abrogated the Concordat of 1801 between Napoleon and Pope Pius VII, by which catholicism had been recognised as the state religion of France.

In 1905 the law was put into operation and the state took over all church property. Priests and bishops were removed from the state payroll and the handling of worship was given over to associations of laymen, called *associations culturelles*.

For a couple of years confusion reigned, until a more tolerant climate, under Aristide Briand, allowed for a compromise. Church buildings were given back to the clergy and the catholic hierarchy was allowed to resume its authority over church affairs. The republic had succeeded in curbing the church's power and position. Yet in one respect the church had gained: the separation of church and state freed it from government control and interference. Though church membership declined over the period, as evidenced by the drop in the number of baptisms, the rise in civil marriages and the fall-off in attendance at worship, thereafter it began to increase. Yet the scars of battle remained; many catholics resented what they termed state persecution, while the republicans still remained suspicious, if not hostile.

THE SOCIALISTS

The 1870s were years of economic depression in France and this increased support for the socialists. But the socialist left were far from united. Some were willing to work within the constitution for better conditions, others (the syndicalists) saw change coming through trade union activity, while the Marxists advocated a class revolution.

The problem for the socialists in the Chamber of Deputies was to provide a united front. Their leader was Jean Jaurès, who believed in destroying the capitalist system by peaceful revolution. The problem facing French socialists in the years before 1914 was essentially that facing all European socialists: work within the system and risk being branded as traitors, or work outside the system for its destruction.

Partly due to socialist pressure, the years between 1875 and 1914 witnessed many reforms that bettered the condition of the masses. In 1874 child labour was prohibited. In 1881 the introduction of tariffs helped to safeguard employment. The same decade also saw the legalisation of trade unions, the achievement of press freedom, and the improvement of wages and working conditions. The socialists were also in favour of educational reforms and the diminution of church authority (p.43).

The main period of reform came after 1900. This was mainly due to the advent of the Waldeck-Rousseau government, a left-wing coalition that included Millerand as minister for commerce, the first socialist in Europe to sit in government. This administration set up a department of labour, which made some progress towards a ten-hour day, and a Public Health Act allocated public money towards improving housing conditions. Despite these reforms, the Assembly continued to obstruct the passage of such worthwhile legislation as the introduction of income tax and old-age pensions until after 1910.

Outside the Assembly there were bitter industrial confrontations. In 1895 the trade unions banded together in the CGT (*Confédération Générale du Travail:* General Confederation of Labour) and adopted the tactics of the syndicalists. A series of 'class warfare' strikes began in 1906. The government brought out troops to break them, and strikers were drafted into the army reserves to be taught army discipline. Bitterness and unrest continued until the outbreak of war in 1914. The call for war against Germany provided a rallying cry for national unity. As the socialist leader, Jules Guesde, put it: 'When your house is on fire, it is no time for controversy. The only thing to do is to take a hand with the buckets.'

FOREIGN POLICY

The one burning issue in French foreign relations was the question of the loss of Alsace-Lorraine. As a constant reminder of this, the monument in Paris to Strasbourg (capital of Alsace) was solemnly draped in black. General Boulanger (p.40) had owed much of his support to his call for revenge against Germany; but it was much easier to talk of vengeance than to take it. France could never hope to defeat the new Germany on her own. Bismarck realised this and ensured that France would remain in diplomatic isolation for twenty years (p.31); he was aided in this by the fact that most powers in Europe were at best suspicious of French republicanism and all it stood for.

For some time after 1871, the French, encouraged by Bismarck, sought compensation in the pursuit of empire overseas. In 1881 Tunisia was seized under the government of Jules Ferry. But when Ferry lost office, his successors abandoned Egypt to the British. On his return to office in 1883, Ferry worked hard to lay the foundations of French control over Madagascar, French Congo and Indo-China (p.96). French colonial ambitions brought clashes with Italy over Tunisia (p.91), with Britain over the Sudan (p.90) and with Germany over Morocco (p.120).

With the fall of Bismarck and the new direction of German policy under Kaiser William II (p.117), it was possible for France to end her diplomatic isolation. First with Russia in a Dual Alliance (p.117), and then with Britain in a Triple Entente, France became part of a powerful group that seemed to encircle and threaten Germany (p.120).

Despite her great expansion overseas and the ending of her isolation, French foreign policy was never consistent or coherent. This was essentially due to the lack of continuity in government. Quick changes of administration handicapped both external and internal policy. In general, however, French foreign relations were more cautious than aggressive; France tried to avoid problems abroad, and, when they did occur, strove to settle them peacefully. Despite this, her overseas acquisitions were enormous and in 1914 her empire was second only to that of Britain. In addition, her empire helped to raise the prestige of the Republic, and provide an outlet for soldiers, missionaries and traders. In Europe, despite French talk, it never did seem likely that France would go to war simply to recover Alsace-Lorraine. And when the country did go to war in 1914, it was not in an offensive to recover the lost provinces, but because it had been provoked by German attack (p.125).

ECONOMIC DEVELOPMENT

The pattern of French agriculture was different from that prevailing in the rest of western Europe. A very large proportion of her slowly growing population remained on the land, which meant that farming continued to be of greater importance than industry. In 1900, 43 per cent of the population engaged in agriculture, compared with 35 per cent in Germany and 9 per cent in Britain. Farms tended to be small and the peasant was the dominant character in agriculture. Except on the large farms near Paris and on the vineyards in the Bordeaux district, there were hardly any landless labourers. The use of machinery did not increase perceptibly, because cheap migrant labour from Spain, Italy and Belgium was more economical for small-scale farming.

French industrial development in the nineteenth century was one of expectations never quite realised. In 1870, France was second only to Britain in industrial production; yet by 1914 she had not grown as rapidly as other continental countries and had been outstripped even by Russia in rate of industrial progress. This was not due to a lack of scientific or technological development —

indeed at times her growth was considerable — but defeat in the Franco-Prussian War of 1870, the payment of the indemnity to Germany, and the severity of the depression from 1882 onwards left France behind other European nations.

The loss of Alsace deprived France of a large textile industry, while the loss of Lorraine deprived her of phosphoric ore, essential for steel production. At times during the nineteenth century disease struck the silk industry and the vineyards. France also suffered from geographical limitations, i.e. the location of minerals remote from the centres of industry. Perhaps the biggest drawback was that the French population increased very slowly compared with the populations of Britain and Germany.

Despite these shortcomings, from about 1900 to the outbreak of war in 1914, French exports and foreign investments rose rapidly, although still not as fast as those of Britain and Germany. Her main exports consisted of fine quality manufactures, such as silks, wines and a great range of artistic goods. To her empire in North Africa and the Far East, France exported machinery, iron and steel products. But the basic problem confronting France's export drive was an overdependence on imports of raw materials, which made her exports less competitive than her European rivals.

CULTURAL ACHIEVEMENTS

Despite internal tensions and an inability to solve her many domestic problems, France's cultural achievements placed her foremost in Europe in art, letters and science.

In painting, especially, where the names of Cézanne, Degas, Gauguin, Manet, Monet and Renoir became household words, France made a revolutionary contribution. In 1874 the French impressionists held their first exhibition, which profoundly affected all subsequent painting. Such composers as Bizet, Debussy and Franck were equal to the best Europe had to offer. In literature, too, France led the field. Prose writers such as Maupassant and Zola, and poets such as Verlaine and Rimbaud ensured that France would remain the cultural centre of Europe. In science the discoveries of Louis Pasteur and the Curies made major contributions to biology, chemistry and physics. In the decades before 1914 Paris became the 'Athens of the West', attracting artists, poets and philosophers from all parts of the civilised world. For these reasons, the period from 1870 to 1914 has come to be regarded by many as *La Belle Époque*.

'Secret' by Renoir.

'The Boats' by Monet.

Study Assignments and Essays

1. Why and how did France become a republic following the collapse of the Second Empire?
2. 'The politics of republican France made impossible any degree of stable government.' Discuss.
3. Consider the following: (i) Boulangism was more a symptom than a cause; (ii) 'The Third Republic needed a strong leader.'
4. Treat of church-state conflict in the Third Republic.
5. 'The two success stories of the Third Republic were her colonial acquisitions and her cultural achievements.' Consider the truth of this statement.
6. Write an essay on two of the following: (i) The Panama Scandal; (ii) The Dreyfus Affair; (iii) The rise of socialism in France 1871–1914; (iv) Economic development in France 1871–1914; (v) French foreign policy 1871–1914.

Tsarist Russia 1855–1914

4

Much has been left in the world that must be destroyed by fire and iron . . .

Lenin

THE REIGN OF ALEXANDER II 1855–81

SINCE 1613 Russia had been ruled by the Romanov family. Russia had no parliament in the nineteenth century, there was pure autocracy, i.e. rule by one man, the tsar, helped by hand-picked ministers and an ever-increasing civil service.

The tsar ruled over a country backward in every respect in comparison with western Europe. Until 1861 the peasants, who made up about 80 per cent of the population, were serfs, the property of the landlord, for whom they had to work three days a week. The landowner had almost the power of life and death over the serf, who was regarded as a mere chattel to be bought, sold or beaten at his master's will.

Alexander II, known as the 'Tsar Liberator', came to the throne on the death of his father, Nicholas I, in 1855. He realised that conces-

TSARIST RUSSIA AND THE RUSSO-JAPANESE WAR, 1904–05

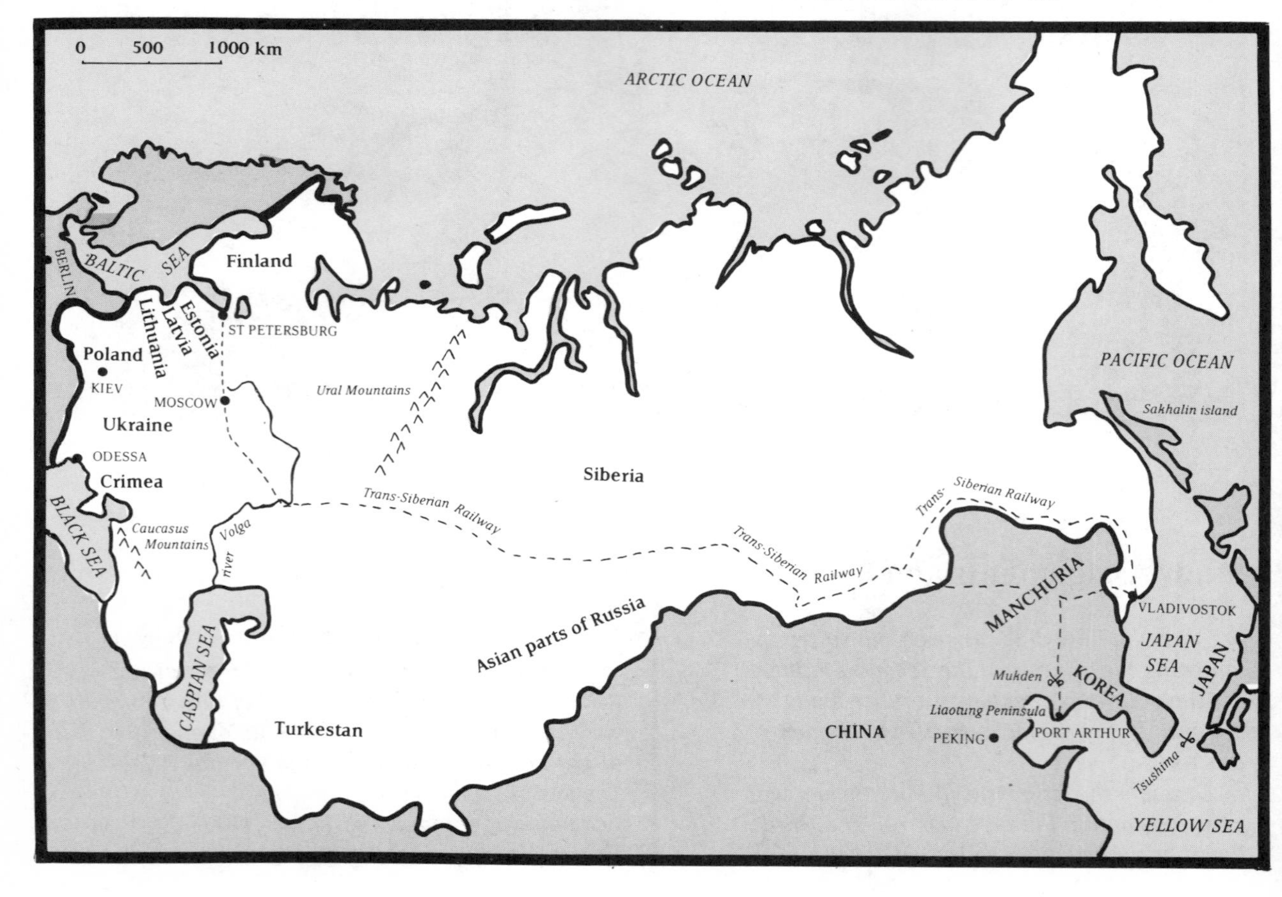

sions must be made. Serfdom, especially, must be abolished, for the Crimean War, in which Russia had just been beaten, seemed to show that a freeman was a better soldier than a serf. On the other hand, the soldier serfs had learnt that masters could be beaten.

The Emancipation of the Serfs 1861

Circumstances were favourable for tackling the peasant problem. The landlords of the fertile Ukraine, who were now entering the world market and exporting grain, discovered that free labour was more efficient than serf labour. Moreover, modern industry was making its first appearance in Russia and mobile labour was needed. It could not come from serfs, who were tied to the land, so in 1861 Alexander issued a decree abolishing serfdom. Legally the peasants were now free citizens and could buy land from their former owners. The government would advance 80 per cent of the money, which the peasants would have to repay over forty-nine years at the rate of 6.5 per cent per annum.

Emancipation was hailed with great rapture but it failed to conciliate the peasants, who had been convinced for centuries that, although they were not personally free, the land belonged to them. 'We are yours but the land is ours,' they said to the landlords. They failed to understand why they were now being called upon to pay for what they already owned. To make matters worse, not all the landlords agreed to sell their property, which meant that, in general, the peasants found themselves with less land to cultivate for themselves after emancipation than they had before. But even where the land was sold, it did not become their own property but was vested in the village *mir* (assembly), responsible to the government for repayments of the redemption debt.

Further Reforms

In 1864, a new system of local government was instituted. Locally elected councils (*zemstva*) took over the control of education, road construction, and public welfare. In the same year the legal system was reformed along western European lines. The courts were made public, trial by jury was instituted, judges were adequately paid to ensure their independence from bribery, and an updated code of laws was introduced.

In the 1870s the pace of reform began to slacken. The Paris Commune (p.21) and the rise of socialism in Bismarck's Germany (p.29), together with the advent of the populist *narodniki* at home, began to frighten Alexander. Instead he turned towards expansion in the Balkans, but this only brought him a diplomatic rebuff at the Congress of Berlin in 1878 (p.107).

The Narodniki

After emancipation of the serfs, some of the landed gentry, many of whom had been educated abroad, developed a curious 'guilt complex': a feeling that they were responsible for Russia's backwardness and poverty. They now swung in the opposite direction and began to idealise the peasant. Together with many university students, they put on peasant dress and, often to the peasants' bewilderment, went out into the countryside to help and teach them. This movement 'to the people' earned them the title *narodniki* (*narod* being the Russian word for 'people').

By 1874 several thousand *narodniki* had gone into the villages to convert the people to socialism. But most peasants were either hostile or uncomprehending and nothing concrete was achieved. Moreover, since the *narodniki* were very conspicuous, the *Okhrana* (the tsar's secret police) rounded up about 1,500 of them and put them on trial. These public trials gave the *narodniki* a greater opportunity to publicise their views. After one such trial in January 1878, a young woman, Vera Zasulich, shot the St Petersburg chief of police, General Trepov.

Alexander II 1855-81
" III 81-94
Nicholas II 94-1917 3 of them

The assassination of Tsar Alexander II in 1881.

This event marked the beginning of a new extreme wing, whose policy was assassination of figures in authority as the only means of action against a brutal autocracy. This group took the name 'People's Will' and, from 1879, made the assassination of the tsar their principal aim. Several attempts on his life failed, but on 1 March 1881 a bomb was thrown at the tsar's carriage as he was returning from a military parade. Alexander was unhurt, but got out of his carriage to enquire after the condition of those who had been injured. A second bomb was thrown that shattered both his legs and seriously mutilated his face and body. Alexander died soon afterwards.

The assassination and its timing were a tragic irony, since Alexander had set up a commission to investigate the causes of popular unrest and the means of alleviating it. The commission had proposed that an assembly of elected representatives from the *zemstva* should be convened to advise the tsar in the preparation of new legislation. Alexander had signed his approval of this proposal on the morning of his assassination. Although it would not have given Russia a constitution and parliament, it would have been a definite step in that direction.

THE REIGN OF ALEXANDER III 1881–94

Alexander II was succeeded by his son, Alexander III. The new tsar was convinced that even limited constitutional reform would make the situation worse, and was determined to crush all opposition. He was much influenced by his former tutor and advisor, Konstantin Pobedonostsev, who believed wholeheartedly in Romanov autocracy and despised western parliamentary democracy. Pobedonostsev contended that the real rulers in western democracies were not the voters but rather those who manipulated a naïve electorate to vote in a certain manner. In 1896 he wrote 'it is sad to think that even in Russia there are men who aspire to the establishment of this falsehood.'

Alexander gave the *Okhrana* additional powers. His father's assassins were hunted down and executed, and relentless war was waged on all terrorists. Censorship became stricter and the universities came under close scrutiny. Pobedonostsev used his authority as procurator of the Holy Synod (lay supervisor of the Orthodox church) to browbeat minority religions, especially the Jews. His position as procurator also gave him a voice in government, which he used to good effect in ensuring the supremacy of the autocracy and the silencing of all opposition.

Since the autocracy depended on the support of the land-owning nobility, steps were taken to strengthen their political and economic position. In 1885 the Nobles State Bank was established to provide credit for the nobility on very favourable terms. In 1890 Alexander passed a law that reduced the representation of the peasants in the *zemstvo* assemblies to 43 per cent. Thus, the nobility, having a 57 per cent majority, could veto any measure of which they disapproved.

The peasants were also brought under the closer supervision of the nobility by the appointment of land captains in each locality. These land captains, chosen from the nobility, had almost dictatorial powers over the peasants' communal life. They could cancel the decisions made in the village *mir*, add items of their choice to the agenda, and remove village elders from their posts if they were considered unreliable. Many land captains carried out their duties justly, but their appointment was a calculated attempt by the autocracy to keep the peasants in bondage, and made it more difficult for them to acquire the knowledge and practice of local self-government. The peasants themselves bitterly resented the system of land captains since it brought back in large degree the condition of tutelage they had known before their emancipation.

Alexander's repressive policies were also extended to the non-Russian peoples of his empire. As the empire had grown steadily outwards, it had incorporated many Asiatic peoples to the south and east, while in the European west, the empire included Finns, Poles, Lithuanians, Estonians, Latvians and Ukrainians (map, p.48).

In the nineteenth century, nationalist movements grew steadily in the European parts of the empire. Alexander's answer to the threat of nationalism among his non-Russian subjects was the policy known as 'Russification'. In effect this meant stamping out all traces of the native culture, such as language, religion and custom, and replacing it with Russian culture. In this way it was believed that these non-Russian peoples would lose their sense of national identity and become entirely Russian. Pobedonostsev exercised a baneful influence over Alexander since he was intensely hostile to Poles, Jews and minority religions. Russification was enforced with special harshness in the Polish part of the empire. The Polish language was banned in the schools and all teaching had to be carried out in Russian. In addition, Polish catholics were not permitted to hold any official office. The Finns and peoples of the Baltic provinces were also subjected to Russification, even though they had never given any significant evidence of disloyalty.

The European part of the Russian empire (especially Poland) contained a high percentage of Jews. They formed a more distinct group, with their own religion and customs, and were proving to be almost immune to Russification. Consequently Alexander singled them out for special attention, and anti-semitism became an active policy. A Jewish girl, Hessia Helfman, had been one of Alexander II's assassins. This fact now became the pretext for a wave of government-inspired pogroms (mass destruction of Jewish property and the killing of Jews) which began in the spring of 1881. 'One third of the Jews of Russia must die, one third emigrate, and one third assimilate,' said Pobedonostsev. In their policy of anti-semitism, the authorities could rely on support at two different levels. In government circles and among the dignitaries of the orthodox church, it was a natural attitude to view the Jews as the killers of Christ. At the level of the illiterate peasantry and among petty officials, there existed a crude class hatred of a thrifty minority who concerned themselves with money, and into whose pockets they believed all their savings vanished.

Some 215 pogroms took place, but although the authorities officially condemned the excesses, they did very little to stop them. In 1882 the 'May Laws' were passed, forbidding Jews to live or acquire property in rural areas. Instead they were to live in certain designated areas and in town ghettos. The ministry of war limited the number of Jews in the medical corps to five per cent, on the grounds that they lowered the standards of sanitation. In 1887 quotas were introduced that kept to a minimum the numbers of Jewish children who could attend secondary school or university. In 1889 all Jews were prohibited from practising law; and in 1890 they were denied a vote in *zemstvo* elections, although they were still required to pay *zemstvo* taxes. In 1894 Jews were refused licences to sell spirits, one of the few occupations left open to them. The harassment of Jews and their reduction to a state of extreme poverty inevitably bred revolutionary ideas among many of them. Being a nation without a state, denied the right of holding property and reduced to the lowest class level, many came to see in the teachings of Marx (who preached the abolition of state, property and class) the only solution to their problems and to the ills of Russian society. For these reasons, Jewish revolutionaries made a significant contribution to the Bolshevik victory in 1917 (p.158).

But despite Alexander III's repressive policies, his reign was not completely negative. In fact the latter years of it witnessed the beginnings of Russian industrial and economic development: railways were built and the country's natural resources were exploited (p.53). In 1894 Alexander, who had been a man of great strength and physique, began to suffer from migraine, insomnia and weakness in the legs. He quickly began to fade and in October died of nephritis.

THE REIGN OF NICHOLAS II 1894–1917

When Alexander's son Nicholas became tsar, he was only twenty-six years of age. He had more sensitivity than his father but too often seemed weak-willed. Pobedonostsev had instilled in him a blind faith in the autocracy, and Nicholas's only policy was to preserve the autocratic regime he had inherited and pass it on intact to his successor. At the age of thirteen Nicholas had been led into the presence of his dying grandfather (p.50) to take his leave of him, and this had left an indelible impression. He therefore continued his father's repressive policies: press censorship, university surveillance and the pogroms. In these, he took the advice of Pobedonostsev, who remained procurator of the Holy Synod until 1905, and influenced the new tsar as much as he had the old.

In 1894 Nicholas married Princess Alice of Hesse-Darmstadt, a grand-daughter of Queen Victoria, who became the Tsarina Alexandra. Although they were a deeply attached couple, their union was to give rise to tragedy as she in time became the dominant influence in his life. Her sincere but misguided interference in matters of state was to prove a major factor in the downfall of the Romanov dynasty (p.158).

The Economy and the Achievements of Witte

From 1870 to the mid-1880s Russian industry developed very slowly, but thereafter a considerable growth occurred. Three factors were responsible for this improvement: (i) the expansion of the railways; (ii) the help of foreign expertise in various industries; and (iii) the role of the state in protecting industries, promoting capital goods industries, and attracting foreign capital.

The man most responsible for the growth of the Russian economy was Count Sergei Witte, the powerful and able minister of finance from 1892 to 1903. Witte, realising that his country was the most backward of the great powers, made the industrialisation of Russia his main objective. Economic strength had to be built up rapidly, and the basis of this was to be the rapid development of railways and heavy industry. The means by which he achieved this has been called 'the Witte System'. It incorporated tariff protection, monetary stability, heavy taxation and foreign investment.

Witte's success was significant. The annual rate of industrial growth was over eight per cent; its basis being the expansion of heavy industry in the Ukraine, stimulated by railway construction. Between 1890 and 1900 the length of track expanded from 30,000 to 53,000 kilometres as new lines were built in the Urals, the Lower Volga region and the Caucasus. But the most ambitious undertaking was the Trans-Siberian railway. It was begun in 1891 and eventually linked St Petersburg and Moscow with Vladivostok on the Pacific. The exploitation of new areas was now possible and large-scale emigration to western Siberia developed. Cotton-growing in Turkestan became feasible as the railway linked together centres of production in a vast network. Railway construction also stimulated the growth of the coal and iron industries and the establishment of large locomotive works.

Foreign capital (mainly French) was attracted to Russia and much of it went into heavy industry. By 1914 Russia was Europe's largest debtor nation, with foreign investment amounting to 2,000 million roubles, but to pay the interest on this debt, further indirect taxes had to be imposed on an already burdened peasantry.

Witte defended the economy and secured a favourable balance of trade by keeping protective tariffs at a high level. He also stimulated agricultural exports by building railways in regions that were supplying grain for export. Witte's policy of high taxation had a dual effect: it encouraged exports by squeezing an agricultural surplus from the peasant, and it provided money for state investment. The following table shows the remarkable growth of the Russian economy between 1860 and 1914.

		Million metric tons			Kilometres
Year	Population (Million)	Coal	Pig iron	Steel	Railway Track
1860		0.3	0.2	—	1,400
1871	80	0.9	0.3	0.2	13,000
1890		6.0	1.1	0.4	30,400
1911	168	26.0	3.5	3.0	75,700
1914	171	26.0	3.5	4.0	75,700

The Growth of Opposition

Although certain progress was being made, real and fundamental discontent remained. Conditions of work were often appalling; accidents in factories were commonplace. In one year alone, 1904, some eleven per cent of the workers in metallurgical factories suffered death or serious injury. The influx of peasants to towns and cities in search of employment created such a huge demand for housing that the majority were forced to live in filthy hovels. Many workers were known as 'corner lodgers' because they rented corners of rooms for themselves and their families. These new illiterate urban poor, uprooted from their rural villages, now found themselves in a strange and hostile urban environment. They suffered emotional deprivation as well as material exploitation and became ready supporters of revolutionary movements.

During the decade between the accession of Nicholas II in 1894 to the Revolution of 1905, three distinct opposition movements developed.

(1) The first movement sprang from Russian liberalism. Initially it drew its strength from the enlightened gentry, but in time it broadened its base to include members of the middle-class professions — professors, doctors and lawyers. In 1901 they set up an illegal opposition group, the Union of Liberation, which had as its objective the ending of autocracy and the creation of

constitutional government by peaceful means. In 1905 they formed themselves into a political party known as the Constitutional Democrats (Kadets).

(2) By the end of the 1880s Marxist ideas had become popular with university students and members of the intelligentsia. This was especially so because of the scientific analysis of society that Marxism offered (p.4), which compared favourably with the vague slogans of other groups. In 1898 Marxists held a secret congress in Minsk and formed a Marxist party. Its leader was George Plekhanov, and it took the name the Russian Social Democratic Labour Party. On the third day of the congress, the police raided it and arrested most of its members.

This set-back led to many disputes within the party: whether it should remain an elite group or create a mass movement, and also what its attitude should be towards the middle-class and the peasantry. One faction, led by Julius Martov, held that a Marxist revolution would have to wait until such time as Russia had fully industrialised and produced a large industrial working class on whom the revolution would be based, as Marx had predicted. Meanwhile, they urged the building up of a mass party and agitation for trade unions and better working conditions.

The other faction, led by Lenin, violently opposed these ideas. They advocated a small elite party of dedicated revolutionaries, who would use the peasantry in a revolution, believing that there was no necessity to wait for capitalism to produce a huge discontented proletariat. Instead, in some crisis, such as an unpopular war, they could seize power. Since most Russian Marxists had been exiled from Russia, the Second Party Congress was held in London in 1903, and it was here that its differences finally came to a head. The party split into two groups. Lenin called his group the majority (*Bolshevik*) and Martov's group the minority (*Menshevik*). However, in Russia itself the Mensheviks, despite their name, continued to have greater support up to 1917.

Born Vladimir Ilyich Ulyanov in 1870 in the town of Simbirsk on the Volga, Lenin was the son of a school inspector. When he was sixteen, his elder brother, Alexander, was executed for his part in a plot to assassinate Tsar Alexander III. In 1897 Lenin was arrested in St Petersburg for Marxist activities, and was sentenced to fourteen months' imprisonment, followed by three years' exile in eastern Siberia. When his term in Siberia ended, he left Russia for Switzerland, where he edited a revolutionary paper, *Iskra* (The Spark), which was smuggled into Russia. In this way Lenin kept in touch with Marxist revolutionaries at home and abroad. His emergence in 1903 as the leader of the Bolsheviks was later to alter the course of Russian history, but for the time being other events were of more importance to the Russian people.

(3) In 1900 the *narodniki* and other peasant groups came together, and from them emerged a new important political force — the social revolutionary movement. Their leader was Victor Chernov, who laid down a policy of immediate revolution without waiting for power to devolve to the bourgeoisie — the policy of the Marxist Social Democrats. After the revolution, land would be distributed to the peasantry. At the end of 1901 they formed the Social Revolutionary Party. It was never as tightly disciplined as the Social Democratic Party, but it was a significant force that could urge the peasants into action. The Social Revolutionaries were more feared by the authorities than the Social Democrats because their policy of assassinating important personages was considered to be more dangerous to the regime than social democrats discussing Marxist theory.

The Russo-Japanese War 1904–05

After her diplomatic defeat at the Congress of Berlin (p.107), Russia turned away from the Balkans and renewed her expansion eastwards toward the Pacific. In 1891 the construction of the single-line Trans-Siberian

Railway began. It ran some 5,000 miles from Moscow to Vladivostok on the Pacific and was practically completed in 1904 (it did not become a double-track until the 1930s). Witte strongly favoured the railway for several reasons. First, he believed, the economic exploitation of Manchuria and the areas around Vladivostok would cause fewer international hostilities than expansion in the eastern Mediterranean, which had brought Russia military defeat in the Crimean War and diplomatic defeat at the Congress of Berlin. Secondly, the Far East offered Russia the prospect of an ice-free (warm-water) port. Thirdly, it was felt that China, being a weak power, could be 'persuaded' to acquiesce in the Russian exploitation of Manchuria and Korea (map, p.48).

But Russia had a rival: Japan. In 1894 Japan had gone to war with China over Korea; and in the Treaty of Shimonoseki the following year had secured from China the island of Formosa (Taiwan), and the Liaotung Peninsula, which contained the important strategic seaport of Port Arthur. Japan also agreed to respect Korean independence, but pressure from Russia and other European powers forced Japan to vacate Port Arthur almost immediately. Both Japan and Russia were now determined to possess Port Arthur (and Korea) as soon as the opportunity presented itself.

In 1898 Russia made the first move when she obtained from China a lease of the Liaotung Peninsula and Port Arthur for 25 years. Then in 1900, while the Boxer Rebellion was in progress in Peking (p.99), Russia occupied Manchuria.

In 1902 Japan made an alliance with Britain that cleared the way for a Japanese conflict with Russia. Britain, having extensive trading interests in the Far East, and fearing Russian penetration in the area, pursued a policy of friendship with Japan, who, she considered, would act as a bulwark against Russian ambitions. For Japan, the alliance with Britain ensured that France would now be deterred from coming to Russia's aid, despite the newly formed Franco-Russian Dual Alliance (p.117).

The Japanese requested that Russian troops be removed from Korea, but Nicholas was in no mood for compromise. In fact the tsar welcomed a war with Japan. His thinking (and that of his advisors) was based on the assumption that a short victorious war would stifle opposition at home and earn prestige for the tsarist regime. In February 1904, the Japanese decided upon a surprise attack on Port Arthur. Russia's Pacific fleet was decisively defeated, and her troops were beaten back in Manchuria and Korea. Port Arthur continued to hold out, but finally surrendered in January 1905.

It seemed incredible that the vast tsarist empire could not defeat the comparatively tiny state of Japan. But the Russian armies were poorly supplied with food and ammunition, because she was conducting a war 5,000 miles from the capital. Furthermore, since the single-line Trans-Siberian Railway had not been completed around Lake Baikal, troops, food and munitions had to be transported over part of the journey by sledge.

At the beginning of March 1905 the Russians suffered a major defeat in the ten-day battle at Mukden in Manchuria. They lost 90,000 men and were forced to retreat from Manchuria. Japan now had complete mastery on land.

Nicholas relied on one last desperate gamble. The Russian Baltic fleet, which in the previous October had been ordered to sail from the Baltic, around Africa, to the Pacific, eventually arrived off Korea in May 1905. There, in the Straits of Tsushima, having got caught in a fog, it was destroyed in a matter of hours by the Japanese navy. Over twenty Russian battleships were destroyed, while a mere handful struggled through to safety in Vladivostok. Not a single Japanese ship had been sunk.

With this annihilating defeat, the tsar accepted the mediation of President Theodore Roosevelt of America and agreed to the Treaty of Portsmouth (New Hampshire) in September 1905. By this treaty Russia was obliged to

The destruction of the Russian Fleet by the Japanese at Tsushima in May 1905.

surrender to Japan, Port Arthur, the Liaotung Peninsula with its railway, and all of Manchuria. She also had to cede the island of Sakhalin, and recognise a Japanese protectorate over Korea (map, p.48).

The Russo-Japanese war weakened and humiliated Russia; for with the exception of the Italian defeat by the Ethiopians at Adowa in 1896 (p.77), it was the first major defeat of a European power by a non-European nation. On the other hand, it started Japan upon the road to becoming a world power. The Far Eastern defeat induced Russia to return again to Europe and the Balkans, but here she was to incur a further rebuff, when the Hapsburgs annexed the Slav province of Bosnia-Herzegovina in 1908 (p.112), and ultimate defeat, when she embarked on World War I (p.117). The more immediate effects, however, were to be found at home, where defeat led directly to the Revolution of 1905.

The 1905 Revolution

By January 1905, public disquiet over the defeats in the Far East was mounting to a serious level. News of the suffering of the ill-equipped soldiers, the primitive medical services and the lack of food had angered the people, who also blamed the war for the rise in food prices.

The workers in the Putilov metallurgical factory in St Petersburg organised a strike, which soon spread to other factories in the city. One of the persistent beliefs among the workers was that the tsar was not fully aware of their suffering, that he was continually misled by his advisors, and that if only he

'Bloody Sunday', January 1905. Father Gapon leading a procession to the Winter Palace is confronted by troops.

could be made aware of their condition, their *Patushka* ('Little Father'), as they affectionately called him, would answer their needs. One of their leaders, Father Georgii Gapon, urged the workers to march to the tsar's Winter Palace and present a petition to him setting out their demands.

On Sunday 22 January 1905, Father Gapon led a procession of 20,000 people to the Winter Palace. The demonstration was peaceful and the petition included requests for such reforms as a shorter working day, better pay for women, free medical aid, and the setting up of a *Duma* (Parliament) as the liberals of the Kadet party had advocated. Nicholas had actually left the palace the previous evening, but the marchers did not know this. Although the crowds sang hymns, and carried crosses, icons and portraits of the tsar, the officials and palace guards panicked at the sight of 20,000 demonstrators. An eye witness recorded:

> The Cossacks at first used their knouts [leather-thonged whips], then the flat of their sabres, and finally they fired. . . . The people, seeing the dead and dying carried away in all directions, the snow on the streets and pavements soaked with blood, cried aloud for vengeance . . . men, women and children fell at each volley, and were carried away in ambulances, sledges and carts. The indignation and fury of every class was aroused.

At least five hundred were killed and thousands wounded, although the official figures given subsequently acknowledged 130 killed and 300 wounded. Nicholas wrote in his diary:

> A painful day . . . many killed and wounded. . . . God, how painful and sad. Mama arrived from town, straight to Mass. . . . Went for a walk.

The day, which became known as 'Bloody Sunday', destroyed the last lingering respect many Russian people had for the tsar. Within days half a million workers were on strike in St Petersburg and Moscow, and a wave of disorder spread throughout Russia. Peasant uprisings erupted, and renewed demands for independence came from Poland and Georgia. The tsar's uncle, the Grand Duke Sergei, was murdered in the Kremlin and the Social Revolutionaries continued to urge the peasants to rise in revolt. In June the crew of the battleship *Potemkin* mutinied, took the ship to a Romanian port and scuttled her.

During this time the middle-class liberals (*zemstvo* leaders and Kadets) continued to press for a *Duma* and other reforms, but the tsar and his ministers revealed themselves as both weak and short-sighted. Although they could not restore order by force, they continued to resist any major reforms.

Meanwhile the Social Democrats had set up *Soviets* in the cities of St Petersburg, Moscow and Odessa. These *Soviets* were workers' councils that took over the running of the strikes and formulated the workers' demands. In September the tsar signed a humiliating peace treaty with Japan. The news sparked off a further wave of unrest; strikes spread even to the professions, and the whole country was brought to a standstill.

In desperation, the tsar turned to Witte (now his chief minister), who strongly advised Nicholas to grant a *Duma* which would satisfy the liberals, and split them off from the Social Revolutionaries and Social Democrats. The tsar had no choice but to agree, for even though the army remained loyal, an attempt to restore order by force would have led to civil war.

On 17 October an imperial manifesto proclaimed the institution of a *Duma*, in the election of which all classes would have a vote; a guarantee that all laws, including decrees of the tsar, would be enacted only with the consent of the *Duma*; and the tsar's autocracy would be replaced by a council of ministers led by a prime minister. This

During Revolution - Presses for a Duma.

imperial announcement, known as the 'October Manifesto', would go a very long way towards turning Russia into a full democracy with a constitutional monarch at its head. Nevertheless, the tsar retained the right to suspend the *Duma*, and continued to hold sole command of the armed forces.

The October Manifesto was received with jubilation in many circles and most striking workers returned to work. This encouraged the tsar to stamp out the remaining unrest with severity, an action which helped to sour the political atmosphere, even before the first *Duma* had opened. The *Soviets* continued their agitation and in December organised a general strike in Moscow. Troops were sent in and more than a thousand people were killed. Special punitive contingents of troops were sent into rebellious areas, particularly in Georgia and Poland and, claiming to defend order, wreaked vengeance on the population. By January 1906, order was restored and executions and flogging-parties dealt ruthlessly with the tsar's enemies.

The effects of the 1905 revolution can only be assessed in the full perspective of Russian history. The October Manifesto did defuse the crisis, but the Social Revolutionaries and Social Democrats had no confidence in the promise of a *Duma*. Their general policy was to ignore it and revert to their underground activities.

Despite the many discussions about revolution in Russia, when it did break out in 1905, it caught the leaders unprepared. Most leading Marxists, with the exception of Leon Trotsky, were in exile and were slow to return. Many of them were engaged in factional rivalry (Mensheviks and Bolsheviks) and at first underestimated the seriousness of the unrest. When Lenin returned in November 1905, he realised that there could be little hope of success while the army remained loyal to the tsar, but he also understood that in any future uprising the *Soviets* would play a crucial role. Meanwhile, Lenin saw the revolution as providing a 'dress rehearsal' for the future socialist revolution and an opportunity to train and recruit new members:

> Immediate operations. Some can undertake to assassinate a spy or blow up a police station; others can attack a bank or expropriate funds for insurrection. Let every squad learn, if only by beating up police. The dozens of sacrifices will be repaid with interest by producing hundreds of experienced fighters who will lead hundreds of thousands tomorrow.

The Dumas

In May 1906, voting took place to elect members to Russia's first parliament. Four days before it met, the tsar once more proclaimed his right to rule as an autocrat:

> To the Emperor of all Russians belongs supreme autocratic power. Submission to his power is commanded by God Himself.

Nicholas saw the *Duma* as little more than a debating chamber or an advisory body. He also dismissed Witte, the only person capable of saving the Romanov dynasty; Nicholas, and particularly his wife Alexandra, had come to dislike the man who had counselled them to make concessions.

Since Lenin had persuaded the Social Democrats to boycott the elections, holding that the *Duma* was nothing but a sham, the Kadets and the Social Revolutionaries dominated it. The first session was stormy. The deputies demanded a full share in government, the release of political prisoners, religious and national rights for minorities and, above all, land for the peasants. The tsar informed them that such demands were inadmissible and dissolved the *Duma*. Russia's first parliament had lasted 73 days.

In dismissing the first *Duma*, Nicholas had declared:

> A cruel disappointment has befallen our expectations. The representatives of the nation, instead of applying themselves to the work of productive legislation, have strayed into spheres beyond their competence.

But he promised:

> In dissolving the *Duma* we confirm our immutable intention of maintaining the institution, and in conformity with this intention we fix 5 March 1907 as the date of the convocation of a new *Duma*.

The tsar now appointed Peter Stolypin as his chief minister, whose first priority was to arrange the elections for the second *Duma*. Stolypin, in an effort to produce a more docile assembly, tightened censorship, banned certain candidates, and used government money to help other candidates. This time the Social Democrats contested the election and succeeded in winning 65 seats (about one-fifth of the total).

The Social Democrats, together with the Social Revolutionaries, other radical peasant groups, and deputies from non-Russian nationalities, all combined to make the second *Duma* more radical than the first. Despite Stolypin's manoeuvrings, the second *Duma* became a further 'cruel disappointment' to the tsar, and from the beginning was in open opposition to the autocracy.

An attempt was made to arrest some of the Social Democrat deputies on the grounds that they were engaged in organising revolutionary cells in the army; but this only provoked a new storm about parliamentary privilege and in June the tsar dissolved the second *Duma*. Lenin, fearing arrest for his alleged part in forming Bolshevik army cells, fled into exile again and remained out of Russia until his historic triumphant return in 1917 (p.161).

Before the third *Duma* was elected, Stolypin, in order to make certain that a conservative parliament would be returned, changed the electoral laws. The system Stolypin devised was extremely complicated, where the value of votes was weighed heavily in favour of landlords and against industrial workers. In practice it meant that one deputy could be elected to the third *Duma* by the votes of 230 landlords, or 1,000 businessmen, or 60,000 peasants, or 125,000 industrial workers. As a result, only 14 Social Democrats got elected. From the government's viewpoint, the *Duma* was at last workable because it was now dominated by moderate Kadets. Despite its conservative character, the third *Duma* was often critical of the tsar. Many of the gentry were enlightened and supported liberal reform. Such independence of spirit won admiration from the Russian people, while the *Duma's* restraint eventually earned it a certain respect from the autocracy. The third *Duma* was able, therefore, to last its full five years in office (1907–11) and was responsible for many reforms.

The composition of the fourth *Duma*, elected in 1912, was very similar to that of its predecessor. It was to be Russia's last *Duma*. The revolutions of 1917 swept aside both the tsarist dynasty and Russia's first steps on the road to parliamentary democracy.

The Work of Stolypin 1906–11

Stolypin was a most controversial figure in Russian political life, disliked by both extremes of left and right. To the workers he was seen as the man who had dissolved two *Dumas* and had changed the electoral laws. He was ruthless in stamping out unrest: in his first year of office, 1,144 people were executed. Yet Stolypin believed that repression alone would never solve Russia's ills. He maintained that the best method of stopping revolution was to prevent it from breaking out. He therefore concentrated his energies on solving the peasant problem; and it was this policy which made him so unpopular with many landlords. Stolypin hoped eventually to institute peasant ownership of the land. If the peasants could be pacified, he argued, Russia would have a guarantee of stability; for a strong class of peasant farmers (*kulaks*) would have a vested interest in maintaining the existing social and political structure of society.

But the obstacles were enormous. It was necessary to transfer land from the village *mir* to the individual peasant; to consolidate the scattered strips of land into single compact farms; to provide the peasant with capital; to teach him more efficient farming; and to end the practice of subdividing holdings at death. If this last objective could be achieved, disinherited younger sons would form a pool of labour available for industry.

Stolypin's policies did bring progress. By 1914 half the peasant lands had become the personal possession of individual holders, although much land still remained in scattered strips. The peasants' Land Bank, which had been formed in 1885 to give credit to peasants purchasing land, now dramatically increased its role. Between 1906 and 1914 it sold four times as much land to the peasants as it had in the previous decade. Peasant migration was also encouraged. The peak years of migration — 1907 to 1909 — saw more than two million peasants migrate to western Siberia, and the region became important for dairy produce and grain.

Stolypin also encouraged the development of industry, and within four years the production of iron and steel had risen by 50 per cent, with a consequent rise in employment. Foreign capital also poured into Russia. French and Belgian capital was invested mainly in the mining and metallurgical industries, while British capital went into the oil and cotton industries. Stolypin's other reforms included extending educational facilities, so that by 1914 almost 50 per cent of all Russian children were literate.

Despite progress, many disquieting features remained: the low level of agricultural productivity, which was rising at only one per cent a year, the harsh conditions of work in mine and factory, and, above all, the rapid rise in population. Despite Stolypin's land reforms, the peasants' problems worsened. The rapid rise in population (171 million in 1914) meant that not enough land was coming on the market to satisfy the land-hungry peasantry. When Stolypin was assassinated in Kiev in 1911, his successor cut down on loans to the peasants and the whole land project lost its momentum.

Russia on the Eve of War

In 1912 an effort was made to pacify industrial workers with modest schemes for state insurance against sickness and industrial accidents. But the same year also witnessed troops shooting down 170 strikers in the Lena goldfields. Widespread unrest followed, mainly instigated by the Bolsheviks, but there was never any danger of the Romanov state collapsing.

In 1913, the tercentenary of the Romanov dynasty was celebrated with protestations of loyalty in St Petersburg and Moscow. It was evident that a fund of popular support for the dynasty still existed. Although there were still immense problems, especially among industrial workers and land-hungry peasants, much progress had been made, and many believed that Russia was slowly but surely moving towards a full parliamentary democracy.

When war broke out in 1914, all groups in Russian society united in a wave of patriotism and anti-German feeling. The capital, St Petersburg, was renamed Petrograd. Only the Bolsheviks declared their unequivocal opposition to the war; their dozen representatives were declared traitors and were exiled to Siberia.

It now seemed that the tsar could at last stand at the head of all classes in defence of Mother Russia. But such unity as the outbreak of war produced was short-lived. Within three years the war had let loose forces that destroyed not only the autocracy but the hopes of a parliamentary democracy as well.

Study Assignments and Essays

1. Consider the following: (i) 'The reforms of Alexander II did more harm than good'; (ii) 'The repression of Alexander III did more harm than good.'

2. 'Despite many problems, Russian economic development under Nicholas II was astonishing.' Discuss.

3. Account for the growth of radical opposition movements in Tsarist Russia up to 1905.

4. To what extent had parliamentary institutions developed in Tsarist Russia by 1914?

5. Compare and contrast the work and achievements of Witte and Stolypin.

6. Write an essay on two of the following: (i) The tactics of Bolshevism and Menshevism; (ii) The origin, course and consequences of the Russo-Japanese war; (iii) The foreign policy of Tsarist Russia between 1870 and 1914; (iv) The origin, course and consequences of the 1905 Revolution; (v) Tsarist Russia in 1914.

Britain 1870 – 1914

5

Wider still and wider shall thy bounds be set; God, who made thee mighty, make thee mightier yet.
A.C. Benson, 'Land of Hope and Glory' (1902).

IN 1870 BRITAIN was the strongest power in the world and the model that most other countries tried to copy. The home of the industrial revolution, her industry, commerce and investments reached out to many parts of the world. She had a great navy and a sizable empire, while at home, although industrialisation had created a new middle class and working class, society was relatively stable.

By 1870 the middle class had secured certain advances through the extension of the franchise and increased representation in parliament, while the working class had gained considerably through the reform of working hours and conditions. Yet, although progress had been made, real power and privilege still remained with the aristocracy.

GOVERNMENT

In 1870 Britain was a constitutional monarchy. Parliament consisted of two

Queen Victoria (seated in carriage) with Tsar Nicholas II and Tsarina Alexandra of Russia and other members of her family at Balmoral in Scotland in 1896.

houses: the House of Commons, elected on a limited franchise, and the House of Lords, composed of hereditary peers. The elected members of parliament were grouped into two large parties, the Conservatives and the Liberals. Traditionally the Conservatives drew their support from the landed class and were opposed to rapid change. They were also associated with imperialism and stressed the importance of expanding the empire (p.85). The Liberal Party, which emerged in the 1860s, derived much of its support from the middle class and was in favour of reforming government and society to meet the needs of the nineteenth and early twentieth centuries.

Yet any definite lines of distinction can be misleading, since the Liberals also engaged in imperial expansion, while the Conservatives did introduce many social reforms. As the century progressed, both parties showed their willingness to adapt to changing circumstances. It was precisely the ruling parties' willingness to expand the electorate and institute reforms to meet the needs of an industrial society that saved Britain from revolution in the nineteenth and twentieth centuries.

POLITICAL REFORMS

By 1870 Britain was on the road to full political and social reform. In 1832, the first Reform Act had given the vote to the upper middle classes, and in 1867 the second Reform Act had extended it to the working classes in towns. Then in 1872 the Liberal prime minister, William E. Gladstone, passed the Ballot Act, which allowed voters to cast their vote in secret in local and general elections. This was a most important step on the road to democracy because, before its enactment, the 'open voting' system meant that employers and landlords could intimidate and bribe their employees or tenants with threats of dismissal or eviction if they did not vote for certain candidates.

In 1884, Gladstone introduced the third Reform Act, which gave the vote to agricultural workers, thus raising the electorate from three million to five million. A separate measure the next year provided for the restructuring of electoral constituencies. During the nineteenth century, as people moved from the countryside into the new industrial areas springing up around mines, factories and ports, the old electoral divisions became increasingly irrelevant. Some rural divisions with a small population could have the same representation in parliament as a new industrial area with a relatively high population. The third Reform Act now redrew electoral divisions on the basis of population, thus ensuring a fairer balance of interests in parliament.

The final step on the road to full democracy came with the triumph of the suffragette movement. In the nineteenth century, Victorian attitudes placed women in a second-class role to men. But with increased educational opportunities and the rise of new female employment opportunities in teaching, nursing and typing, the early twentieth century witnessed the rise of a women's movement seeking the right to vote in parliamentary elections.

Already a start had been made in the Local Government Act of 1888, which allowed women to vote in local elections. Then in 1898 Emmeline Pankhurst and her husband, Richard, founded the Women's Franchise League in Manchester. Five years later (her husband having died meanwhile) Mrs Pankhurst, and her daughter Christabel founded the militant Women's Social and Political Union (WSPU) to campaign for female suffrage. Neither the Conservatives nor the Liberals were in favour of the WSPU's aspirations, but they were welcomed by the newly emerging Labour Party (p.69).

The WSPU adopted a two-pronged approach: public demonstrations and the harassment of government ministers. The former often spilled over into violence, followed by arrest

Procession of arrested suffragettes after a demonstration at Buckingham Palace in 1914.

and imprisonment of the demonstrators. By being sent to jail and being obliged to wear prison clothes and suffer other indignities, the suffragettes hoped to present themselves to the public as martyrs and arouse sympathy for their cause. The policy of harassing government ministers took the form of picketing political meetings, although some women went further by attacking the private property of cabinet members.

In 1909 the suffragettes stepped up their campaign when imprisoned women went on hunger-strike. The authorities, fearing the repercussions that would follow a death by hunger-strike, resorted to force-feeding. But this led to some controversy because it was said to interfere with the moral freedom of the individual and it was soon abandoned.

In November 1910, the suffragettes organised a huge demonstration in London. Inevitably, it became less than peaceful, and many women were roughly treated and were arrested by the police. This incident became known as 'Black Friday' and marked a turning point in the tactics of the suffragette movement.

Already, in 1909, a splinter-group under Christabel Pankhurst had formed the Women's Freedom League, which had initiated the prison hunger-strikes. Now, following 'Black Friday', this more extreme group came to the forefront of the movement. In March

1912, a well-organised campaign of violence began. Private property was attacked, paintings in art galleries were slashed, acid was poured on golf-course greens, telephone wires were cut, and many buildings were burned. Over two hundred women were imprisoned, but they retaliated by going on hunger-strike. This time the government responded by passing the so-called 'Cat and Mouse' Act of 1913. This empowered the authorities to release women from jail when their lives were in danger from the hunger-strike and then imprison them again once they had recovered. The hunger-strikers would have to serve their full sentences in broken periods, and this defeated the whole purpose of the protest.

But the incident that shocked the public and caught the attention of the world's press took place at the Epsom Derby on 4 June 1914, when Emily Wilding Davidson threw herself in front of King George V's horse. Miss Davidson was severely injured and died a few days later. The suffragettes turned her funeral into a mass demonstration, but the government still refused to give women the vote. When war broke out in 1914, Britain was not a complete democracy. The final triumph came, however, in 1918, when the war, and women's role during it, created a climate of opinion favourable for change.

ARMY REFORM

The conditions under which the British soldier fought during the Crimean War (p.10) and the shock defeat of France at the hands of Bismarck's Germany, impelled the British government to introduce a number of reforms in the army to make it more dignified and efficient.

In 1868 the regulation permitting flogging in peacetime was abolished, although it remained in force for 'active service' until 1880. 'Bounty money' for recruits was also abolished. This had been a system whereby young men were offered bribe-money to join the army; and while it did serve to increase the ranks, bounty money generally attracted undesirables, which only served to lower the army's efficiency and morale.

In 1871, despite great opposition, Gladstone succeeded in passing the Army Regulations Bill. This law ended the practice whereby sons of aristocrats could become officers merely by paying a sum of money for the privilege. It had created an aristocratic officer class, many of whom had little ability for the task. The new law now opened the army to all, irrespective of wealth or influence, and ensured that promotion would depend on ability, not on privilege.

One problem of finding suitable recruits stemmed from the fact that, on enlistment, a soldier had to serve for a minimum of twelve years. This naturally inhibited many young men from enlisting, especially since most of their service would be spent abroad in hostile territory under unhygienic and adverse climatic conditions. The Army Enlistment Act, also known as the Short Service Act, allowed men to serve for six years and remain at home on reserve for the following six. This new regulation had the effect of attracting young men who would not otherwise have considered joining the army, and it also built up a trained army in reserve. Another significant improvement in army efficiency came when the old muzzle-loading muskets were replaced by the more modern breech-loading rifles. The cumulative effect of these reforms was that the British army became modern and efficient by nineteenth-century standards, and it played a significant role in Britain's overseas expansion at this time (p.86).

EDUCATIONAL REFORM

Since the Tudor period of the sixteenth century, education in England had developed through the efforts of individuals, charitable organisations and religious bodies. The state, in keeping with the prevailing philosophy of *laissez-faire*, believed that its duty was to govern and that it had no role to play in the economy, nor indeed in education. But as the nineteenth century progressed, it became obvious that private individuals and institutions were not sufficient, and agitation for state involvement in education gathered momentum.

Eventually, the climate of opinion had sufficiently developed to allow Gladstone's Liberal government to introduce William Forster's Elementary Education Act of 1870, making education available to all children between the ages of five and thirteen. Its purpose was not to supplant private institutions; merely to 'fill the gaps'. England and Wales (Scotland had its own system) was divided into school districts. If there was not a school already in the district, the local ratepayers (persons paying a tax on property) were obliged to elect a school board and build a school. In 1880 another act made education compulsory for all up to the age of ten years, and in 1891 it was made free. Then in 1897 the system of 'payment by results' was abolished; and in 1899 the school-leaving age was raised to twelve years. Thus by the end of the century Britain had established free compulsory elementary education, by which the children of the nation were assured of a minimum standard of education that would fit them to work in an industrialised society.

In nineteenth-century Britain, secondary education was enjoyed only by the sons and daughters of the wealthy who could afford to attend public and grammar schools. Those who could attend were limited in their education to a very narrow curriculum, which rarely included anything besides Greek, Latin and mathematics. Only gradually were modern languages, history and geography recognised as an essential part of the curriculum.

Finally in 1902, Balfour's Education Act provided for the financing of secondary schools out of local rates supplemented by government grants. All schools were placed under the control of a Board of Education. In 1907 a scholarship scheme was introduced to help bright children of poor parents to avail of secondary education, while further grants became available for those attending university. Thus, by 1914, Britain had developed an efficient and well-organised system of education at elementary and secondary levels.

CONSTITUTIONAL REFORM

The British parliamentary system consisted of an elected House of Commons and a House of Lords composed of non-elected peers. For a bill to become law, it had to pass through both houses and then be signed by the monarch. Therefore the unelected House of Lords could veto a bill coming from the elected House of Commons. During the nineteenth century the system worked relatively well because there was no fundamental conflict of interests between the two Houses. But in the early twentieth century a gulf opened up between them. By then, Britain had achieved universal male suffrage (p.64) and the new Labour Party was proposing radical social reform. In 1906 a Liberal government, under Sir Henry Campbell-Bannerman, was returned to office, ending (with one brief exception) twenty years of Tory rule.

This government, mindful of the increased electorate and the presence of a new Labour Party, began to introduce a programme of social legislation. In 1909 an Old Age Pension Act gave five shillings a week to all those over seventy years whose income was less than four pounds a week from other sources. The same year the chancellor of the exchequer, David Lloyd George, introduced what was termed a 'People's Budget'. In order to finance social reforms, Lloyd George proposed introducing heavy taxation on the wealthy, such as a supertax, land tax and higher death duties. These taxes would obviously fall most severely on the land-owning aristocracy represented in the House of Lords.

Not surprisingly, the House of Lords rejected the budget by a large majority and precipitated a constitutional deadlock. Prime minister Herbert Asquith, who had succeeded Campbell-Bannerman in 1908, immediately decided to dissolve parliament and call a general election on the issue. In the election campaign the Liberals portrayed the Lords as selfishly trying to avoid taxation, preventing much-needed social reform, and opposing the will of the people as expressed through the elected House of Commons. When the Liberals were returned to office (having secured a majority through the support of the Labour Party and the Irish Home Rule Party), Asquith introduced the Parliament Bill, which contained three main clauses:

1. The House of Lords should not have any power to veto a money bill (such as the Budget).
2. With all other bills, the House of Lords should have the right to apply the veto only on two consecutive occasions; thereafter, the bill would become law with or without the Lords' consent.
3. The maximum duration between general elections should be reduced from seven years to five.

The House of Lords was now prepared to pass the 'People's Budget' but were not prepared to pass the Parliament Bill, which would curb their own power. Asquith went to the new king, George V (Edward VII had died in 1910), and secured an undertaking that he would create several hundred new peers who would vote for the bill in the House of Lords. Realising that the king and the prime minister were determined to win, the Lords reluctantly passed the bill, which became the Parliament Act of 1911.

Almost immediately the government passed the National Insurance Act, which gave financial assistance to those absent from work through illness. It also provided benefits to workers who became unemployed in the building, engineering and shipbuilding industries. At the same time the government passed an act providing for a salary of £400 per week for all members of parliament. Before this, MPs were not paid, and this had prevented excellent candidates from standing for election. This act provided a welcome boost to the Labour Party, which won 42 seats in the 1911 election.

TRADE UNION REFORM

Before 1870, the existence of trade unions was tolerated in Britain, but was not recognised in law. Although the Trade Union Act of 1871 gave them legal recognition, they still suffered from two great disabilities: they were not legally permitted to bargain collectively, and they were not allowed to go on strike. An Act of 1875 removed these two restrictions, and also permitted peaceful picketing. From then until the end of the century many groups formed themselves into unions in order to better their working conditions. At first, only the skilled crafts were organised into unions, but soon union organisation spread downwards to miners and the semi-skilled factory workers, and then to the unskilled labourers as well.

The period up to 1900 also witnessed a great increase in the number of strikes. The most famous of these was the London match-girls' strike of 1888. These girls worked under very poor conditions and many of them suffered from bone deformities due to phosphorus infection. Other famous strikes that caught the public imagination were the gas-workers' strike in favour of an eight-hour day, and the London dockers' strike in 1889 for a basic wage of sixpence an hour plus overtime.

In 1901 the trade union movement suffered a serious setback. Following a strike of railway workers, the Taff Vale Railway Company in

South Wales sued the railway union for loss of earnings during the strike. The court, in giving judgment, ordered that the union should pay £23,000 compensation to the railway company. This ruling meant that, although trade unions still had the legal right to strike, they could now be held liable to their employers for loss of revenue due to strike action. Union leaders realised that all their hard-won gains would be nullified unless the law was changed, but they also knew that the most effective way of doing this was to get their own leaders elected to parliament. The 1906 general election returned twenty-four trade union members to parliament, who influenced the new Liberal government to pass the Trade Disputes Act of 1906. This Act gave trade unions immunity from any claims by employers for damages, such as loss of revenue, caused by strike action.

THE RISE OF LABOUR

The process of industrialisation in the late eighteenth and early nineteenth century had brought into being a new class of people, the middle class or *bourgeoisie*, and the working class or *proletariat* (p.5). The working class continued to grow in numbers and, although they covered a wide spectrum of occupations, their common characteristic was that they performed manual labour in industry. They also were burdened by low wages, poor housing, ill health and negligible educational opportunities.

Many working-class leaders came to believe that their condition was caused by the capitalist system, and so they began to espouse socialism (p.5). In 1881 the Social Democratic Federation (SDF) was founded. It proposed the payment of salaries to members of parliament, the extension of the franchise to women, and the public (state) ownership of mines, factories, transport and banks. Yet the SDF failed to attract sufficient support and gradually lost what little influence it had.

A more successful socialist organistion, the Independent Labour Party (ILP), was formed in 1893 by the Scottish miners' leader Keir Hardie. Elected in 1882 as the first working-class MP, Hardie dedicated his energies to furthering the cause of labour in Britain. He believed that the two big political parties, the Conservatives and the Liberals, would never solve the problems of the working classes. Instead, he hoped that the millions of working people in Britain, who now had the vote (p.64), should elect their own representatives to parliament.

The cause of labour was also taken up by middle-class intellectuals. In 1884 Sidney and Beatrice Webb, together with George Bernard Shaw and H.G. Wells, founded the Fabian Society. Unlike the followers of Marx, who believed in class revolution, the Fabians strove to achieve socialism by gradual and democratic means. Social reforms and equality for all inevitably would come through step-by-step reforms in parliament. The Fabian Society was not a political party; essentially it was a propaganda machine whose members produced books and pamphlets on the ideals of socialism.

In 1900, the SDF, ILP and the Fabians joined together and formed the Labour Representation Committee (LRC) with the distinct aim of getting their members into parliament. Following the court decision in the Taff Vale case (p.68), the trade unions, in an effort to have the decision reversed by parliament, began to turn away from the Liberal Party towards the LRC.

The 1906 election returned the Liberals to power with a large majority, but it also returned twenty-nine members of the LRC, who now adopted the name of Labour Party. The party continued to support the Liberals so long as Liberal reform continued (p.67); meanwhile the party built up its organisation and support in the constituencies. When Asquith formed his wartime coalition in 1915 (p.250), Arthur Henderson became the first Labour MP to attain cabinet rank; then in

1924 Labour won a simple majority and, with Liberal support, formed the first Labour government in British history (p.252).

ECONOMIC DEVELOPMENT

Britain had a number of advantages over her continental rivals. Her island position forced her to develop shipping and trading, her climate was favourable to agriculture, while her religious and political stability created promising conditions for investment and innovation. Britain was the first country to industrialise, and, in the early nineteenth century, was known as 'the workship of the world', enjoying a near monopoly in iron and steel manufacturing and in textiles.

Between 1870 and 1914, however, Britain's economic expansion suffered a relative decline. The rise of serious competition from Germany and the United States and, to a lesser extent, from France and Japan, eroded her previously almost unchallenged position. This was further aggravated by the policies of tariffs and protection pursued to an increasing extent by her continental rivals. Yet Britain did make substantial progress, especially in the export of her traditional products and in the acquisition of new markets in India and the Far East.

Between 1850 and 1914 her overseas investment rose from roughly £400m. to about £4,000m., aiding industrialisation in Russia, Austria-Hungary, the Balkans and Scandinavia, but more particularly outside Europe. By 1914 British investments outside Europe amounted to £688m. in the USA, £587m. in South America, £372m. in Canada, £380m. in Australasia, £365m. in India, and £351m. in South Africa. Thus Britain, a creditor nation, could pay for a huge import bill, especially in chemicals and new manufacturing products, from the interest on her overseas investments.

Britain's growing population, together with increased opportunities for employment in industry, made the country increasingly dependent on imported food. This development was facilitated by improvements in transport (rail and ship) and refrigeration, which enabled huge quantities of meat and wheat to be imported from North America and Australia. Gradually agriculture at home concentrated more on dairy produce and on fruit and market gardening, so that, by 1914, a new balance between domestic and imported foodstuffs had been achieved.

PRE-WAR UNREST

Despite the peaceful evolution of British society through political and social reform, the years before 1914 witnessed serious industrial unrest.

By 1910 Britain's position as a mighty industrial nation was no longer unassailable. The rise of serious competition on the continent (especially from Germany), and from the United States and Japan, caused a decline in her exports and a consequent fall in employment. Moreover, wages in industry were tending to fall behind rising prices, resulting in frequent strikes for better working conditions.

In 1911 a national railway strike almost brought Britain to a standstill. In 1912 the Miners' Federation went on strike for a minimum wage. Over one million workers came out in support in what was the largest single strike to take place in Britain up to that time. In 1913 the three biggest unions — the National Union of Railwaymen, the Miners' Federation and the National Transport Federation — formed the 'Triple Industrial Alliance', representing 1.5 million members, with a view towards combined action through the sympathetic strike. The Triple Alliance formed a formidable threat, not only to employers but to the entire British capitalist system. However, nothing came of the alliance, which on the outbreak of war in 1914, was abandoned in the national interest.

Britain's declaration of war against Germany had the effect of quenching political, social and economic unrest. Industrial discontent ceased, the suffragettes abandoned their violent campaign, and in Ireland Redmond and Carson accepted postponement of the Home Rule issue and civil war was averted.

FOREIGN POLICY

Since the defeat of Napoleon in 1814, Britain mostly had adopted a policy of splendid isolation from European affairs. Her navy 'ruled the waves', she had an empire on which 'the sun never set', and her progress in industrial manufacture made her 'the workshop of the world'. The country seemed to want nothing from anyone, and intervened in European affairs only when it was perceived that her interests were in danger, as in the Crimean War (p.10).

Britain's predominant position during the nineteenth century was based on her industrial supremacy and sea power. France and Russia also had fleets, but Britain adopted a 'two-power standard', which ensured that the strength of her navy was greater than the combined strength of those of her two nearest rivals.

Between 1870 and 1890 Bismarck was careful not to antagonise Britain by building a great navy or engaging in an aggressive colonial policy (p.31). But with the fall of Bismarck and the advent of Kaiser William II, German policy took a new turn, which profoundly influenced Britain's foreign policy. (p.118). Her traditional antagonism towards France and her suspicion of Russian intentions were slowly allayed, while the rise of Germany as an industrial giant with a large navy aroused national jealousy if not hostility. As a result, Britain slowly abandoned her isolationist foreign policy; and in a series of defence and diplomatic agreements (the Anglo-Japanese Alliance, 1902; the Entente Cordiale with France, 1904; the Triple Entente with France and Russia, 1907) came from a 'splendid isolation' in 1870 to a position of war in 1914, in what has been described as a 'Diplomatic Revolution'.

The future King Edward VII as a boy in 1912. The vogue for sailor suits epitomised the role of sea power in Britain's foreign relations.

Study Assignments and Essays

1. *Treat of constitutional and political reform in Britain between 1870 and 1914.*
2. *Treat of the rise of the trade union and labour movements in Britain between 1870 and 1914.*
3. *Analyse the stages by which Britain came from 'splendid isolation' in 1870 to war in 1914.*
4. *'Although Britain suffered a relative decline, her economic achievements between 1870 and 1914 were impressive.' Discuss.*

5. *Treat of any two crises in British history between 1870 and 1914, and analyse how they were resolved.*
6. *Write an essay on two of the following: (i) The fortunes of the Liberal Party 1870–1914; (ii) The suffragette movement; (iii) Social classes in Victorian Britain; (iv) Edwardian England; (v) Britain on the eve of war — a profile.*

The New Italy 1870–1914

6

Italy has a large appetite but small teeth.
Bismarck

POLITICS

THE ITALIAN Constitution allowed for a king and for a government that required a majority in parliament. In theory, therefore, the new kingdom of Italy was a parliamentary democracy under a constitutional monarchy.

During the early years (1870–75) governments were honest and hard-working. They succeeded in completing the country's unification, and laid some foundation for economic development. But in the later 1870s local interests came to the fore and the political system became corrupted by bribery, incompetence and greed. Since the great majority of citizens were poor and uneducated (many were illiterate), the franchise was very restricted. This meant that politicians did not have to take the views of the electorate into account to any significant extent. They devoted themselves instead to political 'horse-trading' — the peddling of offices, honours, gifts and local amenities, in return for support.

Agostino Depretis, who became prime minister in 1876, developed the tactic known in Italy as *trasformismo*, or transforming opponents into supporters by making political deals. On his death in 1887, he was succeeded by Francesco Crispi, who continued the same policy of self-interest. Crispi, with the encouragement of King Humbert I (who reigned from 1878 to his assassination in 1900), wished to make Italy a great power by embarking on colonial adventures in North Africa (p.91). When these led to the disastrous defeat by the Abyssinians at Adowa in 1896, Crispi was obliged to resign.

In the early twentieth century, Giovanni Giolitti came to the fore and under his rule Italy almost became a democracy, in line with most western European states.

ECONOMY AND SOCIETY

The essential economic problem facing the new Italian state was that it was too poor to support national prosperity. In 1861 Italy had a population of 25 million, and could only cope with the problems this population imposed by actively encouraging emigration. By 1900 Italian emigration (mainly to the United States) was running at half a million annually. Despite this, by 1914, her population had risen to 35 million, a fact that inevitably kept living standards very low. In 1906 it was estimated that the average income in Italy was about 70 per cent of that of France.

These social conditions were aggravated by the gulf between northern and southern Italy. The northern half was partially industrialised and had fertile farming land. It had the largest silk manufacturing industry in Europe, and the sulphur and borax deposits in Tuscany and Sardinia were being exploited. In contrast, the southern half had no mineral deposits, had a large amount of marshy land, poor soil and an illiterate peasantry. Over 80 per cent of the southern population were landless labourers, ground down by poverty, dominated by secret societies (such as the Mafia), and terrorised by brigands.

Italy's fundamental problem was economic. She was a poor country, overwhelmingly dependent on a primitive level of agriculture, and having little or no coal or iron necessary for industrialisation and job creation. Successive governments did little to bridge the gap between the two halves. They failed to set up industries and did nothing to educate

ITALY BEFORE 1914

the peasantry in improved methods of agriculture. Instead, various administrations imposed heavy taxes on a people who could ill afford to pay them, and squandered the money on colonial activities in North Africa where prestige, not economic advantage, was the prize (p.91).

The net result of economic and social stress soon evaporated the enthusiasm that had accompanied the *Risorgimento* (p.12). Disillusionment set in; and this, coupled with the strains produced by the Great War, created the conditions necessary for Mussolini to take power in 1922 (p.209).

PROGRESS

Despite the many problems besetting the state and the low level of political life, progress was made in the decades before 1914. Successive governments carried out improvements in communications and public health. Illiteracy was slowly eroded; primary education became compulsory in 1904, and by 1914 over 50 per cent of Italians could read and write. The franchise was also extended. In 1882 Depretis quadrupled the number of voters to take account of improved literacy and an emerging middle class. Universal male suffrage was introduced in 1912.

In 1887 Crispi imposed tariffs to protect home industries, relaxed the penal code and reformed the prisons. Yet the great majority of peasants in the south were untouched by these reforms and a rebellion took place in Sicily in 1893. Mismanagement continued, and financial scandals were more frequent than reforms.

In the opening years of the twentieth century, Giolitti found much that was needed to be done. With the encouragement of the new king, Victor Emmanuel III, he abolished child labour, improved factory conditions of work and legalised trade unions. Giolitti also introduced a system of national insurance (a poor imitation of Bismarck's scheme) to safeguard workers against sickness, accident and old age. By 1914 these improvements had done much to heal the worst excesses of social unrest, but still the south remained poverty-stricken, and anarchist activities and socialist strikes did not diminish the general disquiet.

THE PROBLEM OF THE CHURCH

The unification of Italy meant that the Pope lost all his papal possessions save for the Vatican. He remained a 'voluntary prisoner' and declined to leave the Vatican in protest against the loss of his temporal possessions. Since the people of Italy were catholic, the new government was anxious to reach an agreement. But Pius IX refused to negotiate and declared that loyal catholics should not participate in Italian politics, either as parliamentarians or as voters. The government therefore was obliged to produce its own settlement, known as the Law of Guarantees of 1871. By this the Pope was recognised as owner of the Vatican and all its palaces, and was offered an annual payment of £120,000. The legislation also guaranteed non-interference in all religious appointments in Italy. Pius IX was not appeased and refused the offer. When he died in 1878, his successor, Leo XIII, continued the same policy of non-compliance with the Italian government.

In practice, however, neither the government nor the church stuck rigidly to its position. The government did interfere in ecclesiastical appointments and in the running of church schools, insisting on inspecting them and encouraging parents to reject religious instruction for their children. It also introduced civil marriages. Catholics, on the other hand, found ways of getting round the papal prohibition on voting and sitting in parliament. As the years passed, although the

Vatican found it impossible not to co-operate with the government in many day-to-day matters, the underlying hostility remained, and divided opinion in the country and in parliament.

The tension was eased somewhat in 1905 when Pius X lifted the ban on catholics participating in the political life of the state. His policy was greatly influenced by the growth of Italian socialism and communism since he realised that the presence of loyal catholic influence in parliament would help to obstruct the worst excesses of the socialists.

THE PROBLEM OF SOCIALISM

Poverty and government neglect turned many Italians towards socialism in the late nineteenth century. But because the electorate was so limited, socialists (depending on the poverty-stricken for support) saw no hope of implementing their programme through parliament. As a result, Italian socialism became revolutionary and more akin to socialism in Russia (p.54) than the movements in Britain, France or Germany (p.69,44,29).

In 1894, Crispi, in an effort to crush the socialist threat, banned all socialist societies and publications, and arrested the tiny group of eight socialists who had secured election to parliament. But as Bismarck had discovered in Germany, such measures only served to increase popular support for socialism. The following year, 1895, the socialists won twelve seats in parliament, and in 1896 founded a daily newspaper, *Avanti* (Forward), to disseminate their ideas.

Support continued to grow and in 1900 the socialists won 33 seats in parliament. Giolitti, following Bismarck's example (p.30), introduced social reform to counteract the growing interest in Marxism. But it was division among themselves, and not social reform, that weakened the socialist opposition. The moderates were prepared to use the parliamentary system to win further reforms, and this meant participating in the political intrigues of Italian politics. A more radical grouping, known as the Syndicalists, preferred direct industrial action. In 1904 they organised a general strike in Milan, but it soon collapsed. Again, in 1914 a general strike was organised in central Italy with the object of setting up a breakaway Marxist republic. One of its leaders was Benito Mussolini, who had become editor of *Avanti* in 1912. When war broke out Italian socialists demanded peace, but within a few months Mussolini had changed his attitude. He now demanded that Italy should go to war against Austria to win back *Italia Irredenta*, the Italian-speaking area within the Austrian empire (p.219). His fellow socialists regarded Mussolini as a renegade and expelled him from the Socialist Party. When the war ended, Mussolini formed a new fascist party, which destroyed not only the Italian parliamentary system but Italian socialism as well (p.210).

FOREIGN AND COLONIAL POLICY

Depretis and Crispi neglected the huge social and economic problems confronting the new Italian state. Instead, they wished to win international prestige and an overseas empire. Although unification had been accomplished, they still had to achieve *Italia Irredenta* by securing the return from Austria of part of the Tyrol and Trieste. But the government was too weak to pursue its claims; in fact, it was impossible for Italy to intervene in any region where the great powers had interests (map p.74).

In 1882 Italy became a member of the Triple Alliance with Germany and Austria-Hungary (p.32). It made little sense beyond boosting her prestige because of the association with the great powers and when the war broke out in 1914, Italy abandoned the Alliance. Indeed, when the country did go to war in 1915, it was on the opposite side (p.139).

Italian colonial policy primarily focussed attention on North Africa (p.91). But this only led to a humiliating defeat at Adowa in 1896 when Abyssinian forces routed the Italians (p.92). In 1911 a war against the Ottoman (Turkish) empire for control of Tripoli and Cyrenaica in Libya was more successful. In theory the acquisition of Libya created an Italian empire, but in practice Senussi tribesmen continued to resist, and Italian control was confined to little more than the coastline (map, p.88).

Study Assignments and Essays

1. *'Italian politics after unification left much to be desired.' Discuss.*
2. *'Italian economic development 1870–1914 was almost negligible.' Treat of the social, economic and political factors that account for this.*
3. *Was socialism a danger in Italy in the period 1870–1914?*
4. *'Italian overseas ambitions hindered rather than advanced her domestic development.' Discuss.*
5. *Why may it be said that Italy was not a great power in 1914?*
6. *Write an essay on two of the following: (i) 'The manner of Italian unification laid the seeds of future conflict'; (ii) Relations between the Vatican and the Italian government 1870–1914; (iii) The political, social and economic differences in Italy north and south; (iv) The rule of Crispi; (v) The rule of Giolitti.*

The Hapsburg Empire 1870–1914 7

We reached those last days when we could endure neither our vices nor their remedies.

Titus Livy (59 B.C. – A.D. 17)
on the Decline of Rome

SINCE 1848 the Austrian empire was ruled from its capital at Vienna by the Emperor Franz Joseph of the ancient House of Hapsburg. It was a large multiracial empire sprawling over much of south-central Europe, but although it consisted of eleven nationalities, the Austrians (Germans) and the Magyars (Hungarians) were the two dominant groups. The majority of the remaining groups were of Slav origin, but this is not to say that they were united; in fact they were often quite suspicious of each other. Only one matter kept them together: their determination to secure independence from the Hapsburg empire. The chart (below) shows the relative strengths of the various peoples within the empire.

THE DUAL MONARCHY

By the middle of the nineteenth century, the Hungarians had become the most vocal group in their demand for independence. Their leader, Francis Deák, was willing to compromise and accept independence within

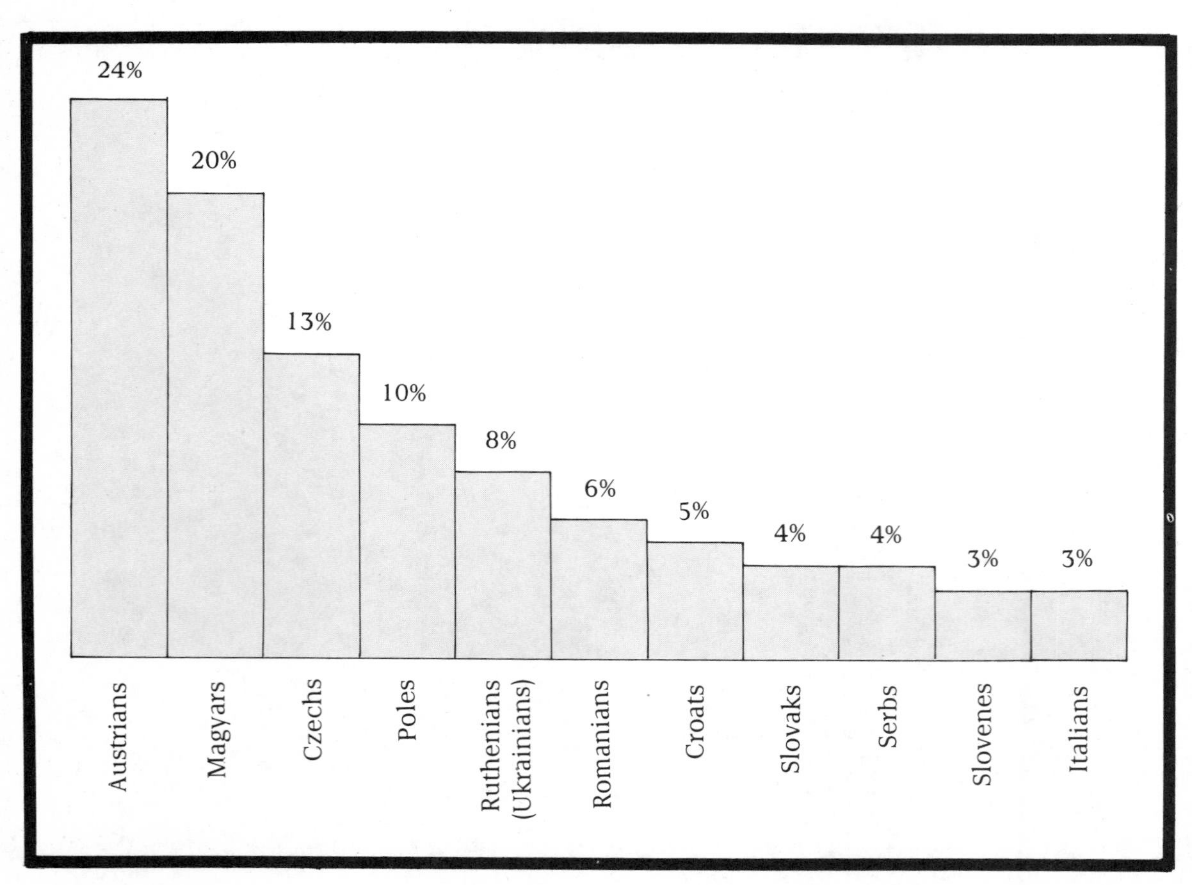

THE HAPSBURG EMPIRE, ITS PEOPLES AND ITS NEIGHBOURS IN 1870

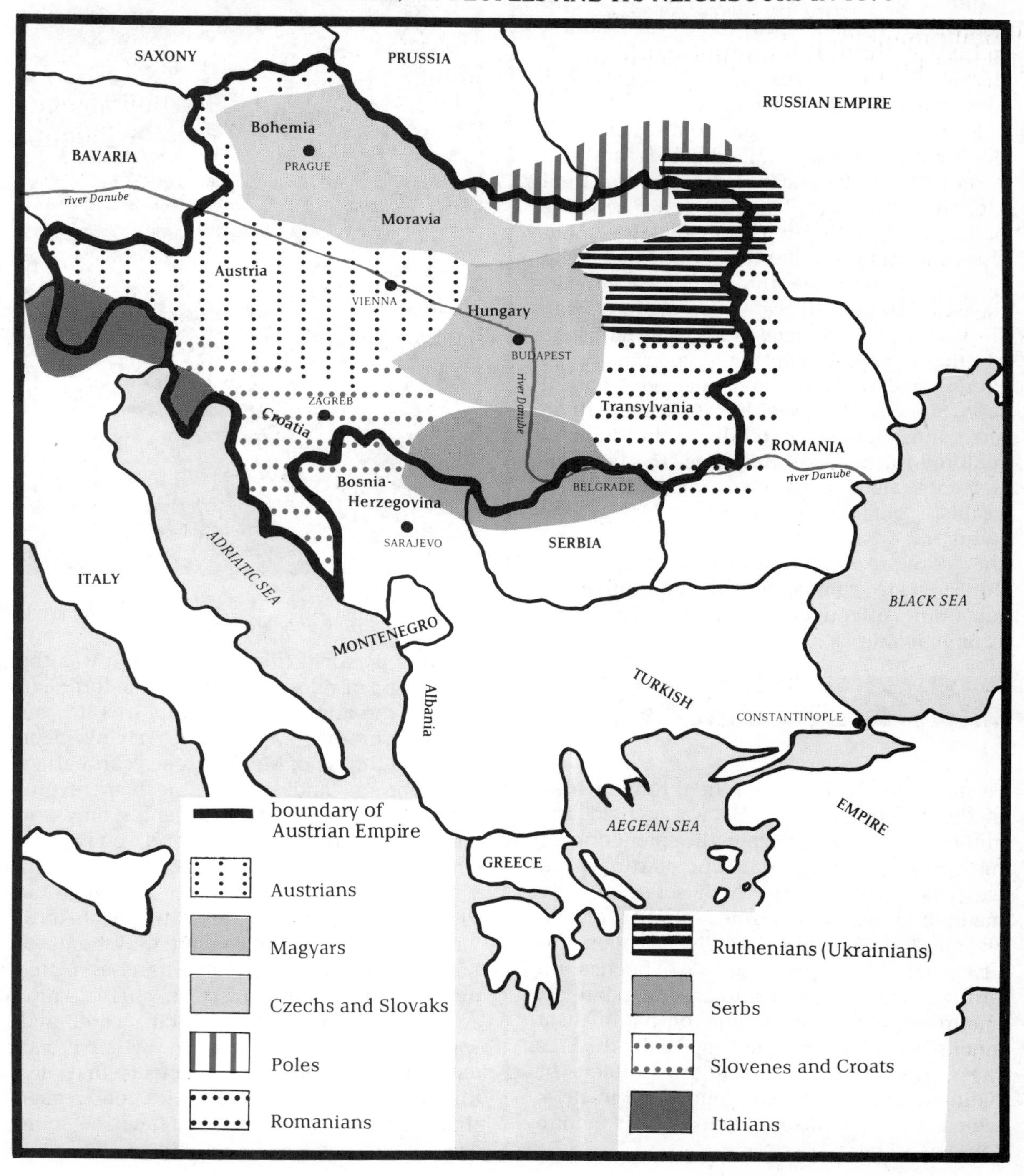

the empire. In 1866 he found an opportunity to press his claims when the Austrians were defeated by Bismarck's forces at Sadowa (p.16). The battle so weakened the Hapsburgs that Emperor Franz Joseph had no option but to accede to Hungarian demands.

By the *Ausgleich*, or compromise, of 1867, the Austrian empire was divided into two parts and was thereafter known as the Dual Monarchy of Austria-Hungary. It had separate parliaments in Vienna and Budapest, but shared a common ruler in Franz Joseph, who remained head of the whole empire. Each parliament shared three departments: war, finance, and foreign relations. The ministers of these departments met alternately in Vienna and Budapest and enacted identical laws. Since Austria was the wealthier partner, she contributed seven-tenths of the finances required for common purposes. The two parliaments also maintained identical tariffs against outside competition. Thus the industrial areas of Austria and Bohemia and the corn-growing areas of Hungary and Transylvania complemented each other by remaining effectively linked in a common economic unit.

THE EMPEROR

Franz Joseph had come to the throne in 1848 at the age of eighteen. He was a rigid and autocratic man who, despite the splendours of his court, lived a spartan life, starting work each day at 5 a.m. His high sense of duty made him regard his role as ruler of the Hapsburg empire as a God-given responsibility. After the *Ausgleich* of 1867, he had no further ideas on how best to accommodate his empire with the rising tide of nationalism among his subject peoples, especially the Slav races. His failure to solve the problem of nationalities finally drove him to war in 1914, which led to the disintegration of his empire four years later.

Emperor Franz Joseph in 1862. He ruled the Hapsburg Empire from 1848 until his death in 1916.

In his personal life, Franz Joseph was the most tragic of rulers. He came to the throne in 1848 in the midst of revolution. In 1867, his younger brother Maximilian, having been given the throne of Mexico three years earlier, was captured and shot by Mexican revolutionaries. In 1889, Franz Joseph's only son and heir, Crown Prince Rudolf, committed suicide with his mistress, Baroness Maria Vetsera, at the Mayerling hunting lodge in the Vienna Woods. In 1898, his wife, Elizabeth of Bavaria, while on holiday on the shores of Lake Geneva in Switzerland, was assassinated by an Italian anarchist. In 1914, Franz Joseph's nephew and heir, Franz Ferdinand, was assassinated at Sarajevo by a Serbian nationalist (p.123), an incident that led directly to World War I. It is with good reason that, following the news of Sarajevo, he could say, 'I have been spared nothing.'

Finally, in November 1916, as his empire was in the throes of war, the 86-year-old Franz Joseph died in a simple iron camp-bed, amid the splendours of the Schönbrunn Palace in Vienna.

AUSTRIAN RULE

The Czech Problem

The Czech people inhabited the former kingdom of Bohemia and the principality of Moravia. Following the *Ausgleich*, the Czechs fell within the Austrian half of the empire. In 1867 they too had demanded self-government, but unlike the Hungarians they were not strong enough to obtain it from a reluctant emperor. For a time they boycotted the *Reichsrat* (Parliament) in Vienna, but soon found it more profitable to return. In 1880 they won the right to use their own Czech language in official business. Nine years later a radical young Czech group came to the fore and demanded that the Czech language be equal to German in all matters within their territory. All educated Czechs understood German, but few Austrians understood Czech, so that if this demand could be won, the Czechs would be well advanced on the road to the complete control of Bohemia. The Czech deputies continuously harassed the government in Vienna, and in 1879 adopted a policy of parliamentary obstruction, such as clattering the desk-lids and throwing bottles of ink. Outside parliament Czechs and Austrians clashed in street battles. Such disruption made effective government in Vienna extremely difficult.

Despite their failure to obtain their own legislature in Prague, the Czechs did succeed in preserving their national identity. During the last quarter of the nineteenth century, a Czech bank, a Czech university and a Czech National Theatre were founded in Prague. The Czechs fought for and obtained Czech schools in which to teach their language and culture. Since the Bohemian part of the empire had a good industrial base, a substantial Czech middle class emerged who were determined to obtain places in administration and in the professions. Nationalist writers and composers not only kept Czech culture alive, but made it flourish. The music of Smetana and Dvořák was distinctively nationalistic, and drew much of its inspiration from Bohemian folk music.

When the Hapsburg empire went to war in 1914, Tomáš Masaryk, a professor of philosophy at the Czech University of Prague, escaped to London and argued the case for independence. He proposed the creation of a new state of Czechs and Slovaks, neighbours with whom the Czechs felt they had far more in common than with the Austrians. Masaryk maintained that the Hapsburg empire was doomed because it was

> . . . an aggregate of nine small nations — quite an artificial state — where the dynasty tries to maintain itself in absolute position by the principle of *divide et impera* [divide and rule], by little concessions now to one nation, now to another; and where the Austrians and Magyars are the favourites.

When the war ended in 1918, Masaryk became president of an independent Czechoslovakia (p.185).

MAGYAR RULE

The Hungarian part of the empire was under-industrialised, consisting for the most part of large landlord estates on which the peasantry found it difficult to rise above subsistence farming. Moreover the latter half of the nineteenth century witnessed a rise in population from thirteen to nineteen million. A social gulf developed between the landowners, who dominated the country, and the mass of Hungarians, who were striving to improve their lot and widen the franchise. Many more Hungarians relieved their plight by emigrating to the United States.

The more radical members of parliament wanted to go further than the *Ausgleich* and achieve total independence from Austria. Controversies raged between Budapest and Vienna, especially over trade relations and Franz Joseph's determination to merge the Hungarian regiments into a common imperial army. Political arguments about the *Ausgleich*, social tension between landlords and peasants, and racial conflicts with the Slavs and Romanians, all contributed towards making the parliament in Budapest as ineffective as that in Vienna. Much-needed reforms never got implemented. The Hungarian authorities were too preoccupied with preserving their positions and maintaining Magyar authority over rival nationalities; consequently, their half of the empire did not develop into anything resembling a genuine parliamentary democracy.

The South Slav Problem

In the Hungarian part of the empire, the Magyars constituted only fifty per cent of the population, but they profited from the disunity of the remaining groups. Yet, like the Austrians, the Magyars faced resentment from one group especially — the Croats. These Slavs lived in the area known as Croatia and had their own capital, Zagreb. Though Deák had promised fair treatment to all national minorities at the time of the *Ausgleich* in 1867, he did not keep his promise. Instead, the Magyars dominated the Budapest parliament and filled almost all official positions. Magyar was the dominant language, and every effort was made to prevent Croatian (and other languages) from being used in official business. The Croatians (and other minorities) were not allowed to own their own schools in which to teach their language and culture. Despite this, the Croats succeeded in founding their own university in Zagreb in 1874.

Just as the Czechs and Slovaks were pushed together under pressure from the dominant Austrians, so also the Slav groups came closer under pressure from Hungarian dominance. The bishop of Zagreb, Josef Strossmayer, until his death in 1905, did much to encourage the movement towards unity among the South Slavs — the Croats, the Slovenes, and the Serbs who already had an independent state on the borders of the empire.

The Slav problem was not the only one facing the Hapsburgs. In Transylvania, the Romanian population was becoming increasingly restless and wished to unite with the independent sate of Romania. But the Slav problem was the most urgent, not only because of their numbers, but because of developments within Serbia. In 1903, following a palace revolution in Belgrade, their pro-Austrian king, Alexander, was replaced by the pro-Russian Peter Karageorgevich (p.112). Thereafter, Serbian calls for the union of all Slavs into a South Slav, or Yugoslav, state were viewed with increasing apprehension by the authorities in Budapest and Vienna.

THE FOREIGN POLICY OF AUSTRIA-HUNGARY

Italian unification deprived the Austro-Hungarian empire of her Italian possessions (p.12). Then the war against Bismarck's Prussia in 1866 left her defeated and isolated (p.16). As a result, the Hapsburgs turned towards the Balkans in the hope of filling the vacuum being created by the receding Turkish empire (p.103). Moreover, since the Danube flowed through her two most important cities, Vienna and Budapest, on its way to the Black Sea, it was tempting to control this vital trade route (map p.79).

Franz Joseph greets the German Kaiser William II on his arrival by train at Vienna in March 1914.

Yet the foreign policy of Austria-Hungary was partly defensive in that it sprang from an anxiety to protect the empire against the racial discontents of her own subjects and those of the Ottoman empire. But Austria-Hungary was also concerned with prestige. The period after 1870 was one of expansion, where most European powers acquired vast territories in Africa and Asia. Austria-Hungary was not a sea-going power. Its only coastline was on the Adriatic Sea, and even its principal river, the Danube, reached the Black Sea through foreign territory. The Hapsburgs, therefore, did not seek an overseas empire, but looked for a modest expansion in the Balkans as an outlet for their amibitions. In 1878, profiting from Turkish weakness, Franz Joseph obtained the right at the Congress of Berlin to occupy Bosnia-Herzegovina; and in 1908, these provinces were fully incorporated into the empire (p.112).

This Hapsburg policy, known as *Drang nach Osten* (Drive to the East), brought the empire into conflict with Russia, whose policy of expansion to the Mediterranean also implied control of the Balkans. As a result of this conflict of interests, the *Dreikaiserbund* was doomed (p.31) and the inevitable consequence was the formation of the Dual Alliance with Germany (p.32). In 1908, when the Hapsburgs annexed the province of Bosnia-Herzegovina, it enlarged the Slav population to seven million within the empire (p.112). More importantly, it enraged an already hostile land-locked Serbia, which coveted the area as an outlet to the Adriatic. Then in 1913 relations worsened further when the Hapsburgs were instrumental in forming the state of Albania (p.113), which completed the process of keeping Serbia from the sea.

By 1914 Hapsburg foreign policy had brought her a bewildering variety of problems. Tied to the kaiser's Germany in a military alliance, at enmity with Russia and in direct conflict with Serbia, Franz Joseph and his advisors became apprehensive and reckless. Then, on 28 June 1914, Franz Ferdinand, heir to the Hapsburg throne, was assassinated in the Bosnian capital, Sarajevo, by a Serbian nationalist. The Hapsburg authorities, concluding that Serbia's continued existence posed a direct threat to the integrity of her multiracial empire, issued an unacceptable ulimatum to Serbia, out of which developed the Great War (p.124) and the collapse of the Hapsburg empire.

Study Assignments and Essays

1. *Treat of the main racial groupings within the Hapsburg empire.*
2. *Why did the* Ausgleich *of 1867 not solve the problems of the Hapsburg empire?*
3. *Compare and contrast Austria's handling of the Czech problem with Hungary's handling of the Croat problem.*
4. *'Economic development within the Hapsburg empire was negligible.' Discuss.*
5. *'Hapsburg foreign policy was a disaster.' Discuss.*
6. *Write an essay on two of the following: (i) The Emperor Franz Joseph; (ii) Nationalism in the Hapsburg empire; (iii) Serbia and the Hapsburg empire; (iv) The Hapsburgs and Germany; (v) The Hapsburgs and the Ottoman empire.*

European Expansion Overseas 1870–1914

8

I would annex the planets if I could....
Cecil Rhodes (1853–1902)

THE LONG process whereby Europeans extended their influence and control over the rest of the world began with the geographical explorations of the fifteenth and sixteenth centuries. Expansion continued, although on a greatly reduced scale, through the seventeenth and eighteenth centuries. From the end of the Napoleonic era in 1815 to about 1870, there was an even greater decline in colonial activity, arising from the belief that in general, colonies were of little importance. But from about 1870 onwards, European powers began to develop a new interest in acquiring colonies in Africa and Asia. Although the chief rivals in this scramble for overseas possessions were Britain, France and Germany, other European nations, together with the United States and Japan, were caught up in the fever of imperialism, so that the period from about 1875 to the outbreak of the Great War is known as the Age of Imperialism.

A German postage stamp commemorates that country's expansion into South-West Africa.

MOTIVES FOR IMPERIALISM

Economic

It is not easy to determine the motives for this new urge to expand, but it must be allowed that the most important reason was economic. European industrialisation was producing a surplus of manufactured goods, which necessitated a search for new markets outside Europe; otherwise, the level of industrial production would drop, causing unemployment and social unrest at home. On the other hand, industrialisation created a need for raw materials, which were in short supply at home, while explorers revealed the vast, unexploited wealth of Africa and Asia. There was a growing demand for cotton, wood and minerals, and specifically non-European products such as tea, coffee, palm oil and rubber. Industrialisation also produced a surplus capital in Europe, and financiers saw in colonial enterprises tremendous opportunities for lucrative investment. To many, it seemed that colonies under one's own political control gave a greater guarantee for new markets, the exploitation of raw materials and the safety of investments.

Social

It has often been suggested that the pressure of overpopulation is one explanation for colonial expansion in this period. Britain, Italy and Germany had growing populations. Although considerable numbers of poorer people emigrated from these countries, the majority of them went to areas with temperate climates (the United States and Australia) and few to the new colonial areas, which were not as suitable for Europeans. At the other end of the scale, however, opportunities for quick advancement for ambitious young men of good education and family existed in army, government and business in the colonies.

Political and Military

As international trade grew, there was a great need for coaling stations and seaports to service this trade. This was especially true of Britain and to a lesser extent of France and Germany.

In addition, by the end of the nineteenth century political tensions and rivalries in Europe were leading to the formation of rival groupings and alliances that were seriously threatening the peace. Each power wished to protect its interests by securing strategic naval bases, thus denying them to rival powers.

Nationalism

However, it could be argued that colonies did not form good markets since they did not require manufactured goods, that sources of food, raw materials and areas of investment could be secured more profitably in independent countries like Russia, South America and the United States. Furthermore, colonial possessions were often troublesome and costly to administer.

The real driving force behind the new imperialism after 1870 may have been the rise of nationalism. As it grew more intense, it found expression and an outlet in overseas expansion. National pride was swelled by raising the flag over hitherto unknown areas of the world. The possession of a colonial empire, it was thought, conferred power and prestige on the mother country. Envy of another power's possession led to rivalry; and rivalry created a scramble for possession, which had the effect of partitioning the remaining areas of the world among the European powers in a relatively short space of time.

For Britain, especially, the acquisition of colonial territory was regarded with pride and received popular approval from the patriotic masses. A. C. Benson's 'Land of Hope and Glory' expresses the pride and patriotism of the age in Britain:

Land of Hope and Glory, Mother of the Free,
How shall we extol thee, who are born of thee?
Wider still and wider shall thy bounds be set;
God who made thee mighty, make thee mightier yet.

Most European countries produced an imperialist literature, which helped to invest colonialism with romance and idealism. The highest point of such literature was represented in the works of Rudyard Kipling, which had an enormous vogue in Britain and her colonies. Not only was it entertaining, it also helped to foster the belief that an advanced and cultured nation had a duty to spread its civilisation to the 'backward' peoples of the world. In a poem, 'The White Man's Burden', written in 1899, Kipling stressed this idea as if it was a divine command:

Take up the White Man's burden –
Ye dare not stoop to less –
Nor call too loud on Freedom
To cloak your weariness;
By all ye cry or whisper,
By all ye leave or do,
The silent, sullen peoples
Shall weigh our Gods and you.

Missionary and Humanitarian

This idea of the 'white man's burden' was often mixed up with Christian missionary zeal and activity. Religious motivation was especially true in relation to French colonialism, since France was the missionary nation *par*

A European missionary and converted native preachers in Uganda.

excellence in the catholic world of the nineteenth century. 'If trade followed the flag, the flag sometimes followed the cassock.'

The humanitarian heritage of the eighteenth-century 'enlightenment' motivated many groups and individuals who worked to suppress the slave trade and to provide medical services and education. Unfortunately, not all imperialists had such high ideals; arrogance, aggression and exploitation, unhappily, were adjuncts of colonialism, especially among the latecomers, who all too often sowed the seeds of twentieth-century racial bitterness.

The Influence of Social Darwinism

Scientists and other thinkers had long speculated about the evolution of man on earth. Charles Darwin, having spent several years on scientific expeditions to South America and the Pacific islands, published his findings in 1859 in *The Origin of Species*. Darwin's conclusion was that the 'fittest' survived because they possessed advantageous characteristics, such as the ability to obtain food, particular skills in combat, elusive speed and camouflage. Species with these advantages would survive longer and would tend to reproduce their own kind. In 1871 Darwin published *The Descent of Man*,

AFRICA IN 1900

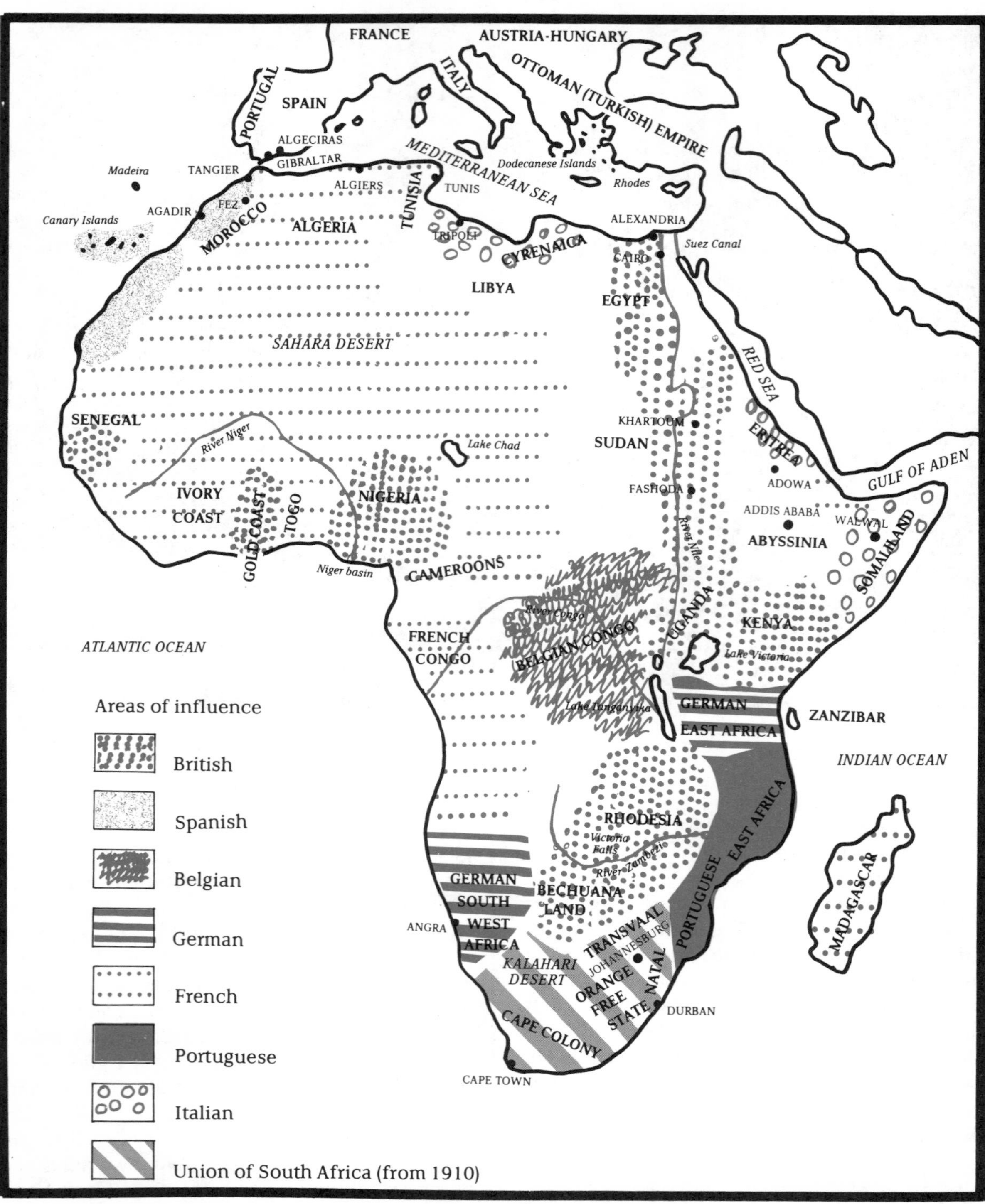

which traced man's descent from animal species through a process of 'natural selection'.

Darwin's theory of life as a struggle for existence met a ready response among late nineteenth-century imperialists, for the idea of 'natural selection' provided a useful excuse for the subjugation of weaker nations and colonial peoples by stronger powers. Racists, who believed in the superiority of one race over another, strongly supported Darwin's thesis and turned it into what is called 'Social Darwinism', or the application of Darwin's 'laws' of nature into laws of societies and nations. These people conveniently ignored the fundamental difference between nature and man. In nature, a non-human species survives in a natural situation of competition, whereas man lives in civilised protective societies and must necessarily co-operate in order to survive.

INDIVIDUAL EXPLORERS

Two important scientific discoveries made it easier for Europeans to conquer Africa. The development of quinine enabled white colonialists to resist the malarial mosquito, and the invention of the Gatling machine-gun gave Europeans a decided advantage over African resistance.

In 1870, except for a few coastal areas, Africa was still the 'dark continent', little known by Europeans, who believed that it was inhabited by primitive negro tribes. Exploration of the interior began late in the eighteenth century when Mungo Park, a young Scottish doctor, tried to discover the source of the Niger. In the 1830s, Richard Lander, an Englishman, further explored the Niger basin, and by 1840 the entire course of this great river was known. In the 1850s Heinrich Barth, a German, explored the area around Lake Chad and gave the world the first accurate description of this area. In East Africa, Richard Burton and John Speke, English explorers, discovered Lake Tanganyika in 1858. The same year Speke discovered Lake Victoria, and six years later he proved that it was also the source of the Nile.

But the greatest and most famous of all African explorers was David Livingstone, a Scottish medical missionary. He began missionary work in Bechuanaland, was the first white man to cross the Kalahari desert, and discovered the Victoria Falls in 1855. His writings, even more than his explorations, were extremely influential, for his reports on the horrors of the slave trade speeded up its abolition in East Africa. Livingstone stressed the need to open up Africa to 'commerce and Christianity', and thus he stimulated widespread interest in the continent.

In 1866 Livingstone began another great journey in Africa and was not heard of for several years. It was widely believed that the world's greatest living explorer was lost. In 1869 the New York *Herald* sent its best reporter, Henry M. Stanley, to Africa with orders to find Livingstone. After enduring many hardships, in November 1871, Stanley wandered into a village on Lake Tanganyika and there found a lone white man. In Stanley's words:

> As I advanced slowly towards him I noticed he was pale, looked wearied, had a grey beard, wore a bluish cap with a faded gold band around it, had on a red sleeved waistcoat, and a pair of grey tweed trousers. I would have run to him, would have embraced him, only I did not know how he would receive me; so I walked deliberately to him, took off my hat, and said: 'Dr Livingstone, I presume?' 'Yes,' he said with a kind smile, lifting his cap slightly. 'I thank God, Doctor, I have been permitted to see you.'

Stanley tried to persuade Livingstone to give up his work and return home, but

Henry Stanley.

Livingstone refused. Instead he travelled west to explore further, and died two years later.

Meanwhile Stanley went on to the Congo, and succeeded in making the dangerous trip down the Congo River to its mouth at the Atlantic. Stanley published his observations in a book, *Through the Dark Continent*, where in thrilling fashion he described his adventures and pointed out the wonderful resources and commercial possibilities of Africa.

Yet, although Stanley's book was widely read, he was unable to secure financial backing for his projects in Britain or the United States. However, he did arouse the interest of King Leopold II of Belgium in the mineral wealth of the Congo river basin. Leopold organised a private commercial company which beguiled the native chiefs into turning over their lands to the company, and the work of exploiting the rubber, palm-oil and ivory markets by slave labour began.

In 1885 Leopold's holdings in Africa were formed into the Congo Free State, into which he poured huge capital. The rewards were rich as rubber exports soared, but this was only achieved through forcing the natives into terribly cruel conditions of work, amounting to inhuman slave labour, which aroused great public indignation. Insistent demands for fundamental reforms, especially after the reports of Roger Casement in 1903, came from both inside and outside Belgium and forced Leopold, in return for financial compensation, to transfer his 'Congo Free State' to the Belgian government in 1908. It then became known as the Belgian Congo, an area eighty times the size of Belgium.

NORTH AFRICA

Britain and France

The Muslim lands along the Mediterranean coast of North Africa were, with the exception of Morocco, subject territories of the Sultan of Turkey. Tripoli, Libya and Egypt were actually parts of the Ottoman empire. Algeria and Tunisia were technically subject, but were in practice free of Turkish control. As a result, the partition of North Africa was carried out under different conditions from those which prevailed in sub-Saharan Africa, where negro tribes lived, or in South Africa where white Boers had settled (map, p.88).

For hundreds of years the North African coastal territories had harboured pirates, who preyed upon shipping and exacted tribute from European nations that used the Mediterranean; and although these activities had declined, they still survived well into the nineteenth century. In 1830 France began the occupation of Algeria as a final step in eliminating piracy in the Mediterranean. Thus, almost by accident, France became a colonising power in North Africa.

France did not follow up this acquisition until 1881 when Tunisia became a French protectorate. From there, the French pushed southwards along the caravan routes, establishing military posts as they proceeded across the Sahara and into western Sudan, eventually linking up with their equatorial possessions, the French Congo and the Ivory Coast. They hoped eventually to extend their possessions right across Africa as far as the Gulf of Aden.

Egypt, officially part of the Ottoman empire, with its own ruler, the Khedive, had loosened many of the bonds tying it to the Sultan and was moving towards full independence. But when the hundred-mile Suez Canal, completed by French engineers and financed from European loans, was opened in 1869, Egypt took on a new significance. Britain regarded the Suez Canal as its lifeline to India, and when the Khedive was unable to meet the interest on his loans in 1875 he was forced to sell his shares in the Suez Canal Company to Britain, which thereby became the largest single shareholder. In 1877 the Khedive again repudiated his debts and this time his chief creditors, Britain and France, set up a 'dual control' of the Khedive's finances. In 1879 the Sultan had the Khedive deposed in favour of Tewfik, his son, who equally resented foreign control, and in 1882 Colonel Arabi Pasha led a violent revolt.

Although the French refused to use force, the British navy bombarded Alexandria, while British troops occupied the country, suppressed the revolt and placed Tewfik under their protection as nominal ruler. This victory enabled Britain to assume sole control in Egypt and appoint a viceroy, Lord Cromer, who held that position until 1907. Under Cromer, Egypt made great material progress; finances were put in order; the administration of justice improved and irrigation works were instituted. In 1883 a local assembly was created and thirty years later it was given some legislative powers.

To the south of Egypt lay the Sudan. The first attempt by Britain to conquer this area ended in disaster, when General Gordon's garrison was annihilated by native troops at Khartoum in 1885. Then in 1898 a French expedition under Captain Jean Marchand, after crossing more than 2,000 miles of almost unexplored wilderness, arrived at Fashoda, a village on the Nile, and claimed the territory for France. Marchand had set out two years previously from Senegal, on the Atlantic, and had proceeded through the French Congo to the upper Nile Valley. The British insisted that the area was in their sphere of influence, and a fortnight later General Kitchener arrived with a much larger expeditionary force (2,000 men) and bigger guns. Marchand refused to lower the French flag, but Kitchener refrained from using force, while both generals sought instructions from home by telegraph.

For a time the two nations stood on the brink of war, but eventually the French renounced all claims to the Nile Valley and in 1899 Marchand and his expedition were withdrawn. Anglo-French relations were at a low ebb, especially among the French imperialists, because Fashoda had effectively stopped their ambition of creating a French empire from west to east across the continent. Nevertheless, Delcassé, the foreign minister who had made the decision, pointed out that it was better to lose the Sudan than to face certain war with Britain over the 'sands of the desert', while facing the German threat in Europe as well.

Italian Ventures

Italy's ambition was to create an empire in North Africa that would earn her a place among the European powers. But she found powerful rivals in France and Britain. France thwarted her ambition to acquire Tunisia in 1881, but Italy went on to seize Eritrea on the Red Sea, and Somaliland on the Indian Ocean. Yet these two areas were of little use to Italy unless she could also occupy Abyssinia (Ethiopia), which lay between them. In 1896 the Italians embarked on a war, but the Abyssinians resisted fiercely and defeated the Italians at the Battle of Adowa. It was a humiliating defeat, and Italy did not attempt any further ventures in North Africa for over a decade (map, p.88).

By the beginning of the twentieth century, France and Britain had taken over all the North African states with the exception of Cyrenaica (Libya), which remained in Turkish hands. In 1911, when the Turks were occupied with problems in the Balkans (p.113), and Britain, France and Germany were distracted with the second Moroccan crisis (p.122), the Italians availed of the opportunity to win prestige in a new colonial adventure and offset the humiliation of Adowa. In September war was declared on the Turks, and the Italians snatched Libya, as well as Rhodes and the Dodecanese Islands. However, success over the Turks did not mean victory. Tribesmen in Libya continued to resist; and the Italians were confined to Tripoli and little more than the coastline.

WEST AFRICA

Meanwhile the French, British and Germans had turned their attention to the Niger region. In 1879 the British founded the United Africa Company for the purposes of trading in the Niger delta. German merchants were busy trying to obtain treaties with the chiefs in northern Nigeria, but before they could get a foothold Britain proclaimed a protectorate over the region in 1885. The first German colony in Africa was established in 1883 at Angra, a semi-desert region on the south-west coast. The next year they acquired the Cameroons, between the French Congo and British Nigeria. Within ten days both the British and the French arrived, but they were too late.

At this stage the great powers agreed to call a conference on African affairs, which met in Berlin in 1885. They declared that their main objectives were to bring European civilisation to the African people and to put an end to the practice of slavery, which could not be achieved other than by direct occupation of African territories. The powers therefore agreed upon certain rules of procedure whereby each would respect the areas of occupation of their rivals. The result was that the continent of Africa, with its 150 million people, was partitioned, despite many conflicting claims, without recourse to war.

EAST AFRICA

In East Africa the rivalry was mainly between Germany and Britain. In 1884 Dr Karl Peters, a German explorer, founded the Society for German Colonisation. Although Bismarck was not enthusiastic, many German firms supported Peters. Finally the Berlin government gave him a charter to form the German East Africa Company, which formed a protectorate over Zanzibar and an area along the East African coast. The British and Germans proceeded to share out the vast hinterland of East Africa. In 1888 the British took over the area now known as Kenya. Then in 1890 they attempted to bring Uganda under their rule. There had been no definite indication at the Berlin conference as to whether this area came within the British or German sphere of influence. Finally in 1894 it was agreed that the British government should declare a protectorate over the area. The East Africans did not welcome British or German rule and neither did the Arabs, who had carried on a profitable trade in negro slaves in East Africa for centuries. Several native risings took place against German and British rule, but they were put down with great harshness.

SOUTH AFRICA AND THE BOERS

British expansion in South Africa brought them into conflict with white people of European origin — the Boers, descendants of Dutch Calvinists who had left the Netherlands in the seventeenth century and had carved out a colony for themselves at the Cape. During the Napoleonic war, Britain had taken Cape Colony from Holland. Then in 1833, when the British insisted that they should free their negro slaves, the Boers, in resentment, moved north in great numbers, and after the 'Great Trek' formed two new states, the Orange Free State and the Transvaal. When Britain tried to gain control of these states, the Boers stubbornly resisted and finally, in the early 1850s, the British government acknowledged their independence.

The discovery of gold and diamonds in Kimberley and the Rand region of the Transvaal, in 1886, brought numerous foreign fortune hunters, *Uitlanders* (outsiders), into the area. One such outsider was the British imperialist Cecil Rhodes. In 1887 he founded the British South Africa Company (it was granted a royal charter in 1889) which acquired the title to a vast area of land which later became known as Rhodesia. In 1890 Rhodes became prime minister of Cape Colony. He dreamed of extending British influence northwards and of building a Cape-to-Cairo railway. The main obstacle to the development of his plans was the Transvaal, the president of which was Paul Kruger, a Boer Calvinist who never tired of showing his hostility to the *Uitlanders*, especially the British.

As the gold mining industry grew, more settlers continued to pour in, creating a thriving town, Johannesburg, around the mines. Before long there were as many *Uitlanders* as male adult Boers and it was estimated that they paid 95 per cent of the government's revenue. Kruger was determined that the *Uitlanders* would have no say in government, and flatly rejected their appeals for voting rights.

The Jameson Raid

In 1895 there were rumours of an *Uitlander* revolt. Rhodes, realising that an insurrection would make his intervention look plausible, prepared for attack. The same year Dr Starr Jameson, a friend and agent of Rhodes, collected a small mounted force on the borders of the Transvaal and waited for the rising to begin. As the year wore on and no uprising occurred, Jameson lost his patience and invaded in the belief that the *Uitlanders* would rise to greet their 'liberators'. But the raid failed to spark off a rising and the news of the invasion caused a sensation in Europe.

THE BOER WAR, 1899–1902

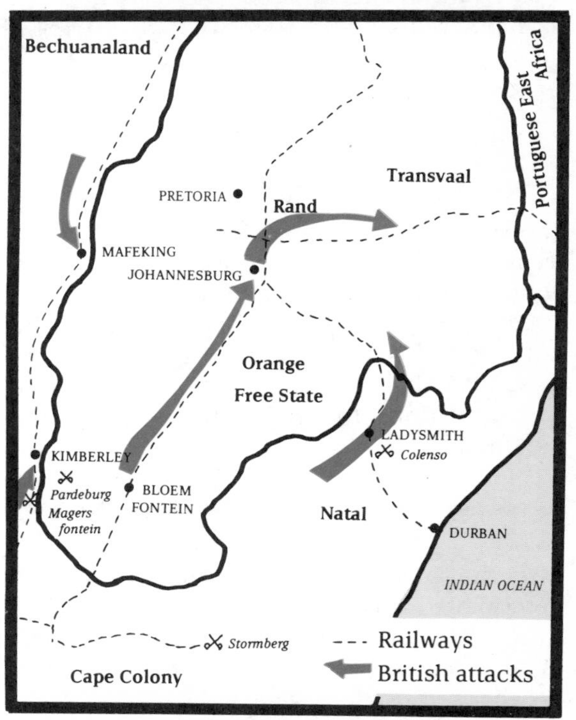

Boer settlers fighting the British at Ladysmith during the Boer War.

The British government disclaimed all knowledge and responsibility and Rhodes was obliged to resign as premier of Cape Colony. The other powers were vocal in their criticism of the British, but they did not go as far as the kaiser, William II, who sent a telegram of congratulations to Kruger, which infuriated the British.

The Boer War

After the Jameson raid, relations continued to deteriorate rapidly until, in October 1899, Kruger declared war, hoping for a quick victory before British reinforcements could arrive.

The Boers had the advantage of fighting in their own country, over terrain they knew intimately and which was eminently suited to guerrilla warfare. Under the leadership of Louis Botha and Christian de Wet, the Boers besieged the British in the towns of Ladysmith, Mafeking and Kimberley and went on to win three battles at Stormberg, Magersfontein and Colenso in 1899. The British, stirred by defeat, poured in an army of 350,000 men under the command of Lord Roberts and Lord Kitchener and quickly redressed the balance. By February 1900, the Boers' main army was encircled and was forced to surrender at Paardeburg. Ladysmith and Mafeking were relieved and the war seemed over; but the Boers thought differently. Outnumbered and ill-equipped, they broke up into small units and resorted to guerrilla warfare.

This 'hit and run' warfare left the superior British army at a decided disadvantage. Kitchener therefore resorted to a systematic comb-out of the entire territory. By using 8,000 block houses, joined by miles of barbed wire, the army cleared the Transvaal of guerrillas, burning their farmsteads and putting their women and children into concentration camps. Over 26,000 died in these camps from neglect, disease and malnutrition. This produced an outcry in Britain; her popularity in Europe sank to a low ebb, and the British government was compelled to make peace with the Boers on favourable terms.

The Settlement

By the Treaty of Vereeniging in 1902, the Boers of the Transvaal and the Orange Free State accepted British sovereignty. In return they received £3 million to rebuild their farmsteads and a promise of self-government in the near future.

When the Liberal government came to power in 1906, the prime minister, Henry Campbell-Bannerman, granted independence to the Boer colonies. In 1910 the two British colonies, Cape Colony and Natal, together with the two Boer colonies, the Transvaal and the Orange Free State, were formed into a confederation known as the Union of South Africa. The first prime minister of the Union was the Boer, Louis Botha, who remained in office until his death in 1919.

COMPARISON OF COLONIAL ACQUISITIONS

In the partition of Africa, Britain had obtained the best share. She had secured all the principal areas that were climatically suitable for European settlement. With one exception, she had completed her all-British route from the Cape to Cairo, and bestrode three of the four great African rivers on which the growth of trade and civilisation largely depended.

The French had secured the largest share in area, though not in population or mineral wealth. Her area of acquisition did however include a portion of the Congo river basin, and Madagascar, the third largest island in the world. Moreover, her North African colonies were ideally situated for her policy of 'assimilation', or treating colonies and their inhabitants as provinces and citizens of France proper. In 1900 France applied 'tariff assimilations' to her North African colonies, which meant that French goods could be imported customs free by the colonies. However, the reverse did not obtain because France only exercised 'a preference for' goods from tariff-assimilated areas. Despite these economic arrangements, the results were very disappointing and French colonial commerce remained negligible. Still, the French, like the British, were motivated by political as well as economic reasons, and they were most effective in their general civilising influence and in the spreading of French culture.

The German experience in Africa was most disappointing. Not one of her colonies contributed more than its expense, nor did any of her colonies prove attractive for German emigrants, who continued to emigrate to the United States. In 1914 the Germans were about to turn their colonies to an alternative use as plantations, which, it was hoped, would supply their needs for rubber, oilseed and cotton, but the outbreak of war ended such schemes, and when it was over, Germany lost all her colonies by the Treaty of Versailles (p.182).

Italian empire-building in North Africa was disastrous. Her defeat at the hands of Abyssinian tribesmen was a national humiliation, which was not erased until Mussolini finally conquered Abyssinia in 1935 (p.219). In theory, Italy's acquisition of Libya was a triumph, because this was one of the last areas still available for the establishment of empire; but it brought no benefits. The struggle with local tribesmen, which continued until 1931, was a continual drain on Italy's limited resources, which could have been put to better use in alleviating the worst excesses of poverty at home (p.73).

ASIA AND THE PACIFIC

India

In the seventeenth century Britain acquired commercial interests in India. She continued to extend her influence and by 1857 British rule was supreme throughout the whole subcontinent. Britain ruled India through a resident viceroy, who had full authority. In 1861 a legislative and executive council, which after 1892 included Indian representatives, was established to assist him. An efficient Indian civil service was also created, although the British held all the key positions. In 1876 the parliament in London enacted that British possessions in India be termed an empire, with Queen Victoria as empress of India. This was the most prized of all British possessions and was termed the 'jewel' in the British crown.

The most important effect of British rule in India was unification. Never before had the entire subcontinent come under a single authority. The introduction of English as an official language also provided a unifying force. The British in India did much to bring law and order and provide protection for life and property. They also put an end to certain socio-religious practices, such as the suicide of widows on their husbands' funeral pyres and the killing of infant girls. Other improvements included the laying of railway and telegraph lines, and the creation of extensive irrigation works that brought fertility to otherwise barren lands.

On the other hand, British rule in India was geared more to the promotion of its own economic interests than to the betterment of Indians. Some 50 per cent of Britain's budgeted outlay on India went on army expenditure, while a mere 15 per cent was expended on schools and hospitals. The majority of India's population were on the verge of starvation, while about 95 per cent remained illiterate. Even the better-educated Indians were treated as second-class citizens, so that by 1915 only 5 per cent of the higher civil servants were Indians. In the nineteenth century this small group could do little, but in the twentieth century Japan's spectacular success showed that non-European races could stand up to the western powers. Then, World War I, and the self-determination policy of Woodrow Wilson, the American president, created the conditions necessary for a demand for independence to arise. This demand was eventually successful on 15 August 1947 when India achieved independence.

The Pacific

Africa was not the only area of imperialist activity in this period. Some few islands in the Pacific had been acquired by the great powers earlier in the century. The French made Tahiti a protectorate in 1843 and New Caledonia became a penal settlement ten years later. The Australians were fearful of French encroachment and called upon the British to forestall them. In this way an Anglo-French protectorate was formed over the New Hebrides. In 1874 the Fiji Islands became a British crown colony.

The western half of New Guinea had long been a Dutch possession; but when German traders appeared in the eastern half, the Australians again urged the British to forestall them. Eventually in 1886 an Anglo-German agreement divided the area, the northern half going to Germany, the southern half to Britain. This agreement also recognised Germany's right to the Bismarck Archipelago,

ASIA AND THE PACIFIC IN 1900

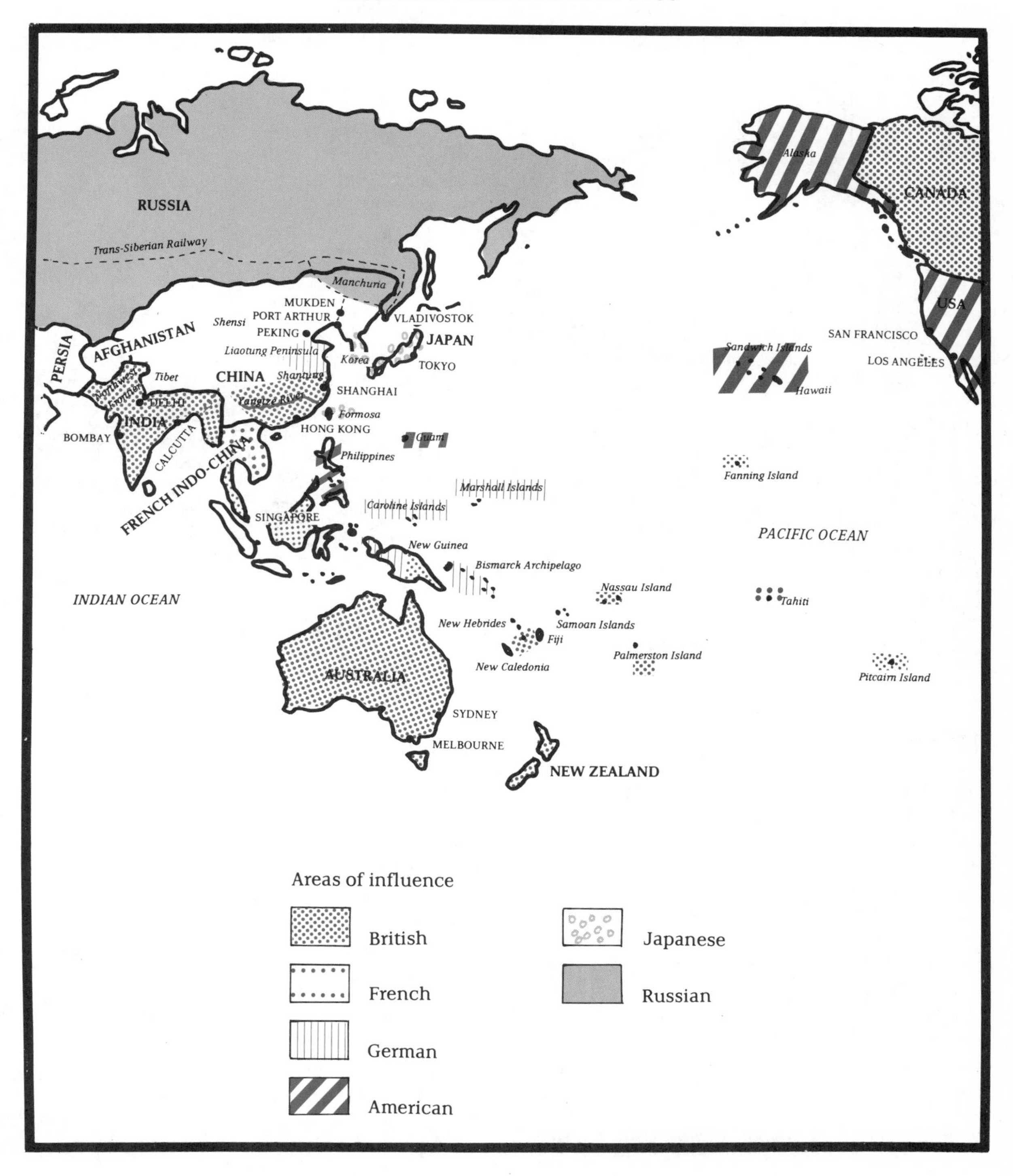

An important British official is greeted on his arrival by elephant at Secunderabad in India.

the Caroline Islands and the Marshall Islands. In 1889 the Samoan group of islands in the South Pacific was divided between the United States, Britain and Germany.

The United States, the only power with a Pacific seaboard, also became involved in taking islands in the Pacific, even though she was ready to denounce European imperialism. By 1900 America had control of the Philippines, Puerto Rico, Guam and the Sandwich Islands (Hawaii).

When a submarine cable was laid between the British dominions of Canada and Australia, it led to the British occupation of several isolated islands: Fanning Island, Pitcairn Island, Nassau Island and Palmerston Island. With the possible exception of the United States, the islands of the Pacific were so far removed from the great powers that it is surprising that they took such an interest in them. For the British, Germans and Americans, their commercial value was the prime motive. The products of these islands (cotton, oils, copra and fruit) were valuable in European and American markets. For the French, their value seemed to have lain solely in their suitability as penal settlements.

The Far East

For centuries the two great nations of the Far East, China and Japan, were almost completely cut off from the outside world. Then in 1853 an American, Commodore Matthew Perry (backed up by a fleet) secured the opening of certain Japanese ports to foreign trade. Within the next few years Britain, France and Russia obtained similar concessions, and Japan experienced an overwhelming dose of western influences.

The inability of the *Samurai* (the old feudal military aristocracy) to withstand western infiltration led to a revolution in 1868. The new rulers (the *Meiji*) set about copying western military tactics and bringing Japan into the nineteenth century. They too aimed at building an empire in the Far East. Japan's first expansive move was centred on Korea. In 1894, China, the nominal ruler of Korea, sent troops to crush a local revolt. Japan, fearing that the Chinese intended to conquer Korea, also sent in troops. War followed. The Japanese were easily victorious and by the Treaty of Shimonoseki in 1895, Korea was detached from China and made independent (Japan annexed it in 1910). Japan also received the island of Formosa and would have taken over the Liaotung Peninsula and Port Arthur had not Russia, backed by France and Germany, intervened. The Japanese felt bitter towards Russia, whom they blamed for having deprived them of the spoils of victory (p.55 and map p.97).

The Treaty of Shimonoseki left China intact, but only because the big powers had intervened to curb Japan. Now the powers themselves rushed in to demand concessions from a China, which, under the Manchu dynasty, was too weak militarily to resist foreign demands.

Russian interests in the Far East were understandable. Despite her enormous size, she was a land-locked country with no outlet to warm waters. Her efforts to gain a free passage through the Black Sea to the Mediterranean had been prevented on several occasions throughout the nineteenth century. After her diplomatic defeat at the Congress of Berlin, Russia's expansion changed direction — to the south-east through Persia and Afghanistan to the Indian Ocean and through the Far East to the Pacific.

In 1891 Russia began building the 5,000 mile railway line from St Petersburg to Vladivostok on the Pacific. In 1898 she obtained a lease of Port Arthur and was allowed to establish fortifications on the Liaotung Peninsula (p.53). The railway ran along the boundary of Manchuria, while a more direct line was permitted to run through Manchuria (via Mukden) to Port Arthur (p.55 and map p.97).

Britain, France and Germany moved in quickly to carve up the 'Chinese Melon' by establishing spheres of influence. The British built railways, and opened mines in the rich Yangtze Valley. Russia got concessions in the north, Germany in the Shantung Peninsula, and France in the south.

In 1899, the United States, fearing that she would be shut out completely, proposed an 'open door' policy; that is, that all powers should compete everywhere in the Far East on equal terms. At first, America's proposal fell upon deaf ears, but gradually her policy came to be accepted. Otherwise China would inevitably have been partitioned on much the same lines as Africa.

Many Chinese deeply resented the exploitation of their country by foreigners, and patriotic societies sprang up to oppose outside domination. One such secret organisation, the Boxers, was organised in 1898 with the object of resisting the foreigner. They held demonstrations, created riots and attacked foreign property. In the province of Shensi, 200 missionaries were killed. Finally they laid siege to the foreign legations in Peking. A six-nation force immediately rushed in troops and put down the rebellion. The great powers used this opportunity to impose even harsher control on China, including the execution of high-ranking Chinese officials and the payment of a huge indemnity.

The consequences of this treatment of the

Chinese were to continue throughout the twentieth century, in the form of enmity towards all foreigners.

EFFECTS OF IMPERIALISM

On European Powers

European expansion overseas between 1870 and 1914 was accomplished without resort to war between the European powers. Nevertheless it did result in several conflicts of interest and heightened tension, which, if not producing war, did contribute, through jealousies and fears, towards the Great War of 1914.

In the 1890s the German Kaiser encouraged the Boers and greatly annoyed the British over episodes such as the Kruger telegram (p.94).

The crisis at Fashoda in 1898 between France and Britain did not lead to war, but it did have the effect of persuading Britain to look for allies, thereby contributing to the formation of the *Entente Cordiale* of 1904 (p.120).

The two crises over Morocco were more serious (p.120). There the kaiser's actions had the effect of drawing France and Britain into closer collaboration and of leaving Germany with a sense of isolation and hurt pride.

On the Colonial Peoples

As the industrial nations of Europe penetrated non-European areas (especially Africa), the whole way of life of the native peoples was affected. The degree of disruption, however, varied because the administration of each area varied from direct rule to token submission of a tribal ruler. In many areas the natives were uprooted from their villages, separated from their families and forced into new types of work in mines and on railway construction.

In effect, the advent of imperialism brought the benefits and the ills of modern civilisation. It brought new diseases, but also improved medicines. It brought the Christian religion, but also sectarian rivalry. It brought modern industry, but also the exploitation of workers in mines and factories. It brought improved agricultural methods, but also forced labour on plantations. The French and Portuguese treated most natives as equals, but the British and Germans drew a definite 'colour line' and lived like exclusive aliens in the midst of native peoples.

On the credit side, imperalism brought roads, canals, ports and railways, which opened up hitherto inaccessible areas, and created a sound infrastructure on which the native peoples could build their economies when they eventually received statehood in the post-1945 era. Imperialism brought modern sanitation, medical facilities and hospitals; and, to a considerable extent, also brought education and Christianity, although these were more properly the result of missionary activity facilitated by imperialism.

Both the catholic and protestant churches engaged in a renewed missionary enterprise in the wake of European imperial expansion overseas. In the catholic church, older institutions, such as the Society for the Propagation of the Faith, were revived, while the Society of Jesus, the Benedictines, Dominicans and Franciscans took on a renewed vigour. New religious societies such as the White Fathers, the Marists, the Holy Ghost Fathers, and the Fathers of the Divine Word were founded specifically to spread Christianity in the new colonial lands.

By 1870 a number of protestant missionary groups were competing with each other and with the catholics for converts in the colonial lands. Most protestant missionary societies working in the age of imperialism — the Baptist Society, the Presbyterian and Congregationalist London Missionary Society, and the Anglican Church Missionary Society —

had been formed in the late eighteenth century.

By 1910 it was estimated that some 41,000 catholic and some 18,000 protestant missionaries were working abroad in non-European lands. Their efforts met with considerable success, as is evidenced from the numbers of practising converts to Christainity.

Numbers of Conversions to Christianity

	Africa	India	China	Korea & Japan
Catholic	3m.	2½m.	1m.	120,000
Protestant	2½m.	1½m.	½m.	86,000
Total	5½m.	4m.	1½m.	¼m.

Another less measurable result of missionary activity was its contribution to the general Europeanisation of the colonial peoples as expressed through dress, language and sport.

Finally, imperialism brought European notions of democracy and nationalism; and when these were expressed through an educated colonial minority, the motive force of independence movements proved irresistible in the post-1945 world. Thus, to a significant degree, European imperialism in Africa and Asia brought with it the seeds of its own destruction.

Study Assignments and Essays

1. *What were the principal motives that led European powers to acquire overseas possessions in the years after 1870?*
2. *Treat of the partition of North Africa and the rivalries and tensions which flowed therefrom.*
3. *'The acquisition of East and West Africa was of little interest to anyone.' Do you agree?*
4. *What were the causes of the Boer War?*
5. *Make a comparative analysis of colonial acquisitions in Africa by the great powers.*
6. *Write an essay on two of the following: (i) The Far East and European imperialism; (ii) The importance of the Pacific in the age of imperialism; (iii) The effects of colonialism on native peoples; (iv) The repercussions in Europe of imperial expansion overseas; (v) Imperialism and Christianity.*

The Eastern Question 1870–1914 9

Those who cannot remember the past are condemned to repeat it.

George Santayana, American philosopher 1863–1952 in *The Life of Reason*

SINCE 1815 the Turkish (Ottoman) empire in Europe, which included the Balkan Peninsula and contained several Christian races of Slav origin, was fast crumbling. By 1870 Greece, Serbia and Romania had attained a certain degree of independence while the tiny state of Montenegro, secure behind her mountain barrier, had never fallen under Turkish authority. But many Slav peoples still remained under oppressive Turkish rule and, as the nineteenth century progressed, they became more and more determined to achieve self-determination.

The question of independence for the Slav peoples under Turkish rule was not a simple matter of ruler versus subject, but was complicated by the attitude of the other European powers. Russia was a great Slav nation whose people were orthodox Christians. The peoples of south-eastern Europe were also Slavs and the vast majority of them were orthodox Christians too. On this account, Russia put forward her claim as protector of her Slav brothers and co-religionists under Turkish rule.

Constantinople, capital of the Turkish Empire, was the gateway from the Black Sea to the Sea of Marmara and the Mediterranean.

This policy, known as Pan-Slavism, had obvious advantages for Russia: since the reign of Catherine the Great in the eighteenth century, Russia, which had no ice-free port, wanted to expand southwards to the Mediterranean on the ruins of the Turkish empire. The Russians certainly wished to extend their power to Constantinople, which guarded the exit from the Black Sea into the Sea of Marmara. From there the way was clear through the Dardanelles to the Aegean Sea, which led directly into the Mediterranean. By claiming to act as the guardian of her Slav cousins and co-religionists, Russia gave to her expansionist policy a degree of respectability, even the aura of a crusade. Yet, despite this, Russia had to move very cautiously in the Balkans, lest she should unduly antagonise the other powers, who regarded her concern for the Balkan Slavs as a mere pretext to conceal an expansionist foreign policy.

Britain, and to a lesser extent France, strongly opposed Russian expansionism, as both powers had commercial investments in the Near and Middle East, including Turkey. Britain, particularly, feared that Russia would get too powerful and perhaps strike at Persia (Iran), Afghanistan, and then at British India. She therefore wished to prop up Turkey, 'the sick man of Europe', because the triumph of Balkan nationalism would essentially mean the emergence of backward states manipulated by Russia. Italy's ambitions lay in North Africa (p.91). She was not concerned with the Balkans except in so far as it concerned the Hapsburg empire. Since Italy had territorial claims on the Hapsburgs (South Tyrol and Istria), events in the Balkans, which might also involve the Hapsburgs, could possibly open up opportunities for her to press claims to *Italia Irredenta* (p.76).

The position of Austria-Hungary was more complex. On the one hand she feared the triumph of Slav nationalism in the Balkans because it might lead to demands for independence from her own Slav subjects (p.82). On the other hand, the Hapsburgs hoped to see the end of Turkish rule in Europe so that they could fill the vacuum created by the receding Turks. Because the unification of Italy had blocked them in the south-west and the unification of Germany had shut them off from the north, they now turned towards the Balkans and the Danube trade route (map p.79).

This Hapsburg policy, known as *Drang nach Osten* (drive to the east) was in direct conflict with Russia's policy of Pan-Slavism. It was this irreconcilable conflict of interests in the Balkans between Russia and Austria-Hungary, compounded by the attitudes of the other powers, which created the 'Eastern Question'. The question was further complicated by racial, religious and traditional rivalries among the Balkan groups themselves, each of which was at a different stage of social and economic development.

THE BALKAN REVOLT 1874–76

In 1874 there were poor harvests in the Balkans, yet the Sultan's tax collectors demanded full payments from the hungry peasants. The following year the people of Bosnia and Herzegovina rose in rebellion and unrest spread rapidly throughout the region. Serbia and Montenegro joined in the uprising, and then the Bulgars, aflame with national spirit, rebelled. None of the great powers wanted war, and Russia, Germany and Austria-Hungary attempted to settle the crises by forcing the Turks to introduce reforms. After meeting in Berlin to discuss the problem, they sent a note to the Sultan urging him to carry out reforms in the hope of making his harsh rule more tolerable to his Christian subjects. The Sultan agreed, but the Balkan peoples, who had experienced 300 years of Turkish oppression, did not believe the Sultan's promises, and the revolt continued.

In May 1876 the three powers again met in

Berlin and this time they presented the Sultan with the Berlin Memorandum, which listed a number of necessary reforms, and threatened intervention if the Turks did not comply. Italy and France also lent their support to the Memorandum, but Britain's prime minister, Benjamin Disraeli, in accordance with his country's policy of propping up Turkey and curtailing Russia, was opposed to intervention and moved British warships to the mouth of the Dardanelles. Disraeli dismissed reports of Turkish atrocities against the Slavs as Russian propaganda. The Sultan, believing that he could count on Britain's support, rejected the Memorandum, and the threatened intervention did not materialise. British policy had ensured that united action to solve the Eastern Question did not take place and Turkish rule in the Balkans continued.

By now the Balkans were in turmoil. In June the Sultan was killed and was replaced by Murad V, but he went insane and after three months was replaced by the wily Abdul Hamid II. The new Sultan unleashed an irregular army known as *Bashi-Bazouks* against the Bulgars. They terrorised the peasant population, murdered thousands of men, women and children, burned towns and villages and stamped out the revolt. On 20 September *The Times* printed a report of a British official who had been sent to investigate the atrocities. He described how, after a Turkish official had forced the people of a Bulgarian village to give up first their arms and then their money, the Turks

> . . . set upon the people and slaughtered them like sheep. A large number of people, probably about 1,000 or 1,200, took refuge in the Church . . . The Turks fired in the windows, and, getting upon the roof, tore off the tiles and threw burning pieces of wood and rags dipped in petroleum among the masses of unhappy human beings inside. At last the door was forced in, the massacre completed, and the inside of the Church burnt.

Slavs throughout the Balkans were calling for vengeance. The mood in Russia was for immediate war against Turkey, but the tsar was reluctant to take that step. Disraeli continued to play down the Bulgarian massacres as mere 'coffee house gossip'. The previous year, 1875, Britain had purchased shares in the Suez Canal (p.91) and now more than ever the British viewed with alarm any extension of Russian influence towards the canal. Gladstone, the Liberal leader, wrote a famous pamphlet, *The Bulgarian Horrors and the Question of the East*, which created an anti-Turkish mood in Britain and made Disraeli's policy of helping Turkey extremely unpopular.

In December 1876 a conference of the powers met in Constantinople to discuss the Balkan problem. Even the British delegate, Lord Salisbury, agreed that the Turks must be forced to introduce reforms. The crafty Sultan announced that a new liberal constitution had been drawn up, safeguarding the rights of all his subjects. But once the conference was over, the Sultan withdrew the constitution, and the peoples of the Balkans continued their struggle.

THE RUSSO-TURKISH WAR 1877–78

In January 1877 Tsar Alexander decided that, in accordance with Pan-Slavism, Russia should take direct military action against Turkey. But since he knew that this would arouse the hostility of Austria-Hungary and Britain, he turned to Bismarck for assurance of support. Bismarck, who had no intention of getting Germany entangled in the Eastern Question, declared in the Reichstag, 'The whole of the Balkans is not worth the bones of a single Pomeranian musketeer.'

Events now moved quickly. Russia managed to secure Hapsburg neutrality by promising not to allow any large Slav state to be formed out of Turkish-controlled territory and by agreeing to allow the Hapsburgs to take over Bosnia-Herzegovina. British fears were assuaged with a Russian declaration that she had no designs on Constantinople and the Dardanelles.

In April 1877 Tsar Alexander declared war on Turkey and Romania gave safe passage to the Russian troops advancing into Bulgaria. In July they were held at Plevna for four months by the heroic defence of the fortress by the Turkish commander, Osman Pasha. In December the fortress, reduced by starvation, surrendered; but the siege had cost the Russians heavy casualties. The way was now open for the capture of Sofia, the chief town of Bulgaria. In January 1878 the Russians captured Adrianople (map p.106). Constantinople looked in danger, but whether the Russians intended to take it was unclear, because their forces were exhausted. By now, British public opinion had swung back to a pro-Turkish policy. Newspapers revived the old scare of the Russian bear, and in music halls people sang enthusiastically:

We don't want to fight,
but, by jingo if we do,
We've got the ships, we've got the men,
we've got the money too.

THE TREATY OF SAN STEFANO

In March 1878 Russia and Turkey agreed to an armistice, which was followed by the signing of the Treaty of San Stefano. By this treaty, Russia took from Turkey part of Armenia (Kars and Batum) on the eastern shores of the Black Sea. She also insisted on taking back from Romania the fertile southern Bessarabia on the western shores of the Black Sea. In compensation, Romania received from Turkey the Dobruja, a relatively barren area between the Danube and the Black Sea. Serbia and Montenegro also had their frontiers extended.

But the most important feature of the treaty was the establishment of a new self-governing principality of Bulgaria, which stretched from the Danube in the north to the Aegean in the south, and from the Black Sea in the east to within fifty miles of the Adriatic in the west. The new Bulgaria, which included Macedonia, was to have a Christian government and a national militia. The prince of Bulgaria was to be freely selected by the Bulgars themselves and would be confirmed by the Sultan. Russia retained the right to station troops in Bulgaria for two years in a supervisory capacity (map p.106).

The Treaty of San Stefano came very near to ending Turkish rule in Europe. It left her remaining possessions reduced to four small semi-detached areas: Bosnia-Herzegovina, Albania, Thessaly and Western Thrace.

Immediately, Britain and Austria-Hungary set afoot moves to destroy the treaty. In Britain it was immediately assumed that the new Bulgaria would give the Russians access to the Aegean and the Mediterranean, and that it was no more than a Russian satellite. In British music halls artists and audiences bellowed in chorus:

We've fought the Bear before,
and while Britons shall be true,
The Russians shall not have Constantinople.

The tsar gave no sign whatever of intending to go any further and take Constantinople and the Dardanelles. But the British government did not point out these details to an incensed public. Instead it brought 7,000 troops from India to Malta. The fleet was already lying off Constantinople and war seemed imminent. Austria-Hungary, though angry about the treaty, was not as warlike as Britain. She had been promised that no big Balkan state would be created; now a new Bulgaria was in existence, which was even larger than the area actually inhabited by the Bulgars. Austria-Hungary had also been promised the right to take the Slav provinces of Bosnia-

THE BALKAN SETTLEMENT PROPOSED BY THE TREATY OF SAN STEFANO (MARCH 1878)

Herzegovina, but the treaty made no mention of this. Austria-Hungary, with British backing, enlisted Bismarck's good offices to call a Congress of the great powers. The German Chancellor, ever anxious to prevent a rift between Russia and Austria-Hungary, which would mean the break-up of the *Dreikaiserbund* — so essential to his policy of keeping France in isolation (p.31) — was glad to oblige. He offered to preside at a congress to be held in Berlin where he professed to be strictly neutral, the 'honest broker' in the proceedings.

The Congress of Berlin 1878

The Congresss of Berlin, which met in June 1878, was a personal triumph for Disraeli (now Lord Beaconsfield). It was he, more than anyone else, who had persuaded the Russians to agree to it and, by the time the Congress had begun, he had concluded secret agreements with Russia, Austria-Hungary and Turkey, which settled the main issues. The final settlement at Berlin merely tidied up the details and formulated them into a treaty. Serbia, Montenegro and Romania became fully independent of the Sultan. Russia retained her gains in Bessarabia and Kars. Romania had to content herself with the Dobruja (map p.108).

The principal part of the agreement concerned 'Big' Bulgaria. The southern part, Macedonia, was returned to Turkey, thus leaving its mixed population of Bulgars, Serbs and Greeks to suffer the terrors of Turkish misrule. However, the major powers were more concerned that the Aegean coastline facing the Straits should not fall into the hands of a state that might become a Russian satellite. The middle section, Eastern Rumelia, was detached from Bulgaria and was given home rule status. It would have a Christian government but was to remain a Turkish province. This arrangement was seen as protecting Constantinople. The area north of Eastern Rumelia, between the Balkan mountains and the Danube, became Bulgaria proper. Since the powers at Berlin regarded this little Bulgaria as a Russian satellite, they saw the Balkan mountains as separating 'Russia' from Turkey.

Meanwhile Disraeli revealed that Britain had received the island of Cyprus from the Sultan in return for a promise to protect Turkey's possessions in Asia:

> In order to enable England to make necessary provision for executing her engagement, His Imperial Majesty the Sultan further consents to assign the Island of Cyprus to be occupied and administered by England.

By another agreement reached before the Congress met, Austria-Hungary was to administer (but not annex) Bosnia-Herzegovina, and also to garrison the Sanjak (district) of Novibazar, a corridor of territory separating Serbia and Montenegro.

The French were compensated when the Congress recognised her acquisitions in North Africa (p.90). Italy's compensation lay in her invitation to the Congress, which implied that she was now recognised as one of the great European powers.

The Congress of Berlin solved, or shelved, the Eastern Question as far as the major powers were concerned. Perhaps Bismarck struck the keynote of the Congress when he declared, 'We are not here to consider the happiness of the Bulgarians, but the peace of Europe.' He was content that he had defused a highly explosive situation where two members of the *Dreikaiserbund* might otherwise have gone to war. Disraeli was equally content and returned from Berlin with 'peace and honour'. But it was an uneasy peace, for many grievances had been created. Russia had suffered a diplomatic defeat for her Balkan policy and turned towards expansion in Asia, which eventually led to her war with Japan in 1904. Serbia was aggrieved at being cut off by the Sanjak from her fellow Slav state, Montenegro, while both Serbia and Montenegro were angered at Austria-Hungary's occupation

THE BALKAN SETTLEMENT IMPLEMENTED BY THE TREATY OF BERLIN (JUNE 1878)

of the Slav provinces of Bosnia-Herzegovina. Romania got a bad bargain in getting the inferior Dobruja in exchange for Bessarabia. The peoples of Macedonia, who were returned to Turkey, were left to the mercy of their overlords until 1912, while the establishment of Eastern Rumelia served no great purpose and only caused another crisis in 1885.

In retrospect, the Congress of Berlin was a turning point in international affairs. That the Congress met in Berlin demonstrated how much European affairs now centred on Germany. Though Bismarck, the 'honest broker', had not asked for any German gains and had secured a peaceful settlement, the outcome was far from satisfactory. The Russians blamed their humiliation on Bismarck's failure to support them and the *Dreikaiserbund* came under heavy strain. Germany drew closer to Austria-Hungary, and the following year saw the formation of the Dual Alliance (Germany and Austria-Hungary) (p.32), which commenced a process that finally led to the division of Europe into two armed camps — a major contribution to the outbreak of World War I.

THE BULGARIAN CRISIS 1885

The new principality of Bulgaria was ruled by a nephew of Tsar Alexander II, Prince Alexander of Battenberg, but the real power behind the prince was Stefan Stambulov, a strong nationalist who had played a leading part in the unsuccessful revolt of 1874–6. At first the prince suspended the constitution and gave his Russian advisers almost total control of the country's army and civil service. But Russian control had the effect of creating strong national feeling, and Bulgaria's gratitude to Russia was replaced by resentment against her interference. In 1882 the prince restored the constitution and Stambulov became president of the *Sobranye* (parliament).

In September 1885 Eastern Rumelia expelled her Turkish governor and proclaimed union with Bulgaria; the great powers were presented with a *fait accompli*. The Bulgarian crisis once again saw Britain and Russia on opposite sides, but this time their roles were reversed. Instead of Bulgaria being a stepping stone for Russian ambitions in the Balkans, she was now a barrier. Consequently, Russia opposed the union. Britain now supported Bulgarian nationalism because it would hinder Russia. The new tsar, Alexander III, held Prince Alexander personally responsible for the anti-Russian feeling in Bulgaria and in July 1886 he arranged a *coup d'état* in which the prince was forced to abdicate. The Bulgarian *Sobranye*, led by Stambulov, was not as easily quelled and offered the throne to Prince Ferdinand of Saxe-Coburg, a German catholic who had served in the Hungarian army. He was naturally acceptable to Germany and Austria-Hungary, but Russia refused to recognise him. The *Sobranye*, angry at the overbearing attitude of the Russians, broke off diplomatic relations with St Petersburg in November 1886.

For a time it seemed as if another war would break out in the Balkans, this time between Russia and Austria-Hungary. But Bismarck, ever anxious to prevent war between the two powers, had the terms of the Dual Alliance of 1879 (p.32) published in February 1888 as a warning to both sides. It warned Russia that Germany would come to the aid of Austria-Hungary if it was attacked by Russia, and for Austria-Hungary it gave public notice that she would have to fight alone if she attacked Russia. Tension relaxed considerably; none of the powers wanted war over Bulgaria. In the Reichstag Bismarck spoke for the great powers when he declared:

> Bulgaria, that little country between the Danube and the Balkan mountains, is not by any means a matter of sufficient importance to justify a European war, from Moscow to the Pyrenees and from

the North Sea to Palermo; at the end of which nobody would know what he had fought for.

THE ARMENIAN MASSACRES 1894

After the Bulgarian crisis, Russia turned away from the Balkans and concentrated on expansion towards Persia, Afghanistan and the Far East, where the warm waters of the Persian Gulf and the Yellow Sea seemed more attainable, even though less valuable, than those of the Mediterranean.

Meanwhile, the Sultan had reverted to despotic rule, and the Ottoman empire stagnated. The next outrage occurred in the Sultan's Asian territory in 1894. Armenia lay some 500 miles to the east of Constantinople, at the south-east corner of the Black Sea. It was inhabited by some two million orthodox Christians who, like their co-religionists in the Balkans, suffered persecution for their faith under Turkish Muslim rule. When an uprising occurred in 1894, the Sultan responded even more fiercely than his predecessor had done in the Balkans in 1874 (p.103), but this time the powers did nothing. Nicholas II, the new tsar of Russia, was unwilling to intervene for several reasons: (a) although the Armenians were orthodox Christians, they were not in communion with the Russian church and the tsar was not particularly interested in their plight; (b) the tsar was afraid that any backing of the Armenians under Turkish rule might encourage his own Armenian subjects to revolt in support of independence; (c) the British were embarrassed about the Turkish atrocities, but the tsar was still smarting over the British stand on Bulgaria; (d) the Russians were expanding eastwards, and the tsar was more interested in Japan's war against China (p.55) than in the plight of the Armenians.

In Germany, the new kaiser, William II, had no intention of helping the Armenians. On the contrary, he was endeavouring to cultivate good relations with Turkey in the hope of forming economic links (p.120) and he sent the Sultan a birthday present. Meanwhile Britain's strong protest to the Sultan was ignored. Then in 1896, in an effort to attract attention to their plight, the Armenians seized the Ottoman Bank in Constantinople, but the Sultan, confident that no power would intervene, ordered a reprisal in which over five thousand Armenians were slaughtered in a three-day massacre. Once again Turkey was saved from a united Christian crusade by the mutual suspicion and hostility of the great powers.

THE REVOLT IN CRETE 1896

The island of Crete in the eastern Mediterranean was mainly inhabited by Greeks but was subject to Turkish rule. Wishing for union with Greece, the orthodox Chrisitians in Crete rebelled in 1894. Two years later the Greeks sent in troops and the conflict developed into open warfare. The Sultan's policy was the same as in Armenia — massacre all enemies. Once again the powers found it difficult to agree, and in April 1897 the Sultan officially declared war on Greece and began the reconquest of Thessaly. Now the powers found common cause and forced an agreement on the Sultan. Crete was given self-government within the Turkish empire. In effect Crete was as good as lost to the Sultan, and in 1913 it was formally incorporated into Greece.

THE REVOLT IN TURKEY 1908

Turkish contact with European ideas of nationalism and constitutional government inevitably led to a movement for reform of the

THE BALKANS, RUSSIA AND THE EAST, 1885–1912

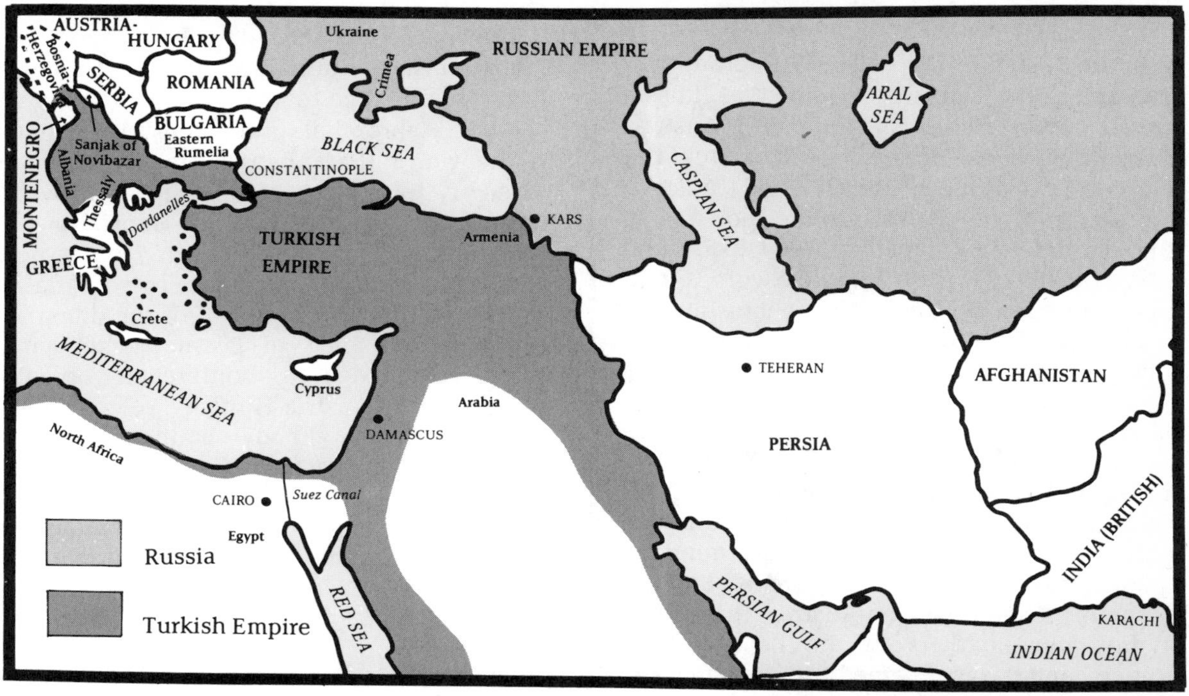

autocratic and backward Ottoman empire. As one Turk put it: 'If we do not hasten to imitate Europe, we must resign ourselves to return to Asia.' A struggle developed within Turkey on this fundamental issue. The Sultan, Abdul Hamid, naturally wished to maintain his autocratic power and bind his Turkish and Arab subjects through their one common link — the Islamic faith. Those who wished to modernise Turkey and imitate Europe were known as the Young Turks. They were ardent nationalists, many of them young army officers, who blamed the backward autocracy for the empire's disintegration.

In 1908 a revolution broke out and the Young Turks demanded a constitution and a parliament elected by universal suffrage. The Sultan conceded and called a parliament, abolished censorship and proclaimed religious toleration for all. The spectacle of a modern democratic Turkey with the Sultan as a constitutional monarch was welcomed by liberal opinion throughout Europe. Yet now a rejuvenated modern Turkey would put the Eastern Question in a new light. No longer would Turkey be the 'sick man of Europe'. This fiercely nationalistic new Turkey might wish to hold on to, even regain, her lost possessions in Europe.

But the Sultan's good intentions lasted for only one year. In 1909 he attempted a counter-coup; it failed and he was promptly deposed in favour of his brother, Mohammed V. Under Mohammed, the Young Turks soon forgot about their liberalism and Turkey reverted to her old ways.

THE BOSNIAN CRISIS 1908

After the Bulgarian crisis of 1885, international tension in the Balkans subsided as Russia turned towards the Far East and Austria-Hungary was held in check by Bismarck. But two events brought Russia and Austria-Hungary into the Balkans once more. First, Russia's defeat by Japan in 1904 (p.55) and the settlement of her disputes with Britain concerning her frontier with Afghanistan and Persia (p.121) turned her attention back towards the Mediterranean. Second, relations between Serbia and Austria-Hungary rapidly deteriorated after 1903. In that year Serbia's pro-Hapsburg king, Alexander Obrenovich, was assassinated; and the new king, Peter Karageorgevich, favoured closer relations with Russia. The Serbian prime minister, Nikola Pashitch, tried to break Serbia's economic dependence on Austria-Hungary by finding new markets in the Balkans, and French capital was obtained for armaments. It was obvious that Serbia was about to step up her campaign for the union of all south Slavs into a new independent state of Yugoslavia.

But if Serbia's ambitions threatened the peace in the Balkans, so did those of Austria-Hungary. With the appointment of Graf von Aehrenthal as foreign minister and Conrad von Hötzendorf as army chief in 1906, a new reckless daring entered Hapsburg diplomacy. Availing of the confusion in Turkey occasioned by the 1908 revolt (p.110) and to forestall any action by the Young Turks in the Balkans, Aehrenthal decided to annex Bosnia-Herzegovina, which had been administered by the Hapsburgs since the Congress of Berlin in 1878 (p.107). In September 1908 Aehrenthal secured the consent to the annexation of the Russian foreign minister, Alexander Izvolsky, on the understanding that Austria-Hungary would support Russia's claim for the opening of the Dardanelles to Russian warships. Izvolsky was given to understand that these agreements would be kept secret until a formal conference of the powers would approve of them.

But no sooner had Izvolsky begun the delicate task of sounding out the attitude of Britain and France to a conference than, on 6 October, Aehrenthal unilaterally announced to the world that Austria-Hungary had annexed the provinces of Bosnia-Herzegovina. Serbia, already resentful of Hapsburg administration of the area since 1878, was now in a warlike mood and called on Russia to intervene militarily on behalf of the one-and-a-half million Slavs of Bosnia-Herzegovina. Russia demanded a conference on the question, but Austria-Hungary rejected this because they had already obtained a promise of military support from Germany. Helmuth von Moltke, the chief of the general staff, with the kaiser's approval, said that Germany would mobilise as soon as Russia did. In March 1909 Germany went further and demanded that Russia should recognise the annexation, and make Serbia do the same. Russia could not be sure of backing from the Triple Entente; Britain had no intention of going to war in Europe on Russia's behalf, and France was non-committal. Thus in March 1909 Russia accepted the situation and the crisis passed. Turkey was compensated by a payment of £2,400,000 and the return to her of the Sanjak of Novibazar.

Ostensibly the crisis was a victory for the central powers: Germany and Austria-Hungary had stood together, whereas the Triple Entente had not. Yet this very fact eventually forced the Triple Entente to draw together, while Germany's backing for Austria-Hungary meant that she would also support her in the next crisis. Far from the Dual Alliance being a defensive one and a check on Hapsburg ambitions (as Bismarck had intended), it was now being interpreted in certain Hapsburg circles as a guarantee of support for a forward Balkan policy. Perhaps the greatest effect of the crisis was on Serbia, where it stimulated bitter anti-Austrian feeling. Her path to the Adriatic was blocked and her dream of forming a union of all southern Slavs (Serbia, Montenegro, Bosnia and Herzegovina) in a Yugoslav state seemed further away than ever.

THE BALKAN WARS 1912–13

The First Balkan War 1912

Despite Turkey's new liberal face, real power rested with a few ambitious army officers, who soon forgot about liberalism and began to suppress the subject peoples as mercilessly as ever, a policy that created anti-Turkish sympathy in Britain.

The Italians, exploiting the British anti-Turkish mood, seized Tripoli in September 1912, and Turkey, faced with a united Slav opposition in the Balkans, had little option but to make peace.

Renewed Turkish persecution forced the Balkan states to cast aside their rivalries and jealousies and, in October 1912, the Balkan League of Serbia, Bulgaria, Montenegro and Greece went to war with Turkey, each hoping to obtain a portion of the territory still under Turkish rule. Everywhere the League was successful. The Bulgarians drove southwards through Thrace and soon were at the gates of Constantinople. The Serbs advanced into Macedonia and won resounding victories in the Sanjak and in Kumanovo. The Greek contribution was mainly naval: her navy blockaded the Turkish coastline and seized the islands, while her land army advanced northwards and took Salonika (map p.115).

When the great powers intervened in December to impose an armistice, Turkish possessions in Europe had been reduced to the four fortresses of Constantinople, Adrianople, Janina and Scutari.

But Turkish defeat led to an internal revolt in which Enver Pasha took control of the government and broke the armistice. However, in the second campaign the Turkish position got worse: Montenegro took Scutari, Bulgaria and Serbia captured Adrianople, and Greece occupied Janina. Only Constantinople and its neighbourhood remained in Turkish hands when fighting stopped in April 1913.

The Treaty of London 1913

There were but two things needed at this stage to put an end to the Ottoman empire in Europe — the harmonious division of the spoils between the states, and the blessing of the great powers upon the arrangement — but neither condition was attainable. When the conference met in London in May, each of the great powers was determined that the new arrangements would conform to its wishes. Because of Bulgaria's independent stand since 1878, Russia had no intention of letting her get control of Constantinople. Britain was determined that Turkey would retain Constantinople and the Dardanelles. Austria-Hungary was resolved that Serbia should not expand to the Adriatic coast.

On 30 May the Treaty of London was concluded. Serbia and Montenegro were obliged to evacuate the Adriatic coastland and a new and independent state of Albania was created, which effectively land-locked Serbia in accordance with the wishes of Austria-Hungary. Constantinople and the Dardanelles coast were left to Turkey in accordance with the (different) wishes of Britain and Russia. The remaining area was divided between Serbia, Greece and Bulgaria. Serbia, in compensation for having lost possessions to Albania, demanded and received a part of northern Macedonia. Greece received southern Macedonia and the key port of Salonika. Bulgaria, having done most of the fighting, was left with

Serbian soldiers receiving orders during the war against Turkey in 1912.

Thrace and a stretch of the Aegean coast that had no proper port.

The Second Balkan War 1913

Bulgaria greatly resented the Greeks getting Salonika and the Serbs being given part of Macedonia, because these areas were to have been part of Bulgaria's share of the spoils.

On 29 June 1913, Bulgaria made a sudden attack upon Serbia. The Greeks and Romanians joined the Serbs, fearing that a Bulgarian victory would jeopardise their own positions. Eventually the Turks (with whom the Serbs and the Greeks were still technically at war) joined in to recover Adrianople. The Bulgarian position was utterly hopeless and within one month an armistice was concluded. The following month, August 1913, the Bulgarians agreed to the terms of the Treaty of Bucharest.

The Treaty of Bucharest 1913

Bulgaria ceded southern Macedonia and the Salonika peninsula to Greece, and northern and central Macedonia to Serbia. To Romania she ceded southern Dobruja, and Turkey took back Adrianople. Bulgaria was left with eastern Macedonia and western Thrace.

The Ottoman empire in Europe had shrunk to a mere toe-hold in the south-east, but it did contain the cities of Adrianople and Constantinople. Serbia had doubled in size, increased her population, and become prouder of her position as the leading Slav state in the Balkans. Anti-Austrian feeling was kept at

THE BALKANS IN 1913, AFTER THE TREATY OF BUCHAREST

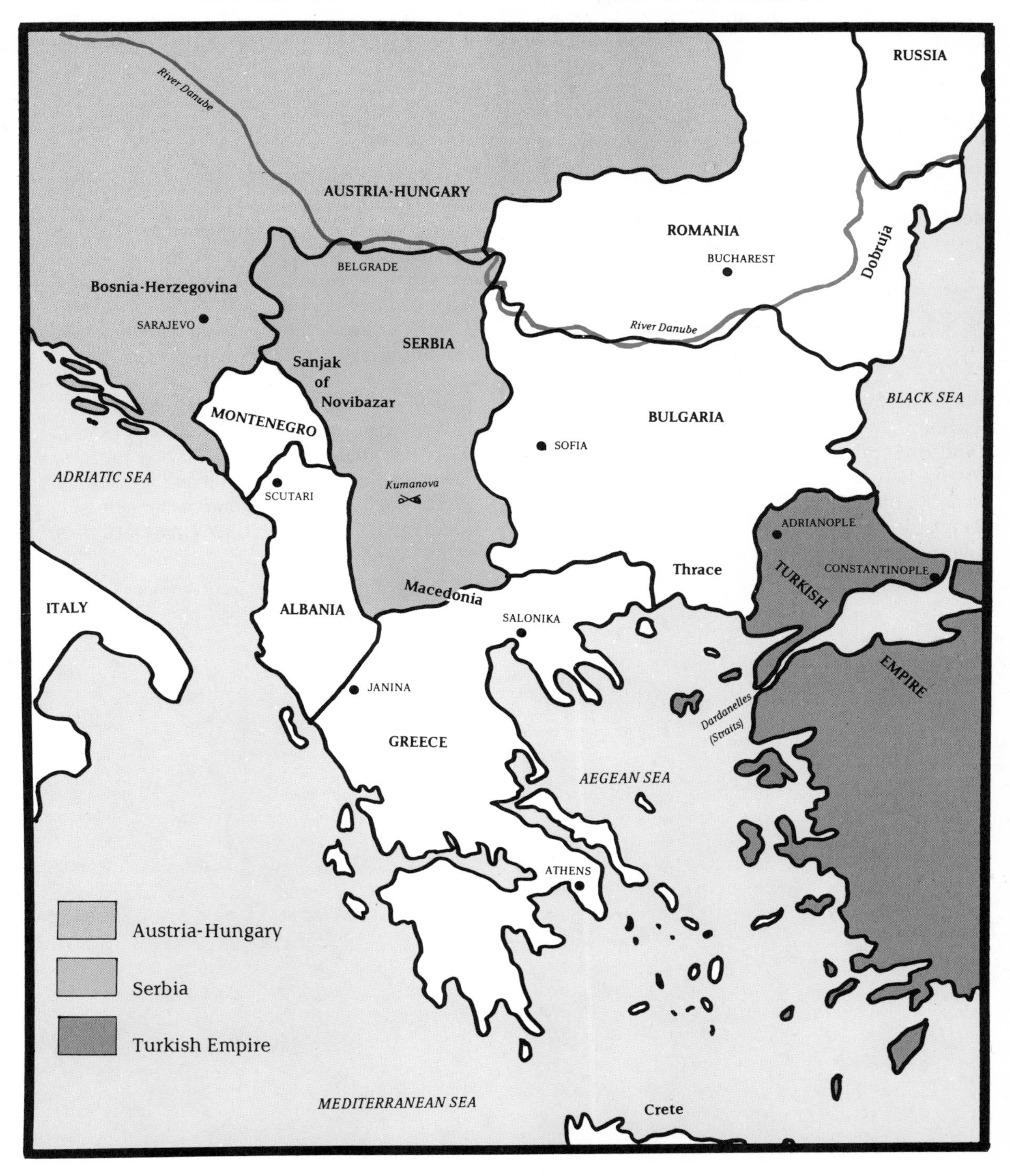

fever-pitch by the 'Unity or Death Society', known as the Black Hand, a fanatical secret society, formed in Belgrade in 1911, whose aim was to unite Serbia with the six million Slavs now under the control of Austria-Hungary. The Hapsburgs believed that if Serbia was not suppressed or even destroyed, she would spearhead a movement for a unified Slav state, which would inevitably mean the disintegration of the multiracial Hapsburg empire.

THE GREAT WAR

When the heir to the Hapsburg throne, Franz Ferdinand, was shot by a member of the Black Hand in Sarajevo in Bosnia on 28 June 1914, Austria-Hungary got her opportunity. She presented Serbia with an ultimatum, so designed to secure rejection by the government in Belgrade. When Austria-Hungary declared war on Serbia, Russia supported Serbia and Germany supported Austria-Hungary (p.125). The Eastern Question had merged into a larger conflict: World War I.

Study Assignments and Essays

1. *Analyse the factors that created the 'Eastern Question'.*
2. *Treat of the causes, course and results of the Russo-Turkish War 1877–78.*
3. *'The Congress of Berlin was a retrograde step in attempting to solve the 'Eastern Question'.' Do you agree?*
4. *Treat of the Balkan Wars 1912–13.*
5. *Write an essay on two of the following: (i) The role of Britain in the Eastern Question; (ii) Turkish rule in the Balkans; (iii) Russia and the Eastern Question; (iv) Nationalism and the Eastern Question; (v) The Eastern Question as a cause of World War I.*

10 International Relations and the Origins of War 1890 –1914

Such is the unity of history that anyone who endeavours to tell a piece of it must feel that his first sentence tears a seamless web.

Frederick William Maitland, 1850–1906

THE LEGACY

THE FALL of Bismarck in 1890 marked a great turning point in international relations. For twenty years he had dominated European diplomacy and had bequeathed to Germany a strong international position: membership of a triple alliance with Austria-Hungary and Italy, a reinsurance treaty with Russia, peaceful accord with Britain, and France successfully confined and isolated. Given careful handling, Bismarck's system was workable, but it was doomed once Kaiser William II took personal control in 1888. Within twenty years Germany's position was reversed — all the more tragic for Germany and the world in that it resulted from a series of blunders rather than from any sinister designs in her foreign policy.

THE FRANCO-RUSSIAN ALLIANCE 1893

William II essentially disliked the complex juggling of Bismarck's foreign relations, preferring a more open style of diplomacy. His foreign policy aimed at friendship with Britain as well as with Austria-Hungary. Accordingly, when the Russians proposed the renewal of the Reinsurance Treaty for six years in March 1890, William declined because it would offend the British. Then in May 1891 the kaiser visited London in the hope of adding Britain to the Triple Alliance, but the British had no wish to get entangled in European affairs.

These moves convinced France and Russia that an Anglo-German alliance was in the offing, and it was their own fear of isolation that brought them together, rather than any anti-German or anti-British motivation. Moreover, France was anxious to end her twenty-year-old isolation, and Russia was acutely aware of the need for French loans for industrialisation (p.53), which might be withheld if an alliance was refused. Finally after two years of negotiation, a military convention was signed in December 1893.

> If France is attacked by Germany, or by Italy supported by Germany, Russia shall employ all her available forces to attack Germany. If Russia is attacked by Germany, or by Austria supported by Germany, France shall apply all her available forces to fight Germany.

The Triple Alliance (Germany, Austria-Hungary and Italy) was now matched by the Dual Alliance between France and Russia. What Bismarck had feared and prevented, a two-front war for Germany, was now a possibility. Yet although this alliance was directed against Germany, the kaiser did not feel threatened; it was a defensive alliance and he had no intention of attacking either France or Russia. But the British viewed the Dual Alliance with apprehension. France and Russia respectively were Britain's main rivals in Africa and Asia and their coming together in a military alliance made Britain look towards Germany to balance this development.

British overtures to Germany were short-lived. Germany wanted Britain to become a full member of the Triple Alliance, but Britain had no intention of involving herself in a continental war on Germany's behalf. On the other hand, Germany had no wish to fight France or Russia on behalf of British imperial interests in Africa or Asia. Furthermore, the kaiser's deepening interest in Africa, and above all, his naval programme (p.92) forced Britain to look elsewhere, a policy that eventually saw Britain and Germany on opposite sides in 1914.

The kaiser's short-sightedness had allowed him to abandon two of Bismarck's principles. He had allowed Russia to go over to France and he had allowed Britain to slip away.

THE NAVAL RACE

Britain now began to feel that her isolation might not be so much splendid as foolish. In 1894 the Japanese war against China (p.99) brought home to Britain that this area was no longer her own preserve. Further embarrassments occurred in South Africa, and the Boer War of 1899–1901 (p.93) revealed that Britain did not have a single ally in Europe. But the real change in British thinking started in 1900. In that year German policy took on a distinct character, which has been variously described as World Policy (*Weltpolitik*) or as a 'place in the sun', befitting a nation of Germany's rank. The flaw in Germany's policy was that she could not play a world role: she was a European power with two hostile neighbours, and the crudeness of her diplomacy merely added Britain to the number of her opponents.

In 1890 the kaiser had declared: 'Our future lies on the water.' He was a great advocate of the notion that sea power is the basis of world power. In 1895 the Kiel Canal, linking the Baltic and the North Seas, was completed. Under the influence of Admiral von Tirpitz, the Navy Laws of 1898, 1900 and 1908 announced great ship-building programmes.

The Germans failed to comprehend the effects that this naval programme would have on British thinking. As Winston Churchill put it: 'The British fleet was a necessity, the German fleet was a luxury.' Germany was already the greatest land power, Britain the greatest sea power; now Germany was aiming to become a major sea power as well. The Germans, failing to appreciate the effects of her naval programme on British attitudes, were inclined to dismiss British fears as exaggerated suspicions and unreasonable anxiety. The British saw in their great navy a guarantee of security for their island position, their world-wide empire and their extensive trading interests. Thus threatened, Britain in 1906 launched the *Dreadnought*, a battleship of an altogether new design. She was capable of 21 knots, and had ten 305 millimetre guns that could fire beyond torpedo range. The *Dreadnought* made all hitherto existing battleships obsolete. But the Germans responded by building battleships to match the *Dreadnought*, and an expensive naval race began.

In 1908 Germany rejected British suggestions that the naval programmes of each power be reduced. Public opinion in Britain now backed the government's naval programme: 'We want eight [*Dreadnoughts*] and we won't wait' became the cry in Britain in 1909 when it was thought that Germany was catching up. Sir John Fisher, Commander of the Royal Navy from 1904 to 1910, was determined that Britannia should continue to rule the waves. He named one of his battleships *Ut Veniant Omnes* (Let them all come) and the naval race went on, arousing fear and suspicion and pushing Germany and Britain farther apart.

THE ARMS RACE

But the naval race between Britain and Germany must be seen as no more than the acute edge of a larger arms race in which all the great powers were involved.

As the industrial revolution spread and the

Diagrammatic representation, in a British magazine, of the expansion of the German navy between 1897 and 1914.

output of coal, iron and steel rose dramatically, so too did the production of arms and armaments. Krupps in Germany was the single greatest armaments firm in Europe. In Britain Armstrong-Whitworth made immense profits from navy contracts. In Sweden Nobel make a fortune from the manufacture of explosives, and in the last thirty years of the century had increased production from 11,000 to 65,000 tonnes. The Schneider firm in France built up an impressive armaments industry, and in the United States, the Carnegie Steel Corporation made vast profits from arms production. These firms were essentially international in that they sold not only to their home governments, but to any power prepared to buy.

By inventing new weapons, these manufacturers drove nations into an ever spiralling arms race where cost was not a factor. Thus, while governments were declaring that war must be avoided, they were arming at an increasing rate. The following table shows the alarming growth of armaments among the six powers of Europe in the period before World War I:

GROWTH OF ARMAMENTS
(cost in dollars per head of population)

	Britain	Germany	France	Russia	Austria-Hungary	Italy
1820	3.74	1.33	3.03	1.34	1.16	1.44
1890	4.03	2.95	4.82	1.32	1.56	2.63
1910	7.56	4.17	6.70	1.91	1.77	3.50
1914	8.53	8.52	7.33	2.58	3.48	3.81

Source: Quincy Wright, *A Study of War* (1965).

THE ENTENTE CORDIALE 1904

After the crisis at Fashoda in 1898 (p. 91), reltions between Britain and France began to improve. At Fashoda France had clearly demonstrated that she was prepared to forgo her interests in Africa to maintain peace with Britain. On the other hand, Britain's deteriorating relationship with Germany prompted her to look more kindly on France. The influence of Edward VII was also useful in promoting good relations with France, and in 1903 he visited Paris for the first time as king. Such Anglo-French *rapprochement* came to fruition in April 1904 with the signing of the Anglo-French *Entente Cordiale* or friendly understanding.

Unlike the Triple and Dual Alliances, it was not directed against any specific enemy — nor indeed was it a military alliance. Essentially the *Entente Cordiale* cleared away obstacles to Anglo-French co-operation by settling outstanding disputes over overseas territories. For instance, Britain agreed to recognise Morocco as a French sphere of influence in return for French recognition of Britain's control over Egypt and the Suez Canal.

THE FIRST MOROCCAN CRISIS (TANGIERS) 1905

Following the *Entente Cordiale*, French involvement in Morocco increased. The kaiser, already hostile to the *entente*, claimed that by a previous arrangement, no change in the status of Morocco could be made without the consent of all the powers. In March 1905, he paid a courtesy call on the Sultan of Morocco in Tangiers. In a bold speech he claimed to defend Morocco's independence and demanded that its affairs be submitted to an international conference. The French had to agree and a conference met at Algeciras, Spain from January to April 1906 (map p.88).

William was surprised to find that only Austria-Hungary supported Germany at the conference. Britain and Russia argued that France had the right to carry out administrative reforms and establish better policing, both of which were badly needed in Morocco. Italy and the United States agreed, although they did not contribute significantly to the argument.

The kaiser had suffered his first major

King Edward VII of England greets spectators at Longchamps racecourse during his visit to Paris in 1903 to promote closer relations with France.

diplomatic defeat. The first Moroccan crisis passed, but only at Germany's expense. In contrast with Germany's rebuff, Britain and France moved closer together, and the *entente* in effect became an alliance.

THE ANGLO-RUSSIAN ENTENTE 1907

The logical outcome of the Moroccan crisis and the cementing of the *entente* was a rapprochement between Britain and France's ally, Russia. For years the British had wanted to settle various questions that had kept them in dispute with Russia. Now, after Russia's defeat by Japan (p.55), the Russians were more willing to negotiate.

In August 1907 the main areas of friction were settled. Tibet was made a buffer state, and the Russians renounced their interests in Afghanistan so that India's North-West frontier was now secure. The main question centred on Persia (Iran). It was agreed to divide it into three zones: the north became a British sphere of interest; the south-east, adjacent to India, also became a British sphere of interest; and the remainder became a neutral zone.

THE DIVISION OF EUROPE

The Anglo-Russian *entente*, like its counterpart, the Anglo-French *entente*, was not an alliance; it was an agreement on the elimination of difficulties. Despite the reversal of her policy of isolation, Britain had not committed herself to an alliance with either

France or Russia, and still retained a certain freedom of choice. Nevertheless, the collective arrangements between all three powers, which became known as the Triple Entente, did complete the division of Europe in two armed camps. On one side stood the Triple Alliance (Germany, Austria-Hungary and Italy) while on the other stood the Triple Entente (Britain, France and Russia).

Within twenty years a diplomatic revolution had occurred in European relations. Britain had emerged as a major factor in Europe; France had surmounted her enforced isolation by Bismarck; and Germany, however unwittingly, had manoeuvred herself from a position of diplomatic strength into a position of encirclement. Germany could now rely only upon Austria-Hungary, an empire beset by huge internal problems (p.78), and upon an Italy that was not just weak but at best a doubtful friend. From 1907 all subsequent crises took on a new dimension since each took place in the context of a Europe divided into two armed camps.

THE SECOND MOROCCAN CRISIS (AGADIR) 1911

In May 1911 the French claimed that their position in Algeria (p.120) was being endangered by unrest in Morocco. They sent in troops and occupied the Moroccan town of Fez, which was under attack from nomadic tribes. The Kaiser again promptly challenged the French, claiming that their action was in breach of the agreement reached at Algeciras in 1906. In July 1911 a German gunboat, the *Panther*, was sent to Agadir, a small port on Morocco's Atlantic coast. For a time feelings ran high as argument and counter-argument flew between the powers. Britain was not so much interested in France as in her own position. She feared that Germany might seize Agadir and build a naval base in opposition to

The Kaiser's 'mailed fist' on Agadir, as depicted in a British cartoon.

her own base at Gibraltar. The tension soon burned itself out. The kaiser was more interested in splitting the *Entente Cordiale* and in getting territorial compensation in Africa than in building a naval base. The Russians were not over-anxious to support France in what they saw as a minor colonial dispute; and even Britain, once her own position was not threatened, failed to give France any firm backing.

In November 1911, after several months of sabre rattling, France and Germany signed the Moroccan Convention. Germany backed down and accepted that Morocco would become a French protectorate. A strip of northern coastline was given to Spain (p.88), and Germany was compensated with two strips of the French Middle Congo, which were now added to the German colony of the Cameroons.

The second Moroccan crisis was of profound significance in the events leading up to the outbreak of war in 1914. Germany, who had wanted no more than to check French ambitions in Morocco, was now portrayed as a warmonger. More important, she had suffered a second major diplomatic defeat. Two crises in North Africa had been defused but only at the expense of Germany. Would Germany give way the next time?

COUNTDOWN TO WAR 1912–14

As a consequence of the naval race between Germany and Britain and the many international tensions, there was a genuine desire to improve relations between the two countries. To this end in 1912 the British government sent their secretary for war, Lord Haldane, to Berlin in an effort to reach an understanding. The Germans offered to drop their new naval building programme in return for a British guarantee of neutrality in any future war involving Germany. The British refused to agree but Haldane promised to 'make no unprovoked attack upon Germany'. This offer, the kaiser declared, was useless since no one would agree about what an 'unprovoked attack' really meant.

The Balkan Wars (p.113) created further tensions between the two nations, but fortunately no great power participated militarily, which meant that, for the most part, the end of the Ottoman empire in Europe was accomplished through the efforts of the Balkan peoples themselves. Nevertheless, the Balkan Wars did bring relations between Austria-Hungary and Russia's friend, Serbia, to breaking point (p.115).

Sarajevo

Archduke Franz Ferdinand, heir to the Hapsburg throne, believed that the problem of the Slavs in his empire could be solved in the same manner as the Hungarian problem had been solved in 1867 (p.79). He advocated a triple monarchy of Austria, Hungary and a Slav state. Independent Serbia bitterly opposed this because, if the Slavs within the Hapsburg empire were satisfied, Serbia's dream of a united all-Slav State under herself would come to nothing.

On 28 June 1914, Franz Ferdinand and his Czech wife, Sophie, paid an official visit to Sarajevo, the main town of Bosnia and capital of Bosnia-Herzegovina, where the army high command had decided to hold its annual manoeuvres. This choice of Bosnia, recently annexed by the Hapsburgs (p.112) and where Slav passions ran high, was deplorably insensitive. Warnings against the archduke's visit had come from many quarters because it was well known that Slav extremist groups intended to assassinate him. But Ferdinand's attitude, expressed to his family one evening at table, was 'I am Inspector General of the Austro-Hungarian armed forces. I must go to Sarajevo. The soldiers would never be able to explain my action.' The archduke had deliberately chosen to visit Sarajevo on St Vitus's Day, the greatest Serbian festival, *Vidoudan*. This day had been celebrated by the Serbs annually since 1389, when the ancient Serbian state had been destroyed by the Turks at the battle of Kossovo.

Despite the explosive situation, security precautions were almost non-existent. There were no soliders lining the streets, despite the fact that some 70,000 soldiers had gathered outside Sarajevo for the army manoeuvres. This left the brunt of security upon the police, who, on their own initiative, instructed their 120 men to turn their faces towards the crowd during the passage of the imperial party. This strategy was woefully inadequate on a route of about four miles.

The imperial cavalcade consisted of six automobiles, and on seing it, many policemen forgot about their instructions. One conspirator, Nedeljko Cabrinovic, actually asked a policeman to point out the car in which the archduke was travelling. The excited policeman pointed to the open car and a few seconds later Cabrinovic hurled a hand-grenade at it. The bomb injured twenty people, including three of the imperial party. Sophie was slightly injured.

After this attempt, the fatal decision was made that the archduke should continue his

HEIR TO AUSTRIA'S THRONE IS SLAIN WITH HIS WIFE BY A BOSNIAN YOUTH TO AVENGE SEIZURE OF HIS COUNTRY

Francis Ferdinand Shot During State Visit to Sarajevo.

TWO ATTACKS IN A DAY

Archduke Saves His Life First Time by Knocking Aside a Bomb Hurled at Auto.

SLAIN IN SECOND ATTEMPT

Lad Dashes at Car as the Royal Couple Return from Town Hall and Kills Both of Them.

LAID TO A SERVIAN PLOT

Archduke Francis Ferdinand and his Consort the Duchess of Hohenberg Slain by Assassin's Bullets.

Newspaper headlines of the assassinations at Sarajevo, 28 June 1914.

drive through the streets of Sarajevo. The only change on the route was made at the archduke's request so that he could visit one of the wounded officers; but no one informed the chauffeurs. The archduke's car was third in the line of six and the driver was about to follow the first two when General Potiorek, the military governor of Bosnia, shouted angrily at him: 'What is this? Stop! You are going the wrong way!' The driver immediately stopped close to the pavement where another assassin, Gavrilo Princip, was standing. Immediately Princip stepped forward and fired his pistol at point blank range. Sophie died first, a bullet aimed at Potiorek penetrating the side of the car and entering her right side. The bullet intended for Ferdinand pierced the right side of his coat collar, severed the jugular vein and came to a stop in his spine. At 11.30 a.m. on 28 June 1914 the heir to the ancient house of Hapsburg, Franz Ferdinand, and his wife Sophie, lay dead in Sarajevo.

Austrian Ultimatum

Immediately after the assassination, Princip attempted to commit suicide but was prevented and arrested. Because he was under twenty, he could not be hanged. Instead he was sentenced to twenty years' hard labour, but died from tuberculosis four years later in an Austrian prison. The group to which Princip belonged was a Serbian terrorist organisation, the Black Hand (p.116), one of many South Slav groups operating against Hapsburg rule.

Although the Black Hand and its members were well known to the Serbian government, there was nothing to show any complicity of the Serbian government in the assassination. Despite this, the Austrian chancellor, Leopold Berchtold, welcomed an excuse for war and claimed that the Serbian government had planned everything. Serbia was the great thorn in the side of Austria-Hungary since her aim of uniting all South Slavs into a Yugoslavia would inevitably signal the end of the multiracial Hapsburg empire (p.116). Now, the opportunity to teach Serbia a lesson was too good to let pass.

On 5 July the kaiser called a meeting of his war council, which promised 'faithful support' if action by Austria-Hungary against Serbia should provoke Russian intervention. Germany hoped that this would frighten off Russia and thus give Austria-Hungary a free hand against Serbia in what was believed would be a local war in the Balkans. But Germany's promise had a quite different effect. The pro-war party in the Austro-Hungarian government had now secured a 'blank cheque' from Germany and was recklessly determined to exploit it to the full. On the other side, Russia, despite the German warning, believed that she could never again let down Serbia, having done so at the time of the Bosnian crisis in 1908 (p.112).

On 23 July Austria-Hungary delivered a ten-point ultimatum to Serbia; it required a reply within forty-eight hours. The ultimatum was so demanding that it was hoped that Serbia would reject it, and thus give Austria-Hungary an excuse for war. The Serbian government, busy with an election campaign, was astounded by the ultimatum, especially since, after a month's delay, they were compelled to reply so quickly. Nevertheless, Serbia did accede to all points in the ultimatum save one: they would not accept the demand that Austrian officials be allowed to enter Serbia and participate in investigating the assassination and in the suppression of all anti-Hapsburg groups such as the Black Hand. Serbia claimed that this would amount to giving up her freedom as an independent state and further declared that if Austria was not satisfied with this, both powers should submit the dispute to international arbitration.

The same day, 25 July, the tsar ordered partial mobilisation of the Russian army and announced that this action was not directed against Germany but was to exert pressure on Austria-Hungary. Thus, Austria-Hungary was determined to crush Serbia, Germany was prepared to back her ally, and Russia was ready to back Serbia. Britain and France had not proclaimed their intentions, which gave the impression that the Triple Entente would not stand firm.

Then on Tuesday 28 July Austrian troops marched into Serbia and shelled Belgrade. The same day, the tsar ordered full mobilisation. This was followed on 31 July by a telegram from the kaiser to the tsar that if Russia did not stop mobilising by 1 August, Germany would declare war. When no reply came from Russia on that day, Germany declared war on Russia.

The German Dilemma and the Schlieffen Plan

Ever since the alliance between Russia and France in 1894, Germany faced the possibility of a two-front war. To overcome this problem, in 1905 the chief of the general staff, Count von Schlieffen, devised a plan which has since borne his name. The plan was based on two broad assumptions: (1) that the French army would attack through Alsace-Lorraine; (2) that Russian mobilisation, owing to her backwardness, would be much slower than that of the French. The plan laid down that a German army would advance to hold the French in Alsace-Lorraine. Meanwhile, the main German army would sweep through Belgium and northern France and swing round to the west of Paris. They would then turn east, and catch the French forces in a pincer movement at the Alsace-Lorraine border (map, p.126).

With France's capitulation, Germany could then transfer the majority of her forces across Germany by rail in time to meet the Russian advance. With the full might of the German army against them, the inferior Russian forces would be easily defeated.

The Schlieffen plan assumed that Germany would wage war on both France and Russia. But now, on 1 August, Germany found herself at war with Russia and not with France. This made the Schlieffen Plan irrelevant; but Germany could not depend on France remaining neutral, especially since Russia had requested France to come to her aid in accordance with the Franco-Russian alliance of 1893 (p.117). On 31 July Germany had asked France what action she would take if Germany went to war with Russia. On 1 August (the day on which Germany declared war on Russia) France replied that she would 'consult' her own interests and immediately began to mobilise. The same day Italy opted out of the Triple Alliance and declared her neutrality.

On 2 August Germany demanded that her troops be allowed to pass through the lowlands of Belgium in accordance with the Schlieffen Plan. When Belgium, neutral since 1831, refused, German troops marched in at 7 a.m. on 4 August with the object of invading France. Up to this point Britain had failed to intimate what action, if any, she was going to take. But now with the violation of Belgian neutrality, to which she was a signatory, Britain immediately demanded that Germany respect that neutrality. The British ambassador spent the afternoon and evening of 4 August pleading with the German chancellor, Bethmann-Hollweg, to evacuate Belgium. But this was impossible, even if the chancellor wished to do so, for the German war machine,

THE SCHLIEFFEN PLAN: GERMANY'S PROPOSED STRATEGY FOR THE RAPID ELIMINATION OF FRANCE, WHICH DID NOT MATERIALISE IN 1914

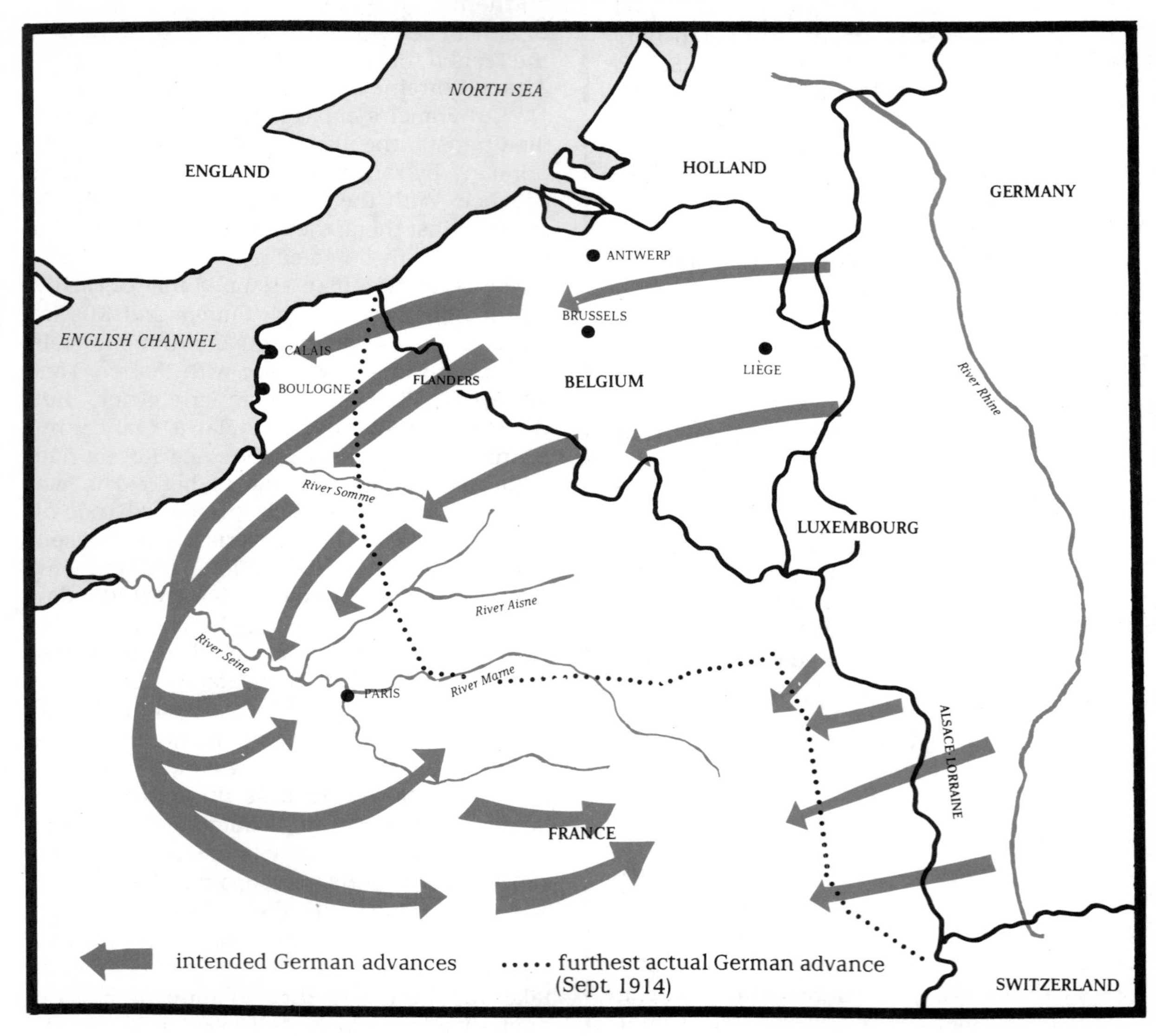

based on action and speed, had clicked into operation and nothing could be done. It was too late. The chancellor deplored the fact that:

> Just for a scrap of paper Great Britain is going to make war on a kindred nation who desired nothing better than to be friends with her.

At midnight on 4 August Britain declared war on Germany. The Great War had begun.

The kaiser had said his troops would be

'home before the leaves fall'; but this was not to be. More prophetically, the British foreign secretary, Sir Edward Grey, said, as he looked out at the street lights being lit over Whitehall: 'The lamps are going out all over Europe; we shall not see them lit again in our lifetime.'

WHY DID WORLD WAR I BREAK OUT?

The events from 28 June to 4 August 1914 explain *how* the Great War came about; it is far more difficult to explain *why* it occurred. Historians have long advanced a multiplicity of causes, and as fresh evidence comes to light some historians tend to place a greater responsibility on German policy. Despite this, no consensus has been, or perhaps ever will be, reached. The division of Europe into two camps obviously trapped its members in a mesh, which made it difficult, if not impossible, to draw back from the brink. The arms race had also created fears and suspicions, and had accustomed European statesmen to thinking in terms of military solutions for political and diplomatic problems. After all, had they not the prime example of Bismarck's highly successful wars of German unification? But the Europe of 1914 was a vastly different Europe from that of 1870, for decades of immense scientific and technological progress could now be put to the service of war, thus making obsolete the weapons of 1870.

There was also the failure of diplomacy; and despite the advances in communication, there was no machinery for an eleventh-hour peacemaking conference. This appears to suggest that the 'will to peace' was lacking and that nations rushed to honour their commitments with too much eagerness and too little apprehension.

A Marxist analysis of the cause of war would claim that capitalism (and imperialism), which is based on competition, inevitably leads to war. Certainly there had been competition for colonies and markets. But Africa and Asia had been taken over without recourse to war, while European businessmen were not clamouring for war. On the contrary, war would only serve to disrupt national economies and international trade. The Marxist explanation of the cause of war, therefore, is not convincing.

The nineteenth century was the great age of nationalism. Germany, Italy, Belgium, and several Balkan states had achieved statehood. Many other nations, most notably the Slavs, Czechs and Poles, were demanding their independence from reluctant empires. National consciousness through educational and other advances had filtered down from the articulate middle classes to the masses; and the nation state seemed to be both the logical and natural order of society. Thus the combination of triumphant nationalism, ready to respond in defence of the nation's honour, with unrequited nationalism, frustrated within dominant empires, created each in its own way the explosive atmosphere of 1914. As Winston Churchill, first lord of the Admiralty, put it: 'the vials of wrath were full.'

Study Assignments and Essays

1. *Was the Franco-Russian Alliance of 1893 inevitable?*
2. *Treat of the Anglo-German naval race, its origins, course and consequences.*
3. *Why may the years 1890–1914 be termed a period of 'armed peace'?*
4. *'In the two Moroccan crises, the kaiser had a good case but handled it disastrously.' Give your reasons for and against this assertion.*
5. *What considerations induced Britain to sign the Anglo-Russian Entente of 1907?*
6. *Write an essay on two of the following: (i) German foreign policy under Kaiser William II; (ii) 'All powers wanted war'; (iii) 'Sarajevo and the division of Europe combined to start the Great War'; (iv) 'Secret diplomacy caused the Great War'; (v) 'The Schlieffen Plan dictated the outbreak of war.'*

The period from the assassination of the Archduke Franz Ferdinand, heir to the Hapsburg empire, at Sarajevo in 1914, to the death of Lenin, the first successful Marxist revolutionary, in 1924, was perhaps the most devastating and far-reaching decade in the history of mankind. The fateful shots at Sarajevo precipitated the Great War, in which all scientific and technological progress — designed for the welfare of humanity — was now used in the service of death and destruction.

World War I differed from all previous wars in almost every respect: in the gigantic size of the individual armies, in the unprecedented numbers of casualties, in the mobilisation of human and material resources, and in the fact that this war was not confined to the battlefield alone, but was waged in the air and at sea, in factories, laboratories, banks and farms.

The war also unleashed factors and forces that brought about the world's first successful communist revolution. The Russian Revolution propounded the doctrines of Karl Marx, which offered a radically different political, economic and philosophical system of society, challenging not only the Judaeo-Christian heritage on which European civilisation was founded, but also the bourgeois capitalism and liberal democracy that had developed in Europe throughout the previous century.

The decade also witnessed the world's greatest peacemaking task when the 'Big Three', Woodrow Wilson, Georges Clemenceau and David Lloyd George, sought to refashion a new Europe from the ashes of the old. A new Europe was constructed, based on national self-determination and liberal democracy, together with machinery for setting in motion general disarmament, and collective security through a League of Nations. But the peace settlement was also based on the principle of victor and vanquished, of guilty and innocent. It was this unhappy combination of idealism and retribution, coupled with the economic dislocation caused by the war, and the alternative of Russian communism, which sowed the seeds of future conflict.

Section Two

War and Revolution 1914–24

World War I 1914–18

11

In wiser days, my darling rosebud, blown
To beauty proud as was your Mother's prime.
In that desired, delayed, incredible time,
You'll ask why I abandoned you, my own,
And the dear heart that was your baby throne,
To dice with death. And oh! they'll give you rhyme
And reason: some will call the thing sublime,
And some decry it in a knowing tone.
So here, while the mad guns curse overhead,
And tired men sigh with mud for couch and floor,
Know that we fools, now with the foolish dead,
Died not for flag, nor King, nor Emperor,
But for a dream, born in a herdsman's shed,
And for the secret Scripture of the poor.

Tom Kettle,
written to his daughter Betty four days before his death in action in 1916.

1914

The armies of Europe went to war almost lightheartedly, believing that they would be, as the kaiser declared, 'home before the leaves fall'. Thinking that war was a glorious thing, where honour could be won, they were almost happy to give their lives for their homelands. Governments and the press extolled the manliness of war which, more than

The glamour of war – children playing soldiers in Trafalgar Square, London, in front of a recruiting poster in 1914.

anything else, helped create a climate of unselfish giving.

Rupert Brooke, the English poet who died on his way to Gallipoli in 1915, glamorises this attitude in his poem, 'The Dead':

Blow out, you bugles, over the rich Dead!
There's none of these so lonely and poor of old,
But, dying, has made us rarer gifts than gold.
These laid the world away; poured out the red
Sweet wine of youth; gave up the years to be
Of work and joy, and that unhoped serene,
That men call age; and those who would have been
Their sons, they gave, their immortality.

The Western Front

German mobilisation went according to plan. Vast numbers of men were transported by trains to the Belgian and Luxembourg borders. But their advance was slowed down by Belgian resistance at the fortresses of Liège and Namur. This gave the French commander in chief, Marshal Joffre, time to move his main forces northwards and further delay the Germans until the British Expeditionary Force (BEF) could be landed on the north coast of France. When the Belgians retreated to Antwerp, their threat to the German right flank and its supplies forced the German general, von Moltke, to transfer eleven divisions to take Antwerp, thus weakening the 'hammer head' of the Schlieffen Plan (p.125).

Meanwhile on the eastern front the Russians had advanced much faster than the Germans had expected. This necessitated the transfer of four more divisions to the east, further weakening von Moltke's chances of a rapid advance. Despite these setbacks, by September one German army had advanced through Belgium and northern France to within twenty miles of Paris (map, p.132).

Since the fall of the capital seemed imminent, the French government fled to Bordeaux and the defence of the city was left to General Gallieni. The French and British troops, which had fallen back in the face of the German advance, now made a stand on the line of the river Marne, a tributary of the Seine.

The Battle of the Marne

General Gallieni rushed all available reinforcements in taxis to the battlefronts. For four days the French and British held off the Germans. They then forced them to fall back on the Aisne river where they commenced to 'dig in' behind barbed wire defences, which were to characterise the next four years of fighting on the western front.

The Battle of the Marne was one of the most decisive battles in world history: it denied the Germans that rapid victory in the west on which the Schlieffen Plan was based, and forced Germany into a two-front war.

Moltke was dismissed for his failure to give Germany that rapid victory which the Schlieffen Plan had appeared to promise. His place as supreme commander of the German Army was taken by Erich von Falkenhayn, whose immediate objective was to race for the channel ports to cut off British reinforcements.

The Germans did manage to take Antwerp in early October, but the dogged resistance of the British and the remnants of the Belgian army, in the month-long Battle of Ypres, saved the channel ports. The failure of the Germans to capture the channel ports was a major setback to their planned strategy of cutting off reinforcements of troops and supplies from Britain. This later proved to be of paramount importance (map, p.132).

The western front was now a stalemate; each side 'dug in', so that by the end of the year an elaborate system of trenches stretched from the North Sea to the Swiss Alps.

THE WESTERN FRONT: THE WAR IN WESTERN EUROPE 1914-18

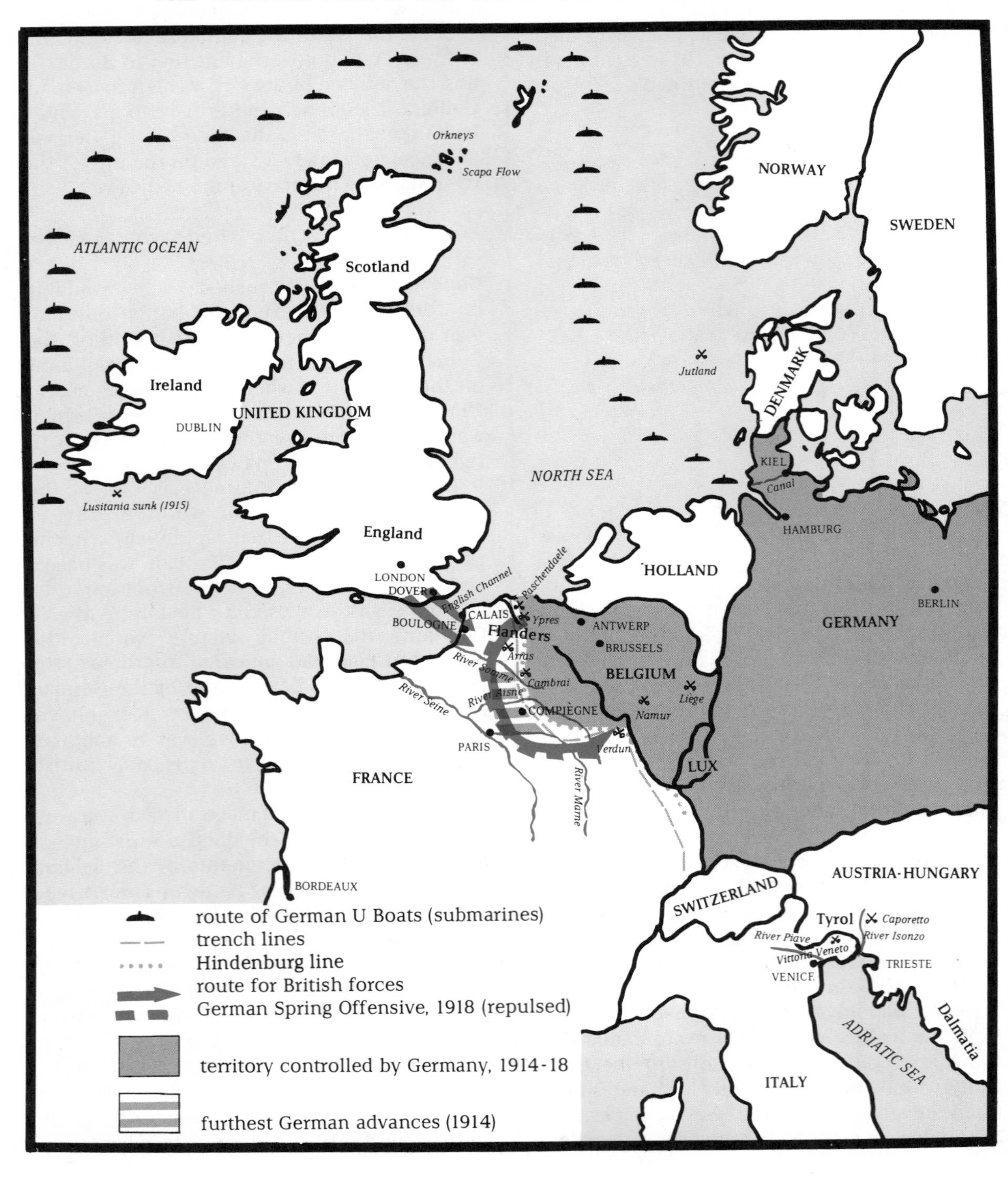

German cavalry advance into Russia.

The Eastern Front

The original plan of the Russian generals was first to crush the Austro-Hungarian army and then concentrate all their forces against Germany. But France's pleas for a second front to relieve the threat to Paris made Russia advance into East Prussia and threaten its capital, Königsberg. This quick Russian advance possibly saved Paris because the Germans were forced to transfer four divisions to the eastern front.

In late August, under General Paul von Hindenburg, Germany inflicted a crushing defeat on Russia at the battle of Tannenberg. One Russian army was almost totally destroyed: 90,000 prisoners of war were taken, together with vast quantities of guns and munitions. Immediately afterwards Hindenburg's chief of staff, Erich von Ludendorff, defeated another Russian army at the Masurian Lakes (map, p.137).

The Russians had more success against Austria-Hungary, whose Slavic peoples sympathised with Russia and Serbia. Austria-Hungary suffered defeats on her Russian and Serbian fronts and, after the first campaign, stalemate set in on the eastern front as well. Germany was forced to concentrate almost all her energies on the western front against Britain and France.

Russian battery in Poland, 1914.

TRENCH WARFARE

Opposing armies now faced each other, from trenches, across 'no man's land'. Against trenches there could be no manoeuvres or brilliant tactics. The trench system gradually sapped the daring and courage of all soldiers because going 'over the top' meant almost certain death by the enemy machine guns. Gradually the trenches became more elaborate:

> To say where the trenches began and where they ended is difficult. We were passing through land that had been retrieved from the enemy. It had been fought for inch by inch, foot by foot. To win it back thousands of lives had been thrown like dice upon a table. There were vast stretches of mud, of fields once cultivated, but now scarred with pits, trenches, rusty barbed wire. The roads were rivers of clay. They were lined with dug-outs, cellars and caves. They looked like the tunnel to coal pits. They were inhabited by a race of Frenchmen, unknown to the Boulevards — men, bearded, caked with clay. What we saw of these cave dwellers was only a few feet of a moat that is cut across France for three hundred miles like a miniature canal.

British troops emerge from the trenches on the Western Front.

From a trench all we could see of the war, all millions of fighting men could see of it — wet walls of clay as narrow as a grave, an arrow pointing to a first-aid dressing station, earthen steps leading to a shelter from sudden death — a shelter deep in the earth reinforced by cement and corrugated iron, and lit by a candle, and overhead the black leaden rain-soaked sky.

(R.H. Davis, *With the French in France and Salonika*)

But if the trenches sapped the soldier's courage, the barbed wire terrified him. He knew that, once caught, he would either be lacerated or mowed down by enemy fire:

What bramble thicket this — grown overnight
on the clean earth — unflowering? In the dusk,
some mad end, loosened, taps upon its pole:
thorns tapping like the ghosts of dead delight.

Wire, barbed wire! — a dour
and monstrous serpent round our lives,
and we're like creatures mesmerised;

it glares at us, all day, malignant, sour.
(R.H. Sauter, 'Barbed Wire')

1915

By 1915 it was apparent that the German lines in France were a fortress that could not be pushed back by a frontal assault. However, French military theory at the time taught that an enemy must be defeated by attacking its forces at the strongest point, and the British were prevailed upon to adopt the doctrine. In theory the BEF was an independent army, but in practice it followed Joffre's orders. Cabinet ministers in every country dared not criticise the generals for fear of damaging the spirit of national unity. Only Lloyd George and Winston Churchill were exceptions to this rule and they advocated the opening up of another front. But when another front (the Dardanelles) was attempted, it was in addition to, and not in place of, the western front.

The Germans behaved a little more sensibly during 1915. The Schlieffen Plan had failed, and Falkenhayn realised that the Allied line in the west could not be pierced; he decided to stand on the defensive in the west while attacking the Russians in the east. He really had little choice because the Austro-Hungarian army could not defeat the Russians, even though they had run out of supplies. The Germans had to go to the help of the Austro-Hungarians and hoped to knock Russia out of the war or, at least, push her armies so far east that she would cease to count as a factor in the war. With Russia out of the war, the Germans hoped that Britain and France would accept a compromise peace in her favour.

When German offensives in the east failed, the German government hinted to Tsar Nicholas that they would be agreeable to peace on the basis of the *status quo*, but Nicholas did not respond. He feared that anything less than total victory might shake his authority and lead to a revolution at home. So Russia drifted on, incapable of winning the war, still more incapable of escaping from it. The generals on each side could not conceive of achieving victory other than by knocking a hole in the enemy lines by bombardment and the sheer weight of numbers; hence they demanded more men, guns and shells. They did not realise that this bombardment would so churn up the ground that infantry advance after it would be slower than ever.

NEW INSTRUMENTS OF WAR

In April 1915 the Germans had used poison gas at Ypres. It had had some initial success, but occasionally the wind blew the gas back on their own lines. The Allies responded by developing gas masks; the Germans were obliged to adopt them too because they had to pass through their own gas as soon as they tried to advance.

At the outbreak of war every army possessed a few aeroplanes that were used for scouting. Later, fighter planes were developed to shoot down the scouter planes; then more fighters were developed to fight the fighters. The Germans started to bomb England in 1915, carrying the bombs in Zeppelins or airships — clumsy monsters that were easily shot down by British fighters. Nevertheless, they caused great confusion in England where the civilian population did not have first-hand experience of the war. However, their real effect was trivial by World War II standards, and only 1,100 people lost their lives from such attacks during the Great War.

The Germans produced one other device that turned out to be more dangerous than poison gas or Zeppelins: the U-boat or submarine. Nevertheless, their cruising range was short and, since the Straits of Dover were closed against them, they had to go around the north of Scotland and could not maintain a blockade of the British Isles for very long.

Since the U-boats had to sink enemy vessels on sight, they did not give a preliminary warning to crews and passengers, who were left to drown. This caused an outcry in the allied countries against German barbarism. When the Germans sank the British liner, the *Lusitania*, off the Irish coast in May 1915, it had over one hundred American citizens on board. American opinion was outraged and President Woodrow Wilson protested strongly to the German government. The chancellor, Bethmann-Hollweg, realising the seriousness of the American protest and knowing that Germany had not got sufficient U-boats to produce a decisive victory, limited the U-boat campaign to appease the Americans (p.147 and map, p.132).

THE DARDANELLES

The episode that made 1915 memorable was the attack on the Dardanelles. In October 1914 Turkey (the Ottoman empire) had entered the war on Germany's side. That she did so defies rationality. Turkey had nothing to gain from the war, even if Germany were victor-

THE EASTERN FRONT, THE DARDANELLES AND THE WAR IN THE MIDDLE EAST

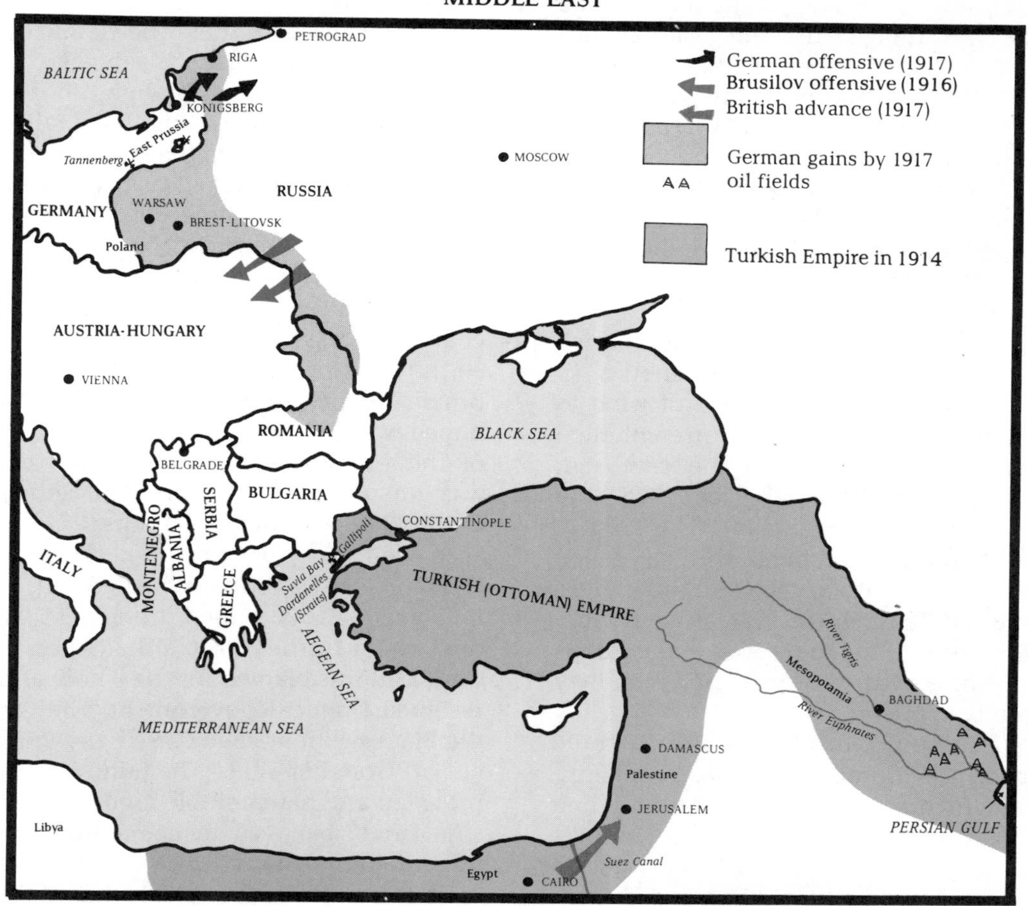

ious. On the contrary, the only remote chance of survival for her crumbling empire was to remain out of war altogether. But Turkey had been bullied by Russia and Britain during the past century, and now the opportunity of striking against both at once was irresistible.

In December 1914 the Russians had sent a desperate appeal to General Kitchener for some British engagement in the eastern Mediterranean that would distract the Turks. Kitchener responded immediately; a diversionary attack was more attractive than deadlock on the western front. In addition, Winston Churchill, as first lord of the Admiralty, saw in it an opportunity for a great amphibious action, using British control of the seas to take the Dardanelles and Constantinople by force. Churchill claimed that the advantage of the Dardanelles operation would far outweight the risks involved. A successful operation, he claimed, would knock Turkey out of the war, provide a lifeline to Russia, relieve the pressure on Serbia, rally the other Balkan states to the Allied cause, and, above all, create a diversionary movement, which would take the pressure off the western front and threaten Germany from another flank.

A preliminary bombardment of the Turkish forts at the mouth of the Dardanelles in November 1914 warned the Turks of what to expect. With German help they strengthened their defences so that when the campaign proper began in the spring of 1915, the element of surprise was lacking. The French, ever fearful of a German break-through, failed to divert sufficient troops to the Dardanelles, while in Britain neither the War Office nor the Admiralty were willing to risk too many troops and battleships in an enterprise of which they did not fully approve.

Despite these drawbacks, the British could have taken the Dardenelles but, mistakenly, they thought they had plenty of time. Their battleships cruised around the Aegean for over a month and entered the Straits only on 18 March. The troops had never rehearsed landing on a hostile coast and had no equipment to help them get ashore. Meanwhile the Turks had gathered together men and munitions and were ready for the attack. Nevertheless, when the attack did come on 25 April, it took the Turks by surprise, and the troops landed; but they were then pinned down on the rocky shore, unable to reach the top of the surrounding hills and move inland. The Turks controlled the hills and raked the troops with shell fire. The Allied troops had no secure rear: only beaches exposed to Turkish shell fire and beyond them the sea.

They then decided on a new attack further up the peninsula at Suvla Bay. On 6 August 20,000 men managed to get ashore almost without loss; only 1,000 Turks barred the way. But instead of taking the initiative and advancing forward, they dug defences. On 8 August they attempted to advance, only to find that the Turks had brought up reinforcements. The attack on Gallipoli had failed.

The expedition to the Dardanelles was brilliant in theory, but disastrous in practice. The general in charge, Sir John French, complained of not having enough shells. In Britain, the Liberal prime minister, Herbert Asquith, fearing a public row, agreed upon a coalition government with the Conservatives — thus ending the last Liberal government in British history. The new government, it was hoped, would bring a more energetic conduct of the war. Instead it produced a pause; it was unsure whether it should retreat from Gallipoli or send in more troops.

In January 1916 the operation in the Dardanelles was finally called off. It had involved 500,000 Allied troops; 55,000 had died and a further 200,000 had been injured. Churchill was blamed for the whole affair and resigned from the government. The Straits to the Black Sea remained closed and Russia was cut off from her allies. The failure of Gallipoli provided an unanswerable argument for those who firmly believed in concentrating everything on the western front.

The year 1915 thus produced no decisive

victory for either side. Public opinion, whipped up by sensational newspaper articles, turned the generals — Kitchener, Joffre and Hindenburg – into demi-gods. Every loyal citizen was expected to have unquestioning faith in these great military leaders. There was as yet no sign of discontent in any country. Only a few socialists and pacifists talked of a compromise peace, but no one was listening to them. Anything short of total victory was regarded as an insult to national honour.

THE MIDDLE EAST

Besides the Dardanelles expedition, the Allies were engaged in several campaigns on the fringes of the Turkish empire. Mesopotamia, between the Tigris and Euphrates rivers, was rich in oil. The British, heavily dependent upon oil, decided to occupy the area in defiance of the Turks, who regarded it as a province of their empire (map, p.137).

The Allies also sent forces to protect the Suez Canal and, from there, aided by T. E. Lawrence ('Lawrence of Arabia', who organised a revolt of the Arabs against the Turks), the Allied forces under General Allenby captured Palestine in 1917.

ITALY GOES TO WAR

When the war started in 1914, Italy, as a member of the Triple Alliance, in theory had been the ally of Germany and Austria-Hungary. Yet she at once declared that going to war did not come within the terms of the alliance and withdrew into neutrality. Throughout the winter of 1914–15 both sides competed for her favour. Germany offered her Austrian territory — the Tyrol and Trieste — if she remained neutral. The Allies offered her much more — not only the Tyrol and Trieste, but Dalmatia and a share of Asia Minor — if she would enter the war on their side. Consequently on 26 April 1915 Italy signed with the Allies the secret Treaty of London, promising to enter the war within one month.

Italy's entry into the war did not bring the expected advantages. Her army had not recovered since the war against Libya in 1912 (p.92). It had plenty of men but little equipment and very few heavy guns. Britain was even obliged to supply Italy with coal. For the next two years Italy fought eleven battles to cross the Isonzo River, which divided her from her claims against Austria, but with little success (map, p.132).

1916

STRATEGIES OF WAR

Although four great powers combined in the allied war effort, so far there had been little co-operation between them. Then on 6 December 1915 a military conference of the Allies was held for the first time, under the presidency of Marshal Joffre. It was proposed that in the following year, 1916, three simultaneous attacks — on the western, eastern, and Italian fronts — should be made against Germany and Austria-Hungary. But the Russians and Italians were so exhausted that they were incapable of mounting any worthwhile offensive on their respective fronts. Only an offensive on the western front seemed a practical proposition.

Joffre's idea was a combined British-French offensive along the valley of the River Somme. General Douglas Haig, the British commander, agreed. It was a strange choice since there was no great prize to be gained nor a vital centre to be threatened; in fact the Germans could fall back, to their own advantage, with better communications and a shorter line (map, p.132).

Joffre and Haig imagined that they had plenty of time in which to execute their plan, which was to send forty French and twenty-five British divisions to attack south and north of the Somme respectively. They considered that the Germans would be battered to pieces; the infantry would then occupy the vacant German positions while the cavalry would go through.

But Falkenhayn also had a plan and got his stroke in first. He did not believe that the war could be won on the eastern front, since victories there would only draw German troops deeper and deeper into Russia without defeating her. For Falkenhayn, the key to victory lay on the western front. He did not choose a spot where victory would bring a strategic advantage; instead he chose one that was a symbol of French pride — the famous French fortress of Verdun in Lorraine. It stood at the head of a useless salient in the French line, had no strategic advantage for either side, but as a symbol of national pride and with its rich historical associations, the French could be relied upon to defend it at whatever cost. Falkenhayn did not intend to break through — it was too far from Paris; but because the French would defend it to the last, he hoped to 'bleed France white' in a war of attrition, and then march on to Paris over the corpses. With France out of the war, he reasoned, Britain would be driven to a compromise peace.

Verdun

On 21 February 1916 the German bombardment of Verdun began. Especially lethal were the 420mm 'Big Bertha' mortars, which wreaked deadly damage. Joffre was prepared to cede Verdun but he was overruled by Aristide Briand, France's prime minister, who realised that it would be impossible to convince French opinion that it was not worth saving; and the consequent damage to morale would be incalculable. 'You may not think losing Verdun a defeat,' he asserted to Joffre, 'but everyone else will. If you surrender Verdun you will be cowards, cowards, and I will sack the lot of you.' France had fallen into Falkenhayn's trap.

Henri Pétain was placed in command of the defence of Verdun and he vowed: 'They shall not pass.' For four months 115 divisions bombarded each other in the most senseless and the longest episode of the entire war. When Falkenhayn abandoned the attack in June, the French had lost 315,000 men and the Germans 281,000. Verdun had not fallen and Pétain's indomitable tenacity made him legendary. It seemed to be a French victory, but in fact it had broken the spirit of the French army and many units were on the verge of mutiny.

The Germans, too, had paid a high price. Just as it had been impossible to convince the French that Verdun was not worth defending, it had also become impossible to convince the Germans that Verdun was not worth capturing, and they too had ceased to count the cost. Verdun was the most senseless episode in a senseless war. There was no prize to be won or lost — only soldiers to be killed.

> *What passing-bells for these who die as cattle?*
> *Only the monstrous anger of the guns.*
> *Only the stuttering rifles' rapid rattle*
> *Can patter out their hasty orisons.*
> *No mockeries now for them; no prayers nor bells,*
> *Nor any voice of mourning save the choirs, —*
> *The shrill, demented choirs of wailing shells;*
> *And bugles calling for them from sad shires.*
>
> (Wilfred Owen, 'Anthem for Doomed Youth')

The Somme

It is generally believed that the offensive at the Somme was started to relieve the pressure on Verdun. This is not true because the attack on Verdun had almost ceased before the Somme offensive began. The motive for the

Dug-outs at Verdun.

Somme offensive arose from Haig's belief that the war could be won there. This view was not shared by many of his junior officers, but they loyally conformed to his enthusiasm. The ordinary British soldier believed that he was about to win a great victory and was unaware of the doubts of his superiors. After Verdun, Joffre was also doubtful; he now believed in the policy of attrition and not in an offensive.

The Somme was unsuitable as an object of attack. The Germans occupied the surrounding hills and so the attackers would have to fight their way upwards out of the valley of the Somme against a concealed enemy. In addition, the Germans had double lines covered with barbed wire; and since the chalk made digging easy, they also had dug-outs forty feet deep, which made them secure from the heaviest enemy bombardment. The British infantry had received only hasty training beforehand; they had been instructed to rely mainly on the bayonet, but when it came to the real war, they never came within reach of the enemy.

The battle opened with five days of heavy bombardment on an eighteen-mile front, which was intended to destroy the enemy front line and barbed wire. Instead, it so heavily cratered the ground that advance by the infantry was almost impossible.

On 1 July, the thirteen British divisions moved forward, but the cratered ground made their progress negligible. The British soldier, weighed down by sixty-six pounds of equipment and struggling across cratered 'no man's land' with no artillery back-up, was mowed down by the Germans, who used the cratered holes as fresh cover for their machine guns when their trenches were destroyed. By the afternoon of the first day of attack, the British had sustained casualties in the order of 20,000 dead and 40,000 wounded. The reward for this slaughter was an advance of about one mile.

It was at the Somme, in September, that the British introduced the tank. These great machines were designed to travel on caterpillar wheels at 2 mph and were intended to break through all obstacles. However, they were too few in number, often stuck fast in the oozing mud or were trundled off in the wrong direction.

Haig and his generals had been so adamant that the break-through would come at the Somme, that they were now reluctant to admit their mistake. Instead, they ordered repeated attacks with the same tragic story — thousands of soldiers killed or maimed. An Australian lieutenant describes their situation:

> We are lousy, stinking, ragged, unshaven, sleepless. I have one puttee, a dead man's helmet, another dead man's gas protector, a dead man's bayonet. My tunic is rotten with other men's blood, and partly spattered with a comrade's brains.

Attacks continued, though on a diminishing scale, until they finally came to an end on 13 November. With the exception of a few miles here and there on the line, there had been no break-through. The British had lost 420,000 men, the French 200,000 and the Germans about 450,000. In all, over one million men died at the Somme in one of the bloodiest battles in world history. Concerning the courage and heroism of the ordinary soldiers in relation to the arrogance and stupidity of their generals, one historian has described it as 'lions led by donkeys'.

Because the Somme was an Allied strategy, it was also an Allied defeat. But more important, it was a defeat for idealism. The soldiers lost faith in their cause, their leaders, in everything except loyalty to their comrades. No longer did the ordinary soldier symbolise the idealism of Rupert Brooke. Now Wilfred Owen's realism took precedence:

Bent double, like old beggars under sacks,
Knock-kneed, coughing like hags, we cursed through sludge,
Till on the haunting flares we turned our backs
And towards our distant rest began to trudge.
Men marched asleep. Many had lost their boots
But limped on, blood-shod. All went lame; all blind;
Drunk with fatigue; deaf even to the hoots
Of tired, outstripped Five-Nines that dropped behind . . .
If you could hear, at every jolt, the blood
Come gargling from the froth-corrupted lungs,
Obscene as cancer, bitter as the cud
Of vile, incurable sores on innocent tongues, —
My friend, you would not tell with such high zest
To children ardent for some desperate glory,
The old Lie: Dulce et decorum est
Pro patria mori.

THE BRUSILOV OFFENSIVE

Meanwhile, the Russian commander, General Brusilov, prepared for an offensive in the east. On 4 June 1916 his army attacked at twenty different points, wherever it happened to find an opening. The Austro-Hungarian front collapsed, but Brusilov had no reserves: they

A Russian soldier threatens two deserters as indiscipline spreads in the tsar's armies.

were engaging the Germans further north. The Germans, realising the serious position of the Austro-Hungarians, rushed reinforcements to the south and defeated the Russians, who were forced into retreat after losing a million men.

This defeat paved the way for the revolution the following year. Since everything had been sacrificed to the army, the weak Russian economy could not now stand up to the pressure placed upon it. Before the war Russia had been an exporter of wheat; now there was a severe shortage of food because the peasants were being conscripted into the army. The administration was too corrupt and inefficient to organise a fair system of rationing. In addition to her huge armies, two million horses had to be fed at the front. As hunger and discontent mounted, Tsar Nicholas II, absent at the front, remained absolute ruler and rejected all suggestions of reform; insteaa he relied on the repressive power of the police and cossacks to keep discontent in check (p.160).

THE WAR AT SEA: JUTLAND

When the war broke out in 1914, the British navy was far superior to the German. The German fleet remained at home for the first two years of war while the British navy kept a close watch from its Scottish bases. Several squadrons of the German navy, scattered throughout the world, were hunted down and destroyed. One such squadron, commanded by Admiral Graf von Spee, inflicted severe damage on British shipping on the coast of South America. Eventually, in December 1914, the British hunted down and destroyed all but one of his squadron at the Falkland Islands. Graf von Spee went down with his vessel.

Britain's trump card against the enemy was to blockade Germany by sea. While Britain's blockade of war materials was accepted under international law, her extension of the blockade to foodstuffs and other non-military goods raised a storm of protest from the neutral nations. But Britain was prepared to incur the displeasure of the unaligned in order to starve Germany into surrender.

The German strategy was not only to break the blockade but to enforce a counter-blockade on Britain which was now the storehouse of supplies for herself and the Allies. On 15 February 1915, Germany announced a blockade of Britain, carried out by submarine attacks on all ships, British and neutral alike. In May 1915 the British liner *Lusitania* was sunk off the Irish coast with a loss of nearly 1,200 lives, including more than a hundred American citizens. Germany now found herself severely censured. The British blockade only interfered with neutral goods, but the German blockade killed neutral civilians. President Wilson protested in the strongest possible manner, and in September, after further sinkings, the Germans, fearing to offend such a powerful neutral, called off their unlimited submarine warfare (p.147).

The only major sea battle of the war was fought at Jutland in May 1916. Vice-Admiral Scheer, in charge of the German high seas fleet, recognised that the British fleet was superior to the German. He therefore hoped to entice British ships into isolated actions and thereby wear it down. Scheer advanced provocatively into the North Sea, and on 31 May set his trap. Rear-admiral Hipper, with his battle cruisers, was to go ahead and lure the British ships on to the main German fleet. From Scapa Flow the British commander in chief, Admiral Jellicoe, sailed south with the grand fleet to take on the Germans in their own trap. The British had twenty-eight Dreadnoughts and nine battle cruisers; the Germans sixteen Dreadnoughts and nine battle cruisers. In all, 250 vessels and 25 admirals were present; there never had been such an array of naval might in recorded history.

Admiral Beatty, commanding the British battle cruisers, engaged Hipper in the early afternoon and, although two of his ships were sunk, Beatty pushed on to the main German fleet. Scheer thought that his chance had come, but Beatty turned away, apparently in flight, and Scheer pursued him. Then at 6.15 pm the main British fleet appeared on the horizon. Scheer saw the danger and immediately turned away. But Jellicoe did not pursue him; he held firmly to the doctrine that it was more important to preserve British ships than to destroy German ones; moreover, he now believed that pursuit would only bring him on to German submarines or mines. (In fact the Germans had neither near the scene of battle.) Half-an-hour later, Scheer's ships suddenly reappeared and the battle was renewed for about fifteen minutes; then Scheer suddenly turned away again. The British were now between the Germans and their home base, but contact had been lost and Jellicoe could only guess at Scheer's route home. He guessed wrongly; Scheer slipped past and got safely home. The battle of Jutland was over (map, p.132).

The British government did not accept Jellicoe's strategy and felt that he should have been more daring. He was replaced by Admiral Beatty in 1917. However, once in command, Beatty also became cautious and recognised that the grand fleet must remain in harbour unless the German fleet came out. But the German fleet did not venture from shore, and so both fleets cancelled out each other. Nevertheless, the British maintained their blockade. The Germans, realising that they could not win by engaging the British, switched to building more U-boats, since they now realised that only an unrestricted submarine campaign could end the British blockade.

CIVILIAN POPULATION AND WAR

The year 1916 also brought home to the civilian populations the grim realities of war. In Britain daylight saving (now called summer time) was introduced and in May compulsory military service became law. For as long as anyone could remember, prices had been stable; now price rises became the order of the day. The people, not understanding the forces at work in producing these rises, blamed the profiteers, the unions; in fact everything but the real cause, which was the fact that when governments start paying their bills with paper money instead of from taxation, inflation will follow.

In some countries bread was rationed; in others, the rise in prices created its own rationing because people could no longer afford to pay. In Germany the fall in agricultural production, arising from the fact that millions of men were taken from the land and drafted into the army, led to a fall in food supplies. This, coupled with a bad harvest in 1916, followed by a bitter winter, meant that turnips became the staple diet in 1916 and the next year. In Britain conditions were not as bad. Bread was never rationed, although flour was adulterated by mixtures of rye, maize and (later) potato.

With the exception of Russia there was as yet little active discontent. Trade union leaders generally co-operated with governments in the smooth running of the economy, while workers were kept relatively quiet with increased wages, which helped to minimise the effects of inflation.

Only in Ireland did nationalistic feelings run sufficiently high to attempt a national uprising. But even here, because of the capture of German arms and confusion among the leaders, the Rising was largely confined to Dublin. On Easter Monday, April 1916, an Irish Republic was proclaimed, but within a week the Rising had collapsed. The leaders were rounded up and executed — an ironic comment on Britain's claim to be fighting against Germany for the freedom of small nations.

CHANGES IN LEADERSHIP

The year 1916 also saw many changes in leadership. General Kitchener was the first to go. On 5 June, while on his way to Russia, his ship, the *Hampshire*, struck a mine off the Orkneys. Kitchener and most of the crew were lost. Falkenhayn was next to topple. Although competent, he lacked glamour; someone with more prestige was needed to cloak the losses at Verdun and the Somme. Moreover, German morale was badly hit when Romania joined the Allies on 27 August. Falkenhayn could not be blamed for this because the Allies had bribed Romania with promises of Hungarian territory; but German opinion had to be given encouragement and this was done by bringing Hindenburg and Ludendorff from the east and placing them in charge on the western front. Falkenhayn was given charge of the Romanian front and conducted it so successfully that before the year had ended practically all Romania was taken by the German armies; but before that happened, British agents had destroyed the oil wells, which were sorely needed by the Germans for the war effort.

Ludendorff, believing that the tactic of fighting for every inch of ground was mistaken, rejected Falkenhayn's previous policy and ordered German troops to cede ground where necessary in order to reduce losses. In fact he went further — he resolved to simplify the German line. This new 'Hindenburg Line', chosen for its advantages instead of being imposed by accident, could be successfully defended by fewer divisions. But successful defence could not achieve victory and Ludendorff too was forced to conclude that only unrestricted submarine warfare could win the war. In this he had Hindenburg's backing (map, p.132).

After Verdun, General Nivelle took over from Joffre as France's supreme commander on the western front.

1917

At the beginning of 1917, essentially nothing had changed. The same European powers were fighting the same European war. But before the year was out, a radically new situation had developed. At one side of Europe was Bolshevism, an entirely new system of thought and government. In the west was the United States, a non-European power that was destined to eclipse all the other powers put together. It was the year of Lenin and President Wilson, both of whom rejected the traditional European standards of political behaviour. Both preached a different kind of utopia. Lenin preached a classless world of communism; Wilson preached a world safe for democracy. It was the birth of the modern world.

AMERICA GOES TO WAR

George Washington, the first president of the United States, had warned the American people never to make permanent alliances with European nations and, for all practical purposes, his advice had been followed until 1917. Americans were proud of their democratic and republican way of life, and very suspicious of those European states that were still ruled by monarchs and riddled with aristocratic privileges.

When Woodrow Wilson became president in 1912, he was mostly concerned with domestic affairs and was a staunch advocate of an isolationist foreign policy. Yet it was the irony of his fate that Wilson would abandon America's traditional role of neutrality and involve her in World War I.

When war broke out in Europe in 1914, Wilson proclaimed American neutrality and urged his people to be neutral in thought, speech and deed. Most Americans regarded the war as irrelevant to their country's interest, something that would be utter folly to become involved in. Yet many Americans had mixed sympathies. Eight million were German-Americans, who saw Germany as saving Europe from the Slavic hordes. Another four million were Irish-Americans with a sense of bitterness against England, and most American Jews hated Russia. On the other side most Americans of older stock were in favour of the *Entente Cordiale*. Language and history created sympathy with Britain, and republican France held a particular place in American hearts. In addition, since the Allies controlled the Atlantic telegraph cables, they were able to feed the United States with Allied propaganda and stories of German atrocities. On balance, it is true to say that the majority of Americans favoured the Allies but had no intention of going to war on their behalf. Why then did America abandon her neutrality and go to war on the side of the Allied powers?

The Interest of Big Business

The war needs of the Allies gave a tremendous boost to American industry. Trade with the Allies soared from $825 million in 1914 to $3,214 million in 1916, which lifted America out of a deep depression. Before the war the United States was a debtor nation, owing money to Europe. By 1917 she was a creditor nation, having lent the Allies huge sums to finance their growing purchases of vital war materials. By 1917 European debts to the United States totalled $2,700,000. American industry had become largely geared to the Allied war needs and an Allied defeat would have been fatal to American prosperity.

American troops in France, 1917.

Freedom of the Seas

But the immediate reason for American entry into the war was the German submarine campaign. This had been suspended after the sinking of the *Lusitania* in 1915, but in January 1917 Germany announced the resumption of unrestricted submarine warfare. U-boats would henceforth sink all ships — passenger and merchant, neutral and belligerent, armed or unarmed — in the war zone. With the German announcement, Wilson immediately broke off diplomatic relations, but did not declare war.

The Zimmermann Telegram

A few days later Germany committed an act that turned the scales of opinion in America. The British secret service (naval intelligence) intercepted a secret telegram from Arthur Zimmermann (the German foreign minister) to Mexico, wherein he proposed that if the United States did declare war on Germany, Mexico could rely on German support to recover all the territory she had lost to America in the Mexican War of 1846. When the British informed America, the press whipped up a wave of anti-German feeling. In March the Russian revolution got rid of the tsarist autocracy. This made the war seem an issue between democracy in Britain, France and Russia, and autocracy in Germany and Austria-Hungary; so the United States could now join the Allies 'to make the world safe for democracy'.

Explaining the necessity for American involvement in the war, President Wilson told Congress in April 1917:

> It is a fearful thing to lead this great peaceful people into war, into the most terrible and disastrous of all wars — Civilisation itself seeming to be in the balance. But the right thing is more precious than peace, and we shall fight for the things nearest to our hearts — for democracy, for the right to have a voice in one's own government, for the rights and liberties of all nations, for a universal domination of right by a concert of free peoples.

THE RUSSIAN REVOLUTION

As the United States was preparing to enter the war, Russia was withdrawing. In early March 1917, as food shortages increased, bread riots followed and the tsar was forced to abdicate. A provisional government was set up and Russia became a republic (p.160). Ironically, the revolution that toppled the tsar was hailed by the Allies, who felt that the new provisional government would prosecute the war more effectively than the inept tsar had done. Moreover, the one autocratic regime in the Allied side was removed so the Allies could more truthfully say that they were fighting the war to make the world safe for democracy.

One man, Lenin, the Bolshevik leader, thought differently. Lenin was not interested in an Allied victory. Instead he wanted to overthrow all existing governments and establish international communism. Immediately Lenin denounced the provisional government and began to prepare for a new revolution. But few people either outside or inside Russia foresaw the coming Bolshevik storm. All eyes were on the west, where General Nivelle was about to launch a French attack on the river Aisne.

THE AISNE

On 9 April the British opened an offensive at Arras to distract attention from Nivelle's preparations. The Canadian troops took Vimy Ridge, one of the few hills on the plains of Flanders, but thereafter the lines settled down as before. The only result of the battle of Arras was 150,000 British casualties and 100,000 German. Meanwhile the Germans had learned of Nivelle's plans for an attack so that by the appointed day, 16 April, they had as many divisions ready as the French. Nivelle's attack failed to dislodge the German machine guns and the infantry went forward and were massacred. The attack continued for two weeks but then it faded out, a miserable failure. Nivelle's hour was over; at the end of April he was replaced by Pétain, who had no faith in the offensive. His policy was to wait until the Americans arrived in sufficient numbers (map, p.132).

THE CONVOY SYSTEM

Meanwhile the German submarines were causing havoc with British shipping. One ship in every four leaving Britain never returned, and neutral ships refused to sail for British ports. The British prime minister, Lloyd George, proposed the convoy system as a solution to the problem. On 26 April he gave the formal order to institute convoys, protected by destroyers. The first convoys sailed on 10 May and soon it became the norm for all trans-

Machine guns among the shellholes and the mud at Paschendaele, 1917 (see p.150).

atlantic shipping. The results were dramatic. Before the convoy system was initiated, the rate of loss of British vessels was 25 per cent. With the convoy system it was reduced to one per cent, and by September the destroyers were sinking submarines faster than the Germans could build them. The institution of the convoy system was Lloyd George's greatest stroke and it ensured that Britain would not be defeated.

German losses, coupled with the British blockade, resulted in strikes on a widespread scale and the sailors at Kiel mutinied. In July the chancellor, Bethmann-Hollweg resigned and an unknown bureaucrat, Georg Michaelis, took his place. He exercised little power and from then on the military increased their importance, as Germany ceased, for all practical purposes, to have a civilian head of state.

In July the Russians launched an offensive against the German lines. They had a few days of success and then were overwhelmed by the German counter-attack, which reached the gates of Riga. Alexander Kerensky, the new socialist prime minister, had hoped to restore Russia's fighting spirit: instead the attack had broken her morale and thousands began to drift home from the front. Kerensky realised that the only hope for Russia was to make a separate peace, but the Allies insisted that Russia stay in the war, and so the country was driven further along the road to another revolution (p.160).

YPRES

Meanwhile, Haig still believed in the efficacy of the frontal assault, despite the tragic lessons of the Somme; he now claimed that the Somme had been the wrong place for an assault. Haig was not sorry that the French were incapable of an offensive because he preferred to work independently, and he looked to the Ypres salient as the place where a break-through could be achieved. He also believed that it was Britain's last chance to win the war before the Americans arrived in strength. Yet Haig never inspected the Ypres salient and disregarded the warning of his intelligence staff about the mud. Marshal Foch, Pétain's chief of staff, said it was impossible to fight both *Boche* and *boue* (Germans and mud), but criticism only made Haig more determined.

On 25 July, with almost a million men crammed into the Ypres salient, the battle began. Heavy rain and shell fire turned the ground into a sea of mud. Men, struggling to advance, sank up to their waists; guns disappeared. Haig sent in tanks, but they too were engulfed by the mud. In mid-August the offensive slackened, but it resumed again in September. There was another attack in October and on 7 November the final attack took the ruined village of Passchendaele. In pushing their line forward five miles, the British had lost over 300,000 men, the Germans 200,000 (map, p.132).

Passchendaele was the last battle in the old style: even the generals now realised that something had gone wrong and this was amply demonstrated at Cambrai. Tanks had been found to be useless in the mud of Flanders, so the tank corps therefore picked Cambrai, some forty miles south of Ypres, where there was dry hard ground. On 20 November, 381 tanks went forward and crossed all three German lines with a loss of 1,500 men as against 10,000 German prisoners. But the success was not exploited; the infantry could not keep up with the tanks and the cavalry was destroyed by German machine-gun fire. The achievement had come to nought.

The desolation of war – Ypres, 1917.

CAPORETTO

Meanwhile if the British were anxious about the fighting spirit of the French, the Germans were equally worried about the Austrians. Ludendorff determined to boost the morale of the Austrians with a victory against the Italians. On 24 October nine Austrian and six German divisions attacked the Italians at

Caporetto on the Isonzo river, and the entire Italian front collapsed. But their very success took the central powers by surprise since they had no transport for the infantry and only horses to move the guns. After falling back 70 miles, the Italians made a stand upon the Piave. The line held and the army recovered its spirit. Yet Caporetto had cost them 200,000 dead, while a further 400,000 had deserted (map, p.132).

In an effort to help Italy, the Allies agreed to set up a Supreme War Council to provide a unified approach. But the council proved to be little more than window-dressing. The Italians continued to run their own front, although with some assistance from France and Britain. There were still two independent armies in France — one under Pétain, the other under Haig.

THE BOLSHEVIK REVOLUTION

One ally was missing from the Supreme War Council. Russia had fallen out of the war. On 25 October the Bolsheviks under Lenin seized all the key positions in Petrograd, stormed the Winter Palace and arrested the provisional government. The same evening the Second All-Russia Congress of Soviets met in Petrograd and was informed that power was in the hands of the Soviets (p.165). Once power had been consolidated in Petrograd, the Soviets negotiated a separate peace with Germany and in December an armistice was signed (p.167).

As the year drew to its close, the Allies' disappointment was manifest. There had been no break-through on the western front: rather, there had been two disastrous failures that had sapped their fighting spirit: Italy seemed to be heading for disaster against Austria-Hungary; and now, Russia was out of the war. There was but one success: on 19 December the British commander, Viscount Allenby, entered Jerusalem and captured it from the Turks — the first Christian master to do so since the Crusades. A few weeks earlier the British, in the famous Balfour Declaration, had announced that Palestine was to become a national homeland for the Jews. Thus, the seeds of future Arab-Israeli conflict were laid (p.330).

1918

WILSON'S FOURTEEN POINTS

In January 1918, in a speech to Congress, President Wilson outlined the general principles on which a fair and lasting peace should be based. It could not be, he declared, a peace imposed by the victors upon the defeated, since this would only serve to continue the cycle of revenge and war. Instead, he believed that this war should be 'a war to end all wars', and that the surest way to avoid conflict was to remove the causes. To this end he outlined his famous *fourteen points* for peace:

1. An end to all secret treaties.
2. Freedom of navigation on the seas.
3. The removal of economic barriers between states.
4. The reduction of armaments to a minimum.
5. Colonial problems to be settled with reference to the wishes and interests of colonial peoples.
6. The evacuation of Russian territory.
7. The restoration of Belgium.
8. The liberation of France and her recovery of Alsace-Lorraine.
9. Italian frontiers to be drawn along clearly recognisable lines of nationality.
10. Self-determination (independence) for the various nations of the Austro-Hungarian empire.
11. Territorial integrity for the Balkan states.

12. The development of independence for the non-Turkish peoples of the Ottoman empire, and free passage for all ships through the Dardanelles.
13. The creation of an independent Poland.
14. The creation of an association of nations, to be known as the League of Nations.

POWERS AT WAR IN 1914

The line up of powers in 1914, at the outbreak of the War.

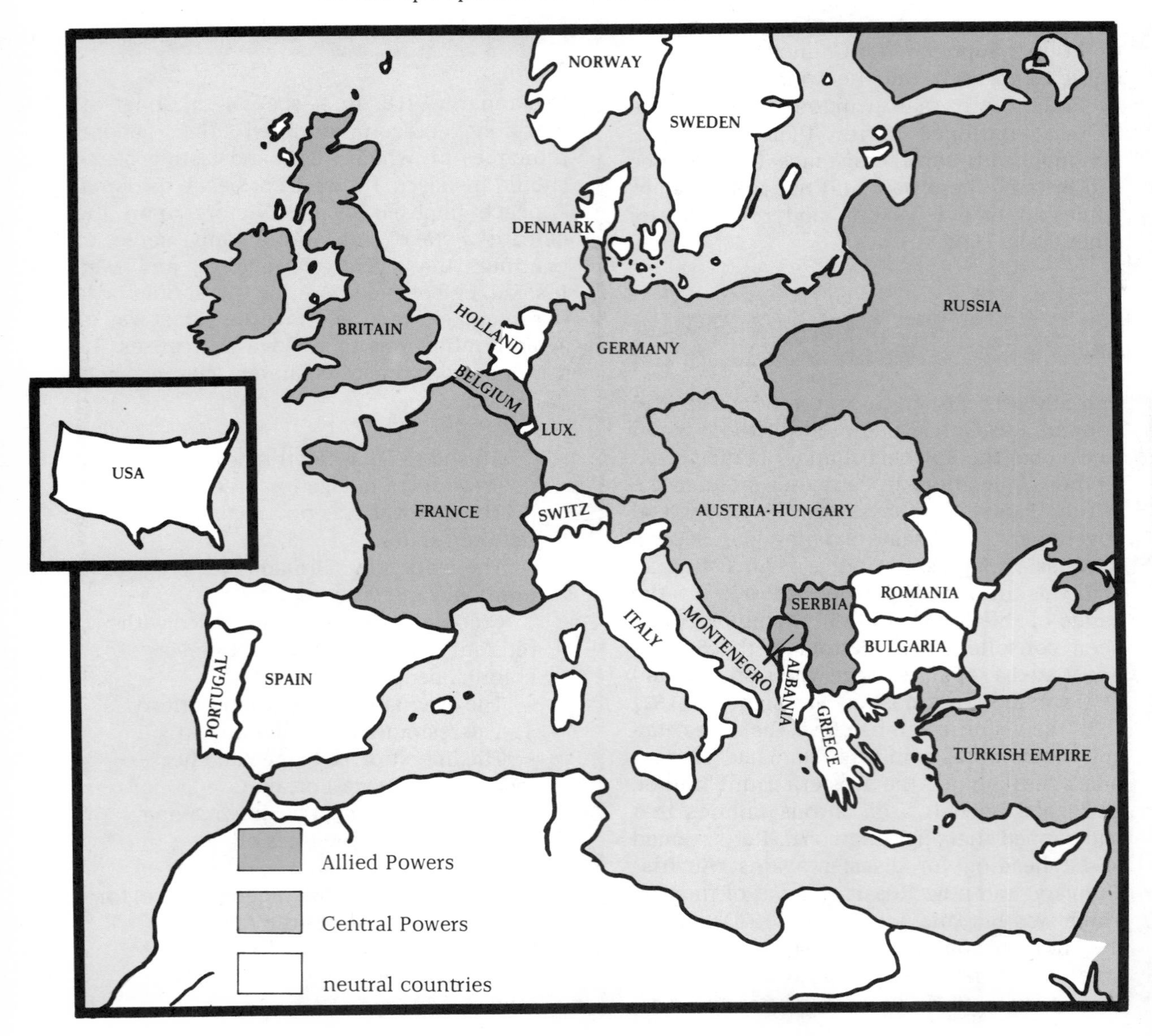

TREATY OF BREST-LITOVSK

Leon Trotsky negotiated peace terms on behalf of the Bolshevik government at a conference with the central powers at Brest-Litovsk. But since the Germans had made such enormous inroads on Russian soil and the Bolsheviks were fighting for survival in a civil war (p.171), the Germans knew they could

POWERS AT WAR IN 1918

The line up of powers towards the end of the War, in 1917-18.

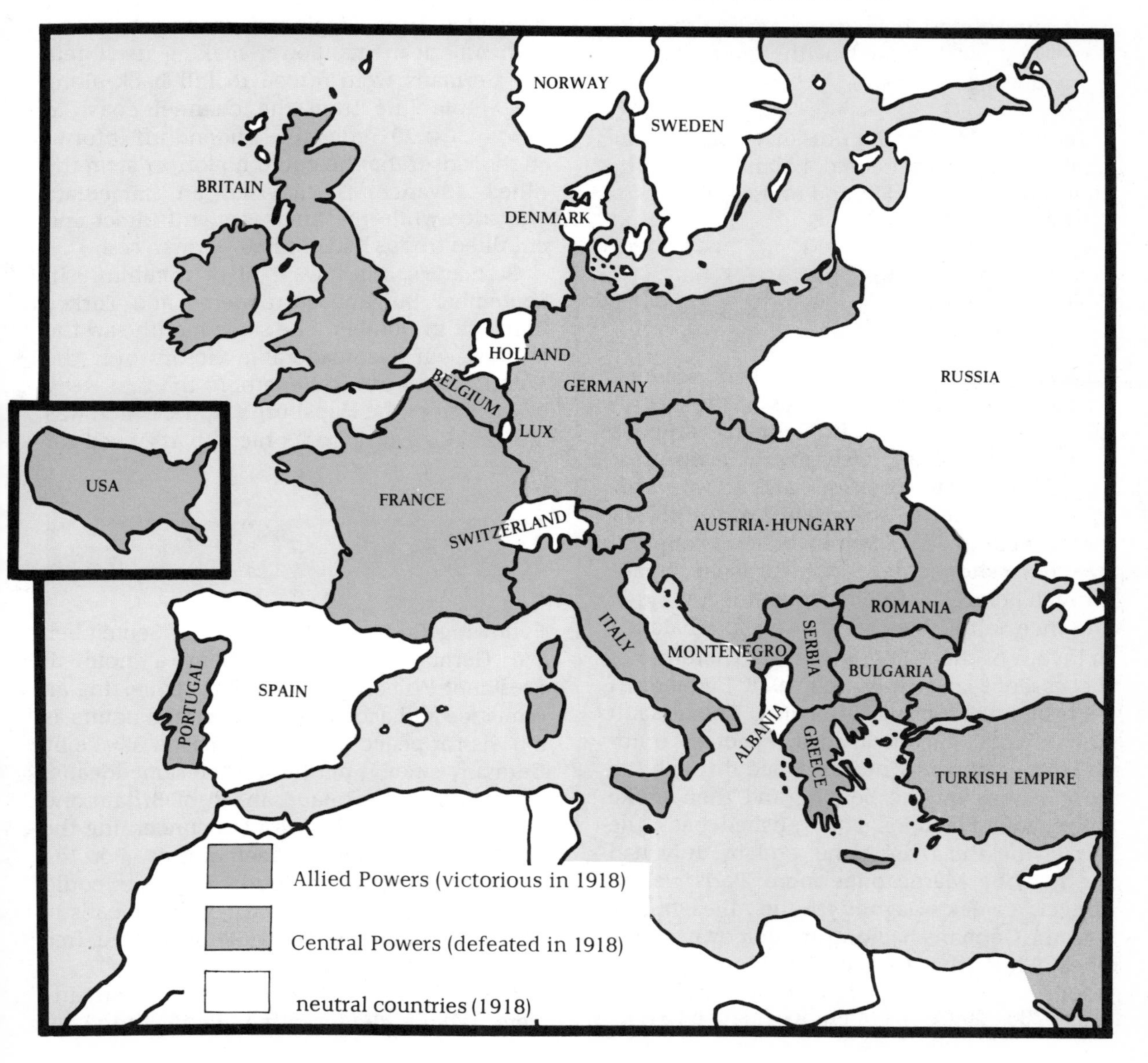

drive a very hard bargain. They demanded all the European land that the tsars had conquered over the previous two centuries; these included the Baltic states of Latvia, Lithuania and Estonia, together with eastern Poland and the Ukraine. Trotsky considered the terms unacceptable, but Lenin insisted that they should sign, since peace at any price was the only course for the fledgling Bolshevik state:

> The soldiers have voted against the war. They have voted with their feet by running away.

In early March the Russians signed the treaty, which surrendered Poland, the Baltic states, the Ukraine, Finland and the Caucasus (p.168 and map, p. 169).

THE LUDENDORFF OFFENSIVE

Russia's exit from the war had enabled Germany to transfer her troops in the east to the western front. But in Germany supplies were running dangerously low as a result of the Allied naval blockade, and it was now essential for her to strike while she still had the strength to do so. Moreover, it was imperative that she achieve the decisive breakthrough before the full impact of the American presence would inevitably swing the balance in favour of the Allies. Speed was therefore of the essence and in March 1918 Ludendorff launched the Spring Offensive. The assault was frenzied, spearheaded by specially trained storm-troopers. They smashed through the British lines on the Somme and then broke through in Flanders. They pushed back the French on the river Aisne, and by July had reached the Marne once more. Paris was in danger. A week of agony for the Allies, but by now the Germans had outrun their own supply lines while the United States, pouring in troops at the rate of 250,000 a month, had some 700,000 troops in France (map, p.132).

When the Germans launched their final attack on 15 July, they had actually crossed the fateful river but had neither the manpower nor the equipment to sustain their advance. Foch, who had been given command of a Franco-American force, not only held but repulsed them, and the attack passed into counter-attack as a second Battle of the Marne. With Foch on the offensive, the Germans began to retreat. This time they were prevented from digging in in trenches, and with American manpower making itself felt, the Germans were forced to fall back along the whole line from the channel coast to Verdun. On 29 September Ludendorff informed the kaiser that he could no longer stem the Allied advance. He advised an immediate armistice while the army was still intact and no Allied troops had entered German soil.

Germany's allies were also crumbling. In September Bulgaria surrendered and Turkey followed in October. The same month saw the Italians win a considerable victory over the Austrians at Vittorio Veneto. In the first week of November the Hapsburg empire, which was fast breaking up into its racial parts, sued for peace.

ARMISTICE

Following Ludendorff's advice in September, the German government sent a note to President Wilson on 4 October, requesting an armistice and accepting his fourteen points as a basis for peace. This was a master stroke by Germany since it put her on the same idealistic level as Wilson, and ahead of Britain and France, who each had doubts concerning the practicality of his fourteen points. For the moment Wilson was jubilant: peace could now be made on the basis of his idealistic points, and a new world would be created, free from war and safe for democracy.

Meanwhile conditions within Germany were rapidly deteriorating. Food shortages,

Compiègne forest, 11 November 1918. Right: *The German delegation's train.* Left: *Foch's train in which the Armistice was signed.*

violent protests and mutinies were bringing her to the verge of revolution. Ludendorff and Hindenburg, realising by 29 September that the war had been lost, had relinquished their power to the Reichstag. The kaiser was persuaded to abidicate and on 8 November he fled to neutral Holland. The following day the chancellor, Prince Maximilian, handed over control of government to Friedrich Ebert, the leader of the Social Democrats. It was his government that signed an armistice on 11 November, on the basis of Wilson's fourteen points, in a railway carriage in the forest of Compiègne in northern France. The Great War was at an end.

These, having life, gave life away:
Is God less generous than they?
The spirit passes and is free:
Dust to the dust; Death takes the clay.

(J. Griffyth Fairfax,
'The Forest of the Dead')

In addition to those killed in action, some 9 million civilians had died from famine and disease, air raids, drownings and massacres, while a further 6 million had died from Spanish influenza.

The war had killed five per cent of the entire population of Europe and had maimed a further fifteen per cent. But no figures can

COUNTING THE COST

Countries	Mobilised Forces	Killed	Wounded
The Allies			
Russia	12,000,000	1,700,000	4,950,000
France	8,410,000	1,358,800	4,266,000
British Empire	8,904,467	908,371	2,090,212
Italy	5,615,000	650,000	947,000
United States	4,355,000	126,000	234,300
Romania	750,000	335,706	120,000
Serbia	707,343	45,000	133,148
Belgium	267,000	13,716	44,684
Greece	230,000	5,000	21,000
Portugal	100,000	7,222	13,751
Montenegro	50,000	3,000	10,000
Total	41,188,810	5,152,815	12,830,095
The Central Powers			
Germany	11,000,000	1,773,700	4,216,058
Austria-Hungary	7,800,000	1,200,000	3,620,000
Turkey	2,850,000	325,000	400,000
Bulgaria	1,200,000	87,500	152,390
Total	22,850,000	3,386,200	8,388,448
Grand Total	64,038,810	8,539,315	21,218,543

(US War Department, February 1924)

ever reveal the sorrow of bereaved families, the broken marriages and careers, the spread of venereal and other diseases, the thousands confined to mental hospitals, and the remaining millions doomed to live out their lives with unforgettable and unspeakable memories of suffering on a scale undreamed of in 1914.

The war had enormous political and economic consequences for Europe and the world. It was, as Lenin said, 'a mighty accelerator of events', which destroyed four empires — the Romanov, Hohenzollern, Hapsburg and Ottoman — while many of the republican states that replaced them soon gave way to left or right-wing totalitarian governments. The war also dislocated the smooth running of the international economy; by 1918 the war was costing the world over £2 million an hour — an expense which was met largely by borrowing and by printing paper money. All this stored up immense economic trouble for the future.

The war also had a levelling effect upon social attitudes and manners. Conscription created a labour shortage in industry and agriculture which was filled by women, while others found employment as bus conductors and as typists. For the first time women commenced earning their own living on a large scale, and this soon reflected itself in their general demeanour; they started to enter licensed premises and order their own drinks; they also wore shorter skirts and cut their hair; and many started 'going out' unescorted, and even marrying without their fathers' permission.

But the greatest consequence of the war was the weakening of Europe from her position as the world's centre of power and influence; and although Europe's eclipse was not finally accomplished until after World War II, that eclipse, and the consequent rise of Soviet Russia and the United States, had each their direct origins in the Great War.

Study Assignments and Essays

1. *'The failure of the Schlieffen Plan was disastrous for Germany.' Discuss.*
2. *'The year 1916 was the worst year of the war.' Explain your answer.*
3. *'The quality of leadership on both sides in World War I left much to be desired.' Discuss.*
4. *Why did the Great War last for over four years?*
5. *'The American entry, more than the Russian exit, was the decisive event of the Great War.' Do you agree? Support your answer.*
6. *Write an essay on two of the following: (i) New instruments of war; (ii) The war at sea; (iii) Italy and the Great War; (iv) Social and economic change during the Great War; (v) Changing attitudes to war, 1914–18.*

The Russian Revolution 1917 12

Like the chewed stump of a fag
We spat their dynasty out.

Vladimir Mayakovsky, 1893–1930,
Russian poet

THE OUTBREAK of war in 1914 led to strong demonstrations of patriotic loyalty to Tsar Nicholas II, and the *Duma* enthusiastically voted war credits. But disillusionment soon followed when it became apparent that Russia was unprepared for war and was incapable of carrying out the necessary planning. The war imposed tremendous strains on her backward economy. Manpower was conscripted indiscriminately and without regard for the needs of agriculture, industry and communications. By 1915, 573 factories and mills had shut down for want of raw materials, fuel and manpower, and 36 blast furnaces were standing idle. The countryside was denuded of horses to serve the army's needs, leaving the peasant with no means of tilling the land. Shcrtages caused prices to rise rapidly, and inflation was made worse by the government's foolishness in printing paper money to pay its debts.

The commander-in-chief of the army was the tsar's uncle, Grand-Duke Nicholas. He was popular with the soldiers, but the army's inherent weakness was beyond his capacity to repair. The soldiers lacked proper military training, while the problems of supplying them from inadequate stores of equipment and munitions in a mobile theatre of war covering vast distances were never overcome.

The offensives of 1914 and 1915 had left one million Russians dead, while a further three million civilians had retreated in the face of German advance, causing a monumental refugee problem. The tsar aggravated the deteriorating situation by committing two serious mistakes. In September 1915 he finally succumbed to the tsarina's goading and dissolved the *Duma*; and two days later he took command at the front in place of his uncle. The government was left mostly in the hands of Alexandra, the hated 'German woman', as she was now called. To make matters worse, Alexandra was very much under the influence of Gregori Rasputin.

RASPUTIN

In 1904 the tsarina had given birth to an only son and heir, Alexis, but it was soon found that he was suffering from the incurable disease of haemophilia. The tsarina was a carrier of the disease through her grandmother, Queen Victoria. This terrible blow made Alexandra so desperate that she was willing to accept aid from anyone who might be in a position to help. In 1905, Gregori Rasputin, a 'holy man' from Siberia, ingratiated himself with Alexandra because of his reputed powers of healing. Rasputin was a strange mixture of cruelty and kindness, viciousness and piety, and led a debauched private life. But he had hypnotic powers of healing and was able to give the tsarevich relief from pain when he lay in agony from internal haemorrhages.

Many accusations of scandal were made against Rasputin, but Nicholas and Alexandra refused to believe them. The tsar was content to accept Rasputin's influence over the tsarina, who believed that her son would not die as long as Rasputin lived.

Rasputin used his influence over the gullible tsarina to have ministers dismissed at will and replaced by men of the worst possible calibre: old, sick and illiterate. The government thus became chaotically incompetent, even ridiculous.

By 1916 Rasputin's influence was almost total; the tsar remained at the front where another offensive had cost Russia a million more casualties. The morale of the army began to crumble. In November, the *Duma* was

Cossack soldiers during World War I.

reconvened, and in December Prince Felix Yussoupov, realising the extent of Rasputin's influence over Alexandra, resolved that he should die.

On the night of 29 December 1916, together with a few of his closest friends, Yussoupov invited Rasputin to the Moika Palace, the Yussoupov family's residence in Petrograd. There Rasputin found a feast of cakes and dainties spread before him. Unknown to him, each cake was dosed with enough cyanide to kill five men instantly. Rasputin ate two cakes and washed them down with two glasses of poisoned madeira — but nothing happened. Yussoupov spent the next two-and-a-half hours talking and singing with the fuddled Rasputin. Finally, in desperation, Yussoupov left the room, returned with a revolver and shot Rasputin in the back at point blank range.

No sooner had Rasputin been pronounced dead by a doctor (who was part of the conspiracy), than he leaped from the floor and threw himself at Yussoupov's throat, who fled in terror from the room. Clambering on all fours, Rasputin pursued him into the darkened courtyard, where he was shot in the head and shoulder by another of the conspirators. He was then beaten to death in the snow, rolled in a curtain, bound with a rope, and pushed through a hole in the ice of the frozen Neva. Three days later when the body was recovered, it was found that the rope binding him was partially freed and his lungs were full of water. Rasputin, poisoned, shot and beaten into unconsciousness, had actually died from drowning.

THE FEBRUARY REVOLUTION 1917

The end for the three-hundred-year-old Romanov dynasty came suddenly. There were about 400,000 workers in Petrograd and by February 1917 they were hungry. On 22 February (the Russian calendar was 13 days behind the west) demonstrators protesting about bread shortages merged with crowds holding a procession celebrating International Women's Day and a strike at the Putilov armaments factory. The following day crowds continued to roam the streets, carrying red flags and shouting 'Down with the German woman'. On 24 February the police opened fire on rioters and the following day forty workers were killed. When the crowds appealed to the military units, the soldiers joined the strikers; this was the fundamental difference between the February Revolution of 1917 and the uprising of 1905.

The president of the *Duma* sent the tsar a stern warning of the need for urgent action, but Nicholas remained astonishingly apathetic. He commented: 'That fat Rodzianko has sent me some nonsense. I shall not even reply.' He did however write to Alexandra, expressing how much he missed his game of patience every evening, and stating his intention of taking up dominoes again in his spare time. All Nicholas did was to dissolve the *Duma*. Its members later met in defiance of the order and elected a provisional committee with the idea of restoring order, but it was too late. Discipline had collapsed and on 27 February the Taurida Palace (where the *Duma* sat) was invaded by workers, who set up a Workers' Soviet, modelled on the Soviet of 1905 (p.58).

Finally, Nicholas decided to return to Petrograd, but the train stopped at Pskov because the railway line further on was in the hands of the rebels. Here on 1 March, for the first time, Nicholas saw the grim reality of his situation, and was persuaded to abdicate in favour of his brother, Grand-Duke Michael. The next day, his brother haughtily rejected the crown of a parliamentary monarch. Thus the Romanov dynasty quietly came to an end and Russia technically became a republic.

THE PROVISIONAL GOVERNMENT

After the tsar's abdication, real power was divided between the provisional committee of the *Duma* and the Soviet of workers' deputies. The provisional committee now formed into a provisional government with Prince Georgi Lvov as prime minister, and included Alexander Kerensky as minister for justice.

From the outset the provisional government realised that its authority was limited because of its formidable rival, the Petrograd Soviet. Despite this, it did make remarkable progress under adverse circumstances in reforming Russian society. It freed political prisoners, and allowed freedom of speech and of the press. The criminal law was reformed, and the death penalty and secret courts were abolished. But it made a fundamental error in not satisfying the great mass of the Russian people on the two burning issues of the day: peace and land. The provisional government continued the war against Germany and Austria-Hungary, since it believed that it had obligations to Britain and France; some of its members hoped to gain prestige by winning the victories that had eluded Nicholas. Thus, to the average soldier, there was no fundamental difference between the new government and the tsarist regime that it had replaced. The new government shelved the problem of land distribution on the grounds that it would first have to hold elections for a constituent assembly, which would then draw up a constitution and give legitimacy to land reform. Until then, its members maintained that they were merely guardians of power, and could not institute any fundamental change until Russia had time to elect a democratic government. Meanwhile they called for patience, greater effort, increased productivity and low wages.

Lenin and the July Rising

When news of the February revolution reached Lenin in neutral Switzerland, he was fearful lest the Bolsheviks should make the mistake of supporting the bourgeois provisional government instead of preparing for the real proletarian revolution. In March 1917 German agents approached Lenin and other exiled Bolsheviks and offered to facilitate their return to Russia on the understanding that they would start another revolution, or at least cause enough disruption to damage the Russian war effort.

Lenin and his party travelled through Germany, Sweden and Finland in a sealed train, arriving at the Finland Station in Petrograd on 3 April 1917. Lenin quickly assumed control of the Petrograd Soviet and in his 'April thesis' outlined a distinct plan of action for Bolshevik victory. There was to be absolutely no co-operation with the provisional government; the revolution of February must only be seen as a first step on the road to the proletarian revolution, which the Bolsheviks would spearhead. Meanwhile they must arouse as much discontent as possible. The soldiers must be incited to demand peace, the workers to demand bread, and the peasants to demand land. Their slogan must be *Peace! Bread! Land!* since these were the things most desired by the masses. If the Bolsheviks could win these discontented groups to their side by offering them what they most needed, then the success of the revolution was assured.

Although he was a determined Marxist, Lenin's blueprint for Bolshevik victory had little, if anything, to do with offering a Marxist state. It was based essentially on a correct analysis of the social conditions and aspirations of the masses in the war-torn Russia of 1917. In general, the provisional government represented the middle classes, and the Soviets represented the masses. But, because of the Soviet presence, the provisional government was obliged to move closer to the people.

On 27 April Prince Lvov invited representatives of the Petrograd Soviet to join the provisional government. On 5 May a new cabinet was formed which included six socialists (Mensheviks and Social Revolutionaries, but not Bolsheviks). The strong man in this cabinet was Alexander Kerensky, who now became minister for war.

Kerensky believed that a new offensive was necessary so that Russia could demand a victorious peace. The offensive started on 18 June, but after some initial success it began to collapse. Troops began to desert in large numbers and between 3 and 5 July half-a-

A Bolshevik poster showing Lenin addressing a workers' rally in 1917.

million people demonstrated in Petrograd, demanding peace and a new government. Violence erupted and 400 were killed. Lenin continued to demand Peace! Bread! Land!, and since the Bolsheviks had secured control of the Petrograd and other Soviets, he added a new slogan — 'All Power to the Soviets'.

On 8 July Lvov resigned and Kerensky became prime minister in a cabinet that now contained a majority of socialists. Kerensky was alarmed at the Bolshevik threat and had some of their leaders arrested, though Lenin escaped arrest by fleeing into Finland, disguised as an engine driver.

The Romanov Family

Kerensky, disturbed by the narrowness of his victory, decided to move the Romanov family from turbulent Petrograd to Tobolsk, an isolated town in western Siberia. At first Kerensky had been hostile to the imperial family but, after interviewing them several times, he became convinced of their sincerity and began to take an interest in their security and future. Their cousin, King George V, had made a tentative offer of asylum in England, but then withdrew it on the pretext that safe passage for the Romanov family could not be guaranteed over U-boat-infested waters.

Riots in Petrograd in July 1917.

Kerensky never discussed the subject of the Romanov family at cabinet meetings. Instead, he personally arranged all the details and supervised the departure of the 'Japanese Red Cross Mission' train, which pulled out of Petrograd with the entire Romanov family, the ladies and gentlemen of their suite, thirty servants and two pet spaniels. In this manner the last tsar of Russia left the capital city that had been built by his ancestor, Peter the Great (map, p.172).

The Kornilov Affair

On 19 July Kerensky appointed General Lavr Kornilov in place of Brusilov as commander in chief of the army. Kornilov managed to stabilise the front after the collapse of the offensive in June. But this decision led to another fatal fiasco. Kornilov believed that Kerensky's government was too weak to deal with the agitation in Petrograd, and he decided to move loyal troops into Petrograd, put down the

The Tsar under guard after his abdication.

agitators, and secure a position for himself in government. Learning of his intention and fearing that Kornilov was planning to set up a military dictatorship, Kerensky dismissed him. But Kornilov refused to recognise the dismissal and continued to march on Petrograd. Alarmed, Kerensky freed the Bolshevik prisoners and used their help in defeating the Kornilov mutiny. The Petrograd Soviet organised the workers into armed defence squads. Railwaymen diverted trains, blocked the lines and removed the rails. Others were sent to persuade Kornilov's troops to abandon him. The workers were victorious and Kornilov's attempt to establish a right-wing military dictatorship ended without bloodshed. Kornilov and his fellow officers were arrested but were not treated harshly.

Kerensky had asked the Bolsheviks to come to the defence of the revolution. This the Bolsheviks most willingly did. But they were not defending the February Revolution, or the provisional government: they were fostering Bolshevism.

By the autumn the Bolsheviks had gained in both membership and popular support. Their numbers now exceeded 200,000 and they had gained control of the factory committees. Their rising support came about essentially because, unlike the other parties, their policies were realistic.

The Bolsheviks, taking their cue from Lenin, urged the immediate seizure of land by the peasants, a rapid conclusion of the war and all power to the Soviets. These ideas won support away from the Social Revolutionaries and the Mensheviks, although it must also be remembered that their power in the countryside was still negligible. The Bolsheviks were also more tightly organised than the other socialist parties. Lenin could count on the unswerving support of his party, a vindication of his insistence, since the congress of 1903 (p.54), on leading a small group of totally dedicated members rather than a large mass party.

THE OCTOBER (BOLSHEVIK) REVOLUTION

On 23 September, Leon Trotsky became chairman of the Petrograd Soviet. Born Lev Bronstein, the son of a wealthy Jewish farmer, Trotsky did more than any other socialist to plan and execute the Bolshevik Revolution. He held that the Bolsheviks were not strong enough to carry through a successful revolution in their own name. Therefore, a rising against Kerensky's government would have to be portrayed as a Soviet action against a counter-revolutionary plot.

Accordingly, the Bolsheviks, working through the Petrograd Soviet, challenged Kerensky's right to order troop movements in the capital. Incensed, Kerensky denounced the Bolsheviks and attempted to arrest Lenin, who had again returned to Petrograd. The Bolsheviks could now claim to be resisting counter-revolution, and on 10 October, at a meeting of the central committee of the Bolshevik Party, a resolution for armed insurrection was passed by ten votes to two. Trotsky was appointed 'organiser of the revolution' and a committee was established to draw up plans for taking all key points in the city. Only the actual date of revolution was left open. Lenin and Trotsky argued that they should strike before the All-Russian congress of Soviets met on 25 October. They feared that a majority of delegates to the congress might not vote for revolution at this time, whereas if a successful revolution was presented to them as a *fait acompli*, it would receive one hundred per cent endorsement. The Bolshevik revolution was therefore fixed for the night of 24 October 1917.

At 2 a.m. the siren of the cruiser *Aurora* gave the signal for the revolution. The Bolshevik Red Guards seized the key points of the capital: the telephone exchange, the telegraph agency, the state bank, the power stations, the railway stations, and the main bridges.

The next morning Kerensky, at the tsar's Winter Palace, now the headquarters of the provisional government, found Petrograd in the grip of the Bolsheviks. He failed to find one loyal regiment of soldiers prepared to dislodge the Red Guards. He then escaped from the capital in a car from the American embassy, but most of his ministers were arrested. At 9 p.m. the *Aurora* fired the shot to signal the start of operations against the Winter Palace. Red Guards rushed from behind the Admiralty Arch at the rear and swarmed into the palace. But it was taken easily and all the Bolsheviks encountered were a troop of women soldiers and a few young officers, the last of Kerensky's bodyguard. Neither at the palace nor at any point in the city did the Bolsheviks meet significant opposition, and the takeover was almost bloodless.

At 11 p.m. the All-Russian Congress of Soviets met and Lenin informed the delegates that the Bolsheviks were in power and ruling in their name. The slogan 'All power to the Soviets' turned out in practice to mean all power to the Bolsheviks.

The congress agreed to the appointment of a *Sovnarkom*, or Council of People's Commissars (Ministers). Russia's new government were all Bolsheviks and it was empowered to rule by decree. Lenin was chairman (prime minister); Trotsky was commissar for foreign affairs; and Josef Stalin became commissar for nationalities.

The Bolshevik Revolution was not a revolution in the accepted sense of that word. Rather, it was a bloodless coup upon a weak and inept provisional government that had failed to identify itself with the soldiers, workers and peasants. As far as the masses were concerned, there was no material difference between the provisional government, which had turned Russia into a republic, and the tsarist autocracy it had overthrown. Russia was still at war, food shortages remained, and Kerensky continued to vacillate on the vexed question of land distribution. In contrast, the Bolsheviks seemed to have something to offer to the masses. 'Peace! Bread! Land!' was an unbeatable slogan. It propelled Lenin and the Bolsheviks into power and, despite Marx's prediction (p.4), made Russia the world's first communist state.

Study Assignments and Essays

1. *What factors led to the February Revolution of 1917?*
2. *'A good hand played badly.' Is this a fair assessment of the part played by Alexander Kerensky?*
3. *'Given the conditions within Europe, the victory of Bolshevism was inevitable.' Do you agree?*
4. *Critically examine the role of Lenin between April 1917 and November 1917.*
5. *'The October Revolution was not a revolution in the accepted sense of that word; rather, it was a*

coup carried out by an armed elite on an exhausted government.' Discuss.

6. *Write an essay on two of the following: (i) The Kornilov affair; (ii) The role of the Petrograd Soviet in 1917; (iii) The significance of the slogan 'Peace! Bread! Land!'; (iv) The timing and importance of the Bolshevik Revolution; (v) The mistakes of the provisional government.*

The Rule of Lenin 1917 –24 13

Do not copy our tactics, but think out for yourselves the reasons why they assumed these particular features, the conditions that gave rise to them and their results.

Lenin, April 1921

BOLSHEVIK REFORMS

WITHIN DAYS of seizing power, the Bolsheviks (who renamed their party the *Communist Party* in March 1918), began to issue a flood of decrees. The Decree on Land began the process of transferring to the poor the lands of the tsars, the orthodox church and the estate owners. The Decree on Peace led to an armistice in December and prepared the way for negotiations with Germany. These two decrees were highly significant because Lenin, realising that most Russians who supported the Bolsheviks wanted active, reforming government, was determined to identify his government with the masses. Other decrees ordered a comprehensive system of national insurance and the nationalisation of banking, foreign trade and major industries. Mortgages were cancelled and private ownership of land in towns was prohibited.

The orthodox church was singled out as a special target for communist attention because of its alliance with the autocracy. In addition to the confiscation of its lands and wealth, it was forbidden to teach religion or carry out marriages (henceforth these would be performed in a civil court).

In theory, the position of women was greatly altered. Decrees were issued asserting their equality with men and enabling them to hold their own property or obtain a divorce. The Julian calendar, which had left Russia thirteen days behind the rest of Europe, was replaced by the Gregorian calendar, bringing Russia into line with the West. All social, military and naval ranks, and all other titles of class distinction, were abolished, in keeping with the communist ideal of a classless society. Henceforth all Russian citizens would be addressed as 'Comrade'.

The Cheka

On 9 November 1917 newspapers opposed to the new government were ordered to cease publication. On 20 December the *Okhrana* was replaced by the All-Russia Extraordinary Commission against Counter-revolution and Sabotage, known as the *Cheka*. In effect this was a secret police force whose task was to destroy all critics of the Bolshevik regime: Social Revolutionaries, Mensheviks, counter-revolutionaries, newspaper editors, strikers, and saboteurs. The *Cheka* had the authority to arrest and even to pass sentence of death. It became the 'eyes and ears' of the Bolsheviks and was used with a more ruthless efficiency than the *Okhrana*.

The Treaty of Brest-Litovsk

In December 1917 the government published the secret treaties made by tsarist Russia, and also concluded an armistice with Germany. The armistice, as Lenin declared, was intended to give the government a breathing space in which to deal with their enemies and to consolidate power. Trotsky, as foreign minister, commenced negotiations with the Germans. But the German government, aware of the Bolsheviks' weakness, was determined to strike a hard bargain, and when it was not getting its demands, it moved troops towards Petrograd. The Bolsheviks had little option but to signal their intention of agreement. The Germans demanded the remainder of Poland, Finland, Lithuania, the Baltic states of Latvia and Estonia, the Ukraine (the bread-basket of Russia), the Crimea and most of the Caucasus — 400,000 square miles of territory with a population of 62 million people. These parts

The Russian delegation at Brest-Litovsk. Trotsky is standing second from the right.

of eastern Europe had been won by the tsars over the previous two centuries. They contained one-third of Russia's agricultural land, one-third of her railways, and three-quarters of her coal and iron reserves.

Many Bolsheviks were aghast at the German terms and were in favour of recommencing the war against Germany since it would be less offensive to them than this humiliation. But Lenin, determined on peace at any price, argued that their first priority was the consolidation of communist power within Russia; they needed peace and time, and only a surrender to German demands would get them that. Otherwise the Bolsheviks would be condemned to repeat the mistakes of the provisional government, giving their enemies within Russia an opportunity to overthrow them. Lenin argued that the success of the communist revolution in Russia would prove to be the spark that would set off the European revolution as well; then, in the context of a communist Europe, national borders would become irrelevant, and German capitalist gains would be undone.

Eventually, despite bitter opposition, Lenin had his way. On 3 March 1918, in the town of Brest-Litovsk, the headquarters of the German eastern front, the Bolshevik delegation, headed by Trotsky, signed the humiliating treaty. Immediately the ceremony was over, one Russian general in the delegation went

THE TREATY OF BREST-LITOVSK

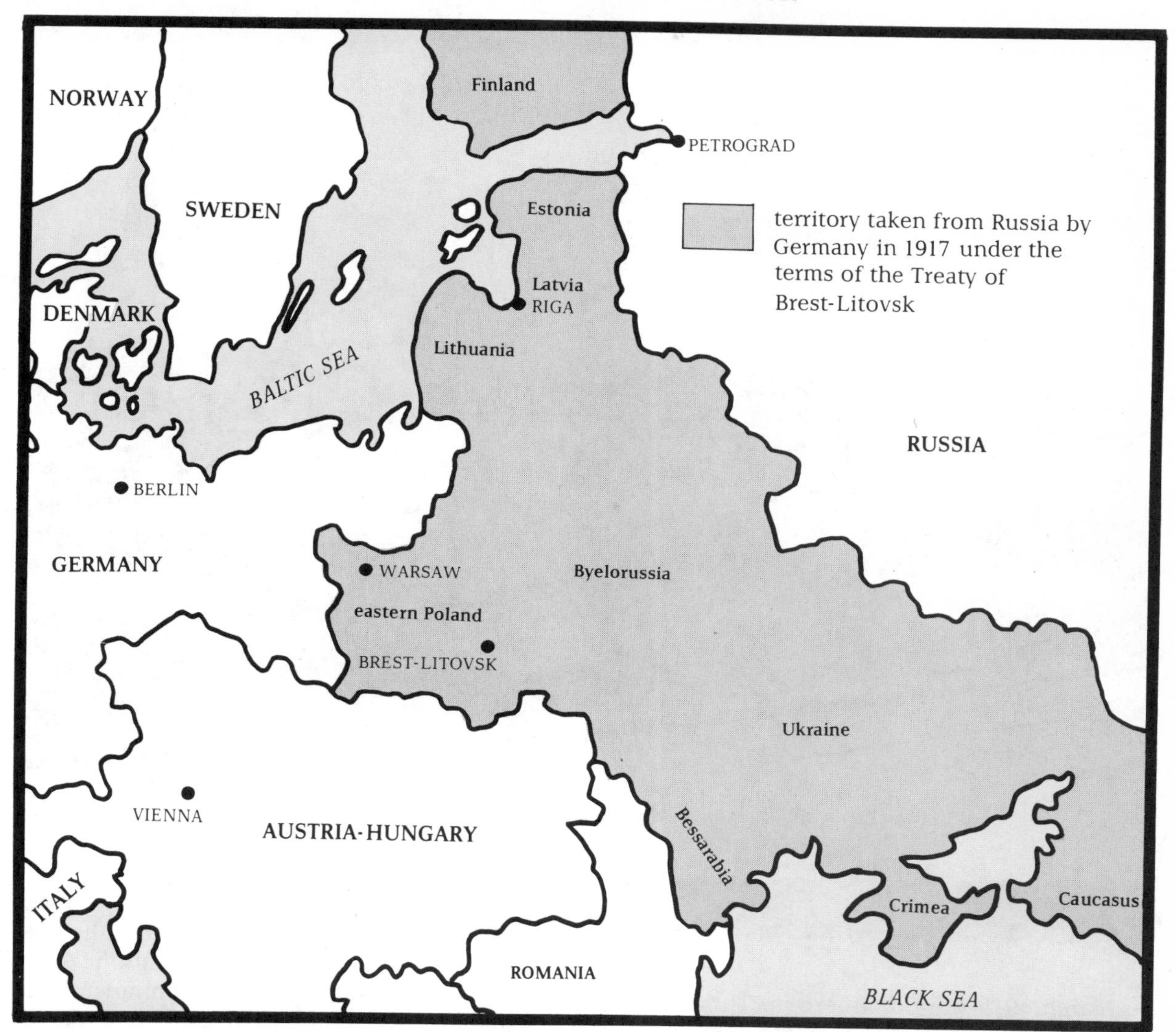

out and shot himself.

In one sense, the treaty was a blessing in disguise for Lenin's regime. By stripping Russia of its western borderlands, the regime could concentrate on containing the opposition within Russia proper, without having to deal with the militant nationalism of the Poles, Finns and Ukrainians as well. But more significantly, there is no doubt that continuing the war against Germany would have aroused such opposition in Russia that the communist regime would have been overthrown. Lenin's wisdom on the matter was in time vindicated and he came to be seen as 'the providential leader of the Communist Party and State without whom the regime would disintegrate.'

Under Lenin, the Kremlin in Moscow became the seat of Soviet government.

THE COMINTERN

In March 1919 the Comintern, or Third International, was established in Moscow to replace the Second International, which had broken up in 1914. The Comintern aimed to spread communism throughout the world. At this stage, Lenin and his colleagues believed that the revolution must be extended if communism was to survive in Russia. Indeed, at the end of World War I, Hungary was for a time in the grip of a communist revolt (p.185); and in Berlin, the left-wing Spartacist uprising (p.193) convinced many that a communist Europe was a distinct possibility.

In 1920 the Comintern laid down strict rules for membership. Learning from the mistakes of the Second International, all socialists who were not also communists were excluded. The Comintern also ensured that all affiliated communist parties from other countries would follow the decisions made in Moscow.

THE SOVIET CONSTITUTION

In December 1922 the former tsarist empire, with the exception of the lands lost at Brest-

Litovsk and through the Treaty of Versailles, was formed into the Union of Soviet Socialist Republics, also known as the USSR or the Soviet Union. The constitution of this union, drawn up in 1923, gave each republic in the union autonomy in local affairs. It provided for the election by indirect and open voting of a Congress of Soviets representing the entire union. This Congress could then elect a central executive committee, consisting of a union council and a council of nationalities. These two councils could then elect the *Praesidium* from its members.

In theory the Praesidium was the supreme authority, but in practice this was not so. Only one political party, the Communist Party, was recognised. It alone could nominate candidates for election to the Congress of Soviets and all elected members had to follow the party policy. Therefore, the highest authority was really that of the top Communist Party officials who were members of its political bureau, the *Politburo*.

CIVIL WAR

A revolt of the Don Cossacks, led by General Kornilov, in December marked the beginning of a civil war, which spread over much of Russia during the following three years. In that war the Bolshevik forces were known as the Reds and all opposition groups were collectively known as the Whites (map, p. 172).

With the exception of the Cossack revolt, however, the first six months of Bolshevik rule witnessed very little organised opposition, mainly because most opponents failed to appreciate the full significance of the Bolshevik takeover. But after the treaty of Brest-Litovsk, anti-Bolshevik groups began to emerge in more definite form. Opponents fell into three main groups: (1) non-Bolshevik politicians, such as Kadets, Social Revolutionaries and Mensheviks; (2) former officers of the tsarist army; and (3) nationalists seeking independence for their particular minority.

Since the nationalists were interested only in their own lands, and the politicians disliked the conservative officers, the military commanders formed the core of the anti-Bolshevik opposition.

The Treaty of Brest-Litovsk came as a severe blow to Britain and France. Now Germany could transfer all her troops from the east to the western front and end the stalemate there with a decisive break-through. In the face of this dilemma, Britain and France decided to intervene in Russia. It has never been made clear what their precise intention was: perhaps it was not obvious to themselves at the time. It has been claimed that their intention was to continue to fight Germany from the east, but this does not bear up to any practical scrutiny. A more plausible explanation is that they intended to overthrow the Bolsheviks and restore the provisional government, which then would reopen the war against Germany. When the war came to an end, however, foreign intervention remained, but at this stage the Allies feared the Comintern with its international connections and potential for world revolution.

In March 1918 British forces landed at Murmansk in northern Russia, and British and French forces in the Black Sea area. In May 1918 a Czech legion (defectors from the Austrian army, on their way to Vladivostok to join other Czech units fighting in France) seized a large section of the Trans-Siberian Railway between the Volga and Irkutsk. The United States, previously unwilling to intervene, decided to go to the rescue of the Czechs; they also dropped their opposition to Japanese intervention and Japanese troops soon landed at Vladivostock (map, p.172).

In August 1918 the Bolsheviks issued a proclamation to the 'toiling masses' of Europe, America and Japan:

> Like a vicious dog loosed from its chain, the whole capitalist press of your

BOLSHEVIK RUSSIA

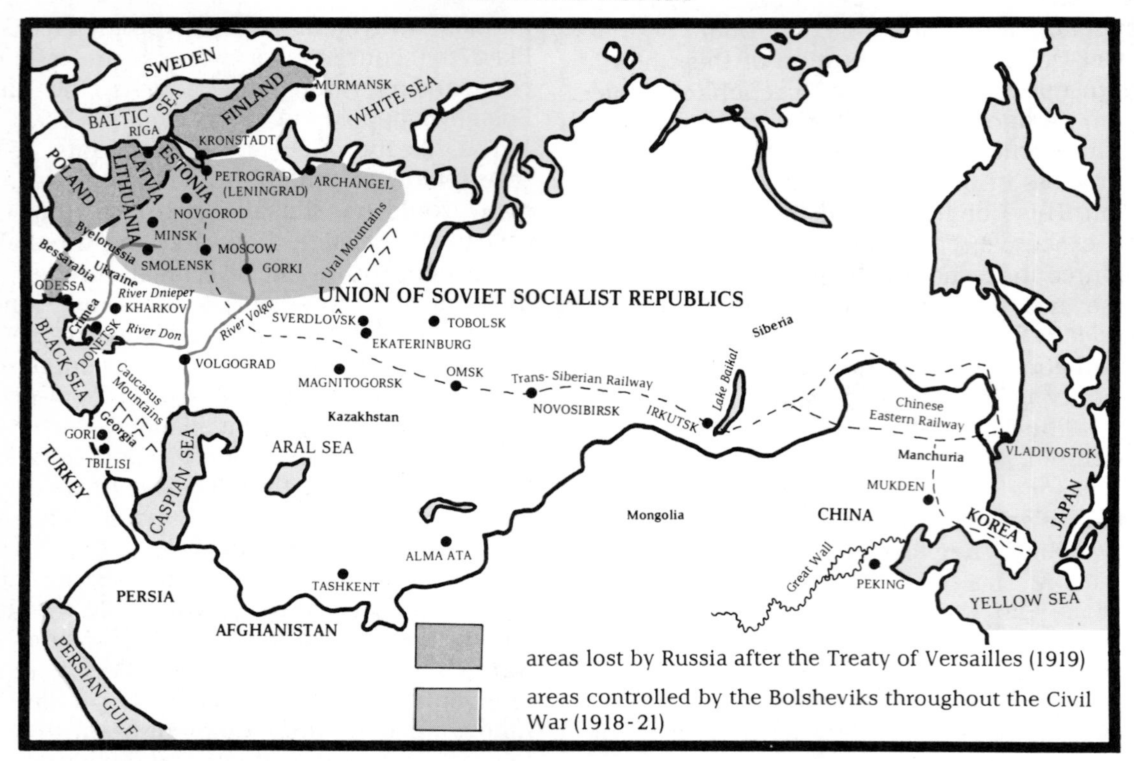

> countries howl for the 'intervention' of your governments in Russian affairs.... The Anglo-French bandits are already shooting Soviet workers on the Murmansk railway... Czechs in the Urals are cutting off the Russian people from bread in order to force workers and peasants to put their necks once more in the noose of the Paris and London stock-exchanges.

The Allied intervention gave the Whites opportunities that they failed to grasp because of their internal disunity and failure to co-ordinate with the Allies.

Yet after the Armistice in November 1918, Allied support dwindled away. In contrast, the Bolsheviks, posing as good patriots, were able to portray themselves as defenders of the homeland against the foreigners.

By the end of 1918 the Bolshevik government found itself close to extinction. It controlled a very small part of Russian territory between Petrograd and Moscow, but its opponents held nearly all the food-growing areas and all exit points from Russia:

1. The forces of General Denikin (who had succeeded Kornilov as head of the anti-Bolshevik forces in the south), together with the French, held the area around the Black Sea.
2. The Japanese were in control from Vladivostok to Lake Baikal.
3. The Americans held part of the Trans-Siberian and Chinese eastern railways.
4. Admiral Kolchak's forces (together with the Czechs) held most of Siberia; his headquarters were at Omsk. In November 1918 he proclaimed himself

'Supreme Ruler of the Russians' and his rule was recognised by the Allies as the legal government of Russia.

5. The head of the anti-Bolshevik forces in the Baltic states, General Yudenich, with British help, had formed an army in Estonia and was preparing to march on Petrograd.

6. A British expeditionary force held Murmansk and Arkhangelsk, where they had established a puppet government.

Opponents of Lenin's rule dreamed of a three-pronged attack that would meet in Moscow (in 1918 the Bolsheviks had moved their seat of government from Petrograd back to the ancient capital). It was hoped that the Whites and Allied forces would converge on the capital from (a) the north — Archangel and Murmansk, (b) the south — Denikin's forces and the French, and (c) the east, Kolchak's forces.

The Red Army

Already in May 1918, Lenin and Trotsky knew that their only hope was to build a dedicated communist army, and to organise food and supplies under an economic programme known as 'war communism' (p.175).

To Trotsky, who became commissar for war, fell the task of organising the new army. He expanded the Bolshevik Red Guards into a Red Army (later the Soviet Army). Trotsky was obliged to enlist many former tsarist officers whose experience he appreciated. However, since he was never fully convinced of their loyalty, he placed a political commissar from the Communist Party over each army commander. These vigilant commissars countersigned every order, maintained morale and indoctrinated the troops in communist ideology. Trotsky endeavoured to recruit as many factory workers as possible, knowing that their loyalty was assured. Through rigid discipline and general conscription, he built the Red Army into the largest and most effec-

Trotsky beside the train he used as his mobile headquarters during the Civil War.

tive fighting force in Russia. Trotsky himself used a train as his moving headquarters during the civil war. The train, which was so long that it took two engines to pull it, carried a printing press, an electric generator, and radio and telegraph equipment, and it enabled Trotsky to keep in touch with developments in the field.

Bolshevik Victory

By the end of 1918 the stage was set for the decisive battles of the civil war. Denikin and his forces struck north and won major victories as he advanced towards Moscow. Kolchak was just as successful, but he was not an able general; the Social Revolutionaries refused to obey him, and many of his officers were his rivals for command. Moreover, swift advance from Omsk was impossible over a vast area lacking in industry and communications. After some advances, in June 1919 Kolchak's forces were rolled back by the Red Army. In November he was again forced to retreat east of Irkutsk; there, after a quarrel, the Czechs handed him over to a revolutionary committee, who had him shot.

Denikin, whose advance on Moscow had been halted in October and who had retreated to the Crimea, became supreme ruler. Yudenich's attempt to take Petrograd was also thwarted and gradually the White dream faded. The three counter-revolutionary forces did not meet and the interventionist forces began to drift home. The last important battles were fought in 1920. The Whites had thought that the land joining the Crimea to the mainland was too strongly held for the Reds to break through, but a major night attack overcame them. Odessa, the last White stronghold, fell, and over 100,000 refugees escaped to eastern Europe. By 1920, all foreign forces had left the Soviet Union except the Japanese, and they eventually departed in October 1922.

Despite the Red Army's successes, 1920 saw another crisis for the Bolsheviks. A new Poland had been created by the Treaty of Versailles (p.187), but the Polish government under General Pilsudski was determined to expand its borders eastwards and re-create the large Poland of the eighteenth century. The Bolsheviks now were facing a traditional enemy of Russia and could again claim to be defending the homeland. Their nationalistic slogans were so effective that they could enlist such ex-tsarist generals as Brusilov to their cause. Despite this, the hard-pressed Red Army could not dislodge the Poles from parts of Byelorussia and the Ukraine, and in March 1921 were forced to sign the Treaty of Riga with Poland (p.187).

When the civil war came to an end, the Bolsheviks were masters of Russia, though many areas still remained outside of their control. The 'Red terror' waged by the *Cheka* and the Red Army had ensured that all bourgeois groups, and even the Social Revolutionaries and Mensheviks, ceased to exist. Communism had brought to Russia a new dictatorship that allowed no opposition. In theory it was the dictatorship of the proletariat; in fact it was the dictatorship of an elite who controlled the Communist Party.

Why had the Bolsheviks won? The first reason was the weakness of the allied intervention; especially when the war in Europe ended, the western governments were more concerned to demobilise their troops than to continue an unpopular war about faraway issues the average voter neither cared about nor really understood. Secondly, the Whites were divided. There could be no great unity of purpose among such disparate groups as monarchists, bourgeois liberals, Social Revolutionaries and Mensheviks. In contrast, the Bolsheviks were a single-minded, dedicated group with one clear purpose in mind — the establishment of a communist Russia.

Thirdly, the Whites were geographically separated by huge distances, which militated against fast and effective tactical coordination. The Bolsheviks controlled the central region, including Moscow and Petrograd, from where they could strike outwards in all directions against a divided enemy. Finally, although atrocities against the peasantry were committed by both sides, the Whites were, if anything, crueller than the Reds. Furthermore, while the peasants hated and resisted the Bolshevik policy of war communism, they also believed that a White victory would mean a return to landlordism and an end to their newly won land ownership. In general, therefore, the peasants sided with the Reds, and their vast numbers ensured a Bolshevik victory (map, p.172).

Execution of the Romanovs

When Nicholas II heard of the Bolshevik victory, he underestimated its significance and did not take alarm. He and his family were occupied in keeping warm — the temperature at Tabolsk (p.162) in December was 68 degrees below zero. Soviet rule did not appear to mean much more than increased restrictions: Nicholas was forbidden to wear his officer's epaulettes; and in March 1918 the family was put on soldiers' rations, which meant parting with ten servants and giving up butter and coffee. What kept them going was the hope that they might be rescued. Strong monarchist organisations had begun to plan to do this, but none succeeded. Nicholas refused to be separated from his family, there were too many groups working at cross purposes, and they eventually accepted Boris Soloviev (Rasputin's son-in-law) as their leader, who absconded with the huge sum of bribe money entrusted to him.

At the end of March 1918 Commissar Vasily Vasilievich Yakovlev arrived with 150 soldiers and took half the family from Tabolsk in peasant carts bound for the railway 200 miles away. They then travelled by train to Omsk, but sixty miles from the city the train was surrounded, and Yakovlev was forced to take his prisoners to Ekaterinburg and hand them over to the custody of the Ural Soviet, the most bitterly anti-monarchist area in Russia.

At Ekaterinburg, the reunited imperial family was incarcerated in 'The House of Special Purpose' where they were closely guarded day and night. On 4 July the guards of the local Soviet were replaced by ten members of the *Cheka*. The Bolshevik government in Moscow had begun to panic because its power was being challenged on all sides: the White armies, interventionist troops, and a Czech legion moving rapidly towards Ekaterinburg. It gave up its plan for a public trial of the tsar and authorised the Ural Soviet to take matters into its own hands.

At midnight on 16 July the imperial family was ordered to dress and assemble in the cellar. Nicholas, Alexandra, their son Alexis, their three daughters Olga, Tatiana and Maria, together with their physician, valet, cook, and maid, were shot by the *Cheka*. Their bodies were taken to a disused mine shaft fourteen miles away, were cut up and burned, and the ashes and residue thrown into the shaft. Eight days later, the Whites took Ekaterinburg.

WAR COMMUNISM

The firm measures the Bolshevik government had taken after seizing power had been intended to transform Russia almost overnight into an egalitarian society. The Supreme Council of National Economy had been set up to organise a state planned economy, where, in accordance with the communist philosophy, people would work for the good of the community rather than out of selfish self-interest. Lenin's vision can be seen in his address to the Congress of Soviets in January 1918:

> The victorious proletariat looks out on a land that has now become a public good, and it will be quite able to organise the new production and consumption on socialist lines. . . . From now on, all the marvels of science and the gains of culture belong to the nation as a whole, and never again will man's brain and human genius be used for oppression and exploitation.

But Lenin had reckoned without the ravages of civil war and the attitude of the peasantry. During the civil war the Whites had controlled most of the food-growing areas, and many workers in the communist-controlled areas were deserting their jobs and going into the countryside in search of food. The peasants, for their part, were not interested in Lenin's idealism. They wanted neither state planning nor any scheme that required them to produce more food, which would be given, without profit, to their 'brothers' in the towns.

To grapple with the deteriorating economic situation, in mid-1918 the government introduced an emergency economic policy known as war communism. Committees of poor peasants were organised all over Russia to requisition grain from the *kulaks* (peasants who owned their farms) to feed the towns and cities. The government believed that the poor peasants would have the required local knowledge and would have little compunction about informing on their wealthier neighbours. But this did not happen and the government was obliged to dispatch Red Guards and the *Cheka* into the villages to requisition grain. The kulaks retaliated by growing just sufficient grain for their own needs (subsistence farming) and no more. An army of officials went into the countryside, exhorting the producers to work harder for the common good and to inform on uncooperative peasants. But officials were met with sullen suspicion and their exhortations fell upon deaf ears. The Red Guards, frustrated in their search for the hidden grain, often committed atrocities, beating the peasants and burning the villages. Many peasant uprisings occurred; industrial output fell to fifteen per cent of its pre-war figure, foreign trade ceased altogether and transport came to a standstill.

By 1920 the Russian economy had suffered the ravages of war, revolution and the policy of war communism. In that year Russia was hit by a severe drought and famine swept the land. Bands of starving children roamed like animals through the countryside and an estimated five million people died of starvation, typhus and cholera. The Soviet government had no option but to appeal to the capitalist world for help. However, they spared themselves the humiliation by prompting the world-renowned Russian writer, Maxim Gorky, to make the appeal on cultural and humanitarian grounds:

> The corn-growing steppes are smitten by failure, caused by the drought. The calamity threatens starvation to millions of Russian people. Gloomy days have come for the country of Tolstoy, Dostoievsky, Pavlov, Glinka and other world prized men and I venture to trust that the cultured European and American people, understanding the tragedy of the Russian people, will . . . immediately succour with bread and medicines . . . Russia's misfortune offers humanitarians a splendid opportunity to demonstrate the vitality of humanitarianism. I think particularly warm sympathy in succouring the Russian people must be shown by those who, during the ignominious war, so passionately preached fratricidal hate, thereby withering the educational efficacy of ideas evolved by mankind in the most arduous labours and so lighty killed by stupidity and cupidity. People who understand the words of agonising pain will forgive the involuntary bitterness of my words. I ask all honest Europeans and American people for prompt aid to the Russian people. Give bread and medicine.

In these devastating conditions the government's popularity reached its lowest point. The peasants especially hated the economic policy of war communism and defied it in every possible way. Workers were going on strike; and even the government regulation of making food, clothing and lodging dependent upon the production of a workers' ration book, had little effect.

The climax of anti-government unrest came in March 1921 when the sailors at Kronstadt naval base mutinied in support of striking factory workers. It had been the revolt of these same sailors that had contributed so much to the revolutions of 1905 and 1917. Now they were rising again, but this time it was not against the tsarist autocracy; it was against the Bolshevik dictatorship. After much bloodshed, the mutiny was suppressed, but it left a deep impression on Lenin. The Bolsheviks had come to power with the support of the armed forces, and Kronstadt had been a valuable ally in 1917. Lenin, as ever the supreme realist, already had acknowledged that war communism was a disaster; now the Kronstadt mutiny gave him the opportunity to convince his more dogmatic colleagues that a change in direction was necessary if they were to remain in power.

THE NEW ECONOMIC POLICY (NEP)

At the Communist Party Congress in 1921 Lenin proposed a new economic policy. It entailed piecemeal relaxations of the government's economic policy, but not of its political policy. Lenin hoped that relaxation would allow time for the Russian masses to be educated in the meaning of communism so that they would come to understand and accept its economic and political philosophy. Meanwhile the NEP would allow the introduction of limited capitalism. The government would continue to control essential industries such as banking, power supplies, heavy industries, transport and foreign trade. All other economic activity, such as small factories and businesses, could operate under private ownership. This led to the emergence of a new bourgeois class called *nepmen*, or small capitalist business men, who were motivated by private profit. Initiative was rewarded, even in state-controlled industries. Piece-work rates, preferential rations and bonuses were instituted for workers.

The NEP also pleased the peasants. Grain requisitioning was abandoned and the peasant was now encouraged to grow a surplus and, after paying a tax on his produce to the government, he could sell the surplus food for personal profit. Gradually industrial and agricultural production increased and the Soviet Union was pulled back from the verge of chaos. Privately owned shops appeared in the cities and by 1924 four-fifths of Russia's smaller factories were privately run. Yet, despite this, the state controlled the essentials of the economy and some 80 per cent of the industrial workforce were employed in state industries.

Lenin's NEP saved the communist regime, but not without encountering fierce opposition from within the party, as many communists argued that the NEP was pushing Russia down the road to full capitalism. These communists were concerned with Marx's theory of communism and did not take into consideration the grim realities of life in Russia in the early 1920s. Lenin, too, was aware of the divergence from communist theory but, unlike his critics, his sense of realism and his overwhelming desire to save the revolution dictated his course of action. His argument was that it was better to risk the dangers inherent in the NEP — of promoting a new bourgeois class inimical to communism — than to face certain defeat under war communism. The Soviet Union, he contended, was not yet ready for communism; therefore the Bolsheviks must 'take one step back in order to take two steps forward at a later stage.' Lenin, therefore, was at one with his critics with regard to the ultimate goal of the revolution; the difference between them was essentially one of tactics. As soon as the economy had improved sufficiently, the temporary expedient of the NEP would be abandoned, to be replaced by Marxist economic principles.

THE DEATH OF LENIN

Lenin did not live to see the abandonment of the NEP. In 1921 and again in 1922 he had suffered strokes which forced him into semi-retirement. Because of his condition, he found it impossible to keep in touch with what was happening in government, and his colleagues began to intrigue for power. In January 1924 Lenin died and was universally mourned by the Russian people. The city of Petrograd, scene of three revolutions, was renamed Leningrad in his memory. His body was embalmed and placed in a wooden mausoleum in Moscow's Red Square. The structure was later replaced with a sombre mausoleum of dark-red granite edged with black, and his embalmed body was placed in a glass sarcophagus, where to this day millions annually file past in tribute to the man whose single-minded dedication, political genius and supreme realism masterminded the world's first successful proletarian revolution.

Study Assignments and Essays

1. *'The humiliation of "Brest-Litovsk" was a necessary prerequisite for Bolshevik success.' Discuss.*
2. *'Early communist reforms were more idealistic than practical.' Discuss the truth or otherwise of this assertion.*
3. *What were the reasons for introducing 'war communism' and why did it prove so disastrous?*
4. *Critically analyse the various forces (motives and tactics) ranged against the Bolsheviks during the Russian civil war.*
5. *Why did the Bolsheviks win the civil war?*
6. *Write an essay on two of the following: (i) The role of Leon Trotsky in the civil war; (ii) The Soviet constitution; (iii) The New Economic Policy; (iv) The role of the peasantry in the civil war; (v) The legacy of Lenin.*

The Peace Treaties

14

Yet when we achieved and the new world dawned, the old men came out again and took our victory to remake in the likeness of the former world they knew. . . .

T.E. Lawrence, 1888–1935

AFTER THE armistice had been signed on 11 November 1918, the Allied powers made arrangements to hold a peace conference, which opened in Paris on 18 January 1919. The conference represented thirty-two powers, but it was dominated by the 'Big Three', Woodrow Wilson, David Lloyd George and Georges Clemenceau. Although the delegates hoped to build a new world free from war, each also had the interests of his own nation to advance.

The French premier, Georges Clemenceau, presided. Known as 'The Tiger' and now seventy-seven years of age, he had lived through two German invasions (1870 and 1914) and was interested primarily in the security of France and the punishment of Germany. His was the voice that made itself heard over all the others and ensured that the 'stamp of France' was embedded on the settlement with Germany. 'Père la Victoire' represented the determination of Frenchmen 'never to let it happen again' — never again would Germans be in a position to invade the fair land of France. Britain was represented by her prime minister, David Lloyd George. A clever politician and skilful diplomat, he had just won an election in December on the slogans 'Hang the kaiser' and 'Make the Germans pay'. Committed to these, he was obliged to demand that Germany must pay for the cost of the war.

The United States was represented by President Woodrow Wilson. Stern and idealistic, Wilson was handicapped by his lack of understanding of European politics and geography, and his unwillingness to compromise his principles. Yet he, more than any of the others, symbolised the hopes of people everywhere that the conflict had been 'a war to end wars' and that a new era of co-operation was about to dawn.

'The Peace Conference', a painting by the Irish artist William Orpen. Shown seated here are Orlando (second left), Wilson (third left), Clemenceau (fourth left) and Lloyd George (fifth left).

Italy was represented by her prime minister, Vittorio Orlando. His chief concern was to receive from the ruins of the Hapsburg empire not only *Italia Irredenta*, but everything promised by the secret Treaty of London in 1915 in return for Italy's entry into the war (p.139). At first one of the 'Big Four', Orlando soon found himself at odds with Wilson, who regarded many of Orlando's territorial claims as a contravention of the principle of self-determination. Orlando soon found himself excluded from the inner cirlce of Wilson, Lloyd George and Clemenceau, and for a time he withdrew his delegation from the conference.

THE PRINCIPLES OF THE PEACE SETTLEMENT

Because the war had been so enormous in its destructiveness, the guiding principle of the settlement was the avoidance of future wars. It seemed logical therefore that the cause of

GERMANY AFTER THE TREATY OF VERSAILLES, 1919-33

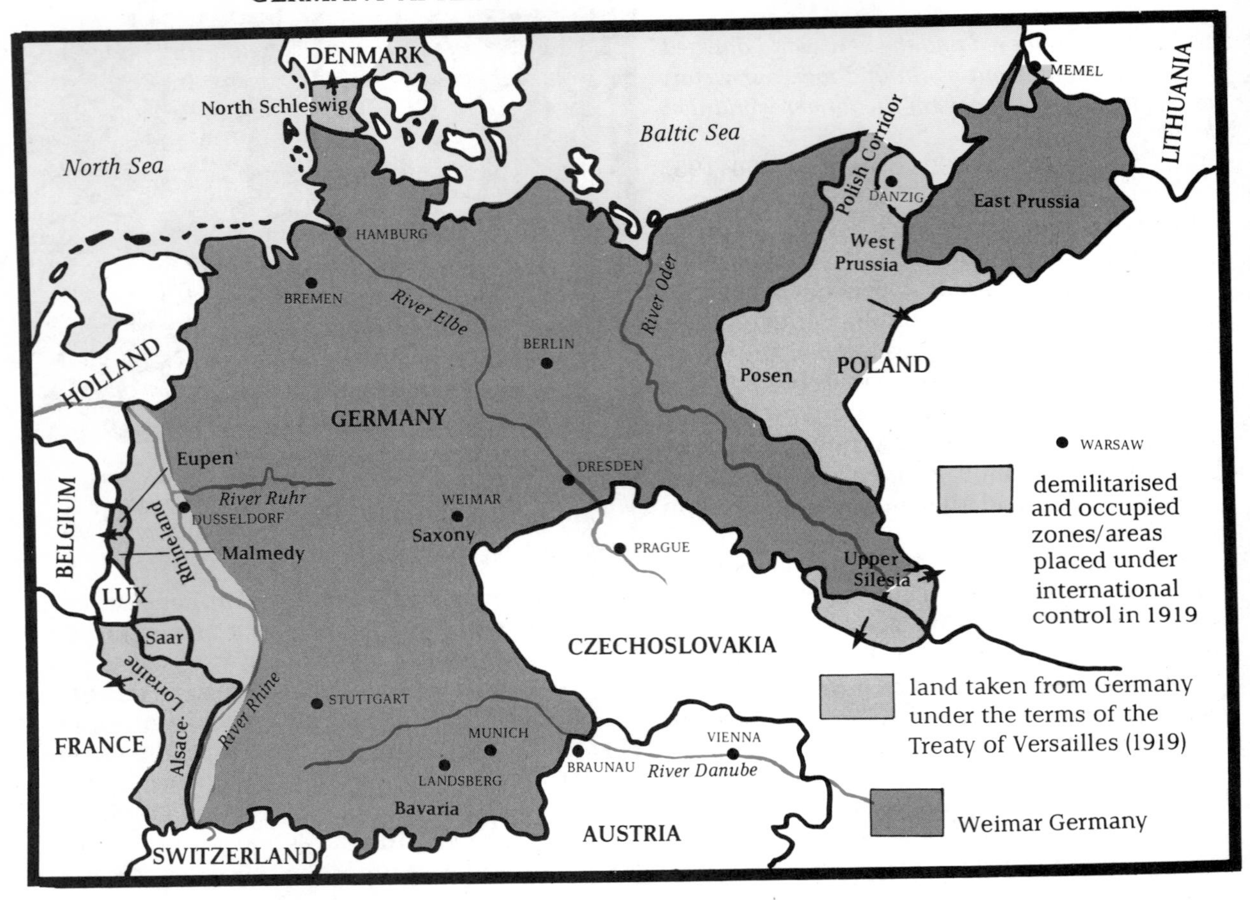

war must be eliminated and that international machinery should be set up to deal with future problems.

Clemenceau argued that since German militarism was the greatest danger to peace, she must be prevented from waging war in the future. There was also general agreement that the existence of empires in Europe, which frustrated national aspirations, had been at the root of the Great War. It was therefore agreed that the new map of Europe should be based on the principle of self-determination, or the nation state.

Wilson proposed setting up a great international body, the League of Nations, which would be a forum for the harmonious direction of world affairs in a new era of peace and co-operation. Since the League was a novel idea, there was some disagreement as to its precise function. One school of thought favoured a 'narrow' League, which would be concerned essentially with preventing future wars. Another favoured a 'broad' League, which would extend its function beyond peacemaking to the social and economic welfare of mankind.

In all, five separate treaties were signed, one with each of the defeated powers — Germany, Austria, Hungary, Bulgaria and Turkey. The major treaty was that signed with Germany — the Treaty of Versailles.

THE TREATY OF VERSAILLES 1919

Although Germany was not allowed to send representatives to the Peace Conference, after receipt of the draft treaty she was allowed to forward written submissions. The Treaty of Versailles, therefore, was not a negotiated treaty but one decided by the victors for the vanquished. In later years Hitler would claim with great effectiveness that since the treaty was a 'dictated' one, its provisions were not binding on Germany (p.283).

Territorial Settlement

By the Treaty of Versailles, Alsace-Lorraine, which had been seized from France in 1871, was returned. Two small areas around Eupen and Malmèdy were given to Belgium. Northern Schleswig, part of the area seized by Germany in the war against Denmark in 1864, went back to Denmark in 1920 after a plebiscite provided for in the treaty.

West Prussia, most of Posen and (after a plebiscite in 1921) a small but valuable part of Upper Silesia went to the newly constructed state of Poland. The loss of West Prussia divided East Prussia from the rest of Germany and was greatly resented by the Germans. The Poles, however, were particularly anxious to acquire this area, which became known as the 'Polish Corridor'; for, in addition to its large Polish population, it also provided an otherwise landlocked Poland with a vital outlet to the Baltic Sea through the port of Danzig. Danzig itself created a further complication as most of its inhabitants were German. A compromise solution was arrived at: Danzig became a free city under League of Nations control; the municipal government remained in German hands while foreign policy, commerce, and the port (customs) were controlled by Poland. The port of Memel in East Prussia was placed under international control in order to guarantee an outlet to the sea for the new state of Lithuania, which seized complete control of it in 1923.

The Saar, a German district with valuable coal deposits, was placed under international control for a period of fifteen years, after which time a plebiscite would determine its future. (In 1935 the people of the Saar region voted overwhelmingly for union with Germany.) Meanwhile the French were to control its mines in compensation for the destruction of her own coalfields by German troops.

The future position of the Rhineland created many problems. Clemenceau claimed that France would be secure only if the Rhineland was taken from Germany altogether. André Tardieu, later prime minister of France, who helped to draw up the treaty, said:

> France has a unique experience of Germany. No one has suffered as she has. . . . What happened in 1914 was possible only for one reason: Germany, because of her mastery over offensive preparations . . . on the left bank of the Rhine thought herself capable of crushing the democracies, France and Belgium, before the latter could receive the aid of the Overseas Democracies, Great Britain, the Dominions, and the United States. It is therefore this possibility which must be done away with, by depriving Germany of the means which permitted her to believe in the success of her plan.

Wilson and Lloyd George would not agree to the permanent detachment of the Rhineland. They argued that to do so would merely create an 'Alsace-Lorraine in reverse' and be a recipe for future Franco-German conflict. Finally a compromise solution was agreed upon: in return for a joint Anglo-American guarantee of military aid in the event of a German attack, France dropped her claim for the permanent detachment of the Rhineland. Instead it would remain part of Germany, but the right (eastern) bank of the Rhine was to be demilitarised for 58 km beyond the river. The Rhineland west of the river was to be occupied by Allied troops for fifteen years, during which period it would be gradually evacuted.

All German colonies were taken from her and were given to the victors as mandated territories, to be administered under the League of Nations (p.276). Her African colonies were divided between Britain, France, Belgium and South Africa, while her Far Eastern possessions were divided between Japan, Australia and New Zealand.

Disarmament

The peacemakers believed that the surest guarantee against war was to remove the means of waging it. For this reason, and in anticipation of general disarmament by all the powers, Germany was disarmed. She was forbidden to conscripit men for service and her army was limited to 100,000 men, who were to serve for a period of twelve years (this stipulation was to ensure that she could not circumvent the limitation of size by creating a high turnover of trained soldiers for a shorter period). Germany was allowed to build six warships, but could have no military aircraft, submarines, tanks or heavy artillery.

All fortresses on the Rhineland were to be demolished. Universities and sporting clubs were forbidden to 'occupy themselves with any military matters' and specifically forbidden to instruct or exercise their members 'in the profession or use of arms'.

Reparations

The Allies had two main reasons for imposing reparations on Germany: to punish her, and to compensate themselves for the cost of the war, which, they claimed, had been caused solely by German militarism. The French and Belgians, who had suffered most, were extremely anxious to impose heavy reparations on Germany. Britain, though not as adamant, was inclined to support the idea, especially since Lloyd George had won the recent general election on the slogan 'Make the Germans pay'. The position of the United States further complicated matters: because she had not suffered any damage at home from the war, she was not interested in making Germany pay but was very interested in getting repayments on the loans she had made to the Allies. In this way a vicious circle was set up; so long as the Allies were going to demand reparations from Germany, America was going to demand repayments of war loans from the Allies; while so long as the Allies had to repay the loans to the United States, they were going to demand reparations from Germany.

No final agreement was reached in the treaty on how much Germany was to pay. The matter was left to a Reparations Commission, which was to present its bill in 1921. Meanwhile Germany was to deliver up most of her merchant navy to the Allies and supply them with coal over a period of years.

War Guilt

The Allied justification for reparations was based on the claim that Germany was solely responsible for starting the war. This 'war guilt' clause, as Article 231 of the treaty came to be called, stated:

> The Allied and Associated Governments affirm and Germany accepts the responsibility of Germany and her allies for causing all the loss and damage to which the Allied and Associated Governments and their nationals have been subjected as a consequence of the war imposed upon them by the aggression of Germany and her allies.

Article 231 was bitterly resented by all Germans and came to be the subject of tremendous propaganda in subsequent German affairs. Moreover, since Germany had only accepted the treaty under compulsion, her people felt that they were morally justified in avoiding payment. The whole question of reparations was to exacerbate political and economic relations between all concerned until the reparations were finally cancelled at the height of the Great Depression, which they had helped to create.

Germany Signs the Treaty

On 28 June 1919, the fifth anniversary of the assassination at Sarajevo, two representatives of the new German republic signed the treaty drawn up by the victorious allies. It was signed at the Palace of Versailles in the same Hall of Mirrors that had witnessed the proclamation of the German empire in 1871 (p.20).

Harold Nicholson, a member of the British delegation, vividly catches the historic moment:

> Through the door at the end appear two ushers with silver chains. They march in single file. After them come four officers of France, Great Britain, America, and Italy. And then, isolated and pitiable, come the two German delegates, Dr Muller, Dr Bell. The silence is terrifying. Their feet upon a strip of parquet between the Savannerie carpets echo hollow and duplicate. They keep their eyes fixed away from those two thousand staring eyes, fixed upon the ceiling. They are deathly pale. They do not appear as representatives of a brutal militarism. The one is thin and pink-lidded: the second fiddle in a Brunswick orchestra. The other is moon-faced and suffering; a *privatdozent* [university lecturer]. It is all most painful. . . .!
>
> There is general tension. They sign. There is general relaxation. Conversation hums again in an undertone. The delegates stand up one by one and pass onwards to the queue which waits by the signature table. Meanwhile, people buzz around the main table getting autographs.
>
> Suddenly from outside comes the crash of guns thundering in salute. It announces to Paris that the second Treaty of Versailles has been signed by Dr Muller and Dr Bell. Through the few open windows comes the sound of distant crowds cheering hoarsely. . . .
>
> We kept our seats while the Germans were conducted like prisoners from the dock, their eyes still fixed upon some distant point on the horizon. . . .
>
> Celebrations in the hotel afterwards. We are given free champagne at the expense of the taxpayer. It is very bad champagne. Go out on to the boulevards afterwards.
>
> To bed sick of life.

The Treaty of Versailles: Some Comments

The Treaty of Versailles was not as punitive as Clemenceau had hoped; neither was it as moderate as Lloyd George had desired; and certainly not as idealistic as Wilson had envisaged. Certain articles deserve special mention because of their controversial nature.

Article 80 stated that Germany and Austria were forbidden to join together. This was a clear denial of the principle of self-determination on which the new Europe was being constructed. Arthur Balfour, the British foreign secretary, believed that they should be allowed to join if they so desired, since it would soften the blow of defeat.

Article 100 took away the German city of Danzig, depriving all its citizens of German nationality, and turned it into a 'free city' within the customs frontiers of the new Poland.

Article 118 obliged Germany to renounce all her 'rights, titles and privileges — whatever their origin' outside Europe. This meant that

The signing of the Peace Treaty in the Hall of Mirrors at the Palace of Versailles, 28 June 1919.

even purely commercial concessions won before 1914 were now lost.

Article 153 laid down that all property and possessions in Egypt of the German empire should pass to the Egyptian government without payment.

Article 156 transferred to Japan all German submarine cables in China 'with all rights, privileges, and properties attaching thereto.'

Article 231, known as the 'war guilt' clause, was the most controversial of all. The case for German reparations arose on 4 November 1918 when Clemenceau and Lloyd George drafted a note to Wilson on the need to extract payment from Germany for the damage caused by her 'invasion' of Allied territory. But later at the Versailles discussion it was found that the word 'invasion' covered only German damage in Belgium, Luxembourg and France — from the Channel to the Vosges Mountains. This would mean that no compensation could be claimed by the remaining allies — Britain, the Dominions and the United States. The final draft of the treaty therefore cut out 'the invasion by Germany of allied territory' and substituted 'the aggression of Germany' since this would cover everything.

But increase in reparations was not the only grievance the Germans had with Article 231.

The Germans never denied 'invasion', seeing its justification in self-defence. But 'aggression' could not be justified and clearly implied war guilt.

One article of the treaty with Germany was never put into effect. Article 227 provided for the trial of the former kaiser 'for a supreme offence against international morality and the sanctity of treaties.' It provided for his trial by five judges, one each from France, Britain, Italy, the United States and Japan. It would be their duty to 'fix the punishment which it considered should be imposed.' On his abdication before the war finally ended, the kaiser slipped across the border into neutral Holland. When the French began to demand his return to stand trial, the Dutch refused. Lloyd George, despite the fact that he had fought and won a general election on the slogan 'Hang the kaiser', was not in favour and refused to back the French demand. Kaiser William II remained safely in exile, cultivating his garden, until his death in 1941.

The last Hapsburg ruler and his wife are crowned in Budapest. Emperor Karl inherited the throne of Austria-Hungary on the death of Franz Joseph in 1916, but he abdicated on 12 November 1918 following the surrender of Germany.

THE TREATIES OF SAINT GERMAIN AND TRIANON

With the defeat of Austria-Hungary, the Dual Monarchy disintegrated as its subject peoples — the Poles, southern Slavs, Czechs and Slovaks — proclaimed their independence and sent representatives to Paris claiming official recognition on the principle of self-determination. This development suited the peacemakers since the principle of self-determination inevitably meant the dissolution of the Hapsburg empire. In this way much of its territory passed into neighbouring states or into new states now officially recognised. Austria and Hungary also split from each other, and so a separate treaty was signed with each of them: the Treaty of Saint Germain with the new Republic of Austria was signed in September 1919, but that with Hungary, the Treaty of Trianon, was not signed until the following June. This was due to the unsettled conditions occasioned by a communist rising in Budapest and the subsequent civil war. Neither Austria nor Hungary was allowed to plead its case. This decision had worse practical results than in the settlement with Germany, because the lands of the former Hapsburg empire, with its mixture of races and frontiers, were more complicated and less familiar to the Allies (map, p.186).

Czechoslovakia

The new state of Czechoslovakia was formed out of part of the territory of the former empire of Austria-Hungary. From the Austrian half came the two rich provinces of Bohemia and Moravia, which contained ten million

CENTRAL EUROPE AND THE EASTERN MEDITERRANEAN, 1919-35

people — two-thirds Czech, but the remaining one-third German-speaking Austrians inhabiting the area known as the Sudetenland. From the Hungarian half came the provinces of Slovakia and Ruthenia, which contained two million peasant Slovaks and one million Magyars, Ruthenians and Poles. This new state of Czechoslovakia was the only multi-racial state deliberately created by the peacemakers. This was because economic and geographic factors took precedence over self-determination.

Yugoslavia

A new state of southern Slavs was formed from the union of Serbia and Montenegro, together with Bosnia-Herzegovina, Slovenia and Dalmatia (from Austria), and Croatia (from Hungary). At first the state was named the 'Kingdom of the Serbs, Croats and Slovenes', but in 1929 it officially became known as Yugoslavia.

Poland

Poland became an independent country for the first time since the eighteenth century, when she had been partitioned between Russia, Prussia and Austria. Her re-creation therefore concerned (a) the Treaty of Versailles, which took from Germany all Polish territory, together with that taken from Russia at Brest-Litovsk, and (b) the Treaty of Saint Germain, which took from Austria the large province of Galicia. The western half of Galicia was inhabited by Poles, but the eastern part was inhabited by Ruthenian peasants who wished to be in the Ukraine, but were subject to Polish landlords. At first Poland's eastern frontier was fixed by the British foreign secretary, Lord Curzon. Known as the 'Curzon line', it excluded eastern Galicia, but the Poles coveted this area because it had formed part of the old Polish kingdom. In 1920 the Poles crossed the Curzon line and in August, with French assistance, defeated the Red Army, which had come to the aid of the Ruthenians, at the Battle of the Vistula. By the Treaty of Riga in 1921, Russia was forced to surrender all land coveted by the Poles (p.174).

Romania

From Austria, Romania received Bukovina, and from Hungary, the rich corn lands of Transylvania and the Banat of Temesvár (a fertile land promised to her when she had joined the Allies in 1915). Transylvania was mostly peopled with Romanian peasants, but the towns were mainly inhabited by Magyars. Romania also annexed Bessarabia from Russia. This was done in order to exclude the Soviet Union from the Balkans.

Italy

Italy received from Austria the Trentino and the South Tyrol as far as the Brenner Pass (which included some Germans in the northern part). She also received the Istrian Peninsula with Trieste and the Dalmatian Islands, to satisy her claims under the Treaty of London of 1915.

Austria

The Treaty of Saint Germain left Austria a small land-locked republic with a population of about six million people. One-third of her German-speaking population was now in other states where they formed disgruntled minorities.

Hungary

The Treaty of Trianon left Hungary small and weak, her population reduced from twenty-one million to seven-and-a-half million. Nearly three million Magyars now found themselves as minorities in surrounding foreign states.

SOVIET RUSSIA

At the time of the peace conferences, the Bolsheviks were consolidating their grip on the lands of the former tsarist empire. Bolshevism was a dreaded concept in the West and Soviet Russia was not invited to attend the Peace Conference. With the cancellation of German gains at Brest-Litovsk, Russia's western frontier had to be fixed. As well as upholding the principle of self-determination, the conference therefore aimed to create out of the western provinces of the former tsarist empire, a *cordon sanitaire* — a series of buffer states — as a protection against Soviet encroachment. Accordingly Finland (1919) and the Baltic provinces of Estonia (1920), Latvia and Lithuania (1921) were recognised as independent states. The only areas regained by Soviet Russia were the Ukraine and the Crimea, while Georgia was also recognised as independent (map, p.186).

THE TREATY OF NEUILLY

The Treaty of Neuilly with Bulgaria was concluded in November 1919. Bulgaria lost a small, but strategically important, area in northern Macedonia to Yugoslavia. In the east she lost western Thrace to Greece, thus cutting off her access to the Aegean Sea, which she had acquired in the Balkan wars. Bulgaria lost very little in territory or population but, like all the defeated powers, was obliged to reduce her armed forces and pay some reparations (map, p.186).

THE TREATY OF SÈVRES AND THE TREATY OF LAUSANNE

The Ottoman empire had already lost the bulk of her European possessions in the Balkan Wars, while Constantinople and most of her Asian territory was occupied by the Allies at the time of the Peace Conference. The Treaty of Sèvres was signed with Turkey in August 1920.

All Turkey's Arab possessions in the Middle East were taken from her and placed under the control of the Allies, who were to 'administer' them as mandated territories under the League of Nations. France received Syria and the Lebanon; Britain received Iraq, Palestine and Transjordan. The Dardanelles was demilitarised and placed under international control. The Sultan was allowed to occupy Constantinople, but only under international supervision. Turkey also had to cede Adrianople to Greece; but what she most fiercely resented was the Greek occupation of Smyrna and the surrounding hinterland, decided on the grounds that most of the population of Smyrna was Greek. The Greeks had secured Allied backing for this move after a wartime understanding (map, p.186).

The presence of Greek troops in Asia Minor aroused Turkish nationalism and, under their patriotic leader Mustafa Kemal, the Turks defied the Allies and the Treaty of Sèvres, which, they held, was punitive. Kemal (later Kemal Atatürk) set up a provisional government in Angora (now Ankara) and succeeded in expelling the Greeks from Asia Minor. This situation was eventually accepted by the powers in 1923 by the Treaty of Lausanne.

THE PEACE SETTLEMENT: AN APPRAISAL

It is easy to criticise the peace settlement; it subsequently became fashionable to say that the seeds of World War II were sown in Paris in 1919. The Germans naturally were its harshest critics. They claimed that their surrender was on the understanding that the peace settlement would correspond with the principles laid down in Wilson's fourteen points for peace, and the Treaty of Versailles clearly had not done so. But it is important to understand the factors limiting the peacemakers in a task of unprecedented proportions.

Before the conference began, certain diplomatic agreements had already been entered into: Constantinople had been promised to the Russians; the Treaty of London had promised Italy, not only *Italia Irredenta*, but part of the Dalmatian coast as well, while Greece and Romania were promised a settlement favourable to their national aspirations. The peacemakers were not always in control of events. The Hapsburg empire had already collapsed and many of its subject peoples (especially the Poles and the Czechs) had proclaimed their independence, in accordance with the principles of self-determination, before the Allies had even settled the armistice terms.

The intricate pattern of racial groupings, especially in the remoter parts of eastern Europe, were not fully known to the conference. Moreover, the war weariness of the Allied peoples and the general clamour for demobilisation left the Allies with reduced power to enforce any decision in the unsettled conditions prevailing in many parts of Europe.

While the peacemakers were deliberating in Paris, the Bolsheviks were consolidating their rule over what had previously been the tsarist empire. Communist risings had occurred in Munich and Budapest and seemed likely to break out in Vienna and Berlin. Social discontent and disillusionment were rife in Italy, while strikes in Britain and France seemed to threaten the social order. In this situation a quick settlement was more important than a good one.

Lastly, the time and place of the conference did not create an environment suitable for such a momentous occasion. The conference opened nine weeks after the armistice that ended the greatest war in history. There had been no time for passions, hatreds, jealousies and fears to cool, leaving the peacemakers open to the charge of vindictiveness. The choice of Paris as the seat of the conference ensured that French influence should bear strongly on the settlement.

Despite its imperfections, the post-war settlement was, in the main, in accordance with the principles of self-determination. For the first time in European history, ninety-seven per cent of Europeans were now living in nation states of their own choice. That three per cent of Europe's population found themselves living as minorities under alien rule was due to the intermingling of peoples and to the desire of the peacemakers to create states of economic and strategic viability. Thus Italy was given the German-speaking south Tyrol because she required a strategic frontier on the Alps. The German-speaking Sudetenland formed part of Czechoslovakia to give that state a mountain frontier with Germany, and also because the Sudetenland formed an integral part of the economic unity of Bohemia (map, p. 186).

The post-war settlement destroyed the old balance of power. Although Germany was reduced in population and size, she was left a potentially powerful state surrounded by small, weak states. While Woodrow Wilson realised this, he hoped that collective security through the League of Nations would replace the balance of power as a more enlightened means of preserving the peace. When the League failed, the peace settlement, with which it was so closely allied, was doomed.

But for the moment there was respite. Statesmen looked forward to the League and to the Disarmament Conference to end for ever the scourge of war. The final passage of Winston Churchill's war memoirs, *The World Crisis*, portrays the hopes and fears of statesmen and ordinary people alike:

> The curtain falls upon the long front in France and Flanders, the soothing hands of Time and Nature, the swift repair of peaceful industry have already almost effaced the crater fields and the battle

lines which in a broad belt from the Vosges to the sea lately blackened the smiling fields of France. The ruins are rebuilt . . . only the cemeteries . . . assail the traveller with the fact that . . . millions . . . shed their blood or perished. . . . Merciful oblivion draws its veils; the crippled limp away; the mourners fall back into the sad twilight of memory. New youth is here to claim its own, and the perennial stream flows on. . . .

Is this the end? Is it to be merely a chapter in a cruel and senseless story? Will a new generation in their turn be immolated to square the black accounts of Teuton and Gaul? Will our children bleed and gasp again in devastated lands? Or will there spring from the very fires of conflict that reconciliation of the three giant combatants, which would unite their genius and secure to each in safety and freedom a share in rebuilding the Glory of Europe?

Study Assignments and Essays

1. *What factors inhibited the peacemakers at Versailles?*
2. *'Germany had justifiable grievances with the Treaty of Versailles.' Discuss.*
3. *'The Treaty of Versailles was tailored to suit France.' Discuss.*
4. *What aspects of the peace treaties contravened the principle of 'self-determination' and why was this the case?*
5. *'The distribution of imperial possessions (Germany and Turkey) had more to do with power politics than with international morality.' Do you agree?*
6. *Write an essay on two of the following: (i) Italy and the peace treaties; (ii) The role of President Wilson at the Paris Peace Conference; (iii) The peace treaties as an antidote to war; (iv) The settlement in eastern Europe; (v) The new map of Europe — its potential for war.*

The end of World War I brought with it the collapse of the old empires. The subject nationalities were liberated and, for the most part, a new state system based on self-determination was established. Within these new nation states, as within older ones, democracy became almost universal, and individual liberties were guaranteed. In addition, a League of Nations was established in 1919 which, it was hoped, would prevent war and preserve peace and democracy in the new age that was about to dawn.

But the war had other consequences. Already in the old tsarist empire, democracy had failed to take root and a novel dictatorship had emerged. A Marxist or communist totalitarian state came into existence, which made a complete break with the past and offered a radically different philosophical, economic and social system from that prevailing in the rest of the world.

In opposition to capitalist democracy on one hand, and communist totalitarianism on the other, a fascist alternative also arose, first in Italy, later in Germany. Imitated in varying degrees in smaller European states and in Japan, fascism developed a totalitarianism as great as that of communism; but unlike its great rival, it was fiercely nationalistic. Moreover, it sought expansion, and believed in force as an instrument of policy.

By 1939, communism had established itself from Vladivostok on the Pacific to the Baltic, fascism held sway in much of eastern and central Europe, and democracy was in retreat. The hopes of the peacemakers of 1919, that a new dawn would emerge, were dead, and mankind was plunged into yet another world war.

Section Three

Democracy, Fascism and Communism 1919–39

The Weimar Republic 1919–33 15

The dignity of an historical epoch depends not upon what proceeds therefrom, but is contained in its very existence . . . each epoch has its own dignity in itself.

Leopold von Ranke, 1795–1886,
German historian

WITH THE abdication of Kaiser William II on 9 November 1918, Prince Maximilian of Baden, the last chancellor of the German empire, handed over the reins of government to Friedrich Ebert, the leader of the Social Democratic Party. That same evening crowds assembled outside the Reichstag in Berlin demanding every type of government, from a socialist dictatorship to a parliamentary democracy. Eventually one of the leaders of the Social Democrats, Philipp Scheidemann, came onto the Reichstag balcony and declared: 'The Hohenzollerns have abdicated. Long live the German Republic.'

The following day a provisional socialist republican government was formed until proper elections to a national assembly could be held. On 11 November this government had to sign the armistice, bringing the Great War to an end. Elections to a national assembly were held on 19 January 1919 and returned a clear majority (75%) of deputies and parties in favour of a republic.

This national assembly met on 9 February in the National Theatre at Weimar in south-east Germany. In choosing Weimar, the assembly was breaking completely with the past. The town, once the home of Goethe and Schiller, symbolised all that was best in German culture and enlightenment, while Berlin was too much associated with Prussian militarism and authoritarianism.

The assembly elected Ebert as the republic's first president and also drew up a constitution, which was ratified on 12 February.

THE WEIMAR CONSTITUTION

The head of state was to be a president, elected by universal suffrage for a seven-year term of office. He was to act on the advice of the government and one of his duties was to appoint the chancellor. Under article 48 he could also suspend the constitution and allow for rule by decree in times of national emergency. (This article was invoked in 1930 (p.204)). The chancellor and his ministers would form the cabinet, which was responsible to the Reichstag, and which therefore would need the support of the majority of its members. (This was in marked contrast with Bismarck's constitution (p.24), where the chancellor was responsible, not to the Reichstag, but to the kaiser alone.)

Parliament was to consist of the Reichstag and the Reichsrat (upper house). The Reichstag was to be elected for a period of four years by secret ballot of all persons over twenty-one years by a system of proportional representation. The Reichsrat was to represent the eighteen states of the republic on a proportional basis of population. For a bill to become law, it would have to pass through both houses and be signed by the president. In the event of a deadlock between the two houses, the Reichstag could override the Reichsrat by a two-thirds majority vote. The constitution also guaranteed the fundamental rights and freedoms associated with other western democracies: freedom of speech, religion, association and the press. There was also provision for referring certain important issues to the people by way of referendum. Powers were enshrined for the nationalisation of industries, although the constitution also recognised the rights of private property.

The success of the new German republic would ultimately rest upon two factors. First,

A Spartacist arrested by the Freikorps.

the ability and willingness of the German people to transfer their allegiance from the authoritarianism and class distinction of Imperial Germany to the liberalism and democracy of the Weimar Republic; and, second, the chancellor's ability to command a clear majority in the Reichstag and so avoid weak and unstable coalitions. From the beginning it was evident that these two conditions would not be met in a sufficient degree to allow republicanism and democracy to take root; but when compounded by other factors, such as reparations payments, the world depression, and the advent of Hitler, the Weimar Republic was doomed.

THE SPARTACIST UPRISING

On the night the republic was proclaimed, Ebert was contacted by Ludendorff's successor as supreme commander of the German army, General Grocner. He offered to place the army at the disposal of the new government in upholding law and order, and especially in putting down communist agitation. In return, Grocner, who already feared what the peace treaty would do to the army, wanted Ebert to guarantee the class structure of the army so that the existing officers' authority could be preserved. Ebert accepted the deal but, nevertheless, the government did vote to dismiss Hindenburg. Furthermore, Ebert authorised his new minister for defence, Gustav Noske, to recruit volunteer forces to keep order. General von Lüttwitz was given command of these irregular forces, which became known as *Freikorps* (Free Corps). In practice, von Lüttwitz encouraged conservative ex-officers of the German army to enrol volunteer recruits of their own. These *Freikorps* were supplied with arms from the regular army depots and constituted a formidable force.

In 1915 the extreme wing of the Social Democratic Party had broken away and formed the Spartacus League. The Spartacists took their name from Spartacus, the man who led the revolt of the slaves in ancient Rome. They, like the Bolsheviks in Russia (p.62), believed that socialists should not partake in the war; rather, they should use the opportunity it presented to instigate a socialist revolution. The Spartacus League was led by Rosa Luxemburg, a Polish Jew with German citizenship, and Karl Liebknecht.

In December 1918 members of the Spartacists formed themselves into the German Communist Party (KPD). During the first week of January 1919, Rosa Luxemburg, believing that the time was ripe for revolution, organised a series of strikes in Berlin. The Spartacists occupied a number of public buildings and hoped that the disturbances would lead to the overthrow of the new government.

But Ebert, helped by the *Freikorps*, acted quickly. On 11 January they moved against the Spartacists and soon brought the city under control. The Spartacists were poorly armed and were unable to offer any worthwhile resistance. When the disturbance came to an end, over one hundred Spartacists and thirteen members of the *Freikorps* had been killed. Rosa Luxemburg and Karl Liebknecht were captured and murdered by the *Freikorps*. Liebknecht's body was delivered to a mortuary, but Luxemburg's body was thrown in a canal and was not found until four months later. Other risings occurred in Bavaria, Bremen, and Düsseldorf, but these too were brutally put down by the *Freikorps*. The Weimar democracy had survived the attack from the undemocratic left, but only with the aid of the undemocratic right (map, p.180).

THE KAPP PUTSCH

When Ebert's government signed the Treaty of Versailles in June 1919, it accepted that the German army would be reduced to 100,000 men (p.182). But the peacemakers also insisted that the bands of irregular troops, such as the *Freikorps*, would have to be brought under control.

When the terms of the treaty became known in Germany, the nationalist right were shocked. They were particularly disillusioned with the Weimar democracy for accepting such humiliating terms. Soon the legend became accepted that the German army had not been defeated but had been stabbed in the back by the 'November Criminals' who had signed the armistice on the basis of the Fourteen Points, which then had been ignored in the treaty. This belief greatly undermined the government's popularity.

In March 1920 one *Freikorps* group attempted a sudden and violent *putsch* in Berlin in the hope of overthrowing the Weimar democracy. It was led by Dr Wolfgang Kapp, a right-wing journalist, and had the support of Lüttwitz and Ludendorff. The government (which had returned from Weimar to Berlin) fled to Dresden and thence to Stuttgart. The minister for defence, Gustav Noske, ordered the army to put down the insurrection, but found to his alarm that the army chiefs were not prepared to move against the *Freikorps*, many of whom had been their comrades in the war. The situation worsened further when Kapp set up a rival government in Berlin, but Ebert and Noske called on the working class to defend the republic against a right-wing coup. Immediately a general strike was called and all public services and commercial life were brought to a halt. With Berlin paralysed, Kapp and his followers found themselves isolated, and within a week, the *putsch* had petered out, a miserable failure. Even the army and police now came to support Ebert because they feared civil war. Kapp fled to Sweden and escaped punishment. Thus the republic was saved, but only through the power of the working class.

In the aftermath of the Kapp *putsch*, the government remained unsteady and adopted a lenient attitude to all those who had been involved. Of the 775 army officers who were implicated, only 48 were dismissed from their positions. It was now obvious that the government was weak and in no position to stand up to the army; but, more important, it was clear that the government could rely on the army to control the left but not to control the right.

THE INVASION OF THE RUHR

By the terms of the Treaty of Versailles, Germany was obliged to pay reparations to the victorious powers for having caused the war (p.182); but the treaty's terms had also reduced Germany's capacity to pay reparations. Territories lost to other countries included over 10 per cent of her arable land, 75 per cent of her iron ore, 68 per cent of her zinc ore and 26 per cent of her coal deposits. Thus when the inter-allied Reparations Commission presented its bill of £6,600 million (plus interest) in April 1921, the Weimar Republic was, in essence, given its death warrant. To make matters worse, Germany was already in debt from her own financing of the war, and this extra astronomical burden made the situation hopeless. If the problem had been solely an economic one, perhaps some compromise solution might have emerged, but the issue had a political dimension as well. France, in particular, saw the reparation payments as not merely an economic compensation for loss, but a device to keep Germany in debt, so that she would remain incapable of ever starting another war against France. The United States too was determined to collect all her debts from Britain and France. Thus American pressure on Britain and France ensured that they would redouble their demands on Germany.

In August 1921 the Weimar government made its first cash payment (of £50 million), but by the end of the year it found that it could not pay any further instalments, because of rapid inflation, and it asked for a moratorium. Lloyd George called for a world economic conference to be held in Genoa in April 1922.

During the conference the Germans and the Soviets met at Rapallo (thirty kilometres away) and on 16 April signed the Treaty of Rapallo (p.240). By this treaty of friendship, the two outcasts of Europe (and non-members of the League of Nations) re-established diplomatic relations. They renounced all financial claims on each other and pledged co-operation. Commercial agreements were also signed, and under the guise of these, Germany was able to circumvent the Versailles clauses on re-armament by producing war materials in the Soviet Union.

When the news of Rapallo reached the British and French at Genoa, they accused the Germans of making political capital out of what was designed to be an economic conference. Consequently, their attitude towards Germany stiffened and France especially became more determined than ever to make Germany pay. Since nothing significant came from the Genoa conference, the German economic situation continued to deteriorate: by July the German mark was worth less than one per cent of its value in 1914. The government succumbed to the temptation of printing more paper money, but this served only to

French troops take over a factory at Essen in the Ruhr, January 1923.

fuel the fires of inflation even further because people lost faith in the currency and panicked. The French had no sympathy for Germany's economic difficulties; in fact, Raymond Poincaré, the French president, accused the German government of deliberately allowing its finances to get out of control in order to avoid payment.

On 9 January 1923, when the Germans had failed to meet their reparations instalment, Poincaré ordered that French troops, in co-operation with the Belgians, should occupy the Ruhr. The ostensible reason was to extract payment by commandeering the industrial produce of the area; but it was also motivated by a desire to weaken further the German economy and if possible to detach the Rhineland from Germany by supporting a separatist movement there. The invasion infuriated German nationalists and embarrassed the government. Chancellor Wilhelm Cuno advised the Ruhr workers to offer passive resistance and to boycott the invaders by refusing to work. The French, unable to operate German machines, responded by ordering mass arrests. They also imposed an economic blockade on the Ruhr and much of the Rhineland. Inevitably, clashes between French soldiers and German civilians occurred, and 132 people were killed (map, p.180).

Berliners buying coins, as paper money is considered worthless.

The Ruhr occupation and its attendant chaos paralysed the German economy and caused runaway inflation. In an attempt to balance its budget, the government printed vast quantities of notes and allowed easy credit. By July one dollar was equal to 160,000 marks; by November it was equal to 4,000 million marks. Printing presses could not keep pace with the outrageous figures. Savings were wiped out and workers demanded to be paid on a daily basis so that they could immediately convert their paper money into goods. As paper money became valueless, a barter economy developed and the whole fabric of life in Germany began to crumble.

The communists staged a rising in Hamburg, but it was suppressed by the police. In August Chancellor Cuno's administration resigned and was replaced by a broad coalition government under Gustav Stresemann. Although he served as chancellor for only a few months, his work as foreign minister made him the dominant politician of the Weimar Republic until his death in 1929.

On assuming the chancellorship, Stresemann immediately ordered an end to passive resistance in the Ruhr and set up a new bank for the issue of controlled amounts of a new currency, the *rentenmark*, which restored a certain amount of confidence. Despite this, discontent continued. A communist revolt occurred in Saxony but petered out. Of far greater importance for the subsequent history of Germany, however, was Adolf Hitler's attempted *putsch* in Bavaria on 14 November (p.201), but this too was put down.

Having asserted the authority of the republic, Stresemann set about putting his policies into practice: settlement of the vexed question of reparations, and the rehabilitation of Germany into the family of nations.

REPARATIONS: THE DAWES PLAN

In January 1924 a committee under the American banker Charles J. Dawes was set up to investigate the problem of reparations payments. In April the Dawes Plan was published; in August Stresemann declared his acceptance of it, and it came into force on 1 September. The plan stated that the invading forces should be withdrawn and the Ruhr returned to Germany. The United States was to give Germany a loan of $800 million to help her economic recovery. The country was to have a two-year moratorium after which reparations at a more modest level would commence. Germany's new currency, the *reichsmark* (issued in August) was to be fixed at twenty to the pound and the bank of issue to be free of government interference.

The influx of foreign capital enabled local authorities to build new schools and hospitals. Gas and electricity were nationalised, but beyond this, Germany chose not to go down the road to socialism. The Weimar Republic was also aided by the brilliant financier Hjalmar Schacht. He was able to borrow more money abroad than was needed for reparations and, by expert juggling, gave the republic an air of financial prosperity. For the next five years Germany enjoyed a superficial prosperity (based on short-term foreign loans) that did much to create an air of tranquillity in domestic affairs.

Yet all was not well beneath the surface of German society. The inflationary crisis had been advantageous to the landed classes and the industrialists since their wealth consisted of land and plant. Yet the middle and working classes had suffered greatly. The savings of the middle classes were wiped out and they were reduced to a near proletarian condition, while the working classes saw the spending power of their wages drastically reduced. In effect inflation had penalised the thrifty saver and had concentrated economic power in the hands of big industrialists. This concentration of economic power continued in the years after the Dawes Plan and there was a trend towards mergers. In 1925 the giant chemical combine, I.G. Farben, came into existence. In 1926 the steel combine of Vereinigte Stahlwerke concentrated many steel firms into one large unit.

The extent of German economic recovery, therefore, was more apparent than real. Even in the peak year of 1928 unemployment was over one-and-a-half million. Germany was living dangerously on foreign loans without much thought of the long-term consequences or of what might happen if those loans stopped. Stresemann warned that Germany was 'dancing on a volcano', but his admonition was ignored.

FOREIGN RELATIONS

The years between 1923 and 1929 are aptly called 'the Stresemann Years', for during that time, first as chancellor and then as foreign minister, Stresemann formulated and put into practice a foreign policy that brought Germany back into the family of nations.

Stresemann was at heart an ardent German nationalist who wished to revise the hated Treaty of Versailles that had crippled and humiliated his country. Yet he was too much of a realist to ignore the fact that Germany could not achieve this on her own; his policy therefore was to have the treaty revised in co-operation with Britain and France. To

Gustav Stresemann, whose political skills, first as German chancellor and then as foreign minister, ensured domestic tranquillity until his death in 1929.

secure their co-operation, he first would have to convince Britain and especially France that a resurgent Germany would not be a threat to France's security or to the peace of Europe. Stresemann's policy was long-term, liable to be misunderstood for cowardice by many Germans, and depended on continued economic and political stability at home and abroad.

The Locarno Pact

One of the great post-war achievements in the field of international affairs was the signing of the Locarno Pact in 1925. It was a victory for confidence in the future over the suspicions of the past, and stood as a monument to its five signatory states: Germany, France, Britain, Italy and Belgium. But especially it was a monument to the greatness of Stresemann and his French counterpart, Aristide Briand, since the Locarno Pact brought the two likely parties to any future European conflict (Germany and France) together in a mutual agreement.

1. The western frontier between Germany and her neighbours, France and Belgium, as set up at Versailles, was accepted by all as final, while the Rhineland should remain demilitarised.

2. Allied troops in the Rhineland would be gradually withdrawn.
3. Germany and France, and Germany and Belgium, agreed to submit any future dispute to arbitration.
4. Germany agreed not to alter her eastern frontiers by force.
5. Germany had the right to alter her eastern frontiers by peaceful negotiation with Czechoslovakia and Poland.

The Locarno Pact renounced war as an instrument of policy and led to the stabilisation of Europe. Stresemann and Briand, in recognition of their courage and efforts, were awarded the Nobel Prize for Peace.

The League of Nations

Following Locarno, there was a general relaxation in international affairs. Germany was fulfilling her treaty obligations by paying reparations; she had accepted the western frontiers, and was prepared to work for change by peaceful means and mutual agreement. As a result of this new climate, Germany was invited to become a member of the League of Nations in 1926, and subsequently was given a permanent seat on the security council. Thus within a few short years after the most horrendous war in history, the victors and the vanquished were acting in concert for the betterment of mankind within a League of Nations.

With Stresemann as foreign minister, Germany pursued a policy known as 'fulfilment'; Germany was prepared to fulfil all her obligations as a full member of the family of nations. Stresemann succeeded in negotiating for the complete evacuation of allied troops from the Rhineland by September 1930. However, the great irritant was the question of reparations.

In October 1928, in exasperation, Stresemann demanded a 'new and final settlement of the reparations question'. A committee, headed by Owen Young, an American businessman, announced such a plan in June 1929. The Young Plan recommended that the total amount of reparations be reduced to £2,000 million and the period of repayment be extended to fifty-nine years. Stresemann accepted the plan, although he was obliged to put it to a referendum. But on 3 October he died suddenly from a heart attack brought on by years of overwork. Three weeks later on 29 October came the Wall Street Crash (p.203). These two events had tragic consequences for Germany. Stresemann's death left a vacuum in German politics just at the time when a strong hand was needed to steer Germany through the depression years sparked off by the Wall Street Crash.

Yet it is doubtful if even Stresemann could have held in check the forces that were about to destroy the Weimar Republic and create in its stead a totalitarian Nazi state. Stresemann's policy was little understood in Gemany during the period of tranquillity (1924–29); it could scarcely be expected to survive during the period of crisis (1929–33). His policy was based on the long-term strategy of a gradual acceptance of German demands. But few Germans were capable of a long-term view during the Stresemann years, and almost none during the crisis years that were about to hit the world in general and Germany in particular.

THE RISE OF HITLER AND THE NAZIS

Adolf Hitler was born on 20 April 1889 at Braunau (near Linz) on the Austro-Bavarian frontier, the son of a customs official in the Austrian government. Born into the lower middle class and bred in ideas of extreme nationalism, he learned to distrust the capitalists and the working class alike.

At the age of nineteen, both parents having died, Hitler moved to Vienna and for the following three years eked out a miserable existence doing odd jobs and living in doss-houses. His only solace appears to have been his devotion to Wagner's operas and Nietzsche's philosophy of the superman. In Vienna Hitler learned to hate internationalism as it was represented by the polyglot of races in the Hapsburg empire (p.78) and to despise the Hapsburgs, socialists, liberals and pacifists. Above all, he learned to hate the Jews with a deep loathing, calling them the 'eternal fissure-fungus of humanity'. He became an ardent German nationalist, adoring Aryan Germans, whom he regarded as the *Herrenvolk* or Master Race.

When the war broke out in 1914, Hitler, although an Austrian citizen, joined a Bavarian regiment and was made a lance-corporal. He served four years on the western front and was wounded and temporarily blinded after a gas attack. He was known to be a brave soldier, especially in his role as dispatch rider, and was decorated on three occasions — once with the Iron Cross for bravery.

When the war ended in 1918, Hitler remained in the army and was stationed in Munich. He was given the task of reporting on fringe political groups springing up at that time. One such group was the German Workers' Party, founded by Anton Drexler in Janury 1919. In September Hitler attended a meeting of the party and was so impressed by what he heard that he decided to join. The ideas enunciated were a strange mixture of German nationalism and a desire to protect the underprivileged from exploitation. Like many Germans, its members believed that their country had not been defeated in the war but had been stabbed in the back by the 'November Criminals', who had betrayed her into surrender. Hitler was asked to speak at one meeting and was so convincing that he was invited to join the organising committee. He resigned from the army and took on the job of publicity and propaganda officer for the party. Soon Hitler made himself the party's indispensable spokesman. His hypnotic power of mass oratory could hold audiences spellbound. More and more people came to listen and many offered financial assistance. In 1920 the party changed its name to the National Socialist German Workers' (Nazi) Party and in 1921 Hitler was elected its leader.

The Nazi Programme

The Nazi programme was a curious mixture of extreme nationalism and vague socialism. It denounced the Versailles Treaty as the source of all German ills; it demanded the union of all German-speaking peoples (including Austrians and all those living in the new states of Czechoslovakia and Poland) into a Greater Germany or *Grossdeutschland*, and the return of her lost colonies. It proposed economic reforms designed to appeal to the lower middle classes and the workers: the abolition of unearned income and an end to land speculation.

The Nazi Party was violently anti-semitic, assailing the Jews as exploiters and traitors; above all, as aliens who should be denied German citizenship. It was anti-communist, declaring that communism was inspired by Jews and diverted the workers from their allegiance to the nation. It condemned the liberalism and democracy of the Weimar republic since these served only to give too much freedom to internal enemies — Jews and communists — to weaken and divide the state.

The Munich Putsch

On 8 November 1923, at the height of the Weimar republic's economic and political crisis, with runaway inflation and occupying forces in the Ruhr (p.197), Hitler and his followers tried to stage a *putsch* in Munich. They took over a beerhall and declared that they were about to set up a new government in Bavaria, from where the revolution would spread to the rest of Germany. Hitler had the backing of General Ludendorff (p.194) and other Bavarian nationalists hostile to the Weimar Republic. However, during the night,

An artist's impression of Hitler addressing a meeting of the National Socialist German Workers (Nazi) Party in 1923.

most of the Bavarian leaders withdrew their support. The next morning Hitler, Ludendorff and about 2,000 supporters set out from the beerhall for the public offices in the centre of Munich. They were confronted by a large force of armed police, who opened fire. The Nazi supporters fled in disorder. Hitler suffered a dislocated shoulder, was arrested, and was brought to trial. The courtroom scene was turned into a personal triumph for Hitler since it gave him an opportunity to make political speeches and articulate what many believed but were too prudent to state openly. The judges gave him the minimum sentence of five years, and recommended an early parole.

Hitler was sent to prison in the Landsberg Fortress and was released after eight months. While in prison he began writing his famous book *Mein Kampf* (My Struggle), which became the political bible of the Nazi Party. In it Hitler looked forward to the creation of a Third Reich in succession to Charlemagne's Holy Roman Empire and Bismarck's Second Empire. It argued that Germany had been betrayed into surrender, forced into paying reparations to Jewish financiers, and was surrounded by enemies. It declared that the Germans were the *Herrenvolk* or master race, superior to all other races and should have *Lebensraum*, or living space, in the east where they could expand and prosper.

The S.A. and the S.S.

When Hitler was released from prison in 1924 he was unable to take an active part in the political life of Germany because the government had banned the Nazi Party (the ban was lifted in 1927). His immediate concern, therefore, was to build up the party and give it an organisational structure. He also concentrated on imposing his philosophy on the party so that it would clearly reflect the ideas enunciated in *Mein Kampf*.

Under Captain Ernst Röhm, a soldier of fortune, a semi-military organisation called *Sturmabteilung* (storm troopers) or S.A., rapidly developed. In 1923 they had acquired a consignment of surplus army dark-brown khaki shirts that had been intended for use in East Africa during the war. These uniforms now turned the S.A. into a distinct organisation, which was also known as 'Brownshirts'. They adopted the emblem of a black swastika (hooked cross) on a white disc, which was worn on a red armband, and they resembled Mussolini's 'Blackshirts' in organisation and methods (p.209).

More frightening than the S.A. were the *Schutzstaffel* or S.S., originally created as a paramilitary bodyguard bound by an oath of loyalty to Hitler. They wore a black-shirted uniform with the emblem of a skull for their badge. This force was eventually placed under Heinrich Himmler, chief of the German Nazi Police (p.222) and became an efficient but ruthless elite, having as its special task the elimination of all opposition to the Nazis.

Externally, however, the years between Hitler's release from prison in 1924 until the summer of 1929 were lean years for him and the Nazis. Since this period coincided with the Stresemann era, the radicalism of the Nazis' programme had little general appeal. In 1924 Nazi membership was a mere 178,000 and even by 1928 they were still relatively insignificant. In the elections of that year, they won only 12 seats, representing as little as 2.5 per cent of the total vote; in contrast, the communists won 54 seats. Thus the Nazis were regarded as no more than a fringe element in German politics and in fact were considered far less dangerous to German democracy than their communist rivals.

Müller's Government and the Depression

The first breakthrough for Hitler came with the referendum on the Young Plan (p.200). This gave him a public platform from which he could denounce the Versailles Treaty and the 'November Criminals' who had 'betrayed' Germany and sacrificed her to the interests of foreign capitalists — mainly Jews — who sought to place the German people under 'permanent interest slavery' in the form of reparations. The tremendous press coverage given to Hitler and the Nazis converted the Nazi Party from a small fringe group into a nationwide organisation of considerable influence. From that moment the great coal and iron magnates of heavy industry began to back Hitler financially, because they realised that, while the party's socialism was not to be taken seriously, its nationalism was impeccable. In fact they began to see the party as a bulwark against the threat of communism.

Following the Wall Street Crash in October 1929, a worldwide depression crippled international trade and commerce and threw millions out of work in every industrial country. In Germany the depression struck with devastating force. Foreign loans and investments immediately dried up and many American short-term loans began to be called in. But many of these loans had been used recklessly for long-term purposes, and American demands now produced a grave crisis that threatened Germany's entire economic system with breakdown. Confidence in the banks began to crack and unemployment increased at an alarming rate.

Unemployment insurance was totally inadequate to cope with the problem. The fund was designed to cater for less than one million people for a three-month period, but in the winter of 1929–30 three million Germans were umemployed. Chancellor Herman Müller headed a coalition government composed mainly of Social Democrats and the German People's Party. At its best it was an uneasy coalition, but in the face of mounting unemployment, it split in March 1930. The Social Democrats wished to increase unemployment insurance but the conservative People's Party objected.

The fall of Müller's government was a turning point in the history of the Weimar Republic: thereafter, no party combination came into existence that could control a majority in the Reichstag. The way was open for the president to exercise his powers under article 48 of the constitution to allow for rule by decree in an emergency. The president of the republic was Paul von Hindenburg, who had been elected to the office on the death of Ebert in 1925. Hindenburg was now eighty-two years old and had fought in the wars of 1866, 1870 and 1914–18. At heart he was a monarchist, who had little regard for democracy and republicanism, and he therefore relied for advice on his military and conservative friends, a policy that was to prove disastrous for the Weimar Republic.

Brüning's Government

With the fall of Müller's government in March 1930, Hindenburg appointed the leader of the Centre Party, Heinrich Brüning, as chancellor, primarily because he had a good war record. Brüning formed a coalition government, made up of members of the centre and conservative parties, which held office until the election in September. This election enabled Brüning to form another coalition government, but his position was greatly weakened by the rise of the extremist parties. The communists increased their seats from 54 to 73, but the most significant result was the rise of the Nazis. From a mere 12 seats, they polled over six million votes and won 107 seats, making them the largest party after the Social Democrats. The undemocratic left and right had won huge support at the expense of the democratic parties. At this juncture Hitler made his demand for a place in the cabinet, but Hindenburg refused, declaring that the best he could offer Hitler was the position of postmaster general so that he could lick stamps!

Brüning's position as chancellor became extremely precarious as the economic situation worsened. He tried to persuade the powers to cancel reparations, but his appeals fell on deaf ears. Eventually in June 1931 the American president, Herbert Hoover, declared a year's moratorium on all international debts. Brüning continued to negotiate for a complete end to reparations, but by the time this was eventually ratified at the Lausanne Conference in July 1932, his government had fallen.

At home Brüning pursued a policy of deflation, which involved a reduction of social services at a time when these were most needed to cushion the unemployed against hardship. It appeared a heartless policy, but Brüning was in dread of adopting a reflationary policy since it would have made the balance of payments deficit even worse and might have led to a loss of confidence in the deutschmark. The example of what had happened in 1923 (p.197) still haunted Germany's leaders, but Brüning's policies made the majority in the Reichstag more hostile, and he was forced to rely on Hindenburg. Between September 1930 and May 1932 (when Brüning fell from office) he invoked article 48 of the constitution, which permitted rule by decree in an emergency. Unemployment soared to six million. The Social Democrats had no policy except to support Brüning lest worse should befall. The communists, while revolutionary in speech, knew that their chances of a successful revolution were still slim. It was Hitler's party that benefited: the landowners, the industrialists and the right wing in general saw in national socialism an opportunity of ending the Weimar Republic and of giving German nationalism what it had never had before — the support of the masses.

Hitler continued to denounce the Treaty of Versailles, the Jews and the Marxists as the root of all his country's ills. His policy of explaining the bewildering economic crisis in terms of the humiliation of Versailles gave countless Germans hope that once the Jews and Marxists were defeated and the hated treaty had been torn up, all Germans could live together in one glorious and prosperous fatherland. *Ein Volk, ein Reich, ein Führer* (one People, one State, one Leader) was an ideal to which many German youths responded with fanatical zeal and devotion. Many others joined the ranks of the communists and street fights between Nazis and communists became a daily occurrence; tensions grew as social misery deepened.

In April 1932 the presidential election fell due. Hitler decided to oppose Hindenburg, but the aged president was re-elected with 19 million votes against 13 million for Hitler. Nevertheless, the campaign had given Hitler the exposure he desired and he was now a national figure.

Brüning ordered the S.S. and the S.A. to be disbanded because he feared Hitler's private armies, but in May he was dismissed from office when Hindenburg learned of his proposal to give land to the unemployed by breaking up large estates in East Prussia. This plan was far too socialistic for Hindenburg.

Von Papen's Government

Hindenburg now appointed a non-party cabinet of aristocrats under the chancellorship of Franz von Papen, a member of the catholic Centre Party. They were dubbed 'the cabinet of barons' and had less support in the Reichstag, where his party was angered by Brüning's abrupt dismissal. Despite von Papen's attempt to pose as the champion of order, the Reichstag rejected him, and he had no option but to ask Hindenburg to dissolve the parliament and call an election in July 1932.

The election proved disastrous for von Papen. From 107 seats, the Nazis jumped to 230 while the communists increased from 79 to 89; out of a total of 608 seats in the Reichstag, the two anti-democratic parties held a majority. Hitler again demanded to be made chancellor since he now had the largest party in the Reichstag, outstripping his nearest rivals, the Social Democrats, by nearly 100 seats. Hindenburg was not prepared to accept Hitler as chancellor, and Hitler would accept nothing less. At the first meeting of the Reichstag, a vote of no confidence in Von Papen's cabinet was passed by 512 votes to 42. The humiliated von Papen was again forced to request another dissolution and a new election was held in November.

In this election the Nazis actually lost a number of seats and were reduced to 196. Von Papen tried to secure the backing of Hitler in the Reichstag, but Hitler demanded the chancellorship for himself. Since von Papen faced the opposition of 90 per cent of the Reichstag, General Kurt von Schleicher prompted Hindenburg to dismiss him and have Schleicher himself appointed chancellor in December.

Hitler becomes Chancellor

In January 1933, von Papen and Hitler, eager for revenge on Schleicher, began negotiations for a joint government. Since Hitler had lost seats in the November election, the conservative classes believed that he would be more amenable to their wishes, and von Papen finally succeeded in persuading Hindenburg to accept Hitler as chancellor in a coalition government. On 30 January 1933 a new government was formed with Hitler as chancellor and von Papen as vice-chancellor.

The conservative classes had put Hitler in power in the mistaken belief that they could control him. They had become convinced that only a regime founded on mass support could

Hitler and Brownshirts campaigning in 1933.

govern Germany, and that only the Nazis had such support. Just three of the eleven-member cabinet were Nazis — Hitler, Wilhelm Frick as minister of the interior (justice), and Hermann Göring, minister without portfolio. In addition, the powers of the president and the majority in the Reichstag would be ranged against Hitler.

But Hitler and the Nazis had no intention of sharing power with anyone. Within a few weeks he demanded a new election, which took place on 5 March. The election campaign was fought against a background of fierce social unrest and street clashes between Nazis and communists. Göring, who was in charge of the police, had 400,000 S.S. and S.A. members drafted into the force so that Nazi terror could be used legally. Hitler claimed that such stern action was needed to save Germany from communism. Then, six days before election day, the Reichstag building was set on fire, and a young Dutchman, Marinus van der Lubbe, was accused of the deed. Van der Lubbe was also accused of being a communist and this gave Hitler the excuse he needed to outlaw the Communist Party and arrest 4,000 of its leaders. More important, Hitler persuaded Hindenburg to issue an edict revoking constitutional guarantees of freedom from arbitrary arrest, freedom of speech and freedom of the press. The edict gave the police extensive powers under Göring's control.

Despite the intimidation and propaganda in the election campaign, the Nazis failed to gain an overall majority. But their 288 seats, together with the 52 seats of the National People's Party, gave Hitler a majority in a Reichstag of 608 seats.

On 23 March Hitler introduced an Enabling Bill that would allow the government to pass laws without reference to the Reichstag. Since the Reichstag was surrounded by hysterical S.S. and S.A. members, most deputies were intimidated into voting for the bill. The Centre Party voted in favour after receiving vague promises that Hitler would revoke the edict of February and respect the rights of the catholic church. Only the Social Democrats voted against, but this was not sufficient to prevent the bill from becoming law. Hitler was now a dictator: the Weimar democracy was dead.

SOME REASONS FOR THE FAILURE OF GERMAN DEMOCRACY

1. The November 1918 revolution was largely the result of defeat in war and was not based on a genuine desire for political and social liberty.

2. The Weimar Republic had no choice but to accept the hated Treaty of Versailles. Democracy became associated with national humiliation and reparations payments. Because the Republic felt that it had to fulfil

the treaty's obligations, it stood condemned in the minds of large sections of the population. Moreover, since the treaty provisions deprived German industry of many outlets for expanding armaments production, the industrialists wished to see it revised. The Weimar Republic was unable to offer this, whereas Hitler promised to tear up the treaty and make Germany great once more.

3. Bismarck had created a German empire that was not a democracy but a strictly organised and largely military regime, through which all sections of society had become accustomed to strong and decisive government. Now, in the moment of their greatest humiliation, the German people were asked to accept democracy in the worst possible climate for it to take root, and transfer their allegiance to drab politicians, unaccustomed to the 'give and take' of parliamentary democracy.

4. The free political system of parliamentary democracy brought to the surface the deep disunity of the German people that had been submerged under the rigid system of Imperial Germany. The religious cleavage between Lutheran and catholic: the historic rivalries between Prussian, Saxon and Bavarian; the social cleavage between the classes — all were intensified under the Weimar system.

5. The republican parties of Weimar were more concerned with establishing orderly society after the dislocation of war than with breaking the power of the ruling classes of the Kaiser's Germany. The class-structured German army remained intact; the teaching profession stayed the same; the civil service carried on, almost independently of the legislature; the judiciary tended to deal lightly with 'offences' caused by right-wing groups; the landowners and industrialists retained their property and power as in the days of the empire. These ruling classes had no love for democratic majorities, which they regarded as 'rule of the masses over the classes'.

6. While the system of proportional representation did not of itself spell the death of democracy, it did lead to a proliferation of parties, none of which could secure an overall majority. It was designed to give a fair representation to all parties, but its very success left them in a state of perpetual frustration, unable to make a decisive electoral breakthrough. Proportional representation ensured that German democracy would become associated with weak coalition governments in a decade when Germany needed strong and decisive government to meet the many political and economic crises with which she was forced to contend.

7. The economic blizzard that struck Germany put six million people out of work and called into question the ability of capitalism and parliamentary democracy to solve the problem. Such widespread disillusionment, together with the fear of communism amongst the ruling classes, created a vacuum in German political life that was filled by Hitler, who sought to transcend the divisions of class, creed and politics, and unite all Germans in emotional faith in the future of the fatherland.

Study Assignments and Essays

1. *'The Spartacist rising and the Kapp* putsch *revealed the fragility of Weimar democracy.' Discuss.*

2. *'The Weimar constitution had within it the seeds of its own destruction.' Discuss.*

3. *Treat of the significance of the Stresemann era 1924–29.*

4. *Account for the importance of the Nazi Party in Weimar Germany.*

5. *Why did German democracy die in 1933?*

6. *Write an essay on two of the following: (i) Cultural achievements in the Weimar Republic; (ii) The invasion of the Ruhr; (iii) Political parties in the Weimar Republic; (iv) The foreign policies of the Weimar Republic; (v) The role of President Hindenburg in the Weimar Republic.*

Mussolini's Italy

16

Italy wants peace and quiet, work and calm; I will give these things with love, if possible, and with force *if necessary.*

Benito Mussolini, 1883–1945.

POST-WAR PROBLEMS

ALTHOUGH ITALY was one of the victorious powers in World War I, her disillusionment was as great as that of the defeated powers. Italy had mobilised five million men, of whom nearly three-quarters of a million were killed. She suffered a humiliating defeat at Caporetto in 1917 (p.150) and, although she had a later success at Vittorio Veneto, it failed to compensate for the many hardships imposed by her involvement in the war.

At the Paris Peace Conference in 1919, Prime Minister Orlando pressed Italy's territorial claims, promised her under the Treaty of London as an inducement to enter the war (p.139). But now the peacemakers, especially Woodrow Wilson, had little time for the intricacies of Italian frontier problems. Italy, however, did receive the Trentino, Istria and Trieste. But her disillusionment centred on the fact that she had failed to secure Dalmatia, which went to Yugoslavia, and the city of Fiume, which was placed under international control (map, p.186).

Fiume was an important port city on the Adriatic and had rail connections with Vienna and Budapest. It was mostly inhabited by Slavs (Croatians) and partly by Italians. When it became clear that the city was not going to be given to Italy, a group of Italian ex-soldiers, led by the fiery soldier poet, Gabriele D'Annunzio, seized the port on 12 September 1919. From then until January 1921, D'Annunzio, with 2,600 ex-soldiers, ruled the city. His rule resembled a comic opera, with parades, flamboyant speeches and flag-waving. None of the powers were sufficiently perturbed to intervene, while the Italian government looked on with sceptical toleration. Eventually the Italian government agreed with Yugoslavia that Fiume should become a free city. It ordered a naval blockade of the city and D'Annunzio and his followers were forced to surrender.

But the biggest problems facing Italy were economic stagnation and social unrest. The war had strained the government's limited finances and the public debt had risen by almost seven hundred per cent. The middle classes suffered from high taxation; inflation wiped out savings, and the value of the lira fell. In 1914, five lire would buy one American dollar, but by 1920 it took twenty-eight lire to do so. Italian imports became very expensive, and since Italy had to import huge quantities of coal, ore and wheat, the cost of living soared. To add further to her problems, some two-and-a-half million demobilised soldiers could not be absorbed into the workforce. These discontented unemployed became an easy prey to ideological exploitation.

To compound Italy's problems, her government proved weak and ineffective in the face of all these difficulties. In 1919 a system of proportional representation was introduced. The two main parties were the Socialist Party and the catholic Popular Party, which not only opposed each other, but were also divided within themselves. The Socialist Party faced the dilemma of all socialists in Europe: whether to function within the parliamentary system, or work for its destruction. In 1921 the extreme wing of the Socialists broke away to form a Communist Party. The Popular Party ranged over a wide spectrum of opinion. Its members included conservative reactionaries at one end and Christian radicals at the other. There was therefore little hope of stable government. In the four years after the war, Italy had five different governments. It was

Benito Mussolini and Blackshirt bodyguards in 1923.

clear that a vacuum existed that a strong, ruthless leader could exploit. That leader emerged in the person of Benito Mussolini.

BACKGROUND TO MUSSOLINI

Mussolini was born in 1883, the son of a blacksmith and a schoolmistress. In 1912 he became editor of the Italian Socialist Party newspaper, *Avanti*. When the war broke out, Mussolini advocated Italy's entry, and he was dismissed from the Socialist Party. When Italy did go to war in 1915, Mussolini joined the army, but was invalided from it two years later.

After the war, Italy faced huge economic and social problems. Following Orlando's failure to secure full Italian demands at Versailles, Mussolini decided that action had to be taken. On 23 March 1919, he summoned a meeting of like-minded followers in Milan and announced the birth of the *Fasci di Combattimento*, or 'Groups for Combat' (also known as 'Blackshirts' because of their uniform). The term originated in the Latin word *fasces*, meaning 'bundles'. The insignia of the lictors (law enforcement officers) of ancient Rome was a bundle of rods (symbolising authority and discipline) bound around an axe with the blade protruding (symbolising the power to administer punishment). Mussolini went back to ancient Rome for a symbol because he wished to be the 'New Caesar' in a new Roman empire.

THE ELEMENTS OF FASCISM

The ideology of fascism arose out of a definite historical situation in post-war Italy. Within fifteen years almost every country in Europe witnessed the rise of parties and groups claiming to be fascist. Unlike communism, which arose from the writings of Karl Marx, fascism did not emerge from the works of any great philosopher. Consequently, statements of fascist doctrine are often vague, and are best explained in terms of what they oppose rather than what they stand for.

1. The principal characteristic of fascism was its opposition to communism; it was at pains to emphasise the opposite of everything communism purported to be. Since communism claimed to be materialistic, fascism claimed to be idealistic. It believed that all actions were motivated by heroism and self-sacrifice, and not by economic forces, as Marxism held. As communism emphasised class loyalty, fascism blurred class divisions and emphasised loyalty to the state and the nation. As communism advocated international class solidarity, fascism became fiercely nationalistic and advocated loyalty to one's country as the supreme good.

2. A second characteristic of fascism was its cult of the infallible leader. In the post-war world of disillusionment and insecurity, there was a great emotional need for a strong leader who would bring his people to safety. Thus, a charismatic leader, backed up by skilful propaganda, could easily seize power from a weak and divided parliament.

3. A third characteristic of fascism was its belief in totalitarianism. Liberalism and democracy were seen as allowing too much freedom to the enemies of the state, such as communists and Jews, who owed allegiance only to their own class and creed. The fascists believed that the good of the nation was su-

THE FASCIST PHILOSOPHY

Fascists are AGAINST	*Fascists are FOR*
Democracy	Nationalism
	Racism
Socialism	Imperialism
	Dictatorship
Communism	Paramilitary organisations
	Self-sufficiency

preme and, since the nation and the state were one, the state must control every act and interest of every individual and group in so far as the good of the nation required it — and, of this good, the state itself would be its own judge.

4. A fourth characteristic of fascism was its economic policy of *autarky*, or self-sufficiency. The Great War had highlighted the dangers of relying on other countries for manufactured food and foodstuffs. Fascist economies therefore strove for self-reliance, which of necessity implied expansionism. Hence Mussolini's policy of making the Mediterranean an 'Italian Lake', and Hitler's policy of *Lebensraum* in the east (p.283).

MUSSOLINI COMES TO POWER

Throughout 1920–21 Mussolini held meetings and gathered more recruits. The communists were organising mass demonstrations and taking over factories in the name of the workers. Mussolini's fascists engaged in street clashes with the communists, and soon the industrialists saw him as a bulwark against the threat of communism. Finance poured in from such big industrialists as Agnelli, the Fiat motor manufacturer, Pirelli, the tyre magnate and the Perroni brothers, the armaments manufacturers.

In the May election of 1921 Mussolini entered into a National Bloc coalition agreement with the prime minister, Giovanni Giolitti, in order to break the power of the left-wing groups. Mussolini and 34 other fascists were elected to a parliament containing 535 seats.

Once in parliament, the fascists repudiated the National Bloc arrangement and Giolitti was forced to resign. The following year saw an increasing deterioration in the ability of parliamentary government to solve Italy's problems. Governments came and went and no prime minister could hold a coalition of parties together for long enough to provide some semblance of stability.

In August 1922, as the economy stagnated and unemployment remained high, the socialists called for a general strike. The government was afraid to take action, but Mussolini, posing as the champion of law and order, offered to break the strike. Mussolini's Blackshirts moved into the affected areas, burned down the offices and printing presses of the socialist agitators, terrorised the workers and forced them to end the strike.

THE ITALIAN FASCIST PROGRAMME

NATIONALISM
Redress wrongs of Versailles;
restore Italy's past grandeur
by
strong central government,
aggressive colonial policy

AUTARKY
The corporate state
to
organise society in
economic units

IMPERIALISM
Create an empire
in the Mediterranean lands
of Europe and North Africa

Despite these tactics, Mussolini gained in stature since many Italians, especially property owners, saw in him a bulwark against strikes and communist agitation. Although Mussolini was obviously not a democrat, the loss of parliamentary democracy, in a land where democracy had but very shallow roots, would be a small price to pay for the restoration of law and order. But two influential institutions in Italy, the monarchy and the church, were dubious of the fascists. Mussolini knew that he would need their friendship or neutrality in any bid for power. Accordingly in September 1922 he declared that he was no longer a republican, that he supported the monarchy and was the friend of the church.

The March on Rome

At the Fascist Party Congress held in October 1922, Mussolini and his party leaders decided that all fascist groups would march on Rome from three separate points to arrive in the capital on 28 October. Their demands would be for a new cabinet with at least six fascist ministers in important posts.

King Victor Emmanuel III and his prime minister Facta, feared confrontation and civil war. Facta asked the king to proclaim a state of emergency, but he refused. Victor Emmanuel feared that in the emergency the troops might be used to stop the fascists; and if the troops switched sides, he would be deposed. The king had lost confidence in parliamentary government, while the Queen Mother, Margherita, was a fervent fascist supporter.

On 27 October Facta resigned and the king asked Mussolini to come to Rome to form a government. Mussolini had set up his headquarters in Milan; being close to the Swiss border, he could easily flee into exile if his plans misfired. On 30 October Mussolini arrived in Rome by train. There was now no need for a march on Rome. Instead, about 25,000 fascists held a victory parade in the capital on the following day.

CONSOLIDATION OF POWER

Ironically, Mussolini's first government was a moderate coalition containing only four fascist ministers. He now had the support of the king, the army, the big industrialists and the landowners, as well as his own fascist followers. Mussolini's first major move towards dictatorial rule was not taken until November 1923. By then his apparent moderation had earned him the confidence of many deputies, so that they saw nothing sinister in his proposal to reform the government.

Arguing that the cabinet could not govern effectively with only 35 fascist deputies in a house of 535, Mussolini proposed a new electoral law that would put an end to weak coalitions. The new law stated that whichever party gained the highest number of votes in the election could automatically claim two-thirds of the seats in the chamber of deputies. This would mean that a stable government could be formed and obviate the necessity of several parties coming together in a weak coalition. Both houses of parliament, the chamber and the senate, readily accepted Mussolini's argument and passed the law by a large majority. Since Mussolini had only 35 deputies in parliament, it was not obvious to the other parties that the fascists would be the first to benefit from the new electoral law. But before the election was called in 1924, three events ensured that Mussolini and his fascist party would gain the most votes.

Following the Corfu incident, whereby Greece was obliged to pay fifty million lire in compensation for the murder of four Italians (p.276), Mussolini's handling of the affair was widely acclaimed by the press and the public. In 1923 Mussolini successfully negotiated with Yugoslavia for the return of Fiume to Italian control. These two international successes greatly enhanced his reputation at home as a leader who could get things done. Then early in 1924 Mussolini transformed his

Cyclists saluting Mussolini at Fascist celebrations in 1923.

Fasci di Combattimento into an official fascist militia with state salaries, and renamed them the Volunteer Militia for National Security (MVSN). During the election in April that year the MVSN used violence and intimidation against left-wing opposition groups. The election gave Mussolini over four-and-a-half million votes, against three million for all other parties. Since Mussolini had secured sixty-four per cent of the votes cast, he could now claim two-thirds of all seats in the chamber of deputies.

The Murder of Matteotti

One of the most outspoken critics of fascism and its methods was the young socialist deputy, Giacomo Matteotti. He particularly denounced the methods that had been used during the April election and challenged the validity of its results. On 10 June 1924 Matteotti was kidnapped by a fascist group under the control of Rossi, head of Mussolini's press bureau. Nothing was heard of Matteotti's fate until a short while later, when his dead body was discovered in a shallow roadside grave on the outskirts of Rome.

There was a public outcry. Fascism, long accused of political intimidation, was now accused of political murder. A substantial group of socialists and other party deputies withdrew from parliament. They were dubbed the 'Aventine Secession' in recollection of the last stand of Caius Gracchus and the Plebs, when in 121 BC they withdrew from Rome to the Aventine Hill in protest against despotic rule. Those who withdrew hoped that by isolating the fascists in parliament, the king would be forced to dismiss Mussolini, but Victor Emmanuel refused to act and the withdrawal from parliament eventually served to strengthen Mussolini's position. The way was now open for dictatorship.

Although the murder of Matteotti had caused a setback to Mussolini's plans, by January 1925 he was sufficiently self-confident to embark on the establishment of a fascist dictatorship. Political parties and their newspapers were suppressed and the fascist party became the only 'legitimate' party in Italy. Mussolini, or *Il Duce* (the Chief) as he liked to be called, became head of the Fascist Grand Council. This council was a type of cabinet, consisting of thirty loyal members selected by Mussolini himself. In 1928 a law gave the Grand Council authority to choose 400 names from lists provided by unions of employers and workers and present them to the electorate for approval. Beyond this the electorate had no further choice.

In 1926 Mussolini made a subservient parliament pass a law giving him power to issue decrees that would have the full force of law. He could now rule by decree, a privilege he used over 100,000 times during his period as dictator of Italy. When this law was passed, the few remaining deputies in parliament withdrew in protest.

In 1928 the franchise was reduced by three million when the right to vote became dependent on membership of a fascist syndicate.

THE CORPORATE STATE

In the early twentieth century, capitalist economies had come under fierce attack from socialism and communism. Mussolini was captivated by the view that a system could be created which at the same time would preserve a basic capitalist structure and end the class struggle. The system was known as *corporatism*; hence in economic terms, Italy became a corporate state. Strikes were forbidden and corporations of workers and employers were set up in six fields of the economy: industry, agriculture, commerce, maritime and air transport, land and inland-waterway transport, and banking. (In 1934 the system was enlarged to twenty-two corporations.) These corporations, representing management and workers, set prices, wages and general conditions of work. Trade unions became both irrelevant and illegal; all disputes were settled by compulsory arbitration. An organisation called *Dopo Lavoro* (after work) provided leisure-time activities and trained workers to be good fascists. The corporations came under the control of a ministry for corporations, and in this way Italy's economic life came under the direction of the fascist state.

In theory the corporate state was attractive since it claimed to bring social justice and real planning to the economy. Moreover, it purported to bring employer and worker into a common endeavour where class conflict would be eliminated. In practice, however, the corporate state created too much bureaucratic bungling, and bribery abounded.

The Economy

Mussolini, expecting a future war, desired that the economy should be self-sufficient in food, in keeping with the policy of *autarky*. This was one reason why he hoped Italy would remain mainly agricultural. Urbanisation was threatening to endanger the food supply of a rapidly growing population. Another hazard was that, as people became urbanised, they began to think and talk too much. Peasants, Mussolini asserted, were more necessary to fascism than urban workers, who might veer towards communism.

In June 1925 Mussolini launched the 'battle for grain', which was intended to make Italy self-sufficient in cereals. High import

taxes were imposed in order to induce people to turn to home production. Cereal production did increase substantially, but at a very high cost. Given the Italian climate, much land was unsuitable for cereal growing so that the output per hectare was relatively low. Many economists claimed that it would be better to grow more profitable cash crops (suitable to the Italian climate) that would earn the foreign currency with which to buy cereals on the world market. But the 'battle for grain' was dear to Mussolini's heart and nothing would deflect him. As a result, the increase in cereal production was achieved at the cost of a high domestic price for foodstuffs and the loss of export markets for other produce no longer produced on land that had been converted to cereal growing. Thus, success in the 'battle for grain' was essentially illusory. Moreover, when war began, imports of fertilisers were greatly reduced, which had a devastating effect on cereal production.

One of Mussolini's more unusual endeavours was his 'battle for births', launched in 1926. With high unemployment, Italy hardly seemed to require a larger population, except perhaps to swell the armed forces or to colonise parts of North Africa. Taxes were imposed on bachelorhood in order to encourage marriage and parenthood. In 1927 a precise target was specified of raising the population from forty to sixty million within twenty-five years. However, despite legislation, and propaganda extolling the virtues of having large families, Italy's birth rate did not increase.

A more genuine victory was won in the 'battle for land reclamation'. The regime allocated huge sums of money to drainage, irrigation, reafforestation and farm building. Count Giuseppe Volpi, acting as minister for finance, successfully persuaded the Americans and British to forgo a large part of the war debts owed them by Italy (Volpi ascribed this achievement to Mussolini). This debt settlement opened the way for the Americans to invest in Italy which was of great benefit to the fascist regime.

A public works programme was initiated and helped to cure the worst excesses of unemployment. The Pontine Marshes near Rome were drained. New motorways (*autostrade*) were built and hydro-electric power was developed. Impressive public buildings, such as railway stations and sports stadiums, were erected. Ancient monuments were reconstructed to remind Italians of the glories of ancient Rome. Many of these ventures certainly helped to encourage tourism and give an appearance of grandeur, but did little to create real wealth or alleviate the condition of many living in poverty, especially in the south.

Mussolini's economic policy from 1925 onwards was dictated more by the need for outward show than by demands of economic welfare. In August 1926 he said: 'I will defend the Italian lira to my last breath — to my last drop of blood.' Accordingly the lira, which stood at one hundred to the pound, was revalued at ninety to the pound. Although this created a strong lira, it also meant that Italian exports became relatively more expensive. This in turn led to depression at home and, by 1932, over one million Italians were unemployed out of a labour force of two-and-a-half million.

It was not until 1936 that Mussolini devalued the lira, but by then the advent of the war against Abyssinia (p.280) was cutting unemployment and stimulating the economy in the short run. On the other hand, Italian intervention in the Spanish Civil War (p.262) and in Albania (p.291) placed a heavy strain on her meagre resources.

Thus, apart from external show, real economic growth between 1925 and 1939 was small. The essential problem facing Italy was its limited natural resources; given this limitation, the programme of *autarky* was doomed to failure.

THE CATHOLIC CHURCH

In his youth Mussolini had been, like most socialists, violently anti-clerical. However, once he founded the fascist movement, he moved towards friendlier relations with the catholic church, which in many ways aided his assumption of power since the church came to see in him an enemy of communism. Mussolini fastened on the deeply rooted sentiments of many Italians, who were disturbed that the rift between church and state, which had its origins in the unification of Italy in 1870 (p.75), has never been healed.

On coming to power, Mussolini showed his goodwill by allowing crucifixes to be displayed in school classrooms and in courtrooms, and permitting the celebration of Mass at public functions. Then in 1925, since he had been married in a civil ceremony, he agreed to a catholic marriage ceremony and allowed his wife and child to be baptised. Finally on 11 February 1929 a treaty signed in the Church of St John Lateran between Mussolini's regime and Pope Pius XI brought the sixty-four-year-old church-state conflict to an end.

The Lateran Treaty had five main points:

1. The Pope was recognised as the sovereign ruler of the Vatican City State, an area of some fifty hectares.
2. The church was to receive ten million pounds in cash and government bonds, in compensation for the loss of the papal states in 1865.
3. The catholic faith was declared the official religion of Italy.
4. The church was given guarantees that the government would not interfere in its work concerning education, marriage, the appointment of bishops, religious orders and church property.
5. The Pope was to relinquish all former territorial claims and recognise the legitimacy of the Italian state.

Pope Pius XI who signed the Lateran Treaty with Mussolini in 1929.

Many devout Italians were overjoyed with the settlement. Mussolini's popularity rose not only in Italy but throughout the catholic world. The Lateran Treaty was to prove one of the few enduring legacies to outlive the fascist era.

Yet the peace it guaranteed was an uneasy one. The issue that caused most friction was the status of the catholic lay organisation, Catholic Action. By 1929 it had 4,000 adult centres and 5,000 youth clubs, and Mussolini became jealous of its strength and independence in a state where fascist control extended into most aspects of life. In 1931 Mussolini accused the organisation of harbouring leaders of the banned Popular Party, and declared that participation in Catholic Action was incompatible with membership of the fascist party. But this merely led to mass resignations from both the fascist party and Catholic Action. Eventually, to the relief of both sides, an uneasy compromise was reached. Catholic Action, although a lay organisation, came more under the control of the bishops, who undertook to appoint lay officers sympathetic to the fascist regime.

Although there were many difficulties up to 1938, the church had not condemned Italian fascism. But in 1938 Mussolini, who had by now come under Hitler's influence (p.289), proclaimed a Racialist Manifesto, setting out reasons for its adoption in Italy. Pope Pius XI, who had already expressed concern about Hitler's racial programme, now condemned anti-semitism as a denial of the brotherhood of man. Mussolini went ahead and brought in a law for the 'Defence of the Italian Race'. Marriage between 'Aryan' Italians and 'Jewish' Italians was forbidden. Jews had to be publicly registered and were forbidden to own important industry; they were also prohibited from certain occupations, such as education and the armed forces. But despite these restrictions, and unlike their fellow Jews in Germany, Italian Jews were relatively safe until 1943 (p.310). This was mainly because Italians were not anti-semitic and the church gave the Jews discreet help.

THE CULT OF THE LEADER

The years after 1926 saw an ever increasing propagation of the myth of the omniscient *Duce*. Mussolini fostered it, not only from vanity but as an instrument of power. Those surrounding him realised that without him they were nothing: the greater he was, the greater they would be. But the most fervent advocate of Mussolini's invincibility was his brother, Arnoldo, who, day after day in the *Popolo d'Italia*, described the *Duce* as a demigod who knew everything, was the greatest statesman in Europe, and had placed his wisdom, heroism and vast intellect at the service of his people.

Mussolini ha sempre ragione (Mussolini is always right) became one of the catchphrases of the regime, while another, stencilled on walls everywhere, was 'Believe, obey, fight'. The press was enlisted in depicting the *Duce* in a diversity of activities: fencing, riding, driving and even playing the violin. He was compared to Aristotle, Kant and St Thomas Aquinas. He was described as the greatest genius in Italian history, greater even than Dante or Michelangelo. *Il Duce's* picture was displayed (often in heroic pose) on all public buildings, and many people had his photograph printed on the head of their writing paper.

Soon Mussolini came to believe, or pretended to believe, that he was almost infallible and needed servants rather than associates. If he asked others for information, he always gave the impression that their answers only confirmed what he had known.

In school, teachers were ordered to magnify this solitary figure, to stress his wonderful courage and brilliant mind, and to teach that to obey him was the highest virtue.

THE NATURE OF THE FASCIST REGIME

Italian fascists claimed to have created a one-party totalitarian state. Despite this claim, and in comparison with Nazi Germany (p.230) and Soviet Russia (p.231), Italy was not quite totalitarian. The monarchy remained, and the church enjoyed a large measure of independence. The Italian people were not fully committed and many of them viewed fascism with as much scepticism as they had previous regimes (p.73). One reason for this was the absence of any definite fascist ideology that people could accept.

One of the basic tenets of Italian fascism was that action was more important than doc-

Blackshirted Fascists march past Il Duce *in October 1935.*

trine. The greatest example of this was to be seen in Mussolini's own demeanour. In addition to being the dictator of Italy, he held nine ministries and claimed to work a fourteen-hour day. He would arrange to leave the lights on in his office until late at night to suggest that he was busy at work, yet his private secretary later revealed that he went to bed each night at 10 pm, and often slept at his desk during the day. To the outside world, however, the fascist regime carefully cultivated the myth of the invincible leader. *Il Duce* was far from being a superman: the footstool on which he often stood when giving speeches was never photographed. He generally appeared on balconies in order to conceal his low stature. By 1939 he suffered from myopia, and a stomach ulcer, which necessitated a milk diet.

Fascism in Italy arose out of a definite historical situation and consisted of a vague and incoherent body of ideas welded together to meet the needs of the moment. It could not be described as totalitarian. Rather, it was a unique type of nationalist dictatorship which perfected the cult of the leader, fed off its own propaganda, and was eventually brought to ruin when it fell under the spell of Nazi totalitarianism (p.316).

FOREIGN POLICY

Despite Mussolini's domestic concerns in the early years of his rule, he managed to write his name on the international scene. In August 1923, following the assassination of four Italians engaged in delimiting the border between Greece and Albania, the world was given its first taste of Mussolini's fascist spirit. He occupied the Greek island of Corfu, which he had long coveted, and reluctantly evacuated it only after receiving heavy compensation (p.276 and map, p.186).

Two weeks after the Corfu incident, Mussolini sent a military officer to govern the city of Fiume on the pretext of restoring order. Since Yugoslavia's ally, France, was distracted with the Ruhr occupation (p.195) and King Alexander of Yugoslavia was an admirer of Mussolini, the Yugoslav government accepted the situation.

In 1930, having consolidated his rule in Italy, Mussolini began a new expansive phase of foreign policy. Soon he was speaking of 'fascism for export', declaring that in another decade all Europe would be fascist. In 1932 he became his own foreign minister and held the position until handing it over to his son-in-law, Count Galeazzo Ciano, in 1936.

With the rise of Hitler, Mussolini feared that he would demand the return of the South Tyrol in a union of all German-speaking peoples (p.283). Accordingly, for a brief period, Mussolini championed the independence of Austria as a buffer between Italy and Germany. In July 1934 when the Austrian chancellor, Engelbert Dollfuss, was murdered by the Nazis, Mussolini immediately rushed troops to the Brenner Pass. This was a clear warning to German and Austrian Nazis that Italy would defend Austrian independence. The warning had its desired effect, and the *putsch* did not materialise (p.289 and map, p.186).

The Annexation of Abyssinia

Abyssinia was the only large African state not ruled by Europeans. It lay between the two Italian colonies of Somaliland and Eritrea. Many Italian nationalists still smarted over the humiliating defeat inflicted on Italy by the Abyssinians at Adowa in 1896 (p.92). The depression years and the inadequacies of the corporate state had diminished Mussolini's image. Therefore a successful war abroad, which would enhance prestige, capture much-needed raw materials and markets, and provide a base for a new Roman empire, seemed an attractive proposition (map, p.88).

There was an important oasis at Walwal on the border between Abyssinia and Italian Somaliland. This oasis was in dispute, and on 5 December 1934 a skirmish broke out: one hundred Abyssinians and more than thirty Italians were killed. Mussolini immediately demanded control of the oasis, together with financial compensation. The Abyssinian emperor, Haile Selassie, referred the matter to the League of Nations for arbitration. But after deliberation, the League merely recommended that the parties concerned should settle the dispute in a peaceful manner.

Mussolini was in no mood for compromise and, on 3 October 1935, Italian troops invaded Abyssinia. Italian forces, backed up by planes, bombs, machine guns and artillery, were greatly superior to the Abyssinian forces with their primitive equipment. World opinion was not unduly disturbed by the war, but when the Italians used poison gas, all sympathy for Italy evaporated. Haile Selassie appealed again to the League of Nations. The League adjudged Italy to be the aggressor and imposed half-hearted economic sanctions, but these had little effect (p.280).

After a seven-month campaign, Italian troops under Marshal Badoglio entered the capital, Addis Ababa, on 5 May 1936. Haile Selassie went into exile in England and Victor Emmanuel was proclaimed emperor of Abyssinia. Mussolini now declared the union of

Abyssinia with Italian Somaliland under the new name of Italian East Africa. Italian gains were short-lived however; during World War II Allied troops drove out the Italians and restored Haile Selassie as emperor on 5 May 1941 (p.305).

Relations with Hitler

One of the most important consequences of the Abyssinian war was its effect on German-Italian relations. Hitler was the only major leader not to have criticised Mussolini's aggression in Abyssinia and, since the two leaders also intervened on the side of Franco in the Spanish Civil War (p.264), it was inevitable that they would now come closer together.

In October 1936 an agreement was reached on the outstanding issue of Austria. The agreement referred to a Rome-Berlin axis around which the affairs of Europe would revolve. In November 1937 the friendship led to Italy joining the Anti-Comintern Pact with Germany and Japan (p.289). But friendship with Hitler had a price; in March 1938 Hitler absorbed Austria into the Third Reich (p.288) without even informing Mussolini. Then in March 1939 when Hitler took over Czechoslovakia (p.290), Mussolini was once again ignored. His immediate reaction was to invade and annex his long-coveted Albania (p.291). Despite Hitler's cavalier attitudes towards Mussolini, the two dictators came closer together in May when the Pact of Steel was signed, in which Italy and Germany promised mutual assistance in any war (p.291).

Mussolini agreed to the pact because the German foreign minister, von Ribbentrop (who had come to Rome to sign the pact with Ciano), promised that Hitler would not go to war for at least three years. But when von Ribbentrop signed the non-aggression pact with the Soviet prime minister, Molotov (Nazi-Soviet Pact, (p.294), Ciano and Mussolini knew that war was imminent. They realised that, despite fascist propaganda, Italy could not mobilise eight million men in a few hours and her aircraft could not blot out the sun. The reality was quite different. The army, one-third of which was serving overseas, was still equipped with nineteenth-century rifles and World War I artillery. In theory the air force had some three thousand planes, but only 980 were ready for action.

Mussolini now hoped to wriggle out of his commitment to Hitler and said that he was ready to join Germany in war on condition that he immediately receive what would have amounted to 17,000 train loads of war material. Ciano wrote in his diary, 'it's enough to kill a bull, if a bull could read.' The demand was impossible and was designed merely as an excuse not to fight. This was obvious to Hitler, who reproached Mussolini with cowardice after his previous promises of support.

When Germany invaded Poland on 1 September, Mussolini told his cabinet that he would not go to war because Hitler's 'treachery' exonerated Italy from the Pact of Steel. Since the word 'neutral' was considered un-fascist, Mussolini coined the term 'non-belligerent' to describe Italy's position.

Study Assignments and Essays

1. Examine the main political, social and economic problems facing Italy in the immediate post-war years.
2. Examine the main features of fascism.
3. Why was it possible for Mussolini to assume dictatorial power in Italy?
4. Treat of Mussolini's economic achievements.
5. Treat of the main features of Mussolini's foreign relations in the inter-war period.
6. Write an essay on two of the following:
(i) Mussolini and the socialists; (ii) Mussolini and the catholic church; (iii) The corporate state; (iv) The cult of the leader in Mussolini's Italy; (v) Italian society on the eve of World War II.

Hitler's Germany 1933–39

Democracy is the breeding ground in which the bacillus of the Marxist world pest can grow and prosper.

Adolf Hitler, *Mein Kampf*

DICTATORSHIP

THE ENABLING Bill that Hitler pushed through parliament in March 1933 allowed him to legislate by decree. The Reichstag now became little more than a rubber stamp. On 14 July Hitler promulgated a 'Law against the New Formation of Parties'. Article 1 stated: 'The sole political party existing in Germany is the National Socialist German Workers' Party.' Article 2 asserted: 'Whoever shall undertake to maintain the organisation of another party, or to found a new party, shall be punished with a sentence of hard labour of up to three years, or of prison between six months and three years.' This law turned Germany into a one-party dictatorship and began the process whereby in a few years it became a totalitarian state, in which every aspect of life — political, economic, social, cultural and religious — was brought within the radius of state control.

THE ARMY

The greatest single obstacle to a Nazi dictatorship was the personnel of the German army (the *Wehrmacht*). Because of the restrictions laid down in the Treaty of Versailles, the German army was circumscribed at every level (p.182); but with the advent of Hitler, the *Wehrmacht* hoped that the restrictions regarding conscription, training and the supply of weapons would be rectified. The officer class of the *Wehrmacht* was still aristocratic and had a special place in German society. Although they had been contemptuous of the Weimar democracy, they were equally disdainful of Hitler a proletarian followers.

Their immediate concern, howeve their weakening position in relation t growing strength of the *Sturmabteilung* (S. 1934 the S.A. had over two million mem while the *Wehrmacht* numbered a n 100,000. It had been supplied with mod weapons and was taking over some dut more suited to the *Wehrmacht*. But what real worried the *Wehrmacht* officers was the fac that the S.A. leader, Captain Röhm, hac proclaimed his intention of merging the S.A. and the *Wehrmacht* into one National Socialist People's Army.

Röhm began openly to criticise Hitler's failure to develop the 'socialist side' of national socialism and suggested that, now that he had gained power, Hitler would turn his back on those who had helped him to win it!

> Adolf is a swine. He will give us all away. He only associates with the reactionaries now, getting matey with the East Prussian generals. They're his cronies now. Adolf knows exactly what I want. I've told him often enough. Not a second edition of the old imperial army. The generals are a lot of old fogeys. I'm the nucleus of the new army.

Hitler was well aware that the *Wehrmacht* would fiercely oppose any merger with the Storm Troops; and while the S.A. had brought him to power, he required the *Wehrmacht* for the future. Hitler therefore chose the *Wehrmacht*.

On 30 June 1934 in what became known as the 'Night of the Long Knives', the S.S. under Himmler, but acting on Hitler's instructions, butchered 150 S.A. members in the Stadelheim Prison in Munich. Röhm and about 250 other S.A. leaders throughout Germany were executed. The S.A., now leaderless, became unimportant, and Himmler's S.S. rose in prominence. The *Wehrmacht* officers and the big industrialists felt more assured about Hitler, and the chances of a *Wehrmacht* revolt against the Nazis receded. Moreover, military conscription was introduced in March 1935. This meant that young men indoctrinated in Nazism filled the army, making it almost impossible for *Wehrmacht* officers to contemplate a coup.

Despite the nazification of the army, Hitler did not fully trust the generals. In November 1937 he called a conference and announced to his generals that Austria and Czechoslovakia were to be absorbed into the Reich. Yet the more cautious generals challenged his plans. Early the following year Hitler decided to restructure the leadership. The minister for war, von Blomberg, the commander in chief, von Fritsch, and fifteen generals were dismissed. Hermann Göring became head of the *Luftwaffe* (air force), Hitler became his own war minister and a new military staff of obsequious officers was appointed to surround him. With the entire armed forces now subservient to his wishes, Hitler's rule was effectively unopposed.

THE FÜHRER

On 2 August 1934 President von Hindenburg died. Hitler now decided to unite the offices of chancellor and president and call himself *Der Führer* (The Leader).

> The *Führer* unites in himself all the sovereign authority of the Reich. . . . We must not speak of the state's authority but of the *Führer's* authority. . . . The authority of the *Führer* is complete and all-embracing; it extends into all fields of national life; it embraces the entire people, which is bound to the *Führer* in loyalty and obedience.
>
> E. Huber, *Constitutional Law of the Great German Reich*

At the same time, Hitler declared himself head of the German armed forces and obliged each member to swear an oath of allegiance:

> I swear by God this sacred oath, that I will yield unconditional obedience to the *Führer* of the German Reich and Volk, Adolf Hitler, the Supreme Commander of the *Wehrmacht*, and as a brave soldier will be ready at any time to lay down my life for this Oath.

Hitler was now the unconditional head of Germany: head of the party, head of the state, head of the armed forces. Having attained this position, he asked that it be ratified by plebiscite. Out of a forty-five million electorate, some thirty-one million voted in favour.

LAW AND ORDER

The two most important organisations in the early years of Nazism were the S.A. and the S.S. But after the 'Night of the Long Knives', Himmler's S.S. became far more influential. It kept watch on all political life in the state. Members were carefully chosen for their physical fitness and racial background, but above all for the undivided devotion to the *Führer*. The S.S. motto was 'my honour is true', which in practice meant absolute loyalty to Hitler.

When Göring was minister of the interior, he established Nazis in key positions in the police and also organised the political police, known as the Gestapo. But Himmler soon became commander of the Gestapo and accordingly appointed his own S.S. to all key positions in the police.

The judicial system lost its independence and came to be an instrument of state policy. Sentences became more severe and the death penalty was extended to a wider range of offences. Special courts were established, staffed only by judges whose Nazi convictions were total. After 1939 the regime increasingly used torture, execution without trial and the concentration camp (p.310).

HITLER AND THE CHURCHES

Hitler's national socialism provided a complete philosophy of life. In one sense Nazi ceremonies and rituals, such as rallies, marching songs, the use of the swastika emblem, special uniforms, and the salute of *'Heil Hitler!'* and *'Sieg Heil!'* with the extended arm and open hand, provided the German people with an alternative religion. Hitler saw Christianity as stemming from Judaism and therefore resolved that it would have no independent place in the future Germany. He declared that, unlike the Italians and the French, who could be heathen and Christian at the same time, the German 'is serious in everything he undertakes' and therefore had to be one thing or the other. 'For our people it is decisive whether they acknowledge the Jewish-Christ-Creed with its effeminate pity ethics, or a strong heroic belief in God in nature, God in our people, in our destiny, in our blood.' In any totalitarian system, no institution can hope to survive outside the all-embracing philosophy of totalitarianism and it was inevitable that the Nazi regime would clash with the churches.

At first the churches were slow to grasp the full meaning of Nazism. Indeed, they had a certain amount of good will for Hitler as the man who would prove a bulwark against the spread of communism.

In 1933 Hitler won the support of German catholics by promising a concordat with the Pope, and although Hitler dissolved the catholic Centre Party on 5 July, Von Papen, as vice-chancellor, signed the Concordat on behalf of Hitler's government on 20 July. By this agreement, catholics in Germany were guaranteed full freedom to practise their religion in public. The church could conduct its own affairs without state interference and could continue its role in education. In return, catholic priests were to keep out of politics. Pius XI was pleased to have reached a satisfactory agreement with Hitler and ordered the German bishops to swear allegiance to the Nazi regime.

Unlike the catholic church, the protestant or evangelical churches in Germany had been already weakened by 300 years of association with government. Besides, protestants were not united in a single church: there were 281 different protestant churches in Germany. Hitler decided to merge them into one national church or *Reichskirche*, and appointed Dr Ludwig Müller as Reich bishop. Many protestants opposed this move, and, led by Pastor Martin Niemöller, formed themselves into a new body, the Confessional Church, which rejected the authority of the *Reichskirche* and the claims of the state to regulate Christian practice. It also rejected the proposal to exclude Christians of Jewish origin from the church, and in 1935 issued a clear warning of the dangers the Nazi government posed to the integrity of the Christian church. The Nazis retaliated by arresting some 800 leading protestant churchmen. Niemöller was also arrested and later was sent to the concentration camp at Dachau. The Nazis confiscated some church property and merged the protestant youth movement with the Hitler Youth. Yet most of the clergy tried to steer a middle course, rejecting the *Reichskirche* but also refusing to join openly with the confessional church.

With the catholic church, the friendly relations occasioned by the Concordat were short-lived. Catholic schools, charities, monasteries, and the catholic press increasingly felt the encroachment of Nazi totalitarianism. It was obvious to Pius XI that the Concordat meant nothing to Hitler's regime. Accordingly he issued an encyclical, *Mit Brennender Sorge* (With Burning Anxiety), to all German catholics on the evils of the Nazi state. The encyclical was smuggled into Germany and was read from the pulpits on

Hitler addresses a Nazi youth rally at Nuremberg.

Palm Sunday, 21 March 1937. The Nazis were taken by surprise and reacted by intensifying their attacks upon the catholic church.

When the war broke out, individual catholic and protestant churchmen played important roles in resisting Nazism. Pastor Gruber's work in assisting Jewish emigration was especially courageous. Cardinal Gallen and Bishop Wurm denounced the Nazi euthanasia programme, and the protestant theologian, Dietrich Bonhoeffer, and the Jesuit priest, Alfred Delp, were both hanged for their alleged association with the conspiracy against Hitler (p.303).

In general, however, the churches failed to react strenuously to the moral dilemma posed by Nazism. But even if they had, it would scarcely have deflected Hitler's regime. The churches for the most part adopted a policy of tacit acceptance and managed to survive.

PROPAGANDA

The Nazis strove to control all aspects of culture and the arts. A Reich Chamber of Culture under Dr Josef Goebbels was established and all artistic creation had to conform to the Nazi theories of life and society. For the Nazis, all intellectual and artistic endeavour must be made in the service of the state. Artists such as Adolf Ziegler and Johannes Beutner glorified the Aryan figure in their work, with paintings of chaste nudes, and peasant girls stripped to the waist working in the fields. Hitler's own particular interest was architecture. He employed Albert Speer to design plans to rebuild Berlin and other cities of the Reich on a monumental and classical scale. The best examples of the Nazi philosophy of architecture were reflected in the gigantic classical columns of the Nuremberg Stadium and the Chancellory in Berlin.

The emerging art of film-making was also employed in the service of Nazi ideals. Leni Riefenstahl produced a memorable film on the Nazi Rally at Nuremberg in 1934 entitled *Triumph of the Will*. Goebbels particularly appreciated the potential of the cinema as a means of indoctrination and propaganda. He had several films produced that glorified the Aryan race and heaped ridicule on 'lesser breeds', such as Jews and Slavs.

In education, creative and independent thought was not allowed. As early as May 1933, students in Berlin were encouraged to take part in a ceremonial burning of 'un-German' books. Jewish and liberal lecturers were dismissed from their university posts. The curriculum was made to conform to Nazi ideals. The student population fell drastically in the years after 1933.

In schools a similar policy prevailed. Teachers were required to belong to the Nazi Teachers' Association and Jews were forbidden to teach. The new emphasis in the school curriculum was on physical education, because intensive physical training 'hardened children for the demands that would be made on them in later years'. History textbooks especially were rewritten to conform to the ideas of anti-semitism, the master race theory and the infallibility of the *Führer*. Children were picked out for their leadership potential and racial purity and were sent to special schools, while older pupils destined for high positions in the Nazi regime were put in special residential schools.

German boys were expected to join the *Pimpfen* (Little Fellows) at six years of age. By the age of ten they were expected to have acquired 'important' knowledge, such as the history of the Nazis, the terms of the Treaty of Versailles and the strategic targets in enemy countries. At ten they progressed to the *Jungvolk* (Young folk) for further education in Nazism. Then at fourteen they entered the *Hitler Jugend* (Hitler Youth), which by 1936 had a membership of six million.

For girls there was the *Bund der Deutschen Mädeln* (League of German Maidens). Here they were taught to honour the Nazi state, give unquestioning obedience, and appreciate the importance of becoming mothers of soldiers of the Reich.

Thus, from an early age, Germans were indoctrinated in absolute loyalty and devotion to the state. The German nation was to be made great in order to fulfil its destiny as the nation of the *Herrenvolk* or Master Race. But to achieve this, it would have to purify itself of all those who were alleged to pollute the race: Germany must be purged of the Jew.

THE JEWS

Anti-semitism was an essential ingredient of Hitler's national socialism, as expressed in *Mein Kampf* and continuously in his speeches.

On the Nazi assumption of power in 1933, the S.A. organised a wave of anti-Jewish violence: window-smashing, looting of premises and assaults on individual Jews. But because the American Jewish community were influential in the world of finance, Dr Schacht, president of the Reichsbank, warned Hitler that Germany's need for foreign borrowing would be jeopardised by anti-Jewish violence. Accordingly Hitler called off the violence for the time being and, instead, the Nazi regime began a systematic drive to circumscribe the 600,000 Jews in their daily lives.

Humiliation of a Jew by the S.A.

In April 1933 a law was passed expelling Jews from the civil service and excluding them from the universities. In October a press law forbade them to work in journalism. Then in November 1935 the infamous Nuremberg Laws 'for the protection of German Blood and Honour' came into effect. These laws forbade intermarriage between Jews and non-Jews, deprived Jews of German citizenship, and obliged them to wear the six-pointed yellow Star of David, as a badge of identification. They could now be easily picked out and held up to public abuse and ridicule. Many Jews considered these laws to be so offensive that they decided to emigrate before worse might befall. Among those who left were the two novelist brothers Heinrich and Thomas Mann and the world-renowned scientist, Albert Einstein.

In 1936 the anti-Jewish campaign was eased because Nazi Germany was hosting the Olympic Games in Berlin. However, when the American negro athlete, Jesse Owens, won four gold medals, Hitler's displeasure was evident.

In 1938 Hitler issued a decree expelling all Polish Jews from Germany. In reprisal, a young Polish Jew, Herschal Gryuszpan, murdered a German diplomat, Erast von Rath, in Paris on 7 November. Immediately the S.S., the Gestapo and the Hitler Youth wreaked vengeance on the Jews. On the night of 9–10 November, known as *Krystallnacht* (Crystal Night) because of the amount of glass that was broken, seven thousand Jewish shops were wrecked, over one hundred synagogues were burned and ninety-one Jews were killed. *Krystallnacht* was the beginning of the end for the Jews. They were now ordered to pay a collective fine of one billion Reichmarks and pay for the damage done to their own property. This was followed up by a decree forbidding them to engage in independent crafts, sales, service and management, while Jewish doctors and lawyers were given three months to liquidate their practices. In effect the decree meant that Jews were no longer able to take any but the most menial job.

When Austria came under Nazi control in 1938, the Austrian Jews met a similar fate. By 1939 some 370,000 Jews and 30,000 others had fled the country. Many more Jews had been sent to concentration camps, together with pacifists, beggars, alcoholics and sexual deviants. But worse was to follow during the war (p.310).

THE ECONOMY

When Hitler came to power in 1933, some six million Germans were unemployed. Indeed, the economic depression and the pool of unemployed it had created had helped bring him to power. Therefore the elimination of unemployment would offer the most convincing reason why he should stay in power.

Hitler's programme had a magic effect. In one year unemployment was down to four million; by 1936 it was reduced to two-and-a-half million; and by 1938 it was non-existent; in fact there was now an influx of foreign workers.

In June 1933 Hitler introduced the Law to Reduce Unemployment whereby the government would become an employer and use its finance to create employment. He also set up a National Labour Service to employ people on a wide range of public works. The Nazi economist, George-Hans Reinhardt, was put in charge of a four-year plan to modernise Germany. A vast road-building programme employing 200,000 men got under way, creating the famous *autobahnen* (highways) network. Railways and other means of communication were also improved, but the greatest achievement occurred in the motor industry. In 1938 the output of motor vehicles was 340,000, or five hundred per cent higher than in 1931. Over one million people were employed in this industry, and in 1939 the first *Volkswagen*, or people's car, was manufactured. Hitler boasted that soon every German would own a car.

However, it was armaments production that did most to end umemployment, since it gave a boost to heavy industry (coal, iron and steel) which had stagnated under the Weimar Republic. The production of submarines, tanks, guns and aeroplanes gave the big industrialists the outlets they required. Their economic objectives ran parallel with the political objectives of the Nazi regime: both had a vested interest in preparing for war.

With the unemployment problem solved, Hitler's next objective was to make Germany self-sufficient in food and essential raw materials. This was prompted by the experience of the Great War, where the Allied blockade, rather than Allied arms, forced Germany to surrender. But here the Nazis were less successful than in their industrial programme. There was a continual flight from the land, mainly caused by better pay and employment prospects in industry. The economic minister, Hjalmar Schacht, clashed with Hitler on economic policy and advocated diverting finance from armaments production to agriculture. This led to the famous controversy over 'guns or butter'. Finally Hitler did release more money to stimulate agriculture. This policy of self-sufficiency, known as *autarky*, was not achieved in the years before 1939. Nevertheless, Germany did

The scene at the opening of a new Volkswagen motor factory in 1938.

succeed in reducing her agricultural imports to 25 per cent of her total needs. Hitler's ultimate answer to the problem of achieving self-sufficiency was bound up with his policy of *Lebensraum* in the east. In 1936 he declared:

> If I had the Ural mountains with their incalculable store of treasures in raw materials, the Ukraine with its tremendous wheat-fields and Siberia with its vast forests, Germany would swim in plenty.

But meanwhile Germany would have to rely on her own resources. Since raw materials were scarce, strict rules were employed to ensure that nothing was wasted. Empty cans, paper and waste fats were saved and recycled into useful products. Scientists were employed to search for synthetic alternatives for rubber, wool, oil, and other imports essential for the war effort.

The main characteristic of Nazi policy towards the economy was *Gleichschaltung*, or regimentation. In 1933 the trade unions were dissolved and workers were obliged to join the Nazi-dominated Labour Front. Employers were given complete authority over their workers, although Nazi officials were also appointed to keep watch on the employers. From 1935 all workers were obliged to carry a labour book that contained their work record and racial background.

The Labour Front organised welfare

A socialist leader is hanged in effigy by Nazi sympathisers in 1935.

schemes and leisure activities through its organisation, 'Strength through Joy'. In this way many German workers were able to enjoy subsidised foreign holidays, sporting activities and cultural programmes. Most of them willingly accepted this paternalistic treatment, which offered fringe benefits in return for the abdication of their former trade union rights.

In the drive for autarky, the consumer came second. Taxation remained high to finance the huge government expenditures necessary to finance public works. Consumer goods were limited to 63 per cent of Germany's total national product, compared with 79 per cent in Britain. Despite this, standards of living rose and by 1939 many people had radios, vacuum cleaners and other electrical appliances.

Apart from the Nazi economic policy, the German economy was helped by a number of external events. When Hitler came to power in 1933, the worst excesses of the world depression had 'bottomed out' and a gradual upturn had begun. In 1937 world trade revived, and the next year when Austria and the Sudetenland were absorbed in the Reich (p.288) their assets and raw materials helped to boost the German economy. The plunder of the Jews, especially after 1938, also added wealth to the exchequer. Yet when war broke out in 1939, German reserves of oil, copper and rubber were still inadequate. Autarky had not been achieved.

THE TOTALITARIAN STATE

Between 1933 and 1939 Hitler and the Nazis turned a democratic Germany into a totalitarian state in which the individual became little more than a cog in the state machine. All organised opposition to Nazism was eliminated. Political parties were banned, trade unions were made illegal, the press and education came under state control, and the churches for the most part were silent.

Individual voices were raised in protest. Some churchmen, democrats and liberals did speak out, but the great majority of Hitler's opponents kept their thoughts to themselves. Most Germans saw Hitler as their saviour. He had saved them from communism, created employment, and given them back their dignity and pride. Perhaps this combination of genuine German patriotism, aroused by Nazi propaganda, together with the Gestapo terror, which threatened any opposition, enabled the Nazis to create a totalitarian state and ensured that when Hitler declared war in 1939, he had a submissive and willing people behind him.

Study Assignments and Essays

1. *Treat of Hitler's regime and the Christian churches between 1933 and 1939.*
2. *Treat of the role of propaganda in Hitler's Germany.*
3. *Treat of the origin and developments of anti-semitism in Hitler's Germany.*
4. *'Economic progress in Hitler's Germany was real and lasting.' Discuss.*
5. *What were the main characteristics of the Nazi totalitarian state established in Germany between 1933 and 1939?*
6. *Write an essay on two of the following: (i) Hitler's assumption of dictatorial power in 1933; (ii) The Night of the Long Knives; (iii) The administration of law and order in Hitler's Germany; (iv) Opposition in Hitler's Germany 1933–39; (v) Youth organisations in Hitler's Germany.*

Stalin's Russia

18

Only an absolute ruler, himself ruled neither by nerves nor by sentiments, could persist in this staggering enterprise in the face of so many adversities.

Isaac Deutscher, *Stalin*

JOSEF VISARIONOVICH Djugashvili, known to the world as Stalin (man of Steel), was born in Georgia in 1879. His father, a former serf, died while Stalin was a boy. His mother intended him for the priesthood and sent him to an ecclesiastical school in Gori and then to the theological college in Tbilisi. In 1899, following a protest in the seminary against the tsar's attempts to 'Russify' the Georgians, Stalin was dismissed. Having rejected religion, and hating the class system because of his peasant origins, it was understandable that he would turn to revolutionary Marxism as an answer to the ills of the tsarist regime.

Stalin joined a revolutionary movement in Georgia and edited a Marxist newspaper. He was arrested and spent two years in various prisons and was then exiled to Siberia, but escaped after a short while. On his return, he organised a Bolshevik group in Georgia and carried out several robberies in order to finance the party (map, p.172).

In 1912 Lenin appointed Stalin to the Bolshevik central committee. The same year he founded the Bolshevik newspaper, *Pravda*, in St Petersburg. He was again exiled to Siberia and was later declared unfit for conscription in the Russian army because of a withered arm. When the February 1917 revolution broke out, Stalin escaped from Siberia and went back to Petrograd. He was elected a member of the Bolshevik *Politburo*, or Political Committee of the party, but when the Bolsheviks seized power in October of the same year, Stalin played a relatively unimportant part.

His first step to prominence was when Lenin, picking his commissars (ministers) to rule Russia, appointed him commissar for nationalities. Stalin's first action as commissar was to grant the Finns their independence. His next was to issue the 'Declaration of the rights of the people of Russia', which prompted Georgia and the Ukraine to declare their independence. Very soon the Bolsheviks realised that they could not afford to be so generous with the non-Russian peoples under their control unless they wanted the complete disintegration of the old tsarist empire. And so Stalin had both Georgia and the Ukraine forcibly reincorporated into the Soviet Union. Nevertheless, he did much to improve the plight of the Asiatic peoples, building schools and hospitals and insisting that their languages be written down. As a result many millions were educated in their own language for the first time.

In 1922 Stalin was elected general secretary of the Communist Party, and this, more than anything else, enabled him eventually to become the sole ruler of Soviet Russia. No one placed much importance on this job, but the role of the party in Russian life was growing. The amateurish approach of 1917 was fast disappearing as full-time officials were taking the place of part-time volunteers in the running of local branches and committees. Stalin appointed his followers as local officials; these in turn elected suitable candidates to local and national councils, and thus in a few years of appointments and dismissals, he controlled a vast network of loyal supporters. However, since he was continuing to play such a minor *public* role, no one realised how powerful he was becoming.

THE STRUGGLE FOR POWER 1924–27

When Lenin died in January 1924 (p.177), there were four potential leaders in the Soviet government: Trotsky, Zinoviev, Kamenev and Stalin. Trotsky, creator of the Red Army and hero of the civil war (p.171), was generally expected to succeed to the leadership. However, at the time of Lenin's death, Trotsky was in the Caucasus recuperating form an illness, and it was Zinoviev who assumed provisional leadership.

Then on 26 January (the eve of Lenin's funeral) a session of the Congress of Soviets decided (a) that Petrograd be renamed Leningrad and (b) that a mass recruitment to the Communist Party be started immediately. This latter decision was highly significant for the future leadership, because Stalin, in his capacity as general secretary of the party, could 'pack' the party with his own supporters and also block the membership of those known to be in support of Trotsky. On 22 May at a meeting of the party's central committee, Krupskaya, Lenin's widow, tried unsuccessfully to have Lenin's 'political will' read to the members. If she had had her way, Stalin would possibly have been demoted from his position as general secretary because Lenin had warned against him in his 'will':

> Comrade Stalin has, having become general secretary, concentrated limitless power in his own hands, and I am not sure that he will always be careful enough in the use of his power.

Kamenev and Zinoviev had no love for Stalin, but they greatly disliked Trotsky because he once had been a Menshevik and also because they feared he might establish a personal dictatorship. They therefore blocked Krupskaya's attempt to publish Lenin's 'will' since they wished to preserve Stalin for their fight against Trotsky.

Stalin proposed that Trotsky should be removed as head of the Red Army (the source of his power) and placed in charge of the electrification of the Soviet Union (an exciting and challenging position, bringing 'old Russia' into the twentieth century). Trotsky, who would never go against the wishes of the party, accepted his new position, although he knew that Stalin had outmanoeuvred him.

Trotsky publicly revealed the existence of Lenin's testament, and for this he was accused of complicity in plots to overthrow Stalin and was voted out of the party and denied any public office. In 1928 Trotsky was exiled to Alma Ata in Soviet Central Asia. There, he published a series of articles bitterly attacking Stalin's government and was soon ordered to leave the Soviet Union. After spending four years in Turkey, Trotsky moved on to France, where he wrote his epic, *History of the Russian Revolution*, but soon the French government ordered him to leave because it was embarrassed by his public attack on Stalin. He then went to Norway but was ordered to leave on the charge that he was implicated in an international plot against Stalin.

Trotsky was invited to Mexico where he continued his inflammatory attacks on Stalin and his regime, claiming that the basic principles of the October Revolution had been betrayed. In August 1940, while reading in his garden, he was killed with a pickaxe by an assassin widely suspected of being an agent of Stalin. Meanwhile Stalin had dispensed with his two former allies, Kamenev and Zinoviev, who had served their purpose. He had them expelled from the *Politburo* and voted out of the party altogether, so that by 1928 Stalin was the undisputed leader of the Soviet Union.

However, while this power struggle was in progress between 1924 and 1927, it was covered over in an ideological debate — that of Trotsky's theory of 'permanent revolution' and Stalin's counter-theory of 'socialism in one country'. Trotsky held that the only hope of communism surviving in the Soviet Union was to export the revolution to the rest of Europe. Only in the context of European communism could Russian communism survive since Soviet Russia was too backward and, surrounded by hostile capitalist powers, would not endure on its own. Stalin argued that fomenting revolution abroad would serve only to antagonise the capitalist powers and give them an excuse to intervene once again in Soviet affairs and perhaps destroy what had been achieved. He held that what the Soviet Union most needed was a period of peace in order to build 'socialism in one country'. Only when socialism had been achieved at home could Soviet Russia think of promoting the cause of international communism.

'SOCIALISM IN ONE COUNTRY'

Stalin was more interested in the future of the Soviet Union, and the need to defend what had already been gained, than in promoting world revolution. His policy had far greater appeal to the ordinary Russian than had Trotsky's. The Russians had had enough of revolution and war since 1914 and Stalin's policy offered them peace. In 1917 the Bolsheviks had seized power and had grimly held on to it during the civil war, in the hope that it would spark off a European revolution. When this had not materialised by 1924, the Bolsheviks found themselves in a cul de sac. Stalin's theory of 'socialism in one country' appeared to offer them a way out. It gave a fresh impetus as well as a new direction to the subsequent history of the Soviet Union. Backward Russia could lead the world if this theory was put into practice. What precisely did it mean?

Stalin justified his proposed new development by appealing to Russian history:

> We must increase the tempo as much as it is within our powers and possibilities. This is dictated to us by our obligations to the working class of the world. To slacken the tempo would mean to fall behind, and those who fall behind get beaten. No, we refuse to be beaten. One feature of the history of the old Russia was the continual beatings she suffered because of her backwardness. She was beaten by the Mongol Khans. She was beaten by the Turkish Beys. She was beaten by the Polish gentry. She was beaten by the British and French capitalists. She was beaten by the Japanese. All beat her, because of her backwardness, military backwardness, cultural backwardness, political backwardness, agricultural backwardness. They beat her because it was profitable and could be done with impunity. Do you remember the words of the poet Nekrasov, 'you are poor and abundant, mighty and impotent, Mother Russia'. Such is the law of the exploiters — to beat the backward and weak. It is the jungle law of capitalism. That is why we must no longer lag behind. . . . We are fifty or a hundred years behind the advanced countries. We must make good this distance in ten years. Either we do it or we shall be crushed. This is what our obligations to the workers and peasants of the USSR dictate to us.

Industrialisation, then, was a means of survival in a hostile capitalist world; Russia must be dragged into the twentieth century or perish. But how could industrialisation be achieved if the vast majority of people lived on small patches of land scarcely producing enough food for themselves, much less enough to feed the increasing numbers of industrial workers? Moreover, the richer peasants, the *kulaks*, kept agricultural prices high, a policy totally against the interests of the industrial workers and the town-dwellers.

Besides these considerations, there was also the fact that the Soviet Union could not industrialise without money; it was impossible to get credit from abroad. The only way was to increase agricultural exports. This could not be done under the existing uneconomic system, where the land was divided into twenty-five million peasant holdings. Everything pointed towards 'collectivisation' of the land. Collective farms were to be large units in which large-scale methods of pro-

Stalin meets workers at a collective farm in Armenia.

duction would be put into operation with the aid of machinery. The peasants would work the collectives under state direction and control. It would mean the end of private ownership and have the added benefit of getting rid of the *kulaks*, a class hostile to Soviet communism. This union of economic necessity and communist theory meant the inevitable liquidation of the *kulaks* and the releasing of peasants from the land so that they might swell the ranks of the workers needed for industrialisation.

Collectivisation

Stalin became obsessed with the idea of collectivisation and saw it as the answer to all Soviet problems. The first move was to declare collectivisaton by example under the first of the famous five-year plans (1928–33) for both agriculture and industry. Soon it became obvious that this was not having the desired effects, so Stalin decided to use force and to wage an all-out war on *kulaks*. 'We must annihilate them as a social class,' he said, and his officials did so with ruthless efficiency. The lucky ones fled the Soviet Union, but the majority were exiled to Siberia where many died from starvation, disease or the bitter cold. Others were sent to enforced labour camps and new industrial sites beyond the Urals. For three years terror and repression reigned. On one side stood the state, embodied in Stalin's officials, backed up by the Red Army and the police; on the other were the *kulaks*, who retaliated by burning their crops and killing their cattle —

preferable to handing them over to the state.

'KILL, it's not ours now!
KILL, the State butchers will do it
if we don't.
KILL, they won't give you meat to
eat in the collective farms.'

Mikhail Sholokhov: *Virgin Soil Upturned*

The following table shows the drastic reduction in livestock and grain during the first five-year plan.

LIVESTOCK
(million)

	1928	1929	1930	1931	1932	1933
Cattle	70.5	67.1	52.5	47.9	40.7	38.4
Pigs	26.0	20.4	13.6	14.4	11.6	12.1
Sheep & goats	146.7	147.0	108.8	77.7	52.1	50.1

GRAIN HARVEST
(million tonnes)

1928	1929	1930	1931	1932	1933
73.3	71.7	83.5	69.5	69.6	68.4

Despite the near-famine conditions that collectivisation created, the policy continued. In 1928 only two per cent of the country's farmland had been collectivised, but by 1932 the figure had reached sixty-two per cent. In 1940 Stalin declared that collectivisation was complete; that 75 million people were now working on 243,000 collective farms and nearly 4,000 state farms. But collectivisation meant a considerable flight from the land into the towns and cities. In 1925 some twenty per cent of the population lived in towns and cities, but by 1939 this figure had risen to thirty per cent.

Collectivisation had been achieved at a terrible cost, the full facts of which may never be revealed. The peasants had gambled that if they refused to grow food, Stalin would abandon the idea of forcing them into collectives. They lost their gamble, for, sooner than give in, Stalin let them starve. Millions died of hunger, malnutrition and disease. Eventually, however, Stalin did make concessions. At first he blamed the problem on the excesses of his officials, and then he announced that the peasant in the collective could have 'a small private allotment not exceeding two-and-a-half acres, and a cow.' This victory for the peasants has been jealously guarded ever since.

Stalin, ignoring the human tragedy that it had caused, claimed that collectivisation was a success because the Soviet Union suffered no more famines. The collectives did grow more food — at least thirty million extra tons of grain. Collectivisation also meant that more modern methods could be applied: tractors and fertilisers were introduced for the first time. Yet the problem of producing sufficient food continued to haunt the Soviet rulers. The peasant had no sense of participation in the collective and reserved his energies for his own private allotment. From the very beginning, the private plot produced a significant proportion of the nation's food and the peasant's income.

Industrialisation

The industrial revolution was comparable to that in agriculture and the heart of this effort was embodied in a series of five-year plans. Soviet Russia was hurled into one gigantic struggle to transform itself into an advanced industrial nation. By a curious irony, the Soviet Union seemed to be mastering its fate at precisely the same time as the capitalist countries were in the depths of economic depression. While unemployment was the scourge of the capitalist West, there was a labour shortage in socialist Russia.

The first five-year plan (1928–33) laid down goals for economic expansion. The emphasis was placed on capital goods: coal, steel, iron and machine tools were to increase their output by three hundred per cent. Consumer goods were scheduled to increase by six hundred per cent.

No foreign capital was available because Lenin had repudiated all the foreign debts of tsarist Russia. The Soviet government found the necessary capital by the ruthless accumulation of profits from the state farms and the limitation of personal consumption. The produce of the state farms was bought at one eighth of its market price, and was sold to the public at a 700 per cent profit. The targets were quite unrealistic and panic and disorganisation occurred because failure to achieve goals might result in charges of idleness or sabotage.

For the second five-year plan (1933–38) more realistic targets were set. As a consequence, and because unskilled workers were becoming more competent, the plan worked more smoothly. However it is difficult to state its precise achievements because most Soviet statistics are either unobtainable or are overstated. Since the period of the second plan coincided with the rise of Nazi Germany, the main concern was armaments production, and many factories were sited beyond the Urals, out of reach of any future German invasion. With the aid of highly paid foreign technicians, excellent growth rates were achieved in the engineering and metalworking sectors; these diminished the Soviet Union's dependence on other countries for her capital goods. The output of coal and electricity also made giant strides, but the increase in the production of oil, iron ore and textiles was disappointing. Moreover, with such emphasis on armaments and capital goods, the production of consumer goods was greatly neglected.

The third five-year plan (1938–41) was cut short by the German invasion in June 1941, but by then the main lines of collectivisation and industrialisation had been well laid down.

During the period of the plans, the Soviet Union underwent a revolution far more tumultuous than that of 1917. The entire workforce was organised in one gigantic effort to achieve the maximum results. In this way were created the vast iron works of Magnitogorsk, the hydroelectric plant on the river Dnieper, the huge dams on the Volga and Don, and the great canals connecting the White Sea with the Baltic and Moscow with the Volga. Large tractor factories were established to revolutionise farming on the collectives. Railways were built in Soviet Asia, machine works in Smolensk and the Moscow region, and a motor plant at Nijni Novgorod. The country's mineral resources were also fully exploited: iron ore at Krivoi Rog, coal in the Donetsk basin and manganese in the Ukraine. Simultaneously towns and cities were rapidly developed. Moscow, Leningrad and Kharkov expanded, as did lesser known places such as Minsk, Tashkent, Vladivostok, Sverdlovsk and Novosibirsk (map, p.172).

This vast development turned Soviet Russia into a great industrial power. Yet when the size of her population is taken into account, the USSR's level of industrialisation falls below that of the western powers.

		Million Tonnes			
	Population (Millions)	**Pig Iron**	**Steel**	**Coal**	**Electricity (million kW)**
Soviet Russia	170	14.9	18.4	164.6	39,600
USA	131	31.9	47.2	395	115,900
Germany	73	18.3	22.7	384	55,000
Britain	47	6.7	10.3	277	30,700

However, when the backward state of tsarist Russia is considered (p.52), it is clear that Soviet Russia's progress was phenomenal. It was brought about by the large-scale planning of the State Planning Commission, working under the direct control of the Communist Party and the Soviet government. The methods used were a combination of ruthless coercion, communist propaganda and incentives. Old Russia was transformed in a few short years and in its stead was created the world's first socialist industrial state.

The Soviet Worker

The Soviet Union was the first country to identify the worker with the national effort, and consequently the majority of workers gave of their best to build the new society. The government bolstered the workers' enthusiasm with constant exhortations from the press, the radio and gigantic advertising hoardings. A constant race ensued to outstrip both their fellow workers and the previous year's production. Prizes and honours were bestowed upon record-breakers. A worker's greatest ambition was to receive the award of the 'Order of Lenin' or the title 'Hero of Socialist Labour'. In 1935 a mining team led by Alexis Stakhanov, with good equipment and easy seams, set up an all-time record by drilling 102 tons of coal in a six-hour shift. Workers in other mines and factories were exhorted to apply his methods; the reward was higher pay and other privileges. The 'Stakhanovite movement' was born.

Education was an essential part of the five-year plans. In a peasant land with no skilled labour to draw from, Stalin had to attract skilled labour from Europe and North America by offering enormous salaries. But he was determined to replace them with native labour as quickly as possible and gave priority to the extension of educational facilities. New universities and technological colleges trained hundreds of thousands of engineers, scientists, doctors and teachers, while all citizens were to have at least elementary education. Stalin also offered incentives — pensions and differential rates — which encouraged the worker to achieve more in an economy that otherwise lacked the profit motive of capitalist countries.

A New Class System

The policy of giving extra-high wages in fields where there was a shortage of skilled labour inevitably led to the creation of a new class structure in the Soviet Union. This was a contradiction of the communist principle of equal pay for all men and women, irrespective of the type of work done.

At the lowest level of society, the peasants and the unskilled workers languished, in the middle were the skilled workers in industry, while the new upper class consisted of scientists, engineers, managers and civil servants. Since this new class owed its position to the state, Stalin hoped that they would support and promote the communist regime in general, and himself in particular. He constantly reminded them that they owed their privileged position to him; but rather than fostering increased efficiency, this had the opposite effect — creating a feeling of insecurity and lack of initiative.

THE GREAT PURGES 1933–38

For a while after the revolution there had been considerable freedom of speech and writing, much more than under the tsars, but Stalin eventually enforced rigid censorship. History was rewritten to exaggerate his own part in the revolution. Stalin tolerated no opposition to his plans for collectivisation and industrialisation. Those who resisted were imprisoned, exiled or shot. Neither did he allow any political opposition, as evidenced by his elimination of Trotsky, Kamenev and Zinoviev. Yet it must be remembered that the first five years of his rule did not witness a reign of terror like that in the aftermath of the French Revolution. Out of the millions who died as the result of the five-year plans, only a minority were deliberately murdered. Most died from carelessness, official callousness or plain inefficiency. The ordinary citizen was relatively safe provided he worked hard and carried out orders. But in 1933 a new black phase of Soviet history began.

On 21 April a resolution was passed by the central committee of the party identifying six categories of 'undesirable' elements:

(i) enemies of communism engaged in fomenting discord in the party
(ii) hypocrites, who at heart wished to sabotage party policy

(iii) those who disregarded party discipline
(iv) bourgeois degenerates
(v) those who served their own ends, such as the over-ambitious and the careerists
(vi) moral degenerates, such as drunkards and idlers.

A Purging Commission was set up to root out these 'undesirables'. Those found guilty were generally imprisoned or deprived of their party membership. By the end of 1933, it is estimated that one-third of the party either had been expelled or had left of their own accord.

During 1934 there was a complete lull in the purging process. This may have been because Hitler had emerged in Germany and Stalin was too preoccupied with readjusting his foreign relations. But on 1 December 1934, a new and more serious round of purges began. On that date Sergei Kirov, leader of the Leningrad Soviet, was assassinated. Kirov was a senior member of the *Politburo* and a likely contender for the leadership.

A young student communist, Nikolayev, admitted to the deed, but it has been suggested that Stalin masterminded the assassination because he feared Kirov's rivalry. In either event, Stalin now used Kirov's death as an excuse for a new wave of purges. While the purges of 1933 concentrated on ordinary party members, this new wave fell on those in high positions: old Bolsheviks of the revolutionary era, Red Army generals suspected of retaining loyalty to Trotsky, and senior officials who might be becoming too powerful. A reign of terror, arrests and executions followed. An important feature of this second phase of purges was the number of people who were prepared to denounce each other.

In August 1936 a third phase began, characterised by a series of public show trials. The prosecutor, Andrei Vyshinsky, accused all suspects of having fomented a plot against

Lavrienti Beria, Chief of Police in Soviet Russia from 1938 until his death in 1954.

the party leaders and the Soviet state. The trials were the brainchild of G.G. Yagoda, the head of the NKVD, the secret police. His tactic was to secure confessions through torture and false promises. While these trials were in progress, a constant barrage of accusation was kept up in the party newspaper, *Pravda*. Headlines such as:

> SPIES: DESPICABLE HIRELINGS OF FASCISM, TRAITORS TO THEIR COUNTRY — SHOOT THEM

were quite common.

Zinoviev and Kamenev were the first to be put on trial and be found guilty. They were shot in the cellars of the Lubyanka prison. Even Yagoda himself did not survive Stalin's suspicion. In 1938 he was accused of having conspired against Stalin, was put on trial and executed. His place was taken by N.I. Yezhov, but he too met the same fate. Stalin dismissed him as the chief of the secret police in

November 1938, had him committed to a lunatic asylum and later had him executed. The new chief of police, Lavrenti Beria, became the most feared man in Soviet Russia and remained in office until even after Stalin's death in 1953 (p.394).

When the purges and show trials ended in 1938, it was clear that the casualties had been immense. In the Red Army, three out of five marshals, including the commander in chief, Tukhachevsky, three of the four full generals, all of the twelve lieutenant-generals, sixty of the sixty-seven corps commanders and 136 of the 199 divisional commanders, were shot. In the navy the purge is said to have been more extreme. In the Communist Party, of the seven men of Lenin's original *Politburo*, only one remained alive in Soviet Russia – Stalin, and one in exile — Trotsky. But Trotsky too would fall victim to Stalin's fear (p.232). Of the twenty-one members of the Central Committee in 1912, only two remained: Stalin and Madame Aleksandra Kollontai. Even Stalin's own cousins and in-laws were victims of the purges; and perhaps most callous of all, his best friend and adviser, Yenukidze. Trotsky wrote from exile: 'Cain what hast thou done to they brother Abel? After this hateful murder, Cain Djugashvili shall be thy name in Russian history.'

Historians have attempted to explain the motives behind the purges, but have reached no satisfactory conclusion. It is said that after his wife's suicide in 1932, Stalin underwent a psychological change and thereafter never trusted anyone. Other explanations focus on the impact of the rise of Hitler's Germany, with its avowed aim of destroying communism and creating *Lebensraum* in the east. Stalin may have feared that in the inevitable war with fascism, his opponents would seize the opportunity to overthrow him, just as he and the Bolsheviks had seized the opportunity of World War I to overthrow the tsarist regime. For the sake of the Soviet Union and for his own sake, Stalin was determined that all opposition (real or imaginary) must be eliminated.

THE SOVIET CONSTITUTION

While the purges were in progress, Stalin introduced a new constitution in 1936. Anxious to appear as a great philosopher-statesman, he declared that his constitution was the only truly democratic one in the world. Everyone over the age of eighteen (except priests and 'bourgeois elements') could vote by secret ballot, but choice was limited to the candidates put forward by the local soviet. The parliament was divided into two houses: the Soviet of the Union, representing the people in proportion to population, and the Soviet of Nationalities, representing the individual states of the USSR. Yet real power remained with the Communist Party and especially with its central committee. Within the central committee, an inner group, the *Politburo*, exercised the greatest power of all. Stalin continued to be general secretary of the Communist Party, personally controlling the entire apparatus. In effect Soviet Russia was Stalin's Russia.

FOREIGN POLICY

One of the basic assumptions underlying the Bolshevik revolution in 1917 was that all Europe would follow the Soviet Union's example. But by 1920 it was obvious that this was not going to happen — at least not in the immediate future. The Bolshevik gamble of seizing power in the hope that it would spark off a European revolution had failed and so they found themselves in a dilemma. Therefore, Soviet foreign policy, after the war of intervention by the capitalist west, was for the most part defensive. The regime would have to defend the revolution in a hostile capitalist world and win a breathing space for itself in order to build and catch up. There was hostility on both sides: the capitalist countries had financed the armed forces of counter-revolution in an attempt to overthrow the new Soviet state, while the Soviets spared no effort to instigate revolution in the capitalist world and also in their colonial lands. Western Europe, however, was split into victors and vanquished, and Lenin saw his opportunity to get a foothold in the capitalist world by a trade treaty with Germany and finally in April 1922 by the Treaty of Rapallo. The two black sheep of Europe had come together in a treaty that greatly alarmed the rest of Europe (p.195).

The Treaty of Rapallo had advantages for the Soviet Union and for German diplomacy. For Soviet Russia it meant that the western powers no longer had the capacity to dominate events in central and eastern Europe. More especially, it meant that Germany would provide the buffer zone between the USSR and the West, but, above all, there could not now be a united capitalist attack upon the Soviet Union. On the German side, Rapallo had the advantage of side-tracking the disarmament clauses of the Treaty of Versailles by allowing its army to train and rearm on Russian soil. The Treaty of Rapallo became the anchor of Soviet foreign policy until 1934, during which time she improved her relations through agreements with many western states.

During the struggle for power after 1924, Trotsky and his followers still believed that exporting the revolution was the only hope of its survival in the Soviet Union, but it was Stalin's policy of 'socialism in one country', backed up by the Treaty of Rapallo, that won the day (p.195).

In 1928, when Stalin commenced his five-year plan, the chaos it created at home meant that he could not afford to arouse hostility abroad. As a result, foreign policy under Maksim Litvinov took on a peace-loving image, and by 1930 the Soviet Union had become an accepted member of international society.

With the rise of Hitler (p.200), Soviet Russia was obliged to recast her foreign policy. Rapallo was now dead and the Soviets were obliged to find a *rapprochement* with the western democracies. In 1934, with the aid of France, she joined the League of Nations and became a firm advocate of the need for collective security. What the Soviet Union feared most of all was to be caught on her own in a war against Nazi Germany.

When the Spanish Civil War broke out in 1936, Stalin aided the anti-Franco forces, although he realised that the triumph of communism in Spain in the midst of a hostile capitalist western Europe was not a practical proposition. His policy therefore was to send sufficient aid to keep the war going in the hope of distracting the fascist powers for as long as possible (p.265).

After the Munich Agreement in September 1938 (p.290), Stalin became convinced that Britain and France were not going to stand up to Hitler's expansion. Worse still, he feared that they might be secretly encouraging him to expand eastwards so that he would destroy communism.

When Hitler absorbed the remainder of Czechoslovakia in March 1939, Stalin realised that the only way to save his country was to come to an agreement with Hitler. The anti-German Litvinov was dismissed and Vyacheslev Molotov took his place as foreign minister. On 23 August 1939 the Nazi-Soviet Pact was signed in Moscow (p.293). It was to last for ten years, during which time both powers agreed to remain neutral in a war in which the other might be engaged. The pact also contained several secret clauses which provided for the partition of Poland, and the recognition of Finland, Bessarabia and the Baltic states as coming within the Soviet sphere of influence (p.294). Stalin was under no illusions that Hitler would respect the ten-year non-aggression pact, but despite this the treaty had its advantages. It meant that the Soviet Union would not have to go to war in

1939. More important, it meant that she could now create a buffer zone against the inevitable attack. But whatever its advantages, the Nazi-Soviet Pact has been described as the most bizarre and cynical pact in modern history. Two irreconcilable systems, fascism and communism, were now in alliance; and despite protestations of anti-fascism during the 1930s, when war broke out in 1939, the Soviet Union was an ally of Nazi Germany.

Study Assignments and Essays

1. *Critically examine the steps by which Stalin came to power in the Soviet Union.*
2. *What was the thinking behind the policy of 'socialism in one country' and what did it entail?*
3. *What were the political, economic and ideological motives for collectivisation?*
4. *Examine the main features of Soviet dustrialisation in the period 1928–39.*
5. *Examine the social (class) structure of Soviet society under Stalin.*
6. *Write an essay on two of the following: (i) Leon Trotsky 1924–33; (ii) Soviet foreign policy under Stalin 1928–39; (iii) The great purges; (iv) The Soviet constitution; (v) The Soviet Union in 1939 — socialist or state capitalist?*

France Between the Wars

19

. . . I will show you something different from either
Your shadow at morning striding behind you
Or your shadow at evening rising to meet you;
I will show you fear in a handful of dust.

T.S. Eliot, *The Waste Land*

DURING THE Great War, French political parties sank their differences and produced a united front against German attack. But with the end of war, the old political divisions re-emerged and were further complicated by a desire for national security and the vexed question of reparation payments. On the right the monarchists had disappeared, while on the left a communist party had been formed. Between 1918 and the destruction of the Third Republic in May 1940, French democracy produced 44 different governments and more than twenty prime ministers. Nevertheless, France clung to the Republic's constitution, dealt with each new crisis as it arose, and retained its reputation as a liberal democracy.

THE BLOC NATIONAL GOVERNMENT 1920–24

The election of November 1919 was dominated by the issues of anti-Germanism and the fear of communism. The right-wing parties won decisively and the seventy-nine-year-old Clemenceau became prime minister of the *bloc national* government. This government was anti-German, anti-communist and in favour of reparations and the rights of property. In January 1920 Clemenceau retired and was succeeded by Alexandre Millerand. In September Millerand became president and Auguste Briand took over as prime minister.

The main problem facing Briand and his government was national defence. American rejection of the League of Nations (p.281) and her failure to ratify the peace treaties had come as a severe shock to France. At Versailles (p.181) France had agreed to abandon her claim to all land west of the Rhine, the Rhine itself and its bridges, in exchange for a joint British and American guarantee of support in the event of a German attack. But this was now cancelled: the United States was in isolation and Britain said her own guarantee was valid only in the context of American support. Now France had neither the Rhine frontier nor the Anglo-American guarantee as security against a resurgent Germany. She felt cheated, alone and vulnerable; and a search for alternative forms of security began. This took two forms.

The first plan was to encircle Germany with a system of alliances, embracing all the states that owed their existence to, or otherwise benefited from, the peace settlement and which, therefore, agreed with France that it should be maintained. France signed military alliances with Belgium in 1920 and with Poland in 1921. Diplomatic ties were also established with Czechoslovakia, Yugoslavia and Romania, and this became known as the 'Little Entente'. But these new alliances were built at the expense of a deterioration in France's relations with her former allies, Britain, Russia and Italy. British public opinion was inclined towards pacifism and her government was more reluctant than ever to make any advance with France, now that France was committed to other European states, a situation that might embroil Britain in Polish or Czech problems. The Soviet Union was alienated by French support for Poland during the Russo-Polish war (p.187), while Italy disliked France joining with Yugoslavia on account of Fiume (p.208).

The second plan was to demand prompt and full payment of annual reparation moneys from Germany. These payments would not only contribute to the country's reconstruction after the ravages of war, but also serve to keep Germany in economic decline. As long as Germany was obliged to pay exorbitant annual sums, she would never be able to rise up and seek revenge against France for the Versailles settlement. Thus, for France, reparations had a security as well as a financial dimension.

In 1921, the Reparations Committee, set up at the peace conference, fixed the sum to be paid by Germany at £6,600 million, payable in annual instalments of £100 million. The Germans could not pay such huge sums in gold, and since payment in goods and services was not acceptable to the French because it would create unemployment at home, the reparations question produced a stalemate. Britain was sympathetic to Germanys' plight, but the bloc national government, led by the anti-German, Raymond Poincaré, was determined that Germany should meet her obligations in full.

In January 1923, when Germany failed to meet her next reparation payments, Poincaré sent troops across the Rhine to occupy the Ruhr coal-mining districts (p.195). Yet this occupation, in which the Belgians also took part, served only to create difficulties for France. From January to August the Ruhr was the scene of undeclared war as the German workers, on orders from Berlin, resorted to passive resistance, which soon led to strikes, sabotage and factory riots. The French imposed martial law and brought in workers from France to replace the strikers. But the French workers were not familiar with the German equipment and had little success in running the industries.

The Ruhr occupation led to a rapid deterioration of the German mark and by November it stood at 400,000 million against the Austrian dollar. In September the German government was forced to resign and Gustav Stresemann became chancellor and foreign minister. Stresemann called off the passive resistance in the Ruhr and resumed the reparation payments (p.195). The British prime minister, Stanley Baldwin, impressed on the United States the need for a new settlement and in January 1924 a committee under Charles G. Dawes was set up to devise a more sensible approach to the problem of reparations. Nevertheless the Ruhr invasion had cost the bloc national government many supporters, and in the 1924 election, a new left-wing government of radicals and socialists took office.

THE CARTEL DES GAUCHES 1924–26

The new coalition of radicals and socialists were known as the *cartel des gauches* (combination of the left). This government adopted a more moderate attitude towards Germany and accepted the Dawes Plan (p.196). In turn, this led to an easing of tension and eventually in October 1924 French and Belgian troops were withdrawn from the Ruhr.

Yet although the policies of the *cartel des gauches* were restoring calm, efforts at security did not stop with earlier treaties. Confidence in the ability of the League of Nations to guarantee French security was seriously undermined by the absence of the United States, so new solutions were sought to the problem of national defence. The first plan put forward was the Draft Treaty of Mutual Assistance. This provided for all member states of the League of Nations to assist a fellow member under attack, but the *obligation* to assist was to be confined to those states in continental Europe in which the attack had taken place. The plan failed because of British objections. Britain argued that because her Dominions occupied a part of every continent, she would become involved in disputes all over the globe.

Perhaps the greatest diplomatic achievement of the *cartel des gauches* was the Locarno Pact of 1925 (p.199). This was a momentous pact in that it brought together the likely parties in any future dispute and ushered in a period of peace and understanding between France and Germany. The problem of the British empire becoming involved in a Euro-

One of many massive concrete forts built along the Maginot Line to protect France's eastern frontier from a German attack.

pean war was overcome by exempting the Dominions from any obligations unless they voluntarily wished to participate.

GOVERNMENT OF NATIONAL UNION 1926–29

The *cartel's* record in foreign affairs was not enough to hold the support of the radicals. When the franc, which had stood at seventy to the pound in 1924, dropped to 250 to the pound in July 1926, the radicals, fearing a complete collapse of the economy, switched their support and the *cartel* fell.

The new government of national union, headed by Poincaré, and formed of a coalition of the radicals and the right wing, immediately secured emergency powers to rule by decree. The franc was devalued to one-fifth of its pre-war value, which stabilised the currency and restored public confidence. Under Poincaré's leadership, good relations with Germany (now a member of the League of Nations) continued. In August 1928 the Pact of Paris (Kellogg-Briand Pact) was signed. This pact, also signed by Germany and the Soviet Union, renounced war as an instrument of national policy. That same year France reduced the period of compulsory military service to twelve months. On the other hand, it was decided to strengthen her eastern frontier by a system of fortifications known as the Maginot Line, running from Longwy (opposite Luxembourg) to the Swiss border (map, p.286).

Poincaré's government gained the confidence of a sufficient number of people to survive the 1928 election. However, Poincaré himself was forced to resign because of ill-health in July 1929, although right-wing governments continued until the next election in 1932.

THE YEARS OF CRISIS 1929–36

The seven years after Poincaré's resignation witnessed a high turnover of governments. The world depression following the Wall Street crash of 1929 came relatively late to France, but it did cause serious distress. French exports, which were largely luxuries, were no longer in demand in other countries. Furthermore, cheap imports from other countries, desperate to sell at any price, hit the home market. Tourism also dried up, and by 1932 unemployment had risen to 433,000, excluding the 600,000 foreign workers who had left France. The government cut salaries, reduced ex-servicemen's pensions, closed down public works and taxed consumer goods.

But these policies failed to get parliamentary support and governments changed rapidly. The worst period was the twenty months between May 1932 and February 1934 when six different governments held office. Such instability served to discredit parliamentary democracy as incompetent, and gave the opportunity for several right-wing (fascist) leagues to gain support and mount a campaign against democracy.

Right-Wing Leagues

Although many anti-democratic right-wing groups came and went during the inter-war period, the four most important were:

1. *Jeunesses Patriotes* (Young Patriots), founded in 1924 by Pierre Taittinger as an anti-communist group. It derived much of its inspiration from Mussolini's fascist movement, and its members wore blue raincoats and berets. By 1933 it claimed to have a membership of 90,000, 6,000 of them in Paris.
2. *Solidarité Française*, founded in 1933 by François Coty, the perfume and talcum-powder tycoon. It had its own journal, *L'Ami du Peuple*, and was violently anti-semitic.
3. *L'Action Française*, founded in 1898 by Charles Maurras and Léon Daudet and still led by them in the 1930s. It was originally set up as a royalist group dedicated to the restoration of the monarchy, but by the 1930s it was a dying force, looking to the past rather than to the future.
4. The *Croix du Feu*, founded in 1927 by Colonel de la Rocque as an organisation for ex-servicemen. It naturally was more military than the other groups and many saw it as a private army. It did have considerable support among the middle classes for almost ten years. This was due to its discipline, its vague programme, and its position as the chief target of socialists and communists.

Membership of the leagues offered those on the right much the same as communism offered those on the left: an opportunity for action, the camaraderie of belonging to an elite, and the charismatic attraction of a leader. Yet, despite their anti-democratic nature, there was never any real danger that the leagues could overthrow the Third Republic and establish a right-wing dictatorship, as had happened in Italy and Germany. The groups never gained a mass following because they failed to unite and also because the depression had not hit France with the same devastation as it had Germany. In fact their various campaigns against democracy might have died out had it not been for the 'Stavisky Affair' in 1934.

The Stavisky Affair

Serge Alexandre Stavisky (1886–1934) was the son of Russian-Jewish parents who had come to France about 1900. He grew up a professional swindler, earning money from the seamy side of Parisian life, but he also ingratiated himself with those in authority, such as police chiefs, judges and government ministers. In 1927 Stavisky had been arrested and charged with the theft of 7 million francs, but he was released on bail pending trial. By 1933, he was still on bail, his trial having been postponed on nineteen occasions with the help of influential friends. In 1933 he overreached himself by floating a loan of 200 million francs worth of fraudulent bonds, allegedly to finance a municipal pawnshop in Bayonne. In December 1933 his scheme collapsed and a warrant was issued for his arrest. However, Stavisky could not be found, until finally on 8 January 1934 he was discovered dead, apparently having committed suicide. Few believed that he had taken his own life; it was more probable that he had been murdered to prevent him from naming his influential protectors.

The prime minister at the time, Camille Chautemps, tried to keep the matter quiet; his brother-in-law was head of the judicial department responsible over the years for not having brought Stavisky to a speedy trial. To make matters worse, Chautemps refused demands for a committee of inquiry to investigate the affair. By this time the rightist leagues were organising large demonstrations in protest against government corruption.

On 27 January Chautemps was forced to resign, and Edouard Daladier took his place. To appease the leftists, Daladier dismissed the prefect of police in Paris, Jean Chiappe, who was well-known for his right-wing sympathies. This further enraged the right. On 6 February, Daladier's first parliamentary appearance as premier, disorder broke out in the Chamber of Deputies, and league demonstrations in Paris turned into a riot. When the police finally restored order, fifteen people had died and 328 were seriously injured. Daladier was forced to resign, and a new national union coalition under Gaston Doumergue, a well known right-winger, took office.

Doumergue's government ordered an investigation into the Stavisky affair. The findings put much of the blame on certain sections of the police and the judiciary, and some seventeen deputies who were found to have had dealings with Stavisky. Public interest was kept at fever pitch when on 21 February Albert Prince, the head of the committee of inquiry, was found fastened to a railway line, badly mutilated. Again, there were charges by the right of corruption, but the mystery was never solved.

The Stavisky affair, and the riots it generated, intensified the bitter struggle between right and left. The right were incensed with the weak and corrupt radical-socialist governments, while the left believed that the leagues had organised the unrest in order to overthrow the Republic. But the most important consequence was the traumatic effect it had on the left. Radicals, socialists and communists realised that they would have to sink their differences in a common front; otherwise a right-wing group, such as the *Croix du Feu*, would overthrow parliamentary government and install itself as a fascist dictatorship. Hitler's rise to power was an obvious example of what could happen in France. Moreover, the Comintern (p.170), on orders from Moscow, had now recast its policy towards national governments. Instead of communists working for the destruction of parliamentary democracy, they were now urged to find common cause with other left-wing groups in an effort to keep fascism at bay.

THE POPULAR FRONT 1936–38

In July 1935 a common front was formed between radicals, socialists and communists and by January 1936 an agreed programme had been formulated. It called for a return to a system of collective security against fascist expansion, the consolidation of the Franco-Soviet pact (p.224), the dissolution of all French right-wing leagues, and extensive measures of economic and social reform. The slogan of the popular front was 'bread, peace and liberty' and was ideally suited to a country beset by so many problems.

When an election was held in June 1936, the *Croix du Feu* refused to run candidates. The combined seats of the popular front came to 380, as against 237 for their opponents, and it formed a government of radicals and socialists, with communist support in the chamber. Léon Blum, a Jewish barrister and socialist, became prime minister.

The new government was immediately embarrassed by a rash of strikes. The victory of the popular front had led many militant workers to believe that far-reaching socialist change was imminent, especially the nationalisation of industry. Beginning in the aircraft factories, sit-down strikes spread from industry to industry, paralysing France's economic life. Blum's first task was to restore industrial peace and reassure employers that they would not be expropriated. He called a conference of employers and union leaders and persuaded employers to make far-reaching concessions. His argument was that if the purchasing power of the masses was increased, economic stagnation would end and both worker and employer would benefit. Accordingly, the agreement provided for an average pay increase of twelve per cent, holidays with pay, and a forty-hour week. To help the peasantry, a wheat board was established to fix a fair price for the producer. These changes marked a turning point in French social history and laid the foundations of a welfare state.

Blum's government devalued the franc by twenty-five per cent in an effort to make French exports more competitive and to encourage tourism, but these measures did not have the desired effect. Devaluation of the franc, coupled with increased government spending, led to inflation; and by the end of 1936 prices had risen by seventeen per cent. Employers distrusted Blum and were reluctant to carry out new investment or expansion; as a result, unemployment remained high. Moreover, the right were still a threat to Blum and, even after the government had the leagues declared illegal, they re-emerged in other guises. The *Croix du Feu* turned itself into a 'constitutional' party, known as the *Parti Social Français*; by 1938 it had a membership of three million. The *Action Française* set up the *Comité Secret d'Action Révolutionnaire* (CSAR) and was also known as the *Cogoulards* (Hoods) because of its secrecy. It was in fact a secret military organisation whose objective was the establishment of a fascist dictatorship to forestall what it saw as the imminent threat of a communist revolution. It received substantial financial backing from big business, especially the tyre manufacturers, Michelin.

But the worst problems facing the popular front government concerned foreign affairs. The outbreak of the Spanish Civil War (p.264) placed the government in a dilemma. They naturally would have liked to aid the republican side against Franco, but it was felt that this would deepen the divisions in French society. The right were in favour of Franco and depicted the left as dupes of the Soviet Union. As the war continued, it made the French radicals reconsider their association with the communists, who had stayed out of government and had exploited the mistakes of the popular front.

By February 1937 the government was under increasing pressure from the extremes of left and right. Industrial peace had not been maintained, and the nationalisation of certain industries had antagonised the right. Blum came to feel that confidence could be restored by calling a halt to reform and cutting government expenditure. But this merely encouraged the extremists to fresh acts of violence. When a communist mob attacked a right-wing meeting at Clichy, the police were forced to open fire and six people were killed. The trade union organisation, *Confédération Générale du Travail* (CGT), called for a national strike. In June Blum was defeated in the Senate on a proposal to enforce foreign exchange controls, and his government resigned.

For the following ten months France experienced a series of different coalitions of the left which served only to demonstrate the inherent instability of French politics. By March 1938, when Hitler's troops marched into Austria, the French government was in disarray. In April the radicals broke from the popular front and supported the formation of a right-wing coalition of national defence under Daladier.

GOVERNMENT OF NATIONAL DEFENCE 1938–40

By 1939, foreign affairs had come to dominate the government's attention. As the war clouds gathered, French defeatism became more apparent. Daladier and his foreign minister, Georges Bonnet, were content to follow Britain's lead in an attempt to appease Hitler (p.258). Only the communists determinedly attacked appeasement. The right wing were not unfavourable to fascism and had previously declared 'better Hitler than Blum'. The newspaper *L'Action Française* declared '*À bas la guerre*' (Down with war). The genuine fear of going to war, coupled with the feeling on the right that France had less to fear from Hitler than from French communism, created a mood of pacifism and defeatism in France, which made Daladier's government incapable of any coherent policy.

On Daladier's return to Paris after Munich in September 1938 (p.290), he was hailed as a hero; the feeling was that he and Neville Chamberlain had averted war. But when Hitler occupied the rest of Czechoslovakia in March 1939, the folly of appeasement became

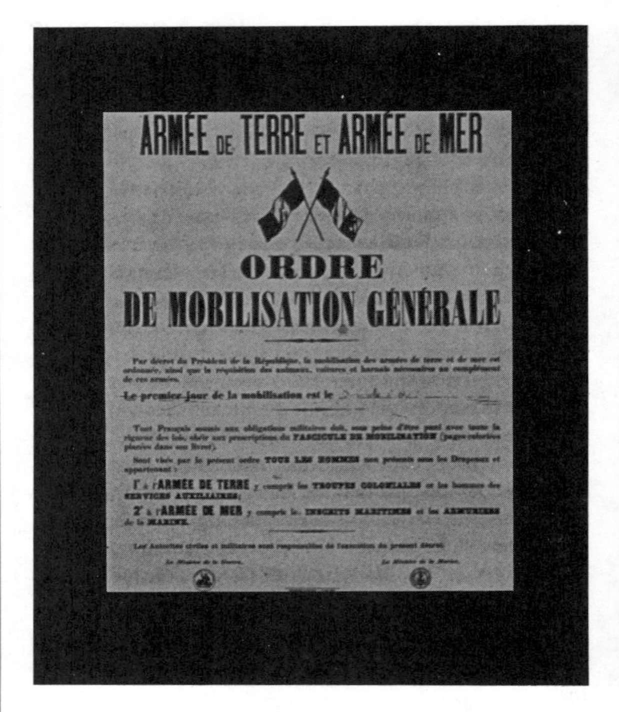

General order of mobilisation issued by the French government in 1939.

obvious. Moreover, the destruction of Czechoslovakia rendered useless the Franco-Polish pact of 1921 (p.242), since both countries were cut off from each other by Hitler's forces. Nevertheless, France (and Britain) guaranteed the independence of Poland, Romania, Greece, and later, Turkey. Daladier was also given power to rule by decree and this enabled him to provide for rearmament.

When Germany and Russia signed the Nazi-Soviet non-aggression pact (p.293) in August 1939, French communists toned down their hostility to Hitler; and when France went to war with Germany on 3 September, the communists denounced it. On 10 May 1940 Hitler attacked on the west and within a month the French had capitulated. On 22 June an armistice was signed (p.303): two-thirds of France came under direct German rule; the remainder, including her colonies, was administered by a puppet government at

Vichy (p.303).

The Third Republic, born out of defeat at the hands of Bismarck in 1870, died in defeat at the hands of Hitler in 1940.

Study Assignments and Essays

1. *What were France's main problems of national defence in the inter-war period and how were they dealt with?*
2. *Treat of the successes and failures of the* cartel des gauches *1924–28.*
3. *Treat of the development of right-wing movements in France in the inter-war years.*
4. *Why would you agree that the period 1929–36 was 'years of crisis' in France?*
5. *Treat of the origin, aims and achievements of the popular front government 1936–38.*
6. *Write an essay on two of the following: (i) The bloc national government 1920–24; (ii) France and the Locarno Pact 1925; (iii) The Stavisky Affair; (iv) The government of national defence 1928–40; (v) France's economic development between the wars.*

Britain Between the Wars

20

This House will in no circumstances fight for its King and Country.

Motion passed by the Oxford Union Society, February 1933.

IN 1914 Britain had entered the war under a Liberal government led by Herbert Asquith (p.69). But in May 1915, following severe criticism of his conduct of the war, Asquith gave in to Tory pressure and formed a coalition government of Liberals, Conservatives and Labour. Discontent continued, however, and finally in December 1916, Asquith himself was replaced as prime minister by his Liberal colleague, David Lloyd George. Although he prosecuted the war with greater drive and was more acceptable to the Conservatives, Lloyd George's assumption of the leadership split the Liberal Party, many of whose members remained loyal to Asquith. Thus, when the war ended in November 1918, party politics were in a state of some confusion.

As soon as the armistice was signed, Lloyd George called an election, hoping to make the most of his current popularity as the man who had led his nation to victory. Andrew Bonar Law, the leader of the Conservative Party, agreed to continue the coalition. A letter of endorsement, signed by him and Lloyd George, was sent to all coalition supporters. Asquith disparagingly called the letter a 'coupon' and the election became known as the 'coupon election'. The coalition won an overwhelming victory, securing 484 seats, but Lloyd George became the prisoner of the Conservatives, who provided 338 of those seats. The largest opposition party was the Labour Party with 63 seats, while Asquith's Liberals secured a mere 28 seats. The Irish parliamentary party, which had played such a decisive role in British politics since 1870, was annihilated at the polls by the new Sinn Féin party, whose members refused to attend Westminster.

LLOYD GEORGE'S GOVERNMENT 1918–22

The coalition government faced serious economic and social problems. Britain's fundamental problem was lack of diversification, and an over-concentration on a few basic industries, such as cotton, shipping and coal. The cotton and shipping markets were now being filled by new competitors such as Japan and the United States. The construction of hydro-electric plants in Scandinavia and oil refineries in the Middle East brought a decline in the demand for British coal as the world moved into the age of oil and electricity. The sharp decline in exports meant that the British economy could not absorb all the four million demobilised troops. Their disillusionment at their jobless homecoming was all the more acute because many of them had believed Lloyd George's promise of November 1918 that post-war Britain would be 'a fit country for heroes to live in'.

The war had stimulated new manufacturing industries — aircraft, motor vehicles, chemicals and optical instruments — but these were insufficient to compensate for the sharp decline in her traditional industries. The result was a high level of unemployment in the older industrial areas such as south Wales and the north of England. By 1920 one-and-a-half million demobilised troops had not found employment; in an effort to alleviate the problem, Lloyd George passed the Unemployment Act. It paid a weekly unemployment 'dole' of twenty shillings to men and eighteen shillings to women, but necessitated raising the rate of income tax, which antagonised many of Lloyd George's Conservative colleagues. To add further to his problem, the new peace treaties and the reparations question claimed much of the prime minister's attention, while nationalism within the empire, especially in Ireland, Egypt and India,

King George V unveils the Cenotaph, London's monument to the dead of World War I, on 11 November 1920. On the gun carriage lies the body of the Unknown Soldier who was buried later that day in Westminster Abbey.

had become a burning issue. In November 1922 Lloyd George called an election, but the Conservatives decided to end the coalition and contest the election independently. The Conservatives won it and Bonar Law became prime minister, but in May 1923 he died and was replaced by Stanley Baldwin.

BALDWIN'S FIRST GOVERNMENT 1923

Baldwin's solution to the unemployment problem was to protect home industries by imposing tariffs on all imported goods, except foodstuffs. His proposals aroused fierce opposition; large sections of the people believed that Britain's position in the world, and its standard of living, was a direct consequence of free trade.

In December 1923 Baldwin called an election on the issue of free trade or protection. The Conservatives won 258 seats, the Liberals (now united) 159, and Labour 191. Baldwin considered the verdict to be a rejection of his policy and resigned. Asquith, the Liberal leader again, was prepared to support Labour in office, and thus Ramsay MacDonald formed the first Labour government in British history.

Stanley Baldwin, leader of the Conservative Party and prime minister of Britain 1923–24, 1924–29 and 1935–37.

THE FIRST LABOUR GOVERNMENT 1924

The advent of a Labour government was hailed as a major victory for the working class: it would have been unthinkable twenty years before. But Labour's lack of experience was a difficulty. MacDonald himself had never held ministerial rank; now he was prime minister. Since it was a minority government depending on Liberal support, it could not put its 'new social order' into operation, lest it antagonise the Liberals. Moreover, Britain's economic problems were too deep-rooted to be dealt with quickly. Only one important measure of social reform was implemented during MacDonald's short stay in government: a Housing Act made possible the building of cheap houses and slum clearances through the provision of generous government grants. MacDonald himself had greater success in foreign affairs (he was foreign secretary as well as premier). His persuasion was chiefly responsible for making the French accept the Dawes Plan, which allowed Germany to pay much-reduced reparations (p.198). MacDonald also extended official recognition to the Bolshevik government in the Soviet

Union, but when he proposed a trade agreement with them the Conservatives and Liberals opposed it fiercely.

In October 1924 the government was defeated on a vote concerning the withdrawal of a prosecution against a communist journal, *The Workers' Weekly*, and MacDonald resigned. A week before the election, the newspaper had published a letter, purporting to come from Zinoviev, head of the Comintern, inciting British communists to undermine the loyalty of the armed forces in Britain. The furore caused by the 'Red Letter', which was almost certainly a forgery, convinced many voters that Labour was 'soft' on communism, and the subsequent election returned Baldwin and the Conservatives with a large majority. Labour fared reasonably well with 151 seats, but the Liberals failed dismally, securing a mere 40 seats. Asquith himself was defeated, but soon afterwards was offered an earldom and retired to the House of Lords. The once-great Liberal Party never recovered and was now replaced by Labour as the main alternative to Conservative rule.

BALDWIN'S SECOND GOVERNMENT 1924–29

The General Strike

The Bank of England impressed upon the government the benefits that would flow from a return to the gold standard, claiming that it would restore Britain's position as the financial centre of the world. In 1925 the chancellor of the exchequer, Winston Churchill, acting on the advice of the Bank of England, restored the gold standard, whereby Britain promised to buy and sell gold to foreign bankers at a fixed rate. The gold standard fixed the pound-dollar ratio at its 1914 value. The effect of this made British exports ten per

Workers demonstrate at Crewe during the General Strike of 1926.

cent more expensive and her external trade declined rapidly. Unemployment soared over the million mark and there was general industrial unrest. The only way exporters could become competitive was to cut wages and introduce a longer working day. The coal miners reacted immediately and with the slogan 'Not a minute on the day, not a penny off the pay', organised the whole trade union movement behind them.

On 1 May 1926 the miners went on strike and a lock-out followed. Then on 3 May, after Baldwin had broken off negotiations, the Trades Union Congress (TUC) proclaimed a general strike. All those workers who were called out — transport, railway, dock, gas, electricity and printing — responded, and some two million employees downed tools. However, there was little disorder and the government's emergency plans worked reasonably well.

The government claimed that the strike had been inspired by communists attempting to destroy the whole economic system. The TUC maintained that it did not wish to cripple the economy, but to secure a better bargaining position.

On 12 May, when it had become clear that the government was not prepared to yield, the TUC decided to call off the general strike, although the miners continued to stay out. Some employers were unwilling to take back prominent strikers and this led to further unrest, but the government immediately intervened, put an end to victimisation and (save for the miners) industry settled down again. The miners continued for a further six months and then, extremely bitter, were obliged to return to longer hours and less pay.

The general strike had clear lessons for both employers and workers. The employers had learned the folly of cutting wages as a means of solving difficulties; many now turned to the notion of linking wages to productivity. The workers had learned that parliamentary pressure and persuasion might bring more speedy results than confrontation.

The Conservative government, claiming to be progressive, now introduced measures of reform. The Unemployment Insurance Act of 1927 ensured that benefits would continue during the entire period of a worker's unemployment. The Equal Franchise Act of 1928 gave the vote to women at 21 years (on the same terms as men). The Local Government Act of 1929 gave more power to local authorities and issued them with grants from the national exchequer.

While the Conservative government firmly held to its belief in private enterprise and abhorred the socialism propounded by Labour, nevertheless it introduced measures of state control in areas where private enterprise could not properly accomplish the task. The Electricity Act of 1926 established a Central Electricity Board to control the generation and distribution of electricity on a national grid. The same year, the BBC (British Broadcasting Corporation) was established and given a monopoly on broadcasting.

THE SECOND LABOUR GOVERNMENT 1929–31

The Equal Franchise Act of 1928 had increased the British electorate by five million and in the election of June 1929 many of them voted Labour. Yet the party still failed to secure an overall majority. Labour won 288 seats, Conservatives 260 and the Liberals held the balance of power with 59.

Ramsay MacDonald became prime minister for the second time in a Labour government with Liberal support, but he was only a few months in office when the Wall Street crash occurred (p.200). Soon the world was in the throes of depression, and Britain, as a manufacturing and exporting nation, was badly hit. Export demand dried up, factories ceased production and ships lay idle. Since 1920 Britain's unemployed had been roughly one million; now, as the depression grew, so did the numbers of unemployed. By the end of 1929 it was nearly two million; by July 1930 it was 2,700,000; and by July 1931 it stood at just under three million.

MacDonald's government started off in 1929 with an optimistic forecast but, as the unemployment figures rose, it seemed helpless to stem the tide. Since it was a minority government, it was hampered by having to rely on Liberal support in the Commons, while the Conservative-dominated House of Lords blocked many bills from becoming law.

The minister of labour, Margaret Bonfield, the first woman to hold cabinet rank, introduced a public works programme to provide jobs, but this had only a minor impact on the huge numbers of unemployed. One junior minister, Sir Oswald Mosley, resigned and started a fascist party. The left wing of the Labour Party demanded full-blooded socialism as the answer to Britain's ills. The rest of the party knew that this was out of the question at this time, and after much wrangling, many extreme socialists were expelled from the party. Yet the Conservatives had no alternative policy to offer except to attack the mounting debt the government was incurring in giving unemployment benefits.

By 1931, the government was spending £120 million a year on the 'dole', to cushion the unemployed from the worst effects of the depression. When the government looked for a loan from the United States, there was no banker there in sympathy with Britain's plight. Americans looked askance at the Labour government giving money to the unemployed, while at home there was no state relief for the twelve million unemployed. Washington, however, would make a loan to the Bank of England provided the government balanced the budget. This could not be achieved without drastically cutting government expenditure in relation to unemployment benefits and salaries. MacDonald agreed to these terms, but his proposed cuts in unemployment benefits split his cabinet and nearly half his government ministers threatened to resign.

In such a crisis it was obvious that an election would not solve anything. Britain's problems had gone beyond party policies. On 23 August 1931 King George V called the leaders of the three parties separately to Buckingham Palace and asked their opinions on how the national crisis could be solved. Sir Herbert Samuel, the deputy Liberal leader (Lloyd George was ill) proposed that a national government drawn from the three parties should be formed. When the other two leaders — Baldwin and MacDonald — met the king, they each approved of Samuel's idea. The question now was which leader would be prime minister. The Liberals said they would serve under MacDonald but not under Baldwin. The Conservatives accepted.

MacDONALD'S NATIONAL GOVERNMENT 1931–35

On 24 August 1931 Ramsay MacDonald formed a national coalition government, with the backing of Conservatives, Liberals and a few Labour members. The great majority of his own parliamentary party, however, repudiated the idea of a national government and went into opposition. They felt that MacDonald, the son of a Scots farm labourer, had betrayed his class in becoming the prisoner of a Conservative-dominated government. Indeed, the thoughts of many Labour followers found expression in the lines the playwright Seán O'Casey later penned of MacDonald:

> *Oh workers on the march, pause here a while, and lay a wreath of part-forgiveness on the lonely grave — forgetting the grey-haired man who did not stay the strife; remembering only the gallant ragged lad of Lossiemouth.*

MacDonald, once Labour's 'disc of gold', was now its renegade. At a meeting of the party he was expelled and Arthur Henderson became leader.

In October 1931 MacDonald called an election to get an endorsement for the national government and its proposed policies. The electorate was warned that unless the government was allowed to cut expenditure, terrible inflationary consequences would follow. Voters accepted the argument and returned the national government with a record 547 seats to 53 for Labour.

The chancellor of the exchequer, Neville Chamberlain, in an effort to balance the budget, heavily increased the taxes on non-essentials such as beer, tobacco and petrol. He also cut unemployment benefit by ten per cent and the salaries of state employees by fifteen per cent. To protect home industry and discourage imports, an Import Duties Act in

Posters for the general election of October 1931.

1932 imposed a ten per cent tariff on certain manufactured goods. Since a large part of Britain's trade was conducted with her dominions and colonies, these tariff retrictions did not apply fully and, at a conference in Ottawa in 1932, a series of preferential agreements was worked out. Britain hoped that Commonwealth countries would help each other by means of imperial preferences. The Ottawa conference agreed to create a common tariff wall around the Commonwealth. Canada and Australia did not like this idea since much of their trade was with countries outside the Commonwealth, and the agreements had only limited success. Even Commonwealth countries were reluctant to abandon self-interest.

Despite government action, Britain's level of unemployment remained seriously high, reaching three million in 1932. The industries worst hit were ship-building and coal mining. Areas such as Tyneside, Clydeside, the north of England and south Wales witnessed serious deprivation and unrest. In an effort to alleviate the terrible conditions, the government was obliged to designate such places as 'depressed areas', entitled to extra welfare schemes.

From about the middle of 1933, a gradual upturn commenced — less perhaps from government action than because home demand began to increase and world trade to pick up. The construction of council and private houses stimulated the building industry, which in turn created demand for electrical products and furniture. The older industries, such as textiles, ship-building and coal mining, continued their long decline and workers began drifting away into the newer industries. Gradually the pay of state employees was restored. The worst excesses of the depression seemed over, although many social and economic problems remained.

BALDWIN'S NATIONAL GOVERNMENT 1935–37

In June 1935 MacDonald resigned in poor health and his place as prime minister was taken by Baldwin. Later in the year an election was called and the national government was returned with a reduced majority.

Baldwin knew that the days of *laissez-faire* were over and that government had a duty to concern itself with economic and social matters to a degree which would have been unthinkable at the turn of the century. 'For good or evil,' he declared, 'the days of non-interference in domestic affairs by government are gone. We are passing into a new era.'

But as the worst excesses of the depression were passing, the focus of government attention was obliged to move from domestic concerns to international problems. The claims of Mussolini and Hitler (p.283), together with civil war in Spain (p.264), made the government realise that Britain could no longer ignore the death of democracy and the revision of the Versailles settlement.

The government's 1932 budget had been the lowest in armaments expenditure of the entire inter-war period. But from 1935 Britain began to spend more on rearmament. This was prompted essentially by the deteriorating international climate, although one side-effect in Britain was the increase in employment generated by armaments production.

The only major domestic problem to face Baldwin's government was the 'abdication crisis' in 1936. In January King George V died and was succeeded by his son, Edward VIII, who as Prince of Wales had become very popular through his interest in sport and his travels throughout the Commonwealth. In the summer of 1936 Edward conveyed his intention of marrying an American, Mrs Wallis Simpson. Not only was Mrs Simpson a commoner, but she had already divorced one husband and was in the process of divorcing a second. The divorce was granted in October and the law permitted her to marry again after six months.

Baldwin and his cabinet were very much opposed to the marriage, which they believed would bring the monarchy into disrepute. Since the time of Henry VIII, the monarch had been the head of the Anglican church, and consequently the Archbishop of Canterbury was equally opposed to the marriage.

In theory it would have been constitutionally possible for the king to marry against the government's wishes. But over the years a constitutional convention had evolved whereby the monarch accepts the advice of the government, and Baldwin was firm in his determination that this should be upheld.

The press remained discreetly silent on the crisis and the general public came to learn of the matter only when the Bishop of Bradford, Dr Blunt, publicly asked for prayers for the king. Immediately, the press and the public began to take sides. Finally, the king decided to abdicate (before he had been crowned) in order to marry Mrs Simpson. On 10 December 1936 Baldwin announced the news in the House of Commons. The following day, parliament passed the Declaration of Abdication Act, which provided for Edward's brother to become king as George VI. Edward went into self-imposed exile and later married Mrs Simpson. They took the titles Duke and Duchess of Windsor. Six months later, in May 1937, Baldwin resigned and was succeeded by Neville Chamberlain.

CHAMBERLAIN'S NATIONAL GOVERNMENT 1937–40

Chamberlain was obliged to devote almost all his energies to foreign affairs. His advisers continually warned him of the dangers arising in Europe, but could offer no solution. In this dilemma, Chamberlain pursued a policy known as 'appeasement', based on the assumption that Hitler and Mussolini were (for the most part) righting the wrongs perpetrated by the Versailles settlement in 1919, and that if they were granted timely concessions, they would not resort to war. This fallacy, as time subsequently proved, rested on the belief that Hitler wished merely to revise Versailles and had no further territorial ambitions. Appeasement could prove successful only if Hitler had limited objectives; but since this was not the case, appeasement did no more than postpone the inevitable conflict. Moreover, it served to convince Hitler that the democracies were weak and ineffective, and encouraged him in the belief that he would not be seriously opposed.

Not everyone in government circles agreed with Chamberlain's policy. His foreign secretary, Anthony Eden, held that appeasement was incompatible with the principle of collective security enshrined in the covenant of the League of Nations (p.274) and claimed that the best deterrent lay in a united front by the League which would also include the Soviet Union. When Chamberlain insisted on appeasement (p.287), Eden resigned.

Despite the official policy of appeasement, the government did take precautionary measures for war, especially during 1939. Aircraft production was increased to six hundred planes a month, and a coastal radar screen was completed, to detect approaching enemy aircraft. Provisions were made for industries to be redirected towards war manufacture, and assurance secured from the TUC that full co-operation would be forthcoming in any redeployment of industrial labour. Then, following the final destruction of Czechoslovakia (p.289), the government introduced general conscription on 26 April.

It was the great irony of Chamberlain's political career that the man who was so much associated with the policy of appeasement was obliged to declare war on Nazi Germany in September 1939. Finally on 10 May 1940 Chamberlain resigned and his national government was replaced by a national coalition under the leadership of Winston Churchill (p.301).

Study Assignments and Essays

1. *What problems faced Lloyd George's coalition government of 1918–22 and how were they dealt with?*
2. *'Baldwin's 1924–29 government was a good administration.' Discuss.*
3. *'The government of Ramsay MacDonald 1929–31 was doomed to failure.' Do you agree? Give reasons.*
4. *Compare and contrast MacDonald's national government of 1931–35 with Baldwin's national government of 1935–37.*
5. *Treat of economic development in Britain in the inter-war period.*
6. *Write an essay on two of the following: (i) The General Strike 1926; (ii) Britain and the Great Depression; (iii) the Abdication Crisis 1936; (iv) Neville Chamberlain; (v) British society 1919–39.*

The Spanish Civil War 1936–39 21

No man is an island, intire of itself; every man is a Peece of the Continent, *a part of the* maine;. . . *any man's death diminishes* me, *because I am involved in* mankinde; *and therefore never send to know for whom the* bell *tolls; it tolls for* thee.

John Donne, 1572–1631

SPANISH PROBLEMS

DURING THE nineteenth century, the once proud Spain lost most of her overseas empire. Her Latin American possessions were broken into eighteen independent states, and in 1898 she lost Cuba, Puerto Rico and the Philippines. The country did not experience an industrial revolution, which meant that no strong middle class emerged. When Europe was convulsed in World War I, Spain remained aloof and cut off from the rest of Europe. But this is not to say that she was a peaceful country. On the contrary, Spanish problems ran so deep, and their attempted solutions were so intractable, that one of the most horrific of all civil wars erupted in that country in 1936.

One serious problem — regionalism — stemmed from her physical features. Since her mountains ran from east to west, trade and communications had not evolved in a north-south direction. Consequently, over the centuries, each area developed its own dialect, dress and customs. A strong sense of regionalism came to dominate the country's peoples, who tended to give their allegiance to their own particular region rather than to Spain as a whole. This separatism was particularly strong in Catalonia and in the Basque region of north-eastern Spain, where strong independence movements arose (map, p.263).

Another problem was economic and social inequality. Since the industrial revolution had almost passed her by, only the iron of Bilbao and the textiles of Barcelona were developed as major industries. Without a strong working class, and having few middle-class liberals, fundamental change could not take place.

But the greatest problem facing Spanish society was created by the land system. In some regions there were enormous estates, *latifundia*, owned by wealthy landlords, while the mass of the peasantry were landless labourers, called *braceros*. Other regions suffered from the opposite problem — *minifundia* — farms too small to support a family.

POLITICS

In the late nineteenth century, Spanish rule alternated between constitutional government and dictatorship. In 1868 the revolution that deposed Queen Isabella II, and the subsequent invitation to Prince Leopold of Hohenzollern, created the misunderstanding between France and Prussia that led directly to the Franco-Prussian war (p.18).

In 1873 Spain became a republic but three years later the monarchy was restored by Isabella's son, Alfonso XII. Then in 1886 a baby, Alfonso XIII, inherited the throne. He was destined to be the last king of Spain, for in 1931 he abdicated and went into exile (p.260).

Between 1873 and 1918 Spain theoretically was a democracy, but the country was dominated by the land-owning and other conservative classes who had no desire to institute economic and social change. Election results were usually falsified by *caciques*, or local political bosses. In this cynical manner Spanish democracy was manipulated by the land-owning class for their own benefit, while army officers enjoyed tax concessions and low-cost travel privileges.

THE DICTATORSHIP OF PRIMO DE RIVERA 1923–30

Between 1918 and 1923 serious social and industrial unrest disrupted Spanish life. In these five years Spain had twelve governments, but all were too weak, or too unwilling, to reform the system. Finally, in September 1923, General Miguel Primo de Rivera seized power with the army's help and proclaimed a military dictatorship. For a time Primo de Rivera's rule looked successful and coal, iron and steel production rose markedly. But Spain's economic improvement was essentially part of the general European recovery after 1923 and was not the result of Primo de Rivera's rule. While he did initiate some reform and started public works programmes, he failed to rectify the real inequalities in Spanish society, fearing that this would displease the great landowners.

In 1928 serious rioting took place. A radical socialist party emerged, determined to end Primo de Rivera's rule and the Spanish monarchy with which it was associated. In 1930, as Spain's problems deepened due to the world depression, Primo de Rivera took the unusual step of asking all army officers to declare their opinion of his military rule. To his amazement they voted for his retirement. Primo de Rivera left immediately for France where he died soon afterwards.

King Alfonso XIII now assumed dictatorial power, but few supported him. In December 1930 a group of republicans attempted a *coup d'état*, claiming that 'a passionate demand for justice surges upwards from the bowels of the Nation. . .' The coup was suppressed, but in the 1931 municipal elections, a substantial majority voted for a republic. To avoid bloodshed, the king left Spain for Rome, and exile.

THE REPUBLIC

The new government was a coalition dominated by republicans and socialists. The first problem it faced was the wave of anticlericalism, in which churches and convents in Madrid and other cities were burned and vandalised. Having restored some semblance of order, the government set about tackling what it saw as the four major problems of Spain: the land, the church, regionalism, and the army.

The Land

The new government suffered by coming to power in a period of world depression. Agricultural prices fell and unemployment rose as land remained uncultivated. A quick solution to the land problem became more urgent than ever. In 1932 an agrarian law laid down that unworked farms of over 56 acres were to be taken over by the Institute of Agrarian Reform, which then would distribute the land to individuals or cooperatives. But the scheme failed because of regional differences and a lack of skilled technicians. Progress was minimal: by 1934 only 12,500 people had been settled.

To make matters worse, the cabinet was so divided that no effective policy could be implemented. The government was essentially urban in outlook and did not fully understand rural problems. The republican wing wished to create peasant ownership of land as in France; the socialists wished to collectivise the land as in the Soviet Union. The problem of Spanish agriculture remained unsolved and the landless labourers of Andalusia turned towards the radical, anarchist-dominated trade union, the *Confederación Nacional de Trabajo* (CNT).

The Church

The catholic church's influence had grown in the late nineteenth century, and it owned railways, banks and huge tracts of land. The republicans disliked the church because it had openly sided with the monarchy. Many members of the government were atheist, and all were anti-clerical, with the exception of Niceto Zamora, the prime minister, and Maura, the minister of the interior.

In its attempt to curb the church's power, the government brought in a new constitution. It provided for the separation of church and state; the ending of payment to priests after two years; the dissolution of religious orders when this was considered necessary; the ending of religious education in schools; the confiscation of church property; and the liberalisation of divorce laws. These terms were a clear challenge to the church and lost the republican government many who otherwise might have supported it. The cabinet split on the issue, Zamora resigned and the Basque deputies withdrew from the Cortes (parliament).

Regionalism

The problem of regionalism ran deep. In 1931 the Catalan party demanded independence and the government was obliged to grant home rule to Catalonia. This infuriated the nationalists and the army. The Basques, too, were agitating for independence and it seemed as if the government might be forced to accept their demands (map, p.263).

The Army

The government knew that it would not be secure unless it curbed the army's power. Press criticism of the army was now permitted and soldiers were no longer immune from the civil law. Since the proportion of officers to ordinary ranks was one-to-ten, a number of officers were compulsorily retired. These were now in a position to plot against the government, and in 1932 General Sanjurjo staged on army revolt at Seville, which ended in failure.

Thus, government action created the worst of both worlds for the Republic. It did not go far enough to satisfy its radical followers and yet it went too far in that it mobilised the conservative forces against the Republic. Divisions within the government also played a part. The radicals attacked government policy, and in September 1934 the socialists deserted, thereby precipitating an election in November.

An unpopular government made it inevitable that the election would produce a swing to the right. A new party emerged, the *Confederación Española de Derechas Autónomas* (CEDA), which claimed to be a mass catholic party set up to resist anti-clerical legislation. It depended for its finance on the great landlords and was therefore no more than a front for the extreme right.

Since the CEDA did not have an overall majority, the radicals formed a centre government with CEDA support. But in October 1934 three CEDA members joined the cabinet. This was the signal for immediate action on the left. Under Largo Caballero, the socialists, afraid of Spain 'going fascist', joined the anarchists in an armed revolt. The uprising was easily crushed, although over 3,000 were killed in Asturias.

The 'October Revolution' marked a turning point in the history of the Spanish Republic. Thereafter middle-ground opinion gave way and polarisation began, reflected in the growing influence of the two extremist groups, the fascists and the communists.

In 1932 a Spanish fascist party, the *Falange Española* (Spanish Phalanx), was founded by José Antonio Primo de Rivera, the son of the former dictator. Another group known as *Juntas de Ofensiva Nacional-Sindicalistas* (JONS) had already been founded by Jiménez Caballero and Omesimo Redonda. In 1934 both groups merged under the name *Falange Española.*

During the 1920s the communists had been an insignificant fringe element, but after the Comintern change of policy in 1934 (p.288) they began to co-operate with other left-wing groups. Their participation in the Asturian uprising increased their prestige because one of the heroines of the rising, Dolores Ibárruri, known as 'La Pasionaria', was a communist.

In the February 1936 election a coalition of left-wing parties known as the popular front won a majority of votes in the Cortes. But in practice a purely republican government ruled because the socialists under Caballero were merely waiting to seize power once the republicans had failed. Since Caballero was afraid of losing support to the anarchists and the communists, his speeches became more extreme, terrifying the middle-classes and driving them to the right. Law and order began to break down. Revolutionaries convicted of crimes were given amnesty, and there was clamour for revenge upon the conservative classes. In May the government made one of its most disastrous decisions when it dismissed President Zamora and had him replaced by Manuel Azaña. This removed the last guarantee of impartial government and made the exercise of power the monopoly of the left.

The government, aware of hostility among the army officers, transferred important generals to posts outside Spain. Goded was sent to the Balearic Isles, Franco to the Canaries, and Mola to Navarre. However, this defensive action was to prove fatal because these generals became conspirators in a plan of action to save 'traditional Spain' from disorder and left-wing domination.

The incident that eventually sparked off the civil war was the assassination of Calvo Sotelo, the leader of the CEDA. On 13 July he was murdered in cold blood by the state police in reprisal for the killing of a young republican by the Falange. The right were convinced that order could be restored only by overthrowing the Republic.

Generalissimo Francisco Franco

The army generals now decided to take action. It was intended that General Sanjurjo would head the army revolt, but when he was killed in a plane crash, leadership passed to General Franco, who later became recognised as 'Generalissimo of all the Armed Forces and Head of the Spanish State'.

Franco was born in El Ferrol in Galicia in 1892. He spent most of his army career fighting the Rifs in Spanish North Africa, where he rose rapidly to the rank of general. Franco's military training and experience made him abhor the destructiveness of the anarchists, his love of Spain made him oppose the separatists, his middle-class birth and way of life made him detest the ideology of the socialists and communists, while his analysis of Spanish problems made him lose faith in parliamentary democracy.

THE CIVIL WAR

On 19 July Franco flew from the Canaries to Morocco, from where he intended to start the revolt with the aid of the Spanish Moroccan army. However, he was unable to ferry his troops to southern Spain because the Spanish navy remained loyal to the government. Franco sent an urgent message to Italy for help, but as Mussolini was slow to reply, he sent another request to Berlin. Hitler saw Franco not so much as a fellow fascist but as an anti-communist, and on 28 July he sent twenty transport planes to airlift the African forces to Spain.

Meanwhile General Mola had taken Pamplona, General Dávila had captured Burgos, and soon Salamanca, Valladolid, Seville, Granada and Córdoba were in rebel hands.

In this early period of the war neither side acted decisively and each lost the opportunity of a quick victory. The republican government, underestimating the seriousness of its plight, refused to arm the workers because that would mean street warfare. On the other side, the army failed to move speedily into position and failed to capture such major cities as Madrid, Barcelona, Valencia, Toledo and Bilbao.

On 6 August Franco arrived in Seville with 10,000 African troops, hoping to end the war

SPAIN DURING THE CIVIL WAR, 1936-39

quickly by capturing Madrid. But republican forces slowed down his advance and when news reached him that the nationalist garrison at Toledo was on the verge of collapse from a republican siege, he was obliged to change direction and go to the relief of the city.

The Siege at Toledo, September 1936

From the beginning of the war nationalists and republicans had been fighting for control of the medieval city of Toledo on the banks of the river Tagus. The nationalists, under immense pressure, retreated within the great stone fortress of the Alcázar. Here General Moscardo, 1,000 army officers and Falangists, together with about 600 women and children and 100 hostages, hoped to hold out. They had a good supply of water, arms and ammunition, but food was scarce and communication with the outside world was cut off. The new republican prime minister, Largo Caballero, came from Madrid to supervise the siege. Despite repeated requests to surrender or at least release the women and children, Moscardo refused.

Eventually the republicans decided to tunnel under the fortress with the intention of planting mines and blowing up the Alcázar. Mining began on 21 September and even though some mines did go off, Moscardo decided to hold out. On 27 September, one of Franco's relief armies under General Varela arrived with artillery, defeated the republicans and lifted the siege. The defence of Toledo passed into nationalist folklore and General Moscardo became a hero.

Reaction in Europe

The Spanish Civil War aroused diverse reactions throughout Europe. In Italy and Germany, where fascism had triumphed, sympathies were naturally on Franco's side and he was seen as the champion of Spain against the scourge of communism. Mussolini sent 50,000 men, over 700 aircraft and 750 tanks. Hitler sent 16,000 men, eleven aircraft squadrons and one tank battalion.

Destruction at Toledo, September 1936.

In France, Blum's radical socialist government favoured the republic whose government was roughly similar to his own. The French premier certainly did not wish to see a fascist Spain on his southern border, but he was afraid that intervention would clearly split further an already divided France (p.247).

In Britain, Baldwin's Conservative government disliked both sides and regretted the end of another democracy. Essentially the government's policy was to restrain others from getting involved lest the conflict should burgeon into a general European war. To this end, Britain proposed a policy of non-involvement and was instrumental in setting up a non-intervention committee to which most

English supporters of the Republican cause on parade during the Civil War.

states sent representatives. But this committee had little practical effect because the totalitarian regimes in Italy, Germany and the Soviet Union ignored its recommendations (p.287).

The Soviet Union pursued an enigmatic policy towards the Spanish civil war. Stalin, realising that the real enemy was not Franco but Hitler and Mussolini, could not afford to side openly with communism in Spain because this would have antagonised Britain and France, with whom he wished to remain on friendly terms in the event of a fascist war against the Soviet Union. Yet Stalin did send aid to the republican side — advisers, raw materials and tanks — while the number of Soviet personnel sent to Spain did not exceed 2,000. Important as such aid was, it was sufficient to keep the republicans in the war, but never enough to give them any possibility of winning. Stalin was devious. Much as he would have liked to see communism triumph in Spain, he was realistic enough to appreciate that an isolated communist Spain would not be tolerated by the western powers, whether fascist or democratic. But he also knew that as long as the war continued, the fascist powers would remain occupied in Spain and would not turn upon the Soviets. Accordingly, Stalin continued to send enough aid to the republican side to keep the war going, while at home he increased the tempo of industrialisation in order to meet the inevitable conflict with fascism (p.235).

Apart from official government reaction, the Spanish Civil War caught the imagination of many idealistic young men and women around the world. For them the war was the good fight for freedom and democracy against the evil of fascism. It particularly attracted writers and poets, fired with the prospect of contributing to the triumph of good over evil. From Britain came young men such as George Orwell, who wrote the novel *Homage to Catalonia*, Philip Toynbee, Stephen Spender and W.H. Auden; from France André Malraux, who later wrote a novel *L'Espoir* (*Days of Hope*); and from America Ernest Hemingway came to Spain as a war correspondent (he later wrote the famous novel *For Whom the Bell Tolls*). From his headquarters in Paris, the young communist Josip Broz (later Marshal Tito of Yugoslavia, (p.340) organised secret routes into Spain. In this way thousands of young people from many lands passed into Spain to fight in the International Brigades.

The Defeat of the Basques 1937

The nationalists now concentrated on the Basque region in north-eastern Spain. On 31 March 1937 General Mola led an attack on Bilbao, but the Basques defended it stubbornly. Eventually superior strength, aided by Hitler's air power, broke their defence and Bilbao fell. On 26 April German bombers destroyed the Basque town of Guernica in one day, leaving 2,500 dead and wounded. (Pablo Picasso recorded for posterity the horror of that day in a celebrated painting, *Guernica*.) By October the whole of the northern coast was in nationalist hands and Basque dreams of independence were over (map, p.263).

The Battle of Teruel, December 1937 — February 1938

Madrid was the key to the whole struggle. Despite the fact that 20,000 nationalists stood at its gates, the republicans held them at bay. Caballero inspired his side to greater and greater efforts. The communists were now becoming the dominant group; their commitment against fascism grew daily. Dolores Ibárruri (La Pasionaria), the colourful communist leader, formed a women's battalion to fight alongside the men and with her famous slogan, *No pasarán* (They shall not pass), inspired the republicans to greater heights.

To relieve the pressure on Madrid, in December 1937 the republicans decided to mount an attack on the nationalist stronghold of Teruel, to the north-east of Madrid. Colonel d'Harcourt with some 18,000 troops held Teruel. The republican offensive was led by the legendary *El Campesino*, who with 100,000 troops began a surprise attack in a blinding snowstorm on 15 December. After fierce house-to-house fighting, the republicans took Teruel. Some 2,500 soldiers and civilians who had hidden in a cave were allowed to leave the city in a gesture of humanity unique in the history of this bitter civil war.

However, when news of the attack on Teruel reached Franco, who was besieging Madrid, he ordered 80,000 troops (backed up by German and Italian tanks and planes) to go to the relief of the city. Since that winter was particularly harsh, the counter-attack did not begin until 15 January 1938. During the following month a fierce battle raged until finally on 18 February the nationalists won control. But by then *El Campesino* and his remaining forces had escaped, leaving behind 14,000 dead and 20,000 wounded.

Teruel showed the decisive influence of the German tanks over the Russian, but, more importantly, the republicans were now in full retreat.

The Battle of the Ebro 1938

In March 1938 Franco decided on a sudden drive towards Valencia. The republicans desperately tried to cut him off at the river Ebro. In the late summer and autumn of 1938 the battle of the Ebro was fiercely contested on both sides. However, Franco's superior air power proved decisive, and republican losses were staggeringly high. The road was now open for the capture of Barcelona, which fell on 29 January 1939 (map, p.263).

The Fall of Madrid, March 1939

From the beginning of the war, Franco had set his sights on the capture of Madrid, the capital and the seat of the republican government. But despite his early objective, Madrid had not fallen. There were several reasons for this. Firstly, Franco and his forces were continually diverted from their task by the need to relieve besieged cities, such as Toledo and Teruel. Secondly, despite requests from the German forces for permission to bomb Madrid, Franco would not agree because he did not want to become master of a ruined city. Thirdly, the republicans, and especially the communists under La Pasionaria, put up a heroic resistance that ensured that Madrid would not fall.

The Battle of Madrid began on 8 November 1936. There was fierce hand-to-hand fighting and heavy casualties on both sides. When the city did not fall, both sides resorted to digging trenches. A stalemate ensued, with neither side able to break through.

Franco's strategy for the following two years was to surround Madrid and starve its inhabitants into surrender. Lack of fuel during the winter and lack of water during the summer created much suffering, but the city continued to hold out. However, time was against its defenders, and as the tide of war turned in Franco's favour during 1938, the situation in Madrid gravely worsened.

On 5 March 1939 the republican government was overthrown by a military *junta* of socialists and anarchists led by Colonel Segismundo Casado, who formed a Council of National Defence. This coup by Casado led to serious division within the anti-Franco forces and over 1,000 were killed in clashes between themselves. Franco had already declared to the republican government that he would accept nothing less than unconditional surrender; as a result, one of the reasons for the coup stemmed from the hope that the *junta* would obtain better surrender terms. But this was not to be; the only concession the *junta* got was permission to leave Spain.

On 28 March Madrid fell to the nationalists, who entered the city with over 200,000 men. Within a few days the remaining cities that were still in republican hands surrendered. On 1 April Franco issued a communiqué: 'Today, after capturing and disarming the Red Army, the nationalist troops have attained their last military objective.' The Spanish civil war was over.

THE COST

The Spanish civil war lasted for two years and 264 days. It resulted in one million deaths from fighting, execution and disease. Some 340,000 republicans decided to go into exile, while a further 250,000 were imprisoned for up to thirty years. About one million were put into penal battalions to clear up the debris. Spain was devastated: her towns and cities were in ruins, much of her land was left uncultivated, and the majority of her roads, railways and bridges were destroyed. To add further to her problems of reconstruction, no outside help was forthcoming because within a few months World War II had begun.

WHY FRANCO WON

Three main factors explain why Franco's nationalists won the civil war. Franco's own contribution was of immense significance. Once the war had started, all groups on the right accepted him as the supreme commander, ensuring a unified front in contrast with their opponents. Franco was a dedicated professional soldier who showed courage, efficiency and patience. For these qualities his troops repaid him with unquestioning loyalty. He also succeeded in gaining valuable aid from Hitler and Mussolini without compromising Spanish sovereignty. Thus, Franco's contribution on the political, military and diplomatic level combined uniquely in an unbeatable formula.

In direct contrast, the republicans were hopelessly divided at every level. When the war started, the CNT and the communists indulged in acts of terrorism which made it impossible for the republican government to organise a war effort. The anarchists refused to accept orders, and saw their current allies as future enemies. The republican forces were little more than the improvised groupings of labour organisations, without the training and discipline of Franco's troops.

The third factor, foreign aid, was the most crucial of all. Although both sides obtained help from abroad, Franco received most. Britain and France decided upon a policy of non-intervention (p.280), leaving the three totalitarian states, Germany, Italy and the Soviet Union, with a monopoly of external support. Stalin sent aid to the republican side, but in quality and quantity it was vastly inferior to that supplied to the nationalists by Mussolini and Hitler. And in the long run, it was this superior ground and air support that proved decisive.

Study Assignments and Essays

1. What were the main problems confronting Spanish society and government up to 1930?
2. Examine the sequence of events in Spain between 1930 and the outbreak of civil war in 1936.
3. What issues were at stake in the Spanish civil war?
4. Examine how the Spanish civil war became international in character.
5. Why did Franco win the Spanish civil war?
6. Write an essay on two of the following:
(i) General Franco; (ii) Famous battles of the Spanish civil war; (iii) Separatist movements in the Spanish civil war; (iv) 'La Pasionaria'; (v) The nature of Spanish fascism.

Eastern Europe Between the Wars 1919–39

22

History is the sextant and compass of states, which tossed by wind and current, would be lost in confusion if they could not fix their position.

Allan Nevins

WITH THE exception of Czechoslovakia, the states of eastern Europe turned to various types of authoritarian rule during the interwar period.

Few, if any, of these countries rested on solid economic foundations, and many lacked a substantial middle class. Democracy proved inadequate to cope with social and economic inequality, and almost inevitably authoritarian rule appeared to be a more attractive means of upholding order. The states of eastern Europe had also to grapple with the problems of racial discontent: the tangle of races and languages throughout this part of the world made it impossible for the peacemakers at Paris to draw boundaries that would satisfy everyone. Inevitably, therefore, every state had at least one minority which found itself on the 'wrong' side of the frontier.

AUSTRIA

The Treaty of St Germain in 1919 left Austria a small land-locked republic shorn of her former territorial possessions (p.185). The two chief parties were the Social Democrats, whose support came mainly from Vienna where one-third of the population lived, and the Christian Socialists, whose conservative support came largely from the countryside. Each party had its own military wing: the Social Democrats had the *Schutzbund* and the Christian Socialists, the *Heimwehr*. When the Nazi Party emerged, it was both a political and military movement, whose aspiration was union with Germany.

In 1932 Engelbert Dollfuss, a Christian Socialist, became chancellor. The following year (as Hitler came to power in Germany) Dollfuss ended parliamentary government by setting up a right-wing Fatherland Front in an attempt to end party strife and keep Austria independent. Later that year the Nazi Party was banned — an edict that infuriated Hitler. In July 1934 Dollfuss was assassinated in an unsuccessful attempt by Austrian Nazis to exterminate the entire government. But when Mussolini moved troops to the Brenner Pass, Hitler did not invade Austria (p.288).

The new chancellor, Kurt von Schuschnigg, attempted to carry on the Fatherland Front. But as the banned Nazis continued to grow and work their way into positions of prominence, Schuschnigg was forced to make concessions. Nazi newspapers were allowed to circulate in Austria and two pro-Nazis were brought into the cabinet.

Then in February 1938, following threats from Hitler, Schuschnigg was obliged to legalise the Nazi Party and appoint a Nazi, Dr Arthur Seyss-Inquart, as minister of the interior in control of the police. The chancellor then announced that a plebiscite would be held, in the belief that Austria would reject union with Germany. But when Hitler massed troops on the border, Schuschnigg lost his nerve, resigned, and Seyss-Inquart became chancellor. Claiming that disorder was imminent, Seyss-Inquart invited German troops to maintain order. Accordingly, on 12 March 1938 German forces marched into Austria, and one month later a plebiscite gave an almost unanimous return in favour of *Anschluss* — the union of Austria and Germany. Austria had lost its independent existence and had become part of Hitler's Third Reich (p.289 and map, p.286).

HUNGARY

When the terms of the Treaty of Trianon (p.185) became known, the walls in Budapest were covered with the slogan *'Nem! Nem! Soha!'* (No! No! Never!). Hungary's initial response was to attempt to recover territory lost to Czechoslovakia, but this proved unsuccessful. Meanwhile the Romanians had invaded Hungary with the object of gaining territory, but after a few months they withdrew.

For the first few months after the war, Béla Kun ruled as a communist dictator in Budapest. But then the Conservatives, representing the great landowners, set up a government under Admiral Horthy and drove out Béla Kun. In theory Horthy was acting as regent for King Carl, the last emperor of Austria-Hungary, who was in exile in Switzerland. But Horthy had no intention of handing over power, and kept informing Carl that the time was not yet ripe for his entry to Budapest. Eventually in 1921, Carl twice secretly returned to Hungary, but on each occasion he was obliged to leave because of the hostility of Horthy and his followers.

Horthy's government stayed conservative under a very limited franchise. The great landholders held sway over a disgruntled peasantry, and unemployment remained high. Horthy's policy was to resist social change at home and to strive to revise the Treaty of Trianon abroad. In 1922 Hungary was admitted to the League of Nations, but when it became obvious that the Treaty of Trianon would not be revised through that channel. Horthy turned to Hitler and Mussolini. He succeeded in obtaining disputed areas from Czechoslovakia in 1938 (p.291 and map, p.286) and from Romania in 1940. For these rewards, Horthy joined forces with Hitler in World War II (p.307).

Tomás Masaryk, first president of Czechoslovakia.

CZECHOSLOVAKIA

The creation of the new state of Czechoslovakia in 1919 was the only deliberate multiracial exception made by the peacemakers at Versailles (p.185).

In 1920 Czechoslovakia adopted a democratic constitution on the French model. Her first president was the Slovak, Tomás Masaryk, who earned an international reputation as a statesman to whom right was more important than might. In 1935 he was succeeded as head of state by Eduard Benes, who was also regarded as a great statesman. Benes remained president until he was forced to resign after the Munich agreement in 1938 (p.291).

The population of Czechoslovakia numbered about fourteen million: seven million Czechs, over three million Germans, two million Slovaks, and substantial minorities of

Hungarians and Ruthenians. Religious differences exacerbated racial differences: most Czechs were protestant and many were anticlerical, while the Slovaks were mainly catholic.

In the Czech area of Bohemia and the German-speaking area of Sudetenland, there was considerable industrialisation and a good standard of education. But in the eastern half of the state, where the Slovaks and Ruthenians lived, there was very little industrial progress and living standards were poor.

In 1919 Hungary declared war on Czechoslovakia in an attempt to recover disputed territory, but her attempts were unsuccessful. At the same time border clashes arose with Poland over the duchy of Teschen (p.279). Despite her internal and external problems, Czechoslovakia did become a stable state. Minority groups were treated far better than in other countries, and the new state fulfilled many of the hopes and ideals of the peacemakers at Versailles (map, p.286).

During the depression years, the Slovaks blamed the Czechs for the country's setbacks, the Ruthenian peasants were resentful about falling agricultural prices, and the Sudeten Germans, hitherto content, now began to get restless. In 1934 Konrad Henlein, with financial backing from Nazi Germany, founded the Sudeten-German Party, which soon became the second-largest party in parliament. From 1936, Nazi propaganda increased and by 1938 most Sudeten Germans believed that their future lay with Germany. At Munich in 1938 Czechoslovakia was abandoned by the democracies and the Sudetenland was incorporated into Germany (p.291). Then in March 1939 Nazi troops marched into Prague, and Czechoslovakia as a separate state ceased to exist (map, p.286).

POLAND

The new Republic of Poland, re-created from parts of the former empires of Germany, Russia and Austria-Hungary, had a population of over 30 million people. It was now sandwiched between Germany and Soviet Russia, and essentially had no natural boundaries. It had suffered wartime devastation, had few natural resources, and had a high level of unemployment.

Marshal Jósef Pilsudski, dictator of Poland 1926–35.

At first the Poles fashioned a democratic constitution, and Jan Paderewski, a world-famous pianist, became the first prime minister. However, democracy fared badly. Under the system of proportional representation, a multiplicity of political parties emerged, which ensured that governments would be both unstable and short-lived.

By 1923 Poland was suffering from inflation, economic stagnation and governmental instability. These conditions continued until May 1926 when Józef Pilsudski, a veteran Polish officer, marched on Warsaw and took over in a *coup*. From then until his death in 1935, he ruled as an unofficial dictator. Marshal Pilsudski made stability and continuity his priorities, and although his regime was not a complete dictatorship, since elections continued to be held, opposition was clearly curtailed and strict censorship imposed. While Pilsudski maintained relative peace within Poland, his regime did nothing to alleviate the social distress caused by high unemployment. Neither was anything done to break up the landlord estates and distribute land to the peasantry.

In international affairs, Poland's policy of settling territorial disputes by recourse to war was not in keeping with the ideals of the peacemakers and the League of Nations. The frontier with Russia was settled only after war (p.333), her dispute with Czechoslovakia over Teschen erupted in violence, and her acquisition of Vilna was achieved by force (p.271).

By 1925, however, Poland had sought security in an alliance with France (p.242) and was in support of strong action when Hitler remilitarised the Rhineland in 1935 (p.285). However, when Hitler made his demands against Czechoslovakia at Munich in 1938 (p.290), Poland was more concerned with acquiring Teschen than with curbing Nazi Germany (map, p.286).

In 1939 Hitler turned his attention to the Polish corridor, and Britain and France gave Poland guarantees of support (p.292). But when the Nazi-Soviet Pact was signed in August, the fate of Poland was sealed. On 1 September Hitler invaded and World War II commenced (p.298).

THE BALKAN STATES

1. The new Kingdom of the Serbs, Croats and Slovenes began its existence with a border dispute with Italy over Fiume (p.208). Internally, a quarrel arose between the dominant orthodox Serbs and the catholic Croats. The kingdom was so divided that in 1929 the Serb king, Alexander, dissolved parliament and abolished all political parties. In an attempt to end the differences between the various groups, the kingdom adopted the name Yugoslavia; but this change was cosmetic and the Croats, especially, continued to demand autonomy within a federal structure. In 1934 Alexander was assassinated by Croatian dissidents at the start of a state visit to France. Thereafter, relations between the Serbs and the Croats became more bitter than ever. Eventually in 1939 Yugoslavia was reorganised along federal lines.

2. Albania had come into existence following the Treaty of London in 1913 (p.113). In 1925 a young Muslim army officer, Ahmed Zogu, became president. But three years later he proclaimed himself King Zog I and ruled his kingdom as a royal dictator. The state was small and backward, but King Zog tried hard to modernise it. His other concern was to resist Italian influence. However, in April 1939 Mussolini sent in troops and occupied Albania, and King Zog went into exile (p.291).

3. The kingdom of Romania under King Carol II almost doubled its pre-war size as a result of the peace treaties in 1919 (p.187). During most of the inter-war years, Romania retained a parliamentary system, but after 1933 the emergence of the Iron Guard, a right-wing anti-semitic group, threatened her fragile democracy. Finally, in 1938 Carol established a dictatorship and set about curbing the activities of the Iron Guard. Meanwhile Romania moved closer to Nazi Germany and away from the Soviet Union.

4. The Treaty of Neuilly in 1919 reduced pre-war Bulgaria and cut her off from access to the Aegean Sea (p.188). Discontent followed and her democratic government under a constitutional monarch, King Boris III, found it increasingly difficult to maintain order. Then, in 1934, the king and the army established a

royal and military dictatorship, which helped the Germans to invade Yugoslavia in 1941 (p.307).

5. At the peace conference, Greece received eastern Thrace, and was allowed to occupy Smyrna for five years, after which a plebiscite would be held. But Greek occupation of Smyrna aroused the Turkish national spirit and in 1921 the Greeks were defeated in a twenty-two-day battle. The following year over a million Greeks were expelled from Asia Minor. Eventually they gave up their claim to Smyrna but kept certain Aegean islands.

In 1924 King Constantine I was forced to abdicate and Greece became a republic under the leadership of Eleutherios Venizelos. In 1935 the monarchy was restored but the following year a military dictatorship under General Joannis Metaxas took control. All political parties were abolished, opponents were persecuted and strict censorship was imposed.

THE BALTIC REPUBLICS

The three Baltic states of Estonia, Lithuania and Latvia were created in 1919 out of the lands of the former tsarist empire. At first they adopted democratic constitutions, but the emergence of fascist and communist agitation soon put an end to their fledgling democracies.

In 1926 Lithuania turned to a national dictator, Antanus Smetona. In 1934 Estonia and Latvia also adopted dictatorial rule. Their independence came to an end in 1940 when Stalin, determined to build a buffer against Nazi expansion, incorporated the Baltic states into the Soviet Union (p.298).

Study Assignments and Essays

1. *Trace the fortunes of the Austrian state from 1919 to 1939.*
2. *Trace the fortunes of the Hungarian state from 1919 to 1939.*
3. *Trace the fortunes of the Czechoslovak state from 1919 to 1939.*
4. *Trace the fortunes of the Baltic states from 1919 to 1939.*
5. *Trace the fortunes of the Balkan states from 1919 to 1939.*
6. *Write an essay on two of the following:*
(i) Democracy in eastern Europe in the inter-war period; (ii) Friction between new European states in the inter-war period; (iii) A comparative analysis between any two eastern European states in the inter-war period; (iv) Poland's internal problems in the inter-war period.

23

The League of Nations

A Living Thing is created.
Woodrow Wilson, at the Paris Peace Conference.

THE CREATION of a general association of nations was a fundamental article of President Woodrow Wilson's fourteen points for peace in 1918. 'Merely to win the war' was not enough, he declared, 'it must be won in such a way as to ensure the future peace of the world.' This could only be achieved, Wilson believed, through a League of Nations, where the representatives of the nations of the world could solve problems around the conference table rather than on the battle-field. Wilson optimistically believed that the moral indignation of a world community of states would be a powerful deterrent against war; and that where any state offended against the peace, the principle of 'collective security' (an attack upon one is an attack upon all) would ensure the speedy resolution of the problem.

FRAMEWORK OF THE LEAGUE

The League's covenant (constitution) had twenty-six articles designed to foster international co-operation, peace and security. The League had four main organs: the Assembly; the Council; the Secretariat; and the Permanent Court of International Justice.

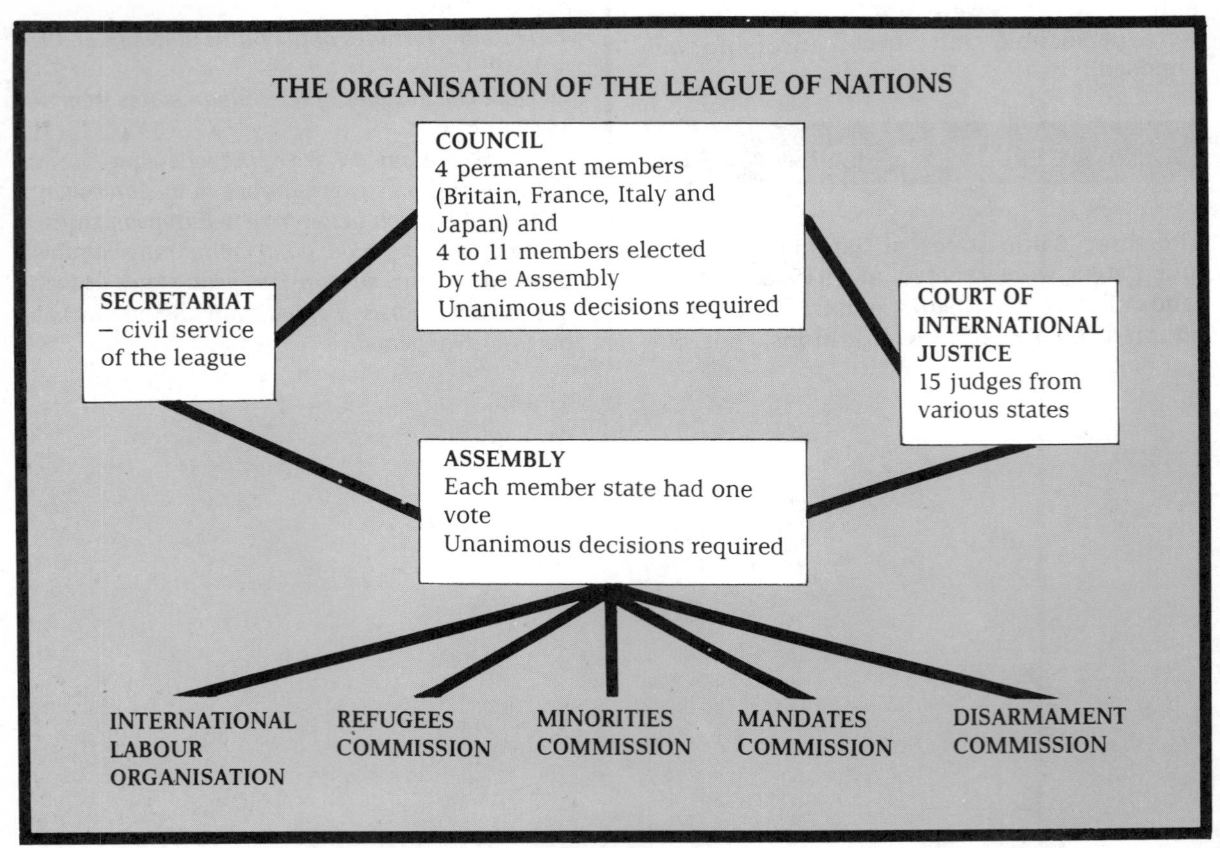

The Assembly met once a year. Each member nation was allowed three representatives, but only one vote. Its decisions had to be unanimous among those voting. The Assembly could debate any matter pertaining to the functions of the League, and essentially served as a world parliament that met to discuss questions of international relations and granted all members an equal right to state their opinions and vote accordingly.

The Council was the chief decision-making body and, as with the Assembly, its decisions had to be by unanimous vote. Its primary function was to arbitrate on disputes that might threaten the peace of the world, but it also adjudicated on minor matters such as frontier adjustments and the right of national minorities. The Council met three times a year and whenever emergencies arose. It consisted of eight members. Britain, France, Italy and Japan were permanent members and the remaining four were elected by the Assembly on a rotation basis; this ensured that every member state would get its turn on the council. In 1926 the number rose to ten, in 1928 to fourteen, and in 1933 to fifteen. Such growth showed the eagerness of the small states to play their part in international decision-making, but since decisions had to be unanimous, an enlarged Council was not necessarily a more efficient one.

The Secretariat peformed the civil service functions of the League: preparing data for conferences, organising meetings and providing a link between the League and national governments. The officials of the Secretariat were drawn from various nationalities. In this way a truly international civil service developed under the leadership of Sir Eric Drummond, the first secretary general of the League, who served in this capacity until 1933. No such international body of officials had existed previously, and it was one of the achievements of the League of Nations that it built up a hard-working and efficient body of officials dedicated to international co-operation.

The Permanent Court of International Justice sat at the Hague in Holland. It had fifteen judges appointed by the Assembly and the Council and drawn from many different nationalities so that the court was international in character. Its function was to give legal advice to the Council, and to arbitrate on cases involving international law. When states in dispute submitted their case to the court, they had to agree in advance that they would accept its verdict.

In addition to its four main organs, the League had several subsidiary bodies, each concerning itself with a specific activity. The International Labour Organisation (ILO) was a successful body and did much good work under its first director, Albert Thomas, a dedicated French socialist. All League members belonged to the ILO, to which governments, employers and employees sent delegates. It debated such matters as workers' compensation, conditions of work, trade union legislation, and women's rights. Although its recommendations were not binding, much was done to improve labour conditions, and it provided a forum where many people of different nationalities and backgrounds could meet, discuss and learn from each other.

The Refugees Commission, under the leadership of the Norwegian Fridtjof Nansen, helped in a practical way with refugees and prisoners of war. Homes were found for White Russians who had fled after the Bolshevik revolution; for over one million Greeks repatriated from Turkish territory; and for some half-a-million Turks who had been moved from Greece.

The Minorities Commission received reports from national minorities on their treatment and welfare. Minority rights consisted of such matters as freedom to practise one's religion and freedom to speak one's own language. The commission was frequently frustrated in its attempts to see that minority rights were respected because sovereign governments often saw the commission's role as an interference in their affairs.

The Mandates Commission supervised sixteen mandated territories and each year reported its findings to the Council; these territories were the former colonial possessions of Germany and Turkey that had been assigned to one or other of the allies under the peace settlement in 1919 (p.182). Each mandatory power had bound itself to administer its mandated territory, not as if it was its own private property, but as a sacred trust for the benefit of the inhabitants in preparation for eventual independence. The work of the Mandates Commission was often frustrating and progress was disappointingly slow. Iraq, a British mandate, reached independent status as early as 1932, but the vast majority of mandates did not become independent until after World War II, and then only after armed struggle with the mandatory powers (p.353).

The Disarmament Commission had the most difficult task of all the League's subsidiary bodies. Article 8 of the covenant pledged member nations to recognise that

> the maintenance of peace required the reduction of national armaments to the lowest point consistent with national safety.

The Treaty of Versailles had required Germany to disarm. The Allied powers had declared that this was but the prelude to general voluntary disarmament by all nations in a world made free from war.

In 1921–22 at a conference in Washington, five naval powers (the United States, Britain, Japan, France, Italy) set limitations on their naval armaments. In 1930, the first three of these powers agreed to further naval limitations. With these two exceptions, there was no disarmament during the inter-war years. The constant argument against disarmament was the need for national security.

In 1932 a general disarmament conference was called which was attended by two non-League members — the Soviet Union and the United States. The USSR was strongly in favour of disarming, but the other powers suspected her motives. First, she herself was very poorly armed; and secondly, since Marxism maintained that war was a product of capitalism, it was good socialist propaganda to preach disarmament. Germany claimed that she was insecure until other states disarmed. When no agreement had been reached by October 1933, Hitler, now chancellor of Germany, withdrew from the disarmament conference and the League. By this time most states were thinking of rearmament and in 1934 the conference simply faded away.

THE SUCCESS OF THE LEAGUE

In its early years the League of Nations did have some success on matters that did not involve any of the great powers. It managed to get co-operation between Germany and Poland over the vexed question of Silesia: following a League plebiscite, the area was partitioned between them. In addition, it provided a high commissioner for the city of Danzig, another trouble spot between Germany and Poland. It also supervised the administration of the Saar region for fifteen years, before it was returned to Germany after a plebiscite (p.181 and map, p.186).

In 1921 the League settled a dispute between Sweden and Finland concerning the Aaland Islands. These islands had strategic importance and were under Finnish control, but many of the inhabitants wished to belong to Sweden. The dispute was submitted to the League. After careful consideration of all the factors, including the previous history of the islands, the League decided in favour of Finland, but the Swedish-speaking inhabitants did achieve home rule. Sweden, which had hoped to secure the islands, protested, but accepted the League's decision (map, p.186).

In August 1923 four Italians were assassinated on Greek territory. The four had been engaged by the Conference of Ambassadors — a council of the four victorious powers in World War I — to decide on the border between Greece and Albania. Mussolini sent an ultimatum to the Greek government demanding a large sum in compensation. When the reply was not to his liking, he ordered the occupation of the Greek island of Corfu. Claiming that Italian 'honour' was involved, he refused to have the matter submitted to the League. Moreover, Mussolini announced that if the League intervened, Italian forces would remain on Corfu. The League wriggled out of the situation by allowing the Conference of Ambassadors (of which Italy was a member) to take the initiative in the matter. The Conference ordered the Greek government to pay fifty million lire in compensation to Italy. On receipt of the compensation, Italian forces were withdrawn from Corfu. Although the solution was not effected by the League, and even though it created bitterness in Greece and allowed Mussolini to get his own way, it did prevent war in the Mediterranean.

The Lithuanians wished to make the ancient city of Vilna the capital of their new state, set up at the peace conference in 1919 (p.188). But the Poles had seized the city in 1920, claiming it on the principle of self-determination. This action was allowed to stand until finally it was taken out of the hands of the League, and in 1923 the Conference of Ambassadors recognised Polish possession of Vilna (map, p.186).

In 1919, Lithuania seized the Baltic port of Memel, but in 1924 accepted the League's proposal that Memel should have home rule within Lithuania (map, p.186).

The Mosul area, on the river Tigris, lay on the frontier between Turkey and Iraq, and had been occupied by the British since 1918. The British were interested in its oil potential and favoured its inclusion in Iraq, which they held as a mandated territory. The inhabitants of the region were Kurds; and the Turks pointed out that since there were other Kurdish people under Turkish rule, they had a better claim than the Arabs of Iraq. The League sent out a neutral commission to study the problem on the spot; but while the study was in progress,

The Angel of Peace sits on a silent gun. Such early optimism by the League's founders was soon dispelled.

the Turks prejudiced their claim by the savagery with which they put down a revolt among their own Kurdish subjects. The League therefore assigned nearly the whole of the disputed area to Iraq. When the Turks protested, the international court at the Hague ruled that under the Treaty of Lausanne (p.188) the Turks had agreed to abide by the decisions of the League Council. Turkey finally accepted the situation in 1926 (map, p.186).

In 1925 Greek troops crossed into Bulgarian territory to avenge the alleged murder of two Greek soldiers by Bulgarians. The Bulgarian government immediately sent a complaint to the League Council. The League acted swiftly. It ordered the Greek troops off Bulgarian territory and instructed the Greek government to pay an indemnity for its act of aggression.

THE LEAGUE IN DECLINE

Although the League had several successes to its credit in the 1920s, only minor powers were in dispute, and thus it could exert its authority in reaching solutions. But when the interests of big powers were at stake, the inadequacies of the League of Nations became painfully obvious.

Germany and the Soviet Union

The Germans at first were not allowed to join the League because the Treaty of Versailles put her outside the 'family of nations'. Since the covenant of the League was written into the treaty, Germany regarded the body as an instrument of France and Britain for maintaining the Versailles settlement. But with the changed international atmosphere following the Locarno Pact of 1925 (p.199), it became possible to accept Germany into the League. Accordingly, in 1926 when passions had sufficiently simmered down, Germany became a full member with a seat on the Council. Gustav Stresemann, posing as the 'good German', had successfully rehabilitated Germany into the family of nations.

Stresemann's death in 1929, the Wall Street Crash the same year and the consequent depression that left six million Germans unemployed, enabled Hitler to come to power on a policy of undoing the hated Versailles settlement. He saw the League as the living symbol of the treaty, which, he claimed, was the source of all Germany's ills. He withdrew Germany from the League in 1933 when the disarmament conference failed to agree on all-round disarmament (p.283).

When the League was set up, communist Russia, like Germany, was also regarded as beyond the pale. The Bolshevik victory had created an unprecedented situation in world affairs. On the one hand the Bolsheviks, fearing encirclement by a hostile capitalist world, denounced the League as a capitalist club. On the other hand the West feared the communist mission of world revolution, and pointed to the existence of the Comintern (p.170) as grounds for their suspicion. They refused to recognise the legitimacy of the Bolshevik regime and did not invite it to join the League. When the Soviet Union eventually joined in 1934 (p.240), it was promised more by the desire to have allies against Hitler than by any conversion to the League's principles.

Manchuria

In the 1920s the Japanese economy was very much dependent upon exports to the United States. But following the Wall Street Crash and the subsequent depression, Japanese exports fell by thirty per cent. The effects on Japan led to internal upheaval, and political power passed into the hands of the military and the industrialists. This right-wing government coveted the large province of Manchuria with its vast resources of coal and other raw materials. Already the Japanese had treaty rights in Manchuria that the Chinese nationalists resented. The coming of the railway to Manchuria had resulted in a great influx of Chinese into the fertile central plain, and by the early 1930s Japan's position seemed to be threatened (map, p.97).

Events came to a head on the night of 18 September 1931 when Japanese troops guarding the railway line at Mukden in Manchuria were murdered. Whoever was responsible, Japan blamed China, and sent in troops to 'protect her interests'. By February 1932 Chinese forces had withdrawn south of the Great Wall and the Japanese conquest of Manchuria was effectively complete. The same month Japan announced the birth of a new state, Manchukuo. Japan claimed that the people of Manchukuo desired to be free of Chinese rule, and all it had done was to help them win their independence. But this claim ignored the fact that the people of Manchukuo were predominantly Chinese, had no love for the Japanese, and that the new state was not independent but a mere puppet of Japan.

The Chinese government appealed to the League of Nations, claiming that Japan had made an unprovoked attack upon the territory

Chinese troops resisting the Japanese takeover of Manchuria, 1931.

of a fellow member, China. The League appointed a commission under Britain's Lord Lytton to enquire into the matter. In October 1932 the Lytton Report found that Japan had not acted (as she had claimed) in self-defence in Manchuria and that the new state of Manchukuo was not an independent state. It recommended that Manchuria should have home rule under China, but that Japan's economic treaty rights should be recognised. The Japanese refused to accept the findings and continued to occupy Manchuria. In February 1933 the Assembly of the League voted to condemn Japan as the aggressor, and the following month Japan left the League.

In the midst of depression the democracies shrank from the prospect of a costly war in the Far East. Moreover, since Britain had extensive possessions and trading interests in the region, she had most to lose by antagonising Japan; indeed her traditional Far Eastern policy had been to maintain friendly relations with Japan. Thus Britain's national interests took precedence over her commitments to the principles of the League of Nations. Many in Britain and France took refuge in the excuse that China, so backward and in a state of internal unrest (communist agitation), scarcely deserved to be called a state. There were others, too, who regarded Japanese domination as preferable to communism in Manchuria.

Ironically, it was two non-League members, the United States and the Soviet Union, who showed the only sign of opposition. The United States protested vigorously against Japanese aggression, but failing to receive any firm support from Britain, did nothing to back up her protests. Soviet Russia, which shared a common frontier with Manchuria and whose relations with Japan had been strained since the war of 1904 (p.54), sought closer ties with China, but beyond this did nothing. Yet fear of the Soviet Union obliged Japan to keep large numbers of troops permanently stationed in Manchuria.

The failure of the League to respond effectively to Japanese aggression upon a fellow League member dealt a serious blow to its moral authority as an instrument of world peace. But worse was to follow.

MUSSOLINI AND HITLER

Between 1935 and 1939 a series of expansive moves by the two fascist dictators was clearly in breach of the peace treaties and the principles of the League. Yet the League failed to act in many of these incidents, and in cases where it did intervene, it did so in such a half-hearted manner that it merely highlighted its own ineffectiveness (p.285).

In October 1935 when Italy, without any declaration of war, invaded Abyssinia, a fellow League member, the League imposed mild economic sanctions, which excluded oil, coal and steel. These were the very commodities Italy most needed, but Britain and France were more concerned with not antagonising Mussolini than with the principles of collective security. Accordingly, when Haile Selassie, the emperor of Abyssinia, addressed the League in Geneva, his appeal fell on deaf ears:

> It is my duty to inform Governments of the deadly peril which threatens them. It is a question of trust in international treaties and of the value of promises to small states that their integrity shall be respected. In a word, international morality is at stake.

In May 1936 Addis Ababa fell, Victor Emmanuel III was proclaimed the new emperor of Abyssinia, and Italy withdrew from the League. Haile Selassie went into exile in England, and two months later, the sanctions were quietly withdrawn. By then, however, most states had lost confidence in the League as an instrument of international peacekeeping.

Meanwhile, on 7 March, Hitler had marched his troops into the Rhineland (p.285), an act expressly forbidden by the Treaty of Versailles (p.181). But the League of Nations merely condemned the Nazi incursion and left it to France and Britain to uphold the guarantees that had been given at Locarno (p.199).

In the summer of 1936 when Spain erupted in civil war, the League adopted a policy of non-intervention, but this did not deter the three dictators, Hitler, Mussolini and Stalin from sending help to the combatants (p.264).

The years 1937 to 1939 saw Hitler take over Austria, Czechoslovakia and Memel (p.288), while both he and Mussolini poured scorn on the League as an instrument for upholding the settlement of 1919. The League had lost the initiative and the fascist axis (Rome-Berlin) was now dictating the pace of events. The democracies and the Soviet Union were too far apart ideologically to find a common cause against fascism. The democracies too were far from united. The United States continued to stand aloof from the League and from all international entanglements. Britain and France pursued opposing policies: France put her trust in her alliances (p.242), while Britain put her faith in appeasement, hoping to satisfy specific grievances by negotiation and revision (p.289).

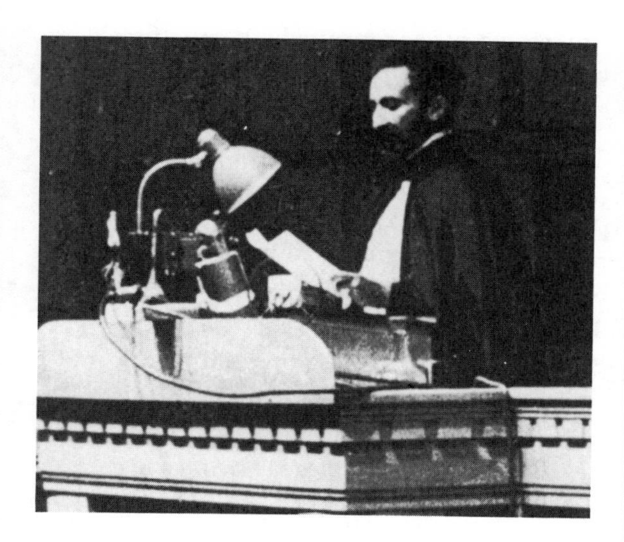

Emperor Haile Selassie appeals to the League of Nations after Mussolini's forces had invaded Abyssinia in October 1935.

Britain and France made no attempt to invoke the covenant of the League in any of the crises between 1937 and 1939; and when they finally declared war on Germany in 1939, they did so as individual powers in support of their treaty obligations to Poland, and not as members of the League of Nations in accordance with the principle of collective security.

The last act of the League was to expel the Soviet Union following her attack upon Finland on 30 November 1939 (p.298); but by then any League action was irrelevant.

Before World War II was over, the main outlines of a new world organisation — the United Nations — had been formulated. Accordingly, on 8 April 1945, the League of Nations officially ceased to exist. It wound up its affairs and transferred its assets to the new United Nations organisation. Thus although Wilson's League of Nations died, the dream that gave birth to it lived on in the United Nations (p.325).

WHY THE LEAGUE FAILED

The League of Nations was born out of the chaos of world war, and since its covenant was written into each of the peace treaties, it became closely associated with the latter, especially in the minds of the defeated powers. Accordingly, those who disliked the peace treaties automatically disliked the League. Moreover, the machinery of the League was primarily designed to maintain the *status quo* and was not sufficiently flexible to make adjustments. For this reason it was often looked upon as a weapon of the victorious powers attempting to make history stand still.

The League had several constitutional defects. The Assembly met only once a year, and the Council three times annually, although it could also meet in emergencies. Since all decisions of the Council had to be unanimous, each member effectively had the power of veto. Thus, hardly anything outside matters of procedure could be decided upon.

A major defect of the League lay in the attitude of the great powers. The United States, the world's greatest power, had retreated into isolation and had never joined the world body. Japan, a founder member, withdrew in March 1933 following her act of aggression on a fellow member, China. Italy, another founder member, also left the League after her conquest of a fellow member state, Abyssinia, in 1935. Germany, not allowed to join at first, secured admission following the Locarno Pact, but soon after Hitler came to power, he withdrew Germany in 1933. The Soviet Union, at first not invited to join, secured admission in 1934 to gain allies against Hitler, but was expelled in December 1939 after attacking Finland.

The only two great powers to remain throughout were Britain and France; but they held divergent views on how the League should maintain world peace and stability.

Britain would not commit herself in advance to action on behalf of a League member, because she preferred to maintain her flexibility and judge each situation as it arose in the light of her own interest. Moreover, she already had large Commonwealth commitments and did not wish to increase her responsibilities. France, ever conscious of her security problems, had hoped for 'collective security' through an international force; but since this did not materialise, she would not agree to disarmament.

But the real weakness of the League lay in its lack of power to enforce its own decisions. Article 12 of the covenant provided for the settlement of disputes by any of three methods: arbitration by a neutral power; settlement in the international court; and inquiry by the Council. But the essential flaw in each of these was that there was no way of forcing any state to *submit* its case for settlement; and even when it did, there was no effective way of compelling a state to *accept* the findings. Article 16 did provide for diplomatic pressure and economic sanctions on an offending state, but this was an impractical answer to the problem since economic sanctions often damage the economies of those applying the sanctions as much as the economy against which they are directed. On the single occasion on which sanctions were imposed, Italy in 1935, they had no effect (p.285).

Thus when Japan, Italy and Germany decided on settling their differences by force, and when the remaining League members failed to apply the principle of collective security, the League as an instrument of international peace was doomed.

Study Assignments and Essays

1. What motives prompted the creation of a League of Nations?
2. Describe in detail the constitution (covenant) and general framework of the League, and examine its defects.
3. Critically examine the successes of the League in the 1920s.
4. Treat of relations between (a) the Soviet Union and the League and (b) Germany and the League.
5. What factors militated against the effective working of the League in the 1930s?
6. Write an essay on two of the following:
(i) President Wilson and the League; (ii) Mussolini and the League; (iii) The role of the League's subsidiary bodies; (iv) The democracies and the League; (v) The failure of the League.

The Road to War 1933–39

24

The generation to which I belong failed in its task.
Léon Blum

THE GREAT POWERS AND HITLER

HITLER'S ACCESSION to power in Germany in 1933 created an entirely new situation in international affairs. He had made no secret of the fact that his avowed aim was to destroy the Treaty of Versailles, unite all German-speaking peoples in a greater Germany or *Grossdeutschland* and extend eastwards to the Ural mountains in pursuance of his twin aims of destroying communism and creating *lebensraum* for the new Germany (p.201).

Despite these ambitious plans, which boded ill for the future of peace in Europe, the reaction of the other powers was muted and varied. In France the government was gravely concerned but, beyond this, said nothing. In Britain official views were mixed. The government regretted the death of German democracy, but took comfort in Hitler's anti-communism. Yet many members of the cabinet held the view that the Treaty of Versailles had been too harsh and needed revision, although preferably by mutual agreement.

In Italy, Mussolini was not as pleased as might be assumed at the emergence of another fascist regime in Europe. The question of the Trentino (South Tyrol) would keep Mussolini and Hitler apart until 1936. This region had many German-speaking inhabitants, and Mussolini feared that Hitler would demand its return. Mussolini's policy accordingly was to support the independence of Austria as a buffer between Italy and Germany.

In the Soviet Union, outwardly at least, Stalin exhibited a desire to be left alone to pursue his domestic programmes (p.233), but it was not long before he had to recast his foreign policy towards the democracies and the League of Nations in his quest for support against the Nazi threat (p.240).

The American president, Franklin D. Roosevelt, though still an isolationist from European affairs, declared that he appreciated the seriousness of Nazi rule and the death of German democracy.

THE GERMAN-POLISH PACT 1934

Hitler's first international act was to withdraw from the League of Nations and the disarmament conference because France had broken the spirit of Locarno. Then on 26 January 1934, he signed a ten-year non-aggression pact with Poland. With one diplomatic move Hitler had detached Poland from the French system of alliances built up around Germany (p.242).

For Hitler, it was simply a case of destroying the Franco-Polish non-aggression pact of 1921. For Poland, the reasons are more complex: Poland had been created at Versailles out of Russian and German possessions and, above all, she feared a Russo-German alliance. She also feared that France might 'do a deal' with Germany in the west in return for German compensation in the east. Whatever the reasons, the German-Polish Pact prompted an immediate change in Soviet foreign policy. Hitherto, Stalin had denounced the League of Nations as a capitalist conspiracy; now he dropped his former antagonism towards the western capitalist democracies and, with French support, the Soviet Union joined the League of Nations in 1934 (p.240).

THE SAAR

In January 1935 the Saar plebiscite was held, as had been agreed under the Treaty of

Germany rearms: cavalry firing from the standing saddle position on practice manoeuvres in 1935, and bombers passing in formation during a demonstration at Nuremberg in 1938.

Versailles (p.181). The Nazis conducted a huge propaganda campaign and, although many Saarlanders did not relish coming under Hitler's sway, there was a ninety per cent vote in favour of a return to Germany. Hitler now became less dependent on the goodwill of France and Britain, and announced his decision to rearm.

GERMANY REARMS

In March 1935 Hitler, claiming that other states had failed to disarm as had been agreed in 1919, declared that Germany would no longer comply with the restrictions placed upon her in the Treaty of Versailles. Conscription was introduced, and the formation of armoured divisions and submarine construction began.

Alarmed, France and the Soviet Union signed a pact of mutual assistance in May 1935. The Soviets also signed a pact with France's ally, Czechoslovakia, which would only become operative if France fulfilled her obligations to Czechoslovakia as well. Stalin had no intention of becoming embroiled in a war against Hitler over Czechoslovakia unless France (and by implication Britain) was also involved.

The Franco-Soviet Pact was immediately used by Hitler to announce general rearmament. As alarm swept through Europe, the British government concluded a separate Anglo-German naval agreement. Britain acceded to the construction of a German navy provided it did not exceed thirty-five per cent of British naval strength: German submarine strength was specifically excluded from these restrictions.

The Anglo-German naval agreement was regarded with dismay in France, while it appeared to Hitler that Britain was prepared to acquiesce in German breaches of the Versailles terms, and this served to encourage him. Accordingly, in 1936 Hermann Göring introduced a four-year plan for the expansion of Germany's land and air forces. Preparations were also begun for the construction of the Siegfried Line along Germany's western frontiers and opposite the French Maginot Line (p.301 and map, p.286).

ABYSSINIA

In October 1935 Mussolini's troops invaded Abyssinia. Britain and France were unwilling to act, fearing that this would drive Mussolini into Hitler's arms. Hitler looked on approvingly because he saw in the distraction an opportunity to remilitarise the Rhineland. The only opposition Mussolini had to face, apart from that of Abyssinia itself, was the token economic sanctions imposed by the League of Nations, which merely served to bring the League into disrepute. In May 1936 Addis Ababa fell, Abyssinia was officially annexed by Italy, and Mussolini withdrew from the League of Nations (p.280).

THE RHINELAND

Article 44 of the Treaty of Versailles stated:

> In case Germany violates in any manner whatever the provisions of Article 42 and 43 [i.e., demilitarisation of the Rhineland] she shall be regarded as committing a hostile act against the powers signatory of the present Treaty and as calculated to disturb the peace of the world.

A demilitarised Rhineland was crucial to French security since it left the industrial heartland of Germany unfortified. But in March 1936, as Mussolini's troops advanced on Addis Ababa, Hitler sent some 35,000 German soldiers into the Rhineland. He justified his action by declaring that the Franco-Russian Pact (p.240) was incompatible with the Locarno Pact (p.199). Hitler immediately offered France and Belgium a twenty-five-year non-agression pact to allay their fears, but they declined the offer. The League of Nations condemned the incursion into the Rhineland, but took no action. Mussolini was too busy in Abyssinia (p.219) to take much notice. France looked to Britain, but the foreign secretary, Anthony Eden, told the House of Commons that in this difficult period they should seek 'a peaceful and agreed solution'. Discussions went on for a few months but no agreement was reached. Hitler had gambled and won.

The principle of a demilitarised Rhineland

THE EXPANSION OF GERMANY UNDER HITLER, 1936-39

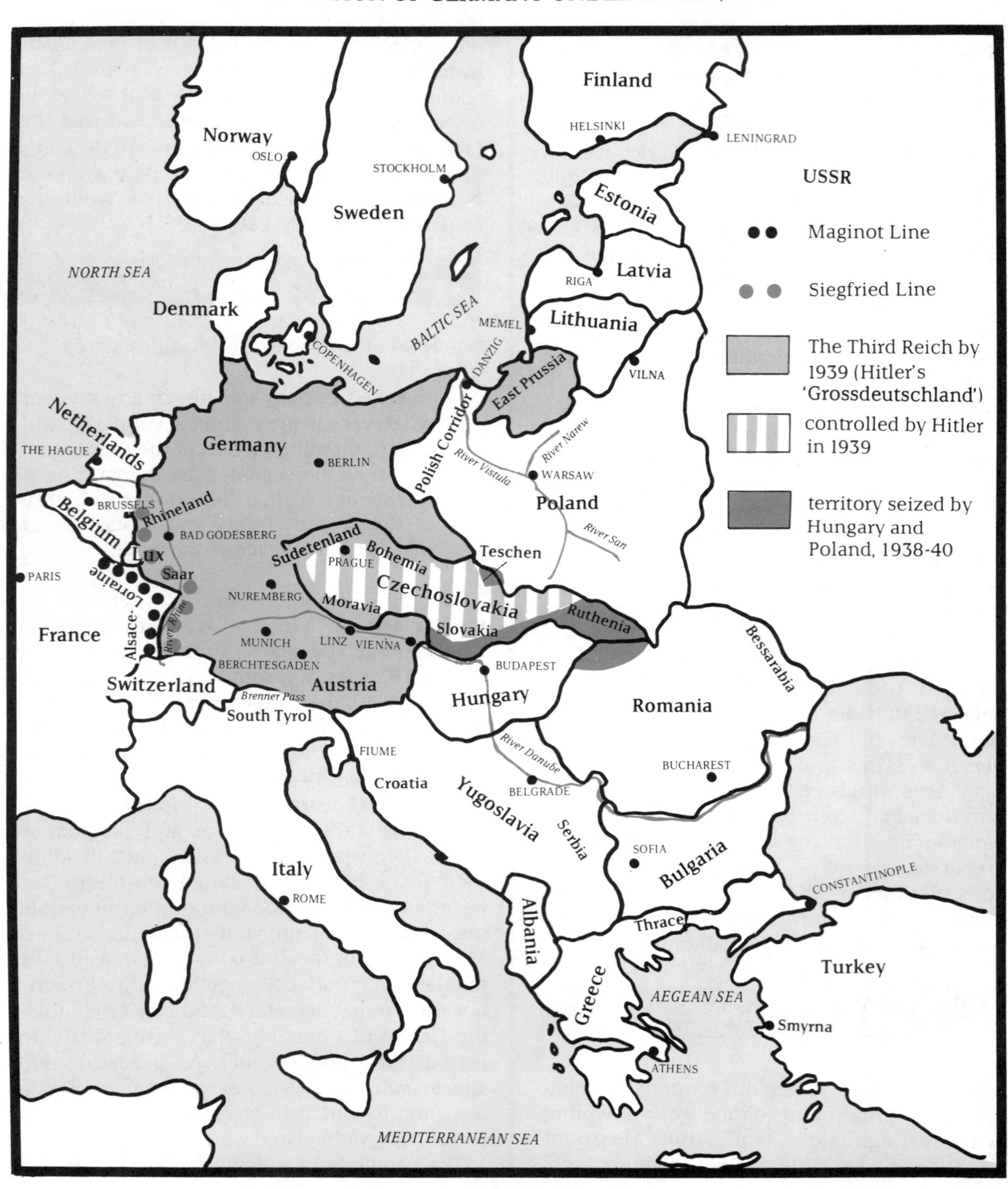

had been the cornerstone of French security, yet Hitler reoccupied the Rhineland unhindered. There could be no united action by Britain, France and the Soviet Union because the British government feared and detested the Russian communist regime and saw fascism as the lesser of two evils. Indeed many saw it as a bulwark against the spread of communism. Moreover, much of Britain's policy throughout the 1930s (p.258). It meant Hitler's demands had a certain justification. Britain felt that timely concessions to Hitler would satisfy him. This policy, known as appeasement, was to characterise British policy throughout the 1930s (p. 000). It meant that fascism got its own way, time after time.

A mood of defeatism now entered French thinking; all her striving for security seemed to have come to nought. The Germans continued building the Siegfried Line to fortify her western frontier. This would mean that in any future war German forces would be poised directly on the French frontier, while conversely the French would be deprived of their former advantage of being able to strike through the demilitarised Rhineland at the industrial heartland of Germany.

Hitler's troops march into Cologne during the reoccupation of the demilitarised Rhineland, in defiance of the Versailles and Locarno treaties.

THE SPANISH CIVIL WAR

In July 1936 the Spanish Civil War broke out. Its causes are complex, but in the totalitarian states of Italy, Germany and the Soviet Union the war was seen as an ideological battle between fascism and communism. Mussolini and Hitler favoured Franco's nationalists. Stalin favoured the communists on the republican side. The British were in sympathy with the republicans, but the presence of communists in their ranks inhibited the British from sending aid. In France the socialist government favoured the republican cause but because of the division of opinion in the country, France remained neutral. All the powers agreed to a scheme for non-intervention, and a pledge to this effect was signed in August 1936.

Despite this, the three totalitarian states ignored the agreement and sent aid to Spain. Then in April 1937 Italy and Germany officially withdrew from the non-intervention agreement and the Soviet Union, using this as an excuse, also pulled out. Eventually, it was the superior aid that Italy and Germany had given to Franco which ensured his final victory (p.268). The non-intervention agreement, the western democracies and the League of Nations had all revealed their inability to influence events. Force was fast becoming the arbiter in international relations.

THE ROME-BERLIN AXIS

The breach between Italy and the democracies over the invasion of Abyssinia (p.280), together with joint Italian and German help to Franco (p.264), brought Mussolini and Hitler together. Gone were the days when Mussolini had displayed contempt for the upstart Germans, 'descendants of people who were illiterate in the days when Rome boasted a Caesar, a Vergil and an Augustus'. Now Mussolini admired the Germans for their 'fine martial spirit' and 'heroic philosophy'. In October 1936 an agreement for Italo-German co-operation was reached. It was referred to by Mussolini as a Rome-Berlin Axis, around which the rest of Europe would revolve.

The agreement included an understanding on the two states' major outstanding difference, Austria. Hitler promised that he would accept the Brenner Pass as the boundary between Italy and Austria. By this he was assuring Mussolini that no claim would be made for the German-speaking population in the South Tyrol in the event of Austria's absorption into the German Reich (p.289).

THE ANTI-COMINTERN PACT

The Comintern had existed since 1919 for the purpose of spreading international communism. In practice it had achieved very little and in 1934 it recast its policy by advising communists to participate in popular front governments in order to prevent the spread of fascism (p.246). But it was the very existence of communist Russia and the Comintern that prompted the fascist powers to sign an anti-Comintern pact. In November 1936 Germany and Japan signed this pact, which was in effect a declaration of hostility towards the Soviet Union. The pact declared that:

> the toleration of interference by the Communist International [Comintern] in the internal affairs of nations not only endangers internal peace and social welfare, but threatens the general peace of the world.

In November, as a logical consequence of the Rome-Berlin Axis, Italy joined the anti-Comintern pact.

AUSTRIA

The union of Austria and Germany had been specifically forbidden by the Treaty of Versailles (p.183), but one of Hitler's stated aims was the union of all German-speaking people in one fatherland.

In 1934 the Austrian chancellor, Engelbert Dollfuss, was assassinated by the Nazis. But Mussolini had immediately moved Italian troops to the border with Austria and had warned Hitler that Italy would stand by Austria. Hitler made no move.

However, by 1938 the Nazi party in Austria was legalised and Dr Arthur Seyss-Inquart, a pro-Nazi, became minister of the interior. As the authority of the chancellor, Schuschnigg, worsened, because of Nazi pressure from within and Hitler's demands from without, Schuschnigg ordered a plebiscite for 13 March to test opinion concerning *Anschluss* or union with Germany.

Immediately Hitler massed troops on the border, demanded that the plebiscite be postponed and that Schuschnigg should resign. Feeling isolated, Schuschnigg gave in and Seyss-Inquart became chancellor. Seyss-Inquart postponed the plebiscite and, declaring that he had uncovered a communist plot, invited German troops into his country to help him maintain order. On 12 March German troops entered Austria (p.269). The next day Hitler visited Vienna and was greeted by Seyss-Inquart.

> In spite of a dictated peace treaty, Germans have found their way to each

> other. Today the entire German people stand united and indivisible. . . . You, my *Führer*, are the Leader of the German nation in its struggle for freedom, honour and right.

From Vienna, Hitler went on to Linz, the town he had left as a schoolboy, and said:

> If providence once called me forth from this town to be the Leader of the Reich, it must . . . have charged me with a mission, and that mission could only be to restore my dear homeland to the German Reich.

In April the Nazis organised their own plebiscite and ninety-nine per cent of those Austrians who voted opted for *Anschluss*. Despite her violation of the Treaty of Versailles, no power was prepared to oppose Germany. The French government was too weak and divided to do anything. The British government took the view that union was desired by most Austrians; and anyhow it was now an accomplished fact, so nothing could be done. The Soviet Union proposed a meeting with Britain, France and the United States to discuss collective security, but the suggestion fell on deaf ears; too many people in these countries still feared communism more than fascism. Even Mussolini, whose policy had been to maintain Austrian independence, remained silent. By 1938 he had distanced himself from Britain and France over Abyssinia (p.280) and Spain (p.264) and had moved closer to Hitler through the Rome-Berlin Axis and the anti-Comintern pact. Moreover, Hitler had guaranteed Mussolini that he would respect the Brenner Pass as the frontier between Austria and Italy. Whether Hitler expected Italian intervention or not, he was extremely grateful to Mussolini for remaining silent, and sent him a telegram:

> *Mussolini, ich werde Ihnen dieses nie vergessen.* (Mussolini, I shall never forget you for this.)

CZECHOSLOVAKIA

Soon after the *Anschluss*, Hitler declared that Czechoslovakia was to be wiped off the map. He knew that any action against Czechoslovakia would have the sympathy of Hungary and Poland, who each had claims on Czech territory (p.271). He also believed that Britain and France would not come to Czechoslovakia's aid because it was geographically cut off and was now almost surrounded by Reich territory. Besides, over three million Germans, living mainly in the Sudetenland, within Czechoslovakia's borders, were appealing to Hitler for protection. Their leader, Konrad Henlein, began campaigning for local autonomy, while Hitler precipitated a crisis by massing troops on the Czech border. The Czechs responded by ordering partial mobilisation and called on France and the Soviet Union for assistance. France was in favour of firm action, but again Britain recommended caution and sent Lord Runciman to Prague to act as a mediator between the Czech government and the Sudetens. Britain hoped that by allowing Hitler to take over the German-speaking areas of Czechoslovakia, he would be appeased and war would be averted. France had great doubts of this policy, but as long as her major ally was not prepared to intervene, she had no option but to agree.

Tension mounted as Hitler, at a Nazi rally at Nuremburg, denounced Czech rule over the Sudetens as intolerable. It looked as if war was about to break out in September 1938, but the British prime minister, Neville Chamberlain, in an effort to preserve the peace, made the first of three visits to Hitler.

The first meeting on 15 September was held at Hitler's retreat at Berchtesgaden in the Bavarian alps. Hitler demanded that all areas with over fifty per cent German inhabitants

Chamberlain with Hitler, reviewing a guard of honour on his arrival at Munich in September 1938.

should be incorporated immediately into the German Reich. Chamberlain agreed and the French followed suit. With great reluctance, and feeling deserted by Britain and France, the Czech government accepted.

A few days later Hitler increased his demands. He now demanded the total annexation of the Sudetenland and also presented the Hungarian and Polish claims to other parts of Czechoslovakia.

Chamberlain made his second visit to Hitler on 22 September, meeting him at Bad Godesberg on the Rhine. No agreement was reached and Chamberlain returned home. The Czechs ordered full mobilisation and deployed their troops along the border. Britain and France also began to mobilise and the Soviet Union placed her air force on the alert. This display made Hitler hesitate, and Mussolini, acting as mediator, proposed a conference of Britain, France, Germany and Italy to settle the problem.

On 29 September, Chamberlain met Hitler at Munich together with Mussolini and Daladier, the French premier. The Soviets were not invited to attend, while the Czechs waited in a nearby hotel to be informed of their fate.

At Munich Hitler repeated his demands made at Bad Godesberg, and Chamberlain and Daladier capitulated. They informed the Czechs that if they did not accept these terms within twelve hours, they could not expect assistance from France or Britain. The Munich Agreement was signed and war was averted. Hitler stated that he had no further territorial claims, while Chamberlain claimed that the agreement meant 'peace for our time'.

When Chamberlain returned home, he was greeted as a hero; there was little doubt that his policy was in accord with the deep-seated pacifism of the British people. Yet a growing minority, led by Winston Churchill, Eden and Duff Cooper, first lord of the Admiralty, were asserting that appeasement was becoming dangerously close to capitulation.

Following the Munich Conference, the Sudetenland passed into German hands while simultaneously Poland seized the Teschen district and Hungary occupied a strip of Slovakia. In all, Czechoslovakia surrendered sixteen thousand square miles of territory, and five million of her population. Moreover, the area ceded to Hitler contained the Czech military defence lines and her new border was now undefended. Nazi Germany increased her territory by over ten thousand square miles and added three-and-a-half million people to the Reich, which now became the largest geographical state in western Europe (map, p.286).

Soon the government of the rump state of Czechoslovakia found that its freedom of action was almost non-existent. The Slovaks demanded more autonomy. In early March 1939 their leaders, Monsignor Tiso and Ferdinand Durcansky, sought Hitler's help for their demands. This was a fatal mistake because Hitler now made them draw up a draft declaration of Slovak independence together with an appeal for German help. With the situation fast deteriorating for Czechoslovakia, the aged president, Emil Hacha, decided to visit Hitler in Berlin on 15 March to see what could be preserved.

Hitler so violently harangued Hacha that the old man fainted. When he recovered, Hitler presented him with an agreement that he was obliged to sign. This put all of Czechoslovakia in Hitler's hands as a means of 'preserving order'. Immediately German troops moved into the Czech provinces of Bohemia and Moravia, while Hungarian troops marched into Ruthenia. On 16 March Tiso requested Hitler to assume a protectorate over Slovakia. Thus the independent state of Czechoslovakia, created at the peace conference in 1919, came to an end. Yet Hitler was able to claim that he had acted legally since he had merely complied with the 'requests' of the Czechs and Slovaks.

Ten days later Hitler seized the port of Memel from Lithuania. Memel lay close to the east Prussian frontier and its hinterland to Germany. Hitler now said that this was his 'final demand'; and though he did not yet realise it, Memel was also his last bloodless territorial acquisition (map, p.286).

THE FATE OF ALBANIA

Since conquering Abyssinia in 1935 (p.219) Mussolini had not added to his new Roman empire. He had, however, contributed significantly to the nationalists in the Spanish civil war (p.264). He also congratulated himself on the role he had played at Munich and in securing for his ally Hungary a part of Slovakia.

Immediately on Hitler's destruction of Czechoslovakia in March 1938, Mussolini decided to take over long-coveted Albania. In April 1939 Italian troops overran the country. King Zog fled to France and Victor Emmanuel was presented with a new crown.

THE PACT OF STEEL

In May Mussolini tied himself further to Hitler's Germany. Ciano, his foreign minister, went to Berlin and signed the Pact of Steel (p.220). This stated that Italy and Germany had an inner affinity between their ideologies and had resolved 'to act side by side' in the task of 'safeguarding the foundations of civilisation'. The pact was dated 22 May 1939 'in the XVIIth year of the Fascist Era'. But as Italy was binding herself closer to Germany, Britain and France were asserting themselves. After the destruction of Czechoslovakia, the bankruptcy of appeasement was all too evident and was now replaced by military guarantees to states in the front line of fascist expansion.

NEW GUARANTEES

The principle on which appeasement had been adopted was that Germany had justifiable grievances against the Treaty of Versailles and that, once its justifiable demands had been met, Nazi Germany would be appeased. But now with the destruction of Czechoslovakia, Hitler was clearly cast in the role of an unprovoked aggressor.

It has been argued that the policy of appeasement had been adopted in order to buy time. In 1938 the military in both Britain and France had advised their respective governments that they were not prepared for a major European war against what everyone considered to be a well-armed Germany. Moreover, since Britain and France were democracies, their governments would have had to take public opinion into account. Memories of the previous war were still very vivid and the great majority of the British and the French wanted peace at any price.

But with the destruction of Czechoslovakia, everything changed. Immediately, Britain and France guaranteed the independence of Poland, Daladier received full powers to arm his forces and the British government introduced conscription.

Speaking in the House of Commons, Chamberlain made the new policy clear:

> In the event of any action which may threaten Polish independence, and which the Polish Government accordingly considered it vital to resist with their national forces, His Majesty's Government would feel themselves bound at once to lend the Polish Government all support in their power. They have given the Polish Government an assurance to this effect. I may add that the French Government have authorised me to make it plain that they stand in the same position in this matter as do His Majesty's Government.

In April Britain and France followed up their guarantee to Poland by issuing similar assurances of support for the independence of Greece and Romania. This was clearly in response to Italy's invasion of Albania (p.291). Hitler replied by renouncing his 1934 non-aggression pact with Poland (p.283) and his 1935 naval agreement with Britain (p.285). Then in May Germany and Italy signed the Pact of Steel (p.291), which guaranteed mutual assistance in any war.

The battle lines were now drawn. Appeasement was dead. Britain and France were prepared to meet force with force. But how realistic were their guarantees to Poland without the aid of the Soviet Union?

THE POSITION OF THE SOVIET UNION

Since the rise of Hitler and Russia's entry into the League of Nations, the Soviet Union had advocated the principle of collective security and had witnessed, with growing dismay, the unimpeded expansion of Hitler's Reich. Stalin advocated a three-power pact of Britain, France and Russia, but mutual mistrust and Polish objections ensured that it would never become a reality. Poland would never consent to the Red Army crossing Polish territory to 'make contact with the enemy'. With a large Russian and Ukrainian population within her borders, she had as much to fear from the Soviet Union as she had from Nazi Germany. As one Polish diplomat put it: 'With Germany we lose our freedom, with Russia we lose our souls.'

Negotiations between Britain, France and the Soviet Union continued until August. They were carried out with a fundamental lack of trust on both sides. Stalin suspected

Soviet foreign minister Molotov signs the Nazi-Soviet Pact in Moscow on 23 August 1939, as Ribbentrop, the German foreign minister, and Stalin look on.

the western democracies of trying to trap him into a war with Hitler so that they would destroy each other. Then with fascism and communism annihilated, Britain and France would step in and impose a new settlement on Europe. For her part, Britain detested communist Russia and was interested in a mere 'cosmetic alliance' in the hope of deterring Hitler. Thus it was that Britain showed no real sense of commitment to a full-scale triple alliance and portrayed this lack of urgency by sending a mission to the Soviet Union *by sea* in August. Negotiations finally broke down on 21 August when Poland adamantly refused to allow the Red Army into Poland in the event of a German attack. But unknown to the democracies, the Soviets were already negotiating with Germany and were on the verge of an agreement.

THE NAZI-SOVIET PACT

Ever since Hitler had come to power, Stalin feared for the safety of Soviet Russia; and though he had sought security in the League of Nations and in various alliances (p.285), he knew that ultimately the best solution was an agreement with Hitler. But Hitler, who hated communism, despised Slavs and had a policy of *Lebensraum* in the east, rebuffed all Soviet overtures. Then, in April 1939, with the end of appeasement, the guarantees of Britain and France to Poland and the enigmatic position of Soviet Russia, the old nightmare of a two-front war for Germany reappeared.

In May Germany informed Moscow that she was ready to negotiate. The same month Litvinov was replaced as Soviet foreign minister by Molotov, which indicated a change in Soviet policy. Litvinov was a Jew, had been fanatically anti-Nazi, and had argued for Soviet co-operation with the West against Hitler. Molotov had no such commitment and was prepared to negotiate with both sides. Molotov kept his German counterpart, von Ribbentrop, waiting until August before an agreement was reached.

Stalin prized Soviet security most of all and had lost faith in the democracies to achieve it for him. Moreover, he wanted to recover the lands lost at Brest-Litovsk (p.167) and at Riga (p.174). Finally on 23 August a Nazi-Soviet Pact (also known as the Molotov-Ribbentrop Pact) was signed in Moscow.

In the pact, which was to last for ten years, both sides pledged to remain neutral in any war involving one of them.

> Both high contracting parties obligate themselves to desist from any act of violence, any aggressive action, and any attack on each other, either individually or jointly with other powers.

The pact contained several secret articles. One such provided for the destruction of Poland and its partition between Nazi Germany and the Soviet Union:

> In the event of a territorial and political arrangement of the areas belonging to the Polish State, the spheres of influence of Germany and the USSR shall be bounded approximately by the line of the Rivers Narew, Vistula and San.

Other articles recognised Finland, Bessarabia and the Baltic states as coming within the Soviet sphere of influence (map, p.286).

The Nazi-Soviet Pact has been described as the most bizarre pact in history. The two irreconcilable systems, fascism and communism, were now in alliance. In essence it was a cynical pact of convenience, which contradicted the anti-Comintern pact (p.288), the Franco-Russian pact (p.240) and the German-Polish pact (p.283). It gave Stalin an opportunity to expand westwards, creating a buffer zone between his country and Nazi Germany. For Hitler the pact ensured the isolation of Poland and ended the possibility of a two-front war against Germany. It also meant that the military effort in France would be impeded by French communists, while the French fascists were already in sympathy with his plans in the east.

Two days after the signing of the Nazi-Soviet pact, Hitler summoned the French ambassador in Berlin. Hitler was making one last effort to persuade France (and Britain also) to stay out of war over Poland. Hitler told Ambassador Coulondre that he had a declaration to make, which he wished him to pass on to Daladier:

> I have no hostility towards France. I personally have renounced Alsace-Lorraine and I have recognised the Franco-German frontier . . . the thought that I should have to go to war with France because of Poland is very painful to me. . . . I shall not attack France but if she starts a conflict, I shall go to the very end . . . I believe that I shall win, and you think you will win. But what is certain is that German and French blood will flow, the blood of two peoples equally courageous. I say again it is extremely painful for me to think we will end up that way. Tell that to M. Daladier, please.

That evening, in a nationwide broadcast, Daladier reiterated that France would stand by commitments to Poland if she were attacked.

THE 'FINAL DEMAND'

At Munich in September 1938 Hitler had said that the Sudetenland was his 'final demand'. But for Germany, the loss of Danzig and the creation of the 'Polish corridor' were the chief irritants of the Treaty of Versailles. In October 1938 Hitler suggested that Poland should cede Danzig to Germany and also allow her to build a road and railway across the corridor. The Poles refused to discuss the question.

Then in March 1939, after the destruction of Czechoslovakia and the surrender of Memel, Hitler said that this was his 'final demand'. But soon he declared that the rectification of the Polish frontier was his 'final demand'. After the signing of the Nazi-Soviet Pact, the fate of Poland was sealed and Hitler set 26 August as the date for attack. But Mussolini, realising what was about to happen, informed Hitler that Italy was not ready for war. Mussolini had lost too much equipment in Spain (p.264) and now sent a request to Hitler for huge stocks of war materials. Hitler was taken aback, but merely decided to postpone the date for invading Poland to 1 September.

During the last week of August pressure mounted on the Poles from all sides, but they held fast. On 29 August Hitler demanded that a representative of the Polish government must come to Berlin within twenty-four hours to conclude the problem of Danzig and the corridor. The Poles stayed silent. On the night of 31 August German soldiers dressed in Polish uniforms attacked a German radio station on the German-Polish frontier at Gleiwitz. Immediately, Hitler declared that Poland had attacked a German frontier post, and at dawn the following morning German troops invaded Poland.

WAR

At first Britain and France appeared to hesitate, issuing an ultimatum to Hitler to withdraw his troops within 48 hours. When the ultimatum was ignored, Britain and France declared war on Germany on 3 September.

Chamberlain, addressing the House of Commons, said:

> This is a sad day for all of us, and to none is it sadder than to me. Everything that I have worked for, everything that I have hoped for, everything that I have believed in during my public life has crashed into ruins. . . . I trust I may live to see the day when Hitlerism has been destroyed and a liberated Europe has been established.

The following day he followed up the declaration of war with a broadcast to the German people:

> He [Hitler] gave his word that he would respect the Locarno Treaty; he broke it. He gave his word that he neither wished nor intended to annex Austria; he broke it. He declared that he would not incorporate the Czechs in the Reich; he did so. He gave his word after Munich that he had no further territorial demands in Europe; he broke it. He gave his word that he wanted no Polish provinces; he broke it. He has sworn to you for years that he was the mortal enemy of Bolshevism; he is now its ally. Can you wonder his word is, for us, not worth the paper it is written on.

Study Assignments and Essays

1. *'The remilitarisation of the Rhineland was the turning point in international relations in the inter-war period.' Discuss.*
2. *Treat of relations between Hitler and Mussolini in the period 1933–39.*
3. *Examine the history and fate of Czechoslovakia in the inter-war period.*
4. *Treat of relations between Hitler and Stalin in the period 1933–39.*
5. *Critically examine the diplomatic position of all European powers in 1939.*
6. *Write an essay on two of the following:*
(i) Hitler's diplomacy, 1933–39; (ii) The place of

Poland in international affairs 1933–39; (iii) Austria, Mussolini and Hitler; (iv) Chamberlain and Hitler; (v) The Nazi-Soviet Pact — its origin and significance.

The efforts of the western democracies to appease Hitler ended in failure and on 1 September 1939 World War II began. At first the Axis powers had an astonishing run of victories, conquering most of Scandinavia, western and southern Europe, and north Africa. Meanwhile, Japan, seeking to create a Pacific empire, clashed with the United States, and both conflicts escalated into global war. The German attack on the Soviet Union threw the Russians into an ill-matched alliance with Britain, France and America. Eventually, in 1945 the Allies destroyed the Axis powers in Europe, while the United States, by dropping two atomic bombs, forced Japan to surrender.

World War II raised as many questions as it solved. Europe lay politically, economically and morally in ruins, while democratic America and communist Russia emerged as superpowers. Once again, as in 1919, dreams of a better future, free from the scourge of war, prompted peace-loving leaders to form a United Nations organisation in the hope that it would create international co-operation. But this was not to be, and the ideological rift between the two superpowers greatly impeded the realisation of the UN's full potential. Europe became the battleground of ideological rivalry, an 'Iron Curtain' cut Europe in half, and a period of 'Cold War' hostility followed.

Meanwhile the 'winds of change' were blowing across former colonial lands. European powers withdrew from empire, and newly independent states emerged, many of them ill-fitted to assume the burdens of nationhood.

Despite manifold problems, the democracies made a remarkable recovery, and a movement for western European unity got under way.

With the death of Stalin in 1953, and despite the Sovietisation of eastern Europe, a thaw in the Cold War opened up a better era. Although division remained, peaceful co-existence became a reality.

Section Four

The Second World War and its Aftermath 1939–66

World War II 1939–45

25

In spite of everything I still believe that people are really good at heart.

Entry for 15 July 1944 from
Anne Frank: The Diary of a Young Girl.

THE INVASION OF POLAND

AT DAWN on 1 September 1939 Hitler launched his 'lightning war' or *blitzkrieg* against Poland. Six heavily armed and mobile *panzer* (armoured and motorised) divisions swept across the Polish plains. Ahead of them the *Luftwaffe's stukas* or dive bombers destroyed towns and cities and wreaked havoc on Polish soldiers and retreating civilian refugees. Behind the *panzers* came the German infantry, combing out pockets of resistance (map, p.300).

Such was the speed and efficiency of the German attack that the Polish air force was destroyed on the ground. Yet the Poles resisted bravely; with no armoured or motorised divisions, they tried, heroically but disastrously, to stop the German tanks with cavalry.

Although Britain and France declared war on Germany on 3 September, there was nothing they could do to help the Poles. The British RAF (Royal Air Force) did not have the fuel capacity to fly over such long distances; and because of the Nazi absorption of Austria and Czechoslovakia (p.288), the French land route to Poland was cut off. The Polish government fled to Romania, and from there to London where it declared itself the 'Polish government in exile'.

Meanwhile the German advance was continuing. On 4 September Nazi troops reached the Vistula. On 27 September, Warsaw, without ammunition, food, water or electricity, surrendered.

At the same time, Soviet forces had advanced from the east. Stalin was astonished at the speed of the German advance into Poland and was anxious to build a buffer zone against any future attack. On 17 September Soviet armies invaded the Ukrainian and Byelorussian areas of eastern Poland (p.174). On 29 September Germany and the Soviet Union signed an agreement partitioning Poland between them, as had been agreed in the Nazi-Soviet Pact (p.293). Once again, Poland ceased to exist as a state (map, p.300).

THE WINTER WAR

Following the partition of Poland, Stalin continued to push the Soviet frontier forward and within a year had incorporated the Baltic States of Latvia, Estonia and Lithuania. On 20 November he demanded from Finland an area of border territory in the Karelian isthmus to complete a defensive system around Leningrad. When the Finns refused, the Soviet Union attacked on 30 November, and for this aggression was expelled from the League of Nations in that body's last official act (p.281).

The Finnish army was one of the weakest in Europe. It was small, had no tanks and little artillery; its air force had only about one hundred planes. Moreover, the Finns stood alone. Their natural ally, Germany, had a pact with the Soviet Union, while Britain and France had poor access to Finland. No one believed, least of all Stalin, that the Finns would hold out for more than a few days.

To the surprise of the world, the Soviet forces encountered enormous difficulties. The Finnish landscape of forests, marshes and lakes was quite unsuitable for mass tank assults, which the Red Army employed, and the Finns put up a brave resistance. Their commander, Field-Marshal Mannerheim, was a capable and determined leader. The Finns were initially successful in holding back the

German forces attack eastwards following the invasion of the Soviet Union in 1941.

Red Army with a line of fortifications, known as the Mannerheim Line. Finnish ski troops caught the attention of the world's press with their swift and unexpected attacks on unwary Soviet units.

In a war of 105 days, known as the 'Winter War', Finland inflicted enormous losses on the Red Army. They captured or destroyed 1,600 Soviet tanks and over 700 aircraft. The Russians lost ten times as many men as the Finns. Nevertheless, it was evident that Finland could not hold out against her mighty neighbour. As a cold winter January set in, the frozen lakes and marshes provided easier passage for the Soviet tanks, and after heavy air bombardment, the Finns were forced to withdraw. The Finnish government now decided to make peace while her army was still intact. On 12 March 1940 the Treaty of Moscow was signed, by which Finland conceded, not only the original Soviet demands, but also the seaport of Vyborg — in all, some 16,000 square miles of territory (map, p.300).

The difficulties that the Soviets had encountered in defeating Finland led the Germans to believe that the Red Army was leaderless and incompetent. This estimate prompted Hitler to attack the Soviet Union in June 1941, even though he had commitments in the west as well (p.303). For the Soviets, the Winter War had gained the desired buffer around Leningrad, but the loss of moral standing for having attacked Finland, and the humiliation of not being able to defeat her within a few days, was a heavy price to pay. Moreover, the Winter War had ensured that

THE EARLY STAGES OF THE SECOND WORLD WAR 1939-40

when Hitler attacked the Soviet Union in 1941, a vengeful Finnish army took the opportunity to attack and recover in a matter of days much of the territory so expensively won by the Soviet Union the previous year.

THE PHONEY WAR

From the defeat of Poland on 5 October 1939 until the offensive against Denmark on 9 April 1940, the powers were technically at war, but no real fighting took place. The period has therefore become known as the 'Phoney War'. The British Expeditionary Force (BEF) had crossed over to France in September and, with French troops, remained behind the Maginot Line. The Germans were content to stay behind the Siegfried Line, and so no fighting took place on the western front.

On 6 October Hitler contacted London and Paris and offered to discuss the European situation, but his offer was immediately rebuffed. Three days later he issued a directive for an attack on the west. It was code-named 'Operation Yellow' and envisaged an attack through the Low Countries, because the Maginot Line extended only as far as the borders of Belgium.

Hitler's objective was to defeat France quickly and then force Britain to sue for peace. However, through a combination of high-ranking army reluctance to attack France at this stage, and bad weather, 'Operation Yellow' had to be postponed several times. Then on 10 January 1940 a German plane was blown off course by high winds and landed in Belgium. Before the pilot could destroy his documents, which included details of 'Operation Yellow', he was captured and the Allies learned of the proposed attack. The Germans were obliged to call off the offensive and draw up new plans.

General Manstein was given the task, which was code-named 'Scythe Sweep'. It envisaged an invasion of Belgium and Holland by one army, and a breakthrough in the Ardennes by another. But before this plan was put into operation, the Germans made a sudden attack on Denmark and Norway.

SCANDINAVIAN DIVERSION

Since supplies of Swedish iron ore were essential for the German war machine, it was imperative to keep the lines of transport communication open. Moreover, the Germans became aware that the Allies intended to seize the Norwegian ports and open a Scandinavian front on Germany's flank. In order to forestall the Allies and keep open the sea lanes along the Norwegian coast, German troops attacked Denmark on 9 April 1940. Within two days Denmark had fallen, and two days later Norway was in the grip of the Nazis. They were helped in their invasion of Norway by Vidkun Quisling, a former minister of defence, who had built up a strong Norwegian fascist party, and who collaborated with the Germans both before and during the invasion. On 14 April the Allies sent troops to Norway, but they were too late. They merely succeeded in gaining footholds at Narvik and Trondheim, and were forced to withdraw by the end of May. The success of the Scandinavian invasion meant that Germany could not be attacked from that flank; but more important, German U-boats could now operate out of the many strategic fjords along Norway's thousand-mile sea coast. The Nazis set up a puppet administration in Oslo under Quisling.

In Britain the unsuccessful attempt to save Norway from falling into Hitler's hands led to general disenchantment with the government. On 10 May Chamberlain resigned and Winston Churchill became prime minister of a national government. On taking office he declared, 'I have nothing to offer but blood, toil, tears and sweat.'

THE ATTACK IN THE WEST

On 10 May the Germans launched a lightning attack on the western front. A few hundred German paratroopers catured the canals in Holland and held the bridges for the advancing tanks and armoured vehicles. The Dutch were defeated in five days. Queen Wilhelmina escaped to England and set up a government in exile. The Dutch navy and merchant marine also went over to Britain, but many thousands of Dutchmen were taken as labourers to Germany.

British and French troops wait on the dunes at Dunkirk to be evacuated to England by ship.

Belgium surrendered on 28 May, although the Belgians later ignored their own surrender and set up a government in exile in London.

One of the principal objects of the Manstein Plan was to let the Allies think that the main attack was coming through the Low Countries as in World War I. But on 10 May German tanks and artillery swept into the Ardennes, and three days later, after crossing the Meuse, came out behind the Allies in Flanders. Then the Germans made a rapid swing to the north and west and on 20 May the first German armoured corps had reached the sea, cutting off the Allies.

Operation 'Scythe Sweep' had worked perfectly and the Allies found themselves trapped in a pincer grip. The encircling Germans took Calais and Boulogne while the retreating Allied troops rushed for Dunkirk, France's northernmost seaport. This was the nearest and only available port remaining, and the Allies hoped to re-embark for England before the Germans closed the trap. In their urgency to re-embark, forty divisions abandoned 60,000 vehicles and 500,000 tonnes of equipment and ammunition. Churchill ordered all available boats and vessels to sail from England to help in the evacuation. Beginning on 27 May a total of 860 vessels took part in a six-day operation and evacuated 338,000 troops (224,000 of them British, 95,000 French, and the remainder Belgian, Dutch and Polish). About 40,000 French soldiers were taken prisoner by the Germans and some 200 vessels were sunk by the bombs of the *Luftwaffe*, although the losses would have been far greater but for the air cover afforded by the RAF.

It has not been satisfactorily answered why the Germans failed to press home their advantage during the evacuation. The main German tank corps had reached the sea near Dunkirk on 24 May, yet Hitler issued a sudden order not to attack until the infantry had joined them. Perhaps he wished to preserve the tank corps for the battle of France, though a more likely explanation may be that he believed that the British had learned a lesson and would now accept the German position in Europe. If this latter explanation is correct, then Hitler made a grave miscalculation. By saving the British forces, he ensured that they would fight another day.

In France all was confusion. The Maginot Line was now obsolete because the German armies were in France. To add to the disorder, thousands of refugees blocked the roads and impeded the movement of troops. General Weygand, the supreme Allied commander, decided to recall the soldiers on the Maginot Line and establish a new front line along the Somme and the Aisne; but with the loss of equipment and the low morale among the troops, the German general, Ewald von Kleist, had little difficulty in breaking through on the Somme on 10 June. On the same day Mussolini joined Hitler and declared war on France; the Italian dictator now believed that the future lay with Nazi Germany. The French government immediately declared Paris an open city; it preferred to surrender the capital than to see it destroyed. On 14 June Paris fell to the Germans; two days later Paul Reynaud, the French premier, resigned and was succeeded by Marshal Pétain, the hero of Verdun (p.140). On 20 June the Italians invaded France in the south-east, but were pinned down by French forces. Despite this, the French position was hopeless and Pétain asked for an armistice.

On 22 June the French signed the armistice in Hitler's presence in the same railway carriage at Compiègne where the Germans had signed the armistice ending the Great War on 11 November 1918. By its terms, about two-thirds of France (including Paris and the industrial north) came under direct German rule. The remaining south and east, together with the French empire, became a puppet state with its headquaters at Vichy, a spa in central France. The Vichy government under Pétain was allowed to retain the French fleet. But on 3 July the British, fearing that the fleet would come under German control, destroyed the bulk of it as it lay at anchor in the Gulf of Oran in Algeria. This operation also killed about a thousand French sailors, and an angry Vichy government broke off relations with Britain (map, p.300).

With the fall of France, nearly two million French prisoners of war came under German control and thousands were taken to work in Germany. Meanwhile Colonel Charles de Gaulle had escaped to Britain. In a broadcast over the BBC on the day of his arrival, he called on the French to resist the Germans. 'France has lost the battle but she has not lost the war,' he declared. De Gaulle later set up the 'Free French Army' and assisted the Allies in several operations before returning as a national hero to France in 1945 (p.319).

THE BATTLE OF BRITAIN

Britain now stood alone. Hitler firmly believed that the war was almost over since Britain would be forced to make peace. However, Churchill, in his speeches in the House of Commons, continued to defy Hitler. In one famous address in June 1940 he made the position clear:

> I expect the Battle of Britain is about to begin. Upon that battle depends the survival of Christian civilization. Upon it depends our own British life, and the long continuity of our institutions and our empire. The whole fury and might of the enemy must very soon be turned upon us... Let us, therefore, brace ourselves to our duties, and so bear ourselves that

> if the British Empire and its Commonwealth last for a thousand years, men will still say, 'This was their finest hour.'

By the first week of July Hitler was convinced that Britain intended to continue the war. He therefore decided on an invasion of Britain 'to eliminate the English mother country as a base from which the war against Germany can be continued.' Britain, however, could not be invaded unless the German navy held a corridor across the channel; and the navy could not accomplish this unless they received full air support. It was thus imperative for Germany's success that her air force win control of the skies. The invasion of Britain would depend upon the outcome of a struggle for control of the air between the *Luftwaffe* and the Royal Air Force.

Britain had made many preparations for the expected attack. The Local Defence Volunteers, later known as the Home Guard ('Dad's Army'), were formed. Barbed wire, anti-tank devices and pillboxes were erected along the coast, and the regular army was put on full alert. But most important, the production of aircraft was given top priority because it was fully realised that air power would play a decisive role.

The Battle of Britain began on 13 August 1940. The Germans, under Göring's expert leadership, had some 2,000 bombers, 1,100 fighters and an adequate supply of trained pilots. Britain had only 1,100 fighters and 1,500 trained pilots, but she had an efficient and valuable radar system that gave advance warning of approaching attack.

Göring had promised that he would win control of the skies in four weeks, and the land invasion of Britain ('Operation Sea Lion') was fixed for 15 September.

At first the Germans concentrated on daylight raids on ports and airfields, using bombers protected by fighters. By mid-September the Germans had lost 1,735 aircraft while Britain had lost 915. Radar gave early warning, anti-aircraft guns and barrage balloons provided some protection, while fighters (Hurricanes and Spitfires) engaged in continuous dogfights in the sky. Lord Beaverbrook was made minister of aircraft production; aircraft factories turned out 600 planes a month, while the German rate of production did not exceed 450. The weather also played havoc with the German bombers because banks of cloud often caused them to be detached from their fighter escorts.

The policy of bombing ports and airfields was not having the desired effect and daylight raids were resulting in heavy losses, so the Germans changed tactics. They now switched to night raids on London and other large cities in an effort to break civilian morale so that the British government would have no option but to capitulate. On sixty-seven nights out of sixty-eight between 7 September and 13 November, London was bombed in attacks that sometimes lasted for six hours. During this period, known as the 'Blitz', London especially, but other cities as well, suffered great damage. During September and October there were some 60,000 casualties in Britain, but morale remained high. The government passed the Emergency Powers Act, which gave the authorities unprecedented control over all persons and property. Churchill continued to infuse a spirit of determination into the people, who responded to his energetic lead.

Although severe restrictions were imposed on everyday life, the government was determined to keep up morale and allow as much normal peacetime activity as possible to continue. In June 1940 the Entertainments National Services Association was formed to provide entertainment for the troops and factory workers. Horse racing continued and radio programmes provided welcome relief. Women played a vital role in the war effort. Many thousands joined the auxiliary military services, while others took jobs in factories and the extended hospital service.

In September Hitler twice postponed 'Operation Sea Lion'. Then in October it was shelved until the spring of 1941, which in effect meant its abandonment. Britain had been saved from invasion by the RAF. Churchill paid tribute: 'Never in the field of human conflict was so much owed by so many to so few.'

German air raids continued, though on a diminished scale, until 16 May 1941, when Hitler had to divert the *Luftwaffe* to the eastern front. He had failed in his aim of forcing Britain to accept, and now turned to his ultimate objective: the creation of *lebensraum* in the east and the destruction of the Soviet Union (p.201). But by this stage the war had also spread to North Africa.

THE WAR IN NORTH AFRICA

With the fall of France imminent in May 1940, Mussolini brought Italy into the war on the German side (p.303). He believed that Germany was unbeatable and hoped that by joining Hitler he could establish his long-cherished Roman empire in the Mediterranean and north Africa. Mussolini particularly coveted French and British Somaliland (bordering on Italian possessions (p.91)) and Egypt. With France and Britain facing defeat at home, the moment seemed opportune. The British position in North Africa looked very precarious as General Wavell, the British commander in the Middle East, commanded no more than 36,000 troops in Egypt and 27,000 in Palestine. The Italian commander, Marshal Graziani, controlled about 250,000 troops in Libya. In September he found little opposition in moving into Egypt, and threatening the British hold on the Suez Canal. A see-saw struggle began, but by December Wavell had cleared the Italians out of Egypt. This success was followed up when he moved into Libya and captured Tobruk on 22 January 1941. His soldiers then moved along the Libyan coast and two weeks later captured Benghazi. But Wavell was unable to follow up these successes because of three developments that adversely affected his conduct of the war:

1. As the Germans went to the aid of the Italians invading Greece, Churchill ordered Wavell to divert troops to Greece. This meant that Wavell could manage to keep only a thin force in North Africa.
2. Churchill ordered Wavell to undertake the reconquest of Abyssinia so that Haile Selassie could be restored to his kingdom (p.280).
3. Hitler sent one of his best generals, Erwin Rommel, with a strong army to rescue the Italians. Rommel (later to become known as the 'Desert Fox') and his *Afrika Korps* tipped the balance in favour of the Axis powers.

On 24 March Rommel opened his attack, and soon Benghazi fell to the Germans. He then moved on to Tobruk but failed to capture the port because the Allies had succeeded in fortifying it. As Rommel advanced on Egypt, Wavell was replaced as commander-in-chief in the Middle East by General Auchinleck. The garrison at Tobruk, supplied by sea from Malta, threatened Rommel's flank and impeded his advance. Rommel was unable to press home for victory because he was obliged to give up many of his reserves for the invasion of the Soviet Union (p.307 and map p.306).

Despite this, he was again on the offensive in January 1942. In May he received fresh supplies of men and tanks; and in June captured Tobruk and drove the British back into Egypt to within seventy miles of Alexandria. Here, at El Alamein, a great decisive battle was about to take place. Alarmed at Rommel's success, Churchill flew to Egypt to assess the situation in the field. Auchinleck was replaced by General Alexander, and General Montgomery arrived with the Eighth Army, later to become known as the 'Desert Rats'.

Montgomery dug in at El Alamein. Throughout the summer he trained his men in 'desert tactics', and equipped them with heavy American tanks that would match Rommel's *panzers*. On 23 October Montgomery opened the offensive against the Germans holding El

NAZI-DOMINATED EUROPE: THE WAR SITUATION IN 1941 - 42

Alamein. The battle lasted for ten days, after which Rommel's lines broke. Montgomery's forces then pursued the *Afrika Korps* across 1,400 miles of desert through Libya. They captured Tripoli, and invaded Tunisia. The campaign lasted for over four months, during which time Rommel was unwell and had little back-up from Hitler, who was engrossed in developments on the Russian front.

On 8 November a joint American and

British force under General Dwight D. Eisenhower landed in French Morocco (p.315). Rommel found himself caught between the two armies in a pincer movement, known as 'Operation Torch', but he received 150,000 reinforcements, ferried across from southern Italy. In January 1943 Montgomery moved all his forces into Tunisia from the east and Eisenhower moved in his forces from the west. By this time Rommel had resigned his command and had returned to Germany. After many desperate battles, Tunis fell to the Allies in May and 250,000 Axis troops were taken prisoner. With North Africa secure, the western entrance to the Mediterranean was clear, and the invasion of Sicily could begin (p.315).

OPERATION BARBAROSSA

Meanwhile, Hitler had put into operation his long-standing aim of invading the Soviet Union. On 18 December 1940, he had issued orders for 'Operation Barbarossa', the code name for this attack, to begin not later than May 1941. This directive began: 'The German armed forces must be prepared, even before the conclusion of the war with England, to crush Soviet Russia in a rapid campaign.'

However, before this could be put into practice, it was imperative to bring the Balkan states under German control in order to protect the southern flank. In October 1940, Mussolini had declared war on Greece, but the Greeks resisted stubbornly and drove the Italians back into Albania. The same month German troops had invaded Romania to 'protect' its oil fields. Hungary, Romania and Bulgaria joined the tripartite pact of Germany, Italy and Japan with its declared objective of establishing a 'New Order', but Yugoslavia defiantly held out: 'Sooner war than the pact, sooner death than slavery.'

In April 1941, Hitler launched a *blitzkrieg* against Yugoslavia. Within three days Belgrade was in ruins and the Germans swept on towards Greece. The Allied troops withdrawn from North Africa (p.305) for service in Greece were easily defeated and forced to evacuate in another 'Dunkirk' from Greece and Crete. It had taken the Nazis less than a week to defeat Yugoslavia and three to overcome Greece. Except for the various resistance movements in operation (p.311), all of south-eastern Europe was now under the control of the Axis powers.

This 'Balkan interlude' meant that Hitler did not start Operation Barbarossa until 22 June 1941. The oil fields of the Caucasus, the fertile Ukraine, and other resources, would give Hitler sufficient material for the final onslaught against Britain. Moreover, victory in the east would destroy communism, push the Russians behind the Urals into Asia, and create *lebensraum* for the Third Reich.

Despite advance notice from secret agents working in Japan, and warnings from Churchill, Stalin still did not believe that Hitler was about to strike. In fact he continued to supply Germany with petrol, wheat, timber, iron ore and manganese under the terms of the Nazi-Soviet Pact of 1939 (p.294).

On 22 June, Hitler, claiming that Russian troops were massing on the frontiers of Germany 'in preparation for an onslaught', sent an army of three million men against the Soviet Union. In addition to Germans, the invading force consisted of Italians, Hungarians, Romanians and Finns. The invasion comprised a three-pronged *blitzkrieg* — against Leningrad in the north, Moscow in the centre, and the Caucasian oil fields in the south. The lightning strike caught the Russians unaware; the *Luftwaffe* bombers destroyed much of the Russian air force on the ground, and with control of the skies, the *Wehrmacht* tanks and armoured divisions drove rapidly and deep into Russian territory.

By 8 September the northern prong under General Leeb had reached the outskirts of Leningrad where it began to lay siege to the city. On 7 August the centre force under

German troops advance past a burning Russian tank during Hitler's blitzkrieg on Russia in 1941.

Generals Guderian and Houth had taken Smolensk, having captured 500,000 prisoners on the way. It then pressed on towards Moscow, and by early December the first German soldiers could see the glistening cupolas the Kremlin in the distance. The southern prong, under General von Rundstedt, took Kiev in the Ukraine, swept into the Crimea, and by 21 November had reached Rostov-on-Don (map, p.306).

By December, Hitler was within an ace of achieving his objective. Yet the seeds of ultimate defeat were beginning to take root, due to five main factors:

1. The Balkan interlude had delayed the offensive by two months, and the Germans were unprepared for such a long campaign during a Russian winter.
2. During the first month of the war in 1939, Stalin had ordered the dismantling of 1,500 factories in European Russia and their removal to the Urals, Siberia and Central Asia, where they were reassembled and began producing vital war materials.
3. Hitler believed that the severity of Stalin's purges in the 1930s (p.237) had left the Red Army demoralised and bereft of worthwhile generals. All that was needed was 'to kick in the door and the whole rotten edifice will fall to the ground'. German estimates put the strength of the Red Army at about 140 divisions, whereas it

comprised 324 divisions, backed up by 12,000 aircraft and 10,000 tanks. In addition two of their marshals, Zhukov and Timoshenko, were brilliant tacticians and created unprecedented problems for the Germans.

Hitler had counted on dealing with a Soviet Union isolated in every respect from the rest of the world. But soon after the invasion, Churchill offered Stalin an Anglo-Russian alliance. This brought much-needed supplies to help the Soviet war effort over the following three years.

On 5 December 1942, as the Germans were at the gates of Leningrad, Moscow and the Caucasus, the Japanese bombed Pearl Harbour (p.312). This brought the United States into the war and it was American might that finally tipped the balance in favour of the Allies.

On 3 December 1941 the Russians under Marshal Zhukov counterattacked in front of Moscow. The Germans formed themselves into a series of defensive blocks called 'hedgehogs' and, supplied from the air, held their positions throughout the long Russian winter.

At Leningrad, the German siege lasted 900 days, but the city refused to surrender, keeping access to the interior across the frozen waters of Lake Ladoga (map, p.306).

With the coming of spring, Hitler and his generals devised a new plan called 'Operation Blue'. It envisaged an all-out drive towards the Volga, the Caspian Sea and the Caucasian oil fields. The capture of the oil fields would have the double advantage of giving the Germans much-needed supplies while, at the same time, depriving the Russian war machine of fuel.

But before Operation Blue could get under way, Timoshenko launched a Russian offensive in the Ukraine on 12 May 1942. It was a disaster for the Russians and in two great battles the Germans captured almost 350,000 Russians and 12,000 tanks.

Encouraged by this success, Hitler now ordered the attack on the Caucasus, which began on 28 June under General Kleist. Rostov-on-Don fell in July, but then Hitler made a fatal error: he split his forces and ordered the Sixth Army under General von Paulus to capture Stalingrad. This city (renamed Volgograd in 1961) had no great strategic significance, but for Hitler it symbolised everything Stalin and the Soviet Union stood for, and it was imperative that it should fall. Equally, Stalin was determined that his city must not yield (map, p.306).

The battle for Stalingrad became the 'Verdun' of World War II and proved to be one of the great turning points in the fortunes of that war.

The battle commenced in August but because of delays and difficulties in keeping supply lines open, the real assault did not begin until 5 September. Stalingrad was defended by 100,000 men under General Zhukov, while von Paulus commanded about 400,000. Although the German bombardment reduced the city to near-rubble, the Russians refused to surrender. Even when the Germans broke into the city, the Russians contested every street in hand-to-hand fighting. By 18 November the Germans were in possession of most of the city, but by this time, Zhukov had re-formed his army, which now consisted of a million men, 900 tanks and 1,115 aircraft. As the harsh winter set in, the Germans found themselves caught in Stalingrad between the Russian forces on the Don and those on the Volga. Von Paulus wished to withdraw (his supplies were cut off) but Hitler was adamant that there should be no retreat from Stalingrad. With supplies cut off and in severe winter conditions, von Paulus and his troops would have to face the surrounding Russian armies.

The counter-offensive began on 19 November and raged for ten weeks. Both sides suffered indescribably until von Paulus surrendered with the remnants of his army on 31 January 1943. The Russians had lost more men at Stalingrad than the Americans lost in the entire war. But for Hitler it was the first major defeat, the beginning of the end.

LIFE IN OCCUPIED EUROPE

By 1942 most of Europe from the Atlantic to Stalingrad and from Norway to North Africa lay under the control of the fascist powers. Hitler proclaimed the establishment of a 'New Order' which would last for a thousand years. It envisaged the German master race ruling the 'lesser' races of Europe. The conquered areas, especially in the east, were to be colonised by Germans, while the indigenous peoples would be cleared out. This task was given to Himmler's S.S. In the first year of the war they removed a million Jews and Poles; but after the invasion of the Soviet Union, vast new possibilities were opened up. A certain proportion of Slavs would be kept for cheap labour while the remainder would be exiled to Siberia and Central Asia. However, the tide of victory turned too quickly from the Nazis for this to take place.

Since the Allies had superior resources, especially after America's entry to the war, the Germans commandeered all raw materials, food and labour within their orbit of control; this was especially evident in the east. In all, about seven million workers were transferred to Germany, while another seven million worked in their native conquered areas.

Nazi rule was essentially dictated by racism. Denmark was allowed her own monarch and parliament because she was a Nordic country. Quisling in Norway and Mussert in Holland collaborated with the Nazis, while in France Pétain ruled a puppet government from Vichy. In contrast, the Slavs were shown little mercy. The inhabitants of Czechoslovakia were brutalised while in Poland and Yugoslavia slave labour and starvation rations were put into operation.

But it was in the treatment of the Jews that Nazism was revealed in all its horror. Already during the 1930s the Jews in Germany had suffered many deprivations (p.225), but with the outbreak of war, and especially after expansion eastwards, where many Jews lived, the persecution grew steadily worse.

Himmler, and the doctrinaire Nazis who advised him, drew up plans for the extermination of all the Jews in Europe as a 'final solution' to the 'Jewish problem'. The S.S. were instructed to round up all Jews. They were taken in batches to remote places, made to dig their own graves, and then were mowed down by machine-gun fire and buried in mass graves. Yet this process was soon seen to be too slow, so mass extermination camps were built, notably at Auschwitz, Treblinka, Belsen and Buchenwald. Here the Jews were given poison gas in chambers disguised as shower rooms. Many others (not all Jews) were shot or used as human guinea pigs for various types of experimentation. Corpses were generally disposed of in huge, specially designed crematoria. At the Nuremberg Trial (p.386) the following testimony was given by the commandant of Auschwitz:

> 'The final solution' meant the complete extermination of all Jews in Europe. In June 1941, I was ordered to establish extermination facilities at Auschwitz. At that time there were already three other camps, Belsen, Treblinka and Wosel. I visited Treblinka to find out how they carried out their extermination. The Commandant told me that he had liquidated 80,000 in the course of half a year. He was principally concerned with the Jews from the Warsaw Ghetto. He used monoxide gas and I do not think that his methods were efficient. So at Auschwitz I used Cyclon B, which is a crystallised prussic acid dropped into the death chamber. It took from three to fifteen minutes to kill people in the chamber. We knew when they were dead because their screaming stopped. After the bodies were removed, our special commandos took the rings and extracted

Jews rounded up in Poland before being taken to a concentration camp.

the gold from the teeth of the corpses. Another improvement that we made over Treblinka was that we built our gas chambers to accommodate 2,000 people at one time. . .

Only when the war came to an end did the appalling facts of the camps become known. It was established that about six million Jews had lost their lives in them.

RESISTANCE MOVEMENTS

Throughout the war, 'underground' resistance movements came into being and were active in the occupied countries. Armed bands sniped at German soldiers and blew up bridges while factory workers sabotaged industrial production whenever they could. At times resistance burst into open warfare. This was particularly the case in Yugoslavia where the 'Partisans' under Josip Broz, Marshal Tito (p.340), waged a successful campaign. Yugoslavia was the only European country to liberate itself. In Poland resistance also amounted to open warfare while her 'government in exile' in London maintained contact through an underground courier service.

France had a variety of resistance movements. The 'Free French' in London maintained contact with their counterparts in France. The 'Maquis' and the 'Organisation de la Résistance Armée' also contributed by every type of sabotage, while the communists were fearless in their opposition to fascism.

Within Germany itself many groups and individuals were opposed to Hitler's policies.

Unlike those who resisted elsewhere, the Germans who refused to yield faced not only danger, but a crisis of conscience. Here resistance meant opposing one's own authorities, which in war could so easily be interpreted as treason. These factors — the high risk and the moral dilemma — plus the fact that many potential enemies of fascism had already been eliminated before the war, meant that resistance within Germany remained weak and ineffective.

The opposition which did arise, however, came from four sources:

On the left, socialists and communists organised underground groups. The most successful of these was the *Rote Kapelle*, which engaged in spying activities.

Members of Hitler's own general staff, most notably Franz Halder and Ludwig Beck, became increasingly disillusioned with Nazi rule and plotted a coup.

Several student groups also emerged. The most notable was the 'White Rose' group in Munich, led by Hans and Sophie Scholl, who were both executed.

The best-remembered group was that known as the 'Kreisau Circle'. It was led by Count von Moltke and included Dietrich Bonhoeffer (p.224), the Lutheran pastor, and Count Klaus von Stauffenberg, who made the unsuccessful assassination attempt on Hitler in July 1944 (p.319).

WAR IN THE PACIFIC

Background to Pearl Harbour

In 1931 Japan had invaded Manchuria (p.278) and had left the League of Nations. In 1936 she had signed the anti-Comintern pact with Germany (later joined by Italy) in common solidarity against communism. The following year Japan had resumed hostilities against China with the intention of bringing all eastern China under control. Then when Hitler invaded western Europe in 1940, Japan turned her attention to French Indo-China (Vietnam, Cambodia, Laos) and the Dutch East Indies, where rice, oil and rubber offered rich rewards for an expansionist policy (map, p.314).

After World War I, the United States retreated into isolation and failed to join the League of Nations (p.281). This mood of isolationism was reinforced in the 1930s by the anti-democratic and aggressive policies of Italy, Germany and Japan.

In 1934 a Senate committee was set up to investigate the circumstances of American entry into World War I. It was headed by Senator Gerald Nye of North Dakota, who presented his findings in 1936. The Nye Report was highly critical of the excessive profits made by industrialists, munitions-makers, ship-builders and bankers, and of the questionable methods they had used in securing lucrative war contracts and in avoiding tax to bolster their profits. The report reached the conclusion that America had gone to war less to defend democracy than to make vast profits for war-time profiteers.

The mood was ripe for the passing of the Neutrality Acts of 1935 and 1936, which prohibited the United States from selling arms or granting loans to *any* belligerent nation, whether victim or aggressor. America had reached the 'high noon' of isolationism where neutrality was not merely a matter of government policy: it was the law of the land.

Yet 1937 also marked the beginning of its end. A small but strong current of opinion had always believed that the United States could not opt out of world affairs. This view was held by President Roosevelt himself, the secretary of state, Cordell Hull, and other prominent Democrats and Republicans. They believed that the surest way of keeping America out of war was for her to play her part in preventing such a war happening in the first place. Furthermore, they contended that science and technology had so reduced the world to a state of interdependence that in a

European conflict the United States inevitably would become embroiled. However, since America was a democracy and public opinion was decidedly opposed to any foreign involvement, Roosevelt knew that he would have to edge his way carefully towards a public realisation of the position.

When war broke out in September 1939, the United States was overwhelmingly on the side of isolation. Despite this, a debate began to gather momentum. Some insisted that if Britain fell, America would not be safe; others claimed that 3,000 miles of Atlantic made the United States immune from danger.

In November 1939 Roosevelt persuaded Congress to amend the Neutrality Acts so that the Allies could get munitions from America on a 'cash and carry' basis, provided that they were carried in the Allies' own ships. After the fall of France in June 1940, Roosevelt realised that Britain would not survive without further aid. Accordingly, he stepped a little further along the road towards intervention by handing over fifty destroyers to the British navy. Yet most Americans were still determined to stay out of the war. In the presidential election campaign of 1940 Roosevelt declared,

> And while I am talking to you, mothers and fathers, I give you one more assurance . . . your boys are not going to be sent into any foreign wars.

But after his re-election (for an unprecedented third time), Roosevelt put before Congress his famous Lend-Lease programme.

> We must be the great arsenal of democracy. The best immediate defence of the United States is the success of Great Britain defending herself.

Roosevelt proposed to Congress that arms be lent to Britain, which could be returned or replaced when the war came to an end. He drove home his argument with the analogy, 'If your neighbour's house is on fire, would you not lend a hose?' A long and, at times, bitter debate followed in Congress, but eventually the bill became law. Throughout 1941, America drew even closer to intervention. German and Italian funds in American banks were frozen and all their consulates were closed.

But the United States was concerned not only with developments in Europe. Throughout the 1930s she had become increasingly apprehensive of the Japanese. The United States had extensive trading interests in the Pacific, the Philippines and China, and saw Japanese expansion as a direct threat. In July 1941, when Japan announced a protectorate over French Indo-China, Roosevelt froze all Japanese credit and cut off American sales of oil and chemicals. Then on 26 November, Cordell Hull sent a demand to the Japanese government to 'withdraw all military, naval, air and police forces from China and French Indo-China.' This demand presented Japan with a dilemma. Should she end her expansionist policy in South-East Asia and the Pacific, where she believed she was entitled to build an empire, or should she continue with expansion and face war with the United States and perhaps Britain as well? Japan chose the latter course.

Pearl Harbour

On 7 December, the Japanese Embassy in Washington requested a meeting with Cordell Hull for 1.45 pm. The Japanese representatives arrived at 2.05 pm. Fifty-five minutes earlier a Japanese task force under the command of Admiral Yamamoto had attacked the main American naval base at Pearl Harbour in the Pacific, destroying five battleships, three destroyers, three light cruisers, and 188 aircraft. The attack also killed 2,960 people. With one blow Japan had crippled the American navy, inflicting her worst defeat in history. The following day Roosevelt addressed Congress:

THE SECOND WORLD WAR AND ITS AFTERMATH IN THE PACIFIC

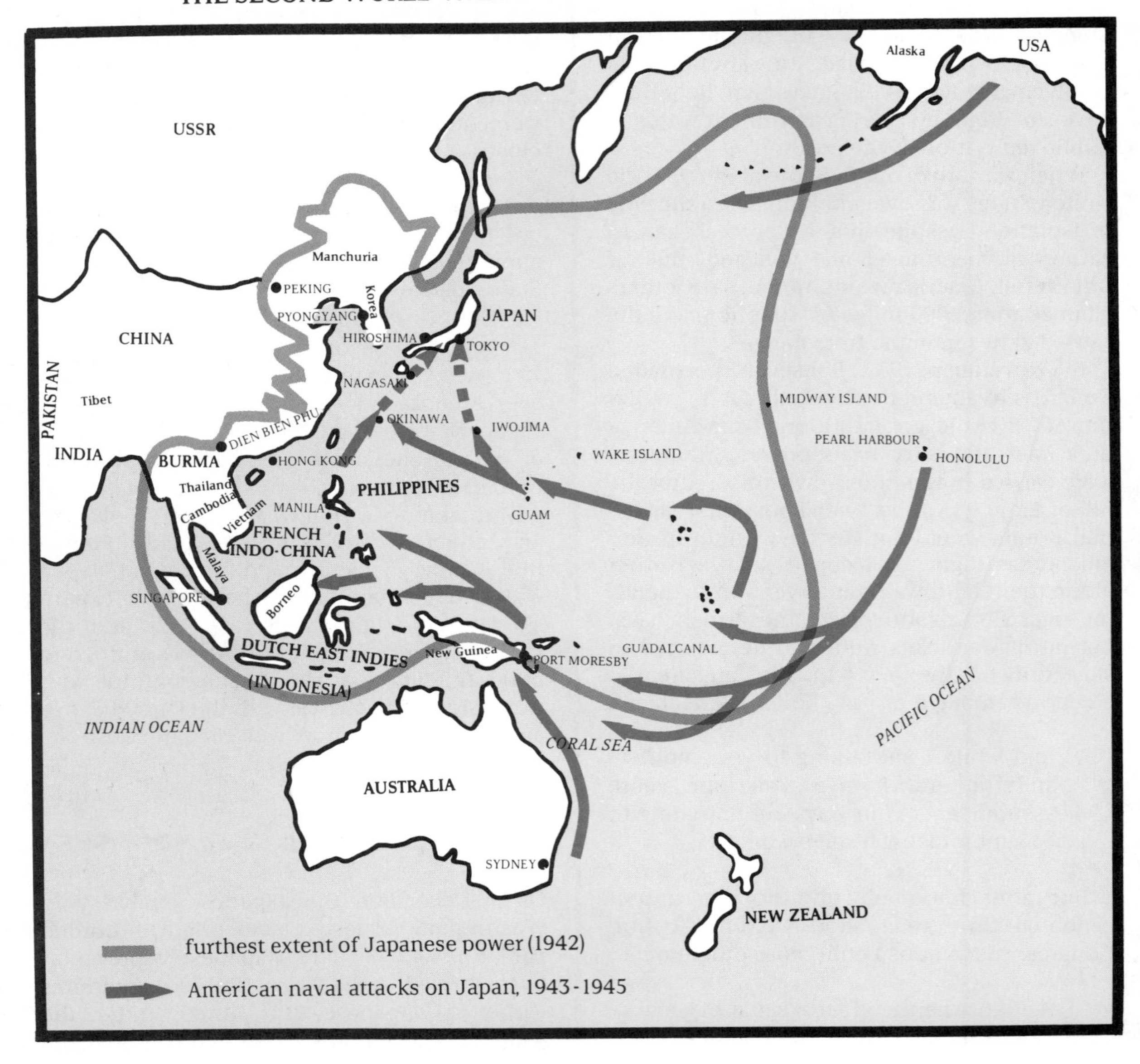

> I ask that Congress declare that since the unprovoked and dastardly attack by Japan on Sunday December 7, a state of war has existed between the United States and the Japanese Empire.

Congress had little hesitation in declaring war and Britain immediately followed suit.

Three days later, on 11 December, Hitler declared war on the United States and Mussolini followed suit. In one sense Hitler was honouring his agreement with Japan, but he had other reasons besides. He had been particularly annoyed with the Lend-Lease programme to Britain, and now, with the American navy crippled, the time was opportune for war. Hitler believed that Roosevelt was the 'elect of the Jews', and a war against the United States would be a crusade against international Jewry, rooted there.

Japanese Expansion

The day following the attack on Pearl Harbour, Japan attacked Hong Kong. The garrison of 12,000 troops put up a stiff resistance but, because of the superior Japanese numbers, it was forced to surrender on Christmas Day. On 9 December the Japanese overran the American bases at Guam and Wake Island. The same day they commenced their attack on the Philippines. A bitter six-month struggle followed until the Japanese were eventually successful; the Americans had lost 30,000 troops and the Filipinos 110,000. By June 1942, the Japanese had also added Malaya, Singapore, Burma, Thailand, the Dutch East Indies and several Pacific islands to their empire. Their expertise in jungle warfare and the speed of their campaign meant that within a few months they had secured an unprecedented run of victories against the Americans.

America's initial loss at Pearl Harbour was a contributing factor, but the Japanese soldiers' philosophical outlook must also be taken into account. They lived by a strict code of honour, which made them commit suicide rather than be taken prisoner. They believed that to die in battle would ensure their entry to heaven; and it was this fanatical zeal which led many *kamikaze* pilots to give their lives as human torpedoes, blowing themselves up with the ships and planes they attacked (p.323).

However, Japan underestimated America's industrial might and her capacity to rise again quickly after the disaster of Pearl Harbour. Yet this did not become apparent for some time because the United States decided that it should first concentrate on the defeat of the Axis powers. Accordingly, the first American action was to aid Britain in the North African campaign (p.307).

CASABLANCA CONFERENCE

In January 1943 Roosevelt and Churchill met at Casablanca in French Morocco to discuss the future conduct of the war in Europe. The Casablanca conference decided that the best approach was to attack through Italy while continuing the bombing campaign of Germany from Britain. Meanwhile supplies would continue to be sent to the Soviet Union for another year until a full-scale landing in France could be undertaken. Stalin was suspicious that the western powers would reach a compromise settlement with Hitler, which would leave the Soviet Union on her own. Roosevelt therefore felt compelled to state unequivocally at Casablanca that the Allied war aim was 'the unconditional surrender of Germany'. The effect of this declaration on Stalin is not known, but it has been argued that its effect on Germany obliged her to fight to the bitter end.

OPERATION HUSKY

On 10 July the invasion of Italy, code name 'Operation Husky', took place. British, American and Canadian troops, under the command of Eisenhower, landed in Sicily. In thirty-nine days they had driven the Axis powers off the island and were poised to land in Italy. While the campaign in Sicily was in progress, the Fascist Grand Council deposed Mussolini on 25 July. After an audience with Victor Emmanuel he was formally dismissed and placed under arrest. When the news broke, people rejoiced in the streets, shouting 'Fascism is dead'. On 3 September Allied troops invaded the mainland of Italy; Marshal Badoglio, the new Italian leader, agreed to surrender (map, p.318).

When news of Mussolini's deposition reached Hitler, he immediately flooded Italy with German troops under General Kesselring. They took control of northern Italy and advanced southwards to meet the Allies. In mid-September they daringly rescued Mussolini from his place of internment and set him up as leader of a fascist republic in northern Italy. Mussolini again declared war on the Allies and Badoglio's government declared war on Germany.

On 1 October the Allies reached Naples but ran into stronger resistance than they had expected. They eventually moved on towards Rome but were held up at the 'Gustav line' near Monte Cassino. For nearly six months the Allies, hampered by wintry conditions, tried unsuccessfully to break through to Rome. It was not until May 1944 that the battle of Monte Cassino was won, when the American air force destroyed this famous fortress monastery that had been used as a stronghold by the Germans (map, p.318).

In order to get around the Gustav line, the Allies made a landing at Anzio, behind the German lines. Twenty thousand Allied troops died, but eventually the Gustav line was broken, and on 4 June the Allies entered Rome, which had been declared an open city.

The Allies pressed on into northern Italy and by December were within 70 miles of the river Po. Yet it was not until April 1945 that the German hold on northern Italy, especially the 'Gothic line' across the Appenines, was finally broken. On 28 April, two days before Hitler's suicide (p.323), Mussolini was captured by his own countrymen and, after a brief trial, was shot, together with his mistress, Clara Petacci, on the shores of Lake Como. Their bodies were taken to Milan and hung up by the ankles outside the main railway station as objects of derision.

The Italian campaign had been costly. Yet it was not in vain. It had eliminated fascist Italy from the war and had obtained a new ally in Badoglio's Italy. More important, it had pinned down some twenty-five German divisions, which would otherwise have been engaged in preventing the liberation of France (p.319).

TEHRAN CONFERENCE

Already in November 1943, as the Italian campaign was in progress, Roosevelt, Churchill and Stalin had met at Tehran to discuss plans for a second front against Germany. Stalin had been calling continually for a second front in order to take the pressure off the Russian front. Churchill suggested an invasion of Germany through the Balkans, but Stalin objected, ostensibly on the grounds that it would be militarily hazardous, but fundamentally because he did not want Allied troops liberating an area that he intended to be a Soviet sphere of influence after the war. The three leaders finally agreed to a landing on the coast of France, 'Operation Overlord', in the spring of 1944.

OPERATION OVERLORD

Throughout that spring the Germans watched and waited as the Allies turned the south of England into one vast military camp in preparation for an invasion of France.

The Germans had placed sixty divisions in France and Rommel was given the task of defending the French coast against invasion. Rommel ordered the beaches and coastal areas to be sown with minefields and studded with stakes in preparation for the inevitable invasion; dug-outs and pillboxes were strengthened and a round-the-clock watch kept for the first sighting of the enemy. The Germans were unsure where the Allied troops would land, but were determined that whatever place was chosen, the invasion would be met with an 'Atlantic Wall'.

General Eisenhower was appointed supreme commander of all Allied forces and Air

Allied troops landing on the Normandy beaches in 1944.

Chief Marshal Tedder acted as his deputy. Air Chief Marshal Leigh-Mallory was given command of all air forces; Admiral Ramsay was given command of all naval forces; and General Montgomery was given command of all land forces during the invasion. General Omar Bradley was placed in command of the American land forces. 'Pluto', an underwater pipeline, was installed to carry oil from the Isle of Wight to the Normandy beaches. Two artificial harbours, called 'mulberries', were constructed of concrete blocks, towed across to Normandy, and linked to the shore by steel roadways.

D-Day was fixed for 6 June when 5,000 ships and landing craft, loaded with troops and equipment, and protected by 1,000 planes, made the crossing from England to Normandy in the greatest armada in history. The first landings on French soil were made by gliders carrying men and equipment who were to seize key positions. The assault forces landed on five beaches, each given a code name, along a sixty-mile line. By nightfall on 6 June the Allies had landed 150,000 troops, but 2,500 men had died in the attempt. By September more than two million men and four million tonnes of supplies had been landed on the Continent (map, p.318).

Rommel's communications were so disrupted by Allied air and naval bombardment that he was fighting a losing battle from the beginning. On 12 June he wrote:

> The material equipment of the Anglo-Americans . . . is far superior. Parachute troops and airborne troops are used in such large numbers and so effectively

THE DEFEAT OF GERMANY, 1943-45

that the troops attacked have a difficult task in defending themselves. . . The Luftwaffe has unfortunately not been able to take action.

On 25 June the Americans took Cherbourg and drove into Brittany, while the British captured Caen on 8 July and advanced through Normandy. German forces were retreating on all fronts: in France, in Italy (p.316) and in the east (p.321).

ASSASSINATION PLOT

A group of German officers came to the conclusion that the only hope for Germany was to negotiate an armistice before enemy troops advancing from east and west entered Germany proper. But they also knew that Hitler would never accept, so they decided to assassinate him.

On 20 July one of the plotters, Colonel von Stauffenberg (p.312), managed to place a bomb concealed in an attaché case under the conference table at Hitler's headquarters at Rastenburg in East Prussia, a little while before Hitler was due to hold a meeting in the same room. However, somebody inadvertently moved the case behind the leg of the table, which greatly reduced the force of the blast. Hitler himself escaped with injuries. He believed that he had been saved by destiny and that this was a sign that he would lead his people to victory. Accordingly, he inflicted terrible vengeance on those who had tried to kill him. Von Stauffenberg and others were executed by firing squad; several hundred suspects (including generals and ambassadors) were rounded up, tortured and killed. Rommel had also been implicated and was arrested. However, in October he was allowed to take poison and then was given a great military funeral.

The unsuccessful assassination attempt meant that the war would continue. In early August an Allied army under the American General George Patton landed in the south of France, advanced up the Rhône valley and linked up with the Allied army in Normandy. Hitler gave orders to destroy Paris, but these were ignored by the commander of the city, General Chaltitz. On 25 August Paris was liberated by the 'Free French' army under General de Gaulle (p.303).

ARNHEM

The Allied command was divided in its views on the most effective way of bringing the war to an end in Germany. Montgomery, who had become a field-marshal, advocated a direct thrust through the Ruhr and on to Berlin. Eisenhower favoured a cautious, slower advance along a broad front in order to consolidate each area as it was won. On 17 September Montgomery's plan was tried in an attempt to secure a crossing of the Rhine. The plan, code-named 'Operation Market Garden', envisaged British and Polish airborne troops landing near the Rhine bridge at Arnhem in Holland. But a reserve division of German *panzers* soon appeared and wreaked havoc on the troops. By 25 September, the Allied forces had to be evacuated; about 3,000 men were killed and about the same number were taken prisoner.

THE BATTLE OF THE BULGE

By December 1944 seventy Allied divisions were ready for the final thrust into Germany. On 15 December Montgomery declared that the Germans were incapable of launching an offensive. Moreover he wished to spend Christmas at home in England before launching the final offensive in the new year. On the morning of 16 December the Germans, under General Von Rundstedt, made an unexpected counter-attack and caught the American forces under Bradley unprepared at their weakest point. Von Rundstedt pushed a huge 'bulge' in the Allied line in the Ardennes region of Northern France in an effort to drive on to the Allied supply base at Antwerp. To add to the confusion, the Germans landed English-speaking German commandos, dressed in American uniforms, behind the Allied lines. After much confusion, and five weeks of heavy fighting, the Allies finally drove the Germans back out of the 'bulge'. When Hitler heard of the failure of this last offensive, he returned from his East Prussian headquarters to his underground bunker in Berlin.

THE RUSSIAN RECOVERY

After the defeat of the German Sixth Army at Stalingrad in January 1943 (p.309), Stalin increased his demands for a second front to take the pressure off the Soviet armies. Stalin was becoming increasingly apprehensive of Anglo-American intentions because the proposed invasion of Europe was not taking place. However, American aid did reach the Soviet Union through Arkhangelsk and the Persian Gulf. Huge supplies of planes, tanks, jeeps and chemicals enabled the Soviet armies to meet the Germans on an equal footing. In the spring of 1943 Soviet armies pushed the Germans back from Moscow and Stalingrad. Then in July the Germans counterattacked at Kursk. In one of the great battles of the war, involving over one million troops and 3,000 tanks, the Germans were defeated after seven days of bloody conflict. In October the Germans surrendered Kiev; and by the end of 1943, they had been almost driven from the Soviet Union (map, p.318).

On 27 January 1944 the 900-day siege of Leningrad was lifted. Some 500,000 Russians had died. Cold, disease and starvation, in addition to the German bombardment, had created unspeakable suffering. The poet Mikhail Dudin describes the scene:

> Ice-bound trams and trolleybuses, broken and grotesquely tangled wires hanging from above — in the dusk hours, figures would pass here and there, pulling a handmade sledge loaded with something swathed like a mummy. This is how the people who died from starvation made their last journey. Or you could see a group of people heaving a big sledge filled with pots and buckets filled with ice-cold water from the Neva or the Fontanka.
>
> It is impossible to list all the heroic deeds performed by the city's defenders. It would take many volumes to tell how Leningrad lived, fought, worked and held out.

The defence of Leningrad is one of great heroic stories in world history. Today on a large 'Boundary Stone', an epitaph by the poet Robert Rozhdestvensky is carved:

> *You*
> *The living*
> *Know*
> *That from this land*
> *We did not mean to go*
> *We made our stand*
> *By the Neva*
> *We did not fear to give*
> *Freely of our lives*
> *That you might live.*

POLAND

In March 1944 the Russians entered Poland. The Polish resistance fighters under General 'Bor' came more to the forefront and this helped the advance of the Red Army. Between 1 August and 3 October they staged an uprising against Nazi rule in Warsaw. The capital was almost completely destroyed and some 200,000 Poles were killed. During this time the Russians did nothing to help the Poles. In fact Stalin denied the use of Russian airfields to British and American planes bringing supplies to Warsaw. It was quickly becoming clear that Stalin wished to weaken the Poles, so that when the Germans were expelled, he could more easily dictate to Poland. Many Poles were increasingly apprehensive of being 'liberated' by the Red Army. In April 1943 the Germans claimed to have discovered the remains of 3,000 Polish officers buried in a mass grave at Katyn forest near Smolensk. The Poles blamed the Russians for this atrocity and now blamed them again for their deliberate failure to come to their aid in Warsaw.

Eventually on 17 January 1945, as the Battle of the Bulge was in progress (p.319), the Russians liberated Warsaw from the Germans. Almost immediately Stalin made it clear that he would not recognise the Polish government-in-exile in London. Instead he set up a communist-dominated Committee of National Liberation in Lublin, although later at Yalta he agreed to a provisional coalition of both groups until free elections could be held.

Meanwhile, the Russian armies had driven back the Germans from Bulgaria, Romania and most of Hungary. They had also entered Austria and were in control of Vienna. At the same time, German forces had moved out of the Baltic provinces. In effect the Red Army was in control of eastern Europe, with the exception of Greece (liberated by the British) and Yugoslavia (liberated mostly by the Slavs themselves) (map, p.318).

This then was the background to the conference held at Yalta, a resort on the Black Sea, in February 1945. With the Soviet armies deep in eastern Europe, and the Allies, recovering from the Battle of the Bulge, not yet across the Rhine, Stalin knew that he was in a commanding position and intended to make the most of it.

YALTA CONFERENCE

Although the 'Big Three', Roosevelt, Churchill and Stalin, were officially allies, each had a different view of future policy concerning Europe and international relations. Stalin was determined to hold on to his gains as a guarantee for his country's safety. Churchill strongly suspected Stalin's intentions and did not wish to see the Red Army making further advances. Roosevelt, already seriously ill, believed that the United States and the Soviet Union could continue in friendship and co-operation after the war and was not prepared to accept Churchill's misgivings about Stalin.

Three issues were discussed at Yalta: the establishment of the United Nations organisation, the future of Germany, and the question of Poland. The first caused no fundamental disagreement. All three leaders agreed that the nations of the world should meet in San Francisco in April to draw up a charter for the United Nations, which was to replace the old League of Nations (p.282). The future of Germany was to be left to a special commission; meanwhile, she was to be defeated, denazified, and democratised. But the question of Poland proved intractable, and revealed the fundamental differences in the grand alliance that eventually led to the Cold War.

Poland had been liberated by the advancing Red Army. Stalin wanted the communist-dominated Lublin Committee to form the new Polish government, while Churchill wished to establish the Polish government-in-exile, which was in London. Finally a compromise solution was agreed upon — a coalition of both groups. More fundamental disagreement arose on the question of Poland's new frontiers. Stalin, wishing to extend his influence as far west as possible, demanded the line of the Oder-Neisse rivers, but no agreement could be reached, so the question of Poland's frontiers was postponed until the peace conference, which followed the war (p.335).

Why was Poland so important to both sides that no agreement could be reached? Consider the two quotations which symbolise the great divide already evident in the grand alliance.

Stalin

'For the Russian people the question of Poland is a question not only of *honour* but also of *security*. Throughout history Poland has been the corridor through which the

The 'Big Three' at Yalta in February 1945: seated, from left to right, are Churchill, Roosevelt and Stalin.

enemy has passed into Russia. It is in Russia's own interest that Poland should be strong and friendly, in a position to shut the door of this corridor by her own force.'

Churchill

'Britain declared war on Germany so that Poland should be free and sovereign . . . our interest in Poland is one of *honour*. Having drawn the sword on behalf of Poland against Hitler's brutal attack, we could never be content with any solution that did not leave Poland a free and independent state.'

The Yalta conference achieved very little except to highlight the fundamentally different outlooks among the Allies, which boded ill for future harmony in post-war Europe.

Roosevelt was not to know the consequences of the Yalta agreements. On 12 April he died and was replaced by his vice-president, Harry S. Truman.

THE INVASION OF GERMANY

After liberating Warsaw, the Russians moved on into Germany. The soldiers were given a propaganda sheet which read:

> Kill. Nothing in Germany is guiltless, neither the living nor yet the unborn. Follow the words of Comrade Stalin and crush forever the fascist beast in its den. Break the racial pride of the German

woman. Take her as your legitimate booty. Kill, you brave soldiers of the victorious Soviet army.

The Germans stood their ground along the line of the Oder. They made a supreme effort but to no avail; the Russians pressed relentlessly on towards Berlin (map, p.318).

On 23 March the Allies crossed the Rhine — Americans in the south, British and Canadians in the north. On 11 April the Americans reached the river Elbe. On 26 April the first American and Russian troops met at Torgau on the Elbe, east of Leipzig.

Berlin

The Battle of Berlin began on 19 April and was fought mainly by Russians and some Americans against the remnants of Hitler's army. The Germans refused to yield a single building without a fierce struggle, but it was all to no avail.

With Berlin in flames, Hitler married Eva Braun, with Joseph Goebbels and Martin Bormann acting as witnesses. Then on 30 April at 3.30 pm Hitler and his wife retired to their apartments in the bunker and committed suicide. On instructions dictated by Hitler beforehand, a few S.S. men carried their bodies up to the chancellory garden, where they were soaked in petrol and burned.

On 2 May the Russians entered Hitler's bunker. The battle for Berlin was over. Two days later German forces in north Germany surrendered to Montgomery. What little authority remained in Germany now passed to Admiral Karl Dönitz, whom Hitler had designated as his successor. On 7 May he surrendered unconditionally to Eisenhower at Rheims and on the following day the Germans in Berlin formally surrenerded to Marshal Zhukov. The war in Europe was over.

THE DEFEAT OF JAPAN

With the defeat of Mussolini and Hitler in Europe, it was now possible to concentrate on the war against Japan.

The brilliant successes of the Japanese in the first six months of the war had expended a considerable amount of their resources. Moreover their attack on Pearl Harbour had not been as devastating as expected, and American industrial might soon made good the loss. The first setback for Japan came in May 1942 when her advance in the direction of Australia was halted at the Coral Sea. Here American carrier forces, aided by the Australian navy, cut off and then turned back a Japanese task force heading for Port Moresby.

Then in June, as the Japanese were moving towards Midway Island, within striking distance of Honolulu, the Americans, having broken the Japanese codes, were waiting. At Midway Island the Americans inflicted a decisive defeat on the Japanese navy, from which it never recovered (map, p.314).

The next major step forward was taken in August when the Americans made a successful landing on Guadalcanal, the most southerly island occupied by the Japanese. Thus, the autumn of 1942 marked a turning point on all fronts: Guadalcanal in the Pacific, Stalingrad (p.309) in the east, and El Alamein (p.305) in North Africa.

The American general, Douglas MacArthur, now devised a strategy known as 'leap-frog'. This meant that American troops would deliberately bypass certain Japanese-held islands, thereby cutting off their supply lines. Throughout 1943 and 1944 this strategy of 'island-hopping' was put into practice; but the Americans were made pay a heavy price by the Japanese, who fought with fanatical zeal (p.315). *Kamikaze* pilots set out with just sufficient fuel to reach their destination, and then flew their bomb-laden planes against their targets. Yet, the Americans made definite progress. In June and October 1944, in two engagements fought off the Philippines, the Japanese navy was effectively destroyed.

Meanwhile the Japanese plan to invade India in March 1944 had ended in failure. The British then invaded Burma and its reconquest was completed in May 1945.

In February American forces landed on Iwo Jima, at a cost of 4,000 lives. This was followed by the capture of Okinawa where 12,000 Americans were killed.

Following their victory in Burma, the British moved on to take Malaya, while the Australians recovered Borneo. Since Japan had lost its navy and air force, the Americans and British were able to make bombing raids upon the Japanese mainland. But despite this, it was clear that Japan would not surrender, and so the new American president, Harry Truman, had to decide how best to bring the war to an end. Since the conquest of Japan would cost the lives of about one million Allies, in addition to Japanese lives, Truman decided to use the new atomic bomb.

On 6 August, a B29 American bomber, the *Enola Gay*, dropped the first atomic bomb on Hiroshima, a city of more than 200,000 inhabitants. Within minutes of the explosion, some 80,000 Japanese were dead and about the same number wounded, many with horrible, incurable burns.

On 8 August the Soviet Union declared war on Japan and invaded Manchuria (Manchukuo). The next day a second atomic bomb was dropped on the city of Nagasaki, killing a further 40,000 people (map, p.314).

The Japanese emperor, Prince Hirohito, now insisted to the military that the war must end and on 14 August Japan asked for peace.

At mid-day on 15 August, in a radio broadcast, the Japanese people heard for the first time the voice of their emperor: 'We have resolved to pave the way for a grand peace for all generations to come by enduring the unendurable and suffering what is insufferable.' On 2 September representatives of the Japanese government signed surrender terms in the presence of General MacArthur on board the battleship *Missouri* in Tokyo Bay. World War II was over.

But the manner of the war's ending gave birth to the Atomic Age, which made obsolete all hitherto existing weapons of war.

> There are deserts of sand, deserts of stone, deserts of ice. But since August 1945 Hiroshima, or more exactly the spot where Hiroshima once stood, has constituted a new, peculiar and original sort of wilderness: An atomic desert, the handiwork of *homo sapiens* and beneath its grey black surface there still remains the echo of his activity and the pitiful remnants of his fellowman.
>
> Robert Jungk, *Children of the Ashes*

Study Assignments and Essays

1. *Why was it possible for Hitler to have such an astonishing run of victories in the first year of World War II?*
2. *Why was 'Operation Barbarossa' doomed to failure?*
3. *'Rather than being an asset, Mussolini was a liability to Hitler's war effort.' Discuss.*
4. *Why were Stalingrad and El Alamein turning points in World War II?*
5. *To what extent was World War II a Russo-German conflict?*
6. *Write an essay on two of the following:*
(i) The United States and World War II; (ii) Life in occupied Europe; (iii) The Battle of Britain; (iv) Technology and World War II; (v) The war in the Pacific.

The United Nations

26

That all men in all lands may live their lives in freedom from fear and want.

UN Declaration

ORIGIN AND GROWTH

ALTHOUGH THE concept of a United Nations organisation could be traced back to Woodrow Wilson's idea of a world parliament in 1918, the UN had its more practical birth in the Atlantic Charter of 1941 (p.314). The ideals of the Charter included self-determination, territorial integrity, equality of opportunity and co-operation, and the abandonment of the use of force in settling international disputes. It was accepted by all nations fighting against the Axis powers and Japan.

From August to October 1944 delegates from the United States, the Soviet Union, the British Commonwealth and the Republic of China met at Dumbarton Oaks, near Washington, to prepare plans for a new international organisation to replace the League of Nations. An outline scheme was drawn up and approved at the Yalta conference in February 1945 (p.321). Following this, a general conference, held in San Francisco from April to June 1945, finalised the arrangements. On 26 June, fifty-one nations signed the charter of the United Nations, which officially came into being on 24 October 1945.

The charter of the UN makes clear that its aims are threefold:

1. The maintenance of peace and security for all peoples throughout the world.
2. The development of friendly relations among nations.
3. The development of international co-operation in economic, social, cultural and humanitarian matters.

The assets, archives and functions of the old League of Nations were transferred to the UN and an impressive new glass-walled building was erected on Manhattan Island, New York, to be its headquarters. The UN adopted a light blue flag emblazoned with a polar map between two olive branches to symbolise international co-operation and peace. The members are required to be 'peace-loving states' and must be willing to assist in any action the UN takes under the terms of its charter.

From its inception, the UN, unlike the old League of Nations, was an international body, and it became even more so as time went on. In 1945 its initial members were the fifty-one represented at San Francisco, but even then it was agreed that others, including the defeated states, might subsequently become eligible for membership. For the next decade, however, on account of the Cold War, only nine additional members were admitted: Afghanistan, Iceland, Sweden, Thailand, Pakistan, Yemen, Burma, Israel, and Indonesia. Then in 1955, as Cold War tensions had greatly abated, a compromise solution was reached whereby sixteen states were admitted en bloc in the belief that their votes would roughly cancel out each other and thereby not upset the balance of power. By 1958 its membership had risen to eighty-two, including Japan and all former allies of Hitler's Germany. With the granting of independence to former colonial lands, membership grew rapidly. By 1962 the United Nations had a truly worldwide membership of 104, and Afro-Asian states had become a majority.

STRUCTURE OF THE UN

The United Nations has seven principal organs and a variety of agencies and commissions.

1. The Security Council

The Security Council is roughly comparable to the cabinet in a national system of govern-

Flags mark an early meeting of the United Nations in 1946, before the construction of its present headquarters in New York.

ment. It had five permanent members (the United States, the Soviet Union, Britain, France and Nationalist China) and ten elected members from the General Assembly. Its essential duty was to preserve the peace and security of all member states and, to this end, it could be summoned at any time in an emergency. Action could only be taken if there was a majority of votes in favour, which had to include the five votes of the permanent members. Any one of the permanent members, therefore, had the power of veto, although abstention did not count as a veto. Because of the post-war divisions between East and West, the Soviet Union used its power of veto to block many decisions. This resulted in the Security Council losing some of its authority, while the General Assembly gained in stature. Since 1950, the General Assembly has been able to bypass the Security Council in the event of deadlock, and recommend action, provided that it can muster a two-thirds majority vote for its decision.

2. The General Assembly

The General Assembly roughly corresponds to the parliament in a national system of government. It is the main debating chamber of the United Nations and can discuss almost any topic. It meets in regular annual sessions (though special sessions can be called) and each member state, irrespective of size, has one vote, although up to five delegates can attend. Resolutions are adopted on a two-thirds majority vote. However, these are only recommendations and are not binding; indeed, they are often ignored. The General Assembly assists the Security Council to elect members to the various subsidiary bodies and also to the Security Council itself. It is also charged with voting for the budget, electing the secretary-general and admitting new member states.

3. The Secretariat

The Secretariat is the international civil service of the UN responsible for its day-to-day administration. It provides information, prepares reports and keeps records for the General Assembly and the Security Council. The staff of the Secretariat is chosen from all nations of the world.

4. The Secretary-General

The chief administrative officer of the UN is the secretary-general. He is recommended by the Security Council to the General Assembly where he is appointed on a simple majority vote. The secretary-general may draw the attention of the Security Council to any problem affecting world peace and may undertake special missions on behalf of any UN bodies. Each year he submits the budget to the General Assembly, which is met by contributions from the member states according to their size and ability to pay. Finally, the secretary-general makes a yearly report to the General Assembly on the running of the United Nations.

The first secretary-general (1946–52) was the Norwegian, Trygve Lie, who had the task of steering the UN through its most difficult period following the end of World War II and the ensuing Cold War. He was followed by Dag Hammarskjöld of Sweden, who was killed in a mysterious air crash on his way to the Congo in 1961 (p.332). His successor was U Thant of Burma, who continued in office until 1966.

The UN was particularly fortunate in that its first three secretaries-general were all men of impeccable integrity and outstanding ability. Moreover, they were nationals of small neutral states, and thus were acceptable as spokesmen for a world organisation.

5. The International Court of Justice

The International Court of Justice is composed of fifteen judges, each from a different country, reflecting the different legal systems of the world. They are elected by the General Assembly and the Security Council, voting separately, and their permanent headquarters is at the Hague, Holland.

The Court gives legal decisions on disputes, such as the interpretation of a treaty or a question of international law, but states are not obliged to submit cases to it. The Court also gives advice and guidance to the General Assembly and the Security Council, but only when requested. Decisions have to be based on a majority of judges, provided that at least nine of them are present. Any judge disagreeing with the majority verdict is entitled to publish his reasons.

6. Trusteeship Council

The Trusteeship Council was responsible for all those remaining territories which were mandates under the League of Nations and had not yet received independence, together with certain other areas that previously were mandated to Japan. (The United States was trustee for the Pacific islands previously mandated to Japan by order of the Security

THE ORGANISATION OF THE UNITED NATIONS

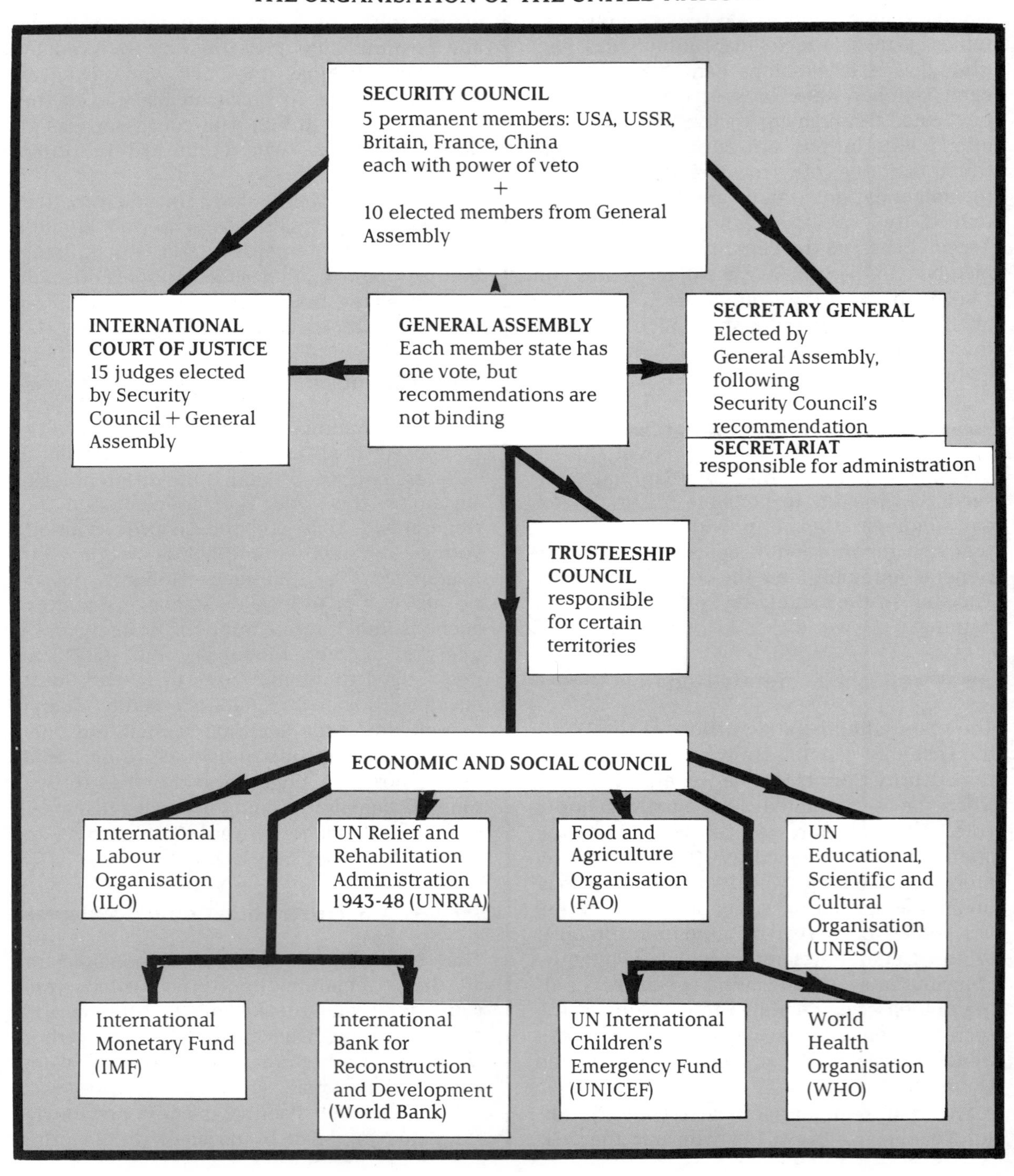

Council, 2 April 1947.)

The Trusteeship Council supervised those powers that administered the trust territories. It received an annual report from the administering power on the progress of the territory towards independence. The inhabitants of a trust territory could complain to the Security Council if they felt that the administering power was abusing its role.

7. The Economic and Social Council (Ecosoc)

The Economic and Social Council consisted of eighteen members elected by the Assembly. Its function was to supervise and co-ordinate a large number of agencies and commissions (some of which pre-dated the UN), dealing mainly with the world's economic and social problems.

The International Labour Organisation (ILO) continued the role originally given it under the League of Nations. It studied working conditions of men and women in different countries, drew up regulations for working conditions in industry and exhorted member states to adopt and abide by them. The ILO also gave technical assistance to new industries in developing countries and had training centres in Geneva and Turin.

In November 1943, the United Nations Relief and Rehabilitation Administration (UNRRA) was established. Its function was to provide immediate aid in food, clothing and medicine, agricultural machinery and transport, in areas liberated from German, Italian and Japanese control. It was financed mainly by the United States and Britain and during the five years of its existence did much valuable work, especially in war-torn Europe and the Far East.

In 1943 the Food and Agriculture Organisation (FAO) was set up to tackle the problems of securing adequate food production for the world's population. When it passed under the control of the UN, it was given a permanent secretariat. Its experts engage in research and the dissemination of information on how to increase food production more cheaply and in sufficient variety.

In 1944 the United Nations Organisation for Educational and Cultural Reconstruction came into being. It later changed its title to the United Nations Educational, Scientific and Cultural Organisation (UNESCO). Its main task is to disseminate scientific and cultural knowledge that would be of educational benefit. UNESCO also reviews textbooks to exclude nationalist propaganda and bias offensive to the dignity and equality of all peoples.

In 1944 at a meeting in Bretton Woods, New Hampshire, a plan devised by the British economist Lord Keynes and by Harry White of the United States Treasury, was accepted by the twenty-eight participating nations. This Bretton Woods agreement provided for the setting up of an International Monetary Fund (IMF) which came into being in March 1946 (p.353). Member states agreed not to make any change in the value of their respective currencies without first consulting the IMF. They were also required to pay into the fund, thereby creating a pool from which a member state could draw up to a certain percentage of its quota in any one year to provide assistance with a balance of payments problem. In this way, the exchange and stability of international currencies came under control.

An International Bank for Reconstruction and Development (World Bank) was also founded. Its initial purpose was to give financial aid to states in their transition from war to peace. After this, its function came to be that of supplying capital for projects in developing countries, such as major irrigation, power supplies and communications.

In 1946 the United Nations International Children's Emergency Fund (UNICEF) was founded, to oversee all aspects of children's welfare. It has aided programmes in child health, welfare, and nutrition and is funded mainly by donations, gifts and other fund-raising schemes throughout the world.

In 1948 the World Health Organisation (WHO) became an agency of the UN. Its function is to unite all nations in a common fight against disease and ill-health. It engages in, and co-ordinates, medical research into many diseases, and provides equipment and trained personnel where needed. It also fixes international standards on drugs and medicines and generally promotes health education.

THE UN AS PEACEKEEPER

When the UN was formed in 1945, it was intended that an international peacekeeping force under the control of the Security Council would maintain peace, while adequate machinery for the open investigation and discussion of disputes took place, which would reach a just and peaceful settlement. But with the onset of the Cold War, the permanent members of the Security Council were unable to reach agreement about this force. Eventually, in 1948, when it became obvious that co-operation was impossible, talks on the formation of a peacekeeping force were finally abandoned.

Palestine

Without a military force of its own, the UN was in danger of becoming as irrelevant as the League of Nations in dealing with outbreaks of violence in the world. This fact was made clear in May 1948 when Britain abruptly abandoned her mandate in Palestine and handed the problem over to the UN (p.371). The solution proposed by the UN was to partition Palestine between Jews and Arabs. War immediately broke out. The UN sent out a Swede, Count Folke Bernadotte, to mediate, but he was assassinated by a Jewish terrorist. The UN had no power to influence events or even prevent disturbance because there could be no unanimity vote in the Security Council. The Jews set up the state of Israel within Palestine (p.373), and the following year it was admitted to the United Nations (map, p.372).

After the experience of the war in Palestine, it became obvious to members of the Security Council that the use of the veto would make it impossible for the UN to achieve its primary aim of keeping world peace. In order to remedy this, the General Assembly attempted to assume greater power than it had been given under the Charter. In January 1950 it passed a resolution that if the use of the veto in the Security Council resulted in no decision being reached in regard to a threat to peace, then the General Assembly could consider the issue, and if a resolution was carried by a two-thirds majority, those states that voted for the resolution could act in accordance with it.

Korea

When World War II ended, the northern half of Korea was occupied by Soviet troops and the southern half by American. But with the onset of the Cold War (p.342) the Russians and Americans were unable to reach agreement on the future of the country. The United States asked the UN to resolve the issue and the General Assembly passed a resolution calling for free elections to establish a united, democratic Korea. The elections were held only in the southern half of the country. The Republic of Korea was proclaimed on 15 August 1948 and was recognised by the UN as the only elected government in Korea. The Soviet Union set up a communist regime in the northern half that was named the People's Democratic Republic of Korea. By 1949 both the Americans and the Russians had withdrawn their forces (map, p.314).

In June 1950 North Korean forces invaded the south; the UN promptly called for their withdrawal, but this was ignored. It was only the temporary absence of the Soviet delegate, Yakov Malik, ostensibly in protest against the continued exclusion of Communist China, that enabled the Security Council to act effectively and make a unanimous call for UN members to assist South Korea with arms and troops.

The Korean war was unique in character and scale among the military and political operations of the UN: in character because it temporarily obliged the UN to take sides in the Cold War; in scale because of the volume and duration of effort required and because of the number of countries that contributed to it. Fourteen nations eventually sent troops to Korea and the total strength of UN service personnel, other than Americans and South Koreans, was about 50,000. But it was the massive American contribution, led by General Douglas MacArthur, that was mainly responsible for driving the North Koreans back and capturing their capital, Pyongyang. Meanwhile Communist China had sent supplies and troops to help the North, and MacArthur demanded permission to bomb supply bases in China. But Truman did not wish to escalate the conflict lest the Cold War should result in full-scale confrontation with the Russians. Accordingly, he felt obliged to replace the uncompromising MacArthur with the more congenial General Matthew Ridgway. Fighting continued until an armistice, signed at Panmunjom in July 1953, brought the Korean war to an end. Both sides agreed to a partition of Korea along the line of the thirty-eighth parallel. The Korean conflict was not only the crisis point in the Cold War (p.342), but the most controversial operation of the UN up to that time.

The Congo

The Congo (now Zaïre) was the scene of the second-largest (and controversial) involvement of the United Nations. In 1960 Belgium granted independence to the Congo. A native government took office with Joseph Kasavubu as president and Patrice Lumumba as premier. But the area of the former Belgian Congo was in essence an artificial creation that had several tribal factions within its borders. Independence was immediately followed by an army mutiny, tribal feuds, and attacks on white settlers. But the most serious development was the attempt of Moïse Tshombe to set up a breakaway state in the rich mining province of Katanga (map, p.355).

On 14 July 1960 the Security Council passed a resolution that authorised the secretary-general 'to provide . . . military assistance . . . until, with the technical assistance of the United Nations, the national security forces might be able, in the opinion of the government, to meet fully their tasks.' The voting in the Council was eight to nil, with Britain, France and Nationalist China abstaining because of their reservations regarding a clause in the resolution that asked Belgium to withdraw her troops.

Within four days the UN had sent 3,500 troops to the Congo, and within two months had sent a further 19,000. But a force of such size was assembled so quickly only after much recourse to improvisation. Wheeled transport remained in short supply in an area of about a million square miles. Several Afro-Asian contingents arrived without such basic commodities as wireless sets, while many European units lacked tropical clothing and tentage. No permanent member of the Security Council sent any ground troops, though many of the units involved were flown to the Congo by the American air force and the British RAF.

Lumumba, who was backed by the Soviet Union, wanted the UN to destroy Tshombe's breakaway regime in Katanga, but the UN declared that it had no mandate to enforce Tshombe's submission. Tension rose as the Russians intimated that they would send aid to Lumumba, but on 6 September the UN forces closed Léopoldville airport to prevent this.

In early September the Congolese army chief of staff, Colonel Mobutu, staged a coup and ousted Lumumba, who was later murdered. After the Soviets had vetoed a Tunisian-Ceylonese motion supporting the UN forces in their task of restoring order, an emergency session of the General Assembly passed a resolution urging Dag Hammarskjöld, as secretary-general, 'to continue to take vigorous action' to seek peaceful solutions to the Congo's internal conflicts, and (in an obvious reference to the Soviet Union) urging that all military aid be channelled through the UN.

In February 1961 the Security Council gave the UN forces a mandate to disarm foreign intruders, meaning especially the many mercenaries, mainly Belgian and French, in Katanga. In September Hammarskjöld was killed in a mysterious air crash while en route to see Tshombe. His successor, U Thant, put forward a new federal proposal in August 1962. Tshombe seemed to accept it in principle, but did nothing to implement it and continued to rebuild his mercenary army. In December the UN forces moved in strength against the mercenary army while Katanga was threatened with UN sanctions. Resistance soon collapsed and early in 1963 Tshombe agreed to end the secession of Katanga.

The Congo affair focused the unease several nations felt about the concept of world affairs being ordered by an organisation that consisted of over 100 nation states, while others questioned the desirability of international peacekeeping arrangements in an age of colonial revolutions. Furthermore, the UN had accumulated huge financial deficits. Over half the member states were in arrears in their subscriptions to the main budget. The special account for the UN Emergency Force that had been in the Sinai Desert ever since the Suez crisis of 1956 (p.374) was being under-subscribed by about a third, while a mere nineteen member states had paid the full annual contribution for the Congo operation. No Soviet bloc state had subscribed to the emergency fund or to the peacekeeping force.

The wars in Korea and in the Congo have been the only conflicts in which a UN force has fought. Thereafter it has strictly limited itself to a peacekeeping role in troubled areas such as Kashmir, Sinai, Cyprus and the Lebanon.

Unfortunately the world situation thwarted the UN in its major role as peacemaker and peacekeeper. Consequently it did not fulfil the high hopes that were expressed on its foundation. Despite this, it did accomplish much, and continues to be a symbol of humanity's eternal yearning for a world at peace.

Study Assignment and Essays

1. *Examine the origin and ideals of the United Nations.*
2. *Examine the structure of the UN with particular reference to its weaknesses.*
3. *Why was there such an emphasis on non-political matters in the UN?*
4. *Examine the role of the UN as peacekeeper.*
5. *Is the UN a truly world-wide organisation?*
6. *Write an essay on two of the following: (1) The United States and the UN; (ii) The Soviet Union and the UN; (iii) The League of Nations and the UN — a comparison and contrast; (iv) The first three secretaries-general of the UN; (v) The changed character of the UN 1945–66.*

27

Soviet Expansion and the Cold War

We have still not found peace and security, and we live in the grip of even worse perils than those we have surmounted.

Winston Churchill, March 1946.

THE POTSDAM CONFERENCE

WHEN THE 'Big Three' met in the Palace of the Hohenzollerns at Potsdam outside Berlin during July and August 1945, only Stalin remained from the Yalta Conference of the previous February (p.321). Roosevelt had died and his place was now taken by Harry S. Truman. Churchill attended the earlier sessions, but when he lost the general election (p.365), he was replaced by the new Labour prime minister, Clement Attlee. Each leader was accompanied by his foreign secretary: Vyacheslav Molotov of Russia, James Byrnes of America, and Anthony Eden, and later Ernest Bevin, of Britain.

As the conference opened, Stalin was in a commanding position because the Red Army was in control of almost all of eastern Europe. Besides, he assumed a certain superiority over the two newcomers, because he was the only remaining link with the decisions that had been made at Yalta.

The Potsdam conference was intended to be the 'Versailles' of World War II, where a new world would be fashioned out of the ruins of the old. But unlike Versailles, where the 'Big Three' were essentially of one mind concerning the need for self-determination and democracy, the leaders at Potsdam were divided on fundamental issues. Truman held a 'one world' view, which sought to further the spread of self-determination and democracy throughout the world. Stalin, on the other hand, viewed self-determination and democracy as bourgeois devices that retarded the growth of class solidarity and world communism. *His* more immediate concerns were to weaken Germany and extract reparations from her, and to extend Soviet influence.

The major question facing the Potsdam Conference was the future of Germany, which had been in a state of utter dislocation since its defeat in April. After much discussion and acrimonious debate, the following decisions were agreed upon:

(a) The Yalta Agreement to divide Germany into four zones was confirmed. Each zone was to be ruled by one of the powers: the Soviet Union, the United States, Britain and France. Berlin, though in the Russian zone, was also to be divided into four zones. Austria was to be split into four zones, with Vienna further divided again, as in the case of Berlin (map, p.334).

(b) The division of Germany was to be temporary until such time as the country could be denazified, demilitarised and democratised.

(c) No central government was to be permitted in Germany unless by agreement of the three powers.

(d) An international court would punish war criminals for 'crimes against humanity' (p.386).

(e) Each occupying power could remove German property from its own zone (as compensation), but not so much as to deny Germans a tolerable standard of living. In addition, the Soviet Union was to get twenty-five per cent of all dismantled industrial equipment in the three western zones, since most German industry was located there; in return, the Soviet zone would supply food and raw materials to the western zones.

The question of Poland, which had proved

CENTRAL AND EASTERN EUROPE AFTER POTSDAM, 1945-47

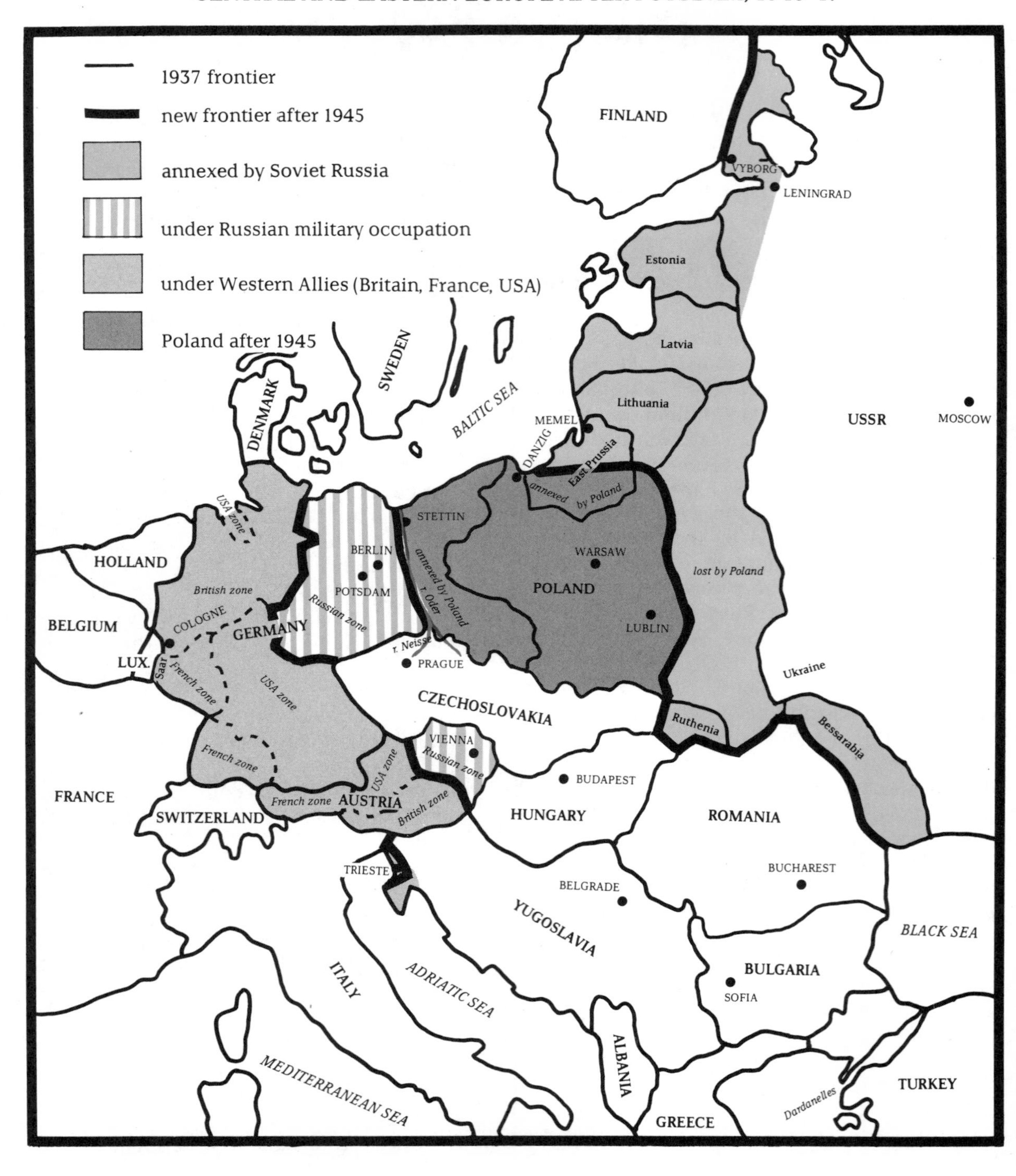

intractable at Yalta (p.321), was considered at Potsdam, but no final agreement was reached. However, Stalin did manage to get two concessions from Truman and Attlee:

(a) The Soviet Union could retain the land taken on her invasion of Poland in 1939. In compensation for her loss of this territory, Poland's western frontier would be moved 200 miles west to the line of the Oder and western Neisse rivers.

(b) Until free elections could be held, the Soviet-backed Lublin Committee of National Liberation was recognised as the legitimate administration, while the London-based Polish government was repudiated.

Beyond these agreements, little was achieved at Potsdam because of the growing deadlock between Stalin and the western leaders. Truman, emboldened by America's successful testing of the atomic bomb in July, decided to shift his policy from compromise to something approaching confrontation. But the bomb never became as significant a factor in Cold War relations as Truman (and Churchill) had expected. Stalin was well aware that the United States would have very few atomic bombs for the foreseeable future and would not permit their use against the Soviet Union, except under the most extraordinary provocation. Nevertheless, the existence of the bomb did inhibit the actions of both east and west and was instrumental in restraining both sides during the Berlin crisis in 1947–49 (p.345).

SOVIET AIMS IN EASTERN EUROPE

Stalin's objective was to ensure that communist governments came to power in the states of eastern Europe. This would advance the spread of communism, guarantee governments that were friendly towards Moscow and create a buffer between the Soviet Union and German territory. Some western commentators have dismissed Stalin's fears of a future renewed German attack as paranoia. But in 1945 only Stalin knew the severe economic weakness of his country and he was distrustful of the West's intentions in Germany. Besides, eastern Europe would be an important aid to Soviet economic recovery and Stalin saw it as a region to be exploited.

In the immediate post-war years Stalin allowed a certain political freedom to non-communist parties in eastern Europe, as long as they posed no threat to the Soviet leadership. In fact, he did not wish to see an immediate takeover by the communists for three principal reasons. First, he feared that precipitate action would arouse the hostility, and perhaps intervention, of the western powers. Second, any immediate attempt at a takeover would be met with hostility because communist parties were in the minority in each eastern European state; furthermore, it would destroy the myth, which Stalin wished to convey to the world, that communism was popular in eastern Europe. Third, Stalin still hoped to resolve the conflict over German reparations (p.336) and even hoped that he would obtain financial aid from the United States.

The orthodox view and the revisionist view of Stalin's long-term objective in eastern Europe tend to differ considerably. The orthodox view sees a predetermined, three-stage pattern of conquest. First, the establishment of coalition governments of communist and non-communist parties. Then a gradual discrimination against non-communist groups and the elevation of communists to all major offices of state. Finally, the elimination of all non-communists from government and the inclusion of the state within the communist bloc.

The revisionist view rejects this and insists that Stalin would have continued to permit coalition governments if western hostility and the Cold War had not forced him to do otherwise.

Both views tend to overlook important factors. The orthodox view presents Stalin as having a predetermined blueprint for the

Sovietisation of eastern Europe, and underestimates, if not ignores, the impact of the Cold War on his perspective. In turn, the revisionist view fails to accept that Stalin saw eastern Europe as coming within the legitimate Soviet sphere of influence. In many respects the onset of the Cold War did determine the timing of the Soviet domination of eastern Europe, but this is not to say that, even in the absence of the Cold War, it would not have happened in any event, even at some future stage.

SOVIETISATION OF EASTERN EUROPE

East German Zone

The Soviets saw the exploitation of Germany as a legitimate means of rebuilding their own economy and also of destroying Germany's war-making potential. They began to strip their zone of industrial plant and material. (This view was shared by the French, who did likewise in their zone.) But, almost from the beginning, the exchange of food and raw materials for industrial equipment between the Soviet and western zones led to acrimony. Each side put different values on the commodities in exchange and arrived at different estimates of what a tolerable standard of living should be for the Germans. The United States maintained that what might have been a tolerable level previously would now have to be revised upwards because of the heavy influx of refugees from the Soviet zone. But the Soviets would not accept this, and stopped the transfer of food from their zone to the western zones. This led the western Allies, in May 1946, to halt the transfer of industrial materials from their zones to the Soviet zone.

Only if both sides had been completely trusting and co-operative could an amicable solution have been reached over the exchange of goods. The western powers, faced with severe food shortages and economic chaos in their zones, stopped sending out reparations and began bringing in food. Meanwhile the East German Communist Party leader, Walter Ulbricht (who had been in exile in Moscow since Hitler's outlawing of the Communist Party (p.221), had returned to the Soviet zone; and though other parties were permitted, Ulbricht's party was clearly favoured by the Soviet authorities.

In 1946 local elections were held in the Soviet zone and the Communist Party fared very badly. This was the signal for the Soviets to eliminate all other political parties except Ulbricht's. Even the German Socialist Party was forced to unite with the communists in the new Socialist Unity Party or *Sozialistische Einheitspartei Deutschlands* in April 1946. In these measures, Stalin's policy towards the Soviet zone was guided by his three-fold desire to keep it weak, to use it to help rebuild Soviet industry, and to prevent the emergence of any group inimical to Soviet control (p.335).

Poland

Since Poland was the key to Soviet security (p.321), the coalition government that Stalin allowed there can only be described as a sham. At the Yalta Conference, Roosevelt and Churchill had pressed Stalin to form a coalition government in Poland. Stalin's response was to permit four members of the Polish government-in-exile in London to join sixteen members of the communist Lublin committee in a new coalition government. At Potsdam (p.334) Stalin agreed that free elections would be held; but subsequently western demands met with stiff opposition. The Poles, predominantly catholic and with a strong antipathy towards Russia and communism, were very likely to reject the Communist Party. Stalin knew this, and declared: 'Any freely elected government would be anti-Soviet and that we cannot permit.'

However, Stalin continued the illusion of

coalition government by allowing the leader of the Polish Peasant Party, Stanislaus Mikolajczyk, to join the government as vice-premier. But because the Peasant Party had been extremely popular with a predominantly peasant population in the inter-war years, Stalin was determined that it would not become a threat to the communists. Accordingly, communist intimidation (and Mikolajczyk's own political blunders) soon split the Peasant Party and rendered it ineffective. In January 1947 Mikolajczyk was dropped from the cabinet and in October he fled to the United States to avoid arrest.

The only other real threat to the communists was the Polish Socialist Workers' Party (RPPS). In 1946 the RPPS challenged the fact that the communists were the leading party in the coalition, and demanded a greater role in government. Twice during 1946, Stalin summoned the leaders of the RPPS to Moscow and compelled them to co-operate with the communists in breaking up the peasant party in return for a promise that the RPPS could retain its separate identity. However, after the Cold War events of 1947–48 (p.343), the RPPS was purged of its independent-minded leadership in September 1948 and four months later was forced to merge with the communists in a new Polish United Workers' Party. But since the communists commanded eight of the eleven seats in the party's *politburo*, the RPPS in effect had lost its identity. However, Stalin continued to suspect the loyalty even of the Polish communists, and in 1949 he appointed a Soviet general, Marshal Rokossovsky, as minister of defence.

Certainly, the Cold War events of 1948 (p. 343) acted as a catalyst in the destruction of the Peasant and Socialist Parties in Poland. But it is extremely unlikely that Stalin would have allowed a peasant party, attached to catholicism and the land, and an independent socialist party to exist indefinitely.

Romania

In its strategic importance to Russia, Romania followed closely behind Poland; and like that country, Romania had a history of hostility towards Russia, and had sided with Hitler until 1944. At Yalta, Stalin's demand that Romania should have a government that was friendly towards the Soviet Union was agreed to by Roosevelt and Churchill. But this soon conflicted with the western demand for free elections and democratic governments in eastern Europe. It was obvious to Stalin (as in the Polish case) that free elections in Romania would not return a government to Moscow's liking. The failure of Stalin and the western leaders to agree on the future of eastern European governments centred on the concept of 'friendly'. When the western leaders spoke of 'friendly' governments, they essentially had in mind governments that would neither attack, nor allow their territories to be used for an attack upon, the Soviet Union. But when Stalin spoke of 'friendly', he unambiguously had in mind 'communist'; for he could never appreciate that any type of government, other than a communist one, could be friendly towards the Soviet Union.

In Romania King Michael had gained widespread popularity when he managed to overthrow the pro-Nazi regime of Marshal Ion Antonescu in 1944 and then declare war on Hitler's Germany. For this reason, Stalin had to proceed slowly so as not to provoke widespread revolt in Romania and further antagonise the West.

But Stalin also knew that the increased popularity of the monarchy would decrease the communists' influence, so in March 1945 he pressed the king to appoint a broad National Democratic Front coalition government, which included three communist ministers. The coalition confiscated all land holdings of over 120 acres and redistributed the land among the peasants. As a result, it was elected by an overwhelming majority in the election of November 1946. But even though the communists could win only sixteen per cent of the seats in parliament, the presence of a Soviet army of occupation gave the communists a power and authority out of keeping with their numbers; and by the spring of 1947, they began to intimidate the other parties.

With the backing of the Soviet army, non-communist party members were accused of being agents of American imperialism and many were sentenced to long terms of imprisonment; in particular the popular Peasant Party was singled out, her leaders imprisoned and the party disbanded. In December 1947 with the Cold War tensions in Europe (p.343), King Michael was forced to abdicate and Romania was declared a people's republic. By March 1948 non-communist parties had been dissolved or forced into a Communist Workers' Party.

Bulgaria

The position of Bulgaria was something of an anomaly. She had allied herself with Hitler's Germany during the war, but had not participated in the attack upon the Soviet Union. And unlike Poland and Romania, she did not have a history of hostility towards Russia; in fact, she owed her liberation from the Turks in 1878 to tsarist Russia (p.104) and her liberation from the Germans in 1944 to the Soviet Union. It was little wonder then that many Bulgarians looked to their mighty Slav neighbour as a protector and benefactor.

The Bulgarians had overthrown their pro-Nazi government in 1944, but the fact that Bulgaria had been a German ally gave the Soviet armies the excuse for invading in 1944 and establishing a Soviet-supported Fatherland Front coalition government in September 1944. Then a Bulgarian army, participating in the final attack on Germany, did much to win Soviet friendship, and in contrast to his policy towards Romania and Hungary, Stalin did not demand reparations from Bulgaria.

At first, the communists in the Fatherland Front coalition held the important offices of state, but this was challenged by Nikola Petkov, leader of the Peasants' Union party, and Kosta Lulchev, leader of the Socialist Party. Encouraged by Anglo-American support, Petkov and Lulchev demanded that the communists should appoint them respectively minister of the interior and minister of justice. Confronted with this challenge to communist control, Stalin decided to eliminate all opposition groups. In July 1946 leadership of the Bulgarian army was transferred from a non-communist minister of the coalition to the entire cabinet, and the army was purged of possible opposition leaders. In September a referendum voted to abolish the monarchy and Bulgaria became a republic. Then in June 1947 as Cold War tensions emerged (p.343), Stalin ordered the elimination of all opposition parties. The Peasants' Union party, as the most direct opponent, was quickly dissolved and Petkov was hanged.

Throughout this period, the leader of the Communist Party was Georgi Dimitrov, who had previously served as general secretary of the Comintern (p.170) at its headquarters in Moscow, and was a close friend of Stalin. Dimitrov, with Soviet backing, forced Lulchev's socialists to merge with his own Communist Party, and ousted the remaining non-communists from government. By 1948 Bulgaria had become a one-party communist state. A new constitution was drawn up on the model of the Soviet Union (p.239) and the nationalisation of industry and the collectivisation of agriculture began. Bulgaria now became the most loyal supporter of Soviet attempts to overthrow Marshal Tito in Yugoslavia (p.340).

Hungary

Because of Hungary's strategic importance, Stalin was anxious to establish a Soviet influence there as quickly as possible. But because he had previously agreed with

Churchill to divide jurisdiction equally between communists and non-communists, Stalin was obliged to bide his time. Accordingly, the Provisional National Government of Democratic Hungary, set up in December 1944, was a true coalition. The communists held only two ministries, trade and agriculture, because this representation was roughly equal to their strength.

However, having a member as minister of agriculture in a peasant land permitted the Communist Party to build up its popularity. Imre Nagy, the minister, expropriated the large Hungarian estates and monastic lands and redistributed the land among 642,000 former landless peasants. Nagy wisely refrained from immediate collectivisation of the land in order to build up support among the peasants. In November 1945 Hungary held its first post-war election. The peasant Smallholders' Party won 60 per cent of the seats, the Communist Party 17 per cent, and the remainder went to a variety of other groups. But before the election, the head of the Allied Central Commission in Hungary, Marshal Kliment Voroshilov, had committed members of the coalition to agree that, no matter what results would follow the election, no party would hold more than half the cabinet posts. This was clearly aimed at curbing the power of the agrarian vote. The new premier was Zoltán Tildy of the Smallholders' Party; one of his two deputy premiers was the communist, Mátyás Rákosi. As a result of Soviet pressure, Nagy was given the ministry of the interior, which also gave him control of the police. But this ministry passed soon to a more ruthless communist, László Rajk, who intimidated or discredited most of the members of the Smallholders' Party.

By 1947 the Smallholders' Party was broken up, Tildy was removed from the premiership, and Rákosi was installed as premier. In June 1948 Rákosi forced the socialists to combine with the communists into a United Workers' Party. Finally in August 1949, the Hungarian People's Republic was proclaimed. Hungary had become a one-party communist state.

Czechoslovakia

Because Stalin had a special friendship with the pre-war Czechoslovak President Eduard Benes (p.270), he permitted the Czechoslovak government-in-exile in London to return to Prague in May 1945. Unlike the Polish government-in-exile (p.336), Benes was anxious not to annoy Stalin and consulted him about the composition of a post-war government. In addition, Benes agreed to the surrender of Ruthenia (the Ruthenians saw themselves as belonging to the Ukraine) (p.185) to the Soviet Union.

Stalin was well disposed towards the people of Czechoslovakia, and since the Communist Party had been popular before the war, he allowed a free election in May 1946.

The communists were returned with 38 per cent of the vote, the socialists gained 18 per cent and the peasant party 16 per cent. A United Front coalition government was formed under the premiership of the communist, Klement Gottwald, who believed that his party could control Czechoslovakia without calling on Soviet aid to eliminate the opposition parties.

For the first year after the election, the Czechoslovak parliament held free and open debate and the press had considerable freedom of expression and criticism. But in the summer of 1947 things changed. Opinion polls had revealed that communist support had decreased while the growth of other parties appeared to weaken, if not threaten, communist domination of the government.

Then in July the Czechoslovak government's acceptance of an invitation to attend a conference on the distribution of American aid under the Marshall Plan (p.344) sounded its death knell. Stalin delivered an ultimatum to the Czechoslovak government to refuse the invitation, and they reluctantly accepted.

Stalin feared that, with American aid,

Czechoslovakia would develop into a western parliamentary democracy and be drawn into the American orbit. Moreover, because of her geographical position, the loss of Czechoslovakia would split eastern Europe in two and render inoperable Soviet control and the free movement of Soviet troops within eastern Europe. In addition, an alignment of Czechoslovakia with the West would give the American-controlled West a common border with the Soviet Union. Finally, if Czechoslovakia was allowed to dilute its communism into a social democracy and leave the Soviet orbit, it would establish a dangerous precedent, which in time would be emulated by other eastern European countries, throwing the entire Soviet defensive system into disarray. Accordingly, Gottwald, on Soviet instructions, ordered the secret police to arrest would-be dissidents. In February 1948, Stalin sent in extra units of the Red Army and assumed control of the country.

In May elections were held but only communists were allowed to stand. On 6 June Benes resigned the presidency since he found it impossible to approve the new communist constitution. Three months later he died in utter disillusionment with Stalinist policies. Perhaps Czechoslovakia would have eventually fallen to the communists, but the death of democratic Czechoslovakia in 1948 was undoubtedly precipitated by superpower rivalry and was one of the contributing factors in the formation of the North Atlantic Treaty Organisation (NATO) (p.348).

Yugoslavia

In Yugoslavia events took a completely different turn from those in the rest of eastern Europe. During 1944, as the Germans were facing enormous difficulties on the eastern and western fronts (p.318), Marshal Tito's forces took Belgrade and went on to liberate Yugoslavia without assistance from the Red Army; and, although Tito established a communist government in Belgrade, he had no intention of taking dictation from Stalin.

Stalin had never envisaged the possibility of a communist state that was not under Moscow's tutelage, but he was determined to end it quickly because the example might be emulated by other eastern European countries. Stalin's strategy was to discredit and bring down Tito's government. When the Cominform, the Communist Information Bureau (p.344), was founded in September 1947, Stalin established its headquarters in Belgrade, partly in order to intimidate and keep watch on Tito and undermine his support within the Yugoslav communist party. Then when Tito refused to industrialise and collectivise according to Soviet plans, Stalin accused him of being anti-Soviet. But the campaign of intimidation was to no avail. Moreover, all attempts to discredit Tito with his own followers failed as the Yugoslav communists, partly because of their Slav nationalism, remained loyal to Tito. Finally, in exasperation, Stalin ordered the Cominform (p.344) to expel Yugoslavia in 1948.

In January 1949 the Council for Mutual Economic Assistance, or Comecon, was founded as a Soviet bloc answer to the Marshall Plan, but also to ensure Yugoslavia's economic isolation. But when Comecon excluded Yugoslavia from eastern European trade, Tito opened up trade with the West, and obtained a loan from the United States that helped him over the period of economic peril.

An important aspect of the rift between Stalin and Tito was the Soviet policy of turning her satellites into suppliers of raw materials and keeping them dependent for manufactured goods on the Soviet Union. The Soviet attempt to delay industrial development in Yugoslavia met with stiff opposition from the Yugoslav leaders, who pointed out that they did not wish to be exporters of raw materials and importers of manufactured goods. However, expulsion from the Cominform and Comecon, despite American aid, did have serious consequences for the Yugoslav

Marshal Tito (right) *and some of his followers in 1945.*

economy. Yugoslavia was a communist state; and though it had been expelled from the communist fold, it still did not wish to have too many close ties with the West. It was thus forced to balance precariously between the 'two worlds' of East and West.

The outcome of this balancing act was the establishment of a new style of socialist economy, which incorporated a mixture of socialist planning and capitalist market forces. The Yugoslavs criticised Soviet socialism. They claimed that state capitalism had created a massive bureaucracy and had deprived the worker of a share in the management of the economy. To reduce their own bureaucracy, the Yugoslavs began a policy of decentralisation through workers' councils and communes; after 1950, most decisions were made by these bodies. The workers' councils became Tito's main propaganda weapon against Stalin's bureaucratic state capitalism and, even though Yugoslav workers did not have full control of the factories, Tito could point out that they had a greater voice in the management of their factories than in any other country.

Unlike the Soviet economy, where there was no competition and where effectiveness was determined by the achievement of production quotas, the Yugoslavs allowed competition between factories, so that effectiveness was determined by the laws of supply and demand, and by profit. The Yugoslavs termed this a socialist market economy, and although it took years to implement, its impact on other eastern European socialist states became damaging to the unity of the Soviet bloc in the 1950s (p.402). No longer did the satellite states accept that the Soviet road was the only one. The Yugoslav experience had shown that there were many roads to socialism.

DIVISION GROWS IN THE COLD WAR

The years between 1945 and 1947 witnessed a growing deterioration in East-West relations. The Sovietisation of eastern Europe, and especially the failure of Stalin to implement agreements on Poland (p.337), did much to exacerbate the situation. But the conflict was not confined to Europe alone. Persia (Iran) was strategically placed in relation to the Soviet Union and the potential of her oil wealth was fully recognised by all the powers. During the war, the country had been occupied in the south by British forces and in the north by Soviet troops. It was agreed that both powers would withdraw after the war. However, in December 1945 the Soviets set up a communist regime in the north. Finally, and only after very strenuous protests by the United States and the UN, the Soviet Union withdrew support, and the puppet regime collapsed.

In Turkey eastern and western interests clashed. Like former Russian heads of state, Stalin considered that control of the Dardanelles was essential for the defence of the Ukraine, and would give the Soviet Union access to the Mediterranean. Stalin proposed a treaty with Turkey that would place control of the Dardanelles jointly in their hands, with no outside power having a say in the matter. Turkey refused this offer and was firmly backed in its decision by Britain and the United States. While these issues were being resolved, in March 1946 Churchill went to Westminster College in Fulton, Missouri, to receive an honorary degree. There he made a famous speech, declaring:

> A shadow has fallen upon the scenes so lately lighted by the Allied victory. Nobody knows what Soviet Russia and its communist international organisation intends to do in the immediate future, or what are the limits, if any, to their expansion and proselytising tendencies. . . . From Stettin in the Baltic to Trieste in the Adriatic, an *iron curtain* has descended across the Continent of Europe. The Communist Party in these Eastern states has been raised to pre-eminence and power far beyond their numbers and are seeking everywhere to obtain totalitarian control. . . . This is certainly not the liberated Europe we fought to build up, nor is it one that contains the essentials of permanent peace.

Churchill warned that many states, including France and Italy, were endangered by the presence of communist parties within their borders. This constituted a growing challenge and peril to Christian civilisation.

But it was the crisis in Greece, and more especially the decisions following from it, that marked the great turning point in East-West relations and the commencement of the 'Cold War' proper.

Following the expulsion of the Axis powers, a pro-western government was set up in Greece. But soon Greek communists, who had played an important part in their country's liberation, staged a revolt and civil war ensued. Greece was geographically cut off from the western powers, surrounded by newly established communist regimes in Albania, Yugoslavia and Bulgaria. Only British forces in Greece stood between the communists and victory. But Britain's Labour government, with enormous post-war difficulties at home, came to realise that she could no longer continue her traditional role as 'policeman of the world'. On 24 February 1947 Britain informed America that 'economic necessity dictates the relinquishment of

British burdens in Greece.' This was the decisive moment when Britain stepped down as a world power and the United States assumed the role of defender of the free world.

The fact that it was Tito, and not Stalin, who gave aid to the Greek communists, was either not known or was purposely misinterpreted by the Truman administration. This may have been so because it was easier to get congressional approval of aid for Greece (and Turkey) if this could be depicted as countering Soviet expansion.

The Truman Doctrine

On 12 March 1947 president Truman asked Congress to vote $400 million economic and military aid to Greece and Turkey:

> I believe it must be the policy of the United States to support free peoples who are resisting attempted subjugation by armed minorities or by outside pressure. I believe we must assist free peoples to work out their own destinies in their own way. I believe that our help should be primarily through economic and financial aid which is essential to economic stability and orderly political progress.

Arthur Vandenberg, chairman of the Senate Foreign Relations Committee, advised Truman 'to scare the hell out of the country' if he wanted congressional approval. The 'Truman Doctrine' was a turning point in post-war international relations since it affirmed that when aggression endangered peace, America's own security was also involved. Thus, the Truman Doctrine committed the United States to a global crusade against anything that could be interpreted as communist expansion. Clearly, the breach in East-West relations had widened considerably; but with the announcement of the Marshall Plan, the economic counterpart of the Truman Doctrine, the break between East and West was complete.

The Marshall Plan

On 5 June 1947, the American secretary of state, George Marshall, announced the American plan for assisting Europe's economic recovery. In Marshall's words, the plan was

> directed not against any country or doctrine, but against hunger, poverty, desperation and chaos.

Marshall went on to explain the plan's economic and political objectives and how it should be implemented:

> Its purpose should be the revival of a working economy in the world so as to permit the emergence of political and social conditions in which free institutions can exist. . . . Before the US Government can proceed much further in its efforts to alleviate the situation and help start the European world on its way to recovery, there must be some agreement among the countries of Europe as to the requirements of the situation and the part those countries themselves will take in order to give proper effect to whatever might be undertaken by the Government . . . the initiative, I think, must come from Europe.

The European Recovery Programme, its official name, was an offer of economic aid to countries on both sides of the Iron Curtain, including the Soviet Union. Marshall was anxious to avoid the sharp ideological tone of the Truman Doctrine and did not want America to be held responsible for the final division of Europe. He was at pains to stress that financial aid was open to all countries, and if Stalin rejected the programme — as indeed he did in July 1947 — the onus for the division of Europe would be shifted to the Soviet Union.

Western European countries were enthusiastic about the Marshall Plan, and the Organisation for European Economic Cooperation (OEEC) was established in April 1948 to administer it.

Meanwhile several eastern European states had expressed their desire to participate in the plan. But the Soviet foreign minister, Molotov, refused on behalf of the Soviet Union and denounced it as a 'repetition of the Truman Doctrine for political pressure through the power of the dollar, a plan for interference in the domestic affairs of other countries.' Moscow rejected the plan because it would increase American influence in Europe and thereby threaten Soviet hegemony in areas she considered essential to her security. Furthermore, Stalin hoped that western Europe would not recover economically because then it would pose no threat to the Soviet Union or to her gains in eastern Europe. Now, with Marshall Aid there was the danger not only of a revived western Europe but of one under American influence as well.

But if Stalin could not influence events in western Europe, he could certainly do so in eastern Europe. If Stalin's satellite states in eastern Europe were allowed to participate in Marshall Aid, there was a grave danger that they would be weaned away from Soviet influence. Czechoslovakia had actually accepted an invitation to a conference (to be held in July) on the distribution of Marshall Aid (p. 339). Stalin now ordered Czechoslovakia not to attend, while Moscow Radio declined the Marshall Plan on behalf of the other eastern European countries. Europe was now firmly divided into two camps.

Realising that there could be no accommodation with Washington after the Truman Doctrine and the Marshall Plan, Stalin launched an all-out drive to bring eastern Europe more firmly under Soviet control. Beginning with Czechoslovakia (p.340), the satellite states were instructed to remove all non-communists from their governments (p.336). Diversity within the communist camp was no longer tolerated as it had been between 1945 and 1947. The Sovietisation of eastern Europe and the creation of a monolithic Soviet bloc was about to become a reality.

George Marshall, American secretary of state and promoter of the Marshall Plan for post-war European recovery.

The Cominform

The Communist International, or Comintern, had been set up by Lenin in 1919 to promote communist revolution throughout the world, but had been disbanded by Stalin during the war as a gesture of good-will towards the western allies.

But following the Truman Doctrine and the Marshall Plan which ushered in the Cold War,

Stalin established a new communist organisation in September 1947. Known as the Communist Information Bureau, or Cominform, its principal aim was to ensure that the eastern satellite states obeyed Moscow strictly and to prevent them from being influenced by western standards of politics and economics. Andrei Zhdanov, the Soviet organiser of Cominform, stated that its purpose was to counteract 'the aggressive and expansionist course to which American imperialism had committed itself since the end of World War II.' Zhdanov instructed communists in the western states to 'take up the standard in defence of the national independence and sovereignty of their countries.' This edict was an attempt to destroy the Marshall Plan in the West and was a signal for western communists to follow an obstructionist course. From November 1947 western Europe was subjected to a number of serious industrial strikes instigated by the communists.

The Coup in Czechoslovakia

In February 1948 the Czechoslovak communists, backed by Soviet troops, staged a coup and established full communist control (p.340). Naturally, this produced a hostile reaction in the West. Truman declared that the Czechoslovak coup proved that the Soviet Union intended to expand 'to the remaining free nations of Europe'. A bill was introduced in the US Congress for universal military training and a return to conscription. This portrayal of the Czechoslovak coup as another step on the Soviet road to world communism has been challenged by revisionist historians. They prefer to see the coup merely as an attempt by Moscow to prevent Czechoslovakia from leaving the Soviet bloc, thereby endangering the security of the Soviet Union (p.340). In support of this thesis, they point to the memoirs of George Kennan, director of policy planning in Truman's administration. Kennan wrote that the coup 'had nothing to do with any Soviet decision to launch its military forces against the West', and that Soviet action 'flowed logically from the inauguration of the Marshall Plan Programme, and was confidently predicted by US government observers six months in advance of the event.'

The Berlin Crisis

In any event, the Czechoslovak coup did heighten tension considerably. In March 1948, Britain, France, Belgium, Holland and Luxembourg signed the 'Treaty of Brussels', which established the Western European Union for collective defence against armed attack on any of its members (p.348).

In addition, a six-power conference (excluding the Soviet Union) took place in London and decided on a plan for a federal form of government for the three western zones in Germany. When the plan was released in a communiqué from London in March, it provoked an angry reaction from the Kremlin. Stalin knew that a successful implementation of this plan would end Soviet hopes of keeping Germany neutralised and weak. A few weeks later, Stalin created a People's Council (later the People's Chamber of the German Democratic Republic) for the Soviet zone, and began restricting western access to Berlin, which though also divided, was entirely within the Soviet zone (map, p.347).

Stalin's strategy was born of the belief that it would divide the western powers and force a retreat on their plans for West Germany. He particularly placed his hopes on France, since he understood French anxieties about the emergence of a strong West Germany. But by this stage, France had moved away from her previously implacable stance towards Germany. Realising that she would get no support in the West for keeping Germany divided and weak, and also realising that a British and American presence in Germany would continue indefinitely on account of the Soviet threat, France now had less reason to fear the unification of the western zones. Accordingly,

Loading food into aircraft for the relief of West Berlin in September 1948.

on 18 June 1948 France agreed to merge her zone with the British and American zones (p.386). Stalin was now confronted with a united and solid western response.

On 20 June the Western powers introduced a new *Deutschmark* to reform Germany's currency and help her economic reconstruction. Stalin realised that this newly sponsored currency would destroy the weak German currency in the Soviet zone. On 24 June he responded by introducing a new German currency in his zone and cut off all road and rail links between Berlin and the western zone. Since western access to Berlin had not been laid down in any formal agreement, Stalin was technically within his rights. His main objective was to use the Berlin crisis as a bargaining weapon to prevent the establishment of a strong West German state under western auspices, but it was also undertaken to test the will of the western powers to uphold West Berlin against the terrible odds placed against them. Moreover a western evacuation of West Berlin would have an additional two-fold benefit: it would end the western 'toehold' in the Soviet zone, and would shatter the confidence of the West German people in the western powers and thereby kill the emergence of the state of West Germany.

Stalin's plan was frustrated. The West took up the challenge with grim determination. A massive air lift, called 'Operation Vittles', was begun, which supplied Berlin's two-and-a-half million beleaguered population with food and supplies. The air lift continued until 12 May

COLD WAR DIVISIONS IN EUROPE SINCE 1948

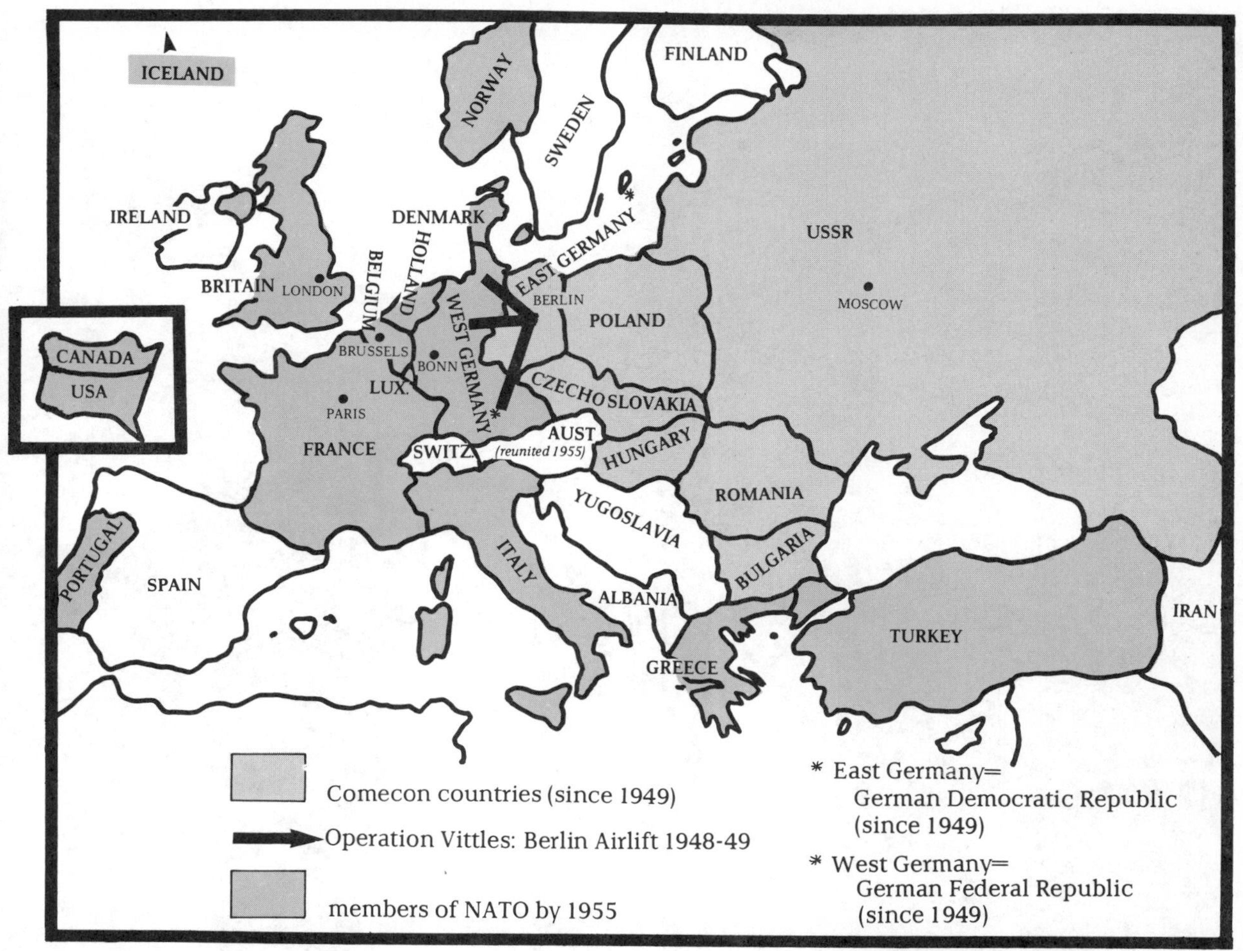

1949, when Stalin, realising that the blockade had not worked, decided to call it off. The Soviet Union capitulated in the face of western determination not to be intimidated. The only way that Stalin could have made the blockade effective was to deny the air corridors to the West. But with American planes flying into Berlin almost continually, Stalin realised that this would mean war.

The Berlin crisis passed, but its effect on the West accelerated the formation of a western military defence system and the establishment of the Federal Republic of West Germany (p.386).

DIVIDED BERLIN

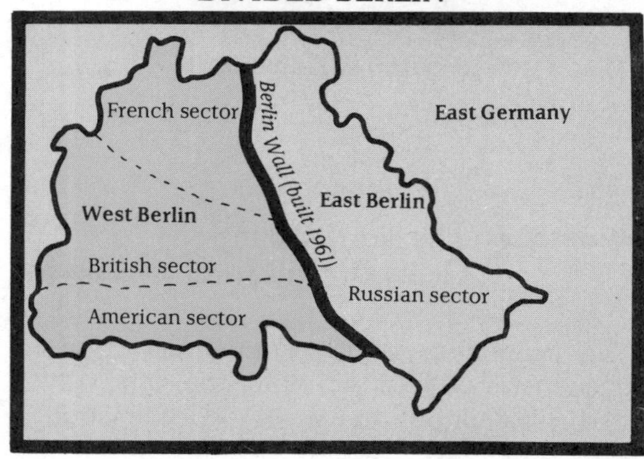

American NATO forces in West Germany in 1952.

The North Atlantic Treaty Organisation

The experience of the communist coup in Czechoslovakia (p.345) and the crisis over Berlin convinced the western powers that a fully integrated western European military alliance, which would also include the United States, was the only answer to the might of Soviet armies now in control of eastern Europe. Already in March 1948 the Brussels Treaty (p.345) had established a western union for co-operation in defence matters, but this was now considered inadequate to deal with the new situation.

Soviet military strength had grown considerably since 1945. In 1948 it was estimated that the Soviet Union had four-and-a-half million men under arms, whereas the western powers had allowed their armies to dwindle significantly. The Soviets also had an air force of 6,000 planes, while the western European powers had about one-sixth of this number. The answer therefore was a military alliance headed by the United States. Accordingly, in April 1949 an agreement was signed in Washington setting up the North Atlantic Treaty Organisation (NATO). It comprised twelve nations: the United States, Britain, France, Italy, Belgium, Holland, Luxembourg, Portugal, Denmark, Norway, Iceland and Canada. (Greece and Turkey joined in 1952 and West Germany in 1955.) (map, p.347)

The keystone of the treaty lay in Article Five, which stated:

> The Parties agree that an armed attack against one or more of them in Europe or North America shall be an attack against them all.

Thus began the return of American military might in western Europe and the division of Europe into two armed camps. Then in 1949 the Soviet Union developed her own nuclear capability and western Europe became even more dependent on American military protection. By 1949, the Iron Curtain that Churchill had described three years before (p.342) had become a grim reality. Nevertheless, a power equilibrium, or balance of terror, had been restored in Europe, which could not be altered without provoking a third world war. Since both sides now portrayed the East-West conflict solely in ideological terms, there could be no compromise. Each had to defend its freedom, either from 'western imperialism' or from 'Soviet communism', not only in Europe but in the world at large. Divided Europe was but the microcosm of a divided world.

The Two Germanys

The creation of the two Germanys was a gradual process. In the eastern zone the Soviet military ordered and implemented a tightly centralised administration which facilitated the Soviet policy of dismantling industrial plants and the general economic plundering of its zone.

Among the western powers, France was determined that a unified and centralised Germany should not arise again. Since she had not been invited to Potsdam, she did not feel herself bound by its decisions. Thus France took the first step towards the division of Germany (p.386).

However, it was the Czechoslovak coup, followed by the Berlin blockade, that finally created the conditions and the determination for the West to establish a West German state, which was immediately followed by the Soviet Union's creation of an East German state.

On 21 May 1949 the West founded the Federal Republic of Germany, which was composed of the territories of the three western zones. The country's first chancellor was Dr Konrad Adenauer, the former mayor of Cologne, who had come to prominence because of his opposition to the Nazis. Adenauer held office until his retirement in 1963 and is considered the architect of West Germany (p.387).

In October 1949 the Soviet Union responded by setting up the German Democratic Republic (GDR) in the eastern zone. The people of East Germany had previously been given the opportunity of voting in an election in which only communist candidates were allowed to stand. From its birth, East Germany was a one-party communist state.

The differences between the two Germanys began to widen significantly (p.388). The 'economic miracle' performed in West Germany is without precedent in any post-war reconstruction, while East Germany stagnated (p.404). The social and economic differences between the two states may be measured by the fact that by 1960, some 17 thousand refugees a month were moving from East to West. To stop this 'stampede', the Berlin Wall was built in 1961 and, though the Cold War in Europe has thawed considerably since Stalin's death in March 1953 (p.394), the Berlin Wall remains as a lasting monument to the continued division of Germany.

Study Assignments and Essays

1. *'The Potsdam Conference was an undisguised victory for the Soviet Union.' Discuss.*

2. *Analyse Soviet aims and tactics in eastern Europe between 1945 and 1948.*

3. *Analyse American aims and tactics in western Europe between 1945 and 1948.*

4. *Trace the emergence of the two German states from the defeat of Hitler in May 1945 to October 1949.*

5. *What factors in post-war Europe led to the formation of NATO?*

6. *Write an essay on two of the following:*
(i) The place of Poland in East-West relations; (ii) Post-war Czechoslovakia; (iii) Marshal Tito; (iv) How real was the 'Iron Curtain'?; (v) The United States and post-war Europe.

Post-War European Developments

28

A society sure of its values needs history only to celebrate the glories of the past, but a society of changing values and consequent confusions also needs history as a utilitarian guide.
Lionel Kachan

THREE MAJOR post-war developments took place in western Europe that, taken together, ushered in a new Europe and had a profound effect on the modern world as well. The first was the pooling of all the abilities and resources of the western powers to reconstruct European societies and economies out of the rubble of 1945. The second was the movement towards decolonisation, whereby the European imperial powers shed their overseas empires. The third was the movement towards the political and economic unity of western Europe.

POST-WAR RECONSTRUCTION

What distinguishes the post-war era from most other periods of economic history is not only its growth but the extent to which this growth was contrived: generated and sustained by governments and the public. M.M. Postan, *An Economic History of Western Europe 1945–1964.*

The economic consequences of World War II were far more serious and widespread than those of the Great War, chiefly because the mobilisation of all available resources for the war effort and the losses from destruction were far greater. In some countries the mobilisation of resources went back much earlier than 1939: the Japanese invasion of Manchuria and the Soviet policy of siting much of her heavy industry beyond the Urals can be interpreted in this way.

Once war broke out in 1939, all governments reacted far more quickly than in 1914. Within months the populations of the belligerents were determined and organised to pursue hostilities to the end. The production of consumer goods was strictly curtailed and their prices controlled. Essential foodstuffs were rationed and only running repairs were allowed to war-damaged factories and buildings. As territories changed hands, especially in eastern Europe, whole industries were uprooted and moved long distances, often with their labour force as well.

When the war ended in 1945, Europe lay in ruins. Millions had died, millions more were homeless. One quarter of all German homes were destroyed and large parts of the great cities of Berlin, Warsaw, Budapest, Belgrade and Leningrad were reduced to rubble. Vast areas of farmland were laid waste. Thousands of acres in Holland were flooded, while huge areas of France were sown with mines. Across this wilderness over twenty million homeless people wandered. Many had been slave labourers or were survivors of the Nazi concentration camps, but the majority were eastern Europeans who did not wish to return to their homelands now that the Soviet Union was in control there. Transport systems, especially rail and road, were disrupted; raw materials and food were in short supply.

In the Far East mines and plantations had been destroyed; this not only affected the livelihood of the inhabitants but greatly impaired the economies of the European powers which had controlled these territories before the war. The division of Europe into eastern and western blocs further distorted the pattern of economic life as the economies of eastern Europe came increasingly under the control of the Soviet Union (p.335).

A two-fold task now confronted the world's

The rebuilding of Europe: new apartments in post-war Berlin.

statesmen in post-war Europe. First, temporary means had to be found to help the war-ravaged countries back to full production for peacetime needs, to resettle their uprooted populations and to fit their economies to a changed European and world setting. Second, an attempt had to be made to establish some form of permanent and stable international economic system to replace the one that had collapsed.

Yet the war had not been all loss: new industries had been developed and many discoveries had been made and these were now turned to peacetime needs. There was a tremendous expansion in the aircraft and motor car industries, in the electrical and electronics industries, and above all in the chemical industry, especially in the field of artificial fibres. Yet while these new developments made a definite contribution towards economic recovery, they do not, of themselves, explain the rapid expansion of the western European economies in the post-war years. The explanation for this can be found in three distinct but related fields: the role of home governments, the field of international co-operation, and American assistance.

The Role of Home Governments

The sheer magnitude of the destruction caused by the war and the need to ration available supplies of food and raw materials forced governments to take a leading economic role where it was obvious that the workings of the free market were no longer sufficient to provide a fair distribution of scarce goods. Political pressures committed many European governments to policies of full employment, which necessitated a greater direction of economic activity than had been attempted before the war, except in the Soviet Union. So serious was the situation that government direction of economic activity in the allocation of capital and scarce raw materials to the channels where they were most needed, for the most part received the acceptance of capitalists and the co-operation of labour.

International Co-operation

The inter-war years had shown that protectionism and a shortage of capital had seriously disrupted international trade. In 1944 the Bretton Woods agreement set up the International Monetary Fund (IMF), which was inaugurated in March 1946. From this fund members could draw up to a certain percentage of their quotas in any one year to help them with their balance of payments problems. A World Bank was also set up whose initial purpose was to aid the transition from war to peace, but later came to supply capital for projects where normal finance would not otherwise be available (p.329).

American Assistance

From the end of the war, American relief poured into Europe, especially to areas where destruction was greatest. But the United States underestimated the time and the amount of relief needed to rehabilitate Europe, especially since Britain was scarcely able to help herself, much less contribute to Europe. During the war Britain had sold over £500 million of her overseas investments and had incurred £2,700 million of debt. By 1947 it was obvious in Washington that exceptional measures were necessary. From this sprang the Marshall Aid programme, to get the European economies back on their feet. The Organisation for European Economic Co-operation (OEEC) was established to administer Marshall Aid. This European recovery programme was extremely successful and by the early 1950s most of the worst problems caused by the war had been solved (p.343).

EUROPE'S RETREAT FROM EMPIRE

We prefer self-government with danger to servitude in tranquillity.
Ghana: the Autobiography of Kwame Nkrumah (1957)

The war that ended in 1945 was more truly a world war than its predecessor, and its effects were deeper and more widespread. The Great War had led to the break-up of empires and the establishment of European states generally along lines of national sentiment. But self-determination was essentially a European phenomenon; and though it had stimulated nationalist movements in the Middle and Far East, the western powers had retained enough power and influence to maintain their overseas empires with only minor concessions to nationalism. But the situation after World War II was radically different.

Historians identify seven broad factors that led to the end of European empires:

1. The national consciousness of peoples previously subject to European imperial rule had grown immensely. This can be seen in the ease with which Japan, a non-European power, had ousted the French from Indo-China, the British from Malaya and Burma, the Dutch from Indonesia, and the Americans from the Philippines (p.315). The Japanese had accomplished this with the slogan 'Asia for the Asians' and, though the indigenous peoples had merely substituted 'one master for another', a lesson had been learned: European powers were far from invincible.
2. With the overthrow of Japanese rule, the British, French and Dutch were too

weak and too preoccupied to repress the demands of their awakened colonial subjects for national independence.

3. The United States, the world's strongest post-war power, was anti-imperialist. Not only had she no imperial past but she contended that imperialism offered an excuse for communist agitation in colonial lands. Communist propaganda portrayed western imperialism as capitalist exploitation; therefore, continued imperial rule would lead to the legitimisation of communist rebellion among the indigenous colonial peoples. In America's eyes therefore, the best way of forestalling the spread of communism was to grant national independence to the indigenous peoples. In the context of the Cold War, this became both imperative and urgent.

4. The United States immediately set the precedent when she recognised the Philippines as an independent republic on 4 July 1946. She gave the Filipino government economic, financial and military aid to rehabilitate her war-torn country and suppress communist guerrillas.

5. Race and colour were important factors. European imperial powers were composed of white peoples; the peoples of their colonies and dominions in Asia and Africa were of coloured races, yellow, brown and black. 'Colour bars', by which natives were excluded from white clubs, hotels and shops, had been common, especially in the British colonies; and the conscious superiority of white administrators had galled the dignity and pride of the indigenous populations. The French (and Portuguese) were exceptions, and tended to treat colonials as equals if they had learned to speak French and had absorbed French 'civilisation'. But the opportunities for integration were very limited for Asians and Africans.

6. A more important factor was what has been termed the 'revolution of expectations'. During the war the peoples of Asia, Africa and Oceania were introduced to modern technology. Many learned to drive jeeps, service aircraft and use modern weapons. The improvements in communications and the development of mass media (wireless telegraphy, radio, magazines, newspapers) made many Asians and Africans vividly aware of the standard of living of the peoples of the industrialised nations. In addition, the manner in which American and European soldiers worked, lived, dressed and ate, on bases throughout the world, gave practical reinforcement to this awareness. Colonial peoples came to realise that other ways of life were possible and that disease, hunger and poverty were not part of the laws of nature. Hence they became eager for a rapid improvement of their situation. Moreover, they were indoctrinated by their own emerging leaders that the only way to achieve this was to secure national independence; everything else would follow as a matter of course.

7. But it was the Cold War that lent special urgency to the process of decolonisation. Marxist doctrine, as developed by Lenin in his *Imperialism: the Highest Stage of Capitalism*, held that imperialism was the last stage of monopoly capitalism, when western powers, having exhausted their home markets, turned to the exploitation of colonial peoples. The theory was not correct: home markets continued to grow, and the new imperialists were the communists themselves (witness the USSR's expansion into eastern Europe and Communist China's expansion into North Korea, Tibet and North Vietnam.)

Despite this, the Marxist-Leninist interpretation constituted an attractive explanation for the backwardness of colonial lands and put the blame squarely on the western capitalist powers. Communist-inspired propaganda spoke challengingly of 'social equality', 'the overthrow of capitalist imperialism' and 'the establishment of socialism'. In addition, Soviet-trained personnel were available to provide leadership for the

POST-COLONIAL AFRICA

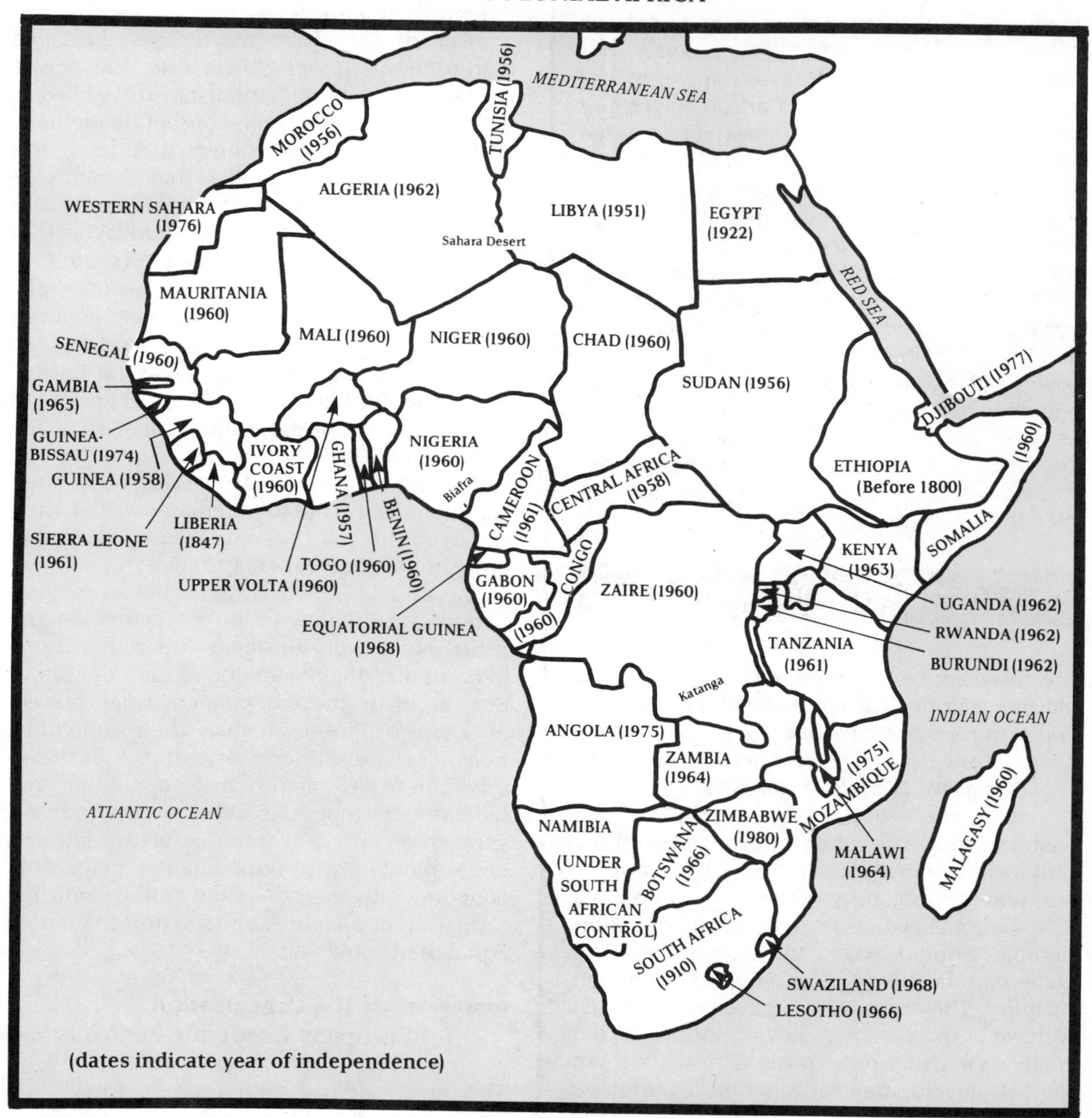

colonial peoples in their struggle for 'freedom and democracy'. As crowning proof of the superiority of communism, the Soviet Union could instance her own recent history: a state backward in every respect under the tsars, she had emerged, within a few decades under communism, as a great industrial and military power; and now, in the name of the communist brotherhood of all workers, stood ready to help colonial people to travel the same road. The fact that Soviet policy was also imperialist was not always apparent; for as the American historian, Carlton Hayes, put it, 'the siren song of its propaganda sounded sweet to peoples emerging from colonialism'.

The new world in the making was, in many respects, clear. European imperialism, which had begun in the sixteenth century, and had revived with astonishing vigour between 1875 and 1914, was about to disappear. European powers, weakened after the war, prompted by the United States, and facing the threat of Soviet expansion in Europe, were increasingly reluctant to maintain their empires by force. As a result, the 'colonial revolution', one of the great epoch-making movements of modern times, was essentially complete by 1966 (p.376).

TOWARDS EUROPEAN UNITY

The creation of a large internal market is indispensable to make it possible for Europeans to take their place in the world again.

Jean Monnet, *Les États-Unis d'Europe ont Commencé: Discours et Allocutions*, 1952–54.

Historians have noted that Europe was united only twice: under Rome in the early centuries and under Christianity in the medieval period. The French Revolution had shown how vulnerable empires were, and how powerful a state can be when it is supported by the people. The romantic movement, which followed the French Revolution, adopted Hegel's view that only in the nation state can the full development of a people's genius be realised. The romantics held that true creativity in the arts was no more than the ability to express this folk genius in the nation state. As the nineteenth century progressed, nationalism continued to gather momentum and was one of the major factors contributing to World War I and the break-up of empires in Europe (p.127).

After the Great War and the peace treaties that followed it (p.179), no one questioned the legitimacy of the nation state. It seemed to be a self-evident fact, on philosophical, political and cultural grounds, that the nation state was the only model that could give expression to man's freedom and dignity. But during and immediately after World War II, a growing number of leaders began to think in earnest of some form of European unity. Many war-time resistance fighters believed that the Europe of nation states had provided a recipe for war, and that the new Europe should be unified and therefore less prone to conflict. In addition, European leaders of the stature of Winston Churchill, Pope Pius XII, Paul-Henri Spaak, Alcide de Gasperi, Robert Schuman and Konrad Adenauer added their voices to the call for some form of European unity in the post-war era (p.358).

The initial spur towards European integration is attributable to three factors: (i) the reality of two non-European superpowers and, in particular, the Soviet domination of eastern Europe, made the independent small powers of western Europe realise their individual weakness and vulnerability; (ii) the desire to incorporate 'Germany' into a united and federated Europe was seen as the best insurance against a recurrence of war with its consequent devastation; (iii) the belief that economic advantages would follow from the formation of a large economic unit that could equal the United States.

The Organisation for European Economic Recovery

The first practical step towards integration was taken in 1947 when the United States asked for the establishment of a common European organisation to plan and supervise the distribution of aid under the Marshall Plan (p.343). As a result seventeen European nations set up the Organisation for European

WESTERN EUROPE: STEPS TOWARDS INTEGRATION SINCE 1949

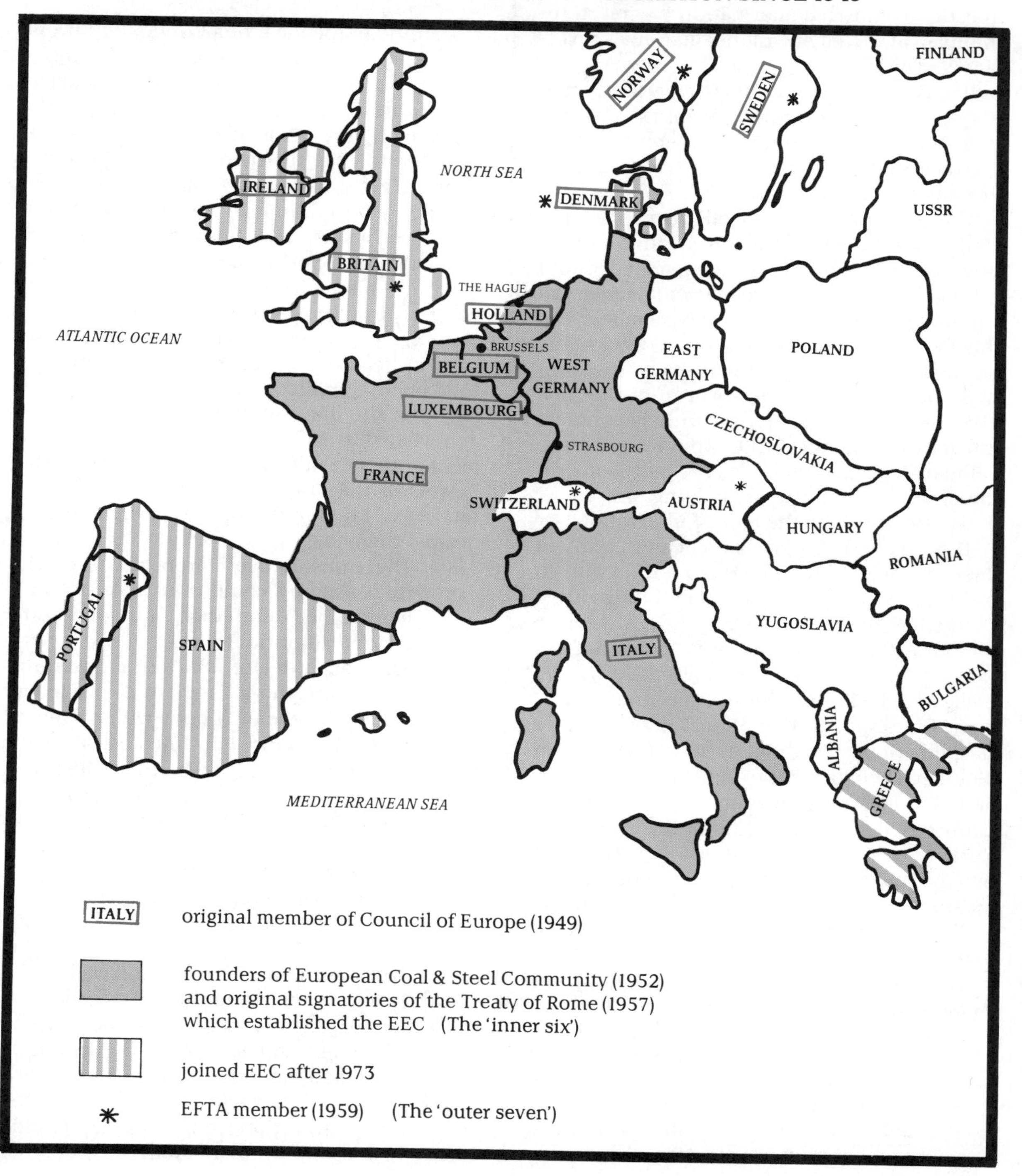

Economic Co-operation (OEEC). There was no question of any member nation having to relinquish any element of her national sovereignty. Thus the OEEC was an international, rather than a supranational, organisation. It played an important role in helping to reduce tariff barriers between its members, and there was a significant expansion of trade across European borders.

These benefits convinced many that the OEEC should be developed further. It was proposed that the OEEC be expanded into a European customs union with common external barriers against all non-members. But this idea was strenuously opposed by Britain, because she did not wish to harm her own trade with the Commonwealth. It became obvious to those who desired further economic integration that the OEEC would not be the vehicle for achieving it. Yet, it had made an important contribution, helping to break down opposition to the idea of integration.

The second major step came with a decision made at the Hague in 1948 to investigate the possibility of setting up a Council of Europe. Following this, a meeting of European federalists was convened in London in May 1948. It was attended by 750 delegates, including Europe's leading statesmen: Churchill (Britain), Spaak (Belgium), de Gasperi (Italy), Schuman and Léon Blum (France). Their aim was to achieve the political and economic unification of Europe. Ten countries signed the statute of the Council of Europe, which held its first meeting at Strasbourg in August 1949. The original ten members were: France, Britain, Italy, Belgium, Holland, Luxembourg, Ireland, Denmark, Norway and Sweden.

The statute set forth the Council's objectives:

> . . . to provide a greater unity between its members for the purpose of safeguarding and realising the ideals and principles which are their common heritage, and facilitating their economic and social progress.

Yet, although the ideal of a Council of Europe had been achieved, attempts to establish some form of political union (even loosely) met with stiff opposition. Britain signed the agreement very reluctantly because of her concern for her partners in the Commonwealth. The British government also regretted that no eastern European states had joined in the discussions and disapproved of the Council's anti-Soviet attitude. However it must be remembered that the communist coup in Czechoslovakia had recently taken place (p.340) and a certain anti-Soviet bias was, at least, understandable. But Britain's fundamental reluctance stemmed from the fact that she did not really belong to Europe and wished to keep free of political entanglements. As a result of British opposition, the powers of the Council of Europe did not extend as far as European integrationists desired them to go.

(i) The Consultative European Assembly in Strasbourg could only make recommendations and had no decision-making authority.

(ii) The Committee of Ministers, consisting of the foreign ministers of the member states, was the only body with power to make decisions. But since the foreign ministers would take their instructions from their individual governments, they would be acting on behalf of individual states and not on behalf of the Council of Europe.

The Council of Europe had no real power and has been described as 'a mere debating society'.

The first president of the Council was Paul-Henri Spaak. When he resigned his office in 1951, he vehemently castigated those who hindered the development of the Council into a truly supranational body: 'if a quarter of the energy spent here in saying "no" were used to say "yes" to something positive, we should not be in the state we are in today.'

Robert Schuman, French foreign minister (left) *in conversation with his British counterpart, Ernest Bevin, in 1950.*

But despite Spaak's harsh words, the Council of Europe continued to make a valuable contribution. Since it could not discuss matters of defence, it developed along other lines, discussing economic, social, scientific, legal and administrative matters as they affected member states. In addition, it soon branched into the questions of social security, medical services, migrant workers, codes of civil and human rights, and education. It also established a Commission of Human Rights where individuals and states may take their complaints for any breaches of the Human Rights Convention. The findings of the Commission were not enforceable, but member states, which were signatories to the Convention of Human Rights, were expected to adhere to its findings.

The European Coal and Steel Community

France, through two of her greatest European integrationists, Robert Schuman and Jean Monnet, took the lead in negotiating a truly supranational body.

On 9 May 1950 Schuman, the French foreign minister, put forward a proposal (known subsequently as the Schuman Plan) for pooling the coal and steel industries of France and Germany under a supranational authority, which would create a 'common market' in these two commodities. Since coal and steel were the basic industries for the production of armaments, their pooling under such an authority would, in the words of Jean Monnet, 'make war between France and Germany not only unthinkable but materially impossible'.

Schuman had spent his youth in Lorraine (then under the kaiser's Germany) and had served in the German army in World War I. In the 1920s he became a French citizen and was elected to the Chamber of Deputies. Schuman was therefore in a better position than many to appreciate the tragedy of Franco-German war, and passionately desired to create a new relationship between the two countries that would make rivalry and hostility impossible.

The heart of the Schuman Plan stated that:

> Europe must be organised on a federal basis. A Franco-German Union is an essential element in it. The French government proposes to place the whole of Franco-German coal and steel production under an international authority open to the participation of Europe by the pooling of basic production and the establishment of a new High Authority, whose decision will be binding on France, Germany and the countries that join them. This proposal will lay the first concrete foundation of the European Federation which is indispensable to the maintenance of peace.

On 18 April 1951 Schuman's proposal came to fruition when France, West Germany, Italy and the Benelux countries (Belgium, Holland and Luxembourg) signed a treaty establishing the European Coal and Steel Community (ECSC). It set up its headquarters in Luxembourg and held its first meeting in August 1952.

Britain refused to join, essentially on the grounds that the high authority of the ECSC had excessive powers because its decisions were binding. Speaking in the House of Commons, Prime Minister Attlee declared:

> We on this side [i.e. the government] are not prepared to accept the principle that the most vital economic forces in this country should be handed over to an authority that is utterly undemocratic and is responsible to nobody.

But besides this, Britain also felt that her links with the Commonwealth and the United States were more important than taking a gamble on an uncertain future in Europe. Moreover, since her own coal and steel industries were flourishing, she did not see any necessity for joining the ECSC.

Despite the absence of Britain, the ECSC, under its first president, Jean Monnet, did much good work. Steel output rose from 42 million tonnes in 1952 to 81 million in 1964. Investment and research increased, unprofitable coal mines in Belgium were closed down, and facilities were made for displaced workers to find employment within the Community.

The European Defence Community

In October 1950, the French premier, René Pleven, proposed that the ECSC should have a military counterpart. To this end, he suggested the formation of a European army made up of contingents from each member state. At this time the Americans were engaged in the Korean War (p.330) and there were fears that the Russians might take this opportunity to make gains in Europe: if not, they were at least expected to help the North Korean communists by heightening tension in Europe so that the Americans would have to divert troops there from Korea. The French were aware that the United States wished to rearm West Germany so that she could play her part in the defence of western Europe. France therefore put forward the Pleven Plan in order to avoid the establishment of an independent West German military force. Many Germans

Jean Monnet, first president of the European Coal and Steel Community, the precursor of the EEC.

supported Pleven because they hoped that a common European army might bring allied occupation of West Germany to an end.

Eventually, the Pleven Plan for a European Defence Community (EDC) was abandoned. With the death of Stalin and the end of the Korean War in 1953, tension in East-West relations decreased; and with it, the need for a common European army. And although the American secretary of state, John Foster Dulles, still threatened to withdraw military aid if the EDC was not established, American pressure diminished after the Korean War.

Even the French had begun to change their minds after their defeat in Vietnam in 1954 and subsequent withdrawal from Indo-China (p.380). French military pride thought that the surrendering of control over their army to the EDC would be yet another humiliation. Furthermore, the new French premier, Pierre Mendès-France, was far less enthusiastic than Pleven. But Britain's refusal to accept the EDC, because of her overseas obligations, was the final blow. France feared an EDC without British forces as a counterweight to those of West Germany. On 30 August 1954 the French National Assembly finally rejected the EDC.

Now the only way to deal with a West German army was to incorporate it into NATO (p.388). As a condition of her membership of

NATO, West Germany agreed to limit her military forces and armaments to levels determined by Britain and France. In addition, British and American forces would continue to keep forces on German soil indefinitely. Thus, with French fears allayed, West German forces joined NATO in 1955.

The European Economic Community

Although efforts to establish a European military union ended in failure, they did not have any repercussions on the movement towards economic unity.

With the impressive progress made in coal and steel by the ECSC, the advocates of further economic integration suggested expanding the ECSC to include free trade in other commodities. With production of coal and steel rising twice as fast amongst the members of the ECSC as in Britain, many former opponents of European economic co-operation now became ardent supporters of further economic unification.

But while the economic arguments were important, political considerations also played their part. The debacle of the Suez crisis (p.374) and the American hostility to the Franco-British attack on Egypt convinced France that an alliance with the United States did not guarantee any special benefit, while the ability of the Soviet Union to crush the Hungarian revolution (p.399) with impunity was further proof that, individually, the nations of western Europe were helpless in a world of superpowers. Finally, the closure of the Suez Canal in 1956 and the cutting off of oil imports to France led to a winter of unheated homes, immobilised automobiles, and run-down industries. There was speculation about what the future held for western industry. Monnet declared that the economic and political life of Europe might in the near future be paralysed if its oil imports from the Middle East were cut off.'

Recognising the weakness of the individual nations of western Europe, the French became firm advocates of a European Economic Community (EEC) and a joint atomic development agency (Euratom).

Spaak was given the task of working out the details. This was so because on 1 January 1948, Belgium, Holland and Luxembourg had formed a customs union known as Benelux; now the objective was to establish an area free of internal tariffs similar to that of Benelux and the United States. Monnet resigned as president of the ECSC in 1955 (p.360) in order to help Spaak develop a more comprehensive plan for European unity.

After several meetings, Spaak's proposals were the basis for an agreement which became the Treaty of Rome, signed on 25 March 1957. This Treaty was signed by the six members of the ECSC and created the European Economic Community (EEC) or Common Market, which came into effect on 1 January 1958. The signatories agreed to:

(i) remove (in stages) all customs duties and trade barriers between themselves. (This was to be completed by 1967.)
(ii) move towards a common level of external tariffs against non-members (in other words, establish a common tariff wall).
(iii) move towards the free movement of goods, capital and labour between the member states.
(iv) establish an agreed common agricultural policy.
(v) establish fair and free competition within the Community.
(vi) establish a European Social Fund to help reduce unemployment and improve the standard of living in disadvantaged areas of the Community.
(vii) establish a European Investment Bank.

Authority in the EEC was vested in four bodies:

(i) The EEC Commission represented the

supranational interest of the Community and made submissions to the Council of Ministers.

(ii) The Council of Ministers was made up of the foreign ministers of the member states and, as such, represented the national interests of their governments. The Council debated and voted on proposals from the Commission.

(iii) The European Parliament was composed of delegates from each of the member states. It could question the Commission members, and force the resignation of the Commission if it had a two-thirds majority of delegates.

(iv) The Court of Justice comprised seven judges appointed by the individual governments. They served for a maximum term of six years and arbitrated on disputes between the member states.

The founders of the EEC realised that the members would not be willing to sacrifice their national interests over their separate economies. For this reason, the EEC sought to strike an equilibrium between the supranational interests of the Commission and the national interests of the Council of Ministers. Decisions were normally reached through a long process of having the Commission submit and re-submit proposals before they were accepted by the Council of Ministers.

During the first few years, this balance worked relatively well. But in the 1960s, Charles de Gaulle's view of the EEC, and its authority, severely reduced the power of the Commission; and thus, hopes for a United States of Europe.

Britain's attitude to the EEC was at best ambivalent. She preferred to maintain her ties with the Commonwealth and America and now proposed the setting up of a larger free trade area to include the EEC. But EEC members were fearful of the British proposal, lest it should keep them from their objective of making the EEC a fully integrated unit. Failing in this, Britain then led the establishment of a European Free Trade Area (EFTA) in 1959. EFTA consisted of Britain, Sweden, Denmark, Norway, Portugal, Switzerland and Austria, who became known as the 'outer seven', as distinct from the 'inner six' of the EEC (map, p.357).

The primary aim of EFTA was to remove trade barriers between member countries; but in practice it had a very limited impact on the redirection of trade in Europe. In fact Austria, Sweden and even Britain traded more with the EEC than they did with EFTA. The whole idea of EFTA was, in the words of one official, 'partly a salvage operation to secure whatever benefits were possible on a smaller and more scattered basis than the EEC envisioned.'

But within a few years Britain's view of herself as a link between the United States and Europe was seriously diluted. The American president, John Kennedy, envisioned a closing of the gap between Europe and his country by tariff reductions. In 1961 the American Trade Expansion Act provided for the reduction of tariffs by 30 to 50 per cent (depending on commodity) on trade between the USA and the EEC. Kennedy wished to see Britain join the EEC, which would enable further tariff reductions to be made. George Ball, the American under-secretary of state for economic affairs, declared:

> So long as Britain remains outside the European Community, she is a force for division rather than cohesion, since she is like a giant lodestone drawing with unequal degrees of force on each member state.

Britain, therefore, with a certain anxiety over her economic future, with a fear that Europe would 'go it alone', and with assurances that America approved, changed her policy on EEC membership. On 10 August 1961 Harold Macmillan's government asked for negotiations to begin. These continued for over a year, and then Charles de Gaulle intervened. On 14 January 1963 he informed the world:

> England in fact is insular, maritime, bound by her trade, her markets, her supplies to countries that are very diverse and often far away. . . . The nature, the structure, the situations that are peculiar to England are very different from those of the continental countries. How can England, as she lives, as she produces, as she trades, be incorporated into the Common Market as it was conceived and as it works?

Two weeks later negotiations for British entry ended. De Gaulle did not want Britain in the EEC for three main reasons: (i) It would destroy French domination; (ii) the EEC had made it possible for France to play a much larger role in the world than would otherwise be the case; (iii) de Gaulle resented the fact that the British had close ties with the United States and therefore would not be true Europeans.

But Britain's own demands were also a stumbling block because she wanted protection for her agriculture and special consideration for the interests of her Commonwealth and EFTA partners. These demands were opposed, for if all members had been given such consideration, the EEC would lose its meaning. In 1967 Britain's prime minister, Harold Wilson, applied again, but was rebuffed. However, de Gaulle's resignation in 1968, and Britain's modified demands, created the necessary conditions for Britain (together with Denmark and Ireland) to join the EEC in January 1973.

In 1965 de Gaulle and Walter Hallstein, head of the Commission, clashed on their respective visions of the EEC. De Gaulle needed the Community's support for his policy of 'grandeur' (p.384) but he did not want to have economic decisions taken out of French hands. Accordingly, a struggle ensued about which of the governing bodies of the EEC should have precedence. Hallstein wished to see a federal Europe and declared that the Parliament had the authority to debate and reject the Community's budget. This de Gaulle opposed as an infringement of the rights of the national governments. Moreover, the French president insisted on keeping real decision-making in the hands of the Council of Ministers.

The impasse was broken in 1966 when the six governments signed the Luxembourg Agreement, which laid down that the Commission must consult individual member states before making any major proposal. Further, the agreement gave each foreign minister the right of veto in the Council, provided that the issue was one affecting a vital national interest. Thus, the conflict with de Gaulle dealt a blow to the supranational concept of Europe, because real authority continued to rest with the Council of Ministers, who take their orders from their respective national governments.

Study Assignments and Essays

1. *Examine the main factors in European recovery after 1945.*
2. *What were the main factors that created the 'colonial revolution' in the post-1945 era?*
3. *Why did European powers (in the main) retreat from empire in the post-1945 era?*
4. *Examine the original role and function of the OEEC.*
5. *Examine the steps leading to the formation of the EEC.*
6. *Write an essay on two of the following: (i) American assistance and European recovery; (ii) Jean Monnet; (iii) Britain and European unity; (iv) The Treaty of Rome, March 1957; (v) The strengths and weaknesses of the EEC.*

Post-War Britain 1945–66

29

No longer Great Britain but Little England.
Edward Arnold.

LABOUR IN POWER 1945–51

WHEN THE war ended in May 1945, Britain had not had a general election since November 1935. One was immediately called for 5 July. The British public had no desire to revert to the austerity of the 1930s, much less to the hardships of the war years. They were looking to the future where a definite Labour programme of full employment, nationalisation and social security seemed more attractive than vague Tory promises. Although the people saw Churchill as a truly great war-time leader, their desire to break with the past ran deep. The election returned Labour with a landslide victory of 393 seats against 213 for the Conservatives and 12 for the Liberals. Clement Attlee formed the first Labour government in British history with an overall majority.

The Welfare State

The main programme of Attlee's government was to institute a welfare state as had been envisaged in the Beveridge Report of 1942.

The heart of the report was the scheme for comprehensive national insurance, which became law in 1946. The National Insurance Act made national insurance compulsory for everyone of working age except married women. From this, benefits were paid for 'interruptions of earnings' caused by sickness, unemployment or old age, but not for losses caused by strike action. Maternity and death grants were paid in the appropriate cases. Furthermore, the act gave a fixed rate of benefit to be revised at five-yearly intervals, in order to keep pace with changes in the cost of living.

The same year, the government passed the Industrial Injuries Act (1946), which gave compensation for those killed or injured at work, and for those suffering from industrial diseases. But the central piece of legislation of the Attlee government was the National Health Service Act of 1946. This provided free medical, dental and ophthalmic treatment for all, and created a national hospital service financed by the state instead of from voluntary subscriptions. The act was not compulsory and anyone who wished to continue with private medicine was free to do so.

Then in 1948 the National Assistance Act set up boards to take responsibility for all those not already covered by the National Insurance Act. These included the dependants of those serving prison sentences, the blind, the deaf, the insane, the deserted, and unmarried mothers.

In 1949 a Legal Aid and Advice Act made it possible for the financially underprivileged who had a 'sound case for litigation' to obtain financial assistance to meet the cost of legal advice and representation.

Thus within four years of taking office, the Labour government had created a structure of welfare that ensured that every category of person would be looked after 'from the cradle to the grave'.

But it was the National Health Service which caught the imagination of the public more than any other aspect of the welfare state. Aneurin Bevan, as minister of health, was regarded as a national hero. The immediate response to the act was overwhelming: medical, dental and optical services were in great demand very quickly. Bevan was obliged to make a special appeal to the public to use the service with restraint and only if in need. Critics of the government's policy, including the Conservative Party and many doctors, seized upon this as an example of how taxpayers' money was being wantonly squandered through the policies of an extravagant socialist government. However, while not condoning the excesses, if not

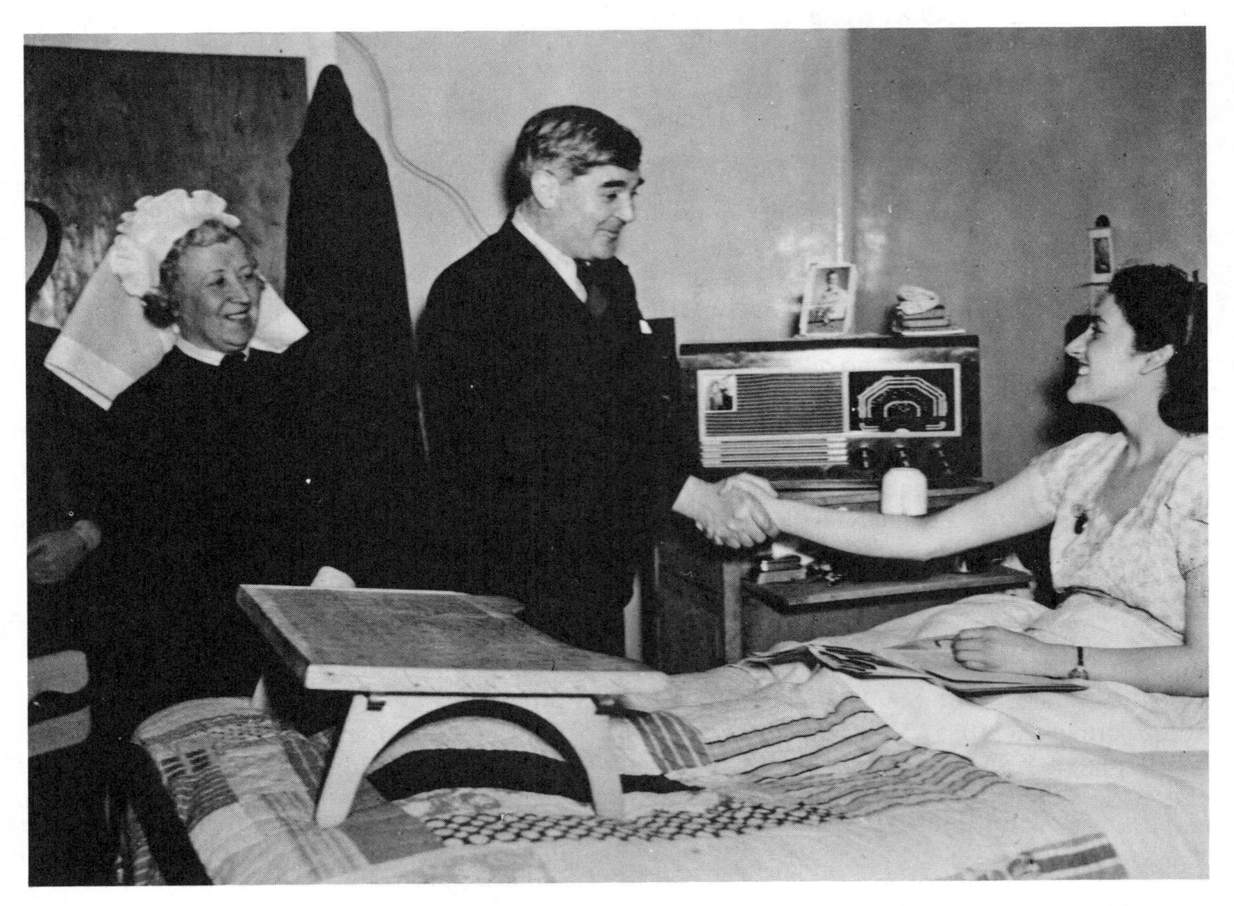

Aneurin Bevan, Labour minister of health, visits a hospital which came under the new National Health Service in 1948.

abuses, the government was quick to point out that most of the demand was the result of years of government neglect of the nation's health.

Nationalisation

A fundamental part of the Labour government's economic policy was its intention to bring key industries under state (public) ownership and control. The Tories claimed that this was 'communism by the back door', but in fact the transition to nationalisation was relatively smooth. The government had extended its control over most aspects of the economy during the war years, so that the break with the past was not as great as it would otherwise have been. Moreover, a certain precedent had been set by the establishment of the Central Electricity Generating Board (1926), the British Broadcasting Corporation (1927), and the British Overseas Airways Corporation (1939). These were public corporations whose chairmen and board members were appointed by the government. They were dependent on the government for financial support, but were not under direct government control.

In 1945 the Bank of England, already acting under government policy, was nationalised.

Between 1946 and 1948 electricity, gas, civil aviation (airlines) and part of the cable and wireless industry, already under some form of local authority or state control, were nationalised. In 1947 the coal industry was placed under the control of the National Coal Board. Persons holding shares in these enterprises were given government bonds in exchange; many mine owners were pleased to be rid of industrial strife and welcomed their compensation.

But when the government attempted to nationalise transport, it met strong opposition from the Tories and the House of Lords. A British Transport Commission was established with control over railways, passenger road transport and long-distance road haulage. When the act was passed, the Tories announced that on their return to office they would revoke it. But even greater opposition was encountered in 1949 when the government proposed to nationalise certain iron and steel firms. These were the industries that had allowed massive unemployment in the 1930s, and there was now a strong demand from Labour and trade union leaders for their nationalisation. However, the war had stimulated the iron and steel industries and the Tories objected to the nationalisation of industries that were flourishing under private control. The Iron and Steel Bill was passed by the Lords on the understanding that its implementation would be postponed until February 1951. However, the process of their nationalisation had hardly begun when the Tories returned to office in October 1951 and promptly repealed the Act. They also denationalised road haulage.

The Decline of the Labour Party

Labour had initiated an enormous rebuilding programme to make good the destruction and neglect of the war years. New towns, such as Crawley and Harlow, were built around London. The bomb sites of London, Liverpool, Manchester and Coventry were cleared and new motorways were begun. Anuerin Bevan, who was responsible for housing as well as health, started an enormous housing programme. However, high costs and the post-war shortage of materials hampered his grand design and a target of 200,000 local authority houses per year was not reached. Bevan was criticised for not allowing private builders to construct more than twenty-five per cent of local authority output.

The winter of 1946–47 was particularly harsh; there was an insufficient supply of coal and transport difficulties exacerbated the problem. There was also a food shortage and the cost of imported foodstuffs rose dramatically. The government had rationed bread in 1946 and now potatoes were included; although both were taken off the ration the following year, the war-time rationing of tea, sugar, bacon, butter, eggs, cheese and meat continued throughout Labour's period of government.

By 1950 the legislative momentum had slackened considerably and popular support for Labour was declining. Many people maintained that nationalisation had not brought any worthwhile benefits, and continued austerity led to public disillusionment. When Attlee called a general election in February 1950, Labour was returned with a slim majority of six.

In October the chancellor of the exchequer, Stafford Cripps, resigned due to ill-health. Then in March 1951 the foreign secretary, Ernest Bevin, also resigned for health reasons. Finally in April the minister of health, Aneurin Bevan, resigned in protest against a cabinet decision to introduce charges in the National Health Service. This cabinet rift greatly weakened the government and in October Attlee called another election. This time the Tories won with a majority of sixteen. Labour went into opposition and remained there until 1964.

CONSERVATIVE RULE 1951–64

The Conservative government under Winston Churchill differed little in foreign policy from

Attlee's administration (p.370). It continued the withdrawal from empire, accepted the principles of NATO and retained close ties with the United States. But in domestic affairs, especially in regard to the welfare state, the main differences between the parties soon became evident, though even here, Tory hostility to the welfare state had mellowed considerably. Instead of dismantling it, they now said they would run it more efficiently. Yet both parties differed on the ideological basis for the welfare state. Labour members saw it as an ideal and had as their objective a full state provision of all services. The Tories merely accepted the welfare state as a temporary necessity; their objective was a sufficient rise in everyone's standard of living so that no citizens would need the state to provide for them. The Conservatives saw themselves as the real party of progress, promoting prosperity, efficiency and private enterprise. They wished to keep nationalisation to a minimum because it created a large bureaucracy and stifled initiative and individual liberty. In keeping with this view, the Tories repealed the Iron and Steel Act and reintroduced private road haulage (p.367).

During the 1950s the electorate came to accept Tory rule and the Conservatives won the following two general elections in 1955 and 1959.

In 1954 rationing came to an end. Wages increased during the 1950s and there was a greater availability of consumer goods. Between 1950 and 1959 the number of private motor cars nearly doubled, the amount of personal savings quadrupled, while the number of television sets increased thirty times to ten million sets. Few people lacked the basic necessities of life — food, clothing, heating and housing. Indeed, it has been argued that more ill-health resulted from overeating than from undernourishment, and while this may be an exaggeration, statistics show that vast sums of money were spent on liquor, tobacco and gambling, while an increasing number of Britons started to go abroad on holiday. Britain had become an affluent society. Yet the implications of this were very serious, for the prevailing affluence, in the long run, depended on increased productivity and the country's continued ability to export manufactured goods and services. The Tory economic philosophy dictated that this could best be achieved by private enterprise, and not by socialist ideas of economic planning.

But during the period of Churchill's government (1951–55), as wages increased, the price of exports rose faster than Britain's competitors, so that her share of the world market declined.

In April 1955 Churchill resigned and his place was taken by Anthony Eden, who led the Tories to an election victory the following month. Eden, however, resigned in ill-health following the Suez debacle (p.374) in January 1957, and Harold Macmillan became prime minister. Then in October 1959 Macmillan led the Tories to their third successive election victory on the slogan 'You've never had it so good!'

During all these years of Tory rule, nothing was done to tackle the basic problem in the economy: Britain's resources were devoted overwhelmingly to the production of consumer goods and she was living beyond her means. The Tories were prepared to take action to tackle only immediate problems, but not the long-term overhaul of the economy. Two such immediate problems were inflation (wages and prices were rising so quickly that money was becoming less valuable) and the balance of payments deficit (Britain was importing more than she was exporting).

Tory governments tried to deal with these problems by deflating the economy. They increased taxes and restricted credit facilities in order to dampen demand, and thus bring imports into line with exports. But when the economy slowed down too much, causing job losses, the Tories reversed the process and reflated the economy. This in turn led to inflation and a balance of payments deficit,

Harold Macmillan, the Conservative prime minister, who won the 1959 general election with the slogan 'You've never had it so good!'

so that the whole 'stop-go' process had to start again.

It was not until the early 1960s that Macmillan's government finally modified the traditional Tory economic policy in favour of government planning of long-term development programmes. In 1961 Lord Robens was placed in charge of the National Coal Board, charged with the task of eliminating all non-productive pits, and introducing modern, efficient methods to the rest of the coal industry. The same year Professor Buchanan was given the task of investigating the problem of roads, and in 1962 his report recommended a set of plans for spending £1,000 million on building motorways. Dr Beeching was given the task of reorganising British Railways and in 1963 produced his report, which recommended the closure of 5,000 miles of track and over half the country's railway stations, and the streamlining of the remainder so that they would make a profit.

Macmillan's government set up a series of committees to investigate a wide range of problems. In 1963 the Robbins Report on Higher Education recommended that the number of universities should be increased from thirty-two to eighty by 1980. Royal Commissions were appointed to study the police and the problems of London local government, and in 1963 an Act was passed setting up the Greater London Council. In the area of economic planning, the government set up a National Economic Development Council and a National Incomes Commission, but these bodies did very little; economic problems continued, with unemployment rising to 800,000 in 1963 — the highest figure in twenty years. As a result, Labour's promise that 'stop-go' economies would end on their return to office continued to gain acceptance with the electorate.

Then in March 1963 a series of revelations suggested that there were serious security risks within the Tory cabinet. In June the minister for war, John Profumo, admitted that he had lied to the House of Commons about his relationship with a girl, Christine Keeler, who was also consorting with the naval attaché of the Soviet Embassy. Profumo resigned, but the scandal badly damaged the standing of Macmillan's government.

At the party conference in October, Harold Macmillan suddenly fell ill and resigned. His place as prime minister was taken by the relatively little-known Sir Alec Douglas-Home. But the fortunes of the party continued to slide and following the general election in October 1964 Labour returned to power.

Labour in Opposition 1951–64

When Labour lost the election in 1951, they could not foresee that it would be the first of three such defeats, and that they would spend thirteen years in opposition. During this period the party was seriously divided.

One such split arose over defence policy and reliance on nuclear arms. In 1955 Aneurin Bevan led a breakaway group of fifty-seven 'Bevanites' who refused to support Labour's policy of an independent nuclear deterrent.

When Attlee resigned after the 1955 election defeat, the leadership passed to Hugh Gaitskell. Thereafter Bevan supported Gaitskell but after the third successive electoral defeat in 1959, the divisions surfaced again. An equally divisive issue concerned the policy of nationalisation. Gaitskell was a moderate socialist and refused to see capitalism and socialism as direct and irreconcilable systems. Rather, he saw a series of infinite gradations between them. Gaitskell proposed deleting from the party's constitution the socialist objective of establishing 'the common ownership of the means of production, distribution and exchange', but this aroused bitter opposition from Labour's left wing.

In 1960 the issue of defence flared up yet again. At the party's annual conference a motion was passed calling for unilateral British nuclear disarmament, but Gaitskell refused to change party policy. This provoked a leadership challenge from Harold Wilson but Gaitskell won the confidence vote. At the 1961 party conference he persuaded delegates to reverse the decision on disarmament. However, he also modified this policy to suggest a willingness to negotiate a gradual movement towards nuclear disarmament, and this did much to reunite the party. In 1963 Gaitskell died suddenly, and Harold Wilson became leader and led Labour to victory in 1964.

LABOUR IN OFFICE 1964–66

On taking office Wilson's government promised to take advantage of the new scientific and technological revolution after the 'thirteen wasted years' of Conservative rule. They also offered a professional approach to the problems of economic growth after the 'stop-go' economic policies of the Tories.

However, the Wilson administration inherited a huge balance of payments deficit, added to an inflation spiral, and had to postpone their plans for economic growth. The government tried to solve the balance of payments deficit by the double policy of placing a fifteen per cent surcharge on imported goods and by encouraging industry to export more manufactured goods.

The problem of inflation could not be solved by the Conservatives' 'stop-go' policy, so the government set up a Prices and Incomes Board to investigate and monitor these two aspects of the economy. However, the Board had no real power to determine prices and incomes and failed to influence events. In fact between October 1964 and the following election in March 1966, prices and incomes rose three times as fast as productivity. Consequently, inflation became even worse than during the previous Tory administration.

BRITISH FOREIGN POLICY SINCE 1945

In 1945 Britain emerged victorious from the war. But unlike her two allies, the United States and the Soviet Union, she had been at war since 1939 (p.295) and had been a great world power for much longer than either of them. Following the war, Britain found herself weak and exhausted while her allies had grown immeasurably. Moreover, the war had accelerated the forces of change throughout the world and for many countries there could now be no going back to a pre-war colonial status. This feeling was especially evident in regions that had come under the control of the Axis powers and Japan. Britain (and the Allies generally) had encouraged the indigenous peoples to fight against the enemy, and these peoples would not now accept the return of their former colonial masters (p.353).

The history of British foreign policy over the next twenty years is the history of her withdrawal from empire; from a position of being a world power to a painful (and at times unwilling) acceptance of her position as a middle-rate power off the coast of Europe.

Labour's post-war foreign minister, Ernest Bevin, was quick to realise the new realities. With the onset of the Cold War (p.342), Bevin moved towards a closer relationship with the United States. It was a policy not without its critics, especially from the left wing of his own party, but also from the Tories, who had not yet accepted that Britain could not pursue a dominant independent path.

The first major instance of Britain's new role came in 1947 when she informed Washington that she could no longer afford the financial and other burdens of supporting Greece and Turkey. This decision led directly to the Truman Doctrine (p.343). Britain stood down from her role as policeman of the free world and America stepped into the breach.

But a more significant symptom of Britain's decline as a world power may be seen in the rapidity with which she lost her overseas empire in the post-war years. In 1942 Churchill had promised India independence after the war, provided that any province of the subcontinent that wished to secede could do so. This was to provide for the Moslem population which would not accept majority Hindu rule. Mahatma Gandhi, the Hindu leader, seeing British power already crumbling before the Germans in North Africa (p.305) and the Japanese in the Far East (p.315) described the offer as 'a post-dated cheque on a failing bank' and refused it.

By 1945 many Indians felt that Britain would not grant any form of independence, now that she had won the war. But Attlee's Labour government was determined to grant Indian independence, and after unsuccessful attempts to preserve Indian unity, decided upon partition. In August 1947 two separate Indian states were established: a Hindu-dominated India and a Moslem-dominated Pakistan.

At the peace settlement in 1919 following World War I, Britain had secured Iraq, Transjordan and Palestine as mandated territories (p.182) and had established protectorates along the south-east coast of Arabia. Between then and the outbreak of World War II only Egypt (1922) and Iraq (1932) had been granted independence, but after 1945 the quest for freedom gathered momentum (p.353). In 1946 Transjordan became independent and three years later changed its name to Jordan, thereby implying its right to Palestinian lands on the west bank of the river Jordan (map, p.372).

But it was the problem of Palestine that proved intractable for Britain. Already in 1917 the then British foreign secretary, Arthur Balfour, in an effort to obtain the support of Jews throughout the world for the allied cause, made the famous 'Balfour Declaration', which promised 'the establishment in Palestine of a national home for the Jewish people'. For some twenty years afterwards this declaration caused little difficulty because less than one in ten Palestinians was Jewish, and few European or American Jews were interested in emigrating to this isolated part of the world. But Nazi persecution of the Jews stimulated an exodus from Europe and by 1945 about 30 per cent of the population of Palestine were Jewish.

Tension between Arab and Jew increased and each side suspected the British of favouring the other. Britain's policy aimed to keep the flow of Jewish immigration into Palestine below 2,000 a month in order to preserve a communal balance between Arab and Jew. But such a policy, coming in the aftermath of Nazi atrocities, was viewed by Jews as intolerable. A Jewish national army, the *Haganah*, stood ready to seize power while Jewish extremist groups, such as the *Irgun Zvai Leumi*, and the 'Stern Gang', waged a war of terrorism against 100,000 British troops.

In February 1947 Attlee's government proposed that Jewish legal immigration should treble and Palestine should be organ-

THE MIDDLE EAST, ISRAEL AND SUEZ, 1948-56

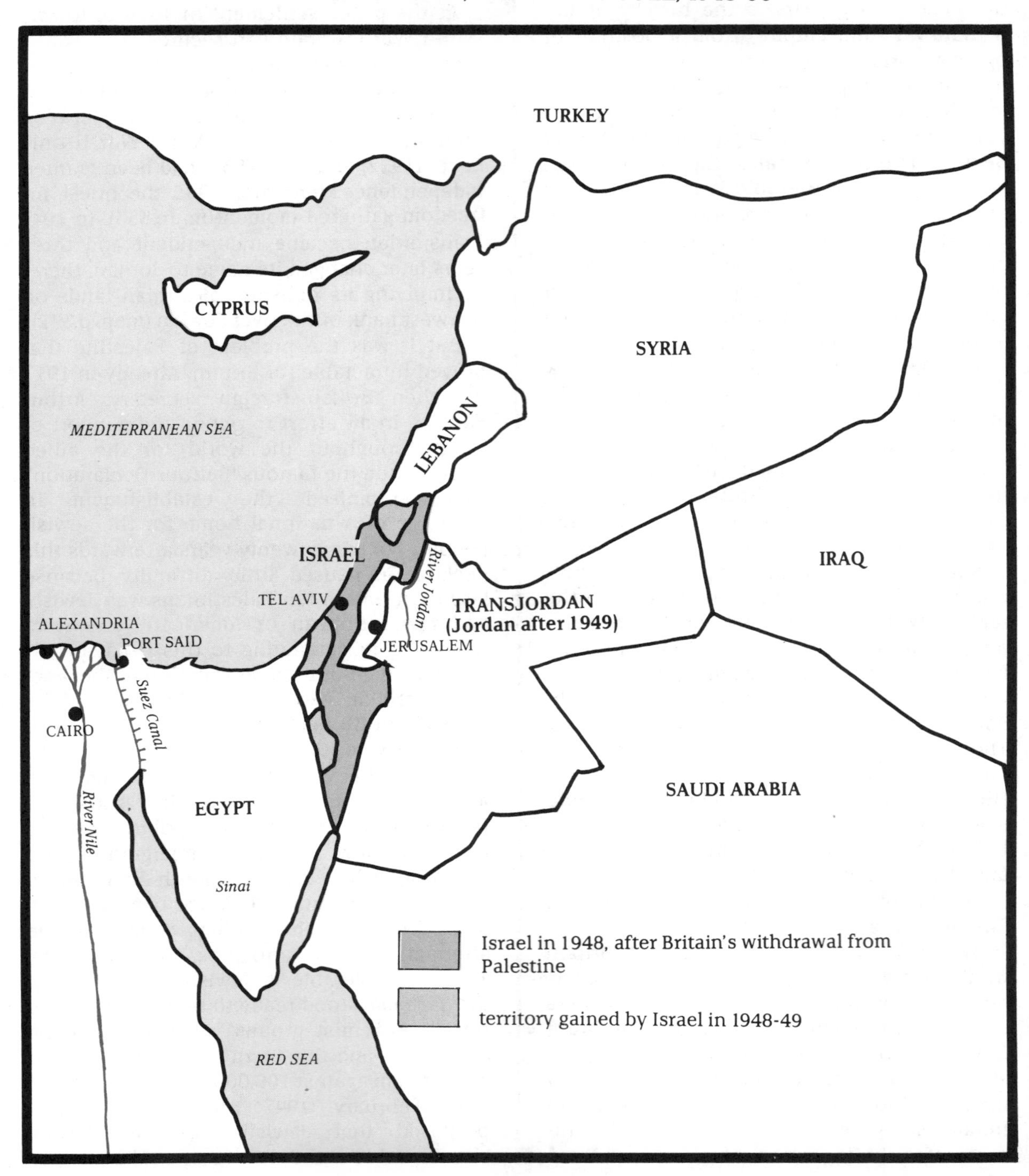

Pandit Nehru, first prime minister of independent India.

ised (for some years) into semi-autonomous zones, pending agreement on a democratic constitution for a two-nation independent Palestine. These proposals were rejected and Britain referred the problem to the United Nations (p.330). In November 1947 the General Assembly passed a resolution in favour of partition; Britain disclaimed all further responsibility for her mandate and announced her intention to withdraw from Palestine by 15 May 1948. As the day approached, Palestine slid into a state of open war. The Jews declared the establishment of the state of Israel with its capital at Tel Aviv. The United States immediately gave the state official recognition, but troops of seven surrounding Arab states attacked the Jewish settlements. Against what appeared to be overwhelming odds, the Jewish forces not only held their own, but extended Israel's borders as well. The UN organised a truce which ran from 11 June to 18 July. More than half of the million Arabs living in Palestine had fled from their homes to surrounding Arab states. The new extended Israel was thus 25 per cent larger than envisaged in the UN partition plan of 1947.

Britain's withdrawal from India and Palestine led to a sizeable reduction in her military commitments and defence expenditure, and released much-needed capital for her domestic welfare programme. However, Britain still had many heavy commitments abroad. In 1949 she helped to create NATO (p.345), and maintained an army of occupation in West Germany. In 1948 she engaged in a war in Malaya against Chinese communists.

In 1951 the government of Iran took over the Anglo-Iranian Oil Company and expelled British personnel. Attlee's government was faced with a dilemma: war or acceptance. Lacking the resources for 'gunboat diplomacy', Britain withdrew from Iran.

When the Tories took office in 1951, the process of withdrawal from overseas commitment was well under way; and during the thirteen years of Tory rule, the greater part of the British empire was dismantled. However, that withdrawal from empire did not take place without friction, and many painful lessons were learned in the process.

In July 1956 President Nasser of Egypt nationalised the Suez Canal. Britain and France had financial interests in the canal (p.91) and it was also the route by which tankers brought the oil of the Middle East to Britain. The Tory prime minister, Sir Anthony Eden, remembered what he regarded as Labour's capitulation to Iran in 1951 and was determined not to repeat the mistake. Furthermore, he saw Nasser in much the same light as he had seen Hitler, and was against any form of appeasement. Eden had not fully accepted that the days of British imperialism were drawing to a close and he believed instinctively that the traditional method of solving colonial problems — the use of force — would still work.

After three months of secret dealing, Britain, France and Israel devised a plan. On 29 October Israel invaded the Sinai peninsula and war commenced with Egypt. Britain and France immediately sent in troops to 'restore order' and 'protect the canal'. On 30 October the British and French issued a joint ultimatum to the Egyptians and Israelis to cease fire and withdraw their forces to a line sixteen kilometres from the canal, which would then be temporarily occupied by an Anglo-French force as a means of protecting the canal. The Israelis (as had been previously arranged) accepted the ultimatum, but the Egyptians ignored it. The following morning British bombers began attacking Egyptian air bases.

World reaction was swift and clear. The United States expressed hostility and the Soviet Union adopted a belligerent stance. In Britain everyone took sides. Two junior government ministers resigned, and the Labour opposition tabled a motion of censure in the House of Commons. Protest meetings were held and many called for Eden's resignation. Others supported the attack on Egypt and the popular press were enthusiastic. But Britain's isolation in the world was sharply brought home at the UN where, in an emergency session in early November, a vote calling for an immediate ceasefire was carried by sixty-four votes to five.

The pound sterling dropped on the international market and Washington refused a loan to help Britain over the crisis. On 5 November the government was told by the chancellor of the exchequer, Harold Macmillan, that continuation of the operation would mean that the pound would have to be devalued. That same evening, the Soviet premier, Nikolai Bulganin, even threatened a rocket attack on London and Paris. It was now obvious that the government was isolated on every front and on 6 November the operation was ended. The Suez Crisis had passed, but the failure was total.

(i) The endeavour cost Britain £250 million. British assets in Egypt were confiscated and some 13,000 British subjects were expelled.
(ii) Each side in the debate in Britain was humiliated. Those who opposed the government's action were humiliated that Britain had launched a war of aggressive imperialism in the guise of

British soldiers and Egyptians in the rubble of Port Said in the Suez zone, November 1956.

'peacekeeper'. Those who supported the government felt humiliated that it had been bungled and had ended in military failure.

(iii) The crisis had a severe effect on Eden's health and he resigned in January 1957. His place was taken by Harold Macmillan, who had the task of restoring party and national morale after the Suez debacle (p.368).

(iv) The crisis was an aberration in the tend of foreign policy since 1945. It was an attempted reversal of the withdrawal from imperial power status; and in its failure it marked the end of the 'gunboat diplomacy' that so often had been successful in the past. The lesson which Labour had known instinctively since 1945 had now been learned by a Tory government.

(v) The Suez crisis had an ironic twist. It soon became apparent that the importance of the canal had become almost obsolete. With the development of large supertankers, it soon became more profitable to ship oil around Africa because they were now too large to go through the Suez Canal.

One lesson Macmillan took from Suez was that Britain must be in a position to act independently of the United States. This idea found expression in the need for Britain to have an independent nuclear capability. Since the Soviet Union had immense conventional forces both inside the USSR and in eastern Europe, and because Britain could not hope to match these, the only answer was the development of a nuclear deterrent independent of America. This, it was argued, would also confer great power status on Britain and give her a respected voice at the conference table.

A costly independent atomic research programme had led to the development of the atomic bomb in 1952, and by 1958 Britain had developed a hydrogen bomb. But military research was advancing, and the superpowers had now developed ballistic missiles armed with nuclear warheads. In contrast, British nuclear capacity, dependent on a bomber force for its delivery, seemed antiquated. Accordingly, in 1957 Macmillan decided that Britain should have her own independent Blue Streak missile capability.

In 1960 the government was obliged to abandon Blue Streak. It had already cost £100 million and its maintenance was proving to be an intolerable burden on the economy. The government decided that it would be better to buy the American Sykbolt missiles instead. But two years later, the Americans abandoned Skybolt because they had now developed Polaris missiles that could be launched from a submarine.

In an effort to maintain some form of British nuclear independence, Macmillan decided to buy Polaris missiles, but Britain would provide her own warheads and submarines. Macmillan argued that Britain had an independent nuclear capability; she had her own warheads and submarines, and could, if she wished, make missiles also, but it was cheaper to buy from the United States.

One important result of this was de Gaulle's attitude. When Macmillan applied for British entry to the Common Market, the French president applied the veto on the grounds that the British were too closely tied to America and would not be good Europeans (p.364). In 1950 Sir Stafford Cripps had declared that Britain's participation in a European federation was not compatible with her Commonwealth ties, her relationship with America and her status as a world power. By 1962 the Commonwealth did not look as important, her relationship with the USA was not very special, and her world power status had greatly diminished with the withdrawal from empire. Now Britain's belated attempt to joint the Common Market (p.363) was rejected by a European Community prospering without her.

By the late 1950s even the African colonies wanted freedom and independence. The Gold Coast had already acquired statehood as Ghana in 1957. Then in February 1960 Macmillan visited South Africa, where he made his famous speech about the 'wind of change' blowing throughout the length of Africa. He fully realised that the tide of history was flowing strongly against empire and the best strategy was for Britain to channel it into a Commonwealth relationship. In rapid succession British colonies in Africa gained independence as Commonwealth members: Nigeria in 1960, Tanganyika and Sierra Leone in 1961, Uganda in 1962, Kenya and Zanzibar in 1963, Nyasaland (Malawi) and Northern Rhodesia (Zambia) in 1964, and Gambia in 1965 (map p.355).

One of the methods by which the Tory government tried to deal with the problem of decolonisation was to create federations in order to maximise economic advantages for the emerging states. Federations were created in South Arabia, Malaysia and the Caribbean, but local nationalism and tribalism, compounded by suspicions and jealousies, made them largely unworkable.

In Africa Britain created two federations which were especially disastrous. On 1 October 1960 Britain granted independence to the Nigerian Federation. It was the largest state in Africa, with a population of over fifty million, made up of some 150 tribes. But three tribes were particularly powerful: the Hausa in the north, the Yoruba in the south-west, and the Ibo in the south-east. The first government was a coalition of Hausa and Ibo. Then early in 1966 a group of Ibo army officers killed the federal prime minister, Sir

Abubakar Tafawa Balewa, and took control. But they in turn were overthrown by the commander in chief of the federal army, General Ironsi, who restored order and abolished the federal government. Ironsi himself was an Ibo and some months later he was killed, and General Gowon took over, restored the federal government and appointed military governors for each region.

Meanwhile, many Ibos living in the north were being massacred and some two million fled from the north to their stronghold in the east. The Ibos formed about two-thirds of the population of the eastern region, which was also the rich oil-producing area with an annual revenue of about £24 million. But a dispute over oil revenues led General Gowon to alter the constitution, divide the eastern region into three and take control of the oil-producing areas away from the Ibos. Then in May 1967 the Ibo leader, Colonel Ojukwu, reacted by declaring the eastern region the independent state of Biafra. Civil war followed. Britain and the Soviet Union sent military equipment to the federal government, and after a year's fighting the Ibos were surrounded and were in danger of being starved into submission. At this point a number of countries began flying in arms to Biafra and various humanitarian organisations airlifted food to the starving Ibos. However, the federal army continued to tighten their control, and in January 1970 Ojukwu fled and Biafra collapsed.

In 1953 Britain had established a Central African Federation in an effort to create a multiracial society and an economic union of Rhodesia and Nyasaland. While the economic advantage of the federation was obvious, the concept of a multiracial society was doomed as long as political power remained in the hands of a white minority, who numbered about five per cent of the population of Southern Rhodesia and about two per cent of Northern Rhodesia and Nyasaland. Black African leaders were extremely suspicious of the federal idea; and when, in 1962, the extreme white racist party, the Rhodesian Front, won the election it spelled the end of the federation.

In 1963 the federation was dissolved. In 1964 Northern Rhodesia became the black independent state of Zambia and Nyasaland became the black independent state of Malawi. The same year Ian Smith became leader of the Rhodesian Front and prime minister of Southern Rhodesia (now known as Zimbabwe) while in Britain, Harold Wilson became prime minister of a new Labour government (p.370). The stage was set for a trial of strength between the advocate of white supremacy and the advocate of majority rule. Negotiations between the two soon broke down. Wilson wanted a speeding up of the process towards black majority rule, while Smith was obviously playing for time and had little intention of surrendering white supremacy. Historians have argued that the turning point came when Wilson injudiciously assured Smith that the British government would never use force to assert its authority in Rhodesia. Encouraged by this assurance, Smith, on 11 November 1965, issued a unilateral declaration of independence (UDI) which placed her, legally at any rate, in rebellion against Britain.

Wilson's government did nothing, except indicate its disapproval and impose economic sanctions, which were also taken up by the UN. However, with the help of white South Africa, Smith's government carried on unperturbed. Then in 1969 the white minority of 220,000 people voted in a referendum to leave the Commonwealth and establish a republic.

The UDI issue was a serious blow to the stability of the Commonwealth, though it continued to survive. Perhaps its very looseness saved it from collapse. It had no political unity and was essentially a multiracial collection of states of various constitutional arrangements, from military dictatorships to parliamentary democracies. As a system of defence, the old empire had now given way to American-dominated alliances, while many Commonwealth states preferred to remain non-aligned. Even the economic ties tended to loosen; many Commonwealth countries began finding their own regional markets while an increasing percentage of Britain's trade was with Europe.

Study Assignments and Essays

1. *Why did Labour secure a landslide victory in the British general election of 1945?*
2. *Analyse the main features of Britain's welfare state.*
3. *Treat of the main features of the British economy under Tory governments from 1951 to 1964.*
4. *What were the main features of British foreign policy under Labour governments from 1945 to 1951 and from 1964 to 1966?*
5. *What were the main features of British foreign policy under Conservative governments from 1951 to 1964?*
6. *Write an essay on two of the following:*
(i) Nationalisation in post-war Britain; (ii) Ernest Bevin; (iii) Harold Macmillan; (iv) Labour in opposition 1951–64; (v) The premiership of Harold Wilson.

The European Democracies 1945–66

30

It is not a question of conservatism or socialism being ascendant. It is that people have voted for change.

Ralf Dahrendorf.

FRANCE 1945–68

IN JUNE 1944 the Free French troops took part in the invasion of Normandy, and on 25 August Charles de Gaulle entered Paris in triumph. He claimed to be president of a republic that Vichy France had not destroyed, but because the communists had played such a major role in resisting Hitler, de Gaulle was obliged to include a few communist leaders in his provisional government.

The first task was to purge all those who had collaborated with fascism. Pétain, as former head of the Vichy government (p.303), was sentenced to death, but because of his age, and record during World War I, the sentence was commuted to life imprisonment in exile. Two thousand collaborators were executed and another five thousand were killed by Frenchmen carrying out personal vendettas.

In October 1945 elections were held for a new constituent assembly. With the pre-war leaders completely discredited, three parties dominated the elections and won 75 per cent of the votes: the communists, the socialists and the MRP *(Mouvement Républicain Populaire* — People's Republican Movement). Yet, the fact that over nine million French citizens failed to vote showed the general political apathy that prevailed in post-war France.

At this juncture two factors saved France from slipping into anarchy. The communists, who had gained immensely because of their war-time resistance and the general reaction against fascism, co-operated with de Gaulle. In one sense, co-operation was an extension of the war-time co-operation and of the military efforts shared by the Soviet Union and the western allies. The communist leaders, Maurice Thorez and Jacques Duclos, were pro-Moscow, but they believed that they could come to power in a left-wing coalition.

Equally important in establishing a degree of national consensus was the existence of a 'Resistance Charter' accepted by the resistance leaders in March 1944. This Charter agreed that major social and economic changes should be undertaken after the war to rid the country of 'economic and financial feudalism'. It also called for the nationalisation of key industries and services, for economic planning, and for the establishment of social and economic democracy.

Constitution-making

The communists and the socialists wanted a constitution that would allow for a strong National Assembly with power to choose and reject the premier. De Gaulle wanted a constitution that would give strong powers to the premier, believing that a strong assembly would be a return to the weak form of government that had bedevilled France under the Third Republic. Since the socialists and communists dominated the Christian democratic MRP, they were able to have their wishes implemented. Accordingly, a constitution giving strong powers to the National Assembly and reducing de Gaulle's power was inevitable. Then on 20 January 1946 de Gaulle, realising that his position would be eroded, suddenly resigned from political life.

The search for a new premier revealed growing divisions. The communists wanted a left-wing coalition of themselves and the socialists with the communist leader, Maurice Thorez, as premier. But the socialists, knowing that the communists would dominate them, wanted a premier who would also be acceptable to the MRP. To break the deadlock, an ineffective leader, Félix Gauin, was appointed. In May 1946 the constitution was put to a national referendum for approval. Largely on account of MRP opposition, it was rejected by the people. As a result of constitutional defeat, an election was called for June. This time the MRP became the largest party in the coalition and its leader, Georges Bidault, was elected premier.

A new constitution was now written, which gave stronger powers to the executive. In November it was put to a referendum, and having been endorsed by the people, the Fourth Republic came into existence.

The Fourth Republic

Coinciding with the national referendum on the constitution, a general election made the communists the largest party once again. Thorez now hoped to be made premier, but by this time not only the MRP but the socialists had come to distrust the communists' intentions. The pre-war socialist leader, Léon Blum, returned from Moscow and made it clear that any communist-dominated coalition would end in dictatorship. Without socialist support, the communists had no hope of obtaining the premiership and were thus obliged in January 1947 to accept the socialist, Paul Ramadier, as premier. The communist strategy now was to keep the tripartite coalition alive, but their attempts to do so were thwarted by three major crises of the Ramadier government: the war in Indo-China, the Cold War, and a labour dispute at home.

1. In 1946 the communist leader, Ho Chi Minh, and his military commander, Vo Nguyen Giap, started a campaign for Vietnamese independence, using the communist guerrilla organisation, the Vietminh.

Until 1947 the French communists supported the government's attempt to reimpose control over Indo-China. But with the advent of Cold War in Europe, they changed their policy. Six days after the enunciation of the Truman Doctrine in March 1947 (p.343), the communists withdrew their support for French control of Indo-China.

The war in fact continued until 1954 when the French army suffered a humiliating defeat at Dien Bien Phu. Following talks in Geneva, the French agreed to leave Indo-China and set up independent states in Vietnam, Laos and Cambodia. Vietnam itself was divided into a communist north and a non-communist south, thereby sowing the seeds of future conflict (map, p.314).

2. At the centre of the conflict among the coalition parties was the question of the Cold War. Before 1947, the coalition tried to adopt a neutral stance between Moscow and Washington, but the deterioration in relations following the Truman Doctrine, and France's need of Marshall Aid, made the continuation of this policy impossible.

Many French politicians recognised the advantage of Marshall Aid and also knew that it emanated from the American fear of communist expansion. Voicing the attitude of many French politicians, Pierre Mendès-France, later to become premier, said: 'We must keep up this indispensable communist scare.'

3. Ramadier's policy of low wages and high prices to promote economic recovery sparked off a massive strike at the nationalised Renault automobile factory in April 1947. Before this, the communists had denounced strikes as anarchist, but now they supported the striking workers. Ramadier put the issue to the national assembly and won a vote of confidence. He then demanded that communist deputies resign, and tripartism came to an end.

Meanwhile the tripartite coalition had made considerable economic changes. A widespread programme of nationalisation included gas, coal, electricity, major banks and insurance companies, the aircraft and petroleum industries. The Renault automobile company was also nationalised, but this was mainly prompted by the fact that it had collaborated with the German occupation.

While Ramadier was receiving American support in his struggle with the communists, de Gaulle made a bid for power. He declared that parliament no longer represented the people and demanded a change in the constitution. In April 1947 he announced the formation of the RPF (*Rassemblement du Peuple Français* — Rally of the French People), which he hoped would be a national movement above the party system. De Gaulle concentrated on attacking communism, holding mass rallies and making grandiose speeches. He posed as the man of destiny who would rescue France from the troubles of the Fourth Republic. However, his call for a referendum was resisted and, for the second time, he resigned from political life. This time, however, he declared that he would only return to politics in the event of a national crisis.

Meanwhile the Fourth Republic continued, and despite political instability, the government of Robert Schuman, the leader of the MRP, had stabilised the situation by 1948. Marshall Aid was used by his colleague Jean Monnet to modernise and re-equip industry, and economic recovery got under way.

The Algerian Crisis

In 1954 a revolt broke out in Algeria. It was led by the 150,000-strong Algerian liberation movement, known as the *Front de la Libération Nationale* (FLN). French society was deeply divided on the issue of Algerian independence. Algeria was part of metropolitan France and was allowed 30 deputies in the French assembly. But more important, some one million of Algeria's population (10 per cent) were French settlers, known as the *colons*. The leaders of the French army in Algeria, Generals Salan and Massu, were determined to win at any cost. After the military disaster at Dien Bien Phu (p.380) in 1954 and the Suez fiasco (p.374) two years later, this was one war they were determined not to lose. They used torture on a large scale against FLN activists, bombed a Tunisian village suspected of being an FLN base, and frequently ignored orders from Paris. Yet though the French were strong enough not to be defeated, they were not sufficiently powerful to win the war. By 1958 some 500,000 French troops were tied up in Algeria, and it was becoming clear that a negotiated settlement would have to be made. But the French right wing and the *colons* were determined to resist this, and set up the *Organisation de l'Armée Secrète* (Secret Army Organisation). The OAS indulged in acts of terrorism against the Algerian people, and the FLN responded in kind.

The French government realised the importance of Algeria after the discovery of oil and natural gas in the Sahara; but despite this, the government came to the conclusion in May 1958 that a settlement should be reached with the Algerian resistance. When this became known to the right-wing elements in the army, they openly revolted, seized power in Algeria and called for the return of de Gaulle to head a new government in France.

De Gaulle, who had almost given up hope of returning to power, now became the focus of attention. As the Algerian situation worsened, it was feared that the French generals in Algeria might also seize power in France. It seemed to many that only de Gaulle could save France from civil war. But de Gaulle was too shrewd to take power immediately: instead he waited for power to be bestowed upon him. On 28 May President Coty called on de Gaulle to save France from civil war, and de Gaulle accepted on condition that he be given complete freedom to draw up a new constitution for approval by a referendum.

On 1 June the National Assembly approved

Charles de Gaulle, president of France, 1958–69.

de Gaulle as premier of France and voted him full powers for six months.

The Fifth Republic

The crisis gave de Gaulle the opportunity to create his preferred constitution. The president was invested with far-reaching powers: he had the right to appoint the premier, dissolve the National Assembly, and had control over defence and foreign policy. He was to be elected by the people for a seven-year term, and could stand again for a second term of office. But the most significant aspect of his powers lay in the fact that the president could consult the people directly by referendum, thus further reducing the importance of parliament.

On 28 September 1958, after de Gaulle had made effective use of television, some 80 per cent of the people approved of the new constitution. The Fifth Republic was born.

In November, elections were held for a reorganised two-house parliament (National Assembly and Senate). The Gaullists formed a new party, the Union for the New Republic (*Union pour la Nouvelle République* — UNR), which became the ruling party. This was made possible by the new, complicated system of voting. France was divided into 465 constituencies. Each party could nominate a single candidate for each constituency, who could be elected on the first ballot only if winning half the votes cast. If he or she failed to do so, a second ballot would have to be taken. This, the Gaullists correctly envisaged, would encourage non-Gaullist candidates, especially communists, to drop out after the first ballot.

In the second ballot, voters who had originally voted for communist candidates now gave their votes to the remaining non-communist candidates, thereby reducing communist representation from 150 deputies to ten. De Gaulle himself was elected president by an overwhelming 78.5 per cent of the vote.

De Gaulle's Solution in Algeria

The overriding initial task was to find a solution to the Algerian war and to bring the army under control. The French people were tired of years of futile colonial wars and alarmed at the cost in lives and resources.

The Algerian question was the supreme test of de Gaulle as a politician, leader and statesman. The army and the *colons* had supported his return to power in the belief he would keep Algeria French. De Gaulle, who had not specifically committed himself, would have liked a victory for the French army, but was realistic enough to accept that this was impossible. His goal was to restore French greatness and dilute American leadership in western European affairs. Therefore, the Algerian question would have to be solved quickly because it was a tiresome distraction from his primary objective.

In September 1959 de Gaulle courageously tackled the problem by offering Algeria self-determination within four years, provided there was a ceasefire. But the offer was refused by an increasingly confident FLN and violently rejected by the French army leaders in Algeria, who now felt betrayed by de Gaulle. General Massu declared that the French army would never leave Algeria, but de Gaulle promptly ordered him home. This led, in January 1960, to an attempted revolt against de Gaulle's policies, but it fizzled out as metropolitan France stood by the president. However, in April 1961, a more serious threat occurred when the OAS, led by two generals, Salan and Jouhand, seized power in Algeria and threatened military action against metropolitan France.

De Gaulle immediately went on television in his general's uniform and appealed directly to military units not to support the generals. The navy and air force and the French public were overwhelmingly on the side of de Gaulle. The rebellion lost support and within a few weeks most of its leaders had been arrested.

The OAS now went underground and made its main objective the assassination of the president. In their view it was the only way of keeping Algeria French. Four major attempts were made on de Gaulle's life, but all were unsuccessful. Meanwhile, the OAS inaugurated a bloody campaign of urban terrorism, but de Gaulle was determined to be rid of the Algerian problem and to bring the army home.

In March 1962 representatives of the FLN and the French government met at Évian-les-Bains to hammer out a solution. It was agreed that Algeria would become a fully independent state on 3 July 1962. The *colons* who wished to remain in Algeria were to be accorded equal rights with Algerians, while those wishing to leave were to be compensated for any loss of property.

The Algerian question was solved, but at a terrible cost in human lives. The FLN leader, Ben Bella, was released from prison and became head of the new Republic of Algeria. Some 10,000 Algerians who had served in the French army were massacred by the new Algerian government. Almost a quarter of a million lives — Algerian, French, soldiers, civilians — had been lost during the eight years of fighting. The OAS continued their terrorist tactics, but within a year, almost 900,000 *colons* had left Algeria. They came mainly to the south of France, where their influx created huge social and economic problems.

De Gaulle had solved the Algerian problem without provoking civil war in France. It was a great achievement, which possibly would have eluded any other French leader. His immense stature and effective leadership had made it possible, though his critics claim that because of his haste to be rid of Algeria, he must share some of the blame for the excesses of both sides.

Foreign Policy

With the Algerian problem solved, de Gaulle could now turn to his goal of making France the leader of Europe. In one sense he believed that as president he personified France (p. 364). Therefore, to increase French prestige and strength, the authority of the president under the constitution would have to be increased further and the power of political parties reduced. He viewed political parties as divisive forces and therefore tried to circumvent them by appealing to the people through national referenda. In 1962 he held a referendum on the question of the direct election of the president and won the support of 67.7 per cent of the voters. De Gaulle now no longer had to please the political parties in the National Assembly in order to stay in power.

De Gaulle nursed a certain resentment against Britain and the United States because of their treatment of him as leader of the Free French during the war. He had been kept out of their deliberations, and had not been recognised as the legal head of the French government in exile; above all, he resented having been left out of the Yalta and Potsdam conferences, which shaped the post-war world.

De Gaulle stood uncompromisingly for French greatness and believed that France had little in common with Britain and the United States. He dismissed as imaginary the American fear of the Soviet threat to western Europe.

Under the Fourth Republic, Robert Schuman and Jean Monnet had done herculean work in integrating western Europe (p.359) France had taken a leading part in creating NATO, the Council of Europe, ECSC and the EEC (p.356). Now, under the Fifth Republic, de Gaulle did not favour closer integration, but preferred a loose association of states in which France would be the dominant member.

In March 1959 de Gaulle began to withdraw French naval units from the NATO Mediterranean command. Then the American 'victory' in the Cuban crisis of 1962 (p.406) and subsequent moves towards *détente* convinced de Gaulle that he had been correct in believing that the Soviet Union did not pose a threat to western Europe.

In order to build up France as an independent 'third force' between the two superpowers, de Gaulle began to develop an independent French nuclear force. In 1960 France exploded her first atomic bomb and in 1968 a hydrogen bomb.

In 1964 de Gaulle refused to sign the nuclear test ban treaty, because it would prevent France from developing an independent nuclear capability; he was not prepared to entrust the security of France to a foreign power. 'We are worthy of better than this,' he declared. In 1965 France left SEATO (p.403), the south-east Asian equivalent of NATO, and ceased to participate in NATO exercises. Then in 1966, France withdrew completely from NATO. Meanwhile, she had built up a *force de frappe* (striking force) of supersonic bombers armed with nuclear bombs, missile-carrying submarines and land-based missiles.

Despite such ostentatious acts of independence, de Gaulle failed to resolve Soviet-west European problems. In 1964 he visited Moscow, and Alexei Kosygin, the Soviet premier, returned the visit. But the Soviets failed to regard France as a superpower and preferred to deal directly with Washington on matters of European and world politics. Nevertheless, de Gaulle did begin the loosening of American-western European ties, and other countries followed suit in the late 1960s and early 1970s.

The Fall of De Gaulle

By the end of 1966, de Gaulle's prestige in France was quite high. He had solved the Algerian problem and had given independence to most French colonies. He had established close relations with West Germany, and was on friendly terms with the Soviet Union. He had asserted France's independence from America and had built an independent nuclear force. Above all, in the Fifth Republic, he had given France a new stable system of government and had exalted her prestige in the world. In 1965 the French people had re-elected de Gaulle for another seven-year term as president.

Yet the end, when it did come, came quickly. By 1968 a new post-war generation had grown up discontented with the spiritual sterility of the consumer society. The student population, which had risen in France to 643,000, was critical of student accommodation, in Paris especially, and of the relevance of academic courses. Unlike their parents, the students regarded de Gaulle as little more than an anachronism. In November 1967 students and teachers staged a sit-in strike at Nanterre, a suburb of Paris. In February 1968 students in Paris went on strike, and under the leadership of Daniel Cohn-Bendit started using 'Molotov cocktails' on the streets. In May huge demonstrations and attempts to take over university buildings led to serious clashes with the police. Charges of police brutality swung public opinion behind the students. At this juncture the workers joined in and led demonstrations against the Gaullist regime. On 17 May ten million workers went on a national strike. De Gaulle, who was on a state visit to Romania, returned swiftly to France.

By now it was obvious that communist militants were directing events, and while many disliked de Gaulle's authoritarian rule, there was a marked lack of rational discussion on what should take its place.

An opportunity therefore existed for de Gaulle to reassert his authority. Having assured himself of the loyalty of the army, he announced on 30 May that he would not resign, and called for the defence of the republic against militant communism. De Gaulle's firm action had the desired effect and soon order was restored.

Although he survived the crisis of May 1968, de Gaulle's prestige was destroyed. The crisis had revealed how far his paternalism and authoritarian rule were removed from the social and economic problems facing the French people. He now tried to recover lost ground by implementing changes in the Senate and by creating regional councils. However, by deciding to put the reforms to the test of referendum, and by declaring that he would regard the outcome as a vote of confidence, he took a decisive risk. In April 1969, while nearly eleven million of the electorate supported the reforms, over twelve million voted against them. De Gaulle, now aged 78, retired to write his memoirs, and in November 1970 he died and was buried at Colombey-les-Deux-Églises.

WEST GERMANY 1948–70

In May 1945 Germany lay in ruins. She was divided into four zones of occupation and had little immediate prospect of helping herself. To add further to her problems, the Soviet Union began stripping her eastern zone of its industrial equipment and demanded reparations from the western zones as well. In addition, some ten million German refugees from German territory lost to Czechoslovakia and Poland streamed into the western zones, making the process of integrating them an urgent necessity.

In this grim situation, the first task of the Allied powers was to provide the basic necessities of life, which was further compounded by the shortage of Germans who were capable of hard work. Three million had been killed, two million were disabled, and several more millions were hospitalised or in prisoner-of-war camps. Output was low, food was scarce, fuel shortages caused hardship, and the many homeless, exacerbated by the influx of refugees from the east, created tremendous accommodation problems. Everything was in short supply and the black market flourished. Since paper currency was not valued, cigarettes became the medium of exchange.

One of the most important and delicate tasks of the military government was the eradication of Nazism. Since more than eight million Germans had been involved in varying degrees in the Nazi Party, it was often not possible to ascertain the degree of involvement of any one individual. In the American zone some 800,000 people were convicted; in the British zone 156,000 were removed from office; and in the Soviet zone (according to official reports) some 500,000 people were dismissed.

Twenty-four top Nazis were returned to a special international court which sat at Nuremberg from November 1945 to August 1946. Twelve Nazis received the death sentence, though two of them (Robert Ley and Göring) committed suicide before the sentence could be carried out. In all, denazification resulted in 600 executions and 4,000 imprisonments, but with the onset of the Cold War, less emphasis came to be placed on punishment. In 1950, 60 per cent of judges and 90 per cent of staff in the foreign office in West Germany had held office during Hitler's rule.

In the western zones, new democratic parties were allowed to come into existence. (1) The Christian Democratic Party (CDU) was a conservative party led by the ex-mayor of Cologne, Konrad Adenauer. The party was somewhat more interdenominational than the old Centre Party (p.25) and stood for general Christian principles. (2) The Social Democratic Party (SPD) was a revival of the party that had played such a prominent role in the Weimar republic (p.192). It was led by Kurt Schumacher and, like all socialist parties, had its Marxist and gradualist wings. (3) The liberal Free Democratic Party (FDP) was an alliance of business and intelligentsia and had much less support than the CDU and SPD. (4) The Communist Party (KPD) was a fringe party and made little progress because it was viewed as a tool of Moscow.

By 1947 the reality of Sovietisation in eastern Europe (p.335) was forcing the western powers to change their policies on Germany. It came to be seen that Germany must be helped to reconstruct herself so that she could act as a bulwark against the spread of communism. In September 1946 the Americans and British announced that they would merge their zones (Bizonia) in an effort to help Germany's recovery. The Soviets and the French were also invited to join the scheme but they refused, each for different reasons: the Soviets because they did not want a united non-communist Germany; and the French because they wanted to keep Germany occupied, weak and divided.

Gradually the West German economy improved; and with Marshall Aid in June, badly needed capital was used for industrial development. A new bank, later to become the Deutsche Bundesbank, was also created.

But the decisive events leading to the creation of a West German state were prompted by the Cold War. The coup in Czechoslovakia in February 1948 led the western powers to agree on establishing a federal state of Bizonia and the French zone (p.346). Then on 20 June they introduced a new *Deutschmark* to reform the currency and help economic recovery. This alarmed Stalin, who knew that the weak German currency in his zone would now be destroyed. His immediate reaction was to close off all links between Berlin and the West, thereby provoking the Berlin Crisis (p.345). But it was this very crisis that accelerated the formation of West Germany.

In June the Allied powers called upon the

German leaders in each state to convene a constituent assembly, and in September they drew up the Basic Law (constitution). Parliament was to consist of two houses. The lower house, the Bundestag, with 500 members, was to be elected by universal suffrage for four years. The upper house, the Bundesrat, with 45 members, was to have representatives from the ten *länder* (states). Unlike the Weimar constitution (p.192), the president was not to be commander in chief of the armed forces, nor was he to have any emergency powers. He was to be elected for five years by the two houses, and one of his chief functions was to appoint the chancellor, who must hold majority backing in the Bundestag.

Important powers were given to a Federal Constitutional Court, which could decide upon the legality of political parties and on breaches of the rule of law. (In 1956 the Court declared the Communist Party illegal.)

In August 1949 the first general election was held since 1933. The Christian Democrats gained 139 seats; the Social Democrats 131, the Free Democrats 52, while the Communists gained only a few. Since no party had an overall majority, the Christian Democrats and the Free Democrats formed a coalition government, with the Christian Democrat leader, Konrad Adenauer, as chancellor.

Born in 1876, the new chancellor was a staunch catholic; he had been dismissed as mayor of Cologne by the Nazis in 1933. During the war years Adenauer was for a time in a concentration camp and was lucky not to have been killed during the American advance across the Rhine in 1945. Since the French occupation of the Ruhr in 1923 (p.243), he had become convinced of the need for an economic alliance between France and Germany, which could be extended later to other states as well. His general policy was liberal economics, after years of state inteference; Christian standards, after years of Nazi terror; international co-operation, after years of national hostility; and, especially, reconciliation with France, after centuries of conflict.

Konrad Adenauer, West German chancellor, 1949–63.

Foreign Affairs

Adenauer's stable government, and his genuine attempt to steer West Germany along a line of democracy, peace and co-operation, led to a quick improvement in his country's international status.

In 1950, at the time of the Korean war, the western powers guaranteed the Federal Republic against attack and increased their forces there. They also relaxed their previous controls on economic development, including limitations of steel output and ship-building.

West Germany under Adenauer was also allowed to join the Council of Europe (p.358) and the OEEC (p.356) and to establish diplomatic relations with other countries.

In 1951 West Germany signed the Treaty of Paris, setting up the ECSC (p.359), and Adenauer's dream of economic unity with France began to take shape. In 1952 the Soviet Union proposed 'a united democratic Germany' which would remain 'neutral and unarmed', but Adenauer refused to negotiate; he preferred to keep close relations with the United States. Both countries despised communism, and the Federal Republic refused to recognise Polish encroachment on East German lands (p.333), or the legality of the East German government on the grounds that it had been imposed on the people by the Soviet Union.

When the idea of a European army (EDC) to defend western Europe was rejected by the French (p.361), West Germany was allowed to contribute troops to NATO. Although she was now allowed to rearm, her forces were placed under the control of the NATO command while other NATO forces continued to be stationed in West Germany (p.362). But the crowning achievement of Adenauer's foreign policy came on 5 May 1955 when the Federal Republic of Germany was recognised by the western powers as a sovereign independent state. Then in September, when Adenauer visited Moscow, the Russians also agreed to recognise the Federal Republic. While in Moscow the chancellor also succeeded in obtaining the release of 10,000 German prisoners-of-war from Soviet camps. Over one million Germans had been deported by the Soviets, and Adenauer claimed that 130,000 were still alive.

In 1956, following a referendum, it was agreed that the Saar should be returned to West Germany. The next year West Germany signed the Treaty of Rome and became a founder member of the Common Market (p.362). In January 1963 she signed a treaty of friendship and collaboration in military, economic, political and cultural matters with France. It was a historic occasion as the age-old animosities between two equally great European nations were buried forever. The signing of the treaty was marked in France by a solemn *Te Deum* in the gothic cathedral of Rheims. Later that year, the 87-year-old Adenauer resigned (p.390).

Economic Development

West Germany's recovery from the ruins of war was an 'economic miracle'. Her minister of economic affairs from 1949 to 1963, Dr Ludwig Erhard (known as 'the wizard'), was the guiding light behind this great achievement. It was based essentially on a unique display of enterprise, good organisation and hard work, in conjunction with Marshall Aid. Erhard's policy was to allow free enterprise its full scope, and Germans responded with enthusiasm. While other western states were nationalising industries, West Germany was handing back state control of industry to private enterprise, and making provision for worker participation in management. A typical example of this was the denationalising of the Volkswagen company, which went on to become the symbol of West German recovery; by 1961 it had exported over one million cars.

Economic development was achieved by holding down domestic consumption in the early years in order to invest resources in capital formation and to concentrate on exports. The government placed increased industrial production over social equalisation in its system of priorities. But because of the booming economy, industrial workers had higher wages and salaries than in any other European country. As a result, harmonious labour relations contributed to further economic growth. Remembering the hyper-inflation of 1923 (p.197) trade unions and workers agreed to observe wage restraints. Worker participation in industry gave employees a considerable say about working conditions which greatly increased morale.

The stream of farm labourers into industry and the huge influx of refugees was another factor in keeping down inflation. Between

1949 and 1962 over three million people entered West Germany from eastern Europe, while a further two million migrant workers from Yugoslavia and Turkey prevented an acute labour shortage.

Between 1950 and 1963 West German exports rose from 8.4 billion marks to 52.3 billion marks, comprising 11 per cent of world exports. During the same period, industrial production rose by 300 per cent. The social services (education, health, housing), paid for out of this wealth, were the best in Europe.

Politics

But the economic prosperity of West Germany also had its political repercussions. The rapid recovery enabled Adenauer to rule in an authoritarian manner. He believed that the failure of the Weimar Republic stemmed from a weak executive and the proliferation of political parties. In effect he believed that the Weimar Republic was 'too democratic' and thus could not function effectively. Adenauer maintained, like de Gaulle, that strong paternalism was the answer, and that a good chancellor should not be impeded by a fractious parliament. His style of leadership came to be known as 'chancellor democracy'. Yet few voices were raised against him as long as economic growth continued and West Germany enjoyed a high status in international affairs.

But the greatest political change brought about by economic prosperity was the attitude of the Social Democratic Party. At first the Social Democrats were led by Kurt Schumacher, who had spent ten years in Nazi concentration camps. Under his leadership, the party favoured German reunification, and opposed close association with the West, the existence of NATO, German rearmament and European unity. In essence, these policies sprang from a Marxist perception of European society; and when they failed to gain any degree of acceptance, younger SPD members began to challenge the party's programme and agitate for a reformist course within a liberal economic state.

During the 1950s the reformist viewpoint came increasingly to the forefront. Then in 1958 Willy Brandt was elected leader of the party. The following year, at the party conference at Bad Godesberg, delegates, by a vote of 324 to 16, dropped all Marxist terminology, rejected nationalisation of industry, approved private property, and accepted NATO and West German rearmament. The dramatic success of the German economy under social capitalism had defeated every argument of Marxism.

The selection of Willy Brandt and the adoption of a reformist programme paid dividends. In the 1961 election the Social Democrats increased their representation in the Bundestag from 169 seats to 190. Adenauer's Christian Democrats fell from 270 seats to 240, but he was still able to form a coalition government with the Free Democrats on condition that he retire before the next election in 1965.

Adenauer was now 85 years old, and many in his own party felt that he had clung on to power for too long and had prevented younger men of talent from coming to the top. But before he retired he became involved in a political crisis that blemished his reputation and his party's as well. In October 1963 the weekly news magazine *Der Spiegel* published an article on the West German army. Adenauer's defence minister, Franz-Josef Strauss, considered that the material was secret military information. He ordered the magazine's office to be searched, and five members of the editorial staff were arrested and charged with treason. When the charges could not be substantiated, the government appeared ridiculous in the eyes of the population. Adenauer refused to accept responsibility for the government's error, but when the Free Democrats in cabinet threatened to resign, he was obliged to dismiss Strauss, and in October 1963, resigned himself.

The *Der Spiegel* incident and Adenauer's retirement from office made the public question the nature of German democracy. It was alleged that Adenauer and, by implication, the Christian Democratic Party, were not fully committed to democracy. Certainly Adenauer had a patrician attitude, and had tried to circumvent the Bundestag as often as possible. He was criticised for paying little attention to education and not moving towards reconciliation with East Germany. However, it may be argued that Adenauer's authoritarian style was exactly what Germany needed in a transitional post-war period. If his government was dull and haughty, it gave Germans security, prosperity and dignity.

Willy Brandt

Adenauer's resignation made the chancellorship of his successor, Ludwig Erhard, much more difficult. Criticism of the Christian Democrats began to grow and it became obvious that many Germans wanted change. Moreover, Erhard was faced with a slowing down in economic growth and his tax increases in the 1966 budget angered the Free Democrats. They withdrew their support and Erhard was obliged to resign in November 1966. The way was now open for the Social Democrats to share power in a coalition with the Christian Democrats. The Christian Democrat Kurt Kiesinger became chancellor and Willy Brandt (mayor of West Berlin since 1957) became foreign minister.

Having adopted the Bad Godesberg programme (p.389), the Social Democrats were now much closer to the Christian Democrats. However, the coalition was an uneasy one because each side saw it as a temporary expedient. In the 1969 election the Social Democrats made a decisive breakthrough and became the largest single party in the Bundestag. They now formed a coalition government with the Free Democrats and Willy Brandt became the fourth federal chancellor.

Unlike Adenauer, Brandt was a firm believer in the need for some form of reconciliation, not only with East Germany but with all communist states in eastern Europe. When he became foreign minister in 1966, he began putting his policy of *Ostpolitik* into operation. The Soviet invasion of Czechoslovakia (p.402) in 1968 was a severe setback to Brandt, but he was not to be deterred. He continued to pursue an *Ostpolitik* and in 1970 signed treaties with the Soviet Union and Poland whereby all sides renounced the use of force, and West Germany accepted the Oder-Neisse line as the *de facto* frontier between Poland and East Germany.

ITALY 1945–66

Before the war had ended the Italians had deposed Mussolini and a new government under Marshal Badoglio took Italy into war on the Allied side.

In June 1944, Badoglio's government was replaced by a coalition cabinet under Ivanoe Bonomi, leader of the Christian Democratic Party. A socialist party emerged with two wings. On one side were those who favoured social democracy, on the other were those who wanted co-operation with the communists. The reaction against fascism had turned the communists into a formidable force with a membership of over two million.

The first problem to be tackled was the future of the monarchy. Its association with fascism had robbed it of much of its prestige and Victor Emmanuel III wisely resigned in favour of his son, Umberto II. However, this was not sufficient to preserve the monarchy. In June 1946 the question was put to national referendum and 54 per cent voted for a republic.

Bonomi's government showed very little will-power. It failed to tackle the problem of economic reconstruction and proved ineffective in rooting out fascist elements in Italian society. Soon a mood of pessimism settled in and the situation seemed ripe for a communist takeover. But the communists, though enjoying immense power and prestige because of their opposition to fascism, failed to move. In any event, a communist bid for power would probably have led to American or British intervention, as the experience in Greece suggests (p.342).

In June 1945 Bonomi's government was replaced by a coalition led by Parri, leader of a party calling itself Radical Action. But his attempts to initiate radical reform lost him the support of the Christian Democrats and his government fell in December 1945.

The Rule of de Gasperi

The next government was a coalition of Christian democrats, socialists and communists, under the premiership of Christian Democrat Alcide de Gasperi. But in 1947 de Gasperi formed a new government from which he excluded the communists. This was made possible by the split in the Socialist Party. The hard-line faction, led by Pietro Nenni, wanted to co-operate with the communists, but the other faction led by Giuseppe Saragat would not accept this. Then in January 1947 Saragat led his wing to form a new party, the Social Democratic Party (PSDI).

In 1948 a constituent assembly drew up a new constitution for the Italian Republic. In the first election under the constitution the Christian Democrats gained an overall majority, winning 305 out of the 574 seats. De Gasperi formed a stable coalition government which lasted for nearly five years. He did not need to form a coalition because he had an overall majority, but he astutely included representatives of the Social Democratic, Liberal and Republican parties, in order to isolate the communists and Nenni's hard-line socialists. He was aided further during the election by an American warning that a socialist-communist element in government would result in no further American aid.

De Gasperi's coalition government had many successes to its credit. He himself was a

Alcide de Gasperi, prime minister of Italy, 1947–53.

firm believer in European unity, and under him Italy became a member of NATO (p.349), the Council of Europe (p.358), and the European Coal and Steel Community (p.360). But despite these external successes, social and economic problems at home tended to erode much of his support. In the 1953 election the Christian Democrats lost 80 seats to two new right-wing parties, the Monarchists and the *Movimento Sociale Italiano* (MSI). De Gasperi could not now form a government and was forced to resign. Thus came to an end a stable period of Italian politics. With meagre resources de Gasperi had reorganised Italian society, preserved democracy, and made Italy a respected member in the family of European nations.

A Decade of Instability

With de Gasperi's departure there followed a long period of instability, as party factions obstructed vital legislation and communist opposition exploited every weakness. In the decade after 1953 Italy had twelve different governments. The Christian Democrats were still the biggest party, but with little more than 40 per cent of the vote they had to rely on other parties to form a coalition.

From 1956 the nature of left-wing opposition began to change. Following Khrushchev's condemnation of Stalin and the Soviet invasion of Hungary (p.399), Italian socialists began to reconsider their attitude. They became increasingly tired of negative opposition and began to moderate their hostility to western parliamentary democracy. In 1962 Nenni's socialists supported the coalition government of Amintore Fanfani, though they did not become part of it. In return for this support, the government promised to nationalise electricity. Another factor in moderating socialism, and increasing its support, was the advent to the papacy of Giovanni Roncalli in 1958. As Pope John XXIII he adopted a conciliatory attitude and many of his pronouncements and encyclicals exemplified a new social awareness in the catholic church.

The Government of Aldo Moro

In the election of 1963 the communists won 166 seats, their highest ever. But despite this, they were confined to opposition. Instead, a coalition of left-wing Christian Democrats was formed under the leadership of Aldo Moro. His government brought back some stability into Italian politics after a decade of instability.

Economic Recovery

Italian economic recovery was retarded by the colossal wartime damage, the return of millions of prisoners-of-war, and inflation. All attempts to reform the currency ended in failure, industry and transport systems often were brought to a standstill, and industrial unrest grew. However, a number of internal and external factors were working in Italy's favour, and she, like West Germany, experienced a minor economic miracle in the 1950s.

(i) Between 1945 and 1950 Italy received $3,500 million in American aid, mainly through the Marshall Plan (p.343). This huge injection of capital enabled Italy to lay the foundations of recovery, and build up export-oriented industries such as car manufacture, office machinery and electrical goods.

(ii) The loss of her colonies saved Italy from the humiliation of defeat suffered by Britain and France (p.374). But more important, it relieved her of the heavy expense involved in futile colonial wars.

(iii) The government policy of state intervention in the economy had beneficial effects on development. In 1947 credit was severely restricted to curb inflation while finance was made readily available to firms with potential for expansion.

(iv) Another important factor was the creation of an efficient energy supply. Italy's fundamental problem, which had hindered economic development since unification in 1870, had been her lack of essential resources, such as coal, gas, oil and iron. But in 1949, oil was discovered in the Po valley, and again in 1953 in Sicily; natural gas was located at Ferrara, near Bologna, and a semi-state body was created to use energy in the national interest.

(v) Cheap labour from rural Italy enabled production costs to be kept relatively low, and Italian exports became more competitive.

(vi) Many Italians sought employment in West Germany and Switzerland and their remittances greatly helped Italian finances. The growth in post-war tourism, especially in the 1950s and 1960s, brought in much-valued foreign currency.

(vii) Italian membership of the EEC (p.362) gave her a wider market for her exports, while the Common Market's regional policy and the European Social Fund helped neglected areas of Italy, especially the south.

These factors, taken together, go a long way to explain Italy's economic recovery. From the 1950s, a surge of industrialisation caused many changes in Italian society. Between 1951 and 1966 the proportion of workers engaged in agriculture fell from 43 per cent to 26 per cent, while those working in industry rose from 31 per cent to 41 per cent. But a more important social change came about through government efforts to bridge the gap between north and south. In 1950 a Southern Development Fund was created by the de Gasperi government to initiate public works in the south. The initiative helped to create employment, but failed to tackle the root cause of southern poverty — lack of industrialisation. In the 1960s, however, the problem was tackled. A large steel works was opened at Taranto in 1965 and an Alfasud car factory was started outside Naples. In addition, the government gave financial incentives to northern Italian firms, such as Pirelli and Fiat, to locate new plants in the south.

Yet despite these efforts, huge social and economic problems remained. The industries that came to the south were essentially capital-intensive, and they failed to create sufficient jobs to alleviate endemic unemployment.

Study Assignments and Essays

1. *What problems faced France's Fourth Republic and how were they dealt with?*
2. *'The Constitution of the Fifth Republic was a realistic response to French problems.' Discuss.*
3. *Trace the establishment of the Federal Republic of Germany between 1945 and 1948.*
4. *Treat of West German economic development in the post-war era.*
5. *Treat of Italian economic development in the post-war era.*
6. *Write an essay on two of the following: (i) The Algerian war; (ii) The foreign policy of Charles de Gaulle; (iii) Konrad Adenauer; (iv) The rule of de Gasperi in Italy, 1948–53; (v) Communist opposition in western democracies.*

The Soviet Bloc After Stalin 1953–66

31

The heart of Lenin's comrade-in-arms and the inspired continuer of Lenin's cause, the wise teacher and leader of the party and the people, has stopped beating.

Pravda 5 March 1953

SOVIET RUSSIA

WHEN STALIN died on 5 March 1953 he left behind a political system by means of which he had operated a thorough and effective dictatorship. In theory, power in the Soviet Union lay with the local soviets, but in practice, it had been concentrated in the hands of a few elite party members led by Stalin. He in turn controlled the party and also the government, which was no more than a civil service carrying out the orders of the party.

Following Stalin's death, his successors were faced with two political problems: (i) should the leader control the party or the party control the leader? and (ii) how far should freedom of speech be allowed to those who disagreed with the government?

On the economic front, Stalin had concentrated on capital (productive) goods, while consumer goods and agricultural development were neglected. His successors were also faced with two economic problems: (i) How far should they develop industry rather than agriculture? and (ii) how far should capital goods, rather than consumer goods, be developed?

In foreign policy Stalin's aim had been to forward the cause of world communism under Soviet direction. His successors were faced with two related problems: (i) How could the advancement of communism be achieved without provoking a nuclear war? and (ii) how could a reduction in hostility towards capitalism be achieved while at the same time maintaining control over communist revolutionary movements throughout the world?

At first the Soviet government was carried on through a five-man collective leadership. Georgi Malenkov became prime minister, Vyacheslav Molotov was in charge of foreign affairs, Nikolai Bulganin took control of the armed forces, Lavrenti Beria was the chief of security and police, and Nikita Khrushchev was appointed secretary of the party.

In practice, however, collective leadership was not working. Beneath the surface a struggle for power was being fought out between those who wished to follow Stalinist lines and those who proposed a new course. In essence, the Stalinists supported the development of heavy industry, rigid social controls, and a continuation of the Cold War. The advocates of the new course stressed the importance of increased production of consumer goods, decentralisation of economic planning, and the achievement of peaceful co-existence with the West.

At first, the collective leadership began to dismantle the system of state terror. Surprisingly, it was Beria who advocated this course, and as a result he gained in popularity. But this relaxation had the effect of letting loose old resentments in East Germany, and workers in East Berlin rose in revolt in June 1953. Immediately unrest spread to other East German towns and the Soviets were obliged to put down the uprisings by military force. The other four now united against Beria whom they regarded as having too much power and new-found popularity. Within a few weeks, Beria disappeared and in December his execution was publicly announced. The reason given in *Pravda* was that Beria had been a capitalist agent.

Malenkov, who was an advocate of the new course in economic affairs, began to allocate more resources to the production of consumer goods. The taking of reparations from East Germany was ended and the use of German prisoners as slave labourers in the USSR was discontinued. But Khrushchev opposed the production of consumer goods being given priority. He wanted priority to be given to agriculture, and needed capital goods, in the form of farm machinery, to achieve this.

Bulganin also opposed Malenkov, but for somewhat different reasons. Bulganin was in charge of the armed forces and he wanted to restore the emphasis on heavy industry, and especially on military hardware.

This combination of Khrushchev and Bulganin proved fatal to Malenkov. In February 1955 he was forced to resign and accept a minor post. Bulganin now became prime minister, and Marshal Zhukov (p.309) became minister for defence.

Molotov, the foreign minister, was basically in favour of a hard-line policy towards the West and tight control of the satellite states. But Khrushchev disagreed with this. In May 1955 he headed a Soviet delegation to meet Tito in Belgrade. In an obvious reference to the breach between Stalin and Tito (p.340), Khrushchev publicly recognised the right of any socialist state to follow its own road to socialism. This 'different roads to socialism' speech was to have significant repercussions in eastern Europe later on (p.397).

Early in 1957 Malenkov and Molotov, who had each suffered defeats at the hands of Khrushchev, were expelled from the collective leadership. Then in October, Khrushchev used his influence in the party to have Zhukov dismissed, and in March 1958 he took over from Bulganin as prime minister.

Although Khrushchev was now the sole leader, as Stalin had been, he was a radically different man. In February 1956, in the middle of his rise to power, Khrushchev had made a dramatic three-hour speech to the twentieth congress of the Communist Party in which he denounced Stalin and Stalinism. He attacked Stalin's failure to prepare for Hitler's inevitable invasion, his draconian economic policies, his purges, and his self-glorification:

> Stalin acted not through persuasion, explanation and patient co-operation with people, but by imposing his concepts and demanding absolute submission to his opinion. Whoever opposed this concept or tried to prove his viewpoint and the correctness of his position was doomed to removal from the leading collective and to subsequent moral and physical annihilation. . . .
>
> Arbitrary behaviour by one person encouraged and permitted arbitrariness in others. Mass arrests and deportations of many thousands of people, execution without trial and without normal investigation created conditions of insecurity, fear and even desperation. . . .
>
> Stalin was a very distrustful man, sickly suspicious; we know this from our work with him. He could look at a man and say: 'Why are your eyes so shifty today?' or 'Why are you turning so much today and avoiding to look me directly in the eyes?' The sickly suspicion created in him a general distrust even toward eminent party workers whom he had known for years. Everywhere and in everything he saw 'enemies', 'two-facers', and 'spies'. Possessing unlimited power, he indulged in great wilfulness and choked a person morally and physically. A situation was created where one could not express one's own will.
>
> When Stalin said that one or another should be arrested, it was necessary to accept on faith that he was an 'enemy of the people'. Meanwhile, Beria's gang, which ran the organs of state security, outdid itself in proving the guilt of the arrested and the truth of materials which it falsified. And what proofs were offered? The confessions of the arrested, and the investigative judges accepted these 'confessions'. And how is it

possible that a person confesses to crimes which he has not committed? Only in one way — because of application of physical methods of pressuring him, tortures, bringing him to a state of unconsciousness, deprivation of his judgement, taking away of his human dignity. In this manner were 'confessions' acquired.

I recall the first days when the conflict between the Soviet Union and Yugoslavia began artificially to be blown up. Once, when I came from Kiev to Moscow, I was invited to visit Stalin, who, pointing to the copy of a letter lately sent to Tito, asked me, 'Have you read this?'

Not waiting for my reply, he answered, 'I will shake my little finger — and there will be no more Tito. He will fall.'

We have dearly paid for this 'shaking of the little finger'. . . .

No matter how much or how little Stalin shook, not only his little finger but everything else that he could shake, Tito did not fall. Why? The reason was that, in this case of disagreement with the Yugoslav comrades, Tito had behind him a state and a people who had gone through a severe school of fighting for liberty and independence, a people who gave support to its leaders.

You see to what Stalin's mania for greatness led. He had completely lost consciousness of reality; he demonstrated his suspicion and haughtiness not only in relation to individuals in the USSR, but in relation to whole parties and nations.

Khrushchev's speech had a dramatic impact inside and outside the Soviet Union. At home, it led to a programme of increased de-Stalinisation, while abroad, the blind adherence of communist parties to Moscow was broken. In Marxist China hostility towards Moscow's leadership of the communist world was soon apparent and in the satellite states the movement for reform gathered pace.

Nikita Khrushchev with party officials inspects the new corn-growing areas of the 'Virgin Lands' project.

De-Stalinisation

In October 1956 control of labour camps was taken out of the hands of the security services and placed under the ministry of the interior.

In economic affairs, the system operated by Stalin throughout the period of the five-year plans was changed so that one ministry in Moscow became responsible for the production of each industrial commodity throughout the Soviet Union. In 1957 this highly centralised system was replaced by a decentralised administration in which each region became responsible for all production in its own area.

But the most far-reaching changes in the economy came in agriculture. It had long been Khrushchev's main interest; he devoted most of his time to it, and he made over 200 speeches on the subject. Hitherto uncultivated lands were made pasturable. In the campaign on the 'Virgin Lands' of Kazakhstan and Siberia, some forty million hectares of arid land was ploughed in an effort to solve the Soviet grain problem. Nevertheless, much of the land brought into cultivation was unsuitable for corn and crop production, and this, coupled with unsuitable climatic conditions, doomed the scheme to failure.

THE SATELLITE STATES

Within four years of Hitler's defeat, the left-wing people's republics in eastern Europe had been replaced by one-party communist dictatorships (p.335).

But while this process was going on, the Communist Information Bureau, or Cominform (p.344) was established in September 1947 to assist in 'the co-ordination of activities' of all communist parties. In practice, however, Cominform was an organisation for the transmission of Stalin's orders to the governments of eastern Europe.

Soon, Stalin decided that many of the local communist leaders were unreliable and conditions became intolerable. In 1949, Wladyslaw Gomulka, first secretary of the Communist Party in Poland, was dismissed and a Russian general, Marshal Rokossovsky, was put into the government as minister for defence (p.336). The same year, a leading Hungarian communist, Rajk, was tried and hanged for alleged conspiracy. Meanwhile the Bulgarian prime minister, Dimitrov, had been advocating a federation of east European states. This proposal was anathema to Stalin because it would have weakened the Soviet grip on her satellites, and would possibly have led to the growth of eastern European nationalism. Stalin invited Dimitrov to visit Moscow for discussions, but while he was there, Dimitrov died.

Such purges of local communist leaders provoked great resentment in eastern Europe. Further ill-felling was caused in 1949 by the Soviet decision to speed up the collectivisation of agriculture in the satellite states. The same year Pope Pius XII excommunicated all communists, and this led to the persecution of catholics in eastern Europe. All these events, together with the continued presence of Soviet troops, restrictions on personal liberty, and the unavailability of consumer goods, combined to produce a permanent state of discontent in the states of eastern Europe. The great mass of people disliked their communist governments, while the communist governments, in turn, resented Soviet control.

Poland

These intolerable conditions, taken in conjunction with Khrushchev's speech attacking Stalin's rule (p.395), led to an explosion in Poland in the summer of 1956.

The Polish government itself was deeply divided. Some of its members were in favour of allowing certain measures of reform, while others were firmly opposed to any basic change and were willing to call on Soviet troops if necessary. But the masses were at breaking point and were prepared to fight if necessary. The Polish party leadership, in an act of defiance, refused to re-elect Rokossovsky to the government. Students and writers came to the fore and played a leading role in voicing the discontent of the masses. Meetings and demonstrations on the streets of Warsaw and other Polish cities gave ample evidence that an explosion was near. Then at the eighth party congress on 19 October 1956, it was proposed to appoint Wladyslaw Gomulka first secretary of the party. This was a clear act of defiance because Gomulka had been dismissed by Stalin in 1949 (p.337). But for most party members, Gomulka was now the saviour, and for the majority of the population, he was far preferable to previous rulers.

The Soviet leaders were alarmed at the turn of events in Poland. Khrushchev and Molotov flew to Warsaw and arrived unannounced at the party congress. They accused the Polish government of anti-Soviet propaganda, but the Poles defied any attempt to interfere in their internal affairs. Meanwhile, mass demonstrations continued in favour of Gomulka, and the Soviet leaders soon came to realise that Polish determination could not be stopped except by Soviet military intervention. Yet this would be fraught with danger and might lead to nationalist revolutions all over eastern Europe.

Gomulka claimed the right of the Polish government to run its internal affairs, but also assured the Soviet leaders that Poland would remain a loyal member of the communist bloc and continue to support Soviet foreign policy. There was by now a growing popular demand for the withdrawal of Soviet troops, but Gomulka resisted this demand in the hope of gaining acceptance of his other demands from Moscow.

Very reluctantly, and now facing a bigger revolt in Hungary (p.399), the Soviet leaders accepted a new Polish government under Gomulka.

At the time, Gomulka was lauded for his responsible leadership, for sparing his country a civil war, and for preventing Soviet intervention. While making concessions to Moscow, he had been able to secure a greater degree of freedom for Poland than was the case in any other satellite state at that time. He also induced the Soviet leaders to cancel Polish debts, and the economy began gradually to improve. Gomulka did not insist on the collectivisation of agriculture because the Polish peasant was deeply attached to his land and any large-scale collectivisation would have led to resistance. The Polish leader also sought an understanding with the catholic church. This was an astute decision: the overwhelming mass of Poles were catholic, and the church enjoyed greater influence in Poland than in any other satellite state.

But Gomulka's popularity soon began to fade. In October 1957, the journal *Po Prostu*, which had played a major role in highlighting the evils of Stalinism in Poland, was suppressed. Leading Polish intellectuals left the party in protest against cultural and intellectual control, and hope gave way to cynicism. The Polish government grew more isolated from the people, but control of the army and police, and a generally apathetic population, ensured that there was no serious threat to Gomulka's leadership. By 1966, the Gomulka regime, once the most liberal in eastern Europe, had become a staunch pillar of the Soviet bloc.

Hungary

The communist regime in Hungary, like others in eastern Europe, had been installed with the help of Soviet troops. The regime had very little support among the masses and barely managed to hold on to power.

Because the communists controlled all organs of state, and because of their brutal policy of terror, there was no active opposition. But following the death of Stalin, a revolutionary situation was bound to arise. Khrushchev's denunciation of Stalin in 1956 weakened the self-confidence of the hardliners of the Hungarian regime.

In July, Stalinist members were dropped from the government and a few minor concessions were made. But the Hungarian people were not to be satisfied with cosmetic changes. They wanted free elections, an end to the collectivisation of farms, and the withdrawal of Soviet troops.

The demonstrations in Poland (p.397) had a great impact on developments in Hungary, and during the second half of October 1956, agitation reached its climax. On 23 October the regime decided to ban all political meetings and demonstrations, and when this directive was ignored, the secret police opened fire on the demonstrators. In protest, the workers joined the struggle, revolutionary committees were set up throughout Hungary, and Hungarian troops who had been sent to quell the disturbances, joined the rebels. They occupied public buildings and centres of production. Cardinal Mindszenty, in prison since 1949 for speaking out against communism, (p.339), was released.

The Soviet-backed leader of the Hungarian regime, Ernö Gerö, decided to call on the Soviet army to put down the demonstrations. This was a serious mistake and most Hungarians interpreted it as a final act of betrayal. The communist regime and party was completely discredited, and the people now desired a non-communist Hungary more than ever.

The focus of attention now turned to Imre Nagy, the ex-leader and liberal communist who had been expelled from the party the previous April. The Soviet leaders concluded that only a communist government led by Nagy could survive without Soviet military backing.

Five days of street battles followed as the security police, backed up by Soviet tanks, were unable to get control of Budapest. On 28 October Soviet tanks withdrew and Nagy formed a government that included two non-communists. Nagy also proposed allowing the establishment of opposition parties, and on 31 October demanded the withdrawal of Soviet troops, Hungary's release from the Warsaw Pact (p.403), and her recognition as a neutral state between East and West.

Such demands confirmed Khrushchev's worst fears about Nagy. Hungary had presented Moscow with an ultimatum which, if acceded to, would herald the beginning of the end of the Soviet bloc.

Immediately, while the attention of the world was focused on Suez as the British began bombing Egyptian airfields (p.374), Soviet troops invaded Hungary. Fighting continued for a few days, but resistance against 6,000 Soviet tanks was hopeless. Nagy and his government sought refuge in the Yugoslav embassy in Budapest. The ruthless suppression continued, and within a few days some three thousand Hungarians had been killed, and the Red Army was in effective control of the country.

The military battle for control of Hungary had been won with Soviet tanks, but the political aim of the intervention was more difficult to attain. The Soviets knew that there was no point in calling on hard-line leaders to form a government because that would provoke mass resistance. On the other hand, liberal or national communists, such as Nagy, could not be trusted. What the Soviets needed was a 'middle of the road' communist leader, mildly acceptable to sufficient Hungarians who would also collaborate with Moscow in keeping Hungary and the Soviet bloc intact. Such a leader was János Kádár, a communist somewhat similar to Gomulka in Poland (p.397).

The task facing Kádár was extremely difficult. Having come to power in controversial circumstances, he was regarded as a Quisling and termed 'a standing affront to national memory and pride'.

Kádár imposed martial law; thousands were arrested and strikes were outlawed. Nagy and his colleagues were induced to leave the Yugoslav embassy but, once outside the building, they were arrested and tried in secret. Later, it was learned that Nagy and some of his colleagues had been executed.

Thousands of Hungarians were deported to the Soviet Union, over 200,000 had fled to the West, and Cardinal Mindszenty was given asylum in the American embassy in Budapest. (He was pardoned by the Hungarian government in 1970.)

The Soviet invasion of Hungary caused a storm of indignation and protest across Europe, but nothing concrete was done to help the Hungarians. At the United Nations, most Asian and Middle East states abstained from voting on a motion that called for a withdrawal of Soviet troops. A few communists in France, Italy and Britain resigned from their parties in disgust, but this was soon forgotten.

A comparative analysis of the Polish and Hungarian risings reveals some interesting facts. Gomulka had come to power in Poland on a wave of opposition to Moscow while Kádár was imposed on Hungary by Soviet might. But despite this, Poland developed a rigid orthodoxy, while by 1966 Hungary had become the most liberal state in the Soviet

Soviet tanks outside the Hungarian parliament in Budapest, November 1956.

bloc. While Gomulka moved towards the re-imposition of tight controls, Kádár concentrated on economic developments and the raising of living standards.

Romania

Inspired by the example of Yugoslavia and encouraged by the apparent softer line from Moscow after Stalin's death, the Romanian communist party leader, Gheorghe Gheorghiu-Dej set his country on an increasingly independent road. This was further prompted by the fact that the Romanians had not accepted the loss of Bessarabia to the Russians after the war (p.334). The pro-Moscow communists in the Romanian leadership were eliminated and an attempt was made to create a diversified economy that was less dependent on the Soviet Union. In 1954 trade with the West was increased and within a year, it amounted to 20 per cent of Romania's total trade (map, p.334).

In 1958 the Soviet troops, who had been stationed on Romanian soil under the Warsaw Pact (p.399), were removed.

In 1963 Khrushchev attempted to make Comecon a supranational economic agency with authority over the economies of each member state. Khrushchev was impressed by the growing economic division of labour in the Common Market and believed that only by achieving a similar divison of labour in Comecon could the communist states keep pace with economic growth in the West. The Romanian leaders were not impressed with Khrushchev's arguments. They knew that a division of labour among Comecon members would relegate their country to a supplier of raw materials (especially oil) to the Soviet Union, and thus hinder her own drive towards industrialisation. In her stand against a supranational Comecon, Romania had the support of China and Yugoslavia, and also received promises of financial aid from the West.

In July 1963 an important decision-making meeting of Comecon members not only defeated supranationalism, but upheld the right of member states to develop independently.

The same year Romania announced support for non-interference in the affairs of other states, and refused to take part in Warsaw Pact military exercises or allow such exercises to take place on her territory. In 1965 Nicolae Ceaușescu became leader. In 1966 he called for the withdrawal of foreign troops from other countries and, in an obvious snub to Moscow, invited the Chinese premier, Chou Enlai, to Bucharest. In 1967 Romania established diplomatic relations with West Germany and in 1968 condemned the invasion of Czechoslovakia.

But despite these manifestations of independence, prompted in the main by a desire to keep free from the Kremlin's control, there was no thought of liberalising the regime. On the contrary, Romania's 'national communism' was more rigid than that in most eastern European states.

Czechoslovakia

Following the death of Stalin, disturbances broke out in Czechoslovakia and the government was obliged to reduce police activity and increase the availability of consumer goods. But the regime stood firm. Under the leadership of Antonín Novotný from 1957, a rigid centralised system was maintained, and even though two communist parties existed, one in the Czech lands and one in Slovakia, the entire state was ruled by a rigid dictatorship from Prague. Economic growth was very limited, due in the main to stringent planning decisions and the partial allocation of scarce resources. But change within the Soviet bloc eroded Novotný's regime. Khrushchev's condemnation of Stalin, his economic decentralisation in the Soviet Union, and the example of Yugoslavia, provided precedents for Czechoslovak reformers to voice their opinions. In addition, the cultural division of the state into Czech and Slovak regions further weakened centralisation.

In 1962 the Slovaks demanded economic decentralisation, pointing to the example of the Soviet Union. In 1963 the Slovak communist party deposed its Stalinist leader, Karol Bacilek, and replaced him with the reformer, Alexander Dubcek. As a result, Novotný and his conservative colleagues began fighting a losing battle against Czech and Slovak reformers.

In 1966 the reformers forced Novotný to accept decentralisation of the economy. This, they claimed, would cure the ills flowing from excessive centralised planning, unwise resource allocation and inattention to consumer goods.

In 1967 Novotný harshly suppressed student demonstrations protesting against dormitory conditions. This further weakened his position with the reformers, who by now had secured a majority in the party's central committee. Accordingly, in December, Dubcek replaced him as chairman of the party. Then in March 1968 he lost his position as president of Czechoslovakia to the moderate, and military hero, General Ludvík Svoboda.

There now commenced the 'Prague spring' as Dubcek's liberal regime freed the press, created a new sense of freedom and dignity, and spoke of accepting the existence of opposition parties. But while the 'Prague spring' made Dubcek immensely popular in Czechoslovakia, the rest of the communist world feared that he was moving towards western parliamentary government.

Despite Dubcek's protestations of loyalty to the Warsaw Pact, the Soviet government was alarmed and in July the soviet leader, Leonid Brezhnev (p.406) warned the Czechoslovaks not to deviate from the socialist path. To complicate matters further, the Polish and East German regimes were becoming equally fearful that the Czechoslovak example would spread to their states. In Warsaw Gomulka was alarmed at student marchers shouting 'We want a Polish Dubcek'; in East Germany, Walter Ulbricht was alarmed that his weak regime would be overthrown.

In late July and early August hurried meetings took place between Soviet and Czechoslovak leaders. The Soviets appeared to accept the Czechoslovak economic programme, but feared that eventually the Czechoslovaks would demand the right to an independent foreign policy similar to Romania's. In their worst fears, the Soviet leaders conjured up visions of an eventual anti-Soviet alliance of Yugoslavia, Romania and Czechoslovakia. When Tito and Ceaușescu were received in Prague in early August, Brezhnev, Gomulka and Ulbricht were convinced that a conspiracy was under way.

On 20 August Soviet and other Warsaw Pact troops invaded Czechoslovakia and replaced Dubcek with the pro-Soviet Gustav Husák. Under Husák liberal reforms were abolished and Soviet troops remained in Czechoslovakia to protect the country against 'imperialism'. In September the Soviet first secretary laid down his view on the invasion of Czechoslovakia. Known as the 'Brezhnev Doctrine', it asserted that interference in another state was justified when its socialist character was threatened.

Yugoslavia

After her expulsion from the Cominform in 1948, Yugoslavia developed independently. The centralised control of the Communist Party was reduced by the establishment of the League of Communists, which gave more power to local communes. Land was restored to many peasants and a degree of private enterprise was allowed. Trade with the West was developed and even American aid was accepted. Many communists in the Soviet bloc criticised Tito for being nothing more than a social democratic leader on the western European model. This charge was erroneous: Tito's mixture of communism and limited capitalism was born of a pragmatic approach to the peculiar political and economic facts of Yugoslav life.

In 1956, following Khrushchev's speech censuring Stalin, attempts were made to heal the rift between the Soviet Union and Yugoslavia (p.340). However, the Soviet invasion of Hungary later that year (p.399) encouraged Tito to maintain more stoutly the principle of national independence. Tito demanded that Khrushchev act against Stalinist-type leaders in eastern Europe, but this was ignored; in fact following the Hungarian intervention, communism became more rigid in the satellite states. In foreign affairs Tito continued a policy of non-alignment. He disapproved equally of Chinese intervention in the Korean War (p.330), Soviet intervention in Czechoslovakia (p.401), and American intervention in Vietnam.

In April 1955 a conference of 29 newly emerged states, mainly Asian and African, had met in Bandung at the invitation of President Sukarno of Indonesia. The object was to present a united front that was independent of the two superpower blocs. Leading figures of this non-aligned group were Chou Enlai of China, Pandit Nehru of India and Marshal Tito.

However, though the Bandung Conference professed non-alignment, its general orientation was anti-western. Yet because of Tito's presence, it did not become as pro-Soviet as it would otherwise have been.

SOVIET FOREIGN AFFAIRS

Soviet foreign policy under Khrushchev took a new and more pragmatic view of the modern world. His great achievement lay in the fact that he fully recognised the 'revolution' that had come about through nuclear weapons and was prepared to tailor Soviet foreign policy accordingly.

In October 1956, at the same congress in which he denounced Stalin, Khrushchev also rejected Lenin's doctrine of the inevitability of war between socialist and capitalist states. He still, however, claimed that the spread and final victory of socialism was inevitable. Because socialism was inherently superior to the contradiction that was capitalism, Khrushchev held that eventually all peoples would choose it. In some countries, full socialism might be achieved by non-violent means rather than by class war. The future, therefore, was with socialism; and in the meantime, he wanted 'peaceful coexistence' with the capitalist world, rather than nuclear war.

The result of the policy of peaceful coexistence meant better relations with the non-communist world and worse relations with China. Mao Tsetung in China accused Khrushchev of 'revisionism'. On the other hand, Khrushchev described Mao as a 'madman determined on nuclear war'.

But despite the 'thaw' in East-West relations following Stalin's death, there were occasions when Khrushchev acted as if the Cold War was still raging. This reaction was essentially due to a series of related events. In 1953 General Eisenhower (p.316) had become the American president and John Foster Dulles his secretary of state. Dulles fully believed that there could be no peace in the world as long as the malevolent force of communism existed. He spoke openly and freely of going to the brink of war in response to Soviet posturing, and declared that 'massive retaliation' would follow any Soviet aggression. The declared policy of the United States, as enunciated by Dulles, was not only to 'contain communism' but if possible to 'roll back communism in Europe and Asia'.

In pursuance of the policy of communist containment, the early 1950s witnessed the formation of a series of treaties and pacts. NATO (p.348) was enlarged by bringing in Greece and Turkey in 1951, and West Germany in 1955. The same year, Greece, Turkey and Yugoslavia formed the Balkan Pact. In 1954 the South-East Asia Treaty Organisation (SEATO) was formed by the USA, Britain, France, Australia, New Zealand, Pakistan, Thailand and the Philippines. In 1955 Britain, Turkey, Iraq, Iran and Pakistan formed the Baghdad Pact for the military defence of the Middle East. The United States signed bilateral treaties with Japan (1952), South Korea (1953), and Formosa (Taiwan) (1954).

The Soviet response to what it saw as encirclement was to form the Soviet bloc countries into a mutual defence organisation known as the Warsaw Pact. Europe was now formally divided into two armed camps, because the Warsaw Pact and NATO mirror-imaged each other.

Thus, ironically, as the Soviets were beginning to talk of 'peaceful coexistence', the world came to be divided more clearly than ever before into opposing alliances. Yet the alliances themselves contributed to the maintenance of peace. First, they gave a degree of stability to international relations. Secondly, they gave the two superpowers considerable control over conflicts *between* their allies; and this reduced the probability of war within their spheres of influence.

The Geneva Summit

Though superpower rivalry had reached the world stage, problems in Europe were still the focal point. Soon after Stalin's death, western leaders put forward the notion of a summit meeting to be followed by a conference of foreign ministers. This was welcomed by Bulganin, then head of the Soviet government, and a summit was arranged for Geneva in November 1955.

The Geneva Summit was attended by Bulganin, Eisenhower, Eden and Edgar Faure of France. The central topic on the agenda was the future of Germany and the control of nuclear weapons. Bulganin wanted American bases removed from western Europe; these, he claimed, were the main military danger to peace. The western powers emphasised the unification of Germany, which, they claimed, was the best guarantee of future peace. They wished American bases to stay because, without them, western Europe would be unable to resist Soviet political and military pressure. They called for free elections to be held for all-Germany; but Bulganin rejected this, knowing that it would mean certain defeat for the communists. Instead, he made a dramatic call for an unconditional ban on all nuclear weapons. The western powers were not prepared to discuss this; without nuclear weapons, the Soviet Union would still have superiority because of its conventional weapons. But more important, since the Soviet proposal did not include any provision for international inspection, the western powers were not prepared to accept a nuclear ban on trust. Yet the Soviets were prepared for an all-round ban on nuclear arms to be implemented on trust. But in the 'closed society' of the Soviet Union and in the vastness of her territory, it would be possible to manufacture and test nuclear devices, whereas in the 'open society' in the West, this would be impossible. Therefore the notion of 'trust' had different implications for each side.

The gulf between the two sides meant that the Geneva Summit ended without agreement either on Germany or armaments reduction. Yet the Summit had not been all loss, for it reflected a new spirit abroad: a new willingness to look for agreement. Khrushchev's visit to Belgrade in 1955 and his recognition of the principle of 'different roads to socialism' (p.396) was evidence of an effort to normalise relations.

In addition, Soviet willingness to conclude a treaty with Austria (the *Staatsvertrag*) was a dramatic step forward on the road to peaceful coexistence. For ten years the Soviets had maintained that the future of Austria could be solved only in the larger context of solving the German problem. Now, suddenly, this policy was reversed. The Soviet Union withdrew her troops from Austria on the agreement that a newly independent Austria would not allow military bases on her soil and would not join any alliance. This agreement was also signed by the United States, Britain and France.

Berlin

The continued refusal of the West to recognise the state of East Germany and the western military presence in West Berlin was an affront to the Soviet Union. Moreover, the division of Berlin was highlighted by the contrast between the drab socialist East Berlin and the bustling, glittering West Berlin. Between 1949 and 1958 over two million East Germans (out of a population of 17 million), many of them young, skilled and professional, escaped into West Germany. By that date, the East German government had almost sealed the frontier with fences, minefields, dogs and armed guards. Yet, despite these measures, a number continued to escape through Berlin. This rejection of communism, for life in the capitalist West, was a continued embarrassment to East Germany; but more important, it was a 'brain drain' of her youth and talent, so badly needed to build up the state.

In 1958 the Soviet Union demanded that the western powers withdraw from West Berlin, and proposed, instead, the setting up of a 'Free Berlin'. The question was put to the West Berliners but 98 per cent of the population voted against it and the western allies stayed.

In 1959 John Foster Dulles (p.360) died and this opened up the possibility of better relations between Washington and Moscow. Later the same year, Khrushchev visited the United States and his meeting with President Eisenhower proved a success. The two leaders agreed that 'all outstanding international questions should be settled . . . by peaceful means through negotiation'.

Khrushchev's meeting with Eisenhower was

Western troops in winter combat dress at the Berlin Wall, erected in 1961.

followed in May 1960 by a meeting in Paris with Macmillan and de Gaulle. But two weeks before, an American spy plane was shot down over Soviet territory. Khrushchev now had a perfect excuse for not reaching an agreement in Paris on a ban on nuclear arms. He said that he could not discuss such matters until the American government gave an assurance that no further spy missions would occur and also apologised for past incursions. Eisenhower gave the required assurance, but made no apology, and Khrushchev hurriedly left Paris and flew to East Berlin. The west feared a sudden and dramatic move in Berlin, but nothing happened and the tension eased.

Khrushchev's return to peaceful coexistence is said to have been prompted by deteriorating Soviet relations with communist China. The Chinese leaders made clear to Khrushchev that any international agreement arrived at in their absence, including one on disarmament, would not be binding on them. In effect, Khrushchev could not win. He could not reach an international agreement since he did not speak for China, yet he could not admit to the West that the communist world was no longer a monolith led by Moscow.

Meanwhile East Germans continued to use Berlin as a gateway to the West. When Khrushchev met the new American president, John Kennedy in Vienna in June 1961, 103,000 East Germans had already gone to the West in that year alone. Khrushchev believed he could frighten the young and inexperienced president by delivering an ultimatum on Berlin. He gave Kennedy the impression that Moscow would risk nuclear war if a solution to the German problem was not forthcoming.

However, he misjudged Kennedy and the temper of America. Whatever Khrushchev may have thought, the Americans were not going to be pushed out of Berlin, Germany, or Europe by Soviet threats. In fact threats made them angry and less inclined to meet the Soviets halfway. In July Khrushchev announced an increase in military expenditure and Kennedy responded by making a similar declaration. Threats and counter-threats followed, but nothing happened. Then suddenly on 13 August 1961 the East German authorities erected a barbed wire fence dividing East and West Berlin. On 17 August they began to build a wall. The division of Berlin and Germany was to remain.

The Cuban Crisis

In 1959 a Marxist revolution in Cuba brought Fidel Castro to power. But American reaction to a tiny communist state on her doorstep was so counter-productive that it threw Castro into the Soviet orbit.

On 8 September 1962 a Soviet missile ship was detected arriving in Cuba. Within a few weeks American spy planes secured photographic evidence that missile sites had been erected. American intelligence reports estimated that the first missiles would be ready for use by 28 October. But on 22 October the United States announced she was about to institute a naval blockade of Cuba. Kennedy made a famous speech to the world stating that the lessons of the 1930s had been that unchecked aggression ultimately leads to war and appealed to Khrushchev to 'move back from the brink of the abyss'. Meanwhile two Soviet ships and a submarine were approaching Cuba, but on 24 October they slowed down, stopped and turned back, thus avoiding confrontation with the American blockade.

On 26 October Khrushchev offered to remove the missiles in return for an American guarantee not to invade Cuba and topple the Marxist regime. On 27 October Kennedy accepted. The following day Khrushchev publicly announced over Radio Moscow that the missiles would be removed and, a few hours later, Kennedy publicly announced over the Voice of America that he accepted the Soviet offer.

The Cuban crisis was the nearest the superpowers had come to war. Both sides fully realised how fragile peace was in a volatile world. The crisis also revealed the outdated methods of communication between Washington and Moscow and the dangers inherent in time lag. To remedy this, a direct telephone link or 'hot line' was installed between the White House and the Kremlin in June 1963. This was followed up in August by the two powers signing a Test Ban Treaty agreeing not to test nuclear weapons in the atmosphere. Thus, the Cuban crisis created a new awareness in Soviet-American relations from which flowed a certain stability based on a 'balance of terror'.

The Fall of Khrushchev and the Rise of Brezhnev

The Cuban crisis was a personal disaster for Khrushchev from which he never recovered. In addition he had presided over the weakening of Soviet control in eastern Europe and had failed to reach agreement with China. Moreover, his colourful and erratic behaviour in foreign affairs was not seen as bringing credit on the Soviet Union.

Added to his failures in foreign and Soviet bloc affairs, Khrushchev's domestic economic policies had been far from successful. Especially disastrous was his 'virgin lands' project, which failed to produce the promised amount of food. Despite a 17 per cent increase in the acreage of crops sown between 1960 and 1963, huge imports of Canadian wheat and bread rationing were necessary in 1963.

In October 1964, while Khrushchev was on holiday in the Crimea, his opponents planned his downfall. Called back for an urgent meeting of the Praesidium, Khrushchev was outvoted by his opponents.

Two days after his removal, *Pravda* denounced Khrushchev's 'hasty decisions and actions divorced from reality'. Although the post-Khrushchev period is often termed the 'Brezhnev era', Leonid Brezhnev as party secretary was never allowed to monopolise power as Stalin and Khrushchev had done. The policies pursued after 1964 were generally the result of collective decisions of the party's fourteen-member *Politburo*.

Under Brezhnev, many of Khrushchev's economic and administrative changes, especially decentralisation, were abandoned, and the Soviet Union became highly centralised once more. In addition, de-Stalinisation was quickly brought to an end as the *Politburo* believed that public criticism of former leaders would serve only to undermine the present leadership.

In cultural matters and in the right of individual dissent, the Brezhnev regime attracted much unfavourable criticism in the West. In 1966 Andrei Siniavsky and Yuli Daniel were sent to forced labour camp for having their creative works published outside the Soviet Union. But the most celebrated victim of Soviet intolerance was Alexander Solzhenitsyn. In 1962 he had been allowed by Khrushchev to publish his famous novel, *One Day in the Life of Ivan Denisovich*, which exposed the existence of Soviet labour camps (p.437), but in 1970, having been awarded the Nobel prize for literature, the Brezhnev regime refused him permission to visit Stockholm to receive the award.

Study Assignments and Essays

1. What were the main domestic changes brought about in the Soviet Union in the years following Stalin's death?
2. What was the significance of Khrushchev's speech in 1956 denouncing Stalin?
3. Examine the principal features of the Polish state in the period 1953–66.
4. What factors led to the Hungarian Rising in October 1956?
5. Why did the 'Polish October', the Hungarian Rising and the 'Prague Spring' each end in failure?
6. Write an essay on two of the following:
(i) National Communism in Romania; (ii) Berlin 1953–66; (iii) Khrushchev's foreign policy; (iv) The 'Brezhnev Doctrine'; (v) Tito's Yugoslavia.

The keynote of the period 1870–1966 was the unprecedented progress made in all branches of science and technology. In biology, the achievements of Darwin and Mendel were built upon by Pasteur, Fleming and others, while medical achievements in combating hitherto fatal diseases continued to surpass each other in rapid succession.

In physics the work of Planck, Rutherford and Einstein revolutionised man's thinking on the nature of matter and led to the new and awful potential of nuclear energy.

Technology, aided by discoveries in physics and chemistry, rapidly developed. The age of 'steam and steel' quickly gave way to the age of 'oil and electricity'. The development of the internal combustion engine and the jet engine created vast transport networks of automobiles, ocean-going liners and aeroplanes. Electricity opened up a revolution in communications with telegraph, telephone, radio and television. Rocket research paved the way for the advent of space programmes and probes to distant planets, while further advances in physics led to the development of electronics. This in turn created a further revolution in technology as man entered the age, not only of space and electronics, but of computerised automation as well.

The far-reaching changes in science and technology were reflected in the cultural and philosophical developments of the period. In literature the romanticism of the early nineteenth century, though continuing in some form after 1870, essentially gave way to realism. In the twentieth century, the experimental work of Joyce, Eliot and O'Neill explored man's subconscious.

In painting, many different directions were pursued. The brilliant colour and free forms of impressionism and fauvism; the intellectual approach of cubism; surrealism's non-objective abandonment of reality — each had their devotees. In music, romantic nationalism and folk music became popular in the late nineteenth century, while the twentieth century witnessed the experimentation of Schoenberg, who in turn influenced the varied work of Stravinsky, Bartók, Copland and Prokofiev.

In sculpture traditional forms were discarded, while in architecture, new materials, such as steel, glass and concrete, allowed scope for the creation of new functional forms.

Viewed as a whole, the arts reflected all the uncertainty and change of the period; for though science could create a better material world, it could not satisfy man's eternal quest for spiritual meaning.

Section Five

Aspects of Contemporary Civilisation 1870–1966

32 Scientific and Technological Advance 1870–1966

For us believing physicists, this separation between past, present and future has the value of mere illusion, however tenacious.

Albert Einstein

BIOLOGY, CHEMISTRY AND MEDICINE

Evolution

IN 1859 Charles Darwin, a natural scientist, published *On the Origin of Species by means of Natural Selection*, which revolutionised man's thinking on the origins and development of life on Earth. Darwin held that in any one species more were born than could live because of limited food supplies and natural dangers. The survivors were those who were better fitted to adapt themselves to their environment.

Darwin, having spent five years exploring islands in the South Pacific, had observed three provable facts, and from them drew two conclusions: (i) all living species have such a reproductive capacity that any one of them could overpopulate the earth if all fertilised eggs developed into mature reproductive animals; (ii) but no species does this. Darwin's deduction from these two facts was that there must be a continuing struggle for existence (survival). (iii) Within each species there was a great deal of individual variation, with no two individuals exactly alike. From this, Darwin deduced that those individuals whose variations and characteristics best fit them to their environment (those that are adaptable) survive into their reproductive years, while those less adaptable die, or survive in fewer numbers. This process is known as the 'survival of the fittest' or the 'survival of the most adaptable'. Those 'fittest' then pass on their characteristics to their offspring.

Heredity

However, what Darwin did not show, because he did not know, was *why* offspring were not *exactly* the same as their parents. The answer to this was provided by an Austrian monk, Gregor Mendel, who discovered the laws of heredity and became the founder of genetics, the study of ways in which inborn characteristics of plants and animals are inherited.

Mendel worked in a monastery garden and, with his training in mathematics and physics, approached the question of heredity scientifically. For eight years he planted peas in his garden, crossing long with short, white-flowered with pink-flowered, until he arrived at the principles of heredity, which he formulated into two basic laws:

(i) Each body cell has two factors, called genes, for each characteristic. These are inherited, one from each parent. When reproductive cells are formed, any one cell gets only one gene from each pair. Mendel's first law, the law of segregation, thus states that any reproductive cell gets only one of each pair of genes.

(ii) Mendel's second law, the law of independent assortment, explains how characteristics are passed from parents to offspring. A child inherits genes for blue eyes and black hair from one parent and genes for brown eyes and red hair from the other. When this child becomes a parent, he or she can pass on all four combinations to the next generations. This law of independent assortment explains why no two children of the same parents inherit the same combination of all characteristics.

In March 1865 Mendel read his paper before the Natural History Society in Brno and published it in 1866. However, his paper was forgotten until 1900. Darwin did not know of Mendel's discoveries, and Mendel died without having his wonderful achievements accepted by the scientific community. However, within a generation, the work of Darwin and Mendel was hailed as a significant advance in man's attempts to understand life.

Bacteria

Not until the seventeenth century was it realised that there were living creatures smaller than the tiny insects that could be seen with the naked eye. In that century a Dutch merchant ground a lens that magnified 200 times. As a result he discovered blood cells under his microscope. His powerful lens just allowed him to see 'germs', as he called them, but what are known today as bacteria.

For generations men had questioned whether or not living creatures could be produced from lifeless, or inorganic matter. Some believed in spontaneous generation, but among those who doubted this was a French chemist, Louis Pasteur. The word *microbe*, from the Greek *mikrós* (small) and *bíos* (life), was popularised by Pasteur when he used it to include plant, animal and bacterial life. Pasteur decided that minute life organisms exist in the atmosphere and in the earth. He believed that these 'micro-organisms' made wine ferment and milk turn sour. Some made food mildew, and some, he believed, were connected with disease. Pasteur discovered that bacteria could be killed by heating their environment to a certain temperature. He experimented with a system that finally succeeded in preserving milk, foodstuffs and beer. This method of killing bacteria and purifying food came to be known as *pasteurising* while his germ theory of disease was a tremendous leap forward in the history of chemistry and medicine.

Antiseptics

While Pasteur was working for the wine industry and delivering the French silk industry from the scourge of silkworms, a Hungarian physician, Dr Ignaz Semmelweiss, made an important contribution to the germ theory, without realising its importance.

Working in the maternity ward of a hospital, Dr Semmelweiss was alarmed that twelve out of every hundred new mothers died from 'child-bed' fever, while mothers giving birth in their own homes scarcely ever got this fever. He came to the conclusion that doctors themselves were carrying the disease into the maternity ward and insisted that his colleagues wash their hands in a solution of chlorinated lime. Immediately the death rate dropped to 1.5 per cent, but Semmelweiss's colleagues were so humiliated by the hand-washing that he was forced to leave the hospital, after which the death rate rose again.

Meanwhile a Scottish surgeon, Joseph Lister, was appalled at the death rate in general hospitals and, like Pasteur, was finally able to prove that germs, and the filth in which germs multiplied, caused infection. As patients with serious wounds always caught infection, in 1864 Lister used an antiseptic (*antí*, against; *sépsis*, putrefaction), carbolic acid, around the wound, and the patient recovered. Soon Lister insisted on spraying the operating room with carbolic acid. This was the beginning of the practice of antisepsis.

A German doctor, Robert Koch, supplemented the work of Pasteur and succeeded in isolating the *bacillus* (from the Latin word meaning 'little rod') that caused anthrax, a disease fatal to warm-blooded animals such as cattle and sheep. Later, he succeeded in isolating the bacillus that caused tuberculosis.

Advance continued in the field of preventive medicine, and the bacilli of other diseases such as diphtheria, typhoid and cholera were eventually isolated.

These three men, Pasteur, Lister and Koch,

laid the foundation for the rapid advance in medicine made in the twentieth century. Before Pasteur's discovery, the average life-span of people living in favourable circumstances was about forty years. Today the average life-span is over seventy years.

After 1900, the scientific practice of medicine progressed rapidly, as a result of developments in bacteriology, microbiology and biochemistry.

In the early decades of the twentieth century, scientists isolated and identified the causes and carriers of many diseases. They developed vaccines for cholera, diphtheria, typhus, tetanus, typhoid fever and yellow fever. Microbiologists connected such fevers as polio and influenza to viruses.

In 1921 insulin was discovered for diabetes, by Frederick Banting and Charles Best of Canada.

In 1935 sulphanilamide drugs were used successfully in treating meningitis and pneumonia. In 1928 Alexander Fleming discovered penicillin but did not use it until 1942. Penicillin came to be known as the wonder drug and proved effective in curing pneumonia, puerperal fever, scarlet fever, meningitis and various sexually transmitted diseases.

In the 1940s cortisone and ACTH proved effective against rheumatism, pneumatic fever and severe burns.

Jonas Salk, working in the late 1940s on the scourge of poliomyelitis (infantile paralysis), discovered a vaccine to control its ravages. In 1954 his 'Salk vaccine' was tested successfully and has been used ever since in controlling the spread of polio.

The application of new discoveries was speeded up during World War II with the result that after the war, medical science advanced rapidly. In 1953 two genetic biologists, James Watson and Francis Crick, constructed a model for a molecule of the substance deoxyribonucleic acid (DNA), which is the main constituent of the chromosomes of all organisms. This knowledge of cell structure encouraged scientists to believe that eventually they would be able not only to control hereditary disease but to predict biological make-up.

Encouraged by successful human kidney transplants, Dr Christiaan Barnard of South Africa carried out the first human heart transplant in 1967. Soon heart and other organ transplants became relatively common throughout the world, though in the case of hearts, factors such as the tendency of human bodies to reject foreign tissue remain to be solved.

PHYSICS

In 1890 a young Polish woman, Marie Sklodowska, enrolled in the Sorbonne in Paris. With her French scientist husband, Pierre Curie, she experimented on an odd element called uranium which appeared to give off a curious radiation. While the Curies were experimenting in the Sorbonne, a German scientist, Wilhelm von Röntgen, made a significant discovery. In 1895 he discovered a new short-wave ray that could penetrate human flesh and leave an imprint on a photographic plate. He called this new ray, X-ray, because he did not know its cause.

Then in 1898 Marie Curie discovered a new element (uranium), which she called polonium in honour of her native Poland, and six months later another new element which she called radium. Experiments with uranium and radium showed that as they threw off tiny particles of matter, their weight and chemical make-up changed. This meant that the atoms of these two elements were constantly disintegrating of their own accord, and releasing an energy called radioactivity.

Meanwhile, a New Zealand scientist, Ernest Rutherford, was beginning to open up the field of sub-atomic physics and to show that the atom itself was not indivisible but was made up of a nucleus and electrons. Two men were now to make important discoveries about energy. In 1899 a German scientist, Max Planck, put forward the notion of the 'quantum theory'. By this he claimed that energy is given off by a vibrating body in little 'packages' or 'quanta', and not in a steady flow as had been believed.

In 1905 a young German scientist, Albert Einstein, published his 'special theory of relativity'. It marked a radical turning point in human thought, after which many of man's most basic concepts would never be the same again.

Until his publication, the common-sense view of time as 'an ordered sequence of moments following one upon another' was accepted by all. According to the eighteenth-century scientist Isaac Newton, 'absolute, true and mathematical time, of itself and from its own nature, flows equally without relation to anything external.' The same was true of space: 'absolute space in its own nature, without relation to anything external, remains similar and immovable.' These Newtonian absolutes had dominated scientific and philosophical thinking for over two centuries, but in his 'special theory of relativity', Einstein showed that an independent absolute time and an independent absolute space were misconceptions. Instead, the dimension of time is related to the three dimensions of space (length, breadth and thickness) in a four-dimensional time-space continuum. Therefore time and space are inextricably linked, are not absolute but relative to the observer.

In 1915 Einstein followed this with his 'general theory of relativity' which demonstrated that space is in fact curved. Einstein showed that the influence of any mass (piece of matter) is such as to 'bend' the space in its vicinity — the amount of bend being equivalent to its gravitational field. Therefore the space around the earth is curved, but the curve is so infinitesimally small as to be almost undetectable. However, when one considers the entire mass of the universe it is just possible, as the American mathematician Kurt Godel suggested in 1949, that space is curved right round upon itself. This would mean that the universe as a whole can be viewed as an enclosed, rotating sphere.

Albert Einstein, whose mathematical discoveries fundamentally altered man's basic concepts of time and space.

But for practical purposes, it was Einstein's formula relating energy and matter that had most effect. In a famous formula, $E = mc^2$, he proved that energy equals mass multiplied by the square of the velocity of light. Since the velocity of light is 186,000 miles per second, it can be seen that a very small amount of matter (mass), when multiplied by the square of this number, will give a stupendous amount of energy. In practical terms this means that one gram of matter when transformed into energy could produce 25 million kilowatt-hours of electricity.

Scientists who had studied the results of smashing atoms had been puzzled to find that some of the mass (the actual material substance) was missing after the nucleus (core) was smashed. But now with Einstein's equation, they could account for this. This missing part had been transformed into energy.

One scientist who explored this released energy was the Italian Enrico Fermi, who won the Nobel prize for physics in 1938. Fermi wished to develop nuclear power that could be used for peaceful purposes. He built a simple nuclear 'reactor' to produce a 'chain reaction' with lumps of uranium surrounded by blocks of graphite to control fissions (separations) within the uranium. The fission released large amounts of controlled energy, largely in the form of heat, in accordance with Einstein's formula $E = mc^2$. Fermi's nuclear reactor, built underneath the football stadium of the University of Chicago, proved that nuclear fission could be controlled.

Following on Fermi's achievement, bigger and more powerful nuclear reactors were built in the post-World War II era and proved to be an immense source of power and energy.

But nuclear energy was not confined to peaceful purposes. The difference between controlled fission and an atomic explosion is the rate of release. In a bomb the chain reaction of fissions is completed in a fraction of a second.

By mid-1945 the atomic bomb had been tested. On 6 August 1945 the first atomic bomb was dropped by parachute and detonated at 1,850 feet above Hiroshima (p.324).

Soon a more terrible bomb was tested. This was the hydrogen bomb, which releases its energy by the fusion (joining together) of hydrogen atoms. This is the same reaction by which the sun generates heat. It takes place only at extreme temperatures of several million degrees. The hydrogen bomb is called 'thermo-nuclear' because the necessary heat for fusion is generated by a small fission bomb inside the hydrogen bomb. The atomic bomb dropped on Hiroshima had the explosive power of 20,000 tons of TNT; a hydrogen bomb has the equivalent of 50 million tons of TNT. Unless man can prevent the use of nuclear arms, the destruction of planet Earth and all life upon it is inevitable.

ELECTRICITY

Although the existence of electricity had been known to the ancient Greeks, it was not until the late eighteenth and early nineteenth centuries that any worthwhile discoveries concerning its nature and use were made. Two Italian scientists were the first to make important discoveries. Luigi Galvani investigated the effects of electrical action and established the basic principles of 'Galvanism', while Alessandro Volta's researches led directly to the electric battery. In 1820 the Dane, Hans Christian Oersted, discovered electromagnetism when he found that current flowing through a wire will move a compass needle that is lying parallel to it. Further discoveries concerning the relationship between electricity and magnetism were made by the French scientist André Ampère, while the German scientist Georg Ohm elaborated a theory concerning the employment of electric current and suggested how electricity could be used for industrial purposes.

COMMUNICATIONS

The commercial exploitation of theoretical knowledge soon became the concern of mechanical inventors. In 1831 the Englishman Michael Faraday showed that electric current could be produced by moving a wire through the lines of force of a magnetic field. His discovery, the first dynamo, became the basis for the electric generator. In 1832 the American Samuel Morse made the first electric telegraph, and in 1876 a Scotsman living in America, Alexander Graham Bell, patented the telephone. In 1879 another American, Thomas Edison, invented the incandescent filament bulb, which ushered in the change from the use of gas or kerosene to electricity for lighting. In 1895 a young Italian scientist, Guglielmo Marconi, revolutionised communications with the invention of a wireless telegraph, which was put into operation across the English Channel in 1898.

Meanwhile Marconi's invention of wireless telegraphy, for which he was awarded the Nobel prize for physics in 1928, led to developments in radio broadcasting. The researches of two British scientists, Thompson and Richardson, and the American, Lee de Forest, who invented the 'three-electrode tube', made this a practical reality after World War I. In 1920 the first radio broadcasting station was put into operation by the Westinghouse Company in America and in 1926 the British Broadcasting Corporation (BBC) was established. The following decade witnessed dramatic progress in the manufacture and use of radio. By 1940 every independent nation in the world had at least one broadcasting station, while in the United States and Europe many millions of homes were in possession of radios.

Another notable advance in communication came with the development of television. In 1928 the Scottish-American physicist John Baird succeeded in transmitting images in combination with colour and sound across the Atlantic. Improvements in and extension of television techniques followed and by 1966 television had become a commonplace in many American and European homes.

In 1927 the radio-telephone helped to speed up communications over very long distances, but atmospheric and other conditions made this communication a little uncertain.

In 1956 transatlantic telephone cables greatly improved the quality of communications, but scientists already saw the need for a much better long-range system.

The Bell Telephone Company suggested that messages could be sent by high-powered ground stations via unmanned stations in space. In July 1962 *Telstar* was sent into orbit and, for the first time in history, television programmes were sent back and forth between Europe and North America. Although the project cost more than $50 million, it was believed that it would be cheaper in the long run than underwater cables, because it was estimated that by 1980 at least 50 cables would be required to handle telephone traffic alone. On the other hand, *Telstar* was an incredibly rapid system of communication capable of sending 1½ million words per minute.

In 1963 a new improved *Telstar* was launched and this was followed by *Relay*. However, both *Telstar* and *Relay* were low-altitude satellites, and scientists went to work on developing a high-altitude twenty-four-hour synchronous satellite timed so that its speed in orbit matched the speed of the point immediately below it on earth. This satellite, *Syncom*, was put into orbit but contact with it was lost. Following this, *Syncom II* was placed in orbit 22,300 miles above the earth, and handled voice, telex and other communications. However, *Syncom II* covered only part of the earth. A second satellite, *Skynet*, was launched into station over the Indian Ocean and a third, *Pacific 3*, was launched over the Pacific Ocean. All three are in synchronous orbit with the earth; all three maintain their positions, and relay messages around the earth.

TRANSPORT

Although the early part of the nineteenth century witnessed a revolution in transport with the development of canals, railways and steamships, the latter half of the century witnessed even greater developments. In 1861 the first steel railway tracks were laid at Crewe in England which made it possible for trains to carry heavier loads and travel at faster speeds. Railway development continued in almost every country up to 1914 and huge projects such as the transcontinental lines in North America and the Trans-Siberian railway were undertaken, which opened up hitherto relatively inaccessible regions of the world.

Transport at a local level was transformed after 1890 by the arrival of the bicycle. But even more significant was the invention of the automobile. Throughout the nineteenth century there had been much experimentation with internal combustion engines and in the late 1870s large stationary engines, worked by local gas, were developed in Germany and Britain. A much more efficient internal engine burning petroleum and fired by compression was developed by the German engineer Rudolf Diesel. After the efficiency of the diesel engine was publicly demonstrated in 1898, its employment became widespread for the generation of electricity, in ocean liners and locomotives. Contemporary with Diesel, another German engineer, Gottlieb Daimler, successfully developed a small light-weight internal combustion gasoline engine. Patents of the Daimler engine were acquired by the Panhard Company in France and the first Panhard automobile appeared in 1894. From this prototype, engineering firms in France, Germany, Britain and America rapidly developed different varieties of automobiles.

The arrival of the automobile made necessary the building of roads and highways, expanded the production of oil and refining, and stimulated a vast rubber industry; and since oil and rubber were non-European products, imperial acquisition was given an increased urgency in the minds of European powers (p.85). In addition, the development of small electric motors made possible the 'self-starter' and led to a rapid increase in automobile production. This was especially the case in America where Henry Ford had introduced the assembly line technique of mass production that was to make cheap cars a possibility. By 1910 America was producing 181,000 cars annually, representing three-fourths of world output.

The internal combustion gasoline engine was applied to uses other then the automobile, and by 1900 motor boats had appeared while Count von Zeppelin commenced experimenting with motor-driven dirigible balloons. But while 'zeppelins' proved practicable, and successful flights were being made by 1906, they were superseded by the heavier aircraft. In 1903 the American brothers, Wilbur and Orville Wright conducted the first aeroplane flight at Kittyhawk, North Carolina. Then in 1909 the French aviator, Louis Blériot, flew a monoplane across the English Channel from Calais to Dover. The age of aviation had arrived.

World War II stimulated the development of more powerful engines, more durable metals, and improved instrumentation and design. In the 1950s, jet engines, pioneered in Britain, began to replace piston engines, and by the 1960s jet-propelled planes, flying at more than 600 mph, dominated long-range passenger service throughout the world.

INDUSTRY

As science progressed, it produced a continuing impact on industry.

Coal and iron had been the basis of the industrial revolution and they remained fundamental in the advance of industrialism. The production of coal and iron rose rapidly, especially in Britain, Germany and the United States, between 1870 and 1914.

In addition the application of the Bessemer and Siemens processes made it easy to produce steel from iron cheaply and in large quantities. Cheap steel in turn made it possible to expand railway construction and build new steamships. As a result, a revolution in ocean transport took place before 1900, as the sailing ship gave way to the faster, bigger and more reliable steamship Cheap steel also made possible a vast variety of machinery; in particular it facilitated the manufacture of improved machine tools, such as the power lathe and the power press, which resulted in better and more precise machines.

The textile industry was revolutionised in 1884 by a French nobleman, Count Willaire de Chardonnet, who patented a process for making a fibre from wood pulp which resembled silk. By 1910 some two-and-a-half million pounds of this 'artificial silk' or 'rayon' was being produced by the Chardonnet process, and much more by the newer British 'viscose' process. Moreover, textiles, old and new, were no longer being dyed by the old natural colouring agents such as indigo, but with a variety of new dyes, often derived from coal tar.

In other fields, innovation proceeded rapidly as one improvement led to another. In 1869 celluloid was first made from wood pulp (cellulose) in America. Then in 1887 George Eastman made the roll film from cellulose. This dramatically improved and speeded the process of photography, made possible the simple camera, and led to the development of the motion picture by Edison and others in 1891.

In 1885 the German-born American Ottmar Mergenthaler invented a machine for setting type, the Linotype, which made it less expensive to produce printed material. And this, coupled with improved methods of making paper from wood pulp, made available cheaper magazines, books and newspapers for an increasingly literate public. Similarly, the typewriter, developed in the 1870s and 1880s, made correspondence easier, and created the new profession of typist, which opened up new possibilities of employment for women.

As the nineteenth century ended, the age of electricity arrived to make possible the supply of many necessities in civilised life. The twentieth century witnessed the progressive use of electricity not only as an industrial motive power but in the production of new comforts in domestic life. Many labour-saving devices, such as milking machines, washing machines and vacuum cleaners, were invented; food preservation was aided by refrigeration, while air cooling and heating appliances made dwelling-houses, offices, shops and factories more congenial for living and working.

Not all inventions were used for peaceful purposes, however. Ships, zeppelins and aircraft were capable of military use and were enlisted in World War I (p.136). In addition, the Swedish chemist Alfred Nobel intended dynamite for peaceful purposes when he introduced it in 1867, but his invention ushered in a new era of high explosives when the military of almost all nations came to realise its potential.

In 1875 the Irish-American John Holland made the first practical submarine, and by 1900 the great powers were adding them to their navies.

In 1884 an American who became a British subject, Sir Hiram Maxim, invented the first truly automatic machine gun, and later an explosive called cordite. His brother, Hudson, developed a smokeless powder and his son, Hiram Percy, invented a silencer for making firearms noiseless.

This range of inventions and technological improvements did not consist of a series of isolated events. In practice they tended to be interconnected.

These developments permitted a dramatic increase in population, a rapid enlargement of cities and a corresponding decline in the rural population. Moreover, the growing cities were linked by rapid transport and instant communication.

Taken together, the scientific, industrial and technological developments in western Europe and the United States between 1870 and 1914 changed the way of life and standards of living of the peoples concerned to a far greater degree than had the cumulative changes of the preceding two centuries.

The new urban masses were better educated and had a longer life expectancy than the generations before 1870. At the same time their coming together in large concentrations made them more accessible to manipulation and more readily influenced by the mass media. Thus while society was becoming more advanced, it was also becoming less stable, as the rootless urban dweller came to replace the old-time peasant as the typical European.

AUTOMATION

During World War I, advanced technology in America began to replace some aspects of manual work. One development that had profound consequences for labour relations and for mass consumption was the system of machine shop management, otherwise known as 'scientific management'. It was originated by Frederick Winslow Taylor, who maintained that knowledge, rather than manual skill, was the key element in production.

After the Great War, the European economies badly needed efficient productive methods and many adopted Taylor's system. Wherever the system was used, it brought about a reduction in the cost of manufactured goods, an increase in wages for workers, and greater profits for employers. As Taylor's system became more widely used, machine operators took the place of unskilled labourers and earned the wages of highly skilled workers. Between the world wars, machine operators became the largest occupational group in every industrialised country.

An extension of Taylor's scientific management was automation, or the use of machines to perform complex tasks with very little human guidance. By 1950 automation took many forms. The most important one was the computer, which stored and produced information for all types of businesses. Computers aided research, made surveys, kept records, calculated payrolls, handled airline reservations, translated languages, and came increasingly to be used in education. In the motor car industry, systems of automation were installed to assemble engine parts. Most other big industries followed suit in an effort to eliminate physical labour and tedious tasks. By 1966 automation had become as important as mechanisation had been in the nineteenth century.

THE SOCIAL SCIENCES

The great advances in science had profound effects upon the non-scientific areas of human behaviour. The 'social scientists' tried to copy the methods of the exact scientists in the expressed hope that sociology, psychology and anthropology (the behavioural sciences) would be able to make generalisations and predictions.

Economics did in fact become more scientific. Aided by improvements in the methods of gathering and interpreting statistics, economists were able to deal effectively with such concepts as 'level of prices', 'index of production', 'gross national product' and 'national income'. As a result, governments and business turned increasingly to economists for an understanding of what was happening, and what might be expected to happen as a result of changes in policy.

Political science and sociology also made progress, but not as great as economics, in the adoption of scientific methods. Both came to use statistics in order to describe and analyse human behaviour. However, they remained descriptive and were scarcely able to keep pace with the rapid political and social change of the twentieth century.

Archaeology also progressed by using new scientific techniques such as carbon-14 dating. This technique enabled archaeologists to expand their knowledge of ancient peoples, of the Mediterranean, India and the Americas. Anthropology made much clearer the evolution of man and also studied surviving 'primitive' peoples who had been brought into contact with modern civilisation.

Psychology seemed to move in two directions. On one hand it developed as a science based on direct observation and laboratory experiments. In Russia, Ivan Pavlov made many experiments with dogs and originated the concept of the 'conditioned reflex'.

Sigmund Freud, father of psychoanalysis.

This approach was carried further by other psychologists, especially the American John B. Watson, who created the 'behaviourist' school of psychology. Another group of psychologists, the Germans Kurt Kaffke, Max Wertheimer and Wolfgang Kohler, gained insights into human actions by studying great apes and other animals. This group developed 'gestalt psychology' which emphasised the wholeness of things as against simple reflexes.

On the other hand, one side of psychology developed into psychiatry, which built up techniques for curing mental illness. The father of psychiatry was the Austrian physician Sigmund Freud, who before 1900 was stressing the part played by the unconscious and subconscious in determining human behaviour. Freud held that these unconscious and subconscious factors were sexual urges, forgotten childhood experiences, and suppressed fears and conflicts. Thus, Freud held that man is only partly rational in his behaviour because many of his actions are conditioned by psychological forces of which he is partly or wholly unaware.

Freud's followers split into different schools of psychiatry. One of his followers, Alfred Adler, developed the notions of the 'inferiority complex' and the 'defence mechanism' to explain ways in which people behave.

Another of Freud's followers, Carl G. Jung, did not accept the importance of the sexual factor in human behaviour. Instead he gave considerable importance to the human soul and to spiritual factors.

Before 1914 there was a trend away from rationalism, not only in the behaviour of individuals but in the behaviour of societies and nations. The Italian sociologist Vilfredo Pareto stressed the non-rational basis of group behaviour. The French engineer George Sorel emphasised the importance of myth in motivating masses of people. Modern advertising was already learning that an appeal to the emotions was more effective than a cold appeal to reason. The rise of nationalist aspirations was interpreted as a non-rational phenomenon.

SPACE EXPLORATION

The first real step towards making space exploration possible came with the practical development of the rocket by the Germans during World War II. Unlike the jet, the rocket does not depend upon the oxygen in the air to provide the fuel. The rocket is completely self-contained and its principle of operation is based on one of Newton's laws of motion which states that 'every action has an equal and opposite reaction.' In a rocket, the container is filled with an explosive (liquid or solid) which is then ignited. The gases from this combustion (burning) expand through an exhaust nozzle, and the heat energy is converted into kinetic energy or motion. The 'push' (action) of the escaping gas forces the rocket forward (reaction). During the war the Germans developed a rocket, the *Vergeltungswaffe* (retaliation weapon). However, this V-1 weapon was too slow and could be easily shot down. The V-2 rocket was developed in 1942, but was not used in warfare until September 1944. The V-2 rocket landed at 3,500 mph, a speed faster than sound so that the explosion occurred before people heard the rocket coming. However, before they could be mass-produced, the war had ended.

As the war drew to a close, the Russians were anxious to capture German rocket scientists who could be used for rocket development in the Soviet Union. The importance of these scientists was not appreciated by the western Allies and consequently the Russians did succeed in winning over a number of them.

After the war the Soviet Union gave top priority to rocket and space flight programmes and on 1 October 1957 announced the successful launching of *Sputnik I* (Fellow Traveller) into orbit around the earth. The world stood amazed at this stupendous achievement and the United States was shocked that she had been beaten into space. A month later, the Russians launched *Sputnik II*, a larger capsule, this time carrying a live dog in orbit around the earth.

In January 1958 America entered the 'space race' by launching *Explorer I*, and the same year Congress created the National Aeronautics and Space Administration (NASA) to handle space science.

In April 1961 the Russians were again first when Yuri Gagarin was the first man to orbit the earth in his spaceship *Vostok I* (East).

The first American spaceman was Alan Shepard who flew 115 miles high in May 1961 but did not orbit the earth. The first American to orbit the earth was John Glenn in the spaceship *Friendship* 7 in February 1962.

During 1962 other American astronauts and Soviet cosmonauts made orbital flights around the earth, and both nations launched satellites with cameras and other equipment to probe outer space.

In 1964 cameras on board the American *Ranger 7* took close-up pictures of the moon, and in July 1964 the American *Mariner 4* took photographs when it passed a mere 6,000 miles from Mars.

The first woman space traveller was the Russian Valentina Tereshkova in *Vostok 6*, the last 'single-seater' spacecraft.

In March 1965 the Russians had yet another 'first' when Alexey Leonov left his spacecraft and floated outside in space.

Although the Russians had scored several spectacular 'firsts', the Americans had designed more manoeuvrable spacecraft. As a result, they scored a major 'first' in late 1965 when two teams of astronauts manoeuvred their two spacecraft nose-to-nose while orbiting the earth. This was followed up in March 1966 when the two-man *Gemini 8* was briefly joined in space to the unmanned *Agena 8*.

In January 1969 the Russians accomplished the first transfer of men in space from one spacecraft to another when *Soyuz 5* (Union) joined *Soyuz 4*.

Lunar Exploration

When President Kennedy assumed office in 1961, he called upon his country to land a man upon the moon and bring him back to Earth 'before this decade is out'. Both the USA and the USSR carried on lunar exploration by camera. In February 1966 the Russians made a 'soft' landing on the moon with *Luna 9*. Before it hit the moon, it transmitted to earth the first on-surface pictures of the moon. Then in April 1966 *Luna 10* made the first lunar orbit. The Americans made their first 'soft' landing

Yuri Gagarin, the first man to orbit the earth, April 1961.

with *Surveyor 1* in June 1966. They followed this in August when *Lunar Orbiter* circled the moon and relayed back pictures of possible landing sites. But the climax came in July 1969 when three astronauts, Armstrong, Collins and Aldrin, were launched into space in *Apollo II.* On 20 July their lunar module touched down on the face of the moon with Armstrong and Aldrin aboard, while Collins continued to orbit in the command module.

On a stainless steel plaque the astronauts left the following message on the moon:

HERE MEN FROM THE PLANET EARTH
FIRST SET FOOT UPON THE MOON
JULY 1969 A.D.
WE CAME IN PEACE FOR ALL MANKIND

TECHNOLOGY AND SOCIETY

Advances in technology gave an increasingly important role to the place of education in industrial society.

In 1860 literacy was a luxury confined to the privileged few; by 1966 it had become a basic economic need for all. Those without education found it difficult, if not impossible, to find employment. Every industrialised country recognised the need to invest in education. Technology demanded experts.

In 1900 few persons were *aware* that inventions then in existence, such as electric light, telephones and automobiles, would radically change society. By 1966 few persons were *unaware* that their living styles had been radically changed by such inventions as the aeroplane, radio, television, and nuclear energy.

The invention of the typewriter and telephone had allowed millions of women to earn an independent living. This trend was accelerated during World War I when a variety of occupations, previously the preserve of men, were thrown open to women (p.156).

After World War II the work-force gained greater economic security as wages increased. Workers constituted a steadily growing middle class which became an important market for business and industry. The proportion of poor declined, but did not disappear. By 1966 even in the Soviet Union, the middle class, composed mainly of bureaucrats, professionals and managers, also showed signs of growth. However, none of the transformations caused by technology came easily because deeply rooted social and political institutions often proved resistant to change. Moreover, as technology changed society, new problems and issues arose.

One such problem was the growing dis parity between the rich industrial nations and the poor underdeveloped nations of the 'Third World'. This inequality was further highlighted by the 'revolution of expectations' in the Third World, which not only accelerated the demand for independence in the post-1945 era (p.353), but was in stark contrast to the reality of hunger, malnutrition and even famine, ever present in the underdeveloped countries. Leaders in the industrialised nations tended to explain the poverty of the Third World in terms of overpopulation, and different motives, attitudes and social institutions. On the other hand, leaders in the Third

World explained their poverty in terms of past colonialism and the continued exploitation of their resources by the developed nations. Whatever may be the cause (and remedies) of world disparities — and they are certainly more complex than the charges levelled by both sides – the vast technological developments in the advanced nations have failed to solve them.

Another result of industrialisation and technological advance was the increasing concentration of population in urban centres. This attraction of people to cities was not new in the twentieth century; but the speed with which cities grew, especially in western Europe and the United States because of migration from rural areas, was greater than at any other time. Each technological advance in agriculture reduced the need for manual labour in the countryside, while each technological advance in industry tended to enlarge industry and attract more people to the centres of work. As a result industrial complexes grew, and with them, extended transport and communication systems.

Growing industrialisation therefore promoted urbanisation. In 1900 only Britain had an urbanised society, with more than half its population living in cities of over 20,000 people. By 1950 every industrial country had become urbanised. In 1900 there were only a few cities with more than one million inhabitants: by 1966 the number had increased to almost one hundred.

Technology changed the very character of these cities. Telegraph poles and telephones, buses and underground rail systems became regular features of most city landscapes. Expanding business and industry encroached on residential areas and forced families to seek dwellings further from city centres. Suburbs grew rapidly and commuting to work became the norm for an increasing proportion of city dwellers.

With increased suburban living, supercities, or immense metropolitan areas, developed in Britain, West Germany, Belgium and Holland. These new developments created the need for efficient transport. Private motor cars enabled people to move independently of public transport and their sales increased. But this led to traffic congestion. In Britain the number of car owners increased more rapidly than roads could be built or improved to accommodate them. In Bonn, skyscraper garages were constructed, while in Belgrade horse-drawn vehicles were forbidden in the streets. Despite measures such as these, the problem of traffic congestion continued and the speed of city traffic fell dramatically in most cities.

Another problem created by technological advance was air and water pollution. The dramatic rise in car users was the main cause of air pollution, though furnaces, apartments, houses, office buildings and industrial plant also discharged large quantities of air pollutants. In order to reduce, or control, the problem, car manufacturers sought lead-free fuels and new power sources for use in cars. City authorities passed legislation regulating the use of heating fuels and some cities reported spectacular success in the late 1960s.

Water pollution also became a serious concern because municipal sewer systems often dumped their waste into major waterways. As a result, more and more water needed for use in homes and industry came from contaminated sources. City authorities were thus faced with the problem of developing more effective methods than the conventional chemicals in order to ensure a clean, hygienic water supply.

Technology, therefore, while advancing civilisation to an unprecedented degree, had also created many problems for man to solve.

Study Assignments and Essays

1. Treat of the contribution made to science by Darwin, Mendel and Pasteur.

2. Treat of medical advances in the twentieth century.

3. Treat of developments in physics between 1870 and 1966.
4. What were the main technological developments in the period 1870–1914?
5. Treat of the 'revolution in communications' during the period 1870–1966.
6. Write an essay on two of the following:
(i) Albert Einstein; (ii) Automation;
(iii) Space exploration; (iv) Technology and war;
(v) Technology and society.

Cultural Developments 1870–1966

33

All art aspires to the condition of music.
Arthur Schopenhauer

PHILOSOPHY

THE SENSATIONAL advances in science in the latter half of the nineteenth century (p.410) led many intellectuals to believe that eventually everything would be explained in the materialistic terms of matter and motion. Accordingly, in philosophy, there was a vogue for materialism, while spiritual concepts were denied or ignored.

For many, Charles Darwin's *Origin of Species* offered a satisfactory explanation of how things came to be. The outstanding philosopher of Darwinian materialism was Herbert Spencer. In 1860 he issued the prospectus of his *Synthetic Philosophy*, a ten-volume work upon which he was engaged until 1896.

In his work, Spencer applied Darwin's principle of evolution to philosophy. He held that everything (organic and inorganic) had evolved naturally by a progression from the simple to the complex. To Spencer, society was an evolving organism, religion was nothing more than the worshiping of ancestral ghosts, and the competition and individualism of capitalism was an example of the 'survival of the fittest'. Before World War I, however, it was becoming evident that most philosophers were moving away from the scientific rationalism of the eighteenth and nineteenth centuries. The non-rational side of man was beginning to gain credence, especially through the researches of Sigmund Freud (p.419).

Despite this, there were attempts in philosophy to keep a place for rationalism. In England, Bertrand Russell tried to bring the exactness of mathematics into his philosophy of 'logical atomism'. Russell held that all language was imprecise, because words can be coloured by emotion, by their cultural meanings, and by their history. He therefore developed a mathematical or symbolic logic which would not depend on words. Russell's work was carried further by the Austrian Ludwig Wittgenstein, who declared that since all philosophical problems were in part linguistic problems, clarification of language was the philosopher's main task. Wittgenstein developed a 'logical positivism' which became so rational that it was practically 'anti-rational' in its insistence that most communication in words is meaningless.

Other philosophers, such as Jacques Maritain in France, propounded a Christian philosophy of life. They harked back to the tradition of Thomas Aquinas and appeared as the defenders of human reason against critics of various sorts.

Marxist philosophers, who were the only kind allowed in the Soviet Union, considered themselves materialistic and deterministic in their viewpoint, and scientific and rational in their procedures. However, by the mid-century, the appeal of Marxism was based on political and economic grounds, and not on intellectual or philosophical arguments.

An important twentieth-century school of philosophy was pragmatism. It was essentially American in origin and was developed by such thinkers as Charles Sanders Peirce, William James and John Dewey. The pragmatists held that a theory was 'true if it works'. In other words, any given belief is true only if it has been found to deal successfully with experience. Conversely, the falsity of any ideal is determined by showing that attempts to verify it in experience have failed. Thus, the pragmatists opposed the traditional philosophical view that the truth of ideas is independent of human experience. Beginning with Plato in ancient Greece, all traditional philosophers held that a theory could be true absolutely, irrespective of whether anyone knew it or not.

William James directed much of his pragmatism towards solving certain individual questions of belief. He insisted upon judging religious views by the latest scientific findings. Dewey, on the other hand, regarded his type of pragmatism as having important applications in society. One such application was in the field of education. Dewey felt that previous educational techniques were aimed primarily at inculcating a mass of factual information into students, without giving them any means of putting it into use. They were filled with the experience of the past rather than prepared to meet the problems of the future. Instead, Dewey proposed that the educational system should develop methods of problem-solving that would fit the student for life in a complex society. Dewey's theories on education started the 'progressive education movement', and were put into practice in many parts of the world.

LITERATURE

In the latter part of the nineteenth century there was a growing trend towards realism in literature. But this is not to say that the romantic tradition of the earlier part of the century died out. On the contrary, many writers remained devotees of romantic idealism.

In England Rudyard Kipling produced many stirring stories and poetical praises of British imperialism. Robert Louis Stevenson, in such works as *Treasure Island*, was also in the romantic tradition. In France, Maurice Barrès, in Italy, Gabriele D'Annunzio and in Ireland, the 'Celtic Twilight' authors — Lady Gregory, W.B. Yeats, George Russell, John M. Synge — all wrote romantic prose and poetry.

However, the predominant trend was towards a realistic treatment of man and society. It was born essentially of the grim realities of industrial change — toil, sorrow, slum-dwelling and inequality. This tendency towards realism had already been evident in the great English novelists of the mid-nineteenth century. Charles Dickens, William Thackeray and George Eliot (although retaining romantic elements) depicted real people occupied with day-to-day problems. Dickens exposed the conditions of the working classes of Victorian England with grim humour; Thackeray bitterly satirised the British upper classes; and Eliot dealt with country people in an age of change.

After 1870, realism came steadily to the fore. In France Gustave Flaubert, in *Madame Bovary*, gave an acutely sordid picture of French country life and human passions. Even more realistic were the works of Émile Zola. In the years after 1871 he produced twenty sombre volumes, *Les Rougon-Macquart*, in which he traced the lives of several generations of a French family, portraying every phase of life and society. Anatole France also produced several realistic novels dealing both with contemporary life and historical events. His novel *Le Crime de Sylvestre Bonnard* (1881) is typical of French realism.

In England, George Meredith employed realism in a psychological analysis of his characters. Thomas Hardy in *The Mayor of Casterbridge, Far from the Madding Crowd,* and *Tess of the D'Urbervilles,* studied the fateful workings of the struggle for existence in village and peasant life in the English countryside of 'Wessex'.

George Bernard Shaw, in such dramas as *Heartbreak House, Pygmalion* and *Saint Joan*, reached the high point of social criticism, as did H.G. Wells in his fantasies and novels, especially in *A Modern Utopia.*

In Norway, the playwright Henrik Ibsen brought realism to the stage in such grim dramas as *An Enemy of the People, Ghosts, A Doll's House, The Wild Duck* and *Pillars of Society*.

In Germany Hermann Sudermann wrote plays about city life, while Gerhart Hauptmann gave a realistic presentation of peasant life.

In Russia a whole galaxy of novelists endowed literature with works, many of them terribly realistic in their portrayals of nobles and peasants, officials and intellectuals, gloomy with a presentiment of future catastrophe. Fyodor Dostoevsky, from his own experience of a tsarist prison in Siberia, wrote *The House of the Dead.* His other great novels, *Crime and Punishment, The Idiot, The Devils,* and *The Brothers Karamazov,* give a unique psychological insight into human motivation and into Russian society between 1864 and 1880.

Maxim Gorky, a friend of Lenin, studied in his novels both the life of Russia and social problems. His autobiographical trilogy, *Childhood, In the World,* and *Reminiscences of my Youth,* paints a graphic picture of the contrasts of Russian life. Anton Chekhov, in his plays *The Seagull, Uncle Vanya, The Three Sisters,* and *The Cherry Orchard,* paints an essentially melancholy picture of Russian life. All his plays, despite flashes of humour, display an overwhelming sense of the tedium and futility of life, as if Chekhov could sense the imminence of social upheaval.

But the greatest of all Russian writers was Lev Tolstoy. His novel *War and Peace* is regarded as one of the greatest in any language, and is an immense and incomparable panorama of Russia and family life during and after the Napoleonic invasion. His other great novel, *Anna Karenina,* gives a detailed view of contemporary life in Russia, and of humanity in general. Above all, it gives a deep psychological insight into the tragic conflict between duty and love, and into the tortured search for the meaning of life.

Although the major trend in European literature was realism, there were countertrends as well. One such trend was towards 'symbolism', which sought not a literary exactness but a suggestive use of words. This was exemplified in France by the poetry of Mallarmé and Verlaine, and in England by the prose of Walter Pater and the verse of Algernon Swinburne. Symbolism later degenerated into 'art for art's sake' in a school known as *fin de siècle* (end of the century). The principal exponent of this was Oscar Wilde, whose extreme affectation and wit may be seen in such plays as *The Importance of Being Earnest.* But by the time of World War I, new winds were beginning to blow.

In 1913 Marcel Proust published in France the first volume of his great novel *A La Recherche du Temps Perdu,* of which the seventh did not appear until after his death in 1922. The work was notable for its delicate psychological analysis of character and for its subtle use of symbol and metaphor. During this time W.B. Yeats in Ireland was producing poetry which also involved myth and symbol. But more significant was James Joyce whose *A Portrait of the Artist as a Young Man* (1916) and *Ulysses* (1922) had a profound influence on later writers. In *Ulysses* Joyce keeps the structure of Homer's epic, *The Odyssey,* but tells the story of a single day (16 June 1904) in Dublin, and does so by reproducing the 'stream of consciousness' of the individual mind with all its leaps, quirks, subconscious associations, preoccupations and obscurities.

Yet more microscopic in their psychological analysis were the works of Virginia Woolf, such as *Mrs Dalloway* (1925) and *To the Lighthouse* (1927).

From the 1920s onwards, novels (except those written purely for entertainment) became even more psychological. Many authors used psychoanalytical techniques to probe or display human motives, and symbols rather than expositions to give insights. But each writer showed his own individual variation. Roger du Gard (France) and Sinclair Lewis (America) were more realistic; André Gide (France) more interested in style; Franz Kafka (Czechoslovakia) more enigmatic in his depiction of the alienation of modern man; Ernest Hemingway (America) more preoccupied with war and violence; William Faulkner (America) more fascinated by symbols; and Graham Greene (Britain) more concerned with sin and salvation.

What was true of literature in the twentieth century was also true of drama. Between 1926 and 1940 the American dramatist Eugene O'Neill was the author of many plays which earned him an international reputation. Essentially his plays were grim portrayals of psychological conflicts within the individual. In *Desire Under the Elms* and *Strange Interlude* O'Neill depicts barbarous and primitive egomania in his characters. In *Mourning Becomes Electra, The Iceman Cometh* and *Long Day's Journey into Night* he adopted Freudian insights to contrast outward respectability with the depravity of one's inmost thoughts.

PAINTING

Unlike literature, painting did not tend towards realism, due to the invention of photography. Since the camera could reproduce a scene with absolute exactness, painters, desiring to surpass the camera, were obliged to strive for something more than accuracy.

The major school of painters after 1870 were the French impressionists. These sought by a skilful use of light, shade and colour to give an impression of how an object looked at a fleeting glance. In one sense impressionism was akin to symbolism in literature in that it sought to suggest reality more vividly than could the accuracy of line and brushwork.

The first great names in the school of impressionism were Claude Monet and Auguste Renoir. Soon they attracted a number of artists to Paris who made that city the world's centre of artistic activity. The most prominent of these were Edgar Degas, Édouard Manet, Paul Gauguin and Vincent van Gogh.

In the early twentieth century there soon appeared a new and more advanced school of painting, known as 'cubism'. Influenced by Paul Cézanne's view that everything in nature is reducible to the 'sphere, the cone, and the cylinder', Pablo Picasso, a young Spanish artist working in Paris, began in 1910 to depict things in geometric form. Other artists, such as Georges Braque, Fernand Léger, and Francis Picabia were moving in the same direction. Their paintings tended to minimise colour and maximise shapes, planes and angles.

By the 1920s the cubists, and especially Picasso, were moving in other directions. Nevertheless, cubism continued to have an influence on later developments in painting and in modern design.

A school of painting contemporary with cubism, and not completely dissimilar, was that known as 'futurism'. In 1909 the Italian poet Filippo Tommaso Marinetti called for a new philosophy of art in keeping with advances in technology. He claimed that there was beauty in such things as 'a racing car rattling along like a machine gun'. Influenced by Marinetti, five Italian painters – Umberto Boccioni, Carlo Carrà, Luigi Russolo, Gino Severini, Giacomo Balla — called for a revolt against tradition and advocated the portrayal of machines and motions. As with the cubists, their subjects were often presented as abstractions; but the real emphasis was on colour, rhythm and movement, which conveyed a sense of excitement. The futurist group broke up during World War I, but their influence on later artists was important.

The same period of experiment also witnessed a variety of other 'schools' of painting, the most important of which were 'fauvism' and 'expressionism'.

Fauvism originated in 1906 as a revolt against impressionism and got its name from some critics who derisively called its adherents *fauves* (wild beasts) on seeing their first major exhibition in Paris. The principal fauves were Henri Matisse, Raoul Dufy, George Rouault and André Derain. They used strong, vivid colours to great effect and tended towards abstraction by distortion of line, form and perspective.

Expressionism was a German school that grew up after 1908 under the leadership of Oskar Kokoschka and Max Pechstein. It sought to express personal emotions ranging from mystic tenderness to physical violence. The method used was heightened colour, distorted figures and the elimination of perspective.

After 1922 a new movement known as surrealism grew out of expressionism. The surrealists were influenced by developments in psychology (p.419) and sought in their paintings to plumb the depths of the subconscious mind. Their paintings brought together unlikely and incongruous objects beautifully and accurately painted so that their effect is often that of a dream or nightmare. The most famous of the surrealist painters were Salvador Dali, Joan Miró, and Jean Arp, while Marc Chagall and Giorgio de Chirico were also influenced by it.

SCULPTURE

Sculpture in the twentieth century witnessed the same tendencies as painting. It moved away from realistic representation and towards abstraction. It frequently used distortions and was much influenced by primitive work such as the wood carvings of Africa or Polynesia.

Before 1914 the most famous sculptor was the Frenchman Auguste Rodin (1840–1917), who was both a realist and a romantic. The blurred outlines of his figures emerging from the rough stone suggest an impressionist influence. His *Man with a Broken Nose* is a realistic work, while his *Thinker* suggests the evolution of man.

The Croatian Ivan Mestrović displayed powerful emotions in his work by the technique of distortion.

But the dominant trend was towards abstraction; and this was shown in the work of the Italian Amadeo Modigliani, who developed a type of cubist sculpture using simple geometric forms.

Even more abstract were the works of an American working in London, Jacob Epstein. His sculptures were met initially with derision but later won increasing appreciation.

By 1950 many 'sculptors' had moved into other media and were producing works in varied materials from cement to scrap iron. These works portrayed form or flight or the appearance of motion, but no longer bore any relationship to natural objects. Some works got their effect by lighting while other works were elaborate mathematical constructs of wire and metal.

Viewed in panorama, modern painting and sculpture expressed all the chaos, confusion, dynamism, uncertainty and change of the twentieth century. It revolutionised design and created exciting decorative effects. It served to express the artist's reaction to the world in which he or she lived. It was used as a medium of propaganda. It communicated mood and emotion, but never ideas, for in the final analysis the viewer is free to interpret in his own way without any assurance that he has unlocked the artist's intention.

ARCHITECTURE

Of all the arts in the period before 1914, architecture was the most diverse. A variety of styles — gothic churches, classical temples, Byzantine basilicas, French châteaux, Swiss chalets, Georgian country homes — were evident in many countries. However, public buildings — banks, courts, memorials, city halls, post offices — continued to be erected in one or other of the western traditions, such as classical, neo-classical, gothic, and Georgian.

Examples of the classical mode are the

Supreme Court building in Washington and the War Cenotaph in London; of the romantic gothic mode, the Anglican cathedral in Liverpool and the Riverside Baptist church in New York; of the Byzantine mode, the Russian war memorial in Leipzig and the shrine of the Immaculate Conception in Washington.

In the twentieth century a definite 'modern' architecture developed, and though it varied in expression, the overall tendency was towards 'functionalism', which may be translated as 'the designing and constructing of buildings to accord with their function' and implies 'the maximum use of vertical to avoid the pressure of space at ground level'.

Many of the newer buildings encompassed vertical lines, wide spans, slim supports, and apparently unsupported elements cantilevered out into space. These characteristics were made possible by the exploration and use of new materials such as steel, aluminium, glass and reinforced concrete.

Generally speaking, most of the larger urban constructions erected after 1930, and more especially after 1945, conform exclusively to the style of functionalism. Many of these huge shells of reinforced concrete and large sheets of glass do not conform to the architectural styles of older buildings in their vicinities. The artistic is disregarded, and without grace or beauty, these buildings have been denigrated as 'glass boxes'.

Yet from the very beginning of twentieth-century functionalism, many architects, while accepting the basic tenets of functionalism, sought to exploit and use all the characteristics of the site and its surroundings to accord with the design and construction of the building.

Four such architects were noted for their rejection of the drabness of the purely box-like designs of functionalism. The American Frank Lloyd Wright advocated 'organic' architecture, whereby the design of the building would conform to its location and thus blend with its natural surroundings. His Imperial Hotel in Tokyo (1922) and his spiralled Guggenheim Museum in New York (1959) are typical examples, while his 'prairie homes' were designed long and low to blend with the flat terrain of the American mid-west. The Brazilian architect Oscar Niemeyer was markedly successful in 'beautifying' functionalism. His best work may be seen in the Palace of the Dawn at Brasilia where straight walls of concrete and glass contrast with the curved columns. The Swiss architect Charles Édouard Jeanneret ('Le Corbusier') designed imaginative buildings, often on stilts to create ground-level space and vistas.

Walter Gropius first won his reputation in 1912 with his factory buildings in Germany. He created the Bauhaus Institute of Architecture, first at Weimar (1914) and later (1915) at Dessau. Basically the Bauhaus sought to unite the arts, technology and industry in order to improve the quality of life. In his institute Gropius taught his students that the ideals of architecture should be clarity, straight lines and functional suitability.

The Bauhaus school also greatly influenced the design of furniture, pottery, painting, sculpture, textile weaving and stage design. Gropius made Germany the centre of an exciting new experiment in living and showed that in art and architecture there need be no contradiction between beauty and function. With the advent of Hitler and the Nazis, Gropius could find no place in Germany for his ideas. He emigrated to America where he became professor of architecture at Harvard University from 1937 to 1952. Gropius designed some of the finest modern buildings in America, including the Grand Central Building in New York.

MUSIC

The music composed in Europe between 1870 and 1914 was a mixture of several styles. In general, however, the romantic dominance of the earlier half of the century continued to influence many composers. Stemming from the romantic tradition, a definite national music arose which drew its inspiration from the legends and folklore of national cultures. Towards the end of the century, a post-romantic era began which in turn led to the 'modern' music of the twentieth century.

Romanticism and Nationalism

The nineteenth century was the great age of romanticism (p.1) and the music of the German Richard Wagner represents its most complete expression. He wrote eleven operas, four before 1850 and seven after, and his influence upon subsequent composers lasted well into the twentieth century. Of his pre-1850 group, two are in the French manner while the other two, *The Flying Dutchman* and *Lohengrin*, are German romantic operas. The seven works after 1850 are cast in a new form invented by Wagner — music drama. The most important of these are *Tristan and Isolde*, *Siegfried*, and the most romantic of all operas, *Götterdämmerung* (the Twilight of the Gods).

The music of the German Johannes Brahms is essentially lyrical and romantic in feeling. He was the most considerable writer of romantic chamber music, a feat that is all the more accomplished since the ideals of romanticism do not readily lend themselves to the restrained and intimate nature of music for small ensemble. Brahms also wrote four symphonies, and much piano music which is romantic in mood and design. As a songwriter, Brahms was one of the outstanding writers of German lieder. Many of his 240 songs reflect the serious side of his nature which flowers into rich romanticism in the 'Magelone' song cycle, and finds a mood of restrained intensity in the 'Four Serious Songs'.

As a native Italian opera composer, Giuseppe Verdi was heir to a tradition stretching back to the early seventeenth century. Verdi's work is usually divided into three groups, the first of which contains fifteen operas between 1839 and 1850. During this period Italy was under the domination of Austria, and the Italian national spirit was clamouring for freedom and independence. In 1842 Verdi produced the famous opera *Nabucco*, which deals with the captivity of the Jews at Babylon, and contains the haunting chorus of the hebrew slaves, 'Go thoughts on wings of gold.' This chorus and its composer became a rallying point for the patriotic spirit of Italians. The second period starts with three outstanding works: *Rigoletto*, *II Trovatore*, and *La Traviata*, and finishes with *Aïda* in 1871. The last period produced two remarkable operas of Verdi's old age, *Otello* and *Falstaff*.

Before the middle of the eighteenth century, Russian music sprang from the liturgy of the Greek orthodox church and a strongly established folk culture. But during that century the westernising policies of Peter the Great and later of his grand-daughter Catherine the Great resulted in the formation of the Russian Imperial Ballet, the music for which was imported from Italy. The first composer to attempt a synthesis between the Russian and western traditions was Mikhail Ivanovich Glinka, whose best-remembered works are his two operas, *A Life for the Tsar* (1836) and *Ruslan and Ludmilla* (1842).

In the middle of the nineteenth century, music in Russia began to develop in separate directions. The western tradition was led by the brothers Anton and Nicholas Rubenstein but since neither composer was influential, the development of Russian music remained with the nationalist school. In 1861 a group of five came together with the aim of promoting Russian music. Mily Balakirev was an outstanding pianist and in 1862 founded the St Petersburg Free School of Music. His handling of the folk idiom is best seen in his overture, *Russia – 1,000 Years*. César Cui is the least-known of the group but he served the cause of the others by promoting their interests and making their works known. Alexander Borodin is best remembered for his opera *Prince Igor* and his symphonic poem *In the Steppes of Central Asia*. Modest Mussorgsky is the best-known of the group, principally because of his operatic masterpiece *Boris Godunov*. Nikolay Rimsky-Korsakov later rewrote much of this opera and also contributed two of his own, *Le Coq d'Or* and *Sadko*.

The greatest of all Russian composers was Peter Ilyich Tchaikovsky, and though he is thoroughly Russian, his outlook was cosmopolitan and his mode of expression international. His famous ballets are *Swan Lake*, *The Nutcracker* and *The Sleeping Beauty*, while his best work is probably the opera *Eugene Onegin*.

Two other composers who each carried the romantic tradition into the twentieth century were Sergei Rachmaninov and Alexander Scriabin. Rachmaninov's best-known works are the symphonies *The Isle of the Dead* and *The Bells*, while Scriabin is best remembered for *The Poem of Ecstasy* and *Prometheus*.

The ancient kingdom of Bohemia (now part of Czechoslovakia) produced two outstanding composers of national music. Bedrich Smetana is generally remembered for his symphonic poems and operas by means of which he celebrated his country's history and natural beauty. Smetana wrote eight operas of which the best-known is *The Bartered Bride*, while of his six poems under the title *Má Vlast* (My Country), the most famous is *From Bohemian Fields and Forests*. Antonín Dvorák was of peasant origin, and the simplicity of his life and his love of nature remained with him even when he became famous. Dvorák's desire to honour his native Bohemia with music is seen in his series of operas, the best-known of which is *Russalka*.

The best-known of the Scandinavian composers is the Norwegian Edvard Grieg. He is also distinctly national and through him Norwegian music became a part of western culture. Although a minor composer, Grieg is chiefly remembered for ten books of *Lyric Pieces* for piano, numerous songs, and two orchestral suites from the incidental music to *Peer Gynt*. In Franz Berwald, Sweden produced a composer of note whose six symphonies stand comparison with the best, while of Danish composers, Niels Gade and Carl Nielsen are the better known. Finland produced an outstanding composer in Jan Sibelius, and though his works reflect his native country, they transcend the bounds of nationalism. His symphonic poems are largely based on a collection of folk tales, known as the *Kalevala*, and Finland's desire for independence from Russia. Among thse are *En Saga*, *The Swan of Tuonela*, the *Karelia Suite*, and *Finlandia*, which was considered so nationalist that the tsarist authorities had it banned.

The national music of Spain has long been renowned for its dance rhythms and the cadence of its melodies. The most important Spanish figure in the latter half of the nineteenth century was Felipe Pedrell. He composed six operas and sought to establish a national school of music. Isaac Albéniz from Catalonia is chiefly remembered for his piano music, in particular the colourful set of pieces entitled *Iberia*, which make much use of Spanish dance rhythms. Enrique Granados, also from Catalonia, was primarily a pianist who captured the flavour of music from all parts of Spain. His main works for the piano are contained in *Danzas Españolas*, and *Goyescas*, which were inspired by the paintings of Goya and are tinged with fervour and melancholy.

In Edward Elgar, England produced her only composer of international stature. His music owes much to Wagner and Brahms and his *Pomp and Circumstance* marches are in the romantic tradition. However, it was with *The Dream of Gerontius*, an oratorio in the English tradition, that he achieved international fame. Meanwhile an important part of London's musical life after the 1870s were the operettas of Gilbert and Sullivan at the Savoy theatre. Such operettas as *The Gondoliers*, *Ruddigore* and *The Pirates of Penzance* are beautifully constructed, and contain many songs which are musical gems in their own right.

Two main types of French opera were inherited from the eighteenth century: grand opera, with its serious subjects, choruses and ballets, and *opéra comique*, which was much more lightweight and allowed spoken dialogue. To these a third was added by the German-born Jacques Offenbach. It is named *opéra bouffe* and is characterised by wit and buffoonery. It includes spoken dialogue and its English equivalent is operetta. Between 1840 and 1880 Offenbach wrote over one hundred such operas, the most famous being *Orpheus in the Underworld*, and *La Belle Hélène*, while *The Tales of Hoffman* is in a more serious vein.

With Charles Gounod and Georges Bizet the tradition of opera passed to French composers. With *Faust*, Gounod, taking the plot from Goethe's drama, wrote the best-known lyric opera of the mid-nineteenth century. But the most outstanding French opera of the period was Bizet's *Carmen*, which is the greatest example of *opéra comique*. Following the Franco-Prussian war of 1870 (p.16) the renaissance in French music gathered momentum. In 1871 the establishment of the National Society for French Music resulted in a marked rise, in quality and quantity, in the composition of works other than opera. Composers concerned with this development may be loosely divided into two groups: those following the German tradition, and those with a nationalistic outlook who sought to re-establish the traditional qualities of French music. The German tradition was established by César Franck (who was in fact Belgian) and carried on by some of his pupils such as Vincent d'Indy and Henri Duparc. Those following national tradition stemmed from Camille Saint-Saëns, who was a prolific composer and wrote in a variety of forms. His most familiar work is *Carnival of the Animals*, while of his thirteen operas, the only one which is still current is *Samson et Delilah*.

Post-Romanticism

At the outset of the twentieth century, music moved from late romanticism into what is termed post-romanticism, the chief characteristics of which are rhythmic complexity and tonal instability. The evolution from romanticism to post-romanticism is seen in the music of south German and Austrian composers: Anton Bruckner, Hugo Wolf and Gustav Mahler.

Bruckner is chiefly remembered as a symphonist and celebrates in his music his unswerving faith in God. Wolf composed opera, chamber music and symphonic poems, but his reputation rests essentially on his songs with piano accompaniment. Mahler was fascinated by the soul of man, by suffering and death, but also by the mystical glory of the natural world. His work consists almost entirely of songs and symphonies. The chief source of inspiration for his vocal music was the anthology of German folk-poems, *Des Knaben Wunderhorn* (the Boys' Magic Horn). Mahler's symphonies represent a vision of the world in its entirety: unrelated events, dislocation, beauty, joy and serenity. These include *Lieder eines fahrenden Gesellen* (Songs of a Wayfarer), *Kindertotenlieder* (Songs on the Death of Children), and *Das Lied von der Erde* (the Song of the Earth).

Post-romanticism in Italy continued to be dominated by opera. The achievement of Giuseppe Verdi in the earlier part of the century was succeeded by a style known as *verismo* (realism). The plots of such operas were concerned with the seamy side of modern life. Two such operas are Pietro Mascagni's *Cavalleria Rusticana* and Ruggiero Leoncavallo's *Pagliacci* (Clowns). Giacomo Puccini's operas were also immensely popular. At the turn of the century he produced such well-known works as *La Bohème*, *Tosca* and *Madame Butterfly*.

Modern Music

In the twentieth century, music displayed conflicting tendencies. Some classical music inherited from the eighteenth century and some romantic music from the nineteenth

A popular dance band of the 1930s.

century continued as a feature of operatic and concert performances. But as the twentieth century progressed, another kind of 'modern music' began to gain acceptance at serious concerts. Young composers began experimenting with dissonance and unusual scales and became more daring in their approach. Already in the late nineteenth century, Claude Debussy in his *L'Après-Midi d'un Faune* had introduced impressionism into his music, and may be called the father of 'modern' music.

In 1910 the Russian Igor Stravinsky caused a sensation with his *Firebird*, and again in 1913 with his *Rite of Spring*. In the ensuing years, a series of composers experimented with the traditional musical forms and techniques, and some even sought to introduce factory sounds or new electronic effects into their music.

Some composers, such as the Russians Dimitri Shostakovich and Sergei Prokofiev, the German Paul Hindemith, and the American Walter Piston, created works that were experimental, though recognisably connected with the older musical tradition. Others, such as the Hungarian Béla Bartók were highly individualistic in their creations. Still others, especially the Austrian Arnold Schoenberg, sought greater freedom for their works, which were subjective, emotionally violent and even neurotic. Schoenberg used the twelve notes of the diatonic scale in a particular way that gave new direction to music. He called his music 'non-tonal' because it had no fixed key and his system was adopted by Stravinsky, Bartók and the American Roger Sessions.

Many composers fitted musical styles to the harmonies and rhythms of native folk music. In England Ralph Vaughan Williams, and in America Charles Ives, helped to promote the revival of national music. But though the romantic and national music continued to inspire and remain popular with concert audiences, the general direction taken by music in the twentieth century was towards primitive rhythms and chaotic dissonances. This was especially true of non-classical music from about 1930 onwards. Historians in attempting to account for this generally attribute it to the reflection of the restlessness and disillusionment of the young of the twentieth century.

Jazz was the most durable of all twentieth-century musical styles, but though its devotees were drawn from many musical cultures, appealing equally to the layman and the professionally trained, it has always been a minority interest among musicians. The elements of jazz are clearly defined.

First, it is a style of *playing* rather than a style of *composition*. Thus the names associated with jazz are not so much composers as performer-interpreters. Secondly, an important constituent of jazz is the element of *improvisation* which distinguishes one performance from another. Largely for this reason, the history of jazz exhibits a startling rapidity of stylistic change.

It originated in America from negro songs. These existed in the form of work songs, play songs in which the 'blues' were prominent, and religious songs which included the spiritual. The term 'blues' refers to an expressive mood, usually one of melancholy, initially associated with negro slavery but transferred in jazz to express the general suffering of mankind. Another negro contribution to jazz was ragtime, a piano music, the leading exponent of which was Scott Joplin.

By 1900 in New Orleans a definite 'jazz style' was fully apparent. This style, which lasted until about 1920, is now known as 'traditional jazz'. It was played in small groups, in which the main instruments were one or two cornets or trumpets, a trombone and a clarinet. During the second half of this traditional period, a more bland style arose. It was performed by white musicians and is known as Dixieland.

In the 1920s the New Orleans musicians moved to Chicago taking their jazz style with them. There they developed an extrovert 'Chicago style' from which dates the introduction of the saxophone into the jazz ensemble. Chief among these players was Louis Armstrong ('Satchmo'), who is generally regarded as one of the foremost of all jazz musicians. W.C. Handy's *St Louis Blues* and George Gershwin's *Rhapsody in Blue* have also become accepted as 'classics' of jazz.

With the development of the phonograph and the radio, jazz became popular in Europe and throughout the world. Even in the Soviet Union, where there was a strong tendency to regard jazz as 'American and degenerate', it eventually had its following among the young.

Jazz also had its many sub-groups: 'hot', 'sweet', 'boogie-woogie'. Each of these in turn enjoyed a certain, if transient, popularity, which seemed to transcend cultural and ideological differences. The 1920s was the period of boogie-woogie, a blues-based piano style. The 1930s was the era of 'swing' and of the 'big band'. During this time, piano-playing gained prominence. It reached a point of sophistication in the playing of Earl Hines and was further developed by Duke Ellington.

Modern jazz developed in the 1950s and started as a reaction against swing and big band. It became known as 'bebop' and one of its main centres was at Minton's Playhouse, a night-club in New York. It produced some outstanding musicians such as Thelonius Monk (piano), Kenny Clarke (drums), Dizzy

Gilespie (trumpet), and Charles Parker (alto sax).

CULTURAL DEVELOPMENTS AFTER 1945

After the horrors of World War II, a cultural pessimism settled across Europe. Many of Europe's intellectuals came to believe that if the land which produced Goethe and Schiller, Bach and Beethoven, could also produce Auschwitz and Dachau, Belsen and Buchenwald, then there was little hope for mankind.

Philosophy

In philosophy the most appropriate response to post-war pessimism was existentialism. Although it had been formulated many years before the war in the works of Soren Kierkegaard, Friedrich Nietzsche and Martin Heidegger, it was only in the post-war climate of disillusionment that it gained a ready acceptance. The existentialists rejected all rational and scientific explanations of the universe and held that the world was absurd and incomprehensible. They claimed that all facts were suspect, that all knowledge was relative, and that the individual was alone and isolated in a meaningless world. The most outstanding exponent of existentialism in the post-war world was the Frenchman Jean-Paul Sartre. He held that man must find his own meaning in this meaningless world; and since God and reason were dead, the individual must adjust himself to his absurd existence. To free oneself from this absurdity, Sartre claimed that one must make choices and act upon them. Acting creates values (essences) and existence is given meaning through commitment; hence human beings are essentially what they make of themselves.

Sartre's own commitment was to communism and this greatly undermined the individualism of existentialism. Moreover, rapid post-war reconstruction led, by the 1950s, to reduced adherence to such a 'meaningless' philosophy. Many intellectuals were no longer able to accept Sartre's pessimistic view of existence, his rejection of bourgeois society and values, and his uncritical commitment to communism.

With the undermining of existentialism, no major movement emerged to replace it for over a decade. In the 1960s a new movement called structuralism emerged. Its adherents held that humanity's choices were determined by the existing structure of the basic units in a society. By understanding the relationship of the various units, truth would emerge. The father of structuralism was the anthropologist Claude Lévi-Strauss. He held that all societies have similar underlying mental structures, apparent in their myths, that guide them. However, Lévi-Strauss never found the key that would unlock these basic components of all societies. Despite this, he has influenced many scholars, in various fields, to search for underlying structures. This has been especially true in the fields of psychology and language studies.

Literature

In literature post-war Europe witnessed the spread of two trends or moods. In the immediate aftermath of the war, a common theme among writers was disgust with European civilisation brought on by fascism and the war, and by the economic and moral poverty of the pre-war period. Such literature was essentially existentialist in that it focused on the bleaker aspects of life — crime, inhumanity, poverty and despair.

Albert Camus, Jean-Paul Sartre, and Simone de Beauvoir (all from France) searched in their works for meaning in what they regarded as an absurd world. They passionately attacked the bourgeoisie, whom they blamed for all the ills of the world, by writing novels the middle class would not understand or enjoy. And although they retained (for the most part) the form and language of the novel, these writers altered the content away from traditional entertaining plots and character portrayal to what they saw as a realistic depiction of sad humanity. Sartre's series of novels known collectively as *The Paths to Liberty* and Camus's *The Stranger* and *The Plague* are in this genre.

One of the most important works of twentieth-century drama was Samuel Beckett's *Waiting for Godot*, which carried the existentialist theme to the point of absurdity. The play in which 'nothing happens, nobody goes, it's awful' presents two decrepit tramps waiting by the roadside for someone (Godot) who will alter their lives by turning up. He never does.

In Germany and Italy literature was committed to eradicating the things in their past that had led to fascism. German writers such as Günter Grass, Heinrich Böll and Wolfgang Borchert described the moral and political degradation of Germany by bringing Germans face-to-face with Nazism. Borchert in *The Man Outside* described the loneliness and despair of a soldier returning home after the war. Grass, in *The Tin Drum*, has a dwarf tell about the moral inadequacies of the bourgeoisie before and during the war. Böll, in *Acquainted With the Night* and *House without Keeper*, focused on the physical and psychological scars wrought by Nazism and war. The most famous of the many German dramatists, Carl Zuckmayer, described anti-Nazi resistance in his plays, *The Devil's General* and *Chorus in the Pyre*.

In Italy writers adopted a bleak realism to paint the moral, political and social inadequacies of Italy before and during the Mussolini period. Carlo Levi's *Christ Stopped at Eboli* depicted the problem of poverty in southern Italy. Others adopted a communist perspective in their works. Elio Vittorini's *Hero of Our Time* has the main character murder his mistress as a logical outcome of his bourgeois social-political upbringing.

In Britain, the first post-war decade produced no new literary movement. Her major writers — George Orwell, Graham Greene, Evelyn Waugh, T.S. Eliot and E.M. Forster — were too individualistic to become part of any new literary school. Communism was not a major influence. On the contrary, George Orwell in *Animal Farm* and in *1984* attacked communism as it had developed in Soviet Russia. Moreover, Britain had not experienced pre-war political and social problems on the scale experienced on the continent, while her post-war welfare state programme (p.365) greatly limited the despair, or need for action, felt by writers in Europe.

However, in the late 1950s Britain did produce a new literary movement of considerable importance. A group of writers, known as the 'angry young men' or 'kitchen-sink school', were alienated by the consumer society and class distinctions the welfare state was producing. Kingsley Amis in *Lucky Jim* poked fun at the class pretensions in British society. Alan Sillitoe in *Saturday Night and Sunday Morning* depicted a working-class world devoid of any real meaning, while John Osborne in *Look Back in Anger* went beyond criticism of class barriers to depict a dehumanised working-class world that had lost all meaning. In the 1960s a new generation, dissatisfied with the reforms of the welfare state and alarmed by the spread of nuclear weapons, turned to a more radical opposition.

Some writers, repelled by this 'new left' opposition, turned in the other direction. Kingsley Amis in *Lucky Jim* attacked political socialism. Doris Lessing wrote of her disillusionment with Marxism in her cycle of novels, *Children of Violence*. Most writers, however, adhered to the 'new left' movement, especially those on the continent such as Herbert Marcuse, György Lukács, and Antonio Gramsci. Their basic theme was man's alienation in a world of plenty. For instance, Marcuse in *One-Dimensional Man* argued that though the mass consumer society satisfied man's material needs, it impoverished his spiritual, intellectual and cultural needs.

In the Soviet Union, literature during Stalin's era was dicated by social realism, which stressed Russian chauvinism, hatred of

Alexander Solzhenytzin after his exile from the Soviet Union.

outsiders, praise for the new Soviet man, and glorification of Stalin. But with the death of Stalin in 1953, Soviet writers were allowed greater freedom of expression. The first great work to break with social realism was Boris Pasternak's *Doctor Zhivago*. But Pasternak's depiction of Zhivago as an apolitical figure was far too inconsistent with Soviet man's commitment to socialism and, as a result, he was refused permission to accept the Nobel prize for literature in 1958.

Despite this, however, Khrushchev's continuing need to check his Stalinist opponents (p.395) led him to support works that exposed the horrors of Stalin's rule. As a result, he approved the publication in 1962 of Alexander Solzhenytsin's *One Day in the Life of Ivan Denisovich*. In this work, Solzhenytsin not only exposed the cruelty of Stalin's rule and the degradation of Soviet labour camps, but also brought to light the skills of one of the most gifted literary figures in post-war Russia. This, and subsequent works such as *The First Circle*, *Cancer Ward*, and *The Gulag Archipelago*, continued to expose the Stalinist regime and also established Solzhenytsin as a world-renowned novelist. A lesser-known novelist, Ilya Ehrenburg, in *The Thaw*, reinforced Solzhenytsin in denouncing the rule of Stalin.

During the Khrushchev years poetry also broke away from social realism. Yevgeny Yevtushenko was highly critical of the Stalin period while the balladeer Bulat Okudzhava was deeply rooted in the Russian tradition, and not in social realism. But the most significant poet was Joseph Brodsky who followed the tradition of Pushkin and Akhmatova. His poetry dealt with the eternal questions of death, loneliness and suffering; but because it had no utilitarian purpose, it was not favoured by the Soviet regime.

Though Khrushchev allowed an unprecedented level of cultural freedom, it was still exceedingly narrow by western standards. Therefore, when the forum provided by Khrushchev proved too limited for the expression of ideas, writers turned to *samizdat*, an underground literature that circulated among intellectuals.

The Brezhnev era brought an end to cultural freedom, and Soviet artists experienced renewed repression. Artists were sent to forced labour camps for publishing outside the Soviet Union while others were forced into exile by the KGB. In fact, by the 1970s, the Soviet Union was unique in that her greatest literary figures were in exile.

Music

The technological revolution of the twentieth century affected post-war avant-garde music with the introduction of electronic devices. The development of these new resources came from France, in the form of 'musique concrète'. Sounds of everyday life were pre-recorded and then manipulated in various combinations, at different speeds, to form a work of art. The first such composition was issued in 1948 by Pierre Schaffer.

Meanwhile the idea that all aspects of a performance may be controlled gave way to a method of composition in which none of them is controlled. The name given to this type of composition is 'aleatory' (from the Latin for 'dice'), though its chief exponent, John Cage, preferred to name it 'indeterminacy'. Cage's method may be seen in *Concert for Piano and Orchestra* (1958), a work that combines percussive sounds, electronic sounds, and aleatory music. The pianist's part is made up of 84 different compositions, which he is free to play in any order, in whole or in part, or not at all.

Side by side with the development of electronic and aleatory music there was a return to large-scale, live, fully composed works which took advantage of avant-garde developments. A strong school of such composers emerged in Poland. Witold Lutoslawski achieved recognition for such atonal works as *Concerto for Orchestra* (1954). Krzysztof Penderecki, the best-known of the younger generation of composers, created intense and dramatic effects from an interesting juxtaposition of sound-masses in such works as *Threnody for the Victims of Hiroshima* (1960) and *St Luke's Passion*. Although certain works of the avant-garde, such as *Le Marteau Sans Maître*, became part of musical history, much 6emained experimental and addressed to a limited audience.

Post-war music for a mass audience was found in the 'pop culture' which arose in the 1960s. 'Rock and roll' was based upon a strong social awareness; and though it made use of traditional tonality, it was much indebted to the new technology with its use of electric instruments, synthesisers, live amplification and use of multi-track recording media. It was given reality by a series of composer-author-performers, and the 'Beatles' were crucial to its development. Their range of composition extended to all forms of pop music combined with elements of chamber music and vaudeville, while their songs combined melodic invention with a precise feeling for tonal harmony. With the break-up of the Beatles, the classical period of pop music came to an end, and since then it continues to exist in a variety of styles.

Cinema

For the general mass of people (and many intellectuals also) the post-war cinema came to replace literature and theatre as their main source of drama. Many artists chose the cinema in an effort to reach a wider audience and because they believed that the creative potential of the cinema was greater than that of the theatre.

In general, the post-war cinema fell into two phases: the Italian realist ascendancy immediately after the war, and the French 'new wave' predominance beginning in the mid-1950s. The Italian realist school had no equal in Europe and graphically revealed the poverty, political corruption and decadence of past and contemporary Italy. Roberto Rossellini in *Rome Open City* (1945) and *Paisa* (1946) fully exploited the possibilities of the cinema to depict Italy's suffering under Nazi occupation in 1943–44. Rossellini's object was not to entertain the audience but to shock them into full realisation. Vittorio De Sica followed Rossellini with *Shoeshine* (1946) in which he depicted society's inhumane treatment of two boys caught up in the post-war black market. This was followed by *The Bicycle Thief* (1948), where De Sica explores the plight of a man in his attempts to recover his stolen bicycle, which he desperately needs in order to take a job as a postman, and the anguish he feels at society's insensitivity to his plight. Luchino Visconti took a Marxist view of society and dealt with the class divisions that inhibit the poor from escaping their condition. In *The Earth Trembles* (1947) he depicted the overpopulation, grinding poverty and violence of rural Italy.

By the mid-1950s, post-war reconstruction and growing prosperity led to a reduced interest in films which dealt only with the harsh brutality and negative aspects of life. As a result, Italian directors such as Federico Fellini began a shift towards a more imaginative style, but by then it was the French cinema that was attracting the attention of Europeans.

During the 1930s French cinema had dominated European film-making; but in the decade after the war, the French cinema had declined considerably. Then in the mid-1950s a group of former film critics turned to film-making and ushered in an era of French dominance once again. Cultural historians generally categorise these new film-makers as the 'new wave', though in fact they differed in approach from each other.

The first commercially successful 'new wave' film was Roger Vadim's *And God Created Woman* (1956). The star was his wife, Brigitte Bardot, who played the part of a sensual 'emancipated' young woman.

Louis Malle concentrated on controversial topics such as poverty, suicide and incest. In his *Lacombe Lucien* a French boy joins the Nazi occupation forces and the audience is made to see how people with no political beliefs became Nazis. Jean-Luc Godard took an ideological view and attacked what he saw as a dehumanised modern world. In *Alphaville* (1964) he attacked the mechanisation of bourgeois life, and in *Weekend* (1967) he attacked its meaninglessness and materialism.

Some French directors made the film an intensely creative process and were concerned with 'film for film's sake' rather than with making a political or social statement. Francois Truffaut concentrated on human relationships and the theme of love. Four of his films however were semi-autobiographical and dealt with social roles – *The 400 Blows*, *Stolen Kisses*, *Bed and Board*, *Love and Run*.

In Germany the first two post-war decades of film-making produced escapist and imitative films that made little contribution to the art of the cinema. But starting in 1965 a renaissance in German cinema began. Schlondorff adapted Robert Musil's novel for his *Young Torless* (1966) in which he juxtaposes the psychological strains of life in a boy's school and life in Nazi Germany.

But perhaps the greatest giant of film-making was Ingmar Bergman, whose individualistic style makes his work difficult to categorise. Bergman's exploration of the nature of interpersonal relations, evil, suffering, death, and the meaning of existence, raised the art of the cinema to unprecedented heights. In one of his greatest films, *The Seventh Seal* (1956), a mediaeval knight gambles with death in order to have time to consider the value of living. In *Wild Strawberries* (1957) an old doctor faces death and tries to determine if his life has been of any use. In *The Virgin Spring* (1959) Bergman treats the subject of youthful innocence, evil and retribution, through the story of a daughter's rape and murder, and how it is avenged by her father in a most brutal manner. In *Persona* (1967) Bergman studies interpersonal relationships through a nurse and a mentally disturbed actress who has refused to speak for years since she believes that life has no meaning.

In the Soviet bloc countries a great outpouring of imaginative cinema began following the death of Stalin. The film industries remained nationalised, but despite this they served as a vehicle for social criticism and ideological debate during the period of de-Stalinisation (p.398).

In Poland, Andrzey Wajda's realist films, *A Generation* (1954), *Canal* (1956) and *Ashes and Diamonds* (1958) established his reputation as one of Europe's major directors. A decade later a number of directors, such as Roman Polanski and Jerzy Skilinowski, emerged but were forced out of Poland by re-Stalinisation (p.407).

In Czechoslovakia the film industry profited greatly from the liberalisation period prior to 1968. A Czechoslovak 'new wave' produced an impressive list of world-renowned directors and films. Vera Chytilova produced *Daisies* (1966) and *The Fruit of Paradise* (1969). Jaromi Jires established his reputation with *The First Cry* (1963), and *The Joke* (1958). Elmar Klos and Jan Kadar co-directed *Shop on Main Street* (1965), and *Adrift* (1971). Kiri Menzel directed *Closely Observed Trains* (1966) and *Capricious Summer* (1967). Milos Forman established himself with *Fireman's Ball* (1967).

With the Soviet crackdown in Czechoslovakia in August 1968 (p.401), Czechoslovak liberalism died and Kadar, Forman and others were forced to flee the country. In Hungary the period after Stalin's death (1953) until the Soviet invasion in 1956 (p.399) allowed sufficient freedom for creative cinema to emerge. Directors aimed at innovation in form and technique and attacked authoritarianism, political terror and bureaucracy. Andras Kovac's *Difficult People* (1964), and Miklos Jancso's *In the Round* (1965) and *Silence and Cry* (1968) were in this vein. In the remaining eastern European countries, with the possible exception of Yugoslavia, films failed to reach the creative heights of western Europe.

CONCLUSION

Thus by the 1960s it was clear that all the arts had changed dramatically from what they had been in the 1870s. A critic from the 1870s would scarcely have recognised as art, much less have understood, much of the painting, sculpture, poetry, or music of the 1960s.

All the arts had come to reflect the uncertainty and tension of their times. Moreover, they were reflecting the industrial society of which they too were a part. But the arts also profited from the great changes that had taken place. Better educational facilities and increased leisure time had opened up the opportunity for many people to enjoy or even practise the arts. In addition, radio, films and television brought within the reach of almost everyone what had previously been available only to an elite. Thus, if motion pictures and television performances were often superficial and tawdry, they also made good drama and music available to millions. Similarly, colour television productions made the art of the past ages, distributed and scattered throughout the world, accessible to vast audiences. In this manner, the modern world was unique in that for the first time the arts of all the ages became accessible to all.

Study Assignments and Essays

1. *What were the main philosophical trends in the period 1870–1966?*
2. *Why was there a growing trend towards realism in literature in the late nineteenth century?*

3. 'In the period 1870–1966, painting developed in many directions.' Discuss.
4. Treat of the main developments in architecture in the period 1870–1966.
5. 'In the period after 1945, the cinema became an "art form" in itself.' Discuss.

6. Write an essay on two of the following:
(i) Literature in the twentieth century; (ii) Sculpture in the twentieth century; (iii) Developments in music 1870–1966; (iv) Existentialism; (v) Cultural trends in the Soviet Bloc, 1945–66.

Glossary of Historical Concepts and Terms

Abdication	Renouncing the throne.
Absolutism	No limit to a ruler's power.
Acculturation	The process whereby a native culture becomes diluted in the face of a stronger culture — usually that of an occupying power.
Amnesty	The granting of a pardon to a political prisoner.
Anarchism	A political belief that advocates the abolition of all organised authority and its replacement by a free association of individuals.
Apartheid	The segregation, on racial grounds, of a particular group from the dominant group.
Appeasement	The granting of limited demands to one's political opponents in order to avoid conflict.
Attrition	The wearing down of an enemy by the sheer weight of numbers.
Autocracy	A system of government where the ultimate authority rests with one person.
Autonomy	Self-government, with or without restrictions.
Bolshevism	A Russian version of communism. The Bolsheviks were the majority group of Marxists who emerged from the split in the Social Democratic Party in 1903.
Bourgeoisie	A term applied by Karl Marx to the middle classes.
Bureaucracy	Government by a centralised administration relying heavily on a vast civil service.
Collective Security	The policy that 'an attack upon one is an attack upon all'.
Collectivisation	The system of forcing farmers to join together and farm their lands communally.
Commissar	The Soviet name for a government minister.
Communism	The political doctrine espoused by Karl Marx, which states that all the means of production, distribution and exchange should be held in common.
Concordat	A treaty between a temporal power and the papacy concerning ecclesiastical affairs.
Confederation	A political organisation consisting of several states loosely connected, yet each with a measure of independence.
Conservatism	The political doctrine which states that changes in society must come very slowly.
Constitutionalism	The practice by which the powers of government are subordinate to a set of fundamental rules, usually set out in a constitution.
Corporate State	A state organised into corporations or large units of similar economic activity, which the state controls.
Demagogy	An appeal to the prejudices of the masses by a

popular leader.

Demilitarised Zone — An area in which military buildings, armaments, personnel or operations are forbidden.

Democracy — A system whereby the ultimate authority rests with the people though the ballot box.

Demography — The science that deals with trends and other factors in population.

Détente — The practice of establishing a friendly understanding with a rival power.

Devaluation — The policy of reducing a currency *vis à vis* other currencies.

Disarmament — A reduction or limitation in the production of the weapons of war.

Existentialism — A modern philosophical school that gained in popularity after World War II. It holds that man's own personal experiences are of fundamental importance, and that man must make personal choices and assume individual responsibility in an absurd world.

Extradition — The returning of an offender to the country of his crime.

Fascism — The political creed founded by Mussolini in 1919, which was characterised by ultra-nationalism, anti-communism, and authoritarianism.

Fifth Column — Term used to describe collaborators with the enemy.

Genocide — The deliberate extermination of a race of people.

Gerrymander — The manipulation of electoral districts in order to gain an undemocratic advantage.

Gold Standard — The international monetary system operating up to 1914, whereby the major currencies (pound sterling, dollar, mark) were valued in terms of gold.

Hegemony — A powerful influence extended by one state over another, yet not extending to annexation.

Imperialism — The practice of a state expanding politically and/or economically beyond its own borders.

Industrialisation — The process whereby the economy moves from an agricultural to an industrial base.

Inflation — A rise in the level of prices with a corresponding fall in the value of money, not due to a rise in imports or in production costs.

Insurrection — An armed revolt against the established order.

Iron Curtain — A metaphor used by Joseph Goebbels, and later adopted by Winston Churchill to describe the division of Europe into the Soviet-dominated East, and the West.

Jingoism	Excessive and bellicose patriotism.
Junker	A Prussian aristocrat and landowner.
Kolkhoz	A collective farm in the Soviet Union.
Kulak	A relatively well-off, land-holding peasant prevalent in Russia before 1928.
Kulturkampf	'Struggle for civilisation'. The term applied to the church-state conflict in Bismarck's Germany.
Laissez-Faire	The absence of state control over the economy.
Lebensraum	'Living space'. The term used by Hitler to denote his intention of expanding eastwards.
Liberalism	The political doctrine that advocates political and economic freedom. It is usually associated with *laissez-faire* capitalism.
Marxism	See communism.
Menshevism	A Russian version of communism. The Mensheviks were the minority group that emerged after the split in the Social Democratic Party in 1903.
Mir	A village commune in tsarist Russia.
Mobilisation	The placing of the armed forces on a war footing.
Nationalisation	The acquisition by the state of any property or means of production in order to use its resources for the benefit of the nation.
Nationalism	The desire of people united by ties of language, race, or religion, to be joined together under a single government.
Nazism	The German version of fascism.
Neutrality	Non-participation in a war between states.
Nihilism	A philosophical outlook that recognises no authority, doubts every value and stands for the freedom of the individual.
Oligarchy	Rule by an elite.
Ostpolitik	West German policy advocating closer ties with the countries of eastern Europe.
Pan-Slavism	The movement to unite and liberate the Slav races of eastern Europe from Turkish control.
Passive Resistance	Non-co-operation with the ruling power in order to gain an objective.
Plebiscite	A direct vote of the adult population of a region in order to decide a matter of fundamental importance, such as self-determination.
Pogrom	A Russian word, first used to describe mass organised attacks upon Jews.
Politburo	The political committee of the Soviet Communist Party.
Political Asylum	The granting of refuge to a non-national.

Proletariat	The Marxist term for the working classes.
Proportional Representation	An electoral system whereby votes are cast in order of preference to ensure a fairer distribution of seats among all parties.
Putsch	A German word meaning revolt or coup.
Quisling	A traitor. Originated during World War II from the collaborationist activities of Vidkun Quisling in Norway.
Radicalism	The belief in extensive political, economic and social reforms, going to the very roots of society.
Rapprochement	The coming together of states, formerly antagonistic, in order to establish better relations.
Referendum	A direct vote of the electorate to give authority, or otherwise, to a government to institute fundamental changes in the law.
Refugee	One who flees his homeland for political reasons.
Republicanism	The belief in having no hereditary ruler, generally associated with democracy.
Revisionism	The modification of a political doctrine in the light of changing circumstances.
Right-Wing	A political term associated with conservative or reactionary parties.
Russification	The process of turning non-Russian people into 'Russians' in thought, language, and allegiance. (See acculturation.)
Sabotage	The deliberate destruction of property, usually for political reasons.
Self-determination	The policy proposed by the American president, Woodrow Wilson, for drawing the political map of Europe according to the wishes of racial groups.
Socialism	The political and economic theory according to which the means of production, distribution and exchange should be owned and controlled by the people.
Suffragette	A female advocate of the movement for women's suffrage (the right to vote).
Syndicalism	A form of socialism that aims at the ownership and control of all industries by the workers.
Totalitarianism	State control over the private and public lives of the population.
Unilateral Declaration	A political declaration taken without the consent of other political parties or partners.
Veto	The right to say no to a political demand. A clause in an agreement that gives 'blocking power' to one group.

Welfare State — A state that provides for the social security (pensions, unemployment benefits, medical services) of all its members.

Zionism — The belief in the establishment of a Jewish state in Palestine.

Suggestions for Further Reading

GENERAL

Derry, T.K. and T.L. Jarman, *The European World, 1870–1971*, Bell, 1968.
Isaac, M.L.R., *A History of Europe*, Edward Arnold, 1970.
Larkin, M., *Gathering Pace*, Macmillan, 1969.
Stokes, J. and G., *Europe and the Modern World 1870–1983*, Longman, 1983.
Tierney, M., *Europe Since 1870*, Fallon, 1984.
Thompson, D., *Europe Since Hitler*, Longman, 1962.

AUSTRIA-HUNGARY

MacCartney, C.A., *The Hapsburg Empire, 1790–1918*, Weidenfeld & Nicolson, 1968.
May, A.J., *The Hapsburg Monarchy, 1866–1914*, Harvard University Press, 1951.
Taylor, A.J.P., *The Hapsburg Monarchy 1809–1918*, Hamish Hamilton, 1948.
Zeman, Z.A.R., *The Break up of the Hapsburg Empire, 1914–1918*, Oxford University Press, 1961.

THE BALKANS

Forster, E.S., *Short History of Modern Greece, 1821–1956*, Methuen, 1957.
Lewis, B., *The Emergence of Modern Turkey*, Oxford University Press, 1965.
Medlicott, W.H., *The Congress of Berlin and After*, Methuen, 1938.
Remak, J., *Sarajevo*, Weidenfeld & Nicolson, 1959.
Seton-Watson, H., *Eastern Europe between the Wars, 1918–1941*, Cambridge University Press, 1945.
Stavrianos, W.H., *The Congress of Berlin and After*, Methuen, 1938.
Temperley, H.W.V., *History of Serbia*, Bell, 1917.

BRITAIN

Cootes, R.J., *Britain Since 1700*, Longman, 1970.
Ensor, R., *England 1870–1914*, Oxford University Press, 1968.
Gilbert, M., *Winston Churchill*, Oxford University Press, 1966.
Hussey, W.D., *The British Empire and Commonwealth*, Cambridge University Press, 1975.
Lane, P., *Trade Unions*, Batsford, 1969.
Lloyd, T.O., *Empire to Welfare State: English History, 1906–1976*, Oxford University Press, 1979.
Mowat, C.L., *Lloyd George*, Oxford University Press, 1966.
Pelling, H., *Modern Britain, 1885–1955*, Sphere Books, 1969.
Reader, W.J., *Life in Victorian Britain*, Batsford, 1964.
Robbin, K., *The Eclipse of a Great Power: Modern Britain, 1870–1975*, Longman, 1983.
Seaman, L.C.B., *Life in Britain between the Wars*, Wayland, 1970.
— *Post Victorian Britain*, Methuen, 1967.
Taylor, A.J.P., *English History, 1914–1945*, Penguin, 1978.
Thompson, D., *England in the Nineteenth Century 1815–1914*, Penguin, 1974.
Wright, C., *The Working Class*, Batsford, 1972.

FRANCE

Brabant, F.H., *The Beginnings of the Third Republic in France*, Macmillan, 1940.
Brogan, D.W., *The Development of Modern France, 1870–1939*, Harper Torchbooks, 1966.
Bury, J.P.T., *France 1814–1940*, University Paperback, 1960.
Cobban, A., *A History of Modern France, Vol. III: 1871–1962*, Penguin, 1977.
Chapman, G., *The Third Republic, 1871–1894*, Macmillan, 1962.

Edwards, S. (ed.), *The Communards of Paris, 1871*, Thames & Hudson, 1973.
Howard, M., *The Franco-Prussian War*, Hart-Davis, 1961.
Lough, J. and M., *An Introduction to Nineteenth Century France*, Longman, 1978.
MacManners, J., *Church and State in France, 1870–1914*, SPCK, 1972.
Thompson, D., *Democracy in France Since 1870*, Oxford University Press, 1964.
Tint, H., *Modern France*, Hamish Hamilton, 1966.
Waght, G., *France in Modern Times*, John Murray, 1960.
Zeldin, T., *France, 1848–1945: Politics and Anger*, Oxford University Press, 1979.

GERMANY

Brandenburg, E., *From Bismarck to World War One*, Oxford University Press, 1927.
Bullock, A., *Hitler and Germany*, Longman, 1966.
Childs, D., *Germany since 1918*, Batsford, 1980.
Corkery, J.F. and R.C. Stone, *The Weimar Republic and the Third Reich*, Heinemann, 1981.
Coveney, D.K., *Bismarck and Europe*, Edward Arnold, 1971.
Craig, G.A., *Germany 1866–1945*, Oxford University Press, 1981.
Elliot, B.J., *Hitler and Germany*, Longman, 1966.
—*Bismarck, the Kaiser and Germany*, Longman, 1972.
Eyck, E., *A History of the Weimar Republic*, Oxford University Press, 1962.
Gray, P., *Weimar Culture*, Secker & Warburg, 1969.
Hiden, J.W., *The Weimar Republic*, Longman, 1974.
Kurtz, H., *The Second Reich: Kaiser Wilhelm II and His Germany*, Macdonald, 1970.
Kochan, L. *The Struggle for Germany, 1914–1918*, Macmillan, 1965.
Shirer, W.L., *The Rise and Fall of the Third Reich*, Secker & Warburg, 1960.
Stone, N., *Hitler*, Hodder and Stoughton, 1982.
Williamson, D.G., *The Third Reich*, Longman, 1982.
Wilson, E. (ed.), *The Road to Dictatorship—Germany, 1918–1933*, Wolfe, 1970.

ITALY

Absolom, R.N.L., *Mussolini and the Rise of Italian Fascism*, Methuen, 1971.
Bayne-Jardine, C.C., *Mussolini and Italy*, Longman, 1966.
Halpern, S.W., *Mussolini and Italian Fascism*, Van Nostrand, 1964.
Leeds, C., *Italy under Mussolini*, Wayland, 1972.
MacSmith, D., *Italy, 1860–1960*, Manchester University Press, 1954.
— *Mussolini*, Granada, 1983.
Purcell, H., *Fascism*, Hamish Hamilton, 1972.
Whyte, A.J., *The Evolution of Modern Italy, 1770–1920*, Blackwell, 1944.

RUSSIA

Carr, E.H., *The Russian Revolution from Lenin to Stalin, 1917–1928*, Macmillan, 1979.
Carrère d'Encausse, H., *Stalin: Order Through Terror*, Longman, 1981.
Deutscher, I., *Stalin — A Political Biography*, Oxford University Press, 1966.
Floyd, D., *Russia in Revolt*, Macdonald, 1969.
Hill, C., *Lenin and the Russian Revolution*, Pelican, 1972.
Jackson, N.C. , *Russia in the Twentieth Century*, Pergamon Press, 1972.
Kennan, G., *Soviet Foreign Policy 1917–1941*, Van Nostrand, 1960.
Kenneth, J., *The Growth of Modern Russia*, Blackie & Sons, 1979.
Kochan, L., *The Making of Modern Russia*, Penguin, 1968.
MacCauley, M., *The Soviet Union Since 1917*, Longman, 1981.
Mann, A., *Stalin*, Allen Lane, 1973.
Mosse, W.E., *Alexander II and the Modernisation of Russia*, Hodder and Stoughton, 1959.

Robottom, J., *Modern Russia*, Longman, 1972.
Seton-Watson, H., *The Decline of Imperial Russia, 1855–1914*, Methuen, 1964.
Sumner, B.N., *A Survey of Russian History*, Methuen, 1944.
Westwood, J.N., *Endurance and Endeavour — Russian History 1812–1980*, Oxford University Press, 1983.

SPAIN

Allison-Peers, E., *The Spanish Tragedy, 1930–1936*, Methuen, 1936.
Carr, R., *Modern Spain, 1875–1980*, Oxford University Press, 1980.
Gibbs, J., *The Spanish Civil War*, Benn, 1973.
Jackson, G., *A Concise History of the Spanish Civil War*, Thames & Hudson, 1980.
Livermole, H.E., *History of Spain*, Allen & Unwin, 1958.
Snellgrove, L.E., *Franco and the Spanish Civil War*, Longman, 1972.
Thomas, H., *The Spanish Civil War*, Penguin, 1977.

IMPERIALISM

Chamberlain, M.E., *The Scramble for Africa*, Longman, 1974.
Horman, A.J., *European Rule in Africa*, Historical Association Pamphlet G. 46.
Lumb, S.V., *Central and Southern Africa*, Cambridge University Press, 1969.
Moon, R.R., *Imperialism and World Politics*, Macmillan, 1926.
Robottom, J., *Modern China*, Longman, 1972.
Shannon, R., *The Crisis of Imperialism, 1865–1915*, Paladin Books, 1974.
Townsend, M.E. and C.A. Peake, *European Colonialism Since 1871*, Lippincott, 1941.
Williams, B., *Modern Japan*, Longman, 1972.

WORLD WAR I

Falls, C., *The First World War*, Longman, 1960.
Gibbons, S.R. and P. Morican, *World War One*, Longman, 1972.
Hoehling, A.A., *The Great War at Sea*, Barker, 1936.
Liddell-Hart, B.H., *A History of the First World War*, Pan Books, 1982.
Lobban, R., *The First World War*, Oxford University Press, 1982.
Parkinson, R., *The Origins of World War One*, Wayland, 1970.
Petrie, C., *The Drift to World War One, 1900–1914*, Benn, 1968.
Selman, R.R., *The First World War*, Methuen, 1970.
Schmitt, B.E., *The Origins of the First World War*, Historical Association, 1958.
Scott, D., *World War One*, Benn, 1971.
Taylor, A.J.P., *The First World War*, Hamish Hamilton, 1963.
— *History of World War I*, Octopus Books, 1974.
Turner, L.C.F., *Origins of the First World War*, Edward Arnold, 1978.

THE PEACE TREATIES, 1919

Ayling, S.E., *Portraits of Power*, Harrap, 1965.
Bloncourt, P., *The Embattled Peace, 1919–1939*, Faber and Faber, 1968.
Bruce, M.G., *From Peace to War, Europe 1911–1939*, Thames & Hudson, 1967.
Hastings, P., *Between the Wars, 1919–1939*, Benn, 1968.
Lederer, J.J., *The Versailles Settlement*, D.C. Heath, 1960.
Nicholson, H., *Peacemaking, 1919*, Constable, 1965.
Watt, R.M., *The Kings Depart*, Pelican, 1972.

WORLD WAR II

Arnold-Foster, M., *The World at War*, Fontana, 1973.
Bayne-Jardine, C.C., *World War Two*, Longman, 1968.
Falls, C., *The Second World War, A Short History*, Methuen, 1950.
Liddell-Hart, B.H., *History of the Second World War*, Pan Books, 1970.
Ray, J., *The Second World War*, Heinemann, 1977.
Savage, K., *The Story of the Second World War*, Oxford University Press, 1957.
Selman, R.R., *The Second World War*, Methuen, 1970.
Trevor-Roper, H.R., *Hitler's War Directive, 1939–1945*, Pan Books, 1966.
— *The Last Days of Hitler*, Macmillan, 1956.
Yass, M., *Hiroshima*, Wayland, 1971.

POST-WAR EUROPE 1945–66

Ayling, S.E., *Portraits of Power*, Harrap, 1965.
Cootes, R.J., *The Making of the Welfare State*, Longman, 1966.
Cowie, L.W., *The Super Powers*, Nelson, 1971.
Elliot, B.F., *Western Europe After Hitler*, Longman, 1972.
Gatzke, W., *The Present in Perspective: A Look at the World Since 1945*, John Murray, 1966.
Hastings, P., *The Cold War*, Benn, 1969.
Jones, R.B., *The Making of Contemporary Europe*, Hodder and Stoughton, 1980.
Lane, P., *A History of Post-War Britain*, Macdonald, 1971.
Laqueur, W., *Europe Since Hitler*, Penguin, 1970.
Miller, A., *The USSR*, Oxford University Press, 1965.
Nicholas, H.G., *The United Nations as a Political Institute*, Oxford University Press, 1971.
Palmer, A., *The Penguin Dictionary of Twentieth Century History 1900–1978*, Penguin, 1979.
Urwin, D.W., *Western Europe Since 1945*, Allen & Unwin, 1972.

INDEX

A

B

C

D

E

F

G

H

I

J

K

L

M

N

O

P

Q

R

S